The Courtesan's Arts

Luis Berrueco (fl. 1727–1749), *Encounter with Four Women*. Municipal Hospital (Ex-Convent of San Juan de Dios), Atlixco, Puebla, Mexico. Courtesy of the Honorable Town Council of Atlixco.

Berrueco's aurally evocative painting depicts St. John of God in a sumptuous bedchamber beseeching four courtesans to leave their profession. The asceticism of the sixteenth-century Portuguese saint, who kneels on the floor wearing only a brown cloak and clutching rosary beads, contrasts sharply with the luxury of the courtesans, whose trappings include clothing made of colorful fabric, pearl bracelets and other jewelry, mirrors, beauty spots, a carpet, and a dressing screen. As a *negrita* servant watches in exasperation, the saint's chanted prayers seem to interrupt a session of music-making in which the courtesans had been playing the Spanish harp and guitar, probably as accompaniment to singing. Ironically, the saint's state of undress, coupled with the particularly luxuriant bed, alludes to the sexual basis of courtesanry while his asceticism highlights the courtesans' acquisition of the art objects and wealth. Following Novohispanic custom, a caption in the corner uses rhyming verse to explain the scenario.

The Courtesan's Arts

Cross-Cultural Perspectives

Edited by
Martha Feldman and Bonnie Gordon

OXFORD
UNIVERSITY PRESS

2006

OXFORD
UNIVERSITY PRESS

Oxford University Press is a department of the University of Oxford.
It furthers the University's objective of excellence in research, scholarship,
and education by publishing worldwide.

Oxford   New York
Auckland   Cape Town   Dar es Salaam   Hong Kong   Karachi
Kuala Lumpur   Madrid   Melbourne   Mexico City   Nairobi
New Delhi   Shanghai   Taipei   Toronto

With offices in
Argentina   Austria   Brazil   Chile   Czech Republic   France   Greece
Guatemala   Hungary   Italy   Japan   Poland   Portugal   Singapore
South Korea   Switzerland   Thailand   Turkey   Ukraine   Vietnam

Oxford is a registered trade mark of Oxford University Press
in the UK and certain other countries.

Published in the United States of America by
Oxford University Press
198 Madison Avenue, New York, NY 10016

Library of Congress Cataloging-in-Publication Data
The courtesan's arts : cross-cultural perspectives / edited by
Martha Feldman and Bonnie Gordon.
p. cm.
Includes bibliographical references and index.
ISBN 978-0-19-517028-3; 978-0-19-517029-0 (pbk.)
1. Courtesans—History—Cross-cultural studies.   I. Feldman, Martha.
II. Gordon, Bonnie, 1968–
HQ111.C68 2006
306.74'2'08621—dc22   2005047340

Visit the Companion Web site at www.oup.com/us/thecourtesanarts
Access with Username: Music2 and Password: Book4416

For
Emily and Rebecca
and
Rebecca and Jonathan

Acknowledgments

This book realizes a dream of many years' standing. We have first to thank the Women's Board of the University of Chicago for making it possible. They gave their most generous support to the project at the conference stage and again at the publication stage. Without their help we could never have done this book in style. Our heartfelt thanks are owed to all of them, as well as to Gretel Braidwood, of Development at the University of Chicago.

We have many others to thank for support in kind. The State University of New York at Stony Brook contributed crucial collaborative support toward making the companion website, as did the Music Department of the University of Chicago. Critical funding toward the conference that brought together the authors included in this volume was provided by the Roger Weiss and Howard Mayer Brown fund of the Department of Music at the University of Chicago, along with funding from the Adelyn Russell Bogert Fund of the Franke Institute for the Humanities, the Committee on South Asian Studies, the Dean of the Humanities, and the Newberry Library Consortium Committee, all of the University of Chicago. Our special thanks to Thomas Christensen and Robert L. Kendrick, past and present chairs, respectively, of the Department of Music at the University of Chicago, as well as the Dean Emeritus of the Humanities Division, Janel Mueller, and the Chair of the Music Department at SUNY Stony Brook, Jody Lochhead.

Martha Feldman's work on the volume was partially supported by a grant for University Teachers from the National Endowment for the Humanities and from the Humanities Division of the University of Chicago, and Bonnie Gordon's likewise by the Bunting Institute of Radcliffe University.

Our editorial assistants helped shorten the making of this book. Martha Feldman's Research Assistant Drew Edward Davies worked with great intelligence through all the early and middle editorial stages of this volume. Cordelia Chenault, Bonnie Gordon's Research Assistant at Stony Brook, lent invaluable assistance on the companion website and illustrations. Additional thanks go to Deborah Heckert, who worked with Bonnie on earlier editorial stages, and especially to Shawn Marie Keener, who worked tirelessly with Martha at the conference stage, wrote a wonderful program essay for the concert of the Newberry Consort, created our website, and stepped in again with great energy and intelligence at the stages of manuscript submission and copyediting. Meredith Ray, our Program Assistant for the conference and now Assistant Professor of Foreign Languages and Literatures at the University of Delaware, was our ace in the hole throughout all the critical phases of conference planning and execution.

Special thanks are due to the Newberry Consort for its superlative work in consulting with Martha Feldman and her seminar, putting together a beautiful concert on April 5, 2002 for the conference, giving permission to include performances on the companion website, and recording other examples separately on short notice. In particular we want to thank the Consort's Director and gambist, Mary Springfels, soprano Ellen Hargis, and violinist David Douglas, as well as harpsichordist David Schrader, lutenist John Lenti, and gambists Craig Trompeter and Ken Perlow. Past managers of the Consort, Fred Liese and Alex Bonus, were helpful through many stages of this project, and most especially has been the present Manager Ken Perlow, who oversaw arrangements for a recent recording of examples for the companion website.

Our most vigorous thanks to the brilliant grand master of kathak dance, Pandit Chitresh Das, Artistic Director of the Chitresh Das Dance Company, and his principal dancer Jaiwanti Pamnani, for a stunning performance-demonstration of kathak dance on April 6, 2002.

We give special thanks also to Andrew Natoli for his skilled mastering of the audio on the companion website. Kelly Foreman helped immensely with locating audio examples, and Miki Keneda, Miho Matsugu, and Janis Mimura helped with various translation issues. The Law Office of Linda Mensch, P.C., as well as Norm Hirschy, Editorial Assistant for Music at Oxford University Press, helped greatly with obtaining permissions for the companion website audio examples.

Carla Zecher of the Center for Renaissance Studies at the Newberry Library was a linchpin in staging the conference that led to this volume. We wish to thank her most particularly as well as the staff of her Center.

We are extremely grateful to those who read the manuscript or portions of it at various stages. Especially encouraging were the initial readers for Oxford University Press, Jane A. Bernstein and an anonymous reader. Judith T. Zeitlin consulted with us repeatedly at all stages in developing the project, which included critical advice on assembling the participants and commenting on the Introduction. Norma Field and Christopher A. Faraone consulted with us often about possible contributors and intellectual directions. Dorothy Ko also consulted with us during the earlier stages of the project. Also invaluable was the extensive reading and advice of our partners, Patricia Barber and Manuel Lerdau. We also thank Patricia for bringing her expertise as a producer and recording artist to our editing of the audio on the companion website.

Martha Feldman wishes to thank all of the members of her research seminar on "The Courtesan's Voice in Early Modern Italy," including Lyndal Andrews, Drew Edward Davies, Dawn De Rycke, Justin Flosi, Shawn Marie Keener, and Courtney Quaintance. Keener's fine essay, "Virtue, Illusion, *Venezianità*: Vocal Bravura and the Early *Cortigiana Onesta*," was sought out by another volume, now published, *Musical Voices of Early Modern Women: Many-Headed Melodies*, ed. Thomasin K. LaMay (Aldershot: Ashgate, 2005).

We owe additional thanks to session chairs Kyeong-Hee Choi, Assistant Professor, East Asian Languages and Civilizations, the University of Chicago; Joan Erdman, anthropologist and performing arts scholar at Columbia College and Research Associate in the

Committee on South Asian Studies at the University of Chicago; James M. Redfield, Professor of Classics; and Elissa Weaver, Professor of Romance Languages and Literatures, both of the University of Chicago. Robert Kendrick and Chika Kinoshita contributed fine papers for the conference but were not able to contribute to the volume.

The administrator of the Music Department at the University of Chicago, Kathy Holmes, provided tireless administrative and budgetary support. Our thanks to her for always making the impossible possible, with sweetness and humor.

The musical examples were expertly prepared by Drew Edward Davies and the index equally so by Melissa Reilly.

Many people traveled long distances to attend the conference as auditors, among them Mary C. Dalton, Kelly Foreman, Eugenio Giusti, and Sheila Schonbrun. We were moved by their special efforts and commitment.

Finally, our warmest thanks to Kim Robinson, Music Editor at Oxford University Press, New York, at the time we contracted this book, who believed in it from the beginning, and her expert Editorial Assistants, Eve Bachrach and later Norm Hirschy, as well as other members of the Oxford team, including Bob Milks, Senior Production Editor, and Suzanne Ryan, the new Music Editor. It is impossible to express enough our gratitude to Bonnie Blackburn, who embraced this project completely and transcended the notion of copyeditor. We often wondered how she could possibly know so much, and thanked the heavens for having her and (less officially) her classicist husband, Leofranc Holford-Strevens, on our project.

Contents

List of Figures

List of Music Examples

A Note about Languages

Authors in this volume use many different languages in their research. Given the forbidding cost and unwieldiness of including the originals in full for all text presented in translation, we have reluctantly adopted a set of principles that limits the amount of non-English material cited while still allowing interested readers to find original sources. In general, we include original languages only in cases that involve questions about meanings of translations (whole texts or specific words) or musical issues, such as the relationship between poetic prosody and music, or questions about how text is set to (or "realized in") music. We have made a few exceptions on a case-by-case basis.

In the endnotes and bibliography we include translations of transliterated Asian texts, adhering to the convention followed by our authors when writing about Asian themes in the English language. We alphabetize East Asian names as last name followed by first name, without comma, except when authors write primarily in English.

Contributors

JAMES DAVIDSON is reader in Ancient History at the University of Warwick. He works on ancient Greek sexuality and cultural history and is a regular contributor to the *London Review of Books*, as well as the *Daily Telegraph* and the *Sunday Times*. He is the author of *Courtesans and Fishcakes: The Consuming Passions of Classical Athens* (1997), translated into German as *Kurtisanen und Meeresfrüchte: Die verzehrenden Leidenschaften im klassichen Athen* (Siedler, 1999). Presently he is completing *The Greeks and Greek Love* for Weidenfeld and Random House (forthcoming, 2006).

DREW EDWARD DAVIES is a Ph.D. candidate in musicology at the University of Chicago. His dissertation, which concerns the reception and refraction of Italianate music in colonial Mexican cathedral culture, is entitled "The Italianized Frontier: Music at Durango Cathedral, *Español* Culture, and the Aesthetics of Devotion in Eighteenth-Century New Spain." The recipient of an Andrew W. Mellon Foundation Dissertation Fellowship, he currently teaches at Northwestern University and serves on the executive board of the "Musicat" project at the Universidad Nacional Autónoma de México. His articles and reviews appear in the volume *Musicology and Globalization*, the *Revista Portuguesa de Musicologia*, *Eighteenth-Century Music*, and *Music Library Association Notes*.

DAWN DE RYCKE, a guitarist, is a Ph.D. candidate in musicology at the University of Chicago. She is a recent Fulbright recipient for dissertation research on civic identity and cathedral music in sixteenth-century Seville, "Music, Liturgy, and Civic Identity: A View from Seville Cathedral, 1495–1600." She has published in the *Journal of the Lute Society of America* and the *Revista Portuguesa de Musicologia*.

LESLEY DOWNER has lived in Japan off and on for about fifteen years since 1978, where she studied womanly arts, such as tea ceremony and flower arrangement. She is the author of *Women of the Pleasure Quarters: The Secret History of the Geisha* (Broadway, 2001). Her other books include *On the Narrow Road: Journey into a Lost Japan*

(Summit Books, 1989), short-listed for the Somerset Maugham Travel Book of the Year award 1988 and televised by WNET; *The Brothers: The Hidden World of Japan's Richest Family* (Random House, 1994), a New York Times "Book of the Year" in 1995, and most recently *Madame Sadayakko: The Geisha who Bewitched the West* (Gotham Books, 2003), the story of the geisha turned actress whom Puccini took as his model for *Madame Butterfly*. As a journalist Downer has written for the *New York Times*, the *Wall Street Journal*, and the *London Sunday Times*. She is currently working on a novel set in nineteenth-century Japan.

CHRISTOPHER A. FARAONE is professor in the Department of Classics at the University of Chicago. He is the author of *Talismans and Trojan Horses: Guardian Statues in Ancient Greek Myth and Ritual* (Oxford University Press, 1992) and *Ancient Greek Love Magic* (Harvard University Press, 1999). He is also co-editor of *Masks of Dionysus* with Thomas H. Carpenter (Cornell University Press, 1993), *Initiation in Ancient Greek Rituals and Narratives: New Critical Perspectives* with David Brooks Dodd (Routledge, 2003), and *Prostitutes and Courtesans in the Ancient World* with Laura McClure (University of Wisconsin Press, forthcoming 2006).

MARTHA FELDMAN is professor of music and the humanities at the University of Chicago. She is the author of *City Culture and the Madrigal at Venice* (University of California Press, 1995), *Opera and Sovereignty: Sentiment, Myth, and Modernity in Eighteenth-Century Italy* (University of Chicago Press, forthcoming 2006), and is currently at work on *The Castrato as Myth*. She is also a volume editor in the series Sixteenth-Century Madrigal (Garland Publishing Inc., 1989–91) and general editor of the six-volume series Critical and Cultural Musicology (Garland and Routledge, 2000–2002). In 1998–99 she was appointed a year-long Getty Scholar at the Getty Center. In 2001 the Royal Musical Association conferred the Dent Medal on her.

JUSTIN FLOSI teaches French and Italian at the University of Chicago, where he is pursuing a Ph.D. in Comparative Literature. In 2003 he was a Mellon Graduate Achievement Fellow. His research interests lie at the intersections of text and music in the early modern period, particularly those of transgressive performers, courtesans, and castrati. An accomplished countertenor, Flosi sings with the Chicago Chorale and the Rockefeller Chapel Choir.

BONNIE GORDON is assistant professor of music at the State University of New York at Stony Brook. She has published on the female voice in early modern Italy and on contemporary female singer/songwriters. Her book *Monteverdi's Unruly Women: The Power of Song in Early Modern Europe* was published in 2004 by Cambridge University Press. She has received awards from the American Association of University Women, the Radcliffe Institute for Advanced Study, and the Mellon Foundation.

AMELIA MACISZEWSKI is an ethnomusicologist, sitarist, and music educator who seeks to create and inhabit spaces where forms of knowledge and human rights weave together with the performing and visual/media arts. She earned the B.Mus. and M.Mus. degrees in Hindustani music and sitar at Viswa-Bharati University (Santiniketan), India, and a Ph.D. in ethnomusicology at the University of Texas at Austin. A disciple of the late sitarist Prof. Suresh Misra, sarode maestro Aashish Khan, and Hindustani vocal diva Dr. Girija Devi, Maciszewski has performed on three continents and has taught music and ethnomusicology on the faculties of the University of Colorado, the University of Alberta, and the University of Pittsburgh. Her work, including documentary films on North India's courtesans, has been supported by a Fulbright IIE Grant, a Killam Postdoctoral Fellowship, and grants from the University of Pittsburgh's Center for Asian Studies.

MIHO MATSUGU is assistant professor in the Department of Chinese and Japanese at Grinnell College. Her dissertation, "The War in *Snow Country*: Aesthetics of Empire, Politics of Literature, and the Struggle of Women," completed at the University of Chicago, is a textual and socio-historical examination of Kawabata Yasunari's *Snow Country* and its geisha heroine Komako. Matsugu received a grant from the University of Chicago and a Twentieth-Century Japan Research Award from the Center for Historical Studies and McKeldin Library at the University of Maryland.

JOSHUA D. PILZER is a doctoral candidate in ethnomusicology at the University of Chicago, focusing on Korean and Japanese folk and popular musics. His dissertation, "My Heart, the Number One: Singing in the Lives of Five Korean Survivors of Japanese Military Sexual Slavery," deals with music and traumatic experience. He undertook fieldwork as a Fulbright scholar in 2002–3 and as a recipient of a Korea Foundation grant in 2003–4. He has also received major funding from the University of Chicago Center for Gender Studies. In 2003 he published "Sŏdosori (Northwestern Korean lyric song) on the Demilitarized Zone: A Study in Music and Teleological Judgment" (*Ethnomusicology*), and in Seoul 2004, with photographer Yajima Tsukasa, he organized the exhibition "Lineages of Separation: Voices and Portraits of Survivors of Japanese Military Sexual Slavery," including songs of Korean survivors.

COURTNEY QUAINTANCE is a Ph.D. candidate in the Department of Romance Languages and Literatures at the University of Chicago. Her dissertation, "Pornography and Patriarchy: Courtesans and Literati in Renaissance Venice," focuses on courtesan satire penned by authors associated with Domenico Venier's literary salon and explores how these writers used the courtesan figure to transmit and negotiate issues of identity. She is the recipient of a Fulbright grant in 2005–6 for research in Venice.

REGULA BURCKHARDT QURESHI is professor of music, Director of the Canadian Centre for Ethnomusicology, and a member of the Program of Religious Studies at the University of Alberta. An anthropologist and performer of Indian and Islamic musical practices, she has published widely on music as expressive culture and musicians as social agents. Her books include *Sufi Music in India and Pakistan: Sound, Context, and Meaning in Qawwali* (Cambridge University Press 1986; University of Chicago Press, 1995) and *Master Musicians of India: Hindustani Musicians Speak* (Routledge, forthcoming). She is also editor of *Music and Marx: Ideas, Practice, Politics* (Routledge, 2002) and a co-editor of *The Muslim Community in North America* (University of Alberta Press, 1983) and *Muslim Families in North America* (University of Alberta

Press, 1991). She has published numerous articles, most recently in *American Ethnologist*, *Ethnomusicology*, *The World of Music*, and the *Journal of Musicology*.

MARGARET F. ROSENTHAL is associate professor of Italian literature at the University of Southern California. A specialist in Venice of the early modern period, she is the author of *The Honest Courtesan: Veronica Franco, Citizen and Writer of Sixteenth-Century Venice* (University of Chicago Press, 1992) and with Ann Rosalind Jones is translator and editor of *Poems and Selected Letters of Veronica Franco* (University of Chicago Press, 1998) and *The Clothing of the Renaissance World: Cesare Vecellio's Costume Book (1590/1598)* (Pennsylvania State University Press, 2006).

GUIDO RUGGIERO, professor and chair of the Department of History at the University of Miami, has published on the history of gender, sex, crime, magic, science, and everyday culture, primarily in Renaissance and early modern Italy. Among other volumes, he has published *Violence in Early Renaissance Venice* (Rutgers University Press, 1980), *The Boundaries of Eros: Sex Crime and Sexuality in Renaissance Venice* (Oxford University Press, 1985), and *Binding Passions: Tales of Magic, Marriage, and Power from the End of the Renaissance* (Oxford University Press, 1993); as well as *Sex and Gender in Historical Perspectives* (1990), *Microhistory and the Lost Peoples of Europe* (1991), and *History from Crime* (1993), all edited with Edward Muir and published by Johns Hopkins University Press. He has also edited *The Blackwell Companion to the Renaissance* (2002), and with Laura Giannetti has edited and translated *Five Comedies from the Italian Renaissance* for Johns Hopkins University Press (2003). In addition he edited the series *Studies in the History of Sexuality* for Oxford University Press (1985–2002) and was a co-editor of the six-volume *Encyclopedia of European Social History* for Scribner's (2002).

TIMON SCREECH is reader in the History of Art and the School of Oriental and African Studies, University of London, where he has taught since 1991. He received his B.A. in Oriental Studies (Japanese) from Oxford University, and his Ph.D. from Harvard University. He is the author of numerous books and articles in English and Japanese on the culture of the Edo period, including the *Sex and the Floating World: Erotic Images in Japan, 1700–1820* (University of Hawai'i Press, 1999), *The Shogun's Painted Culture: Fear and Creativity in the Japanese States, 1760–1829* (Reaktion Books, 2000), and *The Lens within the Heart: The Western Scientific Gaze and Popular Imagery in Later Edo Japan* (University of Hawai'i Press, 2002). His study of the image of England in the Edo period will appear in Japanese in 2006 as *Edo no igirisu netsu*. He is currently completing new editions of Carl Peter Thunberg's *Travels* and Isaac Titsingh's *Illustrations of Japan*.

DORIS M. SRINIVASAN is a visiting scholar in Asian and Asian-American Studies at the State University of New York at Stony Brook. An art historian of pre-colonial South Asian art, her specialties lie in the origins and dawning of early religious imagery and early Sanskrit religious texts. Among her publications are *Many Heads, Arms, and Eyes: Origin, Meaning, and Form of Multiplicity in Indian Art* (E. J. Brill, 1997) and *Mathura: The Cultural Heritage*, of which she is General Editor (American Institute of Indian Studies, New Delhi, 1989), as well as numerous essays and a documentary film on the Hindu ritual Sandhya. She is the recipient of grants and fellowships from the NEH, the Smithsonian Institution, the American Institute of Indian Studies, and the Asian Cultural Council, and was appointed a Getty Scholar in 1999. In 1984–87 she served as President of the American Committee for South Asian Art.

JUDITH T. ZEITLIN is professor of Chinese literature in the Department of East Asian Languages and Civilizations at the University of Chicago. Her publications include *Historian of the Strange: Pu Songling and the Chinese Classical Tale* (Stanford University Press, 1993), *Writing and Materiality in China* (co-editor; Harvard University Press, 2002), and *Thinking with Cases: Specialist Knowledge in Chinese Cultural History* (co-editor, forthcoming). She has recently completed a book-length study on ghosts and gender in Chinese fiction, poetry, and theater, *The Phantom Heroine: Ghosts and Gender in Seventeenth-Century Chinese Literature* (University of Hawai'i Press, forthcoming).

The Courtesan's Arts

Introduction

This volume is an attempt to understand the courtesan and her arts by creating a dialogue about different courtesan cultures. Though hardly a universal phenomenon, courtesanship has recurred in specific times and places, from precolonial India and ancient Greece to imperial China, Renaissance Italy, and Edo Japan. Invariably courtesans have been accompanied by a repertory of rhetorical, gestural, sonic, and visual idioms that complement their sensual power. The essays that follow explore the conditions that have allowed courtesan cultures to evolve and thrive, or caused them to perish. Intimately tied to these conditions are the courtesan's arts. In each case, the factors that motivate, sustain, and destroy courtesan cultures prove to be intimately bound up with the status of courtesans as bearers of artistic traditions and the ways the arts are pressed into service as shapers of culture.

Whether drawn in Lucian's mock salacious tones or instructed by the inventories of the Kamasutra, courtesans have been obscure objects of desire who have fascinated their observers, past and present. Indeed, throughout the world they have tended to go by a common cache of epithets: ambiguous and furtive, veiled but showy, performative, and meretricious. They are gracious and deferential, yet mobile in status and sometimes even in class.

As musicologists, our own fascination with courtesans began with the elusive sounds they generated in early modern Italy, when their music-making formed part of unwritten, hence historically hidden, practices. Working against the mainstream of music history, each of us in our own work met a barrier of musical silence and historical enigma. Yet we also suspected that the arts of courtesans, like their artful ways of living, were indices of deeper, and wider, cultural phenomena. We began looking to other cultures for clues about how to proceed, and as we did so we found ourselves wondering whether, conversely, the history of Italian courtesanship might provide clues about courtesan cultures elsewhere. There was encouragement to be found, at least of a general sort, in the sympathies of writers in other disciplines who had begun to reevaluate cultural practices transmitted through non-traditional means, thriving outside institutional norms, and existing outside the traditional canons of scholarly interest. Indeed, a small number of scholars were already exploring the cultural production and history of courtesans in their own historical/ethnographic domains. Some of these explorations had dealt only with individual courtesans or were mired in narrow disciplinary concerns, but a handful of others were framed within broader—and quite provocative—matrices of social and political practice.

What was lacking was a rigorous cross-cultural study of the phenomenon—doubtless because no single scholar has had the range of analytical and practical skills that such a project would demand. Our hope was to undertake such a study by means of a working group. We presumed from the outset that we would need to start with meaningful collaboration among contributors from different disciplines, and in 2000 we began seeking out scholars from music history, ethnomusicology, East Asian studies, South Asian studies, art history, Italian literature, comparative literature, anthropology, history, and classics. We wanted to find both mature scholars, ready to think broadly and comparatively about a set of shared themes, but also younger scholars who could bring new data and fresh visions to the project. Prior to assembling our group, Feldman led an intensive research seminar in the spring of 2001 with an interdisciplinary team of graduate students who, together with the Newberry Consort, attempted to reconstruct some of the musical and cultural practices of Italian Renaissance courtesans and refine various questions about them.

In April 2002, with strong support from the Women's Board of the University of Chicago, our entire group convened at the University of Chicago and the Newberry Library for a workshop-styled conference and two performances—one on the music of Renaissance courtesans by the Newberry Consort, drawing on work by the University of Chicago seminar,[1] and one on kathak dance of north India by Chitresh Das and Jaiwanti Pamnani, director and member, respectively, of the San Francisco–based Chitresh Das Dance Company. Our goal was this book. To our delight, it turned out that participants were hungry for conversation with one another, each in different ways having long been frustrated by lacunae in their subject matter at levels ranging from the microhistorical to the larger political.

The initial choice to proceed outwards from the instance of early modern Italy had little more rationale than our own areas of expertise. Fortunately, the Italian case proved to be a productive one for initiating the project. Not only is it well studied in some respects, it also opens up a variety of issues that reach both backwards to ancient times, in whose image Renaissance courtesanship was partly fashioned, and forwards to the dilemmas of a post-feudal, capitalistic world, which it adumbrates. Nevertheless, a disclaimer is in order: we never intended early modern Italy to be a yardstick in an old Eurocentric, imperial sense. While in the end we may not have escaped the perils of comparatism (as our collaborators, and now friends, in this volume have been quick to point out), we aimed from the start for something more heuristic. We wanted the friction of widely divergent, even incompatible approaches, disciplinary and theoretical, to challenge seemingly "natural" assumptions. This is not to say that we have overcome the many problems of cultural and linguistic translation that we met along the way either, however much we have bridged certain gaps among us, or have wanted to. But we have agreed that a provisional sense of what courtesanship is has been important to achieving productive dialogue among us, and indeed has been a precondition for it.

The results of this dialogue have at times been surprising, as previously undiscovered, and certainly under-theorized, poetry, music, and other art forms have emerged together with new insights into little-understood practices and conditions. The Sinologist Judith Zeitlin, for example, presents original evidence and interpretations for the music-making that was central to Chinese courtesans of the sixteenth and seventeenth centuries. The Hellenist James Davidson rereads the well-studied courtesan Phryne as a template of the Greek courtesan's status—both an enigmatic reflection of male fantasy and a living, breathing woman with skills and privileges that far exceeded those of her contemporaries. The musicologist Drew Davies explores Italian repertories previously neglected to bring to the fore polarities of high/low and sacred/secular that marked courtesans across wider global spectra. Lesley Downer uses her experience of living within communities of geisha to illuminate some of the tensions between how geisha see themselves and what the world sees in them. Regula Burckhardt Qureshi, in developing ethnographic work within communities of north Indian female musicians, ends by expanding a Marxist approach to inform the relationship between gender and the quasi-mercantile dimension of a once feudally based socioeconomic terrain. Offering close readings of a carefully identified group of texts, Justin Flosi borrows from Nietzsche the concept of distance to elaborate the Neoplatonic precepts of love that were central to courtesans in the Italian Renaissance.

Notwithstanding our varied methods, sources, and perspectives, all of us in this volume are tied together by our engagement in projects of reconstruction—of putting together stories and situations from the barest scraps of history, or the faintest traces of ethnography. From vase paintings to temple drawings, from unwritten song echoed in Renaissance polyphony to the poignant strains heard from descendants of the great courtesan-singers of Lucknow and Benares, we are all about trying to piece together stories. In part this is because even for those who live with them courtesans have been hard to know. They are fundamentally elusive fantasies of the imagination. Yet it is precisely this seductive vagueness, this endless deferral, as Davidson describes it, that has made the courtesan so enticing to her consumers and critics and that keeps even those who vanished thousands of years ago still entangling us in their bright web.

DEFINING COURTESANS

For purposes of this volume, we define courtesanship roughly as the social phenomenon whereby women engage in relatively exclusive exchanges of artistic graces, elevated conversation, and sexual favors with male patrons. Highly educated, creative, and skilled, women who have gone by the epithet "courtesan" and its many linguistic and cultural variants—the Greek *hetaira*, the Italian *cortigiana*, the Chinese *ji*, the Korean *gisaeng*, the Indian *tawa'if*, *ganika*, *devadasi*, and *baiji*—are regularly assigned to special categories within their respective cultures. Above all, their traffic in intellectual and artistic currencies is understood in their own cultural contexts to be wholly interdependent with their commerce in sex. Related to these intersecting spheres, courtesans both reflect and construct the twin realms of pleasure and leisure, at once symbolizing a certain decadence and providing a crucial outlet for it. We thus acknowledge the participation of courtesans in sex trades but instead deal directly here with courtesans' arts and their role in societies that have been strongly marked by the existence of leisure classes.

Approached in this way, courtesans are seen to operate at elite levels where leisure and pleasure have been cultivated, even though most themselves come from lower echelons of society than their patrons do. Often indistinguishable from women born into higher classes, they tend to assume certain upper-class styles and privileges in a performance that crosses and blurs class lines and distinguishes them from other groups designated by cultural/linguistic equivalents (equally rough) to the English-language word "prostitutes." Moreover, though in some sense courtesans stand at the margins of power, theirs is generally a complex marginality in which their close consort with those at the centers of power allows them to slide in and out of agency, control, and influence. Courtesans can often take wealth and status away from their patrons as easily as they help generate it. Dialectically speaking, the rigid hierarchies of class and gender that allow courtesans to flourish make them powerful because they successfully challenge the delineations that keep received social structures in place; but those same hierarchical social structures also deny courtesans full access to privileges guarded at the very highest strata of society. In all of these ways, courtesans and their arts are woven into a dynamic of privilege and constraint that forces a rethinking of the gendering of power. Their artistic practices become means of self-promotion—indeed self-preservation—within systems of freedom and oppression, which in turn involve them and their clients in high-level networks of social and political exchange.

Despite wide variations from these general trends, authors in this volume find that certain tendencies in the social and economic conditions under which courtesan cultures surface repeat themselves with striking frequency, even between those that are temporally and geographically distant from one another: highly stratified societies, often undergoing processes of modernization from feudal to "bourgeois," marked by new forms of mercantilism, accelerated forms of cultural production and circulation, heightened potential for social mobility, and marriage systems that separate love and sexual passion from the institution of matrimony. The establishment of Italian courtesans in early modern cities, for example, allowed them a new mobility tied to their ability to refuse individual clients. During the same time a contraction in the marriage market (which had always been more about politics and power than love) continued to allow courtesans to serve as important escapes from and substitutes for the marital bed, and thus to separate passionate from reproductive sex. Similarly, precolonial Indian ganika (courtesans of the feudal courts) and devadasi (temple goddesses) both filled a problematic sexual role that differed sharply from that of the wife and was necessary for society's self-sustenance. In that world (as Doris Srinivasan stresses) wives were keepers of lineage and courtesans were keepers of culture.

Yet other cases underscore our inability to determine cross-culturally just what courtesans are. Here local etymologies are revealing, as various terms have meant radically different things in different times and places. In early modern Italy, for instance, the verbal kinship between courtier and courtesan (*cortigiano/cortigiana*) had a professional corollary in their shared emphasis on skilled performance at court, or skilled imitations of courtly performances. By contrast, the Greek word *hetaira*, usually translated as "courtesan," is the female counterpart of the male word for "comrade" or "friend" (*hetairos*)—hence the *hetaira* figures as a female companion. The lexicon for women who were skilled in the arts and also offered sexual services extends prodigiously in Chinese, as reflected in graphs built etymologically on woman and entertainer, thus emphasizing female performance (albeit in a variety of ways). And in the many linguistic/cultural regions of the Indian subcontinent a dizzying variety of terms has been used to define the many different kinds of cultivated female performers who have engaged in sex with male patrons over the last millennium and more.[2]

If anything, then, our dialogues have taught us that problems of linguistic and cultural translation are wardens of precious cultural difference, which speak to vast local variations in the profiles and histories that courtesans carry with them. They have also taught us that courtesans will never be wholly known because they are never wholly knowable. Indeed, not just who can be called a courtesan and why, but who has the authority to define her have turned out to be among our central, ongoing questions. In the end what constitutes the courtesan and the culture in which she exists seems to consist less of a set of shared epithets or a priori definable *things* than a relatively commensurate set of phenomena.

That said, we should add that we do not intend this volume to serve as any kind of definitive study of the courtesan. We have intentionally, and inevitably, omitted important historical instances of courtesans that some might regard as falling within our broad purview—the widely studied courtesans of nineteenth-century France, for example (whose fame seems less contingent on intellectual and artistic prowess than does that of the women on whom we focus)[3]—in favor of concentrating on a limited cluster of cases. In keeping with our provisional and deliberately heterogeneous definition, we offer studies that enable us to initiate discussion which can then function as a basis for further inquiry. Among these clusters we have included geisha in an excursus, despite the fact that in the Japanese lexicon and bifurcation of roles there is another category of women who stand in as courtesans, because the focus of geisha on artistic entertainment primarily for the enjoyment of men makes for an interesting contrasting case with our others. Ultimately we do not want to position courtesans in predetermined categories or to foreclose possibilities, but to open them up by looking at specific local manifestations of a phenomenon that cuts across time and space.

FIGURING THE ARTS

The arts have invariably been central to the construction of courtesan cultures and the courtesan has traditionally been a bearer of artistic traditions. In this role courtesans have often been among the best-educated and freest women of their time. For courtesans of the Italian Renaissance and modern India, poetry has occupied a central place, as has music. By contrast, the Kamasutra, probably set down in the third century A.D., lists no fewer than sixty-four arts to be mastered by ancient courtesans as well as the most highly placed women (daughters of kings), arts that include music, magic, carpentry, drawing, and metallurgy; and, as Srinivasan points out, such mastery rendered courtesans custodians of important artistic traditions which they displayed in courtly and aristocratic contexts.[4] Christopher Faraone underscores how ancient Greek sources feature women (clearly hetaerae) using rhetorical arts to spar wittily with the most educated men of their time and even run their own symposia, previously thought to be the province of men. The courtesan culture of the late Ming dynasty in the sixteenth century similarly provided an environment atypical in allowing men and women from different families to socialize freely with one another, as Zeitlin tells us, and one in which poetry and music served as the primary mode of communication between women and their patrons in an otherwise restrictive society. Such situations were often celebrated artistically as part of the courtesan's way of establishing her place in a larger network of exchange. Famed courtesan Jing Pianpian flaunted her own talents with the words "Together we feast deep into the night. / After I've softly tuned the lute, / we sit and tie a lover's knot, / inviting the moon into the room."[5]

For courtesans, art is never an extracurricular activity but one that permeates their lives. Always negotiating a complex dynamic, courtesans are forever producing themselves and being reproduced by the fantasies of their consumers. Our work thus moves between the creations of courtesans' imaginations and imaginings of the courtesan. Glossed differently, we might say that the courtesan exists on the permeable cusp between reality and representation. To borrow again from Davidson, it is therefore "a travesty to treat [her] as a literary figment and equally mistaken to see her as pure unadulterated fact. She . . . belongs to both art and reality, an artfulness in everyday reality, an everyday reality in art." Substituting here an opposition between reality and art for the conventional one between reality and fiction is particularly apt, for courtesans the world over reside in a performative space.

If art and the arts have been key objects for all of the contributors to this volume, the point is not so much to make them reveal historical truths in a conventional sense as to allow us through them to shadow distant cultures, to excavate lost histories in new reimaginings. Srinivasan, for instance, elucidates precolonial courtesans by piecing together a wide variety of artistic and literary sources that describe and thus inscribe the ancient Indian courtesan as a figment of her time. Timon Screech uses poems and pictures to reconstruct the male experience of transit to the courtesan district in seventeenth-century Edo Japan, thereby conjuring up fantasies imposed on courtesans by those who lived beyond the boundaries of the outlying courtesan district, marked by a large gate whose surrounding moats made it look like a stockade.

Through such reconstructions, as each of us queries the complex relationship between "real" courtesans and recoverable fantasies, our project becomes what might seem to some an inherently poststructuralist one, since it lies literally beyond texts. In fact, the reality/art dilemma at its center also applies to a less conventional sense of the "arts" that itself is nontextual, as courtesans consistently relied on artful self-presentation and self-performance. Accordingly, Margaret Rosenthal and Lesley Downer consider ways in which courtesans and geisha, respectively, have used clothes and makeup to create images of themselves as alluring upper-class women. In the first instance, Rosenthal explores the Venetian courtesans' manipulation of dress codes to create a public persona and illuminates the artistic rendition of self-performance that circulated abroad in images commercially marketed in the tourist trade. In the second, Downer reflects on the geisha's intricate practice of creating a highly constructed persona by means of elaborate hairdos, makeup, and kimonos.

Yet as anyone schooled in poststructuralism will declare, a text or performance is rarely read in quite the way its creator intended. Hence the great mystery generated by courtesans but also the façades that conceal longings, furies, and not least suffering. One example exists in our own day among the tawa'if of north India described by Amelia Maciszewski, who openly give the lie to this paradox by using their musical performances to challenge public images of themselves as being "just" sex workers.

The means is telling. As an art form that is performative by nature, music highlights the importance of performance of all kinds and, not surprisingly, occupies a special place among the practices dealt with here. Again, some examples: the courtesan cultures of the Tang dynasty in seventh- to tenth-century China were centered around music, a situation that endured into the modern period of the eighteenth century and beyond. The term "ji," which approximates Western notions of courtesans, is still often translated as "singing girl." And late nineteenth-century Indian courtesans staked their reputations on their vocal talents. As Qureshi explains, their salons were the first venues for Hindustani art music accessible to listeners apart from noble princes and their courts. In other cases, too, music has been a central part of courtesans' cultural performances (not least those of the Italian Renaissance that we ourselves have studied). Repeatedly our authors show that the art of music, sensual and highly intangible, is akin to the art of courtesanship itself.

But musical arts also fuse seamlessly (if in various ways) with rhetoric, theater, poetry, dance, and gesture in virtually every case of courtesanship that we have encountered. Thus the Italian Renaissance is well known for its Neoplatonic understanding of song as a form of heightened speech, the Greek word *mousikē* refers to the agglomeration of what we call poetry, music, and dance, and the songs of certain Indian courtesans depend largely on an elaborate vocabulary of mimed gestures that merge dance with song.

Then too, from music come the many vocal genres discussed here. Even as they remind us of the courtesan's evanescence,[6] these vocal genres give a material presence to the concept of voice that has been so valuable to feminist theorists in recent decades. Some few earlier studies have referred to the "voices" of famed Renaissance courtesans such as Tullia d'Aragona and Veronica Franco, but little has previously been done to describe the effects their sounds actually made—the work of their real material voices—and to puzzle out *what* they sang, as Martha Feldman and Dawn De Rycke do here. Their reconstructive work has broad implications in its insistence on the interaction between oral and written traditions, calling attention to echoes of improvisatory, or at least unwritten, practices of singing that surface in some sixteenth-century printed music. In another work of reconstruction, Zeitlin teases out what courtesans sang in late Ming and early Qing dynasty China, despite the fact that musically notated vocal scores did not make it into print until the late eighteenth century, well after the period about which she writes. All of these studies produce hypothetical traces of the courtesan's song at the same time as they call attention to the courtesan's music as something that continually threatens to elude us.[7]

As music and eros joined in a tantalizing but perilous duet, that elusiveness was the thread that tied courtesans' singing to their bodies. Indeed, Bonnie Gordon shows that received medical and philosophical conceptions of the body understood the movements of the mouth, throat, and diaphragm required for singing to parallel directly the movements of the female genitals and womb imagined to accompany sex and orgasm. Singing thus threatened the chastity of a virtuous woman while it enhanced the erotic capital of a courtesan. Sixteenth-century China saw an interplay between sex and music also based on an embodied notion of the act of singing, which could similarly damn or elevate a young lady. In scenes of singing lessons found in Chinese opera, singing, like dancing, is understood as a means of seduction that gives girls a professional advantage even as it puts them at a moral disadvantage. Confucian scholars, like those of ancient Greece and Renaissance Italy, denigrated as lascivious and seductive the music made by women, but they also celebrated it. The terms for sound and visual allure had been paired together since antiquity to signify the potential that sensual overindulgence carried to topple a ruler's kingdom. And the very word for the singing voice in Chinese is denoted by the throat in a verbal image that makes the voice out as an instrument of flesh. Here too an analogy emerges with the Italian case, where the word for certain ornaments that singers performed translates literally as throat (*gorgia*). Feminine and seductive, singing enhanced the singer's allure.

Prowess in music and other arts allowed courtesans to transcend prescribed gender and class roles, enjoying professional opportunities, wealth, access to civic spaces, and social privileges generally denied other women in their societies. By utilizing rhetoric, music, dance, poetry, fashion, magic, and other arts, courtesans could perform themselves into an existence that exceeded the commodification of their bodies (a trope vulgarized in a recent Hollywood biography of Veronica Franco very loosely based on the work of one of our contributors).[8] As part of this enhanced power and privilege, courtesans have often practiced explicitly male arts. Among these, the ancient Greek hetaera participated in traditionally male games and symposia. And like hetaerae, Italian courtesans were sometimes imagined as coopting male erotic magic.[9] The Italian Franco assumes the province of men by celebrating sexuality with a fierce poetic language, and Italian courtesans were known to wear male bloomers.[10] Japanese courtesans of the seventeenth century might even sport male hairstyles.[11]

Yet, paradoxically, the courtesan, in contrast to a wife, inhabits a space at the margins of dominant patrilineal systems of reproduction because she is reproductively irrelevant. In worlds marked by heterosexual marriage in which men often control all things financial, this irrelevance also puts her outside traditional systems of commerce even though it puts her at the center of economies of pleasure, since love and pleasure traditionally occupy worlds separate from that of marriage. Gaspara Stampa, a sixteenth-century Venetian poet-musician who almost certainly was not a courtesan but whose lifestyle as a free unmarried woman resembled one, stands outside the heterosexual marriage economy that largely dominated the Italian states by virtue of having maintained her own salon for poetry and music and having had two successive lovers. Ancient Greek courtesans managed their own houses, without the aid of men. In Japan, geisha districts are unique spaces in which women rule their world and men serve as mere customers; fathers simply do not exist, even when children enter the geisha's midst, unless a geisha should decide to leave her profession. Courtesans in northern India have typically lacked reference to wider kin and community—a critical and fascinating lack within a society so strongly marked by the caste system. Indeed, until the mid-twentieth century women owned and operated the courtesan salons of India, and the courtesans of Lucknow even inverted patrilineal control over women by making men into service providers and treating patrons as sources of income (as Veena Oldenburg points out).[12] In addition, courtesanship is passed down through matrilineal lines of descent that exist outside of patrilineality and serve to remind us of the way in which lineality can be "strategically invoked or denied" (see Qureshi, chap. 17 in this volume). Today the modern descendants of, and proxies for, what were formerly full-fledged tawa'if operate as small-time entrepreneurs in female-centered family businesses.

Not surprisingly such breaches of normative gender roles, combined with the attraction that courtesans spark, have often led to fierce constraint by the very systems courtesans would seem to have escaped. A violent, ugly side of things lurks beneath the surface of love and pleasure. Far from deterring physical or verbal attacks, attractions to courtesans have often set them in motion, opening courtesans to the consequences of men's ambivalence and, worse, to vilification, fear, and violence. The magic associated with Renaissance courtesans was seen as dangerous, for example, or at least was linked with the ability to entice mad passion and hence lead to the destruction of male wealth. Many courtesans now lost in the annals of history endured gang rapes or mutilations as punishment for presumed misdeeds, and others were tried by the Inquisition for performing heretical incantations (most famously, Veronica Franco).[13] Chinese courtesans and their connoisseurs peppered their poetry with accounts of their vulnerability through tales of bondage and sadism inflicted on them.[14] The repetition of violence against courtesans across time and place follows from their tendency to upset social boundaries. For like other women who exert unruly forces and confuse social categories, courtesans have often found themselves subject to brutal efforts at containment.

Even apart from physical violence, representations of courtesans also reveal a profound ambivalence. Attraction to the courtesan, with her uncanny talents and her ability to reject or accept suitors at will, has easily and often slipped into fear and anxiety. Qureshi describes the two-sided representation of the Indian courtesan who is "the cupbearer of the wine of ecstasy but also the killer who wields the dagger of cruelty." Italian courtesans were addressed in poetry using conventional metaphors of death, killing, and arrows, and were represented in Venetian civic iconography as both the dangerous Venus and the redemptive Madonna. Flosi glosses the effects of such paradoxes by reading the (largely anonymous) poems set to music by Costanzo Festa as moving simultaneously between desire and antipathy, a movement that expresses itself at once as veneration and debasement of a usually unnamed "Madonna" or "Donna" (My Lady, or Lady). In an endless cycle of regress, desire leads to fear, apprehension, and loathing, which leads back to desire.

CONVERGENCES AND DIVERGENCES

Ultimately, we aim to achieve a balance between the empirical and the theoretical that will show both continuities among different courtesanships and discontinuities. At the conference that launched this volume authors were at first struck by similarities between their own objects of study and those of others that lay far apart in time and space. Italianists who heard Zeitlin's paper, for instance, immediately noted parallels in the way sung renditions of elevated poetry used tune patterns applicable to different texts, and in the very elevation of singing high lyric verse within a wider calculus of pleasure. In Italy as in China, too, they noted that centers of pleasure were located amid nascent printing industries, suggesting that in both cases the emergence of publication helped spread and commodify the respective cultures of courtesans.

Notwithstanding such epiphanies—indeed wary of them—authors at the final roundtable resolved to be especially attentive to differences among their cases and to the unique aspects of each culture in working toward this book. Since then many important distinctions have emerged, involving art forms and constructions of the body, kinds and functions of space, forms of modernization, and currencies and forms of exchange.

The last of these opens up an especially revealing domain. All of the women we write about received some form of payment for their services, yet nuances in styles of payment and systems of exchange have varied considerably with time and place. Our Italianists, Greek classicists, and Chinese scholar describe economies based on receiving "gifts" from clients rather than money because only the reciprocal relationship thus implied can mark courtesans' services as offerings returned rather than laying bare what could otherwise be regarded as the services of dispassionate sex workers.[15] In early modern Italy, for instance, courtesans were objects of numerous poems and letters dedicated to them as "gifts" and were sometimes named as dedicatees of books or included in catalogs of female praise. Chinese courtesans expected artistic gifts in the form of poems, paintings, and aria lyrics, and viewed direct payment for service as degrading. At least as a general principle, then, gift exchange is a constant among us. Yet in post-independence India (beginning in 1947) Qureshi encounters a rather different kind of exchange: there the patron/client relationship is modeled on a feudal agrarian culture in which a patron listens to the specific music he wants performed. Since the musician stands in as the (serf-)laborer and the patron as the landholder, support for the musician represents the patron's personal "gift." The production of music is more directly and explicitly tied to this vertical system of class and patronage than appears to be the case elsewhere, particularly in improvised performances that act out submission to a royal patron, thereby dramatizing the power dynamics at play.

Courtesans also engage in different kinds of exchange when it comes to more ephemeral currencies. All forms of courtesanship revolve around desire, yet its consequences, workings, and modes of exchange vary widely from case to case. In Italy and China, discussions of love are particularly prominent, for instance, whereas in India and Japan they seem to occupy a more peripheral place. And while Chinese and Italian courtesans both associated love with music, the latter did so in the Renaissance through Neoplatonic notions that were linked directly to the idea of exchange. Neoplatonic thinking conceived the very act of singing as an exchange of body and soul that was incited as song shot out of the singers' mouth and into the listener's ear. Love in this worldview was peculiarly violent and risky, since falling for the wrong woman, or really any woman, might lead to a shattering loss of self. The Italian case is particularly caught up in the problem of soul loss by losing control of the body, and consequently too with compensating for fears of losing bodily control through an elaborate polishing of the bodily surface, with all its gleaming and luxurious planes. At its best love was consummated in a divine but disembodied exchange of spirits, and at its worst it brought about disease and a life-draining loss of the spiritual self.

Closer to the surface in most courtesan cultures (and not far beneath in the Italian one) lay bodily currencies that come in all kinds of raw and smutty forms. In general, the notion of the body as a form of capital was not so appalling for most contemporaries of courtesans, or at least not so strange, as it sounds to us today. Like the ancient Greeks, early modern Italians bought and sold bodies with none of the moral stigma that we attach to such practices. Even the most sacred marriage debt involved a blatant exchange of young women's bodies in which they gave up authority over their body's use as part of the marriage bargain.[16] Counterintuitively, however (at least for Westerners), the body has often allowed courtesans to trade in the spiritual. Strange as it may sound from our post-Cartesian vantage point, the Italian courtesan sat on the cusp between divinely inspired admiration of beauty and base physical attractions for the body. Admiration of the love object often pushed against sacred texts and concepts, as epitomized in the conflation of courtesan and saint in musical compositions that juxtaposed sacred and secular texts. An instance highlighted by Drew Edward Davies involves representations of the courtesan Barbara Salutati that conflate the sacred and the profane by juxtaposing her with erotically charged passages from the Bible and references to the Immaculate Conception, in effect equating the courtesan with a virtuous saint.

In balancing these poles, sixteenth-century Italians are far from unique. Precolonial Indian courtesans operated rather analogously in a culture that sometimes ascribed to sex a spiritual exchange (and that did not malign sex across the board in the way of Christian traditions). The female life force of the sacred Indian devadasi could render her extraordinarily powerful because she literally took God, and other men who partook of God, into her body and incorporated that divine force into her own fluids, thus inspiring a sacred transformation.[17] Without the Christian contempt for the body, the devadasi is indeed a temptress, yet her sexual attractions and potency are tantamount to godliness. In a Chinese variation on such transformations, the Bodhisattva Guanyin manifests herself in various stories as a beautiful young prostitute who has sex with men in order to free them from desire.[18] A similar situation may or may not have existed in ancient Greece, as the existence of a group of sacred prostitutes who would link sexual exchange to temples, rituals, cults, and worship of Aphrodite is still debated among classical scholars. The most we can say of these women is that ancient Greece saw no real separation between sacred and secular and that accordingly there is evidence for very real connections between courtesans and Aphrodite as their goddess-patron.[19]

The linkage of courtesans to temples brings to the fore another important point of convergences and divergences, namely the array of spaces that courtesans have moved in and out of, including urban centers, salons, theaters, and boudoirs. Pre-colonial Indian classification systems differentiated ganika from devadasi according to their places of practice—the former in the royal courts and the latter in the temples.[20] Despite intersections with the sacred, none of the other courtesans we study have such explicit ties to religious institutions as do devadasi. In a very different use of space, late nineteenth- and early twentieth-century tawa'if managed and organized urban salons that enjoyed increasing prominence. Serving a feudal-mercantile elite of merchants and colonial functionaries, these salons created the illusion of elite gatherings in stark contrast with male-managed stage performances.[21] Italian courtesans also performed at elite domestic salons for exclusive audiences, but they did not have the direct and totalizing patron/client relationships that characterize the tawa'if's salons. In fact, with the first waning of Italian court culture, which took place concurrently with the rise of commercial opera in the mid-seventeenth century, skilled female performers were pushed toward the public stage. In India, to the contrary, the postcolonial, modernizing process did not take place until the mid-twentieth century. When it did, the quasi-feudal patronage system for courtesans entered a phase of rapid demise. But a new kind of postmodern court, created through the global market of grassroots cassette industries and the festivalization phenomenon of which Maciszewski writes, has now emerged for those descendants of courtesans who still make their traditional art, allowing at least some tawa'if to speak in the public sphere to an extraordinarily wide audience.

Chinese and Japanese courtesans differ markedly from one another in the spaces they have inhabited. Although early modern China had pleasure districts in every city, Chinese courtesans were not confined to particular spaces or pleasure quarters but moved in and out of private homes, where they entertained at parties and celebrations, and even went on tours on which they entertained lucky guests on luxury barges. In Japan, by contrast, both courtesans and geisha have worked within carefully confined pleasure quarters. In the Edo period (1603–1867), connoisseurs of courtesans gained access to them in the Yoshiwara (or "New Yoshiwara")—the so-called Floating World—through a long boat journey that enacted a ritual transmigration to a space both physically and metaphorically far away from the real world of the city, and hence a transformation of their visitors.[22] In this alternate reality men escaped normal time as well as space. As Screech explains, the hour 11:00 p.m. literally replayed itself so that a man could arrive in the Yoshiwara at precisely the same moment he had left the city center. Modern geisha, though perhaps not as bound up with a time-out-of-time experience, still work in five very specific districts of Kyoto that constitute little spacetimes unto themselves. Revealingly, those geisha who work at hot springs resorts, located in rural areas and thus totally outside the confines of urban geisha districts, are not considered geisha at all, nor even courtesans, but essentially prostitutes, underscoring how crucial the space of practice is to categorizing geisha.

Perhaps the most striking contrasts among the authors here emerge from issues of modernization, the end of colonialism, and the emergence of globalization as inflected by technology—social transformations that have eroded those class structures that sustained courtesan cultures in the past. The case of Korea is instructive. There the twentieth-century process of modernization, first under the influence of Japanese colonialism and then in the thrall of bourgeois post-Korean-war ideology, led to a bifurcation of the gisaeng—the professional singers closest to our definition of courtesans—into two classes: one a respectable class of desexualized state-sponsored performers and the other a lower class of escorts and prostitutes. This process suggests how interdependent gisaeng culture was with rigid vertical hierarchies and related pre-modern forms of categorization and social structure (and how interdependent it has continued to be in its latter-day transformations). The case of northern India echoes that of Korea. Before Indian independence tawa'if participated actively, as we have seen, in elite entertainments that emanated from feudal and mercantile domains. In this the tawa'if depended on two hierarchically opposed kinds of males (as stressed by Qureshi): elite patrons on the one hand and the socially inferior but highly authoritative professional male musicians who taught and accompanied courtesans on the other. At the same time the freedom of these tawa'if from patrilineal kinship constraints granted them a prominence and influence that were off-limits to most other women. Yet the erasure, or virtual erasure, of tawa'if and other kinds of Indian courtesans by bourgeois nationalist movements makes it clear how thoroughly predicated their marginal lives were on existent class structures, with all their attendant political and economic corollaries, and goes a long way toward explaining why their very survival is so precarious nowadays.

In their much-altered incarnations, both tawa'if and gisaeng have been involved in efforts to revive their art forms, efforts that are aided in turn by the mass media and by national art agencies. Indian tawa'if still exist, but a number of them now perform at festivals organized by a nongovernmental organization (NGO) that presents otherwise denigrated women on the stage in mainstream venues, thus attempting to mitigate the negative associations with the sex trade and with a lower-caste status that plague them elsewhere in life. Except for a very few who live as artists, tawa'if, lacking the intense training that went with their ancestors, are often forced to live as prostitutes in hazardous red-light districts. The Korean gisaeng, on the other hand, have essentially disappeared, while recent years have seen the emergence of women with former gisaeng ties presenting traditional art forms on the concert stage. Also important on the revivalist front are geisha entertainments, in some instances state-subsidized, which, given the norms of Japanese society, continue to fill needs not traditionally met by wives. Yet as Downer points out, geisha working under state subsidies have been turned into mere civil servants who give public performances in exchange for grants, acquiring in the process a bourgeois status that erases the mystique and enigma that otherwise made them enchanting. Who or what, our authors ask, is the postmodern patron? How does the patron of today differ from the one of old? And how does postmodern patronage affect its object?

One answer lies in the domain of cultural tourism. Postcolonial courtesans and their heirs have often found themselves packaged up as tourist spectacles and mobilized for the sake of nationalistic and commercial agendas. Such forms of tourism are not altogether new. We see parallels as far back as the Venetian Renaissance, where courtesans stood as symbols of the city's luxury and glory for the many foreigners who went there. The travelers' albums that feature in Rosenthal's essay reflect the fascination of their northern European owners with Italian material culture, but particularly with women's intricate garments and presumably what lay beneath them; and they show us how such fascination was disseminated and circulated to others who might later join the travel circuit.

What is different in current-day Japan and Korea is that geisha and gisaeng, respectively, have been transformed (differently in each case) into guardians of authentic traditions, though often without the institutional and social contexts that gave rise to their arts in the first place. Tours and vouchers for geisha performances and sightseeing, or for performances by descendants of gisaeng, can easily be secured by Western tourists surfing the web for flavors of the east.[23] In the case of geisha, the organization and control of such encounters translate into a glorification of geisha's artistic practices as national treasures by a state whose relationship to them over past centuries has long been Janus-faced, sometimes elevating and sometimes debasing them. Indeed, Miho Matsugu argues that while Kawabata's 1930s novel *Snow Country* makes the rural geisha a symbol of the beauty of imperial Japan, its enchantment with her is colored with contempt. The Korean case might be considered parallel in some respects. As Joshua Pilzer shows, gisaeng have played crucial roles in the institutionalization of art forms in South Korea. Trained in colonial-era gisaeng schools, gisaeng were retitled "researchers" or "performers" in the postcolonial era, working both at national cultural centers and private institutions of art. But the symbolism has not always worked to their advantage. The 1960s saw the emergence of a sex tourism industry modeled on gisaeng parties that attracted to Korea hundreds of thousands of primarily lower- and middle-class Japanese men who bought sex-tour packages at travel agencies in Japan. And a survey of the same time period shows that about 60 percent of all sex workers in the industry operated near American military bases.[24]

THE ESSAYS

The essays that follow are grouped in six parts. The first part focuses on the central issues of "Spectacle and Performance," taking into account daily life performances, participation in traditional arts, and spectacles of the courtesan's very existence. Davidson raises the curtain on an ancient Greek courtroom in the fourth century B.C., where the courtesan Phryne, skilled in the arts of rhetoric, music, and games, stands accused of impiety. The suspicions she arouses teeter paradoxically on the brink of a near-sacred awe, as Phryne is reviled for having introduced a new god but venerated as an attendant of Aphrodite. Revealingly, her acquittal rides on an abrupt dramatic act: the spectacle of clothes being suddenly torn from her breast by her very defender—an image, Davidson shows, that has been reworked and judged repeatedly in assessing the courtesan throughout the millennia. In a virtuosic melding of history and historiography, Davidson uses this story and its many reworkings to take an intimate look at the hetaera's arts and personal circumstances. Deciphering the nitty-gritty of the historically distant hetaera also leads him to discuss the gift economy in which she circulated and the ways of functioning that differentiated her not just from other women but young men and boys, all of whom were among those who participated in some kind of sex trade.

Writing about the Italian Renaissance, Margaret Rosenthal concentrates on a single but rich genre of evidence, the manuscript of miniature portraits called the "album amicorum" (album of friends), using it to tease out ways in which images of Venetian courtesans were constructed and circulated in touristic representations. In the process she elucidates the daily performances of a courtesan's life. Courtesans, she shows, manipulated gender and class boundaries by making use of Venice's active position in an international trade in luxury goods, a marketplace of used goods, and a street life that allowed courtesans to display their wares both singly and in groups. They did not merely mimic styles of Venetian noblewomen, she argues, but cultivated collective identities and developed individual styles as they selected clothes from a variety of fashions. Because so many Venetians had access to second-hand markets, clothes were deceptive tools for purposes of differentiating social groups. In making use of them, Venetian courtesans became performative prototypes for fashionable women—a problem for a hierarchical, status-conscious society founded in patriarchal marriage conventions, with sumptuary laws that tried to protect class boundaries and a civic ideology founded in shows of decorum and stability.

Turning toward performance in the more traditional, and literal, sense, Zeitlin's essay explores music-making of the *ji* in the late Ming and early Qing periods (ca. 1580–1700) of imperial China. Zeitlin calls on a wide range of recalcitrant evidence, including literary and visual sources, to show how the courtesan learned music, what she sang, and how her music was received by others. The parallels between Chinese and Italian courtesans (noted above) are among the most striking in the volume, with their shared emphasis on a refined style of improvised singing that featured elaborate ornamentation and often involved fitting words to preexistent tunes. Both cultures also reveal blurry lines between actresses and courtesans. Some Chinese courtesans participated in musical theater (or "opera") despite the more widely held preference for solo or "pure" singing of songs that ranged from theatrical to nontheatrical, art song to popular. Yet whatever the style or milieu of the song, the courtesan's art lay in fitting the words to a tune, or "realizing" it (*du qu*). Zeitlin argues that the best courtesans were instrumental in transmitting and generating popular songs as arias. In her coda ("the value of withdrawal"), she demonstrates that courtesans' arias could become not just farewell keepsakes given to departing lovers, but metonyms for the courtesans themselves.

Part II, a case study on "The Courtesan's Voice in Early Modern Italy," includes four writings that function in essence as a single extended essay, offered by participants in Feldman's seminar at the University of Chicago. It will be useful to review some of the historical backdrop of the Italian setting before glossing the essays individually. Courtesans in sixteenth-century Italy, as symbols of elegance and sexual excess, were identified above all with Venice. Fascination with them increased along with travel to the lagoon republic, where foreigners witnessed the so-called honest courtesan (*cortigiana onesta*) in her natural habitat, remarking with surprise that her artistic prowess enabled her to rise to the highest echelons of the nobility. For both foreigners and locals, courtesans sat at the intersection of well-nurtured myths about the republic and its sometimes harsh realities. A center of technological innovation, trade with the east, and print culture, Venice made an ideal marketplace for courtesanship. Unlike most other Italian city states, which were dominated by courts, Venice was run by an oligarchy that formed a broad and flexible patronage base. That in turn allowed individual courtesans to flourish by moving between class lines, at the same time as they thrived on the city's penchant for daily civic performances (formal and informal), becoming paragons for how nonnoble citizens might raise their class level.

Looking beyond Venice to the Italian peninsula as a whole, we find a time and place of massive economic and political unrest. The new vigor of cities and commercial centers led to a new concentration of wealth not just in noble hands but those of citizen bankers and merchants (sometimes foreign). The concurrent vitality of Renaissance humanism brought with it a renewed commitment to the art of self-fashioning, which placed great importance on artistic practices and arts of manners. Castiglione's famous *Il cortegiano* of 1528 exemplifies the investment of the noble class (and those imitating it) in artistic proficiency, and thus helps clarify the courtesans' tendency, and capacity, to emulate the nobility.[25] While courtesans did not generally perform at court per se, they certainly performed with men who did, and "played" with ways of performing at court.

In addition to the social and economic circumstances that helped courtesans flourish, the particular situation of women in this transformative historical moment created particularly fertile ground for their livelihood. The new mercantilism worked progressively to exclude women from the labor force, pushing them back into the domestic sphere.[26] This, combined with economic crisis, led to the tightening of the marriage market noted earlier and a concomitant dowry inflation that made marriage contracts harder and harder to come by, thus rendering courtesanship a necessary course for some. Intercourse with those courtesans, both social and sexual, in turn helped young men make their transitions into marriages, which for noble males did not usually occur until later in life and then only for political and economic reasons.

Let us return, then, to the courtesan's voice as it emerges in part II of this volume. Here the authors work collectively with a variety of evidence in attempting to make some preliminary reconstructions of a virtually lost singing tradition. In these reconstructions, the voice is a central locus of the courtesan's daily performance, both rhetorical and material. Situating the courtesan within dominant Petrarchan and Neoplatonic discourses, Feldman explores the disjoining of physical and corporeal love in contemporaneous writings and the courtesan's refusal to accept that partition. For Feldman, this refusal was not unconnected with the courtesan's voice as an instrument of social and artistic performance, especially with the strictures that accompanied the so-called Counter-Reformation, since, like the voices of other women of her time, hers was knotty at best. A mercurial, dangerous faculty, the voice gave her access to a whole affective realm with overwhelming powers of attraction, yet it also required her own defense.

Feldman's project, like Zeitlin's, involves proposals for reconstructing an unwritten improvisatory tradition from an eclectic and elusive collection of sources. Piecing together snippets from published partbooks and songs in print and manuscript, she reveals some of the ways in which courtesans would have used preexistent melodic phrases and harmonic patterns to sing their poetry (and that of others)—performances that might have been heard from the well-known courtesan Tullia d'Aragona or the free-living *virtuosa* Gaspara Stampa.

Each of the three essays that follow opens out from Feldman's in a different direction. Building on her elucidation of the courtesan's literal and figurative voice, De Rycke considers how a set of four-voice polyphonic compositions, published in Venice by the composer Perissone Cambio in 1547 and dedicated to Gaspara Stampa, might conceal hidden solo traditions. To test the supposition, she transcribes pieces from Perissone's collection from their all-vocal published forms to versions for voice and lute, as Stampa and her courtesan cognates might have done. In a related move, De Rycke reads Perissone's dedication to Stampa for the Petrarchan conventions and metaphors that Feldman explicates by concentrating on a triangle between Perissone, Stampa, and music itself. Love bonds the three together in a nexus symbolized by the perfect cosmic harmony of music. As such the book itself represents the kind of gift exchange discussed above that runs through so many courtesan cultures.

Another sense of voice is treated by Flosi, who encounters matters of address in a large corpus of texts that survive in the madrigal settings of Costanzo Festa from the 1520s and 1530s. In these texts, courtesans appear in a variety of roles: as speaker, subject, object, and even author. Many of the texts react to the courtesans' powers of seduction through the now-familiar dynamic of desire and fear. For Flosi this dynamic is partly caught up in the sheer sounds of the courtesan's voice—but only partly. The critic must also move beyond it to focus on both the metaphoric voices that courtesans are assigned by male poets and the voices that courtesans assume in their own verse. Analyzing various economies of literary exchange, Flosi's essay works with the trope most common to the Petrarchan conventions of Renaissance lyric:[27] love as a paradoxical experience of burning and freezing, adoring and resenting. Like Zeitlin (and Courtney Quaintance later in the volume), Flosi finds such paradoxes repeated not just within given lyrics but across the admixture of elevated and bawdy diction that marks different lyrics across an unwieldy corpus.

Davies works with ambivalent representations of the courtesan's voice as well, but explores indirect mediations of it in repertories for theater and solo harpsichord, as well as in paintings. His discussion of paintings demonstrates through iconographic evidence the role of chordal pieces in courtesans' music, where courtesans could either sing top parts with amateur men on the lower ones or easily adapt such pieces to solo song. Dealing largely with footprints of vernacular traditions, Davies's work supports claims made by Flosi (as well as Guido Ruggiero and Quaintance who follow) that the social register of Italian courtesans was routinely and ambiguously represented as both high and low. Related to such ambiguities of register are the dichotomies of sacred/profane, noted earlier in this introduction, which characterized the courtesan. In a portrait attributed to Domenico Puligo that Davies discusses, the courtesan Barbara Salutati—lover of Niccolò Machiavelli—sings from a partbook that juxtaposes elevated church music with popular street tunes—a contrast, parallel to that of high/low registers, that denotes a woman of many contradictions.

Part III, "Power, Gender, and the Body," explores how various instances of courtesanship depended uniquely on local constructions of gender, the body, and power, and the manipulations by courtesans of those much disputed categories. Srinivasan begins by introducing the precolonial Indian courtesan, situated in opposition to the sexually controlled, uneducated wife. Whereas the two prominent kinds of courtesans, the ganika and the devadasi, were both guardians of important cultural traditions, traditional Hindu constructions of womanhood designated virtuous women as wives whose usefulness lay in their role as procreators and participants in religious ceremonies. Citing a variety of history and fable, Srinivasan nevertheless finds the courtesan's sexuality to be a formidable instrument of power. She argues that the devadasi's power in particular emerged at least partly from her body, since Hindu ascetics required the intervention of a seductive woman for the crucial release of sexual desire and seed.

Like Feldman, Gordon perceives Italian song as trafficking in the immaterial aspects of the spirit as well as the material ones of the body, but provides a specific physiological grounding for the material body in Galenic medical theories. Showing their link to Neoplatonic theories that similarly interweave body and spirit, Gordon argues that the seemingly "immaterial" side of the courtesan—manifested above all in song—was itself material. Contemporary experiences of the bodily mechanics of song, love, and desire turned courtesans' songs into metonyms for their sensuality, located centrally in the actual voice. For Gordon, the metonym was not simply an imagined one of spirit but was truly embodied as matter. For this reason song could serve as embodied sexual and symbolic capital. Yet here too song was dangerous, as her account of the tradition of love treatises (*trattati d'amore*) makes clear. Song could conspire with love in robbing victims of reason, their authors warned, in the worst of cases sending victims into dire states of erotomania.

Quaintance's essay explores the consequences of such dangers in the masses of invective and satire that courtesans provoked from men. In her account, men were implicated in a prodigious power dynamic played out in defamatory texts both public and private, published and unpublished. Male poets, she argues, used the topos of the courtesan to negotiate anxieties about their own social and economic status and their own sexual prowess, each of which affected their positions in a larger struggle for power. In great measure these struggles were fueled by the fact that courtesans in the city were newly able to select clients and dictate appointment times, the more so as their status rose, thus posing challenges to male honor. The problem manifested itself through a recasting of old courtly tropes, codified by Petrarch in the fourteenth century, in the partly new forms of satiric verse, poetic debate, lyric madrigals, and even satiric catalogs and chronicles. Implicated in this phenomenon, much as Gordon emphasizes, is the courtesan's own body, a body that again is at once desired and feared as the cause of men's disease and decline. Ironically, desire for the courtesan's seductive powers causes antipathy; yet as she is defamed she emerges from male texts as a woman who is both deeply alluring and powerful enough to refuse male demands—and so the cycle repeats.

Moving backwards in history, Faraone explores the ways in which Greek hetaerae appropriated male modes and practices in order to accrue power to themselves. In this, he differs from Davidson, who sees in the hetaera a person who is "all girl." But Faraone and Davidson agree that courtesans *can* represent themselves, contrary to some laments in classical studies, even if they arrive at this view through different means. Faraone focuses on courtesans' coopting of the arts of rhetoric, music, and magic, which are otherwise associated almost exclusively with men, and using them as means to assert their own autonomy. Unlike other women in Athens, courtesans could control the production and perhaps even reception of their images. To this end, Faraone focuses on three different kinds of male arts pursued by courtesans: male magic used to drive a young man from his home; a game called *kottabos* that involved the courtesan in an accompanying range of male gestures performed at symposia; and male verbal wit of the rhetorical and poetic kinds.

We next move to an excursus on Japanese geisha (part IV), who are explicitly *not* courtesans but who, as noted above, live lives that parallel those of many women who were. Most pointedly, geisha are women who are always performing themselves into existence. It is this involvement, combined with Japanese traditional arts and their consort with men of power, that relates them historically to courtesans in other cultures.

Yet geisha have always existed in a category separate from courtesans. In ancient imperial Japan up to about the tenth century, the imperial court recognized the skills of female performers in whom they saw shamanistic powers to communicate with gods and spirits, recognizing them as professionals and assigning them special privileges. By the late tenth century they had their own households, often matrilineal, and were seen as part of the court—courtesans, in effect. But the advent in the thirteenth century of the samurai, who viewed courtesans as sexual labor available for commercial exploitation, led to a steep drop in their status and eventually to their being enclosed within special, socially disdained quarters of the city. By the eighteenth century, women in these quarters started to specialize in sex, and at the same time geisha were consolidated as a class that took over the artistic role left behind by women who by then were clearly sex workers.

Downer opens by providing a map of the geisha's household hierarchy and demography, stressing that whatever the rest of the world may think, geisha view themselves as artists, not prostitutes, call girls, or mistresses. While geisha used to be sold into service by their parents, she notes, girls now become geisha because they are attracted to the chic romance of a traditional lifestyle and the status as a cultural symbol that such a lifestyle carries with it. But paradoxically, geisha these days attend less and less to the arts. Good shamisen players, for example, are hard to come by, and male clients no longer participate in the geisha's arts as they once did. The institutional contexts and social practices that would enable female entertainment to flourish as it did in the past, as something highly rarified, elite, and cultivated, no longer exist. It is largely because of their appearance and lifestyle and the traditions they represent that today's geisha serve as national symbols, but without cultivating their traditional arts as intensively as in the past—hence without the very dimension that once gave substance to their style of living.

In response to Downer, Matsugu leafs through the history that has led to the attenuation Downer points up and offers an explanation for the geisha's current-day resistance to being stigmatized as a prostitute. Geisha in this explanation are more connected historically to the sex trade than Downer would allow. And Matsugu finds more insidious forces at work than does Downer, both in the geisha's historical forms and in her current one. According to this account, the geisha's current status as a national symbol evolved only gradually. At various historical moments geisha did brush up against sex work, becoming entertainers who were often exploited and oppressed both by clients and by the state. Only in the past century or so, she writes, did geisha become exclusively prestigious, such that they could *represent* the state. Thus unlike

Downer, who soft-pedals the geisha's involvement in sex in deference to their own claims about themselves, Matsugu stresses that sex work was acknowledged, at least intermittently, in previous centuries as part of the geisha's trade. Among her pieces of evidence she notes that some local governments in the late nineteenth century required that geisha be tested for syphilis. And she underscores that by the 1930s geisha had become instrumental in empire-building, bringing in additional tax revenues and helping to stimulate local economies. Taking the argument up to more recent times, Matsugu points out that geisha have helped modernize and democratize male pleasure, since an expanded group of men emerged in the post-war economy of bourgeois Japan for whom being able to buy an evening of geisha services was a symbolic as well as a practical act. In this context geisha also turned into what Matsugu calls "tokens of authenticity," signaled by the special access required to enter their "flower-and-willow" world. The elite traveler of modernist, interior sensibilities depicted in Kawabata's 1930s autobiographical novel *Snow Country* is swept into a newly beautiful, natural, and sublimely authentic Japan through the poor geisha woman whom he scrutinizes at a hot springs resort.

Discussions of geisha as fantasies of Japanese and Western men lead into part V, devoted to "Fantasies of the Courtesan." The two essays in this section bring to the fore issues surrounding representations and experiences of courtesans that are only touched on elsewhere in the volume. Taking our discussions of Japan back to the Edo Period, Screech explores how men who accessed the female courtesan quarter of the Yoshiwara—the Floating World—were transformed in preparation for their visits through a long journey. Participants in what he calls a "culture of proleptic expectation," they exited everyday life in their transit to the Yoshiwara and on their return to the city were prepared for reentry into normal life. Rather than looking at "real" history, Screech focuses on a male imaginary of the Yoshiwara's mythical world as he takes us through a poetics of the journey via pictures and poems about it. The markers of passage exist in the landscape of the traveler/client: castle turrets, ferries, bridges (the famous Willow Bridge), rivers, embankments, trees, temples, and shrines, each with its own history, memories, associations, symbolism, and meanings. Crucial to understanding the journey was the quarter's prehistory. It had been created in 1657 four kilometers from the city center in a gesture of shogunate "displeasure" that sequestered courtesans in a quarter situated among other places that were deemed impure. Once within the Yoshiwara, however, things were different, for there men attained transcendence and a temporary deliverance from normal time. Screech gives a lyrical account of how the Yoshiwara, and transit to it, posed an alternate but transient reality for the men who frequented it—a temporary "fleeing from home" to a place that, by contrast, was all too permanent for the women who inhabited the district.

Ruggiero approaches fantasy from a different angle—that of positive and negative fantasies about the courtesan's power over men and the story of one woman whose power caused all kinds of trouble. Ruggiero is less interested here in the real lives of courtesans than in how they were imagined and what conflicting imaginings meant for them and those who consorted with them. Reading a varied array of historical documents and literary texts, he shows—reminiscent of Feldman, Quaintance, Qureshi, and others—that the courtesan was both a desired, revered luxury object and an abject dangerous prostitute. His account begins with a microhistory: a legal clash between the Florentine courtesan Giuliana Napolitana and a young Venetian nobleman named Luigi Dolfin. The two were unmatched in inborn status but equal enough in effective status that the courtesan was able to get away with refusing the nobleman his prepaid sex, even in a court of law. Ruggiero uses the tale of Giuliana and Luigi to explore how attraction for the courtesan became fear which then caused her to turn into the "the demeaning, dishonoring whore—a dream/nightmare that haunted the imagination of the Renaissance." In this instance, fear was exacerbated by the courtesan's ability to select and reject the best men and, perhaps even more importantly, by her potential to spark a mad passion that could rob men of their souls. Like the early modern courtesan of Gordon's essay, Ruggiero's can cause soul loss and with it the dissolution of the self.

Part VI, the final section, "Courtesans in the Postcolony," interrogates the contested position of courtesans in Korea and India after colonization when the social structures that had previously held courtesan cultures in place were quickly dissolving. "Postcolony" in our conception denotes a generalized set of sociopolitical conditions accompanied by new idioms and economics of patronage and with them a new imaginary. Pilzer begins the section by considering the role of South Korea's emergent modern sex-and-entertainment industry. Using bibliographic resources and fieldwork, he outlines the historical conditions for the social transformation of gisaeng institutions and the concept of the gisaeng over the course of the twentieth century, glancing briefly back to the Joseon Dynasty beginning in the fourteenth century. Especially critical in the modern phase of this history is the colonial era of Japanese occupation (1910–45), which saw the government disband support of the gisaeng. After that moment, he argues, their roles were split in two, both of which functioned ironically to supply public sites of entertainment for Korea's colonists. One role involved their giving theater performances as part of a new culture of mass media, and the other involved entertaining colonial elites in upscale restaurants and private homes as part of a private room culture. Turning to the postcolonial era, Pilzer then suggests that in more recent times gisaeng have evolved into several discrete entities, including pop performer, sex worker, and national icon. Particularly revealing among the last of these is the revivalist movement of traditional arts produced by women with former gisaeng ties who, rather like geisha, have now become spectacles of national culture on the concert stage.

Our last two essays explore courtesans in modern-day India. Qureshi takes as her axis of inquiry the nationalist bourgeois reform movement that followed Indian independence in 1947, virtually erasing courtesans and their traditions. Where women had previously been the bearers of classical singing traditions, their music was quickly banned as scandalous from All India radio, and in 1952 the Princely States that had supported courtesans up until then were abolished. The salon thereafter functioned as a replacement for the court. Qureshi notes that economically and socially thriving courtesan establishments that were actually run by women endured for some time in northern India. Why then, she asks, did their art and "agency" gradually disappear—and what does this say about how real their agency was all along? To answer these questions, Qureshi expands a Marxist mode-of-production approach in order to "factor in" gender and the quasi-mercantile dimension of a once feudally based socioeconomic scene. Focusing on personal experiences in 1984 with the salon in Lucknow in the feudal heartland of northern India during its twentieth-century heyday, Qureshi demonstrates that courtesan houses were organized along loosely matrilineal lines that always included a prosperous senior woman. In her encounters with those houses, Qureshi freely admits her own complicity in a male patriarchal order by acknowledging her position as a middle-class respectable married woman and a "connoisseur" of Indian music. But she adds a strenuous voice of support for the women she studies too, stressing their difficulties in encountering (and countering) a staunchly patriarchal society and their spirited enactment of rule over their present-day "court"—one in which gesture and improvisation in the arts are key to their success.

In the final essay, Maciszewski examines the adaptation by a group of north Indian tawa'if to changing systems of patronage in the twenty-first century, an adaptation largely grounded in music as a tool for empowerment. Where Qureshi foregrounds the difference between herself and the women she has studied, Maciszewski writes more from a position of solidarity. Her fieldwork centers on the NGO Guria Sanstham "doll help/service collective" dedicated to helping various classes and castes of tawa'if as well as prostitutes—terms that Guria conflates in significant and problematic ways. Guria also serves as an institution for preserving regional performance traditions through a process of festivalization. Maciszewski, through her ethnography of performances in Guria, shows that women from vestigial courtesan communities provide meta-commentaries to and about their extended community. Using the genre of oral literary criticism, they pose challenges to existing social orders. At the same time she finds that surviving courtesan cultures in Muzzafar, Bihar (northern India) display fascinating parallels to these processes, processes she traces through three generations of hereditary singers in a single family, the eldest of whom (recently deceased) practiced a classical and semi-classical, as well as traditional regional repertoire that still evoked the late feudal patronage of her earlier career days. Maciszewski thus shows that the feudal base of courtesan culture, which was central for Srinivasan and palpable still in Qureshi's early ethnography, emerges even in our own day as a vestigial but nevertheless powerful presence.

Each of these final essays confronts remnants of living courtesan cultures in places where sociopolitical structures have enabled them to endure far longer than in Europe. They are each uniquely inflected, revealing in their transformations, and remarkable in their persistence.

It is fitting that this volume should close with the voices of living courtesans and their heirs. They are the historical present of an always elusive past. Far from allowing us to deny the chasm of historical distance, they draw attention to it even as they also suggest the possibility of meaningful relationships across time and space. Moreover, they insist, through their vitality and their very survival, on why we should listen to them as we attend to echoes of their courtesan sisters—because all of them are real people who produced and inspired remarkable art, and for whom art was a way out of hardship, subjugation, and even cruelty. This is the lesson to be learned from the conversations that authors like Downer, Pilzer, Qureshi, and Maciszewski have had with their interlocutors. In those conversations we find resonances between women whose present-day court is made up of media and technology and women whose courts died long before anything like a mass media was constructed. And those resonances tell us that the grand telos of mainstream history, so dependent on hegemonies and texts, will not do, that such a telos is more apt to smother voices like theirs than to listen to them. Meanwhile those women who still survive make public the open secret of the courtesan, whose lives and works have animated a variety of cultures for millennia.

Notes

1. The concert by the Newberry Consort subsequently became the basis for the Italian Renaissance cuts on the companion website included with this volume. See the appendix.

2. For more particulars on these, see Feldman, Davidson, Zeitlin, and the Indianist trio Srinivasan, Qureshi, and Maciszewski, all in this volume.

3. An important memoir is that of Cora Pearl (1837–86), published as *Grand Horizontal: The Erotic Memoirs of a Passionate Lady*, ed. William Blatchford (New York: Stein and Day, 1983).

4. The number 64 runs throughout the *Kamasutra* and connects with number symbolism in other ancient Indian texts. The entire text has sixty-four sections (book 1, chap. 1), there are sixty-four arts to be studied (book 1, chap. 3) and sixty-four arts of love (book 2, chap. 2). On the slipperiness of the number 64 and its mythical connections to other sacred texts and myths see the introduction by Wendy Doniger and Sudhir Kakar to Vatsyayana Mallanaga, *Kamasutra*, trans. Wendy Doniger and Sudhir Kakar (Oxford: Oxford University Press, 2002), xxi–xxv.

5. Paul S. Ropp, "Ambiguous Images of Courtesan Culture in Late Imperial China," in *Writing Women in Late Imperial China*, ed. Ellen Widmer and Kang-i-Sung (Stanford: Stanford University Press, 1997), 21.

6. Extensively cultivated as a scholarly category in feminist writings, the voice has generated histories of its production, use, and intangibility, analyses of its psychoanalytic status, interpretations of its relationship to desire, body, identity, musical ineffability, and so on. See, for instance, Carolyn Abbate, *Unsung Voices: Opera and Musical Narrative in the Nineteenth Century* (Princeton: Princeton University Press, 1991); Vladimir Jankélévitch, *Music and the Ineffable*, trans. Carolyn Abbate (Princeton: Princeton University Press, 2003); Shemeem Burney Abbas, *The Female Voice in Sufi Ritual: Devotional Practices of Pakistan and India*, foreword by Elizabeth Warnock Fernea (Austin: University of Texas Press, 2002); Ellen T. Harris, *Handel as Orpheus: Voice and Desire in the Chamber Cantatas* (Cambridge, MA: Harvard University Press, 2001); Michel Poizat, *The Angel's Cry: Beyond the Pleasure Principle in Opera*, trans. Arthur Denner (Ithaca: Cornell University Press, 1992); idem, *Variations sur la voix* (Paris: Anthropos, 1998); Casey Man Kong Lum, *In Search of a Voice: Karaoke and the Construction of Identity in Chinese America* (Mahwah, NJ: L. Erlbaum Associates, 1996); Susan J. Leonardi and Rebecca A. Pope, *The Diva's Mouth: Body, Voice, Prima Donna Politics* (New Brunswick, NJ: Rutgers University Press, 1996); and *Embodied Voices: Representing Female Vocality in Western Culture*, ed. Leslie C. Dunn and Nancy A. Jones (Cambridge: Cambridge University Press, 1994).

7. A provisional exception is Sheila Schonbrun's "Ambiguous Artists: Music-Making among Italian Renaissance Courtesans (with Particular Reference to Tullia of Aragon, Gaspara Stampa, and Veronica Franco)" (D.M.A. thesis, City University of New York, 1998).

8. The film is *Dangerous Beauty* (Warner Studios, 1998), 111 minutes, directed by Mar-

shall Herskovitz and starring Catherine McCormack, Jacqueline Bisset, Naomi Watts, and Rufus Sewell. It is very loosely based on Margaret F. Rosenthal, *The Honest Courtesan: Veronica Franco, Citizen and Writer of Sixteenth-Century Venice* (University of Chicago Press, 1992). The film was released in England as *The Honest Courtesan* (1999).

9. On courtesans' magic see Christopher A. Faraone, *Talismans and Trojan Horses: Guardian Statues in Ancient Greek Myth and Ritual* (Oxford: Oxford University Press, 1992) and especially *Ancient Greek Love Magic* (Cambridge, MA: Harvard University Press, 1999), as well as Guido Ruggiero, *Binding Passions: Tales of Magic, Marriage, and Power from the End of the Renaissance* (Oxford: Oxford University Press, 1993).

10. See Ann Rosalind Jones, *The Currency of Eros: Women's Love Lyric in Europe, 1540–1620* (Bloomington: University of Indiana Press, 1990).

11. See Cecilia Segawa Seigle, *Yoshiwara: The Glittering World of the Japanese Courtesan* (Honolulu: University of Hawaii Press, 1993).

12. Veena Talwar Oldenburg, "Lifestyle as Resistance: The Case of the Courtesans of Lucknow," *Feminist Studies* 16 (1990): 259–88.

13. See Rosenthal, *The Honest Courtesan*, chap. 4, "Denouncing the Courtesan."

14. Ropp, "Ambiguous Images," 30–41. More recently, instances have even been reported of geisha suffering violence at the hands of their clients.

15. The Chinese case (as well as others) made room for some monetary exchange even if the strong tendency was to try to disguise it. See below, Zeitlin, chap. 3, near n. 25, and chap. Quaintance, chap. 10, near n. 21. For distinctions among aspects of the gift see Seneca, *Moral Essays [= Dialogues]: De Beneficiis*, vol. 1, trans. John W. Basore, Loeb Classical Library (Cambridge, MA; Harvard University Press), who understands in the gift a threefold ensemble of distinct acts that comprises giving, receiving, and reciprocation.

16. See Ruggiero, chap. 15, n. 10.

17. See Srinivasan, chap. 8, 169.

18. Chün-fan Yu, *Kuan-yin: The Chinese Transformation of Avalokiteśvara* (New York: Columbia University Press, 2001), 424 and *passim*.

19. See Davidson, chap. 1.

20. Cf. Srinivasan, chap. 8.

21. See Qureshi, chap. 17, 319.

22. On the technical term for the Yoshiwara as New Yoshiwara in the period under consideration see further in Screech, chap. 14, 255.

23. See, for instance, http://gojapan.about.com/cs/japanesegeisha/a/geisha3.htm and http://japanvisitor.com/jc/gt.html (both accessed January 29, 2005).

24. Geisha too were useful for the Japanese military, who relied on their services to boost morale. See Matsugu, chap. 13, 245.

25. Baldasar Castiglione, *The Book of the Courtier* (1528), trans. George Bull (New York: Penguin Classics, 1986).

26. See especially Samuel K. Cohn, *Women in the Streets: Essays on Sex and Power in Renaissance Italy* (Baltimore: Johns Hopkins University Press, 1996); Christiane Klapisch-Zuber, *Women, Family, and Ritual in Renaissance Italy*, trans. Lydia Cochrane (Chicago: University of Chicago Press, 1987); and Jutta Gisela Sperling, *Convents and the Body Politic in Late Renaissance Venice* (Chicago: University of Chicago Press, 1999), 3.

27. Cf. Feldman, chap. 4, and De Rycke, chap. 5, which also deal with these Petrarchan tropes.

PART I

SPECTACLE AND PERFORMANCE

Making a Spectacle of Her(self)

The Greek Courtesan and the Art of the Present

Thy flattering picture, Phryne, is like thee,
Only in this, that you both painted be.

John Donne, *Epigrams*

JUDGING PHRYNE

It is the year 345 B.C., or thereabouts. A woman is on trial, the courtesan (*hetaira*) Phryne. She is accused of impiety, of introducing a new god, Isodaites, and if proven guilty, she will be condemned to death. The good news is that she is defended by Hyperides. Hyperides is one of the best advocates around and he has produced one of his best speeches for the occasion. Bits of it survive. The bad news is that the judges seem unconvinced nevertheless. Hyperides tries a desperate measure: "He led Phryne herself into view, tore off her underclothes, exposed her breasts and finished his speech with a pitiful finale. He filled the jurors with religious awe and stopped them from condemning to death Aphrodite's representative and attendant, as they indulged their feelings of compassion."[1]

Since that famous docu-fictional trial Phryne has never ceased to take her clothes off. You can see her in St. Petersburg getting skimpy before a famous public dip at the festival of Poseidon on the island of Aegina, as imagined by Henryk Siemiradzki in 1889. If you are quick, you can see her coming out a few minutes later in the Uffizi in Florence, since the scene was the model, supposedly, for Apelles' once very famous painting *Aphrodite Coming out of the Water*, reimagined by Botticelli in ca. 1485. The same event was supposed to have inspired Praxiteles' statue of Aphrodite for the city of Cnidus, often called "the first female nude."[2] The fact that a courtesan had modeled for the image of a goddess provided ammunition for early Christians, especially those of an iconoclastic tendency, such as Arnobius: "And so it was brought to this, that sacred honors were offered to courtesans instead of the immortal gods, and an unhappy system of worship was led astray by the making of statues."[3]

Though never meanwhile forgotten, Phryne enjoyed her second great period of (in)fame in the nineteenth century. She was especially popular in Paris. Saint-Saëns wrote an opera about her, comic, of course; Gustave Boulanger painted her naked slouching on a comfy chair; and in 1861 Jean-Léon Gérôme exhibited "Phryné devant le tribunal," which shows the very moment of revelation: Hyperides whipping off the cloak, the courtesan hiding her face. The picture won instant fame which meant that over 2,200 years after the event, Phryne's trial made it into the New York press, in a satirical version of Gérôme's painting by the cartoonist Bernard Gillam, whose *Phryne before the Chicago Tribunal* was published in *Puck Magazine* on June 4, 1884.

Gérôme's nude Phryne, ideal, unreal, and yet historicized, was a red rag to modernist bulls. Zola hated the color and texture of her skin—"une petite figure nue en caramel"—and thought the gesture of modesty only "exacerbated the nudity, the gesture of a little modern mistress surprised while changing her blouse."[4] Van Gogh agreed with the judgment if not its justification; Phryne lacked the spirituality which comes from calloused hands.[5] Manet published a response in paint two years later, an ancient courtesan transported forwards in time, with her slippers on, and staring out unashamedly: *Olympia*, The Modern, The *Real*.[6] Zola mocked Gérôme's historical accuracy, that "he had had to consult the ancient sources and take the advice of an architect."[7] So evidently did Manet, for "Olympia" is a special name for a courtesan. It was the name of a *hetaira* from Sparta, mother of the philosopher Bion, but since it was the name of the most important sanctuary in Greece, it was a name forbidden to common prostitutes, a name of distinction.[8] By this time the mirroring of images is getting out of control, but I doubt very much that anyone who contributed to the argument was unaware of its resonances, that an image of ancient Phryne was an image whose subject was representation itself. We could say that Gérôme's momentous picture most pointedly raised the question of Phryne's status as Ur-model of the Ur-female nude, and Manet supplied its most momentous answer.

That doesn't quite complete this tale of painted whispers, for a century after *Olympia*, in 1963, the surrealist Paul Delvaux made yet another image of Phryne, naked and full-frontal, but cropped by the painter's lens. She is of the present no longer, in fact she seems to be nowhere definite, and out of time. *Phryne before Her Judges* says the title, but the judges are nowhere to be seen, which means we are in the frame now, part of the painting, its painters and its judges, the producers of this here critical fantastic gaze we see before us.

Maybe you'd like to see these *Phrynes* I am talking about. It's hard to think of a more realistic picture of antiquity than the Siemiradzki. It's almost like a photograph; you really feel as if you're there at the festival watching Phryne disrobe. But they are all really amazing. I am sure you can imagine, though maybe it's a bit frustrating not to have her in front of you here on the page. Hearing about Phryne, what she looks like, from someone who knows someone who claims to have seen her, someone who was present or claims to have been present at that famous trial long before you were born, when all was apparently revealed—that and maybe that alone is the authentic historical experience, the present endlessly deferred.

CONTROVERSIAL COURTESANS

I hope I have demonstrated at least that for Western scholars ancient Greek courtesans come with a whole lot of baggage. The very term "courtesan" is deliberately vague, used for a group of deliberately hard-to-define women of shady reputation who worked or played outside the confines of the brothel (*porneion*), on the one hand, and of respectability on the other, neither immediately available for sex nor completely out of sexual reach. There are a number of grand precipitous narratives in which she has always already got a role; and to make claims about who she is and what she does has meant confirming or challenging those narratives. Some of these issues are reasonably familiar, given extra scale and pomp by the *longue durée* of "Western Civilization," and/or a particular valency by recent intellectual influences on the particular discipline of Classics.

First of all there is the whole question of knowledge. Structuralism and the theory of the Other, especially as developed by Simone de Beauvoir and Edward Said, has had a profound impact on ancient Greek studies. The Greeks are supposed to be very much more of an Us-versus-Them, binary oppositional culture than We are.[9] The Us — the free, male, Greeks — are said to have imposed ideological constructs on the Thems — slaves, "barbarians," women — more forcefully and categorically than other speaking subjects in other times and places. A large number of scholars treat almost everything said about ancient courtesans as simply made up; their voices are *always* the voices of men ventriloquizing; there is *nothing* of them in their representations. To take the evidence seriously can be seen as a sign of weak-mindedness, or even as the indulging of a seductive, romantic, but ultimately misogynist fantasy. But disbelief is not automatically a virtue in the politics of gender, and saying "it's a male invention" is a positive statement, requiring argument and proof. If Phryne makes herself up before she gets painted, then we are guilty of occluding something of her when we insist she is a wholly male production.

Second and not unrelated is the whole question of the oppression of ancient women. The Greek courtesan goes places and does things that other women do not. Her agency or her "capriciousness" is represented as an important part of who she is. But is her agency for real? Does that compromise or modify our theories about ancient woman's place in society? Or is the courtesan when she behaves in an unwomanly fashion simply an honorary man? The grand narratives here are stories about the very origin of "Western" patriarchy, phallocentrism, and pornography, in which as the models, supposedly, for the first female nudes, as penetratees in a supposedly penetration-fixated society, as those closest to power during the "Reign of the Phallus," the Greek courtesans play the role of originary martyrs, blueprints for the many female victims of the objectifying tyranny of male lust.

This may or may not be true but it is complicated by one other thing that the Greeks are famous for, "homosexuality," and in particular the eroticization of the male. Female nudes are vastly outnumbered by images of naked men and youths, citizens now and of the future, many of whom are explicitly depicted as sex objects, their "beauty" (*kallos*) celebrated on ubiquitous vase inscriptions and graffiti — "Leagros is Beautiful" — and not all of whom manage to rise above the objectifying gaze.

This homoerotic gaze was related to political power within the community, in a way not dissimilar to the way that the construction of women as sex objects has been related to the political position of "the fair sex" in other societies — "Don't you worry your pretty little head." For, like many "tribal" polities in Africa and South America, Greek societies (most famously Sparta, Crete, and Athens, at least by the late classical period and probably from a much earlier date) were "age class" societies, in which new citizens were "setted" into year groups (like "Class of 2000") for forty-two years, with power and privilege (e.g., the right to sit on the Council) being assigned according to the "level" or "grade" (like "Sophomore") one's set had reached, resulting in a dominant sequence of four age classes: Pre-pubescent Boys (*Paides*, 18 minus — N.B. pre-modern people generally reached sexual maturity approximately four years later on average than modern people thanks to a diet low in protein, which is why boy sopranos could be much older in the past, and especially before ca. 1800), "beardless" *Meirakia/Neaniskoi* (18 and 19), "bearded" (*Andres*) *Neoi* ("Fresh Men," 20–29), (*Andres*) *Presbutai* ("Seniors," 30–59).

Hence in Athens "Boys" were carefully secluded, like women in a Jane Austen novel, with chaperones and even laws against inappropriate intimacy. The debutants, the *Meirakia/Neaniskoi*, by contrast, who had been age-setted at 18 and who had "come out" into society, were the object of the most intense amatory interest, represented by images like those of beardless Apollo, the archetypical but quite unrealistic "Greek God" of popular imagining. And *Neoi* were considered physically excellent and good for sport and war, but lacking in the kind of common sense that might justify their participation in Councils.[10]

If women are trapped into flirtatiousness, so are young men — to "play the *meirakion*" means exactly that — "to be coquettish." If women are "victims of penetration," so are young men. Boys and men also took their clothes off in public and performed. *Meirakia* too could be courtesans, male mistresses, musicians of dodgy reputation. If Greek men ogled Phryne at the festival of Poseidon, they knew what it was like to be ogled in athletics competitions where they performed naked, in "Pyrrhic" war dances, where they had nothing to hide their modesty but a shield, or simply when they exercised naked in the gymnasium:

> Amazement and confusion reigned when he came in, and a second troop of admirers followed behind him. That men like ourselves should have been affected in this way was not surprising, but I watched the Boys and saw that all of them, even the very youngest, turned and looked at him, as if he were a statue. Chaerephon called me and said "What do you think of the young man [*Neaniskos*], Socrates? Does he not have a beautiful face?" "Most definitely," I said. "But you would consider him quite faceless," he replied, "if he were to volunteer to take his clothes off. For he is the *crème de la crème* in respect of his physique." (Plato, *Charmides* 154cd)

Maybe sex is always gendered, but in ancient Greece sex was also age-classed, which means that here least of all was it a straightforward issue of Us-versus-Them.

The above are perhaps simply starker versions of problems encountered by anyone studying courtesans, but there is one set of controversies that is unique to the study of the Greek *hetaira* and can take outsiders by surprise: a problem about religion and East versus West. There are two apparently contradictory elements in this heated debate. First is the question of "oriental seclusion." A number of texts seem to conjure up a vision of ancient Greece which looks less like Europe and more like Islam, women kept well out of the sight of men to whom they are not related, appearing outside the house only if heavily shrouded and under the veil, embarrassed even to have their names voiced in public.[11] Some scholars, however, take strong exception to this view, arguing that it can only have been an elite practice or an ideal, or that it is a question of separate gendered spheres rather than the seclusion of women.[12] The question has a bearing on the place of courtesans in Greek society — why there was such a longing for a sight of them, why crowds gathered to watch them take a dip — but it is particularly important when discussing images. Some think that most women shown on Greek vases in the company of men off the street (i.e., with cloak, shoes, and walking stick) are prostitutes and courtesans, especially if the women are naked or being offered what looks for all the world like a money bag. Others resist this conclusion more or less comprehensively. It is even argued that money bag or no money bag (and maybe the bag contains a game of knucklebones), these are "normal" women, citizens, wives enjoying a healthy sex life.[13]

There is currently a standoff on this particular debate, with some casually assuming that a particular image is of a courtesan or even of a brothel and others assuming the same scene is a household interior, a picture of domestic bliss. Until some kind of consensus is reached or until at least some ground rules are established upon which we might start to think about constructing a consensus, thousands of images from late archaic and classical Athens (ca. 520–400 B.C.) that may well contain valuable information about ancient Greek courtesans are effectively sequestered.

Apart from the issue of "oriental seclusion" there is the debate, if anything even more heated and marked by even more drastic divergences of opinion, about so-called "sacred prostitution," an umbrella term for a whole range of poorly understood practices linking sexual exchange to temples, rituals, and/or cults.[14] Originally, sacred prostitution in Greece was thought to be a typically eastern phenomenon carried into certain parts of Europe, especially to Corinth, with the cult of Aphrodite — a goddess believed to be strongly influenced by Asiatic goddesses such as Astarte, if not herself an eastern import. Since then a reaction has set in, emphasizing the local origins of "L'Aphrodite *grecque*" and therefore playing down the existence of "eastern elements" in her cult.[15] Now the existence of "sacred prostitution" even in the Near East is under attack, on the grounds that earlier male orientalists had simply allowed their imaginations to run wild, which they sometimes did, and had misunderstood biblical references to "sacreds" both male (the "sodomites" of the King James version) and female; or that, once again, as a discourse of the Other not once, but twice or even three times over (female and "barbarian" and "slaves"), the evidence, which is at first glance both explicit and considerable, though rarely first-hand, must be assessed according to different rules from those that apply in other fields of inquiry.[16]

It is probably wise to avoid the term sacred prostitution altogether. Certainly, so far as the Greek world is concerned, there was no tidy separation between the sacred and the secular (some would say no separation at all), and there is plenty of evidence — literary, archaeological, and epigraphical — not only for general connections between courtesans and their divine *patronne* Aphrodite, not only for obscenity and eroticism in cults, but for actual sexual exchanges in a ritual context. The festival of Poseidon, in which Phryne took on the role of Aphrodite, was probably a winter New Year festival, like the Aphrodite festival celebrated in Thebes with a sex party. In the Theban festival the war magistrates, the Polemarchs, probably fornicated with courtesans, or even with other men's wives, to commemorate the union between the war god Ares and the goddess of love which resulted in the birth of Harmonia (Not "Harmony" exactly, but "Connection," or, better, "[tight, neat, close] Fit") — a symbol of the unity and, especially, of the continuity of the city.[17] We do not know if intercourse, sexual or otherwise, was involved at the Aegina festival, but Phryne seems to have played the role of Aphrodite coming out of the water long before she was represented thus.[18] If the story that she modeled for the goddess's image is made up, it was Phryne's own religious role-playing that inspired it, that is, her performance as Aphrodite in the festival of Aphrodite in front of a large crowd. In other words, Phryne's Aphrodite, the model's Aphrodite, came first.

SHADOW-GRASPING COURTESANS

In one of Plutarch's lives (*Demetrius* 27) we find a story about the wise eighth-century B.C. Pharaoh called Bocchoris: A man had been smitten with love for the courtesan Thonis, but she was too expensive so he sated his desire for her in a dream. Thonis found out and sued for payment. The wise pharaoh resolved the case by ordering the man to bring the sum she had demanded into court. He told Thonis she could have its shadow. Four hundred years later the *hetaira* Lamia found fault with Bocchoris's judgment. Thonis should have gotten the money. For Thonis's desire was not satisfied by the shadow of gold, while her admirer's lust for her had been sated by his imaginings. Did Lamia really say that one day in approximately 300 B.C.? Is that an authentic example of the discourse of an ancient Greek courtesan? Or is she being used as a ventriloquist's dummy by some long-forgotten man, herself now as shadowy as Thonis in a dream? Fabulously expensive, fabulously extravagant, mixing with the most fabulous clients, politicians, and millionaires, kings like Alexander and princes like Demetrius, but as aloof and as invisible as an oriental despot, the Greek courtesan has got us itching with heuristic lust. Clearly she was fabulous, but exactly how fabulous was she?

The powerful acid of postmodern ambivalence and radical doubt has been applied to sources about courtesans to produce a far from doubtful effect, pushing real courtesans to the margins of the real. We are left, like Thonis following Pharaoh's judgment, with no solid gold, only a shadow; nothing, that is, that we can spend. There must at any rate have been a courtesan once who fell inside the looking-glass, who believed the fantasy, who took the stories as seriously as we once did (as ancient men show every sign of doing), who believed the myth and tried to live up to it, the artificial man-made fictionalized *hetaira*, making witty jokes, performing a role which *only men* had imagined, taking her role at the festival of Aphrodite very seriously indeed.

There is another big debate here that we need to juxtapose with the more familiar ones. For modern scholarship itself, feminist, postmodern, positivist, is on trial when it comes to the study of the courtesan. Are we being fair to Phryne? Are we capable of giving her her due? Reading academic work on ancient Greek *hetairai* it is easy to forget that they did in fact exist, something no one has (yet) denied, walking, talking, real-life people, that there was a woman known as Phryne who lived 2,350 years ago in Greece and that she was once put on trial and was not convicted. Putting the Greek courtesan alongside women who performed similar roles in other parts of the world in different times and different contexts is terribly important, therefore, both to rescue her from the sole burden of too many grand Western narratives and to dissipate the force of the linear diachronic flow, maybe even to allow her to pilfer from her sisters (if only by standing next to them) something of the heft and drag that is the property of real persons. The Greek *hetaira* really is difficult to know, but given her history, a little fact-chasing is beginning to look like a radical gesture. A recent document-stuffed study of another Greek Other, the Persians, has demonstrated that the Greeks did not invent things, but were quite happy to misunderstand, modify, or simply decontextualize some salient Persian facts, images, and representations, for, of course, it was the grains of truth that gave negative constructions their cogency.[19] The same in my view is true of ancient courtesans. The sources are not making them up, but we need to be constantly on guard for misdirection, omissions, and other sleights of hand. It is a travesty to treat the Greek courtesan as a literary figment and equally mistaken to see her as pure unadulterated fact. She operates at the intersection and belongs to both art and reality, an artfulness in everyday reality, an everyday reality in art.

COURTESANS IN ATHENS AND THE "MOUSIKĒ-WORKERS"

There are no technical terms for women of more or less easy virtue in Greece, at least none that are used with absolute consistency. The Greek word usually translated as courtesan is *hetaira*, which is related to the masculine *hetairos*—"comrade," "associate," "friend." First and foremost, therefore, a *hetaira* is a woman "who associates," a creature who mixes with men. To be a bit pedantic on the matter of etymology, *hetaira* is probably not, as is often claimed, the feminine form of *hetairos* (*hetaîros*) but of an archaic term *hetaros* (*hétăros*), the pitch-accented *–ai-* being a feminizing element in the word, just as a feminized lion, that is, a "lioness," is *le-ai-na*. The Greeks believed the feminine form was originally an ancient cult title of Aphrodite: Aphrodite Hetaira. Properly speaking, therefore, *hetairos* is the masculine form of *hetaira*, not the other way around. This may seem like the worst kind of academic nit-picking, but just like calling a male ballet dancer a "He-ballerina," calling a male "associate" *hetairos* marks the female "associate" as the primary point of reference. In my view, *hetairai*, like their *patronne* Aphrodite/Venus, represent a kind of quintessential "superfeminine," superseductive, supersoft, structurally most opposed to the masculine of hard Ares/Mars. Unusual images which put them in diametrically opposed male roles and male drag must therefore be seen as perversely confirming that opposition, rather than/as well as undermining it, like showing a ballerina watching the Big Game, with pint glass in hand and a cigar. I am aware that several other scholars have argued the exact opposite, not least in this volume. We might be able to agree that the place of the *hetaira* in the symbolic structure of ancient Greek gender is complicated and involved, but I would like to insist, for the moment, on my part, that the *hetaira* is, in the first place, one hundred and ten per cent girl.

Hetaira is viewed as a nice word, a word "Phryne the *hetaira*" might use of herself. But it can also be seen as a deceitful word, flattering, disguising the dirty reality. It was used, with a qualification, to refer to almost any woman of questionable reputation: on the one hand the "high-fee *hetairai*," or "the awesomely unapproachable [*semnotatai*] *hetairai*," and on the other, "a common [*koinē*] *hetaira*." Despite inconsistencies, we can distinguish several different groups, which are really shadings around points of differentiation along a continuum, groups of women attempting to differentiate themselves from other groups of women or being forced to fit roles assigned to them by madames, lovers, or pimps. This we might call the first of the arts of the courtesan, the art of associating and disassociating, of socializing with distinction. I will come back to that.

The restrictions placed on intimacy between men and decent women, and the Athenian obsession with the terrible and terrifying crime of *moicheia* ("adultery plus," i.e., the sexual burglary of any free woman under your roof), which could result, theoretically, in instant death if you were caught in the act, ceded a broad field of feminine intercourse to the *hetaira*, who is defined first and foremost by the mere fact that she is seen to spend time in the company of, or who associates with, men to whom she is not related.[20] We hear of "married *hetairai*" in monogamous, but not, in fact, married relationships, or as one of several mistresses of a man or of more than one man, of women granting exclusive rights to their company under contract for a period, women who are visited at home and noisily serenaded, women hired as escorts for an evening to accompany men to feasts, women hired on the streets or from a *pornoboskos* ("whore-pasturer") to play the *aulos* (a wind instrument, usually double-reeded, like an oboe or a shawm)[21] or harp, or to sing or dance, or perform acrobatics, sometimes in little pageants.

Hanging over all courtesans, at the opposite end of the scale from the respectable married woman you could commit adultery with, was the dread figure of the "common prostitute" or "whore," a translation of the word pornē, who really belongs in a brothel or on the streets. As the defining Other of the courtesan, the common prostitute, the *pornē* is critical for the courtesan's definition. A *pornē*, the feminine form of *pornos* (a "male whore," most often found in rhetorical vituperation of political enemies), is defined by a whole series of symbolic practices linked to the construction of exchange as promiscuous commodity exchange. The *pornē* derives first and foremost from a legal formula found in the law code of Solon dating back to ca. 600 B.C., which separately defined those women you could have sex with without risking your life, "those who walk to and fro in the open," and "those who sit in a factory [*ergastērion*]."[22]

The one building in Athens so far identified as a brothel, the so-called "Building Z"—lots of small rooms in the red-light district of Ceramicus, evidence of foreign (i.e., slave) women and of the worship of a nighttime Aphrodite—seems literally to have been a cloth factory during at least one of its three phases. The brothel commodified sex through a range of strategies. It was a commercially productive space, a "shop" or a "factory" —one comedy refers to a *kinētērion*, a "sex factory." The women were commodities in the most straightforward sense, that is, purchased slaves pretending to be nothing other than slaves, their agency, autonomy, will, and discretion completely occluded. The women were depersonalized, arranged in a semicircle for the client's selection. Their bodies were open to the gaze. The transaction was immediate, based on a flat-rate pricing system, often the value of a single coin.[23] Above all there was a discourse of "buying" and "selling," in which sex was constructed as a specific isolable product, a thing. The Greeks seem to have been highly self-conscious about the symbolic process of constructing commodities, not least sexual ones. One comedy concerned a woman called Clepsydra, which means stopwatch (a "clepsydra" is a water clock used, like a sand clock, to time speeches). She was said to measure very precisely the time her clients had paid for. One notorious and metaphorically complicated passage in Aristophanes' play *Acharnians* (764–69) has a poor starving man from Athens' hated neighbor, Megara, selling his daughters as if they were simply vaginas ("piggies," *choiroi*) in the marketplace.

Least differentiated from *pornai*—and highly germane to our discussion here— are the *mousourgoi*, "workers of the Muses," which seems to mean practitioners of performing arts, since *mousikē* in Greek refers not just to "music" but to dancing and "poetry" (almost always musical in fact, i.e., songs). Singing and dancing at public festivals ("Tragedy," "Comedy," "Dithyrhamb," etc.) and private drinking parties (*symposia*) were central and ubiquitous elements of Greek culture and society. Philosophers thought a lot about the proper place of *mousikē* in the *polis*, and, especially from ca. 450 B.C. onwards, about the relationship between the "amateur" performances of citizens and the more technically accomplished and commoditized performances of professionals, who alone could do justice to the complex and difficult compositions of the "New Poets" and their notorious "New *Mousikē*."[24] Of these *Mousikē* workers, the lowest on the scale are the aulos girls, the *aulētrides*, apparently almost always slave girls. Their exchanges were very strongly commoditized in terms of space (very much of the streets, "standing at street corners," and so forth), the occlusion of their will (if more than one man required her services, the town officers, Astynomoi, would decide by drawing lots), and the fixing of their price (no more than 2 drachmas). It seems it was their musical, not their sexual services that were on the table, so to speak, for a price, which is an important fact, and they played for women as well as men. We hear of several aulos girls who rose up through the ranks to become illustrious and rich, but it was precisely their rise from such humble origins—"and she was an aulos player"—that aroused comment.[25]

The performances of the *mousikē* workers need to be put in context. The music performed by men in the symposium could be highly varied in form, role-taking, subject matter, and performance structure. The aulos is associated especially—some would say exclusively—with what we might call "broadcast" songs, elegies in simple standard meter (elegiac couplets) and in Ionic dialect. There was no need for any great technical skill on the part of the performer, just the remembering of words (unlike lyre songs, "narrowcast," which could only be performed by those who had had lyre lessons). The aulos was the instrument of collective action par excellence, the instrument to which men marched and worked, the instrument that accompanied tragic and comic choruses.[26] Plutarch states explicitly that in Thebes the aulos was introduced by the founders to promote social cohesion between men: "So they got a lot of aulos thoroughly mixed into work and play, bringing the instrument to a position of dignity and prominence."[27] The aulos brings social harmony, the collectivity of the *polis* even, inside the symposium. Within the symposium every guest was supposed to sing these aulos songs in turn, as they held a branch of myrtle or bay, each guest either finishing off the song of the man before him or starting a new one, passing the baton, so to speak, around the room.[28]

Surviving songs in elegiac meter are rarely mournful or "elegiac" in content, but are often hortatory, politically propagandistic, martial, and/or homo-amatory: the elegiac meter was the medium for getting ideas across, for spreading fame through music that might circulate, like the wine, around the couches of what is sometimes called the "men's room" (*andrōn*). In some cases, such music was clearly designed to circulate around the entire city, going from group to group. As accompanist to these songs, off the streets, through the city from house to house, the aulos girl was therefore an instrument of promiscuous homosociality: "I suggest we dismiss the aulos girl who has just come in," says a guest at Plato's thoroughly homosexual *Symposium* (176e). "She can go and pipe to herself or to the women indoors if she wants, while we have intercourse with ourselves, this day, discursively."

"Pluckers," *psaltriai*, came under the same laws as aulos girls, but seem to have been a cut above. The *hetaira* Habrotonon, who has a starring role in Menander's *Epitrepontes* (*The Arbitration*), is one of these. She is represented simply as the young man's expensive but unused mistress, but she had played, we learn at a critical moment, for a women's festival once. There was a wide range of plucked instruments in the ancient world. The tortoiseshell lyre was the most traditional for amateur aristocratic men.[29] Great poets and performers on the other hand are normally shown with the elaborate wooden cithara, the grand piano of the ancient world. Female "pluckers" seem not to have played either instrument, generally speaking, but rather the triangular harp with up to twenty-two strings. They might also sing occasionally, but rarely strummed. Women also played the sambuca (= *zhambyke*), an ancient Near Eastern type of harp—both these instruments were considered decadent and seductive. There were, however, male *mousikē* workers, young men of dodgy reputation, probably handsome slaves, who had been trained to sing while accompanying themselves on the exalted and difficult cithara. One distinguished Athenian, called Misgolas, was mocked by comic poets for his fondness for these cithara boys; and since he had been seen hanging out with Misgolas who was seen hanging out with cithara boys, aspersions could be cast on the sexual mercenariness of the politician Timarchus.[30] The choreographer (probably a fancy "whore-pasturer") who is a guest and also provides the performers for Xenophon's *Symposium* (4.53–54) at the house of wealthy Callias is sleeping with his beautiful and extremely talented cithara boy as if he were a kind of mistress. Socrates mocks him when he expresses anxiety about men seeking to "corrupt" the boy, as if he were not thoroughly corrupted already. When thinking about male and female musicians we probably need to keep both Socrates' and the pimp's perspectives in our minds.

A very interesting pair of papyri (*P. Berol.* 13049 and 13057) from Egypt of 13 B.C. records an agreement in which for the sum of one hundred drachmas a man called Philios hands over a slave called Narcissus for a year to someone called Eros, all very amatory names, for instruction in a range of different *auloi*, each of them itemized, and for training in a range of standard tunes. There is to be an examination at the end of the period before a small panel of experts to make sure Eros has fulfilled his side of the bargain. A recent study analyzes what seems to have been expected: "the pupil must be able to master seven different instruments, and ones which are not all played in the same way . . . the training of Narcissus as aulos accompanist must allow him to adapt himself musically, through the use of appropriate instruments, to different circumstances of life, which could entail public performances, religious or non-religious, and private, such as banquets, funerals, or even heavy work (such as harvesting or grape-pressing). What is clear is that Narcissus was not prepared to become a virtuoso soloist."[31]

Inasmuch as he was a slave aulos player and a *mousourgos*, the contract for Narcissus the aulos boy is, so far, the best evidence we have for what a contract for the training of an aulos girl must have looked like. But there is lots of more general evidence for this type of slave training. There is even a reference to "schools for aulos girls" in Isocrates' *Antidosis* (4.287) — where "many younger men of a worse nature" are whiling away their time.[32] The pimp Labrax sends Palaestra to a harpist's school, a *ludus fidicinius*, in Plautus' *Rudens*, a version of an older play by the Greek Diphilus, to prepare her for a career in erotic entertainment.[33] She is seen on the way home from there by Plesidippus, who immediately falls in love (and gives Labrax money to purchase her, until Labrax, having been informed of more lucrative business opportunities in Sicily, attempts to abscond). Moreover, a few late archaic/early classical vases seem to depict such establishments. One side of a famous cup attributed to Makron shows two women playing *auloi*, one sitting on a stool, one standing up, interspersed with three bearded men, one of whom (far left) is holding a bag of money (or knucklebones). On the other side a seated woman holding out a floral crown, another item required for drinking parties, and another brandishing *auloi* are interspersed with three beardless youths with staffs, one of whom is disrobed and is gesturing at the wreath-holder's lap, and one of whom (far left) is brandishing a bag of money.[34] What we have here, I think, are places to which anyone could send a slave to get trained up in musical skills and thus increase their profitability, in just the way that Labrax the pimp does in *Rudens*.

Whether slave musicians are best considered musicians that you might presumably or possibly have sex with, or rather as courtesans with a sideline in music, is a difficult question. It is certainly not an either/or question, as some assume (either "they are really just musicians" or "they are really just prostitutes"). Investing in the training of slaves, especially of courtesans, male and female, musical or otherwise, was one of the few really dynamic areas of the ancient economy, an area in which a wise investment might produce dramatic returns. It might cost a lot of money to send a boy or girl to music school for any length of time, and I am sure anyone who contemplated such a thing would calculate extremely carefully the value of his (or indeed her) investment, how best to recoup it and to maximize profit — in the first place, whether it might be better to forget it and just send her to a brothel. One can think of a number of considerations that might affect that calculation: the beauty, skill, age, and popularity of the slave, the hopes for a profitable lover further down the line who might be put off if he or she had been had cheaply by previous clients, the speed with which you needed to recoup the investment, keeping clients happy. But a trained slave was a more or less expensive investment that you more or less looked after, and two conclusions seem certain: one, sexual opportunity was never casually and uncalculatingly assumed to be part of the bargain when you hired someone out to play aulos at a symposium: if they wanted sex too, they would have to pay extra; and two, a slave musician was never completely out of range, unless the owner was completely besotted. We may well have exaggerated the extent to which musicians, even aulos girls, were freely available, but their masters or mistresses were always probably open to bids.

The existence of schools is very interesting, and reveals that the commoditization of such skills (*technai*), the *business* of such skills, had already reached an exceptional level of development in Athens by the early fifth century B.C. Schooling slaves was not the normal way to upgrade them. For most ancient business was small-scale, household-based, and very fragmented. Hence the usual practice was to buy slaves to work alongside you in your own business, and train them in your own trade at no extra cost, as copies or extensions of yourself; and they in their turn would train still more. The most famous example of this phenomenon is the story of Pasio, bought by a banker and then freed, becoming one of the wealthiest men in Athens and even granted citizenship.[35] Pasio in turn bought a slave to work alongside him, and Pasio's son Apollodorus thinks this former slave of a former slave of a banker should have been more grateful: "For I think you all know that if, when he was on sale, he had been bought by a cook [*mageiros*], or a worker in some other *technē*, and learnt his master's *technē*, he would be a long way from the goods he now possesses." Instead it was Apollodorus' father, "a banker, who bought him and educated him in letters and taught him his *technē*."[36] A courtesan once freed may have bought and trained more courtesans in this way, an ex-slave musician more musicians. The original owner may well have supplied the capital or had some other financial interest in the freedwoman's business. In most cases, therefore, it was probably not a matter of private education but personal replication, a matter of educating slaves yourself, not sending them to school. Nor was it a distant Them-and-Us, Master-and-Slave kind of relationship, but a far more close and personal one, Ex-slave and Slave, with the ex-slave's ex-master probably lurking discreetly in the background, with a formal or informal interest in the operation.

Alongside the cithara boy in Xenophon's *Symposium* there is an aulos girl, and a dancing girl who juggles hoops and performs acrobatics through a ring of upright blades. At the end of the evening there is a little musical drama, in which the boy plays Dionysus coming to Ariadne on Naxos. Ariadne appears, dressed as a bride, and takes her place, then the sound of the aulos is heard and Dionysus dances toward her, ending up on her lap embracing her and kissing her. It is probably significant that one of the guests who is under eighteen leaves the room before all this takes place. I don't think the Greeks thought it was acceptable to watch sex shows in symposia, but I do think they watched male and female musicians and dancers, making love in the old sense and engaging in what we might call little erotic pageants; and that on occasion, if you were subtle about it, you might have an opportunity to have sex, real sex, with Ariadne or Dionysus afterwards.

The performance in Xenophon's *Symposium* seems to have been choreographed by the owner, but we get a hint that courtesans themselves might compose. Aristophanes mentions one Charixene, who was known to the later encyclopedias as an "aulos player of olden days and composer of musical pieces; some say a writer of songs as well," "some say a composer of love-stuff" (*erōtika*). Euripides in Aristophanes' *Frogs* is accused by Aeschylus of taking material from "whore songs." He had spoken of a "twelve-trick" star in one of his last plays *Hypsipyle*. Now Aeschylus accuses him of composing songs according to the "twelve-trick of Cyrene," commonly identified as a Corinthian courtesan famous for her sexual skills, but surely, in this context, for her music too. The fancy-pants poet Agathon was shown dressed like Cyrene in another play of Aristophanes.[37] The comparison of two meretricious tragedians to this same Cyrene is probably significant. Cyrene's sexual and musical performances are conflated. Another comic poet makes a similiar fusion of meretriciousness and music: "The other aulos girls are to be seen playing 'Apollo's theme', . . . and 'Zeus's theme'; but the only theme these women play is *The [Grasping] Hawk*."[38] These women I think are piping a silent tune.

Later writers seem to have referred to these sympotic shows as *paignia* from *paizo* "to play" or "play at." The *Oxford Classical Dictionary* calls them "slight often vulgar performances."[39] The mimes (miniature dramatic poems) of the Hellenistic (post-Alexander) courtesan Glauce were referred to as *paignia*. More detail is found in Plutarch's *Table Talk* under the rubric "What sympotic entertainments are most appropriate at dinner?" Not *paignia* evidently: "There are certain mimes," he says, "they call *paignia*," and which "are full of flattery and scandal, unfit to be seen even by the slaves who carry our shoes, if their masters are men of virtue; although the masses even when women and unbearded boys are reclining with them put on representations of words and deeds that are more unsettling than any drunkenness" (712ef; cf. 853a–854d). Later writers traced the *paignion* all the way back to the age of Pericles. The main culprit was a man called Gnesippus (Ath. 638d–639a), mentioned in five or six comedies of the 440s and 430s B.C. The fragments throw some light on the nature of this new type of sex musical. He "sweetened things up on nine strings," he wrote songs for adulterers (*moichoi*) "for calling out women, using sambuca and harp." "A man I would not consider commissioning even for the festival of Adonis," a festival much loved by courtesans. He employed a "female chorus of plucker slaves, who pluck their disgusting tunes [or "limbs," *melē*, a pun] in Lydian fashion."[40]

A large number of works of the Hellenistic period are entitled *paignia*, or *Erotopaegnia*. The great poet Theocritus, who was certainly familiar with the works of Glauce, wrote "mimes" described as "shepherd *paignia*" (Aelian NA 15.19). Theocritus' works are known as Idylls or *Pictures* but they are often in dramatic form, and many are full of "flattery and scandal" too. A good example is the "urban" Idyll *Pharmakeutria*, in which a woman called Simaetha, whom the audience would probably see as a courtesan of some kind, performs a sinister magic ritual to get her boyfriend, a handsome, vain, feckless youth, to come to her. After a series of spells, she describes the course of their relationship, his promises of marriage, the news from the mother of her aulos player that he was seeing someone else. The soloist who performed the short piece would have had quickly to conjure up a particular time and place, a crossroads, a cemetery, at night, and to shift through a whole series of contradictory emotions, sinister passion, anger, love, nostalgia, sorrow, hatred, revenge. I think this is probably a song performed by a *mousourgos* in a symposium, perhaps even by the famous aulos girls Potheinē and Mnesis and the mime actress (*deiktērias*, "exhibitionist") Myrtion whose grand houses in Alexandria scandalized the historian Polybius.[41] Once again courtesan and courtesan culture are conflated as a courtesan performs a meretricious piece about a courtesan doing courtesan things.

THE ART OF AGENCY

Upgrading slaves was serious business, therefore, in the ancient world, perhaps the most dynamic segment of the economy, and one of the most successful initiatives in this area was the business of Nicarete, ex-slave of Charisius of Elis and still attached to his household through her husband, Charisius' cook (*mageiros*). We know so much about her because one of her girls, Neaera, was put on trial, like Phryne and at around the same time (ca. 343–340), and, by a piece of great good fortune, the speech for the prosecution survives, because it was mistakenly included among the works of the great Demosthenes.[42] The speaker (and probably also the true author) was in fact none other than Apollodorus, himself the son of an even more astonishingly successful ex-slave, the banker Pasio mentioned above, a man who knew a thing or two about the slave skills business therefore. Nicarete bought her little girls very young, we are told, and was knowledgeable and skillful in "bringing them up and educating them" (*threpsai, paideusai*).[43] Her girls were not singers, musicians, or dancers, however. What Nicarete produced in the early years of the fourth century B.C. were courtesans of distinction, superstars. We are given a list of seven girls she manufactured, of whom no fewer than six are mentioned elsewhere in speeches, comedies, and anecdotal collections, often alluded to as if everyone would know who they were. One of them, Anteia, according to Athenaeus (13.570e), had a comedy written about her by Eunicus or Philyllius, and gave her name perhaps to comedies by Antiphanes (36–38 K–A) and Alexis. Nicarete was doing something right. If her girls consistently found their way into the antiquarian work called "On the *hetairides* in Athens," compiled by the Hellenistic scholars Aristophanes of Byzantium (ca. 257–180? B.C.), Callistratus, and Apollodorus of Athens, Ammonius of Alexandria, Antiphanes the Younger (all 2d cent. B.C.), and Gorgias of Athens (ca. 1st cent. B.C.) from references in earlier literature, it's because Nicarete put them there.[44]

Her girls attracted numerous rich and powerful lovers and when the time came to sell them, we hear of astronomical sums changing hands. Neaera herself was realized for three thousand drachmas, which would have produced the same kind of effect on most Greeks as something like "a million dollars." One was called Phila (Girlfriend) and a courtesan called Phila was bought for "a lot of money" by Hyperides, the orator who defended Phryne. Having freed her, Hyperides installed her at his house in Eleusis. Later he made her his *oikouros*, mistress of the house(-hold).[45] Pseudo-Plutarch's life of Hyperides (*Moralia* 849d), drawing on the same source, adds the detail that he paid 2,000 drachmas to ransom her, that she was installed "on his own estate" (*en tois idiois ktēmasi*), and that she was from Thebes. The number of famous courtesans (first made into a formal canon in the lists of later commentators on classical literature, that is, "courtesans most often mentioned by great writers," but also famous at the time, since the great writers are writers of public speeches and plays) that existed at any one time was not large—Aristophanes' original list contained the names of only 135 for a period of over a hundred years—and it is quite likely Hyperides' Phila is the same Phila as Nicarete's. Isocrates (15.288) says "two even three thousand drachmas" is the kind of monstrous sum paid by men to free their *hetairai*, so such prices may not have been that unusual. If we assume an average of 2,000 for the other five girls, we get a ballpark total sales figure of 15,000 drachmas, two and a half talents. This was big business and whatever Nicarete received over and above her costs (those not subsidized by admirers) while the girls were under her control must have been dwarfed by the money she received on realization.

Nicarete took a long time to produce her seven girls in the decades after ca. 400 B.C. We are not talking about a large range of girls arranged in a semicircle; this was no "brothel." She seems to have had just two or three under her auspices at any one time, one attracting lovers already perhaps, one still in training. So when she brought Metaneira to Athens to visit one of her admirers, Neaera was also in attendance, though still a little girl. Two of her girls, Anteia and Aristocleia, are both said to have "ceased whoring" in their youth, which probably means they were bought and/or Nicarete was paid for their freedom while they were still under thirty. Once she had got rid of one, she could bring a trainee on the scene and go and scout out another promising little girl who would be sold on in her turn at huge profit maybe a decade later. This final sale was probably how Nicarete made most of her money, and any money she made from them until then would have to have been earned in ways that would not have dented that final huge profit. But what was so special about these girls? What did they learn from watching Nicarete and their older "sisters"?

The short answer is: anything whatsoever that would add to their market value, not excluding learning the entire works of Euripides backwards while performing a cartwheel. But according to the comic poet Alexis, there were two main things involved in the "remodeling" (*anaplattein*) of their protégées by rich courtesans: their dress and appearance, and their "manners" or "ways" (*tropous*).[46] The most straightforward account of how the best type of courtesan behaves is in the late author Lucian's sixth courtesan dialogue, in which Corinna advises her daughter Crobyle to model herself on Lyra. Dress comes first. Lyra dresses up "properly" (*euprepōs*) and is neat and tidy (*eustalēs*). She is cheerful (*phaidra*) but, unlike Crobyle, she isn't too ready to cackle. Rather she smiles sweetly and seductively. She is clever when she is with someone (*prosomilousa dexiōs*) and is not "phony" (*phenakizousa*) if someone visits or accompanies her, nor does she throw herself at men. If ever she takes a fee (*misthōma*) for going out to dinner, she doesn't get drunk—"it makes one a laughingstock and men hate such women"—doesn't fill herself with the *opson* (the dishes you eat with bread), but uses only the tips of her fingers, in silence and not stuffing her cheeks full, and she doesn't gulp down her drink, but takes occasional sips. She doesn't talk more than necessary, doesn't make jokes at the expense of members of the party, and keeps her eye on her paymaster. Whenever it is necessary to go to bed she performs nothing indecent (*aselges*) or casual (*ameles*, "without care").

How true a picture is this of socializing with distinction in Athens half a millennium earlier? The old-fashioned idea of courtesans as educated may be a fantasy, but it is a fantasy based on the ancient sources, which assume that courtesans can read and write letters, quote lines from Homer and tragedy, and compose elaborate pieces of oratory like the funeral speech, ascribed to Pericles' Milesian mistress

Aspasia, in Plato's *Menexenus*.[47] If we doubt that Aspasia was so accomplished a writer, and concede that Plato is being ironic, we do not have to throw the baby out with the bathwater and doubt the evidence for the literacy of courtesans altogether. Courtesans had to look after themselves. They had to manage a household without the close supervision of a man, calculate the value of gifts and expenses, manage long-distance relationships. Reading and writing would have been extremely useful in all of this, and would have reduced the need for too much reliance on unreliable slaves and word of mouth. How did Neaera manage to run a hostel in Megara unless she had picked up from Nicarete, if only by osmosis, some of the basics of dealing with traders and adding up? There may have been good reason why Hyperides chose yet another of Nicarete's girls to run a house on one of his own estates. By taking on such responsibilities themselves, courtesans could free their loving intercourse from the boring and desultory parts of life. How tedious for an Athenian man to be constantly bombarded with letters from his mistress in Corinth asking him to sort out some dispute with the sleevemaker who lived across the road from her. The capable, calculating courtesan is viewed by ancient sources as a contradiction of the carefree amorous courtesan, or as the truth behind the façade. But as soon as we think about practicalities, we can see that they are two sides of the same coin. The calculating courtesan, sorting herself out, frees the carefree courtesan for the business of pleasant intercourse with men.

DEXIOTĒS

One of Nicarete's girls, Metaneira, made witticisms, we are told. Hegesander of Delphi (mid-second century B.C.?) recorded two of her jokes at the expense of the poverty of the professional gate-crasher, the *parasitos* Democles known as Lagunion (ap. Athenaeus 13.584f). Perhaps little Neaera heard Metaneira in action when she accompanied her to Athens in the 380s B.C., when the orator Lysias was having her initiated into the Mysteries.

Greek jokes are of the "you-had-to-be-there" type and lose a little of their magic in the retelling. They usually follow the form "Someone nicknamed Tripper fell over and ended up with his head on a plate of red snappers and she said 'The Tripper tripped, the biter bit.'" Nothing is more controversial than taking seriously the authenticity of the wisecracking courtesan, whose jokes were recounted in several anecdotal collections.[48] Scholars construct elaborate theories to explain these jokes as completely male productions put into the mouths of courtesans to make a political point, just as Plato is making a point by putting a seductive piece of oratory in the mouth of Aspasia.

Since contemporary courtesans featured in comedies, sometimes even played by male actors in the dramatic festivals, they may indeed have had lines written for them, but we cannot just assume that the courtesans' well-attested wittiness is a fiction, or that a fictional wit can be separated in some kind of bell jar from the real wit who happens to share her name and biography. It is by no means impossible that among the jokes ascribed to the witty *hetairas* are some that are authentic and original, maybe just one or two, maybe the vast majority. This may at first seem ridiculous—how can a joke heard once one night two and a half thousand years ago possibly have survived intact?—but the Greeks not only recalled single lines from tragedies and laughed when Aristophanes parodied them years later, but celebrated clever jokes made by amateurs, especially if they involved a pun on a line in poetry.

Therefore, although a joke is indeed a flimsy thing and anecdotes tend to wander, we should not play down the importance of the classical symposium as a theater of discursive performance. Jokes were events, recorded in the very earliest prose literature, such as Ion of Chios's eyewitness account of a series of witticisms made by Sophocles during a symposium. At the end of Aristophanes' *Wasps* (1259, 1426–43), Bdelycleon recommends that his father learn some jokes to tell at a symposium. Xenophon takes care to record one of his own witty comments at a banquet in his histories. The jokes of Stratonicus the musician were collected by Alexander's historian Callisthenes. Philip of Macedon was said to have paid a fortune for the jokes of a group of wits called the Sixty (Ath. 14.614d; cf. 6.260b). There was certainly a question of taste and timing. Philip's young son Alexander (the Great) made barbed asides at the expense of another boy during the visit of Athenian ambassadors. This was held against the boy by one of the ambassadors, Demosthenes, whose rival Aeschines rebuked him in turn for rebuking someone so young. In contrast, the boy in Xenophon's *Symposium* makes no such jokes and comports himself like a quiet little angel.[49] Jokes must be dexterous and nimble (*epidexios, eutrapelos*), says Aristotle, Alexander's tutor, and should not expose the victim to ridicule.[50]

Among the good *hetaira*'s qualities mentioned by Lucian is *prosomilousa dexiōs*, that is, talking to someone in a clever fashion. Acclaim would be attached to a good one-liner, especially if it came from the mouth of a courtesan at the expense of a *parasitos* who was there precisely to earn his supper as the butt. A witty, erudite, and appropriate comment delivered off the cuff, from a normally quiet woman sitting on the edge of your couch, would, it seems to me, have been just the thing to make an impact on men well known to mix with *hetairas*: Lysias, Hyperides, the comic poets Xenoclides and Diphilus. I am sure Nicarete hoped that Neaera would pick that much up from Metaneira in Athens.

In conclusion, we should accept that a majority of the famous courtesans were clever enough to be capable of looking after themselves at least, to read and write a little, to manage minor transactions; that courtesans were expected to be witty; that a few met that expectation magnificently; that a good joke would be remembered and celebrated; that among the many jokes of courtesans that are recorded, some are more or less authentic.

CHARIS

Courtesans, who are what common prostitutes are not, are shown striving hard to avoid anything that reeks of the sexual marketplace, avoiding cash, avoiding even the smell of bronze on their hands after handling a mirror, clinging fiercely to the language of love (*philia*) and friendship (not customers but "intimate friends," *philoi*). In practice this involves the art of *charis*, "grace," the same word found in "charismatic" and "eucharist," an extremely difficult word to pin down, sometimes implying

gratitude, at other times miraculous, unlooked-for altruism, but also fawning, ingra-
tiating, or (especially in the aorist form of the verb, *charisasthai*) something like "putting out" — "she graced me." *Charis* is, then, "an adornment of social relationships or
moral qualities — gold on silver, as Homer said, or the icing on the cake, as we might
say. But as adornment it is functional, not superfluous and merely decorative. The
pleasure of *charis* is the spur to social activity, the engine of morality, the reward of
altruism."[51] Aristophanes is more down to earth: "Many make passes at Comedy, but
she puts out (*charisasthai*) for only a few" (*Knights* 515).

We can see something of this art of *charis* in Xenophon's account of Socrates'
visit to the house of Alcibiades' mistress, Theodote. Socrates is sure that Theodote
has learned how to charm (*charizesthai*) her "friends" "with a certain eye contact"
(*emblepousa*) and learned "that you need to make sure someone who pays you lots of
attention has been assiduously charmed (*kecharistai*)." The jolt of "assiduous" and
"charm" is fully intended, I think. This may involve congratulations on a success
and visits full of concern if he falls sick, a very prominent motif in all pre-modern
relationships of affection. Theodote must gradually build up the gracious exchanges,
asking her boyfriends for small things and paying them back by graciously favoring
(*charizomenēn*) in the same manner. She must not force-feed them on these courte-
sies, however, for she would most delight them (*charizoio*) if she gives what she's got
when they are feeling the lack of it. She should keep them keen "by being manifestly
reluctant to favor them (*charizesthai*), by running away until they are really begging
for it." For Theodote, at least, there is more to "putting out" than sex.[52] Personhood
is constructed through one's performance of subjectivity, one's mastery of what we
might call the game of agency, a game forced on courtesans, a game of choosing when
they didn't always have much choice, for men wanted to be loved for themselves, not
for their money. All this sometimes seems terribly remote and complicated, but we
understand the logic of it every day of our lives. We can see it, for instance, in one
parochial example that has become famous in the UK, when the comedian Caroline
Aherne in the guise of "Mrs. Merton" asked Debbie McGee during an interview "So,
what attracted you to the millionaire Paul Daniels?" It's as subtle, and as lacking in
subtlety, as that.

The associating/disassociating courtesan played a vital role in relationships between men. She was exclusive and might by her society define rank. The names
mentioned at Neaera's trial read like a Who's Who. The vast sums spent on her
might be well spent if it meant keeping her out of the hands of those beneath you.
She was light and trivial and helped to create a playful space where men who might
otherwise be deadly enemies could come together one evening and not talk about
politics and war. Of course this homosocial function might backfire, when men used
women to get at men, and courtesans like Neaera and Phryne found themselves
caught in the crossfire, the games of trivial pleasantry suddenly exposed as battles of
deadly earnest.

But *charis* is more than a one-way street. Hyperides began his speech on Phryne's
behalf by declaring that he himself was one of her hopeless devotees under the spell
of *erōs*. If not, it might seem that his speech was itself a service, a commodity, a payment for services rendered. Both sides of an exchange were implicated by its nature.
The insane sums spent on courtesans also functioned as a kind of potlatch. They

were a symbol of uncalculating passion, that extravagant generosity which is the mark of true love, an extravagant subjectivity. Men too had an interest in not being seen as whore clients, keeping their relationships even with ladies of shady reputation shady and out of the marketplace. Men of decency did not visit brothels. One of Stratonicus' more revealing witticisms tells how the musical wit was seen looking around shiftily as he emerged from the gates of the city of Heraclea: "I am ashamed to be seen," he said, "as if I were leaving a brothel." It is noticeable that the only "inn-cum-brothel" known from Athens, the one labeled "Building Z" by the archaeologists in Ceramicus, the "red-light district," has a hidden entrance, right under the city walls.[53] And there were some fancy rooms found there for guests and plenty of vessels for drinking and socializing, which belies the impression given by the comic poets that it was a question of a quick in and out. A depersonalized transaction depersonalized both parties. If she was a thing to you, you were a thing also, though you of course could choose whether or not to enter the space of commodification, while she could never leave.

THE PERSUASIVENESS OF PHRYNE

Yes the modeling of manners, yes the glory of an off-the-cuff remark. But of course the first art the courtesans taught their protégées, according to Alexis, the foremost thing they were famous for, was their appearance. Numerous sources describe their extraordinary beauty and also their obsession with mirrors, clothes of the latest fashion, in the best-quality colors, the jewels, very expensive items in themselves, which they sought from admirers and the way they upgraded them with added gold, a nice way of keeping control of one's looks and still being a grateful recipient. This is why Socrates visits Theodote—not to hear her jokes or explore with her the ironies of gift exchange. Someone had said: "the beauty of the woman defeats words (*kreitton logou*)." Then we will have to go sightseeing, replies Socrates, for "mere listeners are never going to get a proper understanding of that which defeats words." When they arrive she is already under the gaze, sitting for a painter. Socrates reflects on the obligations of viewer to viewed and of viewed to viewer.[54]

The phrase "defeats words" brings us back full circle to Phryne in a courtroom. For Phryne's famous disrobement is not just about nudity and nakedness, timelessness and history, piety and impiety. It is also about two different kinds of *peithō*, "persuasion" in Jane Austen's sense—not persuading but "persuasiveness"—one kind for the spectatorship of the eyes, the other for the audience of the ears, the argument of the voice and the argument of the vision, speech versus painting, the literary versus the visual arts. This is certainly what made Phryne's trial such a *cause célèbre* from antiquity to Gérôme via Rousseau. For "Phryne was saved not by the eloquence of Hyperides, marvelous though it was, but by the sight of her exquisite body, which she further revealed by drawing aside her tunic."[55] The earliest reference depicts an old courtesan teaching those too young to remember how Phryne, "most distinguished of us *hetairas*," went to each judge in turn, clasping him by the right hand and weeping. This is probably the seed of the story, a plea for mercy, a walkabout, a gesture of supplication with or without a little garment-rending.[56] The tale of the orator's violent exposure is not only more melodramatic, however, it also serves to turn the event into a contest between the noisy persuasion of the greatest speech of a great orator and the silent persuasion of the "most beautiful woman in the world." When words fail him, Phryne's cogent beauty rides to her rescue, which means that in a manner of speaking Phryne saves herself.

CONCLUSION

As many have noticed, the literature on courtesans is strongly characterized by its nostalgic antiquarian flavor.[57] But this is just another side of the coin from the contemporary sources which use her as a trope of contemporaneity. The vanishing beauty of the courtesan, as passing as the morning glories in a Dutch still life, has always configured a particular kind of modernity, city life, urbanity, terribly vivid, but fragile, brief, a present always with an eye on the time, a present distinguished not only from the past but from the future, a future from which it knows it will be looked back on with nostalgia, the latest fashion until the next big thing, not just a moment, but a moment captured for posterity, always latently elegiac, a bygone, shortly. Over time the courtesan configures an era and all its fractals, her floruit, the floruit of those she knew, a famous occasion, a few minutes, an event—not just modern, but instant, the time when someone fell over and she said . . , the time when she went to the festival of Poseidon and . . ., the time when she was on trial and Hyperides . . . , *the time when.* She is always in that respect a calendar girl, hodiernal, a beauty of Today. But her construction of a contemporaneity, soon to be lost forever, is a reflection, perhaps, of her evanescence in the present, the rare glimpse she once gave of an unapproachable world, a *monde*, peeped at through a keyhole, a body beneath its petticoats and draperies, shockingly exposed in a courtroom or in a gallery, the shock of nakedness, lending frisson to the shock of Now. That's what Manet put his finger on and used to pull his viewers into the present, a well-dressed courtesan's shocking modernity when surprised by a naked lens, not quite nude, not quite naked, with just a touch of fashion, or rather of a passing fashionability.

Notes

1. Hermippus 68aI (Wehrli) ap. Athenaeus 13.590e f.; cf. ibid. 590de, 591f; [Plutarch] *Hyperides* 849e, Harpocration s.v. "Euthias"; Alciphron *Letters of the Courtesans* 3–5 (1.30–32); Anon. *De sublimitate* 34.3; Quintilian 10.5.2. For the trial, see Laura McClure, *Courtesans at Table: Gender and Greek Literary Culture in Athenaeus* (London: Routledge, 2003), 132–36; Craig Cooper, "Hyperides and the Trial of Phryne," *Phoenix* 49 (1995): 303–18; and Robert Parker, *Athenian Religion* (Oxford: Clarendon Press, 1996), 162–3 with n. 34 and 214–17. McClure's recent book, a kind of commentary on the collection of much earlier snippets of literature gathered in Athenaeus, book 13, now provides by far the most up-to-date and accessible guide to the literature and scholarship on ancient courtesans, although her emphasis is very much on courtesans as a trope. It does contain some errors, however; cf. James Davidson, "*Liaisons Dangereuses*: Aphrodite and the Hetaera," *Journal of Hellenic Studies* 124 (2004): 169–73.

2. McClure, *Courtesans at Table*, 130–32.

3. Arnobius, *Adversus Gentes* 6.13.

4. Émile Zola, "Lettres de Paris: L'école française de peinture de 1878," *Le Messager de l'Europe*, July 1878.

5. Vincent van Gogh to Theo van Gogh, in *The Complete Letters of Vincent van Gogh* (Boston: Bullfinch, 1991), no. 117, Amsterdam, January 9, 1878.

6. T. J. Clark, *The Painting of Modern Life: Paris and the Art of Manet and His Followers* (Princeton: Princeton University Press, 1984), 79–146; cf. Judith Ryan, "More Seductive than Phryne: Baudelaire, Gérôme, Rilke, and the Problem of Autonomous Art," *Proceedings of the Modern Language Association* 108 (1993): 1128–41.

7. Émile Zola, "Nos peintres au Champ de Mars," in *La Situation*, July 1, 1867.

8. Athenaeus 13.587c, 591f; McClure, *Courtesans at Table*, 62. Since there are several courtesans named after religious festivals, the problem seems to have been specifically with slave girls, as the passage, *pace* McClure, makes clear.

9. The most drastic use of this idea is to be found in Paul Cartledge, *The Greeks: A Portrait of Self and Others*, 2d ed. (Oxford: Oxford University Press, 2002), with a new preface which falls a little short of a full-scale recantation.

10. I have discussed this at length in James Davidson, "Revolutions in Human Time: Age-Class in Athens and the Greekness of Greek Revolutions," forthcoming in *Rethinking Revolutions*, ed. Robin Osborne and Simon Goldhill (Cambridge: Cambridge University Press, 2005).

11. On this feature, see now Lloyd Llewellyn-Jones, *Aphrodite's Tortoise: The Veiled Woman of Ancient Greece* (Swansea: Classical Press of Wales, 2003), very much alive to the East-versus-West debate.

12. E.g., Bruce Thornton, "Greek Appetite and Its Discontents," *Arion*, 3rd ser. 7, no. 3 (2000): 153–66.

13. This is a recurrent theme of Sîan Lewis, *The Athenian Woman: An Iconographic Handbook* (London: Routledge, 2002).

14. McClure, *Courtesans at Table*, 137–65, provides all the evidence, but believes it not "solid," 140.

15. Vinciane Pirenne-Delforge, *L'Aphrodite grecque: Contribution à l'étude de ses cultes et de sa personnalité dans la pantheon archaïque et classique*, Kernos Suppl. 4 (Liège: Centre International d'Étude de la Religion Grecque Antique, 1994).

16. See, for instance, Mary Beard and John Henderson, "With This Body I Thee Worship: Sacred Prostitution in Antiquity," *Gender and History* 9 (1997): 480–503; Fay Glinister, "The Rapino Bronze, the Touta Marouca, and Sacred Prostitution in Early Central Italy," in *The Epigraphic Landscape of Roman Italy*, ed. Alison E. Cooley, BICS Suppl. 73 (London: Institute of Classical Studies, University of London, 2000), 19–38; and various articles in *Prostitutes and Courtesans in the Ancient World*, ed. Christopher A. Faraone and Laura K. McClure (Madison: Wisconsin University Press, forthcoming 2006). Cf. Leslie Kurke, "Pindar and the Prostitutes," *Arion* 42 (1996): 49–75; and Davidson, "*Liaisons Dangereuses.*"

17. McClure, *Courtesans at Table*, trivializes the cult of the goddess: "perhaps not much more than a special symposium" (142). Pirenne-Delforge, *L'Aphrodite*, plays down the links to courtesans and indeed the "*porneion*" (74–80, 97–8, 176–8, 281–6).

18. Pirenne-Delforge, *L'Aphrodite*: "Phryné joua à l'Aphrodite Anadyomène" (177, n. 41).

19. Pierre Briant, *From Cyrus to Alexander* (Winona Lake, IN: Einsenbrauns, 2002).

20. James N. Davidson, *Courtesans and Fishcakes: The Consuming Passions of Classical Athens* (London: HarperCollins, 1997), chap. 4.

21. M. L. West, *Ancient Greek Music* (Oxford: Clarendon Press, 1992), 81–109.

22. [Demosthenes] 59.67; cf. Lysias 10.19 and Plutarch *Solon* 23.1. The phrase is found in

whole or in part in at least two separate laws; Eberhard Ruschenbusch, *Solōnos Nomoi: Die Fragmente des Solonischen Gesetzeswerkes*, Historia Einzelschriften, vol. 9 (Wiesbaden: Steiner, 1966), Frr. 29 and 30; cf. Michael Hillgruber, *Die zehnte Rede des Lysias*, Untersuchungen zur antiken Literatur und Geschichte, vol. 29 (Berlin: de Gruyter, 1988), 77–79.

23. Eupolis 99.27 K–A; Xenarchus 4 K–A; and Philemon 3 K–A; cf. Eubulus 67 and 82 K–A.

24. See now the essays in *Music and the Muses: The Culture of Mousike in the Classical Athenian City*, ed. Penelope Murray and Peter Wilson (Oxford: Oxford University Press, 2004) and *Performance Culture and Athenian Democracy*, ed. Simon Goldhill and Robin Osborne (Cambridge: Cambridge University Press, 1999).

25. Davidson, *Courtesans and Fishcakes*, 80–83.

26. Peter Wilson, "The *Aulos* in Athens," in *Performance Culture and Athenian Democracy*, ed. Goldhill and Osborne, 58–95. It is amazing that the aulos girls, about whom there is more data than any other professional musicians, have been so neglected by the burgeoning scholarship on musical performance.

27. Plutarch *Pelopidas* 19.1, with Aristoula Georgiadou, *Plutarch's Pelopidas: A Historical and Philological Commentary*, Beiträge zur Altertumskunde, vol. 105 (Stuttgart and Leipzig: Teubner, 1997), ad loc. for further notes and references.

28. John G. Landels, *Music in Ancient Greece and Rome* (London: Routledge, 1999), 115–16.

29. Plato *Laws* 809e, 812d; *Lysis* 209b; Aristophanes *Frogs* 1284–97. In general see West, *Ancient Greek Music*, chap. 3, esp. p. 69, and for the aristocratic lyre, 25–6, Plutarch *Alcibiades* 2.5. Alcibiades despises the aulos and praises the lyre because it does not destroy the face and leaves it "fitting for a free man." McDowell ad Aristophanes *Wasps* 959: "Learning to play the lyre was part of the traditional education of an Athenian gentleman. It is a symbol of artistic and intellectual activity; the opposite is digging" (citing also *Knights* 987–96 and *Clouds* 964); cf. fr. 232, Plutarch *Themistocles* 2.3: Themistocles was of low birth . . . "So, later, in the midst of the pastimes called liberal and sophisticated he was mocked by those who supposed themselves educated and was compelled to defend himself in vulgar fashion. He said he didn't know how to tune a lyre or attempt the plucking little harp, but he did know how to make a paltry inglorious city into a great and glorious one." Players tried to play quickly; see Plato *Charmides* 159c.

30. Aeschines 1.41 and the comic fragments cited by Athenaeus 8.339ac.

31. Daniel Delattre, "Contrat d'apprentissage d'un joueur d'*auloi*," in *Instruments, musiques et musiciens de l'antiquité classique*, ed. Arthur Muller, Ateliers 4 (Lille: Université Charles-de-Gaulle, 1995), 55–69, at 67.

32. Isocrates 4.287; cf. Liddle and Scott, *Greek–English Lexicon* (*LSJ*) with Suppl. s.v. *aulētērion*.

33. Plautus *Rudens* 43.

34. Makron (attrib. Beazley) BM E61 = Beazley Archive 204827. Other examples are a column krater in Taranto ascribed by Beazley to the Pig Painter = BA 206436, "Woman Seated, Playing Pipes, Draped Man with Purse Leaning on Staff, Woman with Pipes Case, Box and Lyre Suspended," and Rhodes, Archaeological Museum, 12887 = BA 214766, early classical pelike, Hephaistos Painter (attrib. Beazley), "Domestic, woman with lyre seated on chair, draped youth with purse, leaning on staff, sponge (?) suspended."

35. Jeremy Trevett, *Apollodoros, the Son of Pasion* (Oxford: Clarendon Press, 1992).

36. For this and other references to upgrading skills, Demosthenes 36.43; 45.71–2; [Aristotle] *Oeconomica* 1.4.1 1344a.

37. *Etymologicum Magnum* 367.12; Hesychius (ε 5413); Aristophanes *Frogs* 1301 and 1325–28; Suda s.vv. *Dodekamēchanon* = delta, 1442; *Hetairai Korinthiai* = epsilon, 3266; West,

Ancient Greek Music, 354; cf. Pherecrates 155 K–A. Kenneth Dover, in his edition of Aristophanes, *Frogs* (Oxford: Clarendon Press, 1993), suggests, ad l.1327, that the twelve-trick thing was her vagina.

38. Epicrates 2 K–A.

39. William Beare, in *Oxford Classical Dictionary*, 3d ed. (Oxford: Oxford University Press, 1996) s.v. "mime," and in general see James Davidson, "Gnesippus *Paigniagraphos*: The Comic Poets and the Erotic Mime," in *The Rivals of Aristophanes: Studies in Athenian Old Comedy*, ed. John Wilkins and David Harvey (London: Duckworth, 2000), 41–64.

40. Chionides 4 K–A, Eupolis 148 K–A, Cratinus 17 K–A, 276 K–A. Kassel–Austin, ad Chionides 4, propose that the punning allusion to "plucking songs" implies either spoiling (*disperdere*, Meineke) or tearing to pieces like a critic (*lacerare*), but given the emphasis on Gnesippus' use of stringed instruments, it is surely much better to see a reference to harps, as *LSJ* s.v. *tillō* suggest; cf. *psallō*. For Glauce see A. S. F. Gow ad Theocritus 4.31, Hedylus X (Gow–Page), Aelian *NA* 5.29.

41. Polybius 14.11.2 ap. Ath. 13.576f; cf. D. Ogden, *Polygamy, Prostitutes, and Death: The Hellenistic Dynasties* (London: Duckworth, 1999), 223–6 with notes.

42. K. A. Kapparis, *Apollodorus "Against Neaira"* [D. 59] (Berlin: de Gruyter, 1999); Debra Hamel, *Trying Neaira: The True Story of a Courtesan's Scandalous Life in Ancient Greece* (New Haven: Yale University Press, 2003); Davidson, "Liaisons Dangereuses."

43. [Demosthenes] 59.18.

44. Athenaeus 13.567a, 583de, 586ab, 586f, 591cd 596f; see Jacoby's commentary on *FGrHist* 347–51; Ogden. *Polygamy*, 228, n. 43.

45. Idomeneus, *FGrHist* 338 F 14 ap. Ath. 590cd, probably from his book *On the Demagogues in Athens*; see Jacoby's commentary.

46. Alexis 103 K–A = Athenaeus 13. 568ad.

47. Again the evidence is collected by McClure, *Courtesans at Table*, 79–105, and studied as a trope ("the marginal or low other turns the tables on an interlocutor of equal or higher status," 105), but I am not at all sure that the awesome *semnai hetairai* really were "marginal or low" others, in the symbolic universe of the symposium, which cannot be said of the *parasitoi*; cf. Davidson, "Liaisons Dangereuses."

48. Leslie Kurke, "Gender, Politics, and Subversion in the *Chreiai* of Machon," *Proceedings of the Cambridge Philosophical Society* 48 (2002): 20–65.

49. Aeschines 1.168 with Aeschines, *Against Timarchos*, trans. N. R. E. Fisher (Oxford: Clarendon Press, 2001), ad loc. Cf. Aelian, *Varia Historia* 3.32. Silvia Milanezi, "Laughter as Dessert: On Athenaeus' Book Fourteen, 613–16," in *Athenaeus and His World: Reading Greek Culture in the Roman Empire*, ed. David Braund and John Wilkins (Exeter: University of Exeter Press, 2000), 400–412, esp. 405–6.

50. Aristotle *Nicomachean Ethics* 1128a33.

51. Bonnie MacLachlan, *The Age of Grace: Charis in Early Greek Poetry* (Princeton: Princeton University Press, 1993), 149.

52. Xenophon *Cyropaedia*, 5.1.18, 6.1.31–2; cf. *Memorabilia* 3.11.10.

53. Athenaeus 351d; Davidson, *Courtesans and Fishcakes*, 72, 83–91; cf. Ray Laurence, *Roman Pompeii: Space and Society* (London: Routledge, 1994), 73: "The brothels are sited in streets that are not through-routes and were isolated from the main areas of social activity."

54. Xenophon *Memorabilia* 3.11.

55. Quintilian 2.15.9; cf. Alciphron Letters 4 (1.31.4).

56. Posidippus (fl. 289 B.C. –?), *Ephesian Woman* 13 K–A ap. Ath. 13.591ef.

57. For Athenaeus' nostalgia, see Davidson, "Pleasure and Pedantry in Athenaeus," in *Athenaeus and His World*, 292–303, 570–71.

Cutting a Good Figure

The Fashions of Venetian Courtesans in the
Illustrated Albums of Early Modern Travelers

CONSUMING THE COURTESAN

In this essay I argue that Venetian courtesans were not transgressors of dress codes but fashion trendsetters who played artfully with the visual boundaries separating women into distinct groups. My principal evidence consists of three unpublished miniature albums in manuscript dating from the 1570s to the 1590s that display courtesans and other women in various states of dress. Rather than mere mimicry of the styles of Venetian noblewomen by courtesans, these manuscripts show that courtesans selected clothing from many different groups of women both as a tool for collective identification and to create highly individualized styles. They also show that certain courtesans not only negotiated social freedoms as writers and musicians but managed as a collective to attract to the lagoon republic foreign visitors who hoped to witness them in action during annual festivals.[1] Visitors often purchased visual representations of courtesans' dress in the Venetian marketplace and then placed them, together with colored miniatures of other Venetian fashions of both men and women, in personal albums as memories of their visit.[2]

The colored miniatures in travelers' albums required a trained eye capable of un-raveling the many social identities present in the courtesans' fashionable ensembles since courtesans took advantage of the fact that clothing was a useful but highly deceptive tool for social differentiation. Unlike women of the upper social ranks, who were required to display their identities with regard to their marital status alone, courtesans were relatively free to pick and choose from the clothing available to them and cobble together personal identities. Doing so became easier with the fluid social structure of sixteenth-century Venice, where wealth no longer belonged, as it once had in the fourteenth and fifteenth centuries, to one privileged social register but was located in and attainable through the many sumptuous objects that the city produced and traded. Principal among these was cloth, which courtesans wore on their persons to advertise not just their city's splendor but themselves as individuals. In this specific sense, the Venetian courtesan was the prototype for the fashionable

woman. She displayed a style that was individual, with unusual color choices and decorative trims, while adhering to conventional sartorial limits, thus revealing a mastery over her own body (fig. 2.1). The fabric is striped in matching colors of gold and green. Her overgarment, with revers turned back, is held together in front with a silk sash that accentuates the line of the garment, and the gold braid and buttons on the sleeves are inspired by Spanish military garb. An entrepreneur of the self, the courtesan knew well how to advance in the social echelons of Venetian life by adapting to the vagaries of custom.

Cesare Vecellio indexes this phenomenon in his famous costume books printed in Venice in 1590 and 1598, providing extensive commentary, often critical, on the dress of his fellow Venetian citizens. Profiting from a direct knowledge of the city as a mecca of trade, a center of publishing, and a meeting point between the East and the West, Vecellio brings to the reader a mine of information about material culture—art, textiles, and world trade systems. When describing the figures of the "Venetian Noblewomen and Others, at Home and Outdoors in the Winter," he notes that courtesans, both indoors and outside on the Venetian thoroughfares, match the refinement of Venetian noblewomen but can nonetheless be distinguished from them by their physical demeanor and by the "laws" that restrict their display of luxury goods:

far more than others, courtesans in their houses present themselves as elegant and well turned out . . . they can be recognized easily by the way they carry themselves, for at home and outdoors they behave very boldly, showing not only their faces but a lot of their breast, whitened and painted, and most of the embroidered stockings that cover their legs. But a difference is visible between these women and honorable women in their dress and in their accessories, since courtesans cannot wear pearls, as honorable women do, according to the carefully designed laws in place in the city of Venice, though some of them . . . do wear them. And they also wear the dress shown here, just as virtuous women of good reputation do.[3]

The three illustrated manuscript albums I deal with were all owned by northern European travelers and selected as evidence for their particular interest in Italian—especially Venetian—women's dress. Like other early modern travelers, their owners were fascinated with different types of ephemera: manuscript decoration and changing styles of clothing, manners, and customs. A predecessor of the printed Renaissance costume book, colored albums, called *alba amicorum* or "albums of friends," depict fashions in clothing and daily scenes of regional life. Images are assembled on individual folios together with witty mottoes, emblems, and heraldic shields, and organized throughout by geographical region (country and city) and social ranks of figures represented. Unlike printed costume books these collections were personalized according to the preferences of the individual collector, and only later added to private holdings of the elite northern families to which the students returned. Of course, the very idea of assembling a fashion album as a stable collection of memories is a contradiction since an album of memories suggests a degree of permanence while fashion involves endless change.[4]

Album miniatures were painted directly into the bound album and dated but rarely signed by their artists. The people of each city were summed up by brightly colored, conventionalized images of the clothing worn by their officials and citizens. In cities such as Padua and Venice, travelers consulted individual drawings and watercolors of local costume available in printers' and stationers' shops and directly from artists, and had them painted into their albums. Signatures of friends and distinguished academists are often included on the same folio with illustrations, creating a kind of temporal diary that records for posterity the owner's peregrinations and experiences. Personalizing their albums according to economic means, taste, and experience, the owners often adorned their books over many years. They were small-format books that could travel with their owners like prints, easily transportable from place to place.

From one album to the next, images were often duplicated with only subtle variations in pose, gesture, color, and fabric type, even though the albums' owners come from different European countries.[5] These duplications suggest that originally there were prototype drawings for illustrations, now lost, from which buyers could pick and choose. Such prototypes were probably kept in print shops, stationery stores, or the "workshops" of itinerant painters who moved around in various urban locales. Padua and Venice are important in this regard, as in the sixteenth century both were not only university locales but also centers of manuscript illumination, publishing, printmaking, and fashion.

The album of a Nuremberg university student who studied in Padua, Sigismund

FIGURE 2.2. "Gentildonna Venetiana." British Library, MS Egerton 1191, fol. 61.

Ortels (MS Egerton 1911, of 1575–77), contains a wide assortment of Venetian and Paduan noblewomen's and courtesans' dress and the luxury goods—textiles and jewels—that they used to adorn their gowns (figs. 2.2 and 2.3).[6] Rather than a mere travel album, Ortels's compilation is a highly personalized collection of memories, containing numerous coats of arms, signatures, learned mottoes, and witty poems and quips, written in the hands of his fellow students.[7] His interests, and those of other university students and their friends, in clothing, habits, and languages of other lands, and modes of self-expression and definition, expressed an awareness of their global world.[8] The album Yale 457 was apparently commissioned by a French patron and similarly dates to 1575–76.[9] Represented in a portrait medallion at the front of the book, its patron is identified by his coat of arms as a member of the de la Houssaye de la Morandais family of Brittany. A third album from 1595, Los Angeles 91.71—an authentic *album amicorum*—was owned, unlike the Ortels or French albums, by a Hungarian military officer who took his bound manuscript onto the battlefield, where he collected the signatures of his comrades-in-arms, most likely after the miniatures had already been designed and painted.

Album miniatures raise many questions in relation to representations of courtesans: How was the courtesan's dress legible to other countries and social groups? How

FIGURE 2.3. "Cortegiana Venetiana." British Library, MS Egerton 1191, fol. 62.

did she function within a system of cultural tourism? Was the courtesan a fashion trendsetter, and what might that mean in a larger sense? A study of these visual representations makes it clear that it is necessary to look beyond the commonly held notion that courtesans were simply code breakers, for beneath their transgressive demeanor lies a much more tangled net of realities that both defy and reinstate social boundaries.

VENICE AND THE FASHIONABLE COURTESAN

In the early modern period Venice was the principal European center of technological innovation in manufacturing and in the production of luxury goods such as textiles (especially silk and wool), sugar, paper, lace, soap, and glass.[10] The city's geographic location facilitated its ability to dominate land-based trade, as it was highly accessible to northern European cities through a number of Alpine passes and to the rest of Italy via the roads and rivers of the alluvial plain of northern Italy. In addition, the medieval manufacturing guilds of Venice, more numerous there than anywhere else in Italy, continued to expand throughout the sixteenth century. Venice was no longer just a distribution point between West and East as it had been in the late fifteenth and early sixteenth centuries, but controlled the movement of luxury goods from the Middle East to northern Europe, and luxury goods produced in the Veneto region even supplanted goods from the Levant.

The demand of Renaissance Italians for consumable, often luxury goods, constituted not merely an economic force but a social one.[11] Tourists, many of whom were also merchants, traveled great distances to witness the material wealth of the Venetian Republic and take part in its splendid ceremonies and festivities. At specific times of the year, sumptuous objects bought and traded in the open-air markets, fairs, and public auctions were displayed.[12] At these times elite Venetian women and high-ranking courtesans advertised to tourists, and to one another, the elegance and distinctive nature of Venetian dress as they descended upon the piazzas to rent, buy, or trade clothing and goods in the city's public markets. Patricia Allerston's illuminating research into the "supply mechanisms" and uses of clothing in early modern Venice has revealed that while the high costs of clothes imposed limits on the numbers of Venetians who could afford them, the second-hand clothing industry helped individuals acquire clothes that they could otherwise not have owned:

> Clothes could be bought new and second-hand from the workshops of guild-registered dealers . . . in the Ghetto, at market stalls, from peddlers passing through the streets, as well as in taverns. They could also be bought directly from public auctions, which probably proved a cheaper alternative, unless they were rigged by unscrupulous dealers . . . Yet, if buying was out of the question, clothes could also be hired on short-term rental agreements.[13]

With her clothes, the courtesan played with the visual demarcations that divided women into groups according to the stages of their life cycle and their marital status: maiden (*donzella*, fig. 2.4), married woman (*sposa*, fig. 2.5), or widow (*vedova*, fig. 2.6).

That courtesans wore styles of clothing similar to those of women from more privileged social groups does not necessarily mean that these are the only groups to which courtesans aspired. Allerston argues, apropos the story of the early seventeenth-century Venetian courtesan Pasquetta, that donning her luxurious clothing allowed her, and other courtesans like her, to "advertise their success." In addition, luxurious clothing was a way for courtesans to take advantage of a hybrid, "chaotic, dynamic and densely populated" city such as Venice. The courtesan thereby exposed the very notion of fashion as it was newly defined in the sixteenth century—fashion as endless change, pretense, performative counterfeit, and social subversion.[14]

How fast did Venetian women's fashions change during the sixteenth century and how much did courtesans keep up with these changes? Costume historians locate the most significant shifts in the large transformations in women's silhouettes as taking place approximately every twenty years. These transformations mainly affected the décolleté, the length of the bodice, the shape of the sleeves, and the coiffure. Doretta Davanzo Poli charts these changes specifically for Venetian dress: by the late 1540s to the late 1550s, the low-neckline bodice is very rigid and opens almost immediately below the breast, stopping at the waist, and often descending

FIGURE 2.4. "Donzella
Padoana." British Library, MS
Egerton 1191, fol. 82.

below it into a V. The neckline is wide and square and the gown's skirt is gathered
into soft folds. Detachable sleeves are streamlined and edged with richly embroidered cuffs. The coiffure is composed of curls that dangle onto the forehead. In the
1550s this silhouette changes when the bodice becomes pointed and extremely rigid,
maintained by structural supports known as "costelle" or small pieces of ribbed cot-
ton fabric that hold the bodice open in the front as the décolleté falls well below
the breast and shoulders. This exposed neckline is covered with a "bavaro"—a neck
piece, sometimes made of richly embroidered fabric, or a neck ruff in a fan shape. As
the century draws to an end, the ruff becomes increasingly large. The overskirt is
tightly gathered and ends in a long train. The coiffure consists of hair pulled to the
back, formed into small "crowns" decorated with gold and silver and fresh flowers.
Small curls frame the face or are pulled into nets or head veils.[15] All of these changes
are documented through the 1570s in Davanzo Poli's essay, but extend until the 1590s
in the dress of both noblewomen and courtesans, who, according to Vecellio, prefer
to dress as married women:

> Courtesans who wish to get ahead by feigning respectability go around dressed as
> widows or married women. Most courtesans dress as young virgins anyway. In fact,

FIGURE 2.5. "Sposa." British
Library, MS Egerton 1191,
fol. 65.

they button themselves up even more than virgins do. But a compromise must
eventually be reached between the wearing of a mantle that hides their bodies
and their need to be seen, at least to some extent. Finally, courtesans are forced to
open up at the neck, and one recognizes at once who they are, for the lack of pearls
speaks loud and clear. Courtesans are prohibited from wearing pearls. Indeed, in
order to remedy this situation, some arrange to be accompanied by a love-protector,
borrowing his name as if the two of them were married. In this way courtesans feel
free to wear things forbidden to them by law.[16]

Which features of the noblewoman's dress distinguish her from the Venetian
courtesan? If we compare figs. 2.10–2.12 with the earlier miniatures in figs. 2.1 and
2.3, it is evident that many of the attributes commonly held as the signatures of the
courtesan—naked breasts, extremely high platform shoes, pearls, and male breeches—were not universal. As the miniature of the Venetian noblewoman of the 1570s
makes clear (fig. 2.2), she is the one who bares her breasts in keeping with the fashion
of the day, not the courtesan. In this sense, clothes were deceptive tools for differentiating Venetian social groups because *many* Venetians, given the second-hand
market, had access to extremely expensive clothes that crossed social and gender

FIGURE 2.6. "Vedova
Venetiana." British Library,
MS Egerton 1191, fol. 64.

lines. Courtesans in particular must have profited greatly from this market, as their multiple identities in manuscript albums clearly reveal.

Differentiating courtesans from noblewomen based on clothing depended greatly upon seeing them in action. And yet not all travelers were pleased to see them at all. The Calvinist John Cheke, for example, who attended the University of Padua, wrote this note to Secretary Petre on 22 July 1554: "Here is a country much esteemed in opinion, of which yet being unskilled, he [Cheke] cannot judge certainly without rashness, else at first sight he would say that neither for private order, nor yet common behaviour, is it anything to be compared to their own supposed barbarous country. 'Courtesan in honor, haunting of evil houses noble; breaking of a marriage a sport; murder in Gentleman, Magnanimity; Robbery, Finesse if it be clean conveyed, for the spying is judged the fault and not the stealing."[17] By contrast, Fynes Moryson, a Cambridge graduate who wandered Europe in the 1590s, applauded the dress of all Venetian women with the utmost enthusiasm:

FIGURE 2.7. "Gentildonna Venetiana come vano fora di casa." Los Angeles County Museum of Art, M.91.71.93.

The women in general are delighted with mixed and light colors. The women of Venice wear choppiness or shoos three or foure hand-bredths high, so as the lowest of them seeme higher than the tallest men, and for this cause they cannot goe in the streetes without leaning upon the shoulder of an old woman. They have another old woman to beare up the traine of their gowne, & they are not attended with any man, but only with old women . . . The women of Venice weare gownes, leaving all of the necke and brest bare, and they are closed before with a lace, so open, as a mean may see the linen which they lap about their bodies, to make them seeme fat, the Italians most loving fat women. They shew their naked necks and breasts, and likewise their dugges, bound up and swelling with linen, and all made white by art.

Moryson later reminds the reader that this breast-baring is not practiced by noble-women elsewhere in Italy ("And Gentlewomen in generall, wear gownes loose be-hind, with a close collar, hiding all nakednesse"),[18] emphasizing the fact that Vene-tian courtesans have much more freedom of movement in and outside the city when compared to other women: "While Curtizans walke and ride in Coaches at liberty, and freely saluted and honored by all men passing by them, theire wives and virgins are locked up at home, watched by their wemen attending them abroad, have their faces covered with a vaile not to be seene, and it is death by private reveng for any man to salute them or make the least shewe of love to them."[19]

FIGURE 2.8. "Una Donzella
Venetiana." Yale 457, "Mores
Italiae," fol. 97.

Moryson also makes a special note of the veil worn by women of the nobility, which sets them apart, he claims, from courtesans and lower-ranking women.
As is evident in figs. 2.3 and 2.10, though, the courtesan also had a veil which she
could raise to reveal her face and breasts beneath. Her gestures are what give her
away in public, even when she disguises herself as a married woman, a maiden, or a
widow. Indeed, Vecellio warns his reader that Venetian courtesans (prostitutes, he
calls them) manipulate sartorial distinctions for their own designs (see figs. 2.11 and
2.12):

> We said earlier that prostitutes who want to gain credit by means of feigned modesty
> wear widows' clothing, and that of married women, especially in the color worn by
> brides. Formerly, most of them went about dressed as maidens, a custom still in ef-
> fect but with greater modesty. So as not to be completely enclosed and covered by
> their long veils and yet not allowed to be visible, they are forced to reveal themselves
> slightly, so they cannot fail to be recognized by this gesture. And because they are
> forbidden to wear pearls, they reveal themselves as prostitutes when they expose
> their bare necks. So to make up for this, these unfortunate women use a *bertone* (as
> they are called), who plays the role of a husband for them and permits them the use
> of luxury goods, and under this pretext they can avail themselves of everything that

FIGURE 2.9. "Gentildonna Venetiana." Yale 457, "Mores Italiae," fol. 49.

the laws generally forbid them. Their gowns are of *brocatello* of various colors,[20] and embroidered at the greatest expense they can afford. They wear Roman-style shoes inside their mules, and these are the courtesans of highest standing. But those who openly and in public places practice this infamous profession, wear silk doublets with gold ties or embroidery of some kind, and also skirts, which they cover with tied up cloths or silk aprons. On their heads they wear a short gauze veil, and in this style they go flirting throughout the city, and easily recognized by everybody, they are easily targeted by everyone with gestures and words.[21]

But Vecellio also reminds his reader that the courtesan could not dress as another at all times. She had to be noticeable to the public world. If donning others' clothes successfully camouflaged her identity, lifting her veil and peering out into the world did not. For after all, the Venetian courtesan was a woman who needed to be seen as she expertly navigated through the circuitous waterways of the city and the shifting boundaries separating women into groups. This she did by cutting a good figure.

Miniature and costume book illustrations demonstrate vividly that the dress of Venetian women, and courtesans in particular, was much less circumscribed and codified than imagined by foreign travelers, for whom women's dress, far less than

men's, must have been an extremely confusing spectacle. Illustrated albums, sometimes produced on a yearly basis, were able to register subtle changes in fashions
faster than printed costume books (even if both grouped images by gender and social
status). Vecellio admits despite himself that fast-changing fashions make him anxious: will his coverage of 1590 be obsolete by the new edition of 1598? And, if fashions transform at such an alarming rate, how will he ever provide accurate coverage?
The main culprits, more than shifting trends in fabric production and cuts of clothes,
he contends, are Venetian women as a whole, with their vain, obsessive need to "stay
in fashion": "Because women's clothing is very subject to change and is as variable as
the phases of the moon, it's not possible in one description to say all that can be said
about it. Indeed, it's rather to be feared that even as I am describing a style, women
are turning to another one, so that it's impossible for me to capture it all."[22]

His and other costume books represent a nostalgic desire to return to a mythi-
cally well-ordered society where social ranks were not only distinct and legible to
others but also harmonious. In his world, to the contrary, Venetian women of middle
and lower ranks intermingled with men in the public spaces much more frequently

FIGURE 2.11. Cesare Vecellio, "Cortigiane moderne" (1590)

than previously thought, especially from 1540 to 1630, when working women were a visibly active part of public life.[23]

We might ask, then, whose nostalgia for order it really was: that of the artist who followed the models laid out in the costume books, or created new drawings not available in print; the Venetians who hung on to and publicized abroad notions of unchallenged social order; or the foreign travelers who acquired miniatures to take home as mementos? Because the miniatures adhere to a hierarchical ordering system, they reinforce an idealized image of Venice and its territories. Courtesan-poets like Veronica Franco might take advantage of travelers' praise of their fame and skills, but they nonetheless helped promote the notion that the Republic was unusually flexible and tolerant regarding women.[24]

Still, Venetian civic authorities, like Vecellio and others, were periodically troubled in the sixteenth century by the courtesan's ability to destabilize the boundaries

FIGURE 2.12. Cesare
Vecellio, "Meretrici
publiche" (1590).

between the material surfaces of the body and a person's interior, and by the deep
transformations of selfhood that fast changes in fashion allowed. Changing fashion
could index the frivolity, instability, and fickleness of women. And if fashionable
clothing allowed new identities,[25] they might be hard to alter since clothes were a
sign of one's inner "habits." As Stallybrass and Jones argue, clothes "constitute[d] subjects through their power as material memories" and "a worn world of social relations
put upon the wearers' body."[26] Illustrated miniatures reveal for album owners not just
memories of luxurious surfaces but memories of those who wore them.

Courtesans' manipulation of women's dress codes relied upon the personal
touches they added and their use of gesture. More than in the printed costume
books, where color and performativity are less apparent, brightly colored miniatures
depict courtesans in action, so to speak, as they display their individual tastes in color
and fabric. Flaps intended to be raised by the viewer conceal what lies beneath their

gowns, recalling erotic scenes of courtship and seduction in carriages and gondolas. Indeed, scenes of flirtation abound in travelers' illustrated albums.

THE FESTIVAL OF THE SENSA: WITNESSING THE COURTESAN AND CARRYING HER NORTH

In his travel chronicle, John Evelyn reported with dazzled amazement that the Feast of the Ascension (the "Sensa") was more splendid than any ceremony he had ever witnessed, focusing much of his comment on the dress of Venetian women:

> It was now Ascension-week, and the great mart, or fair, of the whole year was kept, everybody at liberty and jolly; the noblemen stalking with their ladies on choppines . . . The truth is, their garb is very odd, as seeming always in masquerade; their other habits also totally different from other nations . . . And many times in the cities (as at Padua) I have seene Curtizans (in plaine English, whores) in the time of shroving, appareled like men, in carnation or light colored doublets and breeches, and so playing with the racket at Tennis with yong men, at which time of shroving, the Women no lesse than Men, (and that honourable women in honourable company,) goe masked and appareled like men all the afternoone about the streetes, even from Christmasse holydaies to the first day of Lent. The Women wearing Mens breeches, have them open all before, and most part behind, only buttoned with gold or silver buttons: And the Curtizans make all the forpart of their gownes in like manner open, to avoide wrinckling.[27]

A fifteen-day fair that culminated in the ritual ceremony of the Marriage of Venice to the Sea, the Sensa took place in May leading up to Ascension Day (fig. 2.13). In this period, piazza San Marco became a free-trade zone where all craft controls were suspended, thereby allowing mercers, goldsmiths, foreign fabric makers, and used clothing dealers to set up improvised shops, carts, and stalls to sell their wares.[28] Venetian guilds played a special civic role on such ceremonial occasions. Many trades concerned with the production and sale of luxury items—paintings, furniture, textiles, carpets, mirrors, and objects of glass, gold, and silver—displayed their wares while shops were ordered to remain closed.[29] It was also the only time during the year that foreign artists were allowed to sell their works in Venice without incurring fines such as those famously levied on Albrecht Dürer. Historians have noted, however, that "it was not an occasion for major international trading as the Champagne fairs of France were. Instead, it was an opportunity for shoppers to purchase small gifts and various other ornaments."[30]

During the Sensa, while male tourists purchased and traded goods such as prints, drawings, painted miniatures, fabrics, silver and gold objects, lace, and embroideries in the free-trade zone in piazza San Marco, courtesans acquired or rented clothing and art objects to decorate their homes.[31] It is likely that the drawing prototypes for album watercolor miniatures created by local and itinerant artists were available for consultation and purchase from the many *cartolerie* and print dealers' shops that lined the Frezzaria and Mercerie—the two main commercial thoroughfares stretching from piazza San Marco to the Rialto district—both especially famous, as Vecellio notes, for luxurious fabrics:

FIGURE 2.13. Cesare
Vecellio, "Nobile ornata alle
feste" (1590).

These lovely fabrics were invented here in Venice by Messer Bartholomeo Bontem-
pele, at the sign of the Chalice, who, when he exhibits these materials of his own
design, demonstrates his brilliant skill, for which, added to his incredible liberality
and generosity, he is much loved by the Venetian nobility, and by many princes of
Italy, especially the most serene Duke of Mantua. In his shop, to which many great
lords and princes send orders, and even as far as the seraglio of the Great Turk, can
be seen all sorts of brocades woven with gold and silver.[32]

So, too, Evelyn waxed eloquently on the beauty of the fabrics he saw lining these
streets:

Hence, I passed through the Merceria, one of the most delicious streets in the
world for the sweetness of it, and is all the way on both sides tapestried as it were
with cloth of gold, rich damasks and other silks, which the shops expose and hang
before their houses from the first floor, and with that variety that for near half the
year spent chiefly in this city, I hardly remember to have seen the same piece twice
exposed.

Evelyn reports a curious confusion when he remarks that both Venetian courtesans and "citizens" cover their bodies with veils made "of a certain glittering taffeta, or lustree, out of which they now and then dart a glance of their eye, the whole face being otherwise entirely hid with it; but go abroade barefaced. To the corner of these virgin-veils hang broad but flat tassels of curious *point de Venise*" (adding that the veils of married women are black).[33]

Lina Urban argues that the fair had specifically "strong associations for women."[34] And Allerston sees the Sensa as an opportunity for Venetians of all social groups and registers to share "access to the famous shopping streets and squares of Venice . . . where luxury fabrics and trimmings were displayed for all to see. Most sectors of society also participated in the city's festive occasions . . . which . . . required additional adornment." In the absence of clearly-defined clothing codes, courtesans' specific attire during these periods of the year can be regarded as a form of "collective identification."[35]

Such identifications were translated and circulated in the many drawings that served as models for manuscript miniatures. Circulating widely along a German/ Italian axis, specifically from Venice to Nuremberg ("the Venice of the North") and northwards to Frankfurt and Antwerp, trade in the drawings extended commercial relations between businessmen and German merchants that dated from the Middle Ages. The Germanic area, according to Crouzet Pavan, was, like the northern Italian plain, a "natural outlet for Venetian trade." Through the Brenner pass, merchants and travelers made their way to Augsburg, Ulm, and eventually Flanders. Another, more easterly, route went through Tarvisio to Salzburg, then on toward Prague or Nuremberg.[36] As early as the late fifteenth century, fabrics produced in Venice stunned English and German travelers, who also remarked on the sheer abundance of goods that were contained in the German warehouses in Venice (the Fondaco dei Tedeschi). The Milanese cleric Pietro Casola noted the variety and splendor of the objects to be found in the German warehouses:

> Indeed, it seems as if all the world flocks there, and that human beings have concentrated there all their force for trading. I was taken to various warehouses, beginning with that of the Germans . . . I see that the special products for which other cities are famous are all to be found there . . . and who could count the many shops so well furnished that they also seem warehouses, with so many cloths of every make—tapestry, brocades and texture, silks of every kind . . . These things stupefy the beholder, and cannot be fully described to those who have not seen them . . .[37]

Rather than transport the fabrics back north, university students such as Ortels had their own clothing made while in Padua, and they purchased costume miniatures of the clothing of others that were highly transportable. Slightly over three inches high, painted in jewel-like tones in watercolor or gouache, they were the sixteenth-century equivalent of modern-day postcards, linked to a desire for knowledge about the customs of countries, including newly formed nations, and used to advertise the places and people encountered in travel. German university students' desire to collect painted miniatures was widespread not only among the nobility but also among the middle social registers. Like prints, miniatures were not unique art objects but reproducible ones, often produced in a series. Similarly too, Venice's sophisticated

FIGURE 2.14. "Cortegiana Venetiana." Los Angeles County Museum of Art, M. 91.71.100.

technologies allowed for the quick dissemination of miniature images much as those technologies made for rapid reproduction of printed costume books. Miniatures came into direct contact with a Venetian marketplace where goods were bought, traded, and bartered, but the market no longer drew clear distinctions between art objects and non-art objects, between the fine arts of painting, sculpture, and architecture, on the one hand, and decorative and applied arts, on the other. As products of a market economy, art objects were no longer supposed to be so much unique as typical, even copyable.[38] (See fig. 2.14.) Nor were they any longer purchased solely through patrons or artist agents but acquired at public auctions, from printer dealers, and assembled in the public domain.

There is a striking relationship between the styles of dress, fabric types, gestures, and poses of individuals depicted in these albums and the numerous costume books printed in Europe from 1562 to 1600. But costume books were composed of woodcuts or engravings produced in multiple printed copies, which laid claim to a more thorough and accurate representation of regional styles of clothing. Sometimes printed costume books were hand-colored (whether in small octavo or large-scale luxury formats), and most contained, with the exception of Vecellio, very brief commentary in the form of titles, short poems, or prose. At times, the illustrated *album amicorum* predated the more widely consulted printed costume books by as much as twenty years and, for this reason, contains much useful information about fashion trends, local customs, and social behaviors that were not recorded in printed costume books.[39]

The representation of Venetian courtesans' dress in colored travel albums demonstrates the extent to which a courtesan created her own style out of the pieces of others. She was able to manipulate traditional systems of dress which marked women according to the dictates of age, marital status, and their city or regional identity. In a largely pre-literate society, people learned to "read" the value of textiles and the meaning of their cut as signs of profession, wealth, and social status. To dress was to be invested with a public identity systematized by fixed clothes. Venetian courtesans, especially the higher ranked *cortigiane oneste* (honored courtesans), confounded that reading because they assembled a distinct identity largely from others. While costume books attempted over the course of the sixteenth century to classify courtesans' dress according to specific signs (male breeches, platform shoes, exposed breasts, wearing pearls at their neck despite sumptuary laws prohibiting them from doing so), the illustrated *album amicorum* reveals instead that many women, not just Venetian courtesans, exposed their bodies, towered dangerously above their male companions, and peered from behind silk mesh veils.

Notes

I am very grateful to a number of institutions for their research materials and assistance. My greatest debt is to the Getty Research Institute and its staff, who have provided me over the years with the use of the GRI library, photo collection, and technical expertise. At different stages in this project, I delivered lectures and received valuable comments from the participants: at the GRI in 1997, at the University of Wisconsin in 1998, and at the History of the Book seminar directed by Peter Stallybrass at the University of Pennsylvania in 2003. Sandra Rosenbaum, Associate Curator of the Doris Stein Research and Design Center, Los Angeles County Museum of Art, first introduced to me the *album amicorum* in that collection and has instructed me on the history of Italian dress in the printed costume book.

1. On the many musical skills of Venetian courtesans, see below, chaps. 4, 5, and 9, and the literature cited therein. On the Venetian courtesan as a published writer, see Ann Rosalind Jones, *The Currency of Eros: Women's Love Lyric in Europe, 1540–1620* (Bloomington: University of Indiana Press, 1990), and Margaret F. Rosenthal, *The Honest Courtesan: Veronica Franco, Citizen and Writer in Sixteenth-Century Venice* (Chicago: University of Chicago Press, 1992).

2. On the intersection of art objects, conspicuous consumption, and consumerism see *Art Markets in Europe, 1400–1800*, ed. Michael North and David Ormond (Aldershot: Ashgate, 1998); Giovanni Levi, "Comportements, resources, process: Avant la 'revolution' de la consummation," in *Jeux d'échelles: La micro-analyse à l'expérience*, ed. Jacques Revel (Paris: Seuil-Gallimard, 1996), 187–207; *Subject and Object in Renaissance Culture*, ed. Margreta de Grazia, Maureen Quilligan, and Peter Stallybrass (Cambridge: Cambridge University Press, 1996); and Patricia F. Brown, "Behind the Walls: The Material Culture of Venetian Elites," in *Venice Reconsidered: The History and Civilization of an Italian City-state*, ed. John Martin and Dennis Romano (Baltimore: Johns Hopkins University Press, 2000), 295–338.

3. Cesare Vecellio, *Degli habiti antichi, et moderni di diverse parti del mondo* (Venice, 1590), 143. I have translated this text in collaboration with Ann Rosalind Jones as part of a forthcoming book on the subject.

4. The illustrated travel album originated in Germany when university students began collecting signatures and drawings by their friends and itinerant artists, and from teachers with whom they studied. While no equivalent tradition of compiling autograph albums existed in Italy in the early modern period, Italians were at the forefront in the production of the printed costume book, which was at times hand-colored. On the practice of painting prints, see Susan Dackerman, *Painted Prints: The Revelation of Color in Northern Renaissance and Baroque Engravings, Etchings and Woodcuts* (University Park, PA: Pennsylvania State University Press and the Baltimore Museum of Art, 2002); see especially plate 34, "Costumes of the World," 180–81, from Jost Amman's costume book of 1577.

5. The albums have been selected out of many hundreds that survive because they have a preponderance of Italian images, particularly of Venice. The first is British Library, Egerton MS 1191 (hereafter Egerton 1191), dated to 1575–77, with 127 folios (87 blank), 55 with coats of arms and 37 with miniature illustrations, plus 116 mottoes in various languages. The second is Yale University, Beinecke Rare Book and Manuscript Library, MS 457, "Mores Italiae," of 1575 (hereafter Yale 457), with 105 watercolor drawings of Italian costumes and scenes of daily life and two maps of Venice (but no autographs, coats of arms, or mottoes). The third is Los Angeles County Museum of Art, Doris Stein Research and Design Center, MS 91.71 (hereafter Los Angeles 91.71), owned by a military officer and compiled in 1595 during the siege of Gran (Estergom, Hungary), with 101 full-page miniatures in brown ink with colored gold highlights, 17 coats of arms on versos (5 in pencil outline and 12 hand-colored), plus 24 signatures with mottoes in various languages.

6. The folio in fig. 2.2 of a Venetian noblewoman is very much like the 1595 "Cortegiana Padoana" (Los Angeles 91.71, fol. 61), where a Paduan courtesan wears a similar gown and overgarment with pendant sleeves enriched with braid or metallic ribbon. Her bodice is rounded with cross-striping. A standing lace collar frames her neck and a long billowing veil falls from the back of her head, held in place with a jeweled pin. Over one arm is draped a fur pelt and in her other hand she carries a glove—all signs of luxury and social prestige. It is interesting to note that the British Library noblewoman's breasts are completely exposed, whereas the Paduan courtesan's are not.

7. In Augsburg, for example, there were a large number of painters of coats of arms such as Matthias Kager, Hans Karg, and Anton Ramsler. German artists earned at least part of their livelihood with such work. Phrases in a number of the albums such as "haec pingi feci" or "curavi" or "hab ich hierin malen lassen" (I had this painted here) occur on only a very few folios but the folios are never signed by the artists themselves. Ortels was a student in the German "nation"—a kind of "corporation of scholars" from German-speaking lands at the University of Padua. Foreign students had to matriculate within one month of arrival at the University and within fourteen days had to sign the ledger of their corresponding nation (headed by a consiliarus with a treasurer and secretary beneath him), to which they paid dues and taxes. I have found Ortels's name listed in the university matriculation archives in Padua for the year 1575. The shorter album Egerton 1192, owned by Paul Behaim (one of Ortels's close friends), contains many interesting illustrations of Venetian dress. The Behaims of Nuremberg are well represented in the manuscript holdings of the British Library, which contains numerous *alba amicorum* kept by three generations of the family over the period 1574–1640.

8. On the global interests of European travelers, see Bronwen Wilson, "'The Eye of Italy': The Image of Venice and Venetians in Sixteenth-Century Prints" (Ph.D. diss., Northwestern University, 1999), 144–219.

9. For a description of this album, see Barbara A. Shailor, *Catalogue of Medieval and Re-*

naissance Manuscripts in the Beinecke Rare Book and Manuscript Library, Yale University (Binghamton, NY: Medieval and Renaissance Texts & Studies, 1984–92). Unfortunately, since the album was cut and rebound in the nineteenth century and each leaf is stuck fast to a thick paper with a gold fillet which trims the edges on all sides, it is impossible to judge whether the album once contained autographs and other formal characteristics of the *album amicorum*.

10. For a useful exploration of the production of luxury goods in Venice in this period, and especially glassmaking, see W. Patrick McCray, *Glassmaking in Renaissance Venice: The Fragile Craft* (Aldershot: Ashgate, 1999).

11. On the demand for goods for consumption as a social, not merely economic, force in Venetian society, see ibid., 26–32.

12. On the sale of second-hand goods in the Venetian public fairs, auctions during festival time, and at other times, see Patricia Allerston, "The Market in Second-Hand Clothes and Furnishings in Venice, c. 1500–c.1650" (D.Phil. diss., European University Institute, Florence, 1996), and Jack Hinton, "By Sale, by Gift," *Journal of Design History* 15 (2002): 245–60. Allerston notes that a proclamation of November 1575 included a two-month total ban on trading in used goods made of cloth because of the outbreak of the plague (283).

13. Patricia Allerston, "Clothing and Early Modern Venetian Society," *Continuity and Change* 15 (2000): 367–90, at pp. 376–77, with extensive bibliography on the market activities during the Sensa trade fair and other Venetian events that attracted foreign visitors (390, n. 113).

14. Ibid., 380.

15. Doretta Davanzo Poli, "Le cortigiane e la moda," in *Il Gioco dell'Amore: Le cortigiane di Venezia dal Trecento al Settecento. Catalogo della mostra*, ed. Alfredo Bruno (Milan: Berenice, 1990), 98–103; and eadem, "Abbigliamento Veneto: Attraverso un'iconografia datata: 1517–1571," in *Paris Bordone e il suo tempo: Atti del Convegno Internazionale di Studi* (Treviso: Canova, 1985), 243–53.

16. Vecellio, *Habiti antichi*, 137.

17. For this quote, see Kenneth R. Bartlett, *The English in Italy, 1525–1558: A Study in Culture and Politics* (Geneva: Slatkine, 1991), 146.

18. Fynes Moryson, *An Itinerary Containing His Ten Yeeres Travell*, 4 vols. (Glasgow: J. MacLehose, 1907–8), 220–21.

19. Ibid., 410.

20. *Brocatello* is a heavy fabric frequently combining linen and silk. The pattern, which is created on the warp, appears raised. It is not the same as brocade, for which is it sometimes mistaken.

22. Vecellio, *Habiti antichi*, 138.

23. Ibid., 100.

24. See Monica Chojnacka, *Working Women of Early Modern Venice* (Baltimore: Johns Hopkins University Press, 2001), 78 and passim.

25. On reading courtesans' portraits see Patricia Simons, "Portraiture, Portrayal, and Idealization: Ambiguous Individualism in Representations of Renaissance Women," in *Language and Images of Renaissance Italy*, ed. Alison Brown (Oxford: Clarendon Press, 1995), 263–311. Simons claims that the courtesan "has too often been conflated with the 'ideal portrait,' as though the arousal of sensuality is visually embodied only when the model's profession overtly allows it or when an idealization excuses sexual fantasy" (288). She speaks about collecting images of beautiful women (including Veronica Franco in Yale 457) as examples of "anonymous referentiality, an understanding, in a visual and marketing sense, that the images reported particular, localized women" (298).

26. Some printed costume books used flaps (like paper dolls) to conceal and then uncover what lies beneath, which in the case of courtesans is often male breeches, or extra-high platform shoes.

27. Ann Rosalind Jones and Peter Stallybrass, *Renaissance Clothing and the Materials of Memory* (Cambridge: Cambridge University Press, 2000), 4.

27. *The Diary of John Evelyn*, ed. Austin Dobson, 3 vols. (London: Macmillan, 1906), 1:295–97.

28. On Ascension festivities see Bianca Tamassia Mazzarotto, *Le feste veneziane* (Florence: Sansoni, 1961), 180–91. Henry Wotton wrote that in 1617 the Ascension festival was "a poor show of gondola, by reason of a decree in Senate against the courtesans, that none of them shall be rowed con due remi [with two oars]; a decree made at the suit of all of the gentlewomen, who before were indistinguishable abroad from those baggaes" (quoted in Wilson, "'The Eye of Italy,'" 98).

29. Lina Padoan Urban discusses the history of the Sensa fair in "La festa della Sensa nelle arti e nell'iconografia," *Studi veneziani* 10 (1968): 291–353, as beginning in Venice in 1180 because of the great numbers of pilgrims embarking for the Holy Land. She also shows that the Sensa was often a showcase for painters, especially in the eighteenth century (331, n. 185). See also Patricia Fortini Brown, *The Renaissance in Venice: A World Apart* (London: George Weidenfeld & Nicolson, 1997), 88–90, who discusses Jost Amman's "The Feast of the Sensa," a woodcut with watercolor of ca. 1560.

30. Bronwen Wilson notes in "'Il bel sesso e l'austero Senato': The Coronation of Dogaressa Morosina Morosini Grimani," *Renaissance Quarterly* 52 (1999): 73–139, that "festivities in Renaissance Venice were the principal events at which patrician women appeared in public" (78–9).

31. Tintoretto and his brother exhibited their paintings on the *Mercerie* for sale and self-advertisement.

32. Vecellio, *Habiti antichi*, 139.

33. *The Diary of John Evelyn*, 297.

34. Lina Urban, "La festa della Sensa," explains that women were the only ones allowed into the church of San Marco to view the relics on the eve of the Sensa. The fair also provided them with the opportunity to purchase household items and objects of personal adornment. Female servants, in particular, especially girls who were trying to accumulate items for their trousseaux, seem to have looked forward to and attended the Sensa.

35. Allerston, "Clothing," 348.

36. Elizabeth Crouzet-Pavan, *Venice Triumphant: The Horizons of a Myth* (Baltimore: Johns Hopkins University Press, 1999), 120.

37. Pietro Casola, *Canon Pietro Casola's Pilgrimage to Jerusalem in the year 1494*, ed. M. Margaret Newett (Manchester: Manchester University Press, 1907), 14–15.

38. There are similarities of pose and type between this miniature that of fig. 2.3.

39. As Wilson notes in "Il bel sesso," 81, Venetian costume books capitalized on the potential for confusing courtesans with patrician women, notably Giacomo Franco's *Habiti delle donne veneziane* (1610), a book of engravings. For a general consideration of printed costume books, see J. Olian, "Sixteenth-Century Costume Books," *Dress* 3 (1977), 20–48; John L. Nevinson, "Origin and Early History of the Fashion Plate," *United States National Museum Bulletin* 250, Paper 60 (Washington, DC: Smithsonian Press, 1967), 65–92.

CHAPTER 3

"Notes of Flesh" and the Courtesan's Song in Seventeenth-Century China

The period of the late Ming and early Qing dynasties, roughly 1580–1700, is widely recognized as one of the pinnacles of Chinese courtesan culture and the arts. Pleasure districts could be found in virtually every city and town across the empire, including the capital Beijing to the north, but the focus of elite courtesan culture lay in Jiangnan, in the metropolises of the Yangzi River Delta, particularly Suzhou, Hangzhou, and the former capital Nanjing, where economic and cultural capital was concentrated (see the map in fig. 3.1). Although merchants constituted one major new clientele, the most celebrated courtesans owed their reputations in large part to patronage by leading men of letters, who, in turn, derived their status from competing in the civil service examinations and from their achievements in the literary sphere.

Music-making, especially song, was indispensable to the social and sexual activities of the entertainment quarter, as it had been since the eighth century, when a musical and distinctively Chinese courtesan culture first coalesced. The components of that culture were several: (1) literary prowess, particularly in poetry, as a fundamental qualification for male elite status and as an integral part of elite social life; (2) a particularly close connection between verse forms and song because of the tonal qualities of the Chinese language; (3) involvement of the pleasure quarters in setting fashion in music, with courtesans as the transmitters of new popular types of music to the elite; and (4) the emergence of new verse forms keyed to song arising out of this creative exchange between courtesans and male literati.[1]

Classical Chinese has an extensive lexicon designating women with skill in the arts whose services could include sex, but the most frequent term is *ji*. Although in modern Chinese this character simply means "prostitute," etymologically *ji* (妓) combines the graph for woman (女) and the graph for entertainer (伎), and the function of a *ji* as a performer remained vital into the twentieth century. In her study of Song dynasty courtesans (tenth to thirteenth centuries), Beverly Bossler notes that

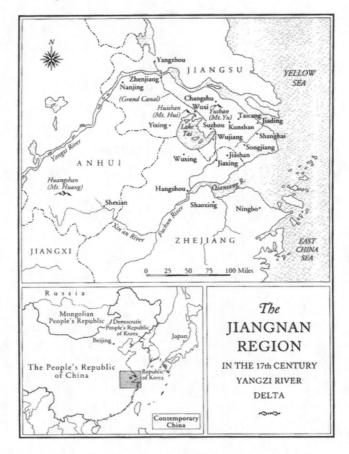

FIGURE 3.1. Map of seventeenth-century Jiangnan.

the word *ji* generally referred to the upper range of "the class of female entertainers"; even so the term covered a multiplicity of roles and hierarchies. Part of what a *ji* could offer, at least during the Song period, Bossler argues, was sexual companionship, yet a *ji* "was first and foremost a performing artist." Even a low-class *ji* therefore "was not one who exclusively sold her sexual favors, but one who approached the banquet table and began to sing without having been invited."[2]

The expectation that, at a minimum, the entertainment a *ji* provided would include song is one reason such women are still often referred to as "singing girls" in translations of Chinese literature, in part as a euphemistic heritage from the missionary writers on China, but also because English lacks any nuanced ground between the high of "courtesan" and the low of "prostitute."[3] In lieu of the orientalist "singing girl," "courtesan" remains the best English approximation for *ji* and related terms prior to the modern period.

By the late Ming (1580–1644), the compound *ming-ji* (literally "renowned *ji*") had come into common currency to distinguish the uppermost stratum of the profession, but the boundaries and terminology between echelons of courtesans were always slippery, mutable, and subjective. For instance, the 1616 preface to *Stylish Verses from the Green Bower*, a book of poetry by courtesans (Green Bower being a literary term for a courtesan establishment), reserves the term *ji* for "those celestial creatures of innate seductive beauty and penetrating intelligence," distinguishing them from common prostitutes—"those women who lean in doorways, proffering smiles at all comers indiscriminately."[4] Yet the collection also incorporates large chunks from a book labeled *The Classic of Whoring*, juxtaposing cynical and idealized views of courtesans on the same page.

Physical mobility also characterizes the spatial and social horizons of the courtesan in the late Ming and early Qing. Courtesans had a gift for blurring the boundaries between public and private, written and oral media. A courtesan was not confined to the pleasure quarter. She was invited into private homes to entertain at parties and celebrations. She could go on tours of different cities and entertain on her own boat or those of her clients. In her retirement, she might be hired to teach singing and dancing within a household to the master's private troupe of household entertainers or even to his wives and daughters. Until the reforms of 1723–35, courtesans, like actors and other entertainers, were, at least in theory, a hereditary caste with base legal status, but this status could be changed if a courtesan were taken into a household on a more long-term basis as a concubine. Such unions were not always permanent, however, and concubines sometimes reverted to the courtesan life. In any event, the courtesan's relatively mobile status meant that the musical culture she was involved in shaping had a wider geographic and social currency, extending beyond any specific entertainment quarter.

James Davidson's discussion of the ancient Greek hetaera emphasizes the importance of a courtesan receiving "gifts" rather than payments from her clients because this shadowy and easily manipulated distinction implies that she, in turn, bestows her favors voluntarily as a return gift, rather than fulfilling a set payment for service.[5] In the Chinese case, the gift economy was likewise all-important in constituting the relations between a courtesan and her literati clients, but it was also expected that some of the gifts she received be of a literary (or artistic) nature—a poem, a painting, the lyrics to an aria—and that the courtesan be able to reciprocate in kind—by matching the poem, adding to the painting, or singing the song. All of this contributed to the fantasy of parity between a courtesan and her lover, of favors freely exchanged, and was the *sine qua non* for romance in the Chinese tradition.

The ability to participate in this gift-giving also determined the status of a courtesan because such literary exchanges were fundamental to the status and social life of her literati patrons. Despite (or because of) the increasing commercialization of the sixteenth and seventeenth centuries, direct payment for service or objects accorded high cultural value was considered déclassé or even degrading and had to be disguised. For a courtesan and her client, the illusion of the disinterested gift was naturally even more crucial. As *Stylish Verses in the Green Bower* puts it: "Even a single word or a single object received from a beautiful woman is precious—how could a man not respond in kind?" This statement is neatly punctured by a quotation from *The Classic of Whoring* on the same page: "When she sends a letter, it's like issuing a summons for money; when she sends a handkerchief or fan, it's like hurling a brick to extract precious jade."[6]

In recent years, scholars interested in recouping Ming and Qing courtesans as significant cultural agents have explored their poetry, and to some extent their painting, to find traces of genuine self-expression rather than mere signs of professional expertise. While none would deny the centrality of song to the courtesan's arts, this aspect of the courtesan's cultural production has tended to drop out of the equation.[7] The history of performance is always hard to reconstruct, of course, but in the Chinese case, it is especially so because music relied primarily on oral transmission, and musically notated vocal scores were not published until the late eighteenth century.[8]

A more serious obstacle has been discomfort with the extent to which music and sex were intertwined in the courtesan world. The idealizing impulse evident in much contemporary scholarship extends a cultural bias in the historical sources themselves. To prove that a courtesan was truly cultured, her gifts as a poet rather than a musical performer were most important. Because of the supreme valuation of the written word and the exaltation of literary authorship in China, the most celebrated courtesans through the ages have tended to be those skilled in writing verse, whose poetic output has at least in part been preserved on paper.

This essay attempts to reevaluate the courtesans' role in cultural production, but addresses the relation of top courtesans to music-making through the creative dimensions *and* the professional business of pleasure integral to their careers as musicians. I begin with an exploration of the erotic connotations of the female voice in China to explore why courtesans specialized in singing. I then sketch the dominant genres and performance styles of the courtesan's repertory in the late sixteenth and seventeenth centuries. Finally, I explore the courtesan's vocal training and the complex value invested in her songs through a close reading of the singing lesson scene dramatized in one of the most famous plays of the period, *Peach Blossom Fan*.

MUSIC AND EROTICISM

Music and eroticism have long been linked in the Chinese calculus of pleasure. The terms *sheng* (sound, denoting music) and *se* (visual allure, denoting beautiful women) were paired from antiquity as a metonym for the sensual overindulgence of rulers at court that could topple their kingdoms. As Joseph Lam asserts: "Music made by women is singled out by Confucian scholars as particularly corruptive because it seduces not only with sound but also with the physical presence of female performers."[9] The cover illustration of a miscellany published in 1610 offers the perfect witty correlative for music as foreplay (fig. 3.2). A courtesan is seated on the lap of her lover, his two legs straddling hers. They are playing a "duet": a pipa is stretched across her lap, a xiao flute at her lips. It seems as though it is the man who is plucking the pipa and the woman who is playing the flute, but a closer look reveals that each of them is simultaneously playing both instruments. Only one hand on the pipa belongs to the man: his other hand fingers the flute as his arm encircles her; the woman is touching the flute with one hand as she presses down on the pipa strings with the other. Adding to the piquancy of the picture are the double entendres involved: "blowing the xiao" is a flowery term for fellatio, while "zither strings" is a poetic locution for the

FIGURE 3.2. Cover page of *Tempering the Reed Pipe in a Jade Valley.*

clitoris.[10] In the context of the image on the cover, then, even the miscellany's title suggests the titillating interplay of sex and music: *Tempering the Reed Pipe in the Jade Valley (Yugu tiaohuang).*[11]

Some singing ability and a repertory of songs were minimal requirements for a courtesan. In a comic opera of 1618, two courtesans on the make, who have "mastered dancing but not yet singing," complain: "We've got the 'looks' (*se*) but not the 'sound' (*sheng*) . . . For girls like us, singing is number one: only then can we entice men and arouse their desires."[12] Their solution is to seek out a fashionable singing master, who agrees to teach them some popular songs while strumming on a pipa. "Gain some accomplishment at singing / and those notes that 'wind sinuously round the rafters' will boost your reputation and price. / At banquets they'll love you to death / and wherever you go, you'll steal all the men."[13]

Singing was fundamental to the courtesan's arts in China not only because song was a social and sexual lubricant and the lyrics were appreciated for their literary and sentimental value, but because singing itself, when offered as entertainment at banquets or other settings, was culturally gendered as feminine. To perform a song was to submit oneself to the gaze as well as the ears of another, and there was a perpetual tendency for the audience to conflate the physical beauty of the singer with the acoustic beauty of the song. Already in the late twelfth century, the writer Wang Zhuo had complained that people of his time prized only the female voice. (In fact, lists of famous singers from earlier times attest that a preference for female singers had probably predominated in the past as well.)[14] Wang associated this preference with "plaintive and seductive"—hence feminine—lyrics that his fellow literati liked to write. He cites the story of one man of letters who refused to listen to an elderly male singer, despite his reputed excellence: "A singer must be a person lovely as jade, with rosy lips, white teeth, and a complexion like ice. In communicating the private meaning of the lyrics, the words must sound charming with a waver in the voice, the syllables as round and lustrous as a string of pearls. This old man may be an expert singer, but what can be done about his snowy whiskers?"[15] Yet while Wang's point was to disparage the "vulgarity" of such an attitude, his view was not the majority one.

Certain conceptions of the voice may have strengthened the sense of singing as an integral part of the body that produced the sound. Not disembodied as in European languages, the singing voice in Chinese is commonly denoted by "throat." The poetic equivalent in Classical Chinese to "good voice" in English, especially in descriptions of women, is "a throat for singing" (*ge hou*).

Even more striking is the metonymic appellation of the voice as an instrument of flesh. An eightfold classification of musical instruments based on the material they were fashioned of had developed in early antiquity. In this system, bells are "metal," flutes are "bamboo," while lutes are "silk" (the material used for the strings), and so on. The human voice did not figure in the original eight categories, but in a later collection of witty anecdotes from the fifth century, the term "flesh" was coined in a dialogue between a general and his aide on the superiority of the human voice over other instruments. The general inquires: "'When I'm listening to performers, stringed instruments don't sound as good as bamboo, bamboo instruments don't sound as good as flesh. Why would that be?'" Replies his aide: "'Because you're getting closer with each one to what is natural.'"[16]

From the ninth century on, the aphorism "String is inferior to bamboo, bamboo is inferior to flesh" is ubiquitous in disquisitions on singing.[17] Pan Zhiheng, one of our best sources for late Ming entertainment culture, even coins the term "notes of flesh" (*rou-yin*) for singing to match "notes of bamboo" (*zhu-yin*), denoting flute accompaniment. Pan links the "naturalness" of the voice to its affective power, placing his lyrical discussion on song within the discourse on emotion or love so fashionable in this period. "At their most subtle, 'notes of flesh' will make the soul melt, and make one perish from emotion. If 'notes of flesh' are performed and the listener doesn't perish, then the heights of emotion that flesh is capable of have not been scaled."[18]

But it is Li Yu who, in his 1671 discussion on how to train female singers and dancers, explicitly linked this aphorism to a gendered discourse on the "natural" qualities of the female voice and the physical attractions of the female body and face:

Even the most exquisite male voice only stands on par with string and bamboo; it still remains "string of flesh," "bamboo of flesh." How do I know this? Observe that when someone praises the beauty of a male voice, they either say "It's as fine as a stringed instrument," or "It's as clear as a bamboo instrument." But when it comes to a woman's voice, then it is praised purely because it is flesh. The saying goes: "A song-lyric must come from a beauty's mouth." I say: "She doesn't *have* to be a beauty." It doesn't matter whether she's pretty or ugly. Any girl who's gifted at singing will produce a sound that is extremely different from that of a man. . . . There's never been a case of a good-looking woman whose voice is not worth listening to. You just need to teach her some method, and direct her in artistry. She simply needs to develop her innate talent: just don't let her go against her own nature.[19]

Although at one point Li Yu notes that "the program of study for music is the same for men and women," he emphasizes throughout the essay that a chief point of studying music for women is to enhance their appearance and deportment. As he puts it bluntly: "What's important for a man in playing an instrument is the sound, for a woman it's her looks."[20]

THE PERFORMING REPERTORY AND
VOCAL STYLE OF COURTESANS

The courtesan's performing repertory in the sixteenth and seventeenth centuries was closely linked to the dominance of operatic forms of entertainment in this period. All traditional Chinese drama is musical theater, which is why it is often called "opera," with intricately crafted verse sung as arias interspersed with dialogue declaimed in colloquial language. During the late Ming and early Qing, the passion for opera was at its height among the elite. Literary men, some from the highest echelons of officialdom, turned their hands to libretto-writing, and the richer ones even maintained household troupes to stage their own works and those of their friends. Salon performances of operas (sometimes full plays, but more often excerpted scenes) were ubiquitous fare at banquets in private homes and at court. The most common public venues, even in cities, were the performances given on temple stages during festivals. Although commercial urban theaters had thrived during the twelfth to fourteenth centuries, they had disappeared by the mid-fifteenth, and only gradually started coming back into fashion in selected cities during the late seventeenth.

For salon-type performances, although permanent stages in private residences were not unheard of, all that was necessary to demarcate a stage was a rug, with an area to the back or the side to serve as a combination backstage/green room from which the actors could make their entrances and exits. The easily improvised and versatile nature of performance space, along with the absence of elaborate scenery, meant that, in principle, almost any location could double as a stage. It is not surprising therefore that during the late Ming operas were sometimes staged in courtesan houses too, though serving as a theater was never their primary function. The question is whether courtesans generally participated in these productions as actresses or instead made up the audience along with their clients.

Historically, the line between courtesan and actress was a blurry one. Our main source for top courtesans of the Yuan dynasty (1264–1368), for example, the *Green Bower Collection*, primarily involves actresses connected with the stage. By the late sixteenth century, however, the two professions had essentially bifurcated, although there was still some movement of women from one profession to the other.[21] There were exceptions, of course. The famous late Ming courtesan Ma Xianglan was said "to have trained her maids on the model of an acting troupe, and often had them perform at her establishment to entertain guests."[22] This information is provided in Xianglan's biography as something worthy of note, rather than as something typical, however, and the wording of the entry acknowledges a tacit difference between the acting troupe model and its courtesan imitation. Zhang Dai, elite chronicler and connoisseur of the late Ming entertainment world, recalled attending a matinee performance that an opera troupe gave in the Nanjing pleasure quarter; that very evening he watched the courtesans who had been members in the afternoon audience perform scenes from the same opera in emulation. Zhang asserts that "Nanjing courtesans considered putting on plays to be a stylish activity and they took it very seriously," and he was pleased to be enlisted as their coach.[23] In my view, Zhang Dai's recollection suggests above all an enthusiasm on the part of courtesans to mount amateur theatricals, echoing the vogue for such pastimes in certain late Ming literati circles.[24]

The theory that sees top courtesans as theatrical amateurs, who sometimes put on plays in their establishments but mainly left full-scale theatrical productions to professional acting troupes (as their literati clients did), may be one way to reconcile the contradiction between Zhang Dai's account and Yu Huai's 1693 memoir of the Nanjing pleasure quarter, another of our best sources for late Ming courtesan culture. In his *Miscellaneous Records of the Wooden Bridge District*, Yu Huai says that acting troupes frequently gave performances in the quarter at night,[25] but that a top courtesan considered performing plays on stage to be deeply humiliating. What she preferred was an intimate party with a few clients who were knowledgeable about music, and even then she had to be strenuously coaxed before she would sing. Those privileged to be present would be overwhelmed by the beauty of her voice and willingly paid "ten times the price" for this exclusive pleasure.[26] He describes only one courtesan who was also celebrated as an actress, for her skill at performing plays on stage; she is the only one, too, who is mentioned in conjunction with theatrical role types.[27] Most of the information he provides about stage performers instead concerns male actors, who were also regular participants at parties in the quarter.

Instead of acting on stage, then, courtesans specialized in the performing practice known as "pure singing" (*qingchang*).[28] This entailed singing dramatic arias without the lines of dialogue interspersed in full play texts, without theatrical make-up or costume, with minimal props (such as a fan) and minimal instrumental accompaniment (such as a set of clappers, a flute, or a stringed instrument), and with few or none of the elaborate dance steps and gestures customarily performed on stage. Another equally important segment of the courtesan's repertory were "independent" or "free-standing" arias (*san-qu*), which were never performed except as pure singing.[29] Independent arias were largely on sentimental themes, and were closely associated with the activities of the pleasure quarter. The independent aria is sometimes

FIGURE 3.3. Yu Zhiding, "Qiao Zhiyuan's Three Delights."

translated as "art song" to distinguish it from the more colloquial "popular song" (*xiao-qu*, literally "minor *qu*"), the third indispensable segment of the courtesan's singing repertory.

Three female musicians in fashionable headdresses are engaged in a "pure singing" performance in a 1676 hand scroll painted by the society portraitist Yu Zhiding and entitled "Qiao Yuanzhi's Three Delights" (fig. 3.3). The phrase "Three Delights" alludes to a certain sixth-century aristocrat's passion for wine, books, and music, and the painting flatteringly portrays its modern subject, the debonair Qiao Yuanzhi, lolling on a couch in his study, book in hand and wine cup at his elbow, savoring the music. The singer, who is seated, as is usual in pictures of pure singing, holds a fan in her right hand and gestures theatrically with her right sleeve as she glances at the flute player accompanying her; a bowed-*qin* player completes the trio. Although the musicians are included in the portrait as idealized "emblems" of the male subject's interests and personality, rather than as likenesses of real women or of a real performance, it is safe to assume that they portray courtesans, or possibly household entertainers, since it would have been unseemly to depict family members in the intimate act of performing music for a male listener.[30]

The term "pure singing" and the elegant vocal style it implies were closely associated with *kun qu* (kun-style opera, which originated in Kun shan, outside the city of Suzhou). *Kun qu*, with its emphasis on vocal refinement and elaborate ornamentation, was particularly suited to salon performance because it avoided the noisy percussion of competing opera styles and favored the plaintive and soft sounds of the *dizi* flute as its leading instrumental accompaniment. The pure singing of independent arias by a coterie of professional male music masters, literati, and courtesans during the 1560s and 1570s is the matrix out of which the musical system of *kun qu* had originally coalesced, but it quickly spread to the performance of full-fledged opera.[31] By the early seventeenth century, *kun qu* had become the reigning operatic mode for elites across the country, who extolled the elegance of *kun qu* and disparaged the vulgarity of competing styles. Top courtesans, keenly sensitive to the status differential of the music they performed, naturally specialized in *kun qu*; and pure singing—always considered a more refined and prestigious activity than acting on stage—remained a favored pastime in literati/courtesan circles.

REALIZING THE TUNE

The salient compositional feature of the Chinese aria form (*qu*) is that of writing new words to a pre-existing melody, identified by a tune title. This mode of versification required the poet to observe the individual rules governing rhyme, meter, and word tone prescribed for each tune pattern, which were codified in manuals that could be consulted for "filling in" new lyrics, as this act of composition came to be called. (Popular songs composed to tune formulas, much fewer in number, also became known by certain titles, but they had freer prosodic structures.) Well-known patterns were reused hundreds or even thousands of times for new songs whose content (as opposed to form) would have nothing to do with the original tune title. The melodies were mainly transmitted orally and understood to be highly mutable over time. As Wang Jide, author of an important seventeenth-century treatise on opera, says flatly: "The tunes of an age change every thirty years."[32] The verses, on the other hand, were easily preserved through publication and could continue to be read (or adapted to new melodies) long after the original music had disappeared.

The model of filling in new lyrics to pre-existing, abstract melodic patterns sounds straightforward, but it took considerable skill and effort to make such verses work in actual performance. From what we know about the composition of full-length operas for the late seventeenth-century stage, for instance, a literary playwright had to work extensively with a musical advisor to adjust his aria lyrics to conform fully to the melodies. Isabel Wong observes that the process of creating a *kun qu* opera typically required the "collective efforts of several groups of specialists": (1) a poet-playwright to compose the verse, (2) a "music master" who was also a singer and familiar with all the tunes in the repertory to ensure that words and melody fit properly, a process she terms "tune accommodation," and (3) a singer-actor skilled in *kun qu* singing techniques and ornamentation to realize the music in performance.[33] In the case of independent arias in the *kun qu* style, a similar, if much more streamlined process must have been required.

Stephen West notes that Yuan dynasty courtesans were for the most part illiterate, but by the late sixteenth century, in keeping with the greater emphasis on education for upper-class women, courtesanry required at least some literacy. What are omitted in accounts of the courtesan singing her client's verse are precisely the kinds of adjustments of words and melody necessary to make lyrics and music fit together, and thus to bridge the gap between text and performance. The technical Chinese musical term for this kind of activity is *du qu*, which may be imperfectly translated into English as "realizing the tune."

The phrase *du qu* means either "to perform a song" (in which case it is pronounced *du qu*) or "to fashion a song by fitting new words to a pre-existing tune" (in which case it is pronounced *duo qu*).[34] Both ways of "realizing the tune" required serious skill and understanding of music to execute, and both activities had one of the other in it. To perform a new song from written lyrics inevitably meant making prosodic and musical adjustments. Fashioning a song by fitting new words to an existing tune pattern demanded even more effort. Particularly challenging was the method of *ji qu* (developing a "composite tune"), which involved piecing together individual lines from separate tune patterns in the same mode to create a patchwork melody with a new title.[35]

Wong notes that the music masters charged with the task of "tune accommodation" "usually came from the ranks of singing teachers, professional actors, or *dizi* (flute) players. . . and . . . from a lower stratum of society than the playwright-poet."[36] I suspect that courtesans, who were also trained as professional musicians and came from lower social strata than poets, must have frequently assumed responsibility for tune accommodation in addition to that of singer-performer—much like the Venetian courtesans discussed by Feldman, De Rycke, and Davies in this volume—especially with independent arias written for courtesans by their clients. To be sure, courtesan-singers must sometimes have relied on the intermediary services of music masters, who might also have doubled as accompanists in performance. But a good deal of the fun and prowess in the courtesan's world came from displays of extemporaneous improvisation and repartee, from participation in games and contests invented on the spot. A top courtesan-singer would have been expected to render an impromptu performance of her lover's verses, and for that she would have been capable of modifying the words and the tune on her own.

The skill of courtesans in the late Ming and early Qing in singing new arias to her clients' verses—"realizing the tune"—required literary skill and musical knowledge of the aria verse form, then, not only a good voice and good memory. Some courtesans who excelled both at versification and singing were able to craft their own lyrics to arias, although few of these survive. Wang Duanshu's enormous anthology *Classic Verse by Renowned Women*, published in 1667, is our best source for independent aria lyrics by courtesans. Wang, a well-known writer in her own right, was the daughter of a famous man of letters and a respectable married woman, but her omnivorous interest in women's writing extended to the literary efforts of courtesans as well. The focus of her anthology was mainstream genres of poetry, but she did include two chapters of aria lyrics, one of which is entirely by courtesans. Wang was sufficiently broad-minded to include a salacious aria credited to an unnamed "Courtesan from Chu" and subtitled "Sent to a Friend." The aria involves a set of ribald double entendres about a common mode of transporting heavy loads, in which bundles were tied on either side of a pole placed across the shoulders:

When tying on the load of love,
The moment it's lifted onto the shoulders is the hardest of all.
Even if the porter is a man of iron, it will crush the thighs and make them sore,
It will make one pant till the mouth is parched.
And still one worries that the rope will snap mid-route . . .

In her comment, Wang marvels that this piece had become famous and earned the praise of literati since "the aria is certainly witty enough in a minor way but it presents a great impediment to public morals." Yet she could still condone compositions of this sort as part of their author's profession: "Women in the quarter need arias like this or they'll be unable to arouse the erotic thoughts of men."[37]

Generally speaking, Wang's evaluations in this chapter reinforce the truism that the independent aria was principally considered a performance genre. Her comments on two arias by the famous sixteenth-century courtesan Jing Pianpian seem deliberately to blur the boundary between composition and performance:

> Experts at "realizing the tune" always lower their voice to make it more bewitching. True mastery lies not in forcing and interrupting but in passing smoothly from tune pattern to tune pattern in accord with the rhythm. Pianpian's first aria, "A Red Candle on a Silver Stand," is like a stringed instrument played without a single string broken;[38] the feeling is sad and calm. Her second aria, "My Heart Flutters as I Face You," is like a duet in which "bamboo" and "flesh" exquisitely follow each other and the mood is never shattered. Raising a wine cup and turning your head to look at her, what more would you need?[39]

Living some decades after Pianpian, Wang could never have heard her sing, so her evocation of the courtesan is mainly imaginary, conjured up through reading the lyrics and the tune titles. The implication is that the written aria text must be able to invoke in the reader the compensatory *sensation* of witnessing a performance (hence the emphasis on *looking* as well as listening). Wang cunningly describes the two arias in terms of voice and instruments to give an impression of how they would sound in concert, but the description is in fact metaphorical, meant to convey the musicality and expressiveness of Pianpian's skill as a writer.

AUTHORSHIP, PUBLICATION, AND MEMORY

One reason for the spread of southern forms of courtesan culture across the empire during the late Ming was that the cities of Nanjing, Hangzhou, and Suzhou, the locales of the most famous pleasure districts, were also centers of the publishing industry. Books about the courtesan world geared to the contemporary market were produced in rapid succession from the 1610s to the 1640s by literati editors capitalizing on their familiarity with the quarter. All of them include a large selection of lyrics to independent arias and popular songs and are important sources for understanding how flexible notions of authorship may be related to collaborative performance practices in a courtesan context.

Two such publications are *Seductive Courtesans of Suzhou* (1617), compiled by Zhou Zhibiao, and a sequel, *Seductive Courtesans of Nanjing* (1618), compiled by Li Yunxiang in the following year.[40] Both are examples of parodic "flower registers" in which courtesans were ranked according to the grading system for the top examination candidates and then paired with a specific flower.[41] The Suzhou volume singles out three courtesans as top singers, one of whom, Liang Xiaopian, is portrayed in the act of "realizing a tune" (fig. 3.4). In the illustration, Xiaopian is draped elegantly but

FIGURE 3.4. "Realizing the music." From Zhou Zhibiao, *Wuji baimei* (1617).

casually against a chair, in a relaxed sensuous pose that no respectable woman would ever be pictured in. An exposed arm dangles across the back of the chair; the hand of the other is raised, propped up against her thigh, as though she were beating time to the music. On a stool facing her is another woman, a maid or perhaps a fellow courtesan, who is accompanying her, a flat drum on her lap and a drumstick in one hand, a clapper in the other. She may be setting the tempo before starting to sing, or perhaps even beating out a tricky rhythm in the midst of fitting new words to a tune. It seems to be a rehearsal since no audience is present in the illustration and Xiaopian's mouth is not even open (although the small rosebud mouth preferred for female beauty meant that women singing are seldom pictured with open mouths).[42] *Categories of Flowers*, a huge late Ming compendium on courtesans, includes a similar picture of a courtesan "realizing the tune," but here she is performing for an intimate drinking party of literati clients, who are watching her avidly as servant-boys heat and pour out the wine (fig. 3.5).[43]

FIGURE 3.5.   Courtesan singing at a party as one servant boy
heats wine and another pours it. From *Categories of Flowers*,
seventeenth century.

The entry for Xiaopian includes a poem, the lyrics to an aria, and the words to a
popular song. Both the poem and the aria pay tribute to her singing. The aria is ut-
tered in the voice of a man propositioning a courtesan: its formulaic quality and trite
allusions may be signposts of impromptu oral composition and performance, where
seduction was clearly the point:

To the tune "Perfume of Hanging Branches"
Her figure is charmingly slender.
She always magically understands a lover's heart.[44]
Her singing has the elegance of "White Snow."[45]
It's no lie to say the notes "wind sinuously 'round the rafters."
In the Green Bower, it's rare to find her match.

The popular song, conversely, is a proposition from a woman to a man. It is an example of a "mountain song," an unaccompanied type of folk song originating in the rural areas around Suzhou that became fashionable among the urban populace during the late Ming. As is common in this kind of song, the speaker refers to herself as "Jie" (older sister) and to her lover as "Lang" (young man). The freshness and directness of the language, the reliance on double entendres, and build-up to a punch line are also typical of the genre:

> *Jie* has these feelings of hers,
> And *Lang* has these feelings of his.
> Now take those feelings of yours
> and come touch these feelings of mine.
> I'm not afraid that one set of feelings is soft,
> and one set of feelings is hard.
> I'm just afraid that what's hard are your intentions,
> And what's soft are your feelings.

The interplay between "hard" and "soft" in the song implies a double entendre, especially because the images are more physical in the original: the word I translate as "feelings" is literally "heart" (*xin*) and "intentions" is "gut" (*du chang*). The difficulty is figuring out precisely what is meant, especially because in the original no personal pronouns are used in the last four lines. "Heart of the flower" (*hua xin*) is a bawdy term for the female genitals. Though no comparable usage can be definitively traced for "gut," it might, as the proverbial bodily seat of nefarious intentions, connote the male genitals.

Neither one of the *Seductive Courtesans* collections provides authorial attribution for the verses in the courtesan entries, contrary to the fixation on authorship in anthologies, which resort to place-keepers like "Anonymous" when the author is truly unknown. In this respect, the two *Seductive Courtesans* collections differ from an anthology like *Stylish Verses from the Green Bower*, in which every verse is assigned the name of a courtesan author. The *Seductive Courtesans* collections also differ from the many anecdotal or individual literary collections that included verse to or about specific courtesans by male literati, which likewise identify the authorship of each individual piece. Even within the entries in the *Seductive Courtesans* collections, in contrast to the unassigned authorship and polyphony of the verse selections, general comments are clearly labeled with the compiler's pseudonym.

From the content of the verse included in the two *Seductive Courtesans* collections, as the entry for the singer Liang Xiaopian suggests, many poems and arias appear to have been written in tribute to a courtesan by a male admirer; others, particularly the popular songs, are written in a female voice, often addressing a male lover. Some of the verse is purposefully vague—the sentiments it espouses could be voiced by either sex in a love affair. Kathryn Lowry notes that most popular songs are couched in a woman's voice, and one major difference between independent aria and popular song is that the former tend to be written in the third person, the latter in the first person.[46] Since there is a long tradition of men writing poetry in a woman's voice in China, however, a first-person feminine voice is by no means a definitive sign of female authorship. Conversely, since women writers were accustomed to depicting the beauty of other women, and perhaps even their own, adulatory descriptions of a feminine body or face need not be a definitive sign of male authorship either.[47]

In his biography of a Nanjing actress, Pan Zhiheng appends two tributary poems about her physical charms and musical talents: one that he composed and one composed by her good friend, a Nanjing courtesan who was known as a poet. Both may have been composed at one of the parties at the "House of Twin Beauties" that the three of them attended in 1609. The poems are similar in style, and without the authorial attributions Pan provides it would be impossible to determine that one was written by a man and the other by a woman.[48]

My hypothesis is that this very promiscuity of provenance in the *Seductive Courtesans* collections may be a key to the kinds of loose collaborative and improvisational types of music-making and versifying that went on in early seventeenth-century courtesan houses.[49] The collections do not designate poetic authors in each entry or specify circumstances of composition. Lowry's theory that the collections included compositions both written to and by courtesans is plausible.[50] But the real point is that authorship is not actually what is at stake here. If top courtesans excelled at performing their lovers' verse to music, and sometimes their own, and were also instrumental in transmitting and generating popular songs and arias, then at least a portion of the pieces clustered under the entry of a particular courtesan should be understood as characteristic of her *performing* repertory, and certainly of her performing cohort and milieu. The courtesan's singing is a frequent topic of the poems and arias, helping to keep the performance context of these offerings constantly in the foreground.

Important for my argument is the high density of arias and popular songs in these collections, since other verse forms, while chanted aloud, were not actually sung in this period. Furthermore, unlike more prestigious genres of poetry, which carried clear expectations of having an "author," arias, especially arias presented in a courtesan context, were more likely to remain anonymous or to have false attributions. When it came to popular songs, the concept of authorship was not even really applicable.

Lowry argues that the boundaries between arias and popular songs were quite permeable during the late Ming and that tune types were actually very flexible. Her research shows that at least in the case of popular songs, verses with very different prosodic forms could share the same tune title, and popular songs could sometimes even share the same tune title with arias.[51] I interpret her findings to indicate that tunes and lyrics were continually mutating in performance through improvisation. Crucial to bringing about such mutations were courtesans who functioned as a principal "artery" for absorbing new folk tunes into urban culture through popular song and disseminating them across the country.[52]

The anthologies of Feng Menglong help shed some light on contemporary attitudes toward the "authorship" of arias and popular song arising from a pleasure quarter milieu. Writer, editor, playwright, and publisher, Feng was a crucial figure in the early seventeenth-century publication of arias and popular songs and can be linked with both the *Seductive Courtesans* collections. In the Suzhou collection, Zhou Zhibiao calls him "a friend," and details Feng's liaison with the courtesan ranked sixth in the volume. Feng was directly involved in the compilation of the Nanjing collection, for which he wrote a preface, and where his comments are appended to many entries.[53]

In 1627, Feng published an anthology of arias mainly written to or about courtesans, *The Celestial Air Played Anew*, which included many of his own compositions. In it, he notes that "older generations did not wish to be known as the authors of arias, and although many of their arias were in wide circulation, we don't know from whose hand they came."[54] He scoffs at a 1616 anthology of arias also assembled by Zhou Zhibiao, *An Elegant Collection of Kun-Style Songs*, which did provide names of authors for the arias, but often "recklessly mismatched them."[55] The problem of unknown or faulty attributions for arias, especially those of earlier periods, is also raised in *Love Lyrics of Stylistic Brilliance*, a collection compiled by Zhang Xu in the 1620s, which showcased arias by literati written to courtesans.[56] Both Feng Menglong's and Zhang Xu's anthologies present themselves as novel endeavors to apply the rigorous standards of authorial attribution demanded of prestigious collections of verse to compilations of arias composed and performed in the courtesan world. At the same time, both men directed their anthologies to an audience of "reader-singers" and adopted various organizational and typographical strategies meant to facilitate singing so that the literary value they were championing for the arias did not entirely eclipse their performance value.

The absence of authorial attribution in the *Seductive Courtesans* collections is consistent with the editorial practice of anthologies of popular songs from the 1610s or 1620s, notably *Hanging Branches* and *Mountain Songs*, both compiled by Feng Menglong. Only in a handful of cases are actual authors given for literary imitations inspired by a certain song, but courtesans are occasionally noted as sources from whom Feng learned a song. The most extensive account in *Hanging Branches* concerns two songs that he got from his "good friend" Feng Xi (no relation), a famous courtesan ranked as "Magnus" in *Seductive Courtesans of Suzhou*. On the night before she was to be married, she invited him to come bid her farewell. The hour grew late. As he was about to leave, he asked whether there was anything she had left unsaid. She replied that she remembered two popular songs she had never divulged to him. And then she sang them for him. Feng Menglong prints the texts of the two songs, which are quite witty, and then waxes melancholy that he never saw her again: "Ah, this face as pink and lovely as a peach flower has long vanished, becoming the stuff of dreams. But whenever I read the lyrics of these songs, I faintly hear her voice 'winding sinuously round the rafters.'"[57]

The songs are a parting gift that Feng Xi bestows on her friend Feng Menglong, whose interest in collecting and publishing popular songs would have been common knowledge in the pleasure quarter.[58] As befits a popular song, she uses the language of "remembering" rather than composing (though this would not rule out her having shaped or modified the words and music); and he credits her as the person who "passed on" the songs to him, not as their author. But even when all he has before him are the written texts (presumably that one of them had transcribed), the songs are indelibly stamped with her performing presence and his memory of the occasion upon which he heard them. As this instance suggests, it is all too easy for writers on courtesans to slip into nostalgia, but Feng Menglong quickly follows this emotional outburst with witty imitations of Feng Xi's first song written by himself and his literati friends, which are among the few songs in the collection presented as the work of named "authors."[59] Still, their efforts pale in comparison with Feng Xi's, the written texts of whose songs serve as a reminder of a whole sensory past, which lingers in the memory like an elusive scent or color.

LEARNING TO SING

Singing skill, as we have seen throughout this essay, was highly profitable to a courtesan and her establishment, and training in the vocal arts was consequently regarded as an important investment. Singing in a performance context may have been culturally coded as feminine, but the main arbiters of musical taste (the amateurs) and the most prestigious singing teachers (the professionals) were certainly men. Studying with a top music master was understood as one major avenue to a successful career as a courtesan, whose reputation, at least at the outset, might be partially contingent upon the renown of her teacher. Pan Zhiheng's biography of the courtesan Xu Pian, for instance, names the four male teachers of different arts with whom she studied simultaneously: one for calligraphy, one for the *qin*, one for poetry, and one for singing arias.[60] Liang Xiaopian, the courtesan who illustrated "realizing the tune" in the *Seductive Courtesans of Suzhou*, is said to have studied the art of the aria with a certain Gong Muxi. His numerous students acknowledged him as "the best music master in the south" and Xiaopian as "the best among them."[61]

A dubious honor perhaps. The remainder of the passage damns as much as it defends her: "Who says that a girl who sings is not worth speaking of?"[62] The line implies that in a girl a talent for singing is ordinarily regarded as a sign of her lack of virtue. Therefore what wins her fame and increases her value in her profession as courtesan is precisely what makes her *not* otherwise "worth speaking of."

Despite the greater prestige of male music masters, becoming a singing teacher was one possible source of livelihood open to a courtesan past her prime. A courtesan who left the profession and married might even coach her husband's maids in singing or eventually teach her granddaughters.[63] We know that extensive training was required to gain the vocal expertise necessary for a top courtesan. Unfortunately, most sources are too terse or formulaic to provide any details on how courtesans were actually trained in singing. One place to find at least imaginative representations of such training sessions, however, are the scenes from operas in which courtesans or palace entertainers are being tutored. Such scenes became stock components of operas, no doubt because they helped vary the spectacle and incorporated into the plot the operatic injunction to sing. Although dramatized singing lessons can be found as early as the fifteenth century, the vogue for such scenes was launched by Liang Chenyu's famous historical drama *Washing Silk Clothes* (ca. 1572), said to be the first opera written expressly for *kun qu* performance. This opera features a scene entitled "Instruction in the Arts" where the Queen of Yue teaches the palace lady Xi Shi to sing and dance so that she will be fully equipped to seduce their enemy, the King of Wu, and help topple his kingdom.[64]

The best-known and most complex of the singing lesson scenes appears in Kong Shangren's *Peach Blossom Fan*. First completed and performed in 1699, *Peach Blossom*

Fan is a historical drama about the fall of the Ming dynasty some fifty years earlier, which centers much of the action on the pleasure quarter in Nanjing. Virtually all the characters in the play are based on historical figures, including the courtesans, music masters, and other denizens of the demi-monde. The scene in question is our first introduction to the heroine, a budding courtesan named Li Xiangjun, whose career has not yet been launched. The date is 1643, the year prior to the dynasty's collapse. The setting is the house in the Nanjing pleasure quarter in which Xiangjun lives with her adoptive mother, the courtesan Li Zhenli, who is grooming her to enter their profession. A patron of theirs, a politician and man of letters named Yang Wencong, has just come to call, in part because he's interested in finding a mistress for a friend of his, the hero of the play, a famous late Ming literary figure named Hou Fangyu. Yang first admires Xiangjun's beauty, then immediately inquires as to her skill in the arts. Her mother answers that she has hired a singing master to teach her how to sing arias and that she has already learned half of Tang Xianzu's famous opera *Peony Pavilion*, one of the most famous romances of all time and a classic of the *kun qu* repertory. Then she calls her daughter over.

> ZHENLI: Child, Mr. Yang is no outsider. Take out your songbook and quickly practice a few arias. After your teacher has corrected you on these, you'll be ready to start on some new tunes.

> XIANGJUN (frowning): How can I practice singing in front of a guest?

> ZHENLI: What a silly thing to say! For those of us in the entertainer ranks, singing and dancing are what put food on the table! If you won't apply yourself to singing, what are you going to do with yourself? [*Xiangjun looks at her songbook.*][65]

The scene makes it clear that Xiangjun, as befits a high-class courtesan, is being trained in the elegant "pure singing" style rather than in the performance of full-fledged operas on stage. What Xiangjun sings for her teacher Su Kunsheng are two arias from the famous garden scene in *Peony Pavilion*, where the well-born heroine experiences her first carnal dream of love. Since Xiangjun omits all the interspersed dialogue written into the arias in the original play, however, the book she is consulting could not have been a full playtext, but is most likely a collection of arias meant primarily for singing.

The lesson proper begins with the teacher asking Xiangjun the usual formula employed in scenes of this sort: "Do you have the arias you learned yesterday down cold?"[66] When she replies that she has, he asks her to begin (companion website track 1).

> XIANGJUN: [*seated opposite SU, sings to the tune "Black Gossamer Robe" from* Peony Pavilion]:

> "See how deepest purple, brightest scarlet
> open their beauty only to dry well crumbling.
> 'Bright the morn, lovely the scene,'
> listless and lost the heart"[67]

> SU: Wrong! Wrong! "Lovely" gets an individual beat and so does "lost." You can't just slur them together. Take it from the top again.

XIANGJUN:

" 'Bright the morn, lovely the scene.'
—where is the garden 'gay with joyous cries' "?
streaking the dawn, close-curled at dusk,
rosy clouds frame emerald pavilion;
fine threads of rain

SU: Wrong again! "Fine threads" is the climax point (*wutou*); it should be sung from inside the throat.[68]

Wutou is a much discussed technical term in the traditional prescriptive literature on the vocal art of the aria. As Marjory Liu explains, a *wutou* "in effect . . . brings together in two or three words within a line or a song a concentration of literary-musical components that signifies an aesthetic climax. That is to say, a choice grouping of key words, usually in lyrical style each representing a different specific speech tone, coinciding with melodic and rhythmic highlights collectively constitutes a *wutou*."[69] The lingering emotional effect a *wutou* is thus supposed to create makes the interruption of the acoustic pleasure in the singing lesson just cited particularly jarring for a knowledgeable audience.

One important point of the musical jargon in *Peach Blossom Fan* is not only to convey the teacher's professional expertise, but to bolster Xiangjun's credentials as a seriously trained singer, important if she is to succeed as a courtesan. And it works. After she finishes the second aria from *Peony Pavilion* ("My Darling Girl"; companion website track 2), Yang Wencong is impressed. "How delightful that your daughter is so gifted. She'll become a famous courtesan, don't you worry!"[70] And he promptly proposes to arrange a union with his friend Hou Fangyu.

CODA: THE VALUE OF WITHDRAWAL

A number of recent interpretations of this scene emphasize that this technical treatment of singing pedagogy suppresses and distorts the romantic meaning of the lyrics the courtesan sings.[71] Indeed the possibilities for irony are even greater, since the emphasis on learning a craft not only undermines the meaning of the lyrics the performer sings, but undermines the affective power of her voice to transport the listener.

The historical nucleus of this scene from *Peach Blossom Fan* derives from the biography of Li Xiangjun that Hou Fangyu wrote between 1650 and 1652 describing their former relationship and a letter covering some of the same ground.[72] In the biography, he mentions that she would "invite him to compose poems for her and then reciprocate by singing them."[73] There is more here than meets the eye. He uses the word *shi*, which refers to the genre of poetry that was chanted, not sung, and therefore never written to pre-existent tunes as arias were.[74] Several short poems that he is thought to have written for her appear in his only extant collection of verse.[75] Although we do not know whether these are the poems she actually performed for him, it is clear that none would have been singable. Unfortunately, Hou gives no indication of how Xiangjun was able to sing his poems, but they would have needed first to be set to music, by rewriting and expanding the words to conform to an existing tune pattern.[76] In this case, "realizing the tune" would have required an unusual degree of literary and musical effort on her part.

Hou's biography of Xiangjun also notes that she was exceptionally skilled at singing arias from another famous opera, *The Pipa*, but that she was extremely reluctant to perform them. When at last she does sing them for him, this initial reticence lends her rendition that much more power and weight. He recounts her passionate farewell at the riverbank upon his departure from Nanjing, in which she sang from *The Pipa* to see him off, knowing their relationship was over. Hou had come to Nanjing to sit for the triennial provincial exams, and, as was customary, had taken a mistress from among the courtesans in the famous pleasure quarter directly across the river from the examination compound; now having failed the examination, it was time to take his leave of the city and of her. The transient course of such an affair was entirely predictable.

Yet Xiangjun interjects a deeper meaning into the standard farewell by choosing this particular opera from her repertory and drawing a historical analogy to warn him against aligning himself with the evil political faction then in power. "We cannot expect to see each other again, so I hope you will always take care of yourself. Don't forget the arias I have sung from *The Pipa*! I will never sing them again!"[77] We know Xiangjun's words only through the remembered speech that Hou Fangyu includes in his idealized biography, but it is still worth pondering the two possible meanings of her last two lines. Why should he not forget the arias she has just sung?

On a superficial level, she is simply reinforcing the seriousness of her message: I will no longer be around to advise you, so you must engrave my words, underscored by these arias, in your memory. In this reading, "I will never sing them again" implies "I will never sing them again *for you*." On a deeper level, however, the arias become a substitute for her person, the injunction not to forget them replacing the more expected plea at a parting of lovers, "Don't forget *me*." Her performance of these arias is a farewell keepsake she bestows upon him, the rarity of her gift imbuing it with correspondingly greater value. In keeping with such a logic, a second interpretation of her last line is possible: "I will never sing them again *for anyone*."

As we have seen throughout this essay, one of the most important currencies at a courtesan's disposal was her performance of song. The dilemma that Li Xiangjun faced at the riverbank was how to turn the seemingly most commonplace and banal gesture in a courtesan's repertory—singing arias for her lover—into a truly valuable thing, one that could adequately express the integrity of her feelings for him and repay his favor. Her solution was to withdraw these arias permanently from circulation from that moment on. Only in this way could she claim "ownership" of them and present them to her lover as "his" forever.

The symbolism of this musical resolve anticipates the grand gesture for which she became famous: her principled refusal of the princely sum of 300 taels to join the household of a wealthy and powerful member of the evil faction that she had warned her lover against. It is for this act of fidelity that Hou Fangyu wrote her biography and that she is featured as the heroine of *Peach Blossom Fan*.[78]

Notes

My deep thanks to Kathryn Lowry, Patrick Hanan, Martha Feldman, Bonnie Gordon, Wilt Idema, and Zhou Yuan for help with this essay.

1. For this argument, see, for example, *The Lotus Boat: The Origins of Chinese Tz'u Poetry in T'ang Popular Culture* (New York: Columbia University Press, 1984).

2. Beverly Bossler, "Shifting Identities: Courtesans and Literati in Song China," *Harvard Journal of Asiatic Studies* 62 (2002), 6–7.

3. Although the term "singing girl" (*ge nü*) can be traced back to the eighth century, neither this term nor the related term "singing courtesan" (*ge ji*) is common in seventeenth-century sources. The translation "sing-song girl" is a pidgin corruption of the southern (Wu) dialect pronunciation for *xiansheng* (here meaning "courtesan," but ordinarily meaning "master" or "teacher") and has nothing to do with singing.

4. *Qinglou yunyu*, comp. Zhang Mengzheng (Hangzhou, 1616); facsimile ed. in *Zhongguo gudai banhua congkan erbian* (Shanghai: Shanghai guji chubanshe, 1994), 4:1. Unless otherwise indicated, all translations are my own.

5. James Davidson, *Courtesans and Fishcakes: The Consuming Passions of Classical Athens* (New York: HarperPerennial, 1999), 124.

6. *Qinglou yunyu*, 230.

7. The exceptions are: Kathryn Lowry, "Transmission of Popular Song in the Late Ming" (Ph.D. diss., Harvard University, 1996); Dai Ning, "Ming Qing shiqi Qinhuai qinglou yinyue wenhua chutan," *Zhongguo yinyuexue jikan* 1997, no. 3, pp. 40–54; and Oki Yasushi's work, including *Chūgoku yūri kūkan: Min Shin shinwai gijo no sekai* (Tokyo: Seidosha, 2002), and idem, *Fū Bōryū sanka no kenkyū* (Tokyo: Keisō shobō, 2003).

8. Publication of opera arias with the full *gong chi* method of musical notation began with Ye Tang, *Nashuying qupu* (1791), but was still aimed at amateur rather than professional singers.

9. Joseph S. C. Lam, "The Presence and Absence of Female Musicians and Music in China," in *Women and Confucian Cultures in Premodern China, Korea, and Japan*, ed. Dorothy Ko et al. (Berkeley: University of California Press, 2003), 97.

10. For the sexual meaning of these terms, see W. L. Idema and Stephen West, *The Moon and the Zither: The Story of the Western Wing* (Berkeley: University of California Press, 1991), 147 and 151.

11. In *Shanben xiqu congkan*, vol. 2, compiled by Wang Qiugui (Taipei: Xuesheng shuju, 1984–87). *Yugu tiaohuang* is the title on the cover page, but elsewhere the title is printed as *Yugu xinhuang* (New Pipes in the Jade Valley). *Gu* (valley) is sometimes a poetic double entendre for the vagina.

12. Sun Zhongling, *Dongguo ji*, scene 8, 16b–17a, in *Guben xiqu congkan*, 2d ser. (Shanghai: Shangwu yinshuguan, 1955).

13. Ibid., 17b. The locus classicus for this cliché praising female singing appears in an early philosophical text: a beggar woman who sings for a living passes through a city gate; the lingering notes are said to "wind sinuously round the rafters" and to be audible for three days. See *The Book of Lieh-tzu*, trans. A. C. Graham (New York: Columbia University Press, 1990), 109.

14. See, for instance, the section on song in Duan Anjie, *Yuefu zalu* (ca. 894), which lists a few male singers but concentrates mainly on female ones. *Zhongguo gudian xiqu lunzhu jicheng* (Beijing: Zhongguo xiju chubanshe, 1959), 1:46–48 (henceforth, *Xiqu lunzhu*).

15. Wang Zhuo, *Biji manzhi*, in *Xiqu lunzhu* 1:111.

16. *Shih-shuo hsin-yü*, trans. Richard B. Mather (Minneapolis: University of Minnesota Press, 1976), 205.

17. The aphorism is cited, inter alia, in: Duan Anjie, *Yuefu zalu*, *Xiqu lunzhu*, 1:47; Yannan zhiyan (pseud.), *Changlun*, *Xiqu lunzhu*, 1:159; Wang Jide, *Qulü*, *Xiqu lunzhu*, 4:160; Pan Zhiheng, *Pan Zhiheng quhua*, ed. Wang Xiaoyi (Beijing: Zhongguo xiju chubanshe, 1988), 19.

18. *Pan Zhiheng quhua*, 28; for another instance of the phrase "notes of flesh," see ibid., 8.

19. Li Yu, *Xianqing ouji*, ed. Shan Mianheng (Hangzhou: Zhejiang guji chubanshe, 1999), 3. 139.

20. Ibid., 3. 138.

21. Wang Anqi, *Mingdai chuanqi juchang ji qi yishu* (Taipei: Xuesheng shuju, 1985), 87.

22. Qian Qianyi, *Liechao shiji xiaozhuan* (Beijing: Zhonghua shuju, 1983), 2:765. For additional evidence for performances by Ma Xianglan and her troupe, see Wang Anqi, *Mingdai xiqu wulun* (Taipei: Da'an chubanshe, 1990), 10.

23. Zhang Dai, *Tao'an mengyi* (Shanghai: Shanghai guji chubanshe, 1982), 69–70.

24. On the fashion for amateur theatrical performances in the late Ming and the backlash against it, see Sophie Ann Justine Volpp, *Worldly Stage: The Figure of the Theater in Seventeenth-Century China* (Cambridge, MA: Harvard Asia Center Publications, forthcoming).

25. Yu Huai, *Banqiao zaji*, ed. Li Jintang (Shanghai: Shanghai guji chubanshe, 2000), 11.8; in English as *A Feast of Mist and Flowers: The Gay Quarters of Nanking at the End of the Ming*, trans. Howard S. Levy (Yokohama: privately published, 1966).

26. Yu Huai, *Banqiao zaji*, 11.

27. Ibid., 22.

28. Dai Ning, "Ming Qing shiqi Qinhuai," 43; Wang Anqi, *Mingdai chuanqi*, 87–94; Fu Xueyi, *Kunqu yinyue xinshang mantan* (Beijing: Renmin yinyue chubanshe, 1996), 8–10. The term "pure" connotes cool and quiet as opposed to noisy and hot.

29. *Quxie*, vol. 4:4; 54b–55a in *Sanqu congkan*, compiled Ren Zhongmin (Taipei: Zhonghua shuju, 1964).

30. See Richard Vinograd, *Boundaries of the Self: Chinese Portraits, 1600–1900* (Cambridge: Cambridge University Press, 1992), 11; 53.

31. Wang Xiaoyi, "Pan Zhiheng xiqu pinglun chutan," in *Shuoshi xuewei lunwen ji: xiqu juan* (Beijing: Wenhua yishu chubanshe, 1985), 124–25.

32. Wang Jide, "*Qu lü*," in *Xiqu lunzhu*, 4:117.

33. Isabel Wong, "Kunqu," in the *Garland Encyclopedia of World Music*, vol. 7, ed. Robert C. Provine *et al.* (New York: Garland, 2002), 293.

34. In "Transmission of Popular Song," Lowry translates *duoqu* as "to realize or unfold a tune" (48) and later defines the phrase as meaning "to shape a song in accordance with the score, or often (since there is no musical notation for sixteenth-century popular songs till more than 150 years later) in accordance with the conventional notion of a tune, a tune type" (51).

35. On the composite tune method, or what musicologists call "centonization," see Marjory Bong-Ray Liu, "Tradition and Change in *Kunqu* Opera" (Ph.D. diss., University of California at Los Angeles, 1976), 64–65; 67. "Patchwork melodies" is Rulan Chao Pian's term in *Song Dynasty Musical Sources and Their Interpretation* (Cambridge, MA: Harvard University Press, 1967), 36.

36. Wong, "Kunqu," 293.

37. Wang Duanshu, *Mingyuan shiwei* (Qing edition), 38.4a–4b. The same aria, credited to "A Courtesan from Hubei" ("Qizhou ji"), also appears in Feng Menglong's 1627 anthology *Taixia xinzou*, in *Feng Menglong quanji*, ed. Wei Tongxian (Shanghai: Shanghai guji chubanshe, 1993), 15:14. 742–43.

38. *Si*, the character translated as "string," is commonly punned with its homophone to mean "thoughts of longing."

39. Wang Duanshu, *Minyuan shiwei*, 38.5a. The second aria, "My heart flutters," is taken from *Stylish Verses from the Green Bower*, one of Wang's principal sources for works by courtesans.

40. Both compilers published these books under pseudonyms. For the identification of Wangyuzi as Zhou Zhibiao, see Lowry, "Transmission of Popular Song," 242; and *Zhongguo quxue dacidian* (Hangzhou: Zhejiang jiaoyu chubanshe, 1997), 657. For the identification of Weilinzi as Li Yunxiang, see Hanan, *The Chinese Vernacular Story* (Cambridge, MA: Harvard University Press, 1981), 89.

41. On "flower registers," see Dorothy Ko, "The Bound Foot and the Written Word," in *Writing Women in Late Imperial China*, ed. Ellen Widmer and Kang-I Sun Chang (Stanford: Stanford University Press, 1997), 74–100, and Goyama Kiwamu, "Kaan, kabo kō," *Bungaku runshū* 35 (1989), 12.

42. Along the same lines, Li Yu (*Xianqing ouji*, 3. 138) advises that a woman looks best playing the *xiao* flute because it makes her mouth appear attractively smaller. This is why, he says, pictures of beautiful women like to portray them playing this particular instrument (see fig. 3.1) and why a woman should never play the shawm, which distorts the face.

43. On this compendium, *Huapin jian*, compiled by Qingtiao yishi (pseud.), see Mao Wenfang, *Wu.xingbie.guankan: Mingmo Qingchu wenhua shuxie xintan* (Taibei: Xuesheng shuju, 2001), 384–92.

44. Literally, "penetrates the magic rhinoceros horn," a common poetic cliché for erotic love and mutual understanding between lovers.

45. "White Snow" is an ancient tune title that also figures in the title of an important early fourteenth-century collection of independent arias.

46. Lowry, "Transmission of Popular Song."

47. Ko, "The Written Word," 90–95.

48. *Pan Zhiheng quhua*, 127. Both poems are literary songs in the *yuefu* style rather than popular songs or arias. Pan doesn't specify what sort of establishment the "House of Twin Beauties" (*Shuangyan lou*) was, presumably a courtesan house, a restaurant, or a wineshop, all of which could employ the word *lou* (storied building) in their name.

49. Martha Feldman makes a similar argument about the Italian Renaissance in "Authors and Anonyms: Recovering the Anonymous Subject in Cinquecento Vernacular Objects," in *Music and the Cultures of Print*, ed. Kate van Orden (New York: Garland, 2000), 166–99.

50. Lowry, "Transmission of Popular Song," 242.

51. Ibid. 3–5 and chap. 3.

52. "Artery" is the phrase used by Dai Ning in "Ming Qing shiqi Qinhuai"; for a more extended version of this argument see Oki Yasushi, "Sokucho shu 'Guazhi'er' ni tsuite," *Tōyō bunka kenkyūjo* 107 (1988): 95–96.

53. Hanan, *The Chinese Vernacular Story*, 89–90.

54. *Taixia xinzou*, in *Feng Menglong quanji*, 15:7. Only three of the arias in this collection are by women, only one of whom is a courtesan.

55. Ibid.

56. *Caibi qingci*, in *Shanben*, 75:14–15.

57. Feng Menglong, comp., *Guazhi'er*, in *Ming Qing min'ge shidiao ji* (Shanghai: Shanghai guji chubanshe, 1987), 1:4. 107–8.

58. In the same collection, Feng Menglong describes how a female musician named Ayuan, a pipa player who is also an expert at "pure singing" and skilled at "making new music," comes to see him to give him the words to some of her songs when she hears that he is expanding an earlier edition of such material (*Guazhi'er* 3.85).

59. For a translation and discussion of these songs, see Lowry, "Transmission of Popular

Song," 191–200. Lowry suggests that Feng Xi sings this particular song because the words express her own feelings about her imminent marriage.

60. *Pan Zhiheng quhua,* 110.

61. *Wuji baimei* 2.11a–b; list of top singers 2.48b.

62. Zhou Zhibiao, *Wuji baimei,* 2.11b.

63. See Yu Huai, *Banqiao zaji,* 27–28, 17, and Wu Weiye, "Linhuai laoji xing," in *Wu Meicun shi xuan,* ed. Wang Tang (Hong Kong: Sanlian shudian, 1987), 149–51.

64. Liang Chenyu, *Huansha ji jiao zhu,* ed. Zhang Shenshi et al. (Beijing: Zhonghua shuju, 1994), scene 25, 142–47. Other notable examples include an aria suite from Ma Xianglan's lost opera, in *Qunyin leixuan,* comp. Hu Wenhuan, *Shanben* 38.18, 947, and Zhou Youdun, *Mudan pin,* in *Ming Zhouxian wang yuefu sanzhong,* 3b.

65. Kong Shangren, *Taohua shan* (Beijing: Renmin chubanshe, 1980), 17.

66. Ibid., 17.

67. Lines from *Peony Pavilion* translated by Cyril Birch, *The Peony Pavilion* (Bloomington: Indiana University Press, 1980), 44.

68. Ibid.

69. Liu, "Tradition and Change in *Kun qu* Opera," 136.

70. Kong, *Taohua shan,* 18.

71. For example, Wai-yee Li, "The Representation of History in *Peach Blossom Fan,*" *Journal of the American Oriental Society* 115 (1995): 421–33; Tina Lu, *Persons, Roles, and Minds: Identity in* Peony Pavilion *and* Peach Blossom Fan (Stanford: Stanford University Press, 2001), 161; and Stephen Owen, "'I Don't Want to Act as Emperor Anymore,'" in *Trauma and Transcendence in Early Qing Literature,* ed. W. L. Idema et al. (Cambridge, MA: Harvard Asia Center Publications, 2005).

72. *Hou Fangyu ji jiaojian,* ed. Wang Shulin (Zhengzhou: Zhongzhou guji chubanshe, 1992), 112–14; 262–64.

73. *Hou Fangyu ji,* 262.

74. In his letter, he refers to the *xiao shi* ("little poems") that he wrote for her, but does not mention her having sung them for him.

75. Hou Fangyu, *Siyitang shiji* (Shanghai: Saoye shanfang, undated facsimile edition), chap. 2. One of these is the poem he inscribes on the fan on their "wedding night" in *Peach Blossom Fan.* For the list of poems, see *Hou Fangyu ji,* 114, n. 8. His extant literary corpus preserves no lyrics to arias or *ci,* which makes it more plausible that the verses he gave her were actually "poems," not the lyrics to arias.

76. For a *ci* song-lyric whose lines are altered to conform to an aria tune pattern so that it can be sung, see the treatment of Li Bai's "Qingping diao" in scene 24 of Hong Sheng, *Changsheng dian* (Beijing: Renmin wenxue, 1986), 126.

77. Hou Fangyu, "Li ji zhuan," 263.

78. After this essay went to press, I discovered that although *The Classic of Whoring* incorporated into *Stylish Verses from the Green Bower* does not survive as an independent book, the identical content circulated verbatim in late Ming daily-use encyclopedias under headings such as "Regulations of the Green Bower" (in *Santai wanyong zhengzong* 21.294–348) or "Secret Mechanisms of Romance" (in *Wuju wanbao quanshu* 10.250–266 and *Miaojin wangbao quanshu* 24.306–334), all reprinted in *Chūgoku nichiyo ruisho shusei* (Tokyo: Kyuko Shoin, 1999–2000). On these "brothel treatises," which were also included in drama miscellanies, see Yuming He, "Productive Space: Performance Texts in the Late Ming" (Ph.D. diss., University of California at Berkeley, 2003), 99–102.

PART II

A CASE STUDY:
THE COURTESAN'S VOICE
IN EARLY MODERN ITALY

Introduction

When the twelfth-century courtier and churchman Walter Map exclaimed on the baffling nature of the court, he drew attention to a clutch of problems: "'What the court is, God knows, I know not,' it is so 'changeable and various.'"[1] The same condition that exasperated Map endured into early modern Europe, from the macrocosmic variations in a court's residence and personnel to the microcosmic mutability of the courtier's own selfhood. The efficacy of courtiership depended on the courtier's versatility in serving whoever his prince happened to be with whatever manner of courtesy, skill, and style was needed, whether in warfare, arts, letters, speech, or manners.

Courtiership is an arresting framework in which to consider the place of the courtesan's music in early modern Italy, specifically the high-brow realm of the *cortigiana onesta*, the so-called honest (or "honored") courtesan whose demeanor and values most closely resembled those of courtiers and court ladies (called "donne di palazzo"). By the sixteenth century, the courtier's arts of service, transposed from the court to the city, were adapted by the Italian *cortigiana*. Courtesanship was arguably a late urban variant of the courtly patronage system, subject to and product of much the same demands. Indeed the verbal kinship of courtier and courtesan—shot through Indo-European languages—recalls this professional continuity, rooted in courtly service through skilled performance: the ability to be many things to many people. Often the most exalted courtesans claimed fame and sometimes fortune precisely through this adaptive ability.[2]

But in the computations of history, the kinship breaks down there. Where Italian courtiers can be tracked and counted in a calculus of social relations still perceptible at the prospect of history, high-placed courtesans thrived in a social field that was and remains inherently elusive, prone to erasures that are part documentary, part intrinsic to the courtesan's condition.

The essays in this part of our volume, written by a research team at the University of Chicago,[3] set out to recuperate some musical practices of courtesans in early modern Italy and explore how their ephemeral nature relates to various cultural conditions that allowed courtesanship to thrive. What emerge are different valences of the courtesan's voice: the voice as an index of social tensions, class positions, and rhetorical efficacy, the voice as the grain of courtesan-like sensuality, but also as a workaday instrument that improvises song, sings polyphony, sounds to a plucked lute or keyboard, crafts its accompaniments, and declaims its own verse. In my essay the voice is as tangible in popular philosophy and anxious politicized discourse as it is intangible in historical remains. I propose some ways it can be heard, which are then taken up variously by other members of our team: Dawn De Rycke by looking at partbooks as bearers of courtesans' song, Justin Flosi in his search for hidden courtesan voices and social networks in madrigal texts of the 1520s and 1530s, and Drew Edward Davies in finding new repertorial evidence of courtesan-like ambiguities, high and low, sacred and secular. Different in our projects, we nevertheless agree on two essential points. First, we see the courtesan's success in negotiating her social world as crucially bound up with her abilities as a cultural performer—a mistress of manners brandishing choice clothes and jewels, fine verse, wise thoughts, witticisms, and sensual speech and music. On this view, the success of Italian courtesanship depended not so much on a litany of traits, signs, or products that the courtesan bore or made as on the *efficacy* of her actions. What counted most was the effectiveness of her performances. In this sense she was the true Renaissance woman—a rhetorical being, more *verba* than *res*, and dangerously so. Second, we understand the voice as a particularly critical instrument in the performative repertory of Italian courtesans, critical not just to their ability to "give performances" but to the way in which they functioned as actors shaping their positions in social life. However much the courtesan's voice has vanished from the records of history along with other ephemera of oral traditions, it sat center stage in the unstable field of her self-production and holds the key to a phenomenal dimension of early modern courtesanship.[4]

Notes

1. Quoted by Peter Burke, "The Courtier," chap. 4 in *Renaissance Characters*, ed. Eugenio Garin, trans. Lydia G. Cochrane (Chicago: University of Chicago Press, 1988), 98.

2. See Margaret F. Rosenthal, *The Honest Courtesan: Veronica Franco, Citizen and Writer in Sixteenth-Century Venice* (Chicago: University of Chicago Press, 1992), and Ann Rosalind Jones, *The Currency of Eros: Women's Love Lyric in Europe, 1540–1620* (Bloomington: University of Indiana Press, 1990).

3. See the Introduction to this volume, p. 4.

4. Wider contextual implications of early modern Italian courtesanship are taken up by Gordon, Ruggiero, and Quaintance later in this volume.

The Courtesan's Voice

*Petrarchan Lovers, Pop Philosophy,
and Oral Traditions*

COURTING MUSIC

Like the *donna angelicata* (the revered woman) of Petrarch's lyric canon, so immensely popular in the sixteenth century, courtesans were often reproached by abject lovers but also venerated by them. A painting by Parrasio Michel of ca. 1560 (fig. 4.1) condenses this double status of the courtesan by presenting her in a performative guise. She gazes heavenward as she sings to the lute but with breasts exposed and is attended by a secularized Cupid who stands in as both son of Venus (herself a stand-in for the courtesan) and the Roman God of Love deployed so prolifically in sacred and secular images.

As the site of this doubleness, the courtesan was also the quintessential object of a generalized male way of encountering women. In Petrarchan glosses she was the lyric obsession that marked the poet's lost youth, his sweet error, the cause of his tears and singing and his loss of reason. But more often than other women, she could suffer when the balance tipped toward viewing her as the cruel, unattainable lady. When that happened her reputation could be put on the line. And as a woman who conversed and sang when other women often could not, her voice then became the locus of an irresoluble paradox—madonna or a whore, lady or harlot? Small wonder, then, that as the voice was increasingly added to the courtesans' wares in the sixteenth century, the female voice became a general blazon of courtesan-like disrepute—the more so as singing styles increasingly favored solo virtuosity. By the 1540s, when reactionary religious leanings had intensified debates about female propriety, "singing" itself became a watchword for female impropriety, something from which courtesans' uses of courtly singing could profit but which could also damn them, and exclude them from legitimate social life.[1] Thus, for example, where the humanist Pietro Bembo exalted the place of singing for women as well as for men in his 1505 dialogue on love *Gli asolani*, in 1541 he admonished his teenage daughter not to play a musical instrument, since doing so was "a thing for vain and frivolous women."[2] No longer was it clear by the mid-sixteenth century whether courtesans

FIGURE 4.1. Courtesan with lute, oil painting by Parassio Michel.
Szépművészeti Múzeum, Budapest

might sing as beautifully as noblewomen, or whether "honest" women who sang turned into courtesans.

The mercurial place of singing in female self-production and reception of the time has long bewildered scholars. Further on in this volume Bonnie Gordon shows that the popular tradition of sixteenth-century love treatises aggravated confusions over courtesans' singing in their own day, since love was conceived as spiritually uplifting yet threatening to self and society. Bembo's own dialogue on love, which initiated the tradition, spells out the dilemma. Staged during a wedding at the court of the ex-Cypriot queen Caterina Cornaro at Asolo, the queen's ladies-in-waiting charm their guests with song, then join conversations among those who dispute the Neoplatonic musical theories of Marsilio Ficino. Love emerges as the desire for beauty, and beauty in turn as a grace that results from harmony: the better proportioned the parts of the body or the virtues of the soul, the more beautiful each may be. Access to bodily beauty is given mainly through sight, whereas access to the beauty of the soul is attained solely through hearing. As the soul reawakens to its divine origins, music becomes a means of ascent to God,[3] valorized for its power to enrapture the soul.[4]

But the dialogue soon turns to a more worldly mood, even while invoking the Neoplatonic notion of sympathetic vibrations: when two lutes are well tuned and one of them is plucked, the other lute will immediately respond at pitch. The same thing happens to two loving souls who make sweet matching harmonies, even when distant from one another.[5]

As Bembo's fusion of music and eros was propelled through a veritable explosion of vernacular writings on love, language, music, and beauty issued in the second quarter of the sixteenth century, tensions between the spiritual and the worldly became their chief burden. Popularly the claim was still that music was a medium of love and the lover one who had to be skilled in music,[6] with loftier Neoplatonic philosophy linking the faculty of hearing with the spiritual side of love. It was de rigueur at mid-century to spiritualize love in popular love dialogues like Giuseppe Betussi's *Il raverta* (Venice 1544). Yet inevitably the ambivalent nexus between love and music was unloosed, as the two slipped perilously from spirit to body and back. Along that continuum, Betussi, for example, proposed a series of gradations from intellectual love wholly devoid of sensuality to corporeal love devoid of intellect, even as, paradoxically, he glossed them as "the two Venuses."[7] Between these poles, Betussi imagined female protagonists—emblematic of courtesans—who figured radical cosmic stretches from immaterial to material, spiritual to physical. The same divide marked Bernardino Tomitano's *Ragionamenti della lingua toscana* (Conversations on the Tuscan Tongue) (Venice, 1545), which personified music and verse as "a most sweet procuress who, with the enticements of her sweetnesses, lures the soul into that happiness with the state of loving an unknown ('un non so che')."[8] When beautifully sung, poetry was a female "temptress" ("lusinghiera"), he added, furtively gathering souls for some spectral place in a world beyond.

At stake in these discourses was less how music inflected the status of love than how it inflected the status of lovers. Love theories generally made music an asset to lovers, even as it made the practice of making music a liability for women. Not surprisingly, therefore, the single dialogue on love written by a woman, Tullia d'Aragona's *Dialogo della infinità d'amore* (Dialogue on the Infinity of Love) (Venice, 1547), effaced music altogether—along with her own status as a courtesan—when it went about comparing the virtues of spiritual and mundane love.[9] Significantly, the *Dialogo* did much to help legitimize her intellectual standing, not least by using the famed Florentine literato Benedetto Varchi as her foil but also by appropriating his Aristotelian discourse on love and reshaping it to fashion her own virtuosic apologia endorsing physical love. "Virtuous love," she wrote, could encompass physical as well as spiritual love because humans, being made of intellect and matter, needed both kinds.

Tullia d'Aragona's total omission of music in a work that defends physical love is striking given that she herself was a poet, lutenist, and singer, and owned a considerable library of music books, in addition to her many books in Italian and Latin.[10] According to an admirer at the Ferrarese court, her sight-reading of music was proficient enough that she could "sing from the book any motet or chanson,"[11] and as she played the lute, she surely accompanied her own verse in monodic arrangements too. But her music, like that of other women of her time, could be met with distrust. She had been publicly excoriated for accompanying elderly clients, who danced barefoot the *rosina* and *pavana* to the tune of her lute.[12] At a chilly moment in her *Dialogo* Tullia tells Varchi that he's trying to "slip out of the argument, get away, and pay [her] with a song."[13]

If song was a useful currency in Tullia's own trade, it was just as useful for beating Varchi at his own game. For song was cheap and dangerous from the Aristotelian heights of Varchi's argument, not least in the nervous Counter-Reformational climate (so-called) of the 1540s. Polyphonic singing was deemed less dangerous for women than solo singing because it regulated the rhythmic pacing of declamation, made lavish ornamentation musically harder to incorporate and easier to put under metrical controls, and in general discouraged excessive ostentation by virtue of collective delivery. But even polyphonic singing and lute-playing could be seen as risky. When Bembo admonished his daughter not to play a musical instrument, only eight years had passed since the brilliant, notorious Pietro Aretino published his vituperative satire on prostitutes, *I ragionamenti* of 1533, and invective literature was flooding from Venetian presses.[14] Indeed in his first book of letters published in 1537 Aretino declared that "the sounds, songs, and letters that women know are the keys that open the doors to their modesty."[15] Even more blunt were several satiric verses addressed some years later by the poet and music-lover Girolamo Fenaruolo to Adrian Willaert, choir master of St. Mark's: "Never is there found a woman so rare nor so chaste that if she were to sing she would not soon become a whore."[16]

This demotion of song to a tool of self-display makes a striking contrast to Castiglione's humanistic endorsement of song for courtiers and court ladies in 1528. But by the 1540s fashions for solo song had traveled from the northern Italian courts to the salons of mercantile cities where they were no longer festishized in print as they had been in the early part of the century. When the venal polygraph Antonfrancesco Doni (an Aretino knock-off) wrote in his *Dialogo della musica* (Venice, 1544) about his first encounter with the salons of Venice, he had seven male interlocutors adorning with conversation and music the society of a woman named Selvaggia, ambiguously presented as an urbane courtesan or a courtly libertine woman. "Honored" and "indebted," as she calls herself in courtly rhetoric, Selvaggia thrives among men who praise, adore, and sing with her. At last they serenade her with four solo monodies accompanied by the "lyre" (*lira*) on sonnets whose music is unwritten, unlike all the other music in the *Dialogo*.

THE COURTESAN'S SONG

At issue in all of this is women's self-display in unwritten solo song. Such singing and playing went on primarily in the cultured salons where women—some, or perhaps most, courtesans—were typically admitted for their poetic prowess, complemented with singing to their own accompaniment.[17] The Venetian academist Domenico Venier rhapsodized about an otherwise little-known singer named Franceschina Bel-

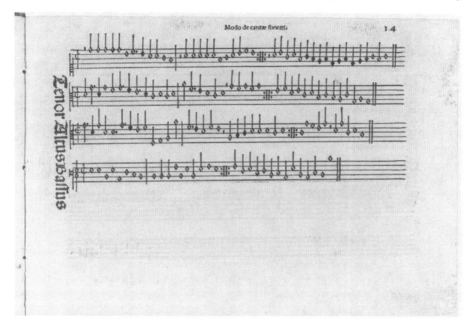

FIGURE 4.2. Ottaviano Petrucci, "Modo de cantar sonetti."
Libro quarto de frottole (Venice, 1505).

lamano, making her hand into a metonym for her song: "With various words, now this, now that string / Does the lovely hand ["la bella mano"] touch on the hollow wood, / Miraculously tuning her song to its sound" (no. 68, vv. 9–11).[18] And virtually all the other women who make an appearance at Venier's prestigious salon were singers too.

Anecdotal evidence suggests that the singing of courtesans and other soloists utilized melodic formulas that were committed to memory and performed over chord or bass patterns.[19] Examples of these oral practices survive in some of the frottola books printed by Ottaviano Petrucci between 1504 and 1514, books of vernacular songs in three- or usually four-voice format, and explicitly so in Book 4 of 1505 (undated but dateable), which printed different "modi" ("modes" or "melodies") for particular poetic forms.[20] Figure 4.2 shows in facsimile the "modo de cantar sonetti" (mode for singing sonnets) as printed in Petrucci's Book 4, transmitted without words since any sonnet can be sung to it.

The layout of the four voices makes it obvious that the printed format was merely the basis for whatever arrangement a given performer or group of performers would choose to make. Not only is no text given, but the parts (tenor, altus, and bassus, respectively, beneath the unnamed cantus) have no obvious means of being realized. They are nothing more than a spare three phrases each, each phrase sixteen minims long (or eight semibreves) with shared consonances and phrase endings and a repeat sign after the second phrase. Unlike the syntactic parsing of poetry in polyphonic madrigals of the 1540s, such monodies appear to have been based almost entirely on a principle of matching poetic lines to musical phrases. That this was the case throughout the sixteenth century is suggested by prints and songs that appear well into the later sixteenth century and beyond. Seventy years after Petrucci's print was made, the Florentine lutenist Cosimo Bottegari compiled a manuscript (the "Bottegari Lutebook") including *modi* of a very similar kind (some texted and some untexted), and the same was true three years later of tunes in the Neapolitan print *Aeri raccolti* edited by Rocco Rodio.[21]

Using a combination of practical knowledge and historical fantasy, we can picture Tullia d'Aragona declaiming one of the sonnets she wrote to her mentor and lover Girolamo Muzio, a courtier, soldier, and writer at the court of Ferrara (the probable pattern of musical phrases is shown in capital letters):

A Fiamma gentil che da gl'interni lumi
B con dolce folgorar in me discendi,
B il mio intenso affetto lietamente prendi,
C com'è usanza a tuoi santi costumi;

Gentle flame that descends in me
from internal lights with a sweet burning,
take my intense affection with joy,
as you are used to doing,

A poi che con alta tua luce m'allumi
B e sì soavemente il cor m'accendi,
B ch'ardendo lieto vive e lo difendi,
C che forza di vil foco nol consumi.

since with your great light you illumine me
and so sweetly ignite my heart
that, burning, it lives happily and you defend it,
for the force of a terrible fire does not consume it.

A E con la lingua far che 'l rozo ingegno,
B caldo dal caldo tuo, cerchi inalzarsi
C per cantar tue virtuti in mille parti;

And with language you let my rough talent,
warmed by your ardor, seek to awaken itself
to sing your virtues in a thousand places.

A io spero ancor a l'età tarda farsi
B noto che fosti tal, che stil più degno

C uopo era, e che mi fu gloria l'amarti.

I still hope in old age to make it
known that such were you that a more worthy style
was needed, and that it was an honor for me to love you.

Published in her *Rime* in 1547, the sonnet weaves praise of Muzio, as the true author who taught her to write and "sing," into praise of herself as his worthy and glorious pupil.[22]

Tullia claims by suggestion that his honor is hers, since it was *she* who learned to sing of his virtues, and who can therefore take the credit through her act of proclaiming them. Elaborating on the theme, she declares with all too specious modesty that the great Muzio is no common man but a "flame," "gentle" yet so overwhelming that only he can protect her from the threat of the "terrible fire" he ignites in her. But eros pales beside the fire of fame: it was his flame that gave her voice, and with it now lit, she sings to her own glory of his virtues and his love for her. This is much the way love strikes Petrarch in his famous canzone 23, "Nel dolce tempo della prima etade," which declares that Love and his lady transformed him "into what I am, turning me from a living man into a green laurel"—transformed him, that is, into a poet crowned with the laurel wreath that bestows fame on the poet laureate.[23] Yet Tullia puts the fire back in the torch of fame. Inverting directly Petrarch's last lines—"But I have certainly been a flame lit by a lovely glance and I have been the bird that rises highest in the air raising her whom in my words I honor" ("ma fui ben

EXAMPLE 4.1. Sonnet setting in frottola style by Paulo Scotti, published in 1511 in the second book of frottole for voice and lute arranged by Franciscus Bossinensis.

fiamma d'un bel guardo accense, et fui l'uccel che più per l'aere poggia alzando lei che ne' miei detti onoro")—she eroticizes Petrarch, claiming not just that it is her lover who has raised her to write and sing with honor, but that it was his ardor for her that motivated and thus honors her, and that will allow her to be honored (like a poet laureate) in old age. The direction of the Petrarchan urge to write is reversed here too, the man inspiring the woman (and the woman showing up the man).[24]

In ex. 4.1 I give a simple setting by Paulo Scotti, published in 1511 in the second book of frottole for voice and lute arranged by Franciscus Bossinensis, of Petrarch's sonnet "O tempo, o ciel involubil" (no. 355), which represents the kind of *modo* Tullia could have used to sing her own poem (replacing Petrarch's poem with hers). Highly recitational, the music, like Petrucci's "modo de cantar sonetti," is merely a skeletal starting point for the elaborated repetitions of phrases that singers turned out in performance. It could just as easily have served as a *modo* for new texts as the untexted *modo* of Petrucci did (cf. fig. 4.2). Like all other such *modi*, this one limits itself to several phrases of music that match the sonnet's two quatrains and two tercets in the pattern ABBC, ABBC, ABC, ABC.[25] The three phrases array themselves by step around a Dorian tonality on g that lifts off from g' to a' (phrase A), moves down to pause on f♯' (phrase B), and finally rises from f♯' back to g' (phrase C)—overall an initiating, medial, and final phrase that form together a kind of structural mordent.

Imagine Tullia offering her own sonnet in praise of her lover to the ears and hearts of fellow academists, stirring up a lather of ornaments through each successive quatrain and tercet. (See the different renderings of phrase 3, compared with Scotto's melody, at the endings of the quatrains and the sestet in ex. 4.2a–d.) At first she might have held back all but a little tugging at the cadences—some pathetic rubato here, a seductive mordent there (e.g., "costumi," which ends the first quatrain, ex. 4.2b). By the second quatrain one might suppose more extravagant diminutions, delicious runs and turns over sustained notes on phrases like "soavemente 'l cor," a trill seasoned with a turn at the cadence at "il cor m'accendi" (verse 6) and still more on the culminating "nol consumi" that ends the octave (verse 8, ex. 4.2c). Only at the end of the sonnet might there have been a really frothy surface (ex. 4.2d).[26]

We have little idea how luxuriant the ornaments produced by female monodists (or any solo singers from the mid-sixteenth century) actually were.[27] Ornamented examples of polyphony and monophonic examples in ornamentation treatises of the mid- to later sixteenth century tend largely to avoid leaps in embellished passages, instead favoring scalewise "diminution" (runs and figuration). But these were largely written for students by male teachers and published for a public of amateur music-lovers. They are more prescriptive than descriptive, and steer toward normative practice over the arresting extravagance that courtesans may have ventured.

There are at least modest examples of extensive runs and leaps in written-out monodies from the early to mid-sixteenth century, suggesting that the degree of luxuriance depended on the poem sung and the self-presentation of the singer. An example from the late fifteenth- to early sixteenth-century frottola repertory is the anonymous *Ayme sospiri*, which exists in an unornamented manuscript version of ca. 1460–70 as well as an ornamented version in Petrucci's book 4, performable like all such pieces in either a vocal version or an instrumental version.[28] Other cousins to improvised *modi* and ornamented frottole include various through-composed, treble-dominated polyphonic madrigals. Some were included in lutebooks, like the lute-accompanied solo madrigal by Hippolito Tromboncino *Io son ferito, ahi lasso* shown in facsimile in fig. 4.3. The madrigal comes from the "Bottegari Lutebook" dated 1574 and shows a vocal part ornamented throughout, albeit in a relatively measured and reserved way. Other written-out ornaments found their way into genres of repertories printed in partbooks. Among them are the *madrigali ariosi*, "song-like" madrigals

EXAMPLE 4.2(A–D). Paulo Scotti's melody for phrase 3 of Ex. 4.1, compared with proposed ornamentation for Tullia d'Aragona to use in declaiming verses 4, 8, and 14 of her sonnet "Fiamma gentil che da gl'interni lumi." Ornamentation by Martha Feldman.

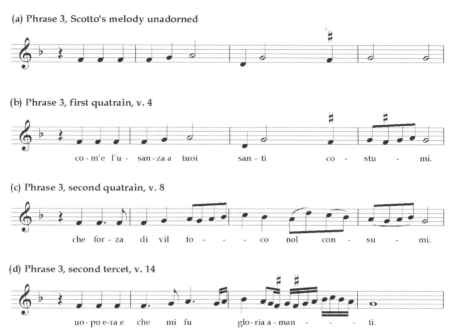

(a) Phrase 3, Scotto's melody unadorned

(b) Phrase 3, first quatrain, v. 4

co - m'e l'u - san-za a   tuoi   san - ti   co -   stu –   mi.

(c) Phrase 3, second quatrain, v. 8

che for - za   di vil   fo – –   co   nol   con -   su –   mi.

(d) Phrase 3, second tercet, v. 14

uo - po e-ra e   che   mi fu   glo - ria a - man –   –   – ti.

evocative of oral traditions that were linked with practices of reciting *ottava* (eight-line) stanzas from Lodovico Ariosto's epic *Orlando furioso* and then codified and printed in written polyphonic form by the Roman Antonio Barré between 1555 and 1562; and what Alfred Einstein dubbed "pseudo-monodies," madrigals that mimic solo improvisations by supplying buyers with written-out runs and decorations in the treble part of a four-voice texture supported by relatively plain chords in the accompanying parts beneath.[29]

Pseudo-monodies make it especially clear that crucial to the seductive bravura of the *cantatrice* was delivery and embellishment, whether prepared or improvised. An archetypal example is a setting by the Venetian Baldissera Donato of the anonymous poem "Dolce mio ben, dolce colomba mia," published in his four-voice madrigal book in Venice in 1568 (companion website track 3).[30] While the lower voices are largely chordal, the soprano is replete with ornamentation of a sort that was otherwise rarely notated before the early seventeenth-century monodies of Giulio Caccini and Sigismondo d'India. The piece has an intriguingly flexible metrical feel and lithe style of embellishment, both suggestive in imagining how courtesans like Tullia d'Aragona might have sung. As the dialect poet Andrea Calmo wrote in praise of a female friend (filtering a sensual libertine style through the local patois then fashionable among literati), "Oh, what a beautiful voice, what style, what runs and divisions, what sweetness, enough to soften the cruelest, hardest, most wicked heart in the world! How excellent the

FIGURE 4.3. Hippolito Tromboncino, *Io son ferito*. Lute song with written-out
vocal ornamentation from the Bottegari Lutebook.

words, the subject, the meaning, so acute, so elegant that poetry itself lags behind . . ."
("[O]himè che bela vose, che maniera, che gorza, che diminution, che suavitae da far
indolcir cuori crudeli, severi e maligni al mondo! Mo le sorte de le parole, del sugieto,
del significato tanto eccellente, tanto arguto, tanto doto, che la poesia istessa ghe
perderave . . .").[31]

In the mid-sixteenth century, with the onset of severe anxieties in response to the
Protestant Reformation, there were growing proscriptions against display and indeco-
rousness for women of the nobility and the class-conscious "bourgeoisie" (as Rosenthal points out). When courtesans declaimed poems like Tullia's, they were brokering
their class status as it crossed with the axis of gender. Envoicing their physical love
with a view to crafting idealized portraits of female sensuality, they also joined in an
energetic process of social differentiation that saw fast development in the mercantile
culture of sixteenth-century Venice. To that end, they required not just fine things
and fine skills, but the flair of a distinctive personal style.[32] They needed above all
to capture the untranslatable and ephemeral power of song, for only beyond the
reach of script could song attain that most esteemed, elusive, and mystical appellation of "*aria*," an ineffable expressive power endowed with the Neoplatonic force located in the realm of the suprasensual. In the words of the organist, madrigalist, and
polygraph Girolamo Parabosco, rhapsodizing over the poet-singer Gaspara Stampa,

"What shall I say of that angelic voice, which sometimes strikes the air ("l'aria") with its divine accents, making such a sweet harmony that it not only seems to everyone who is worthy of hearing it as if a Siren's… but infuses spirit and life into the coldest stones and makes them weep with sweetness?"[33]

Stampa was the unchallenged lyric heroine of her time, authoress of a then unpublished canzoniere (known among cognoscenti) that translates the Petrarchan idiom of poetic self-creation and narration into a female voice.[34] An acclaimed lutenist–singer, she was an underground legend in literary and musical circles of her time—this despite having avoided publication (if not partly because of it)—and had gained and given entrée to the most prestigious literary and musical salons in Venice.

Stampa has been the object of an enduring controversy that has made her out as a courtesan on one side and roundly denied it on the other. Her relatively free lifestyle (free by mid- to late sixteenth-century standards) is well known. She was born in 1524 to a wealthy mercantile family in Padua and moved as a child to Venice, along with her mother and siblings. Living there as an unmarried woman, she began composing poetry and performing song to her own lute accompaniments in private salons. By her own poetic account she had two liaisons, most famously with the neglectful, quasi-feudal Count Collaltino of Collalto. But unlike known and professed courtesans such as Tullia or the later sixteenth-century Veronica Franco, she voiced her *canzoniere* predominantly in a pastoral mode imitative of Petrarch and seemingly resisted publication.[35] Perissone Cambio's setting of the anonymous Petrarchan imitation "Non di terrestre donna il chiaro viso," printed in a book dedicated to Stampa in 1547 (see the essay following by De Rycke), might remind us of Stampa's last canzone (table 4.1 below), which is not pastoral but an encomium of a deceased nun.

> Non di terrestre donna il chiaro viso
> Che m'arde e strugg'il cor, non l'aurea testa,
> Non de gli occhi sereni i rai lucenti,
> Né le labbra di rose e 'l dolce riso,
> Non la divina angelica modesta
> Voce onde s'odon sì soave accenti,
> Ma di celeste dea tal che finire
> Ne lei per morte può nel mio martire.

> No earthly woman's, the fair face
> That enflames and melts my heart, nor the golden hair,
> Nor the limpid eyes' sparkling rays,
> Nor the rosy lips and gentle laugh,
> Nor the divine, angelic, modest
> Voice that makes such soft sounds,
> But a celestial goddess's, so that not even death
> Can end my torments.[36]

Where "Non di terrestre" praises its subject for her "golden crown" ("l'aurea testa") and "divine, angelic, modest voice," quoting Petrarch's depiction of a celestial Laura in his sonnet "Ripensando a quell ch'oggi il ciel onora" (no. 343, vv. 20 and 3–4, respectively), Stampa's "Alma celeste" (see below, table 4.1) eulogizes the nun as a bride of god, referring to Heaven where the deceased "lived always with her first Love [God] in delightful ways" ("in dilettose tempre" in other contexts could mean "in" or "with charming *modi*"), and thus lamenting the fate of the nun's mortal brethren who struggle for mastery over their bodily senses. Behind the image of Petrarch's Marian-styled madonna Laura with which Stampa endows the nun lies the whispered suggestion of Stampa herself, as a repentant Mary Magdalen imploring heaven's grace.

I will forgo a summary of the copious evidence adduced as proof and disproof of Stampa's courtesanship in controversies that raged between 1913 and 1920 and have reared their head on various occasions since. More interesting for my purposes is the fact that her ambiguous position has given observers room over a good four hundred and fifty years to make of Stampa what they would. Alfred Einstein—more knowledgeable than anyone on Italian secular music—typified the staunch patriarchalism that underwrote the twentieth-century vision of such a woman, collapsing her into a master narrative in which virtually all female musicians were fallen women.

One way she undoubtedly did resemble courtesans, though, was in the style of her repertory, produced by fleshing out her own melodies from skeletal melodic formulas used for Petrarch's verse, or by making up new material.[37] Indeed Lynn Hooker has produced evidence that Stampa elaborated melodic formulas in singing to her lute, as I have speculated Tullia did. Hooker notes that Stampa's only two canzoni share the exact same versification scheme with Petrarch's canzone *Chiare fresche e dolci acque*, the obvious model for Stampa's *Chiaro e famoso mare*. (See table 4.1, with the first two stanzas of each poem and lexical/thematic correspondences italicized.) She also cites a letter to Stampa from the Friulian religious reformer Orazio Brunetti, who begs for reentry into Stampa's salon, pleading that he has missed her marvelous singing and especially her rendition of Petrarch's *Chiare fresche*.

Canzone stanzas were the least regular of the fixed poetic forms, and therefore the least amenable to being sung to melodic formulas. Singers could utilize stock melodic phrases for them, apt for seven- or eleven-syllable lines and for beginnings, middles, and endings of pieces, so long as they ordered the phrases to match a given canzone's individual formal scheme. That meant stitching together the phrases with due attention to the length and form of the piedi and sirima, the idiosyncrasies of the rhyme scheme, including its placement of rhymed couplets, the need for opening gambits, expressive high points, and cadential closure, as well as the need for melodic continuity. The mere fact that all three of Stampa's canzoni share the exact same poetic form, down to the last syllable and rhyme scheme, makes it quite likely that she performed them all using the same or a similar succession of melodic phrases.

Since Stampa's singing lay largely beyond the reach of script, we can only dream of her intoning the words of *Chiare fresche* or *Chiaro e famoso mare* to her lute. Yet there is some written evidence linking *Chiare fresche* with formulaic oral declamation, at least by association. *Chiare fresche* was set as a multi-voiced madrigal cycle by Jacques Arcadelt and printed in 1555 in Barré's first collection of *madrigali ariosi*. The cycle is polyphonic, but as James Haar has shown, it is laced throughout with a melodic formula that migrates from voice to voice and seems to have been widely associated with orally transmitted traditions of declaiming Ariosto's *ottave*.[38] To evoke something of this spirit, the Newberry Consort has performed Arcadelt's setting of Petrarch's *Chiare fresche* substituting for the latter Stampa's *Chiaro e famoso mare*

TABLE 4.1. Comparison of first two stanzas of Petrarch's canzone no. 23 with the only two canzoni by Gaspara Stampa (Stampa, *Rime*, no. 68 and no. 299)

Verse numbers and rhyme scheme	Petrarca, *Chiare fresche*, no. 126	Stampa, *Rime*, no. 68 (corresponding verses)	Stampa, *Rime*, no. 299 (corresponding verses)
1 a	*Chiare fresche e dolci acque*	*Chiaro e famoso mare*	Alma celeste e pura,
2 b	*Ove le belle membra*	*Sovra 'l cui nobil dosso*	che, casta e verginella
3 C	*Pose colei che sola a me par donna*	*si posò 'l mio signor, mentre Amor volle;*	stata tanto fra noi, se gita al cielo
4 a	*Gentil ramo ove piacque*	*rive onorate e care*	dov'or sovra misura
5 b	*(con sospir mi rimembra)*	*(con sospir dir lo posso)*	ti stai lucente e bella,
6 C	*a lei di fare al bel fianco colonna*	*che 'l petto mio vedeste spesso molle;*	di più perfetto accesa e maggior zelo,
7 c	*erba et fior che la gonna*	*soave lido e colle,*	perché nel mortal velo
8 d	*leggiadra ricoverse*	*che con fiato amoroso*	rade volte altrui lice
9 e	*co l'angelica seno*	*udisti le mie note,*	unir perfettamente
10 e	*aere sacra sereno*	*d'ira e di sdegno vote,*	al suo Fattor la mente,
11 D	*ove Amor co' begli occhi il cor m'aperse:*	*colme d'ogni diletto e di riposo;*	sì triste è del nostro arbor la radice
12 f	*date udienzia insieme*	*udite tutti intenti*	e sì forte n'atterra
13 F	*a le dolente mie parole estreme.*	*Il suon or degli acerbi miei lamenti.*	Questa del senso perigliosa guerra;
	[five more stanzas]	[five more stanzas]	
1 a	*S'egli è pur mio destino,*	*I' dico che dal giorno*	Tu vagheggi or beata
2 b	*e 'l cielo in ciò s'adopra,*	*che fece diparite*	quell'infinito Sole,
3 C	*ch'Amor quest'occhi lagrimando chiuda,*	*l'idolo, ond'avean pace i miei sospiri,*	di cui questo altro sole è picciol raggio;
4 a	*qualche grazia il meschino*	*tolti mi fûr d'attorno*	e la voglia appagata
5 b	*corpo fra voi ricopra,*	*tutti i ben d'esta vita;*	hai sì, ch'altro non vuole,
6 C	*e torni l'alma al proprio albergo ignuda;*	*e restai preda eternal de martiri:*	giunta a l'ultimo fin di suo viaggio;
7 C	*la morte fia men cruda*	*e, perch'io pur m'àdiri*	e la noia e l'oltraggio
8 c	*se questa spene porto*	*e chiami Amor ingrate*	e l'ombra di quell male,
9 e	*a quell dubioso passo,*	*che m'involò sì tosto*	che sostenesti in vita,
10 e	*ché lo spirito lasso*	*il ben ch'or sta discosto,*	è per sempre sbandita
11 D	*non poria mai in più riposato porto*	*non per questo a pietade è mal tornado;*	salita in parte, ove dolor non sale,
12 f	*nè in più tranquilla fossa*	*e tien l'usate tempre,*	ove si vive sempre
13 F	*fuggi la carne travagliata et l'ossa.*	*perch'io mi sfaccia e mi lamenti sempre.*	Col primo Amor in dilettose tempre.
	[five more stanzas]	[five more stanzas]	[five more stanzas]

The table is based on unpublished research by Lynn Hooker.

(companion website track 4). Soprano Ellen Hargis sings the lyrics attended by a viol ensemble, thus replacing the masculine voice of Petrarch's model with the feminine voice of one whose faith (*fede*) will be sung in a thousand pages (*in mille carte*). At the same time the viol players replace Stampa's own lute with a hypothetical consort of admiring accompanists.[39] With another leap of historical imagination we can conceive Stampa singing these canzoni as lute-accompanied monodies, perhaps varying a specific formula like the one James Haar distilled from Arcadelt's cycle to make a simulacrum of what Brunetti so sorely missed hearing when he found himself barred from her salon.[44]

At this high echelon of poetizing and vocalizing, women like Tullia d'Aragona and Gaspara Stampa needed more than just good vocal timbre, agility, and other technical skills to achieve fame. Above all they needed a distinctive *modo* and that special personal style that would render the voice untranscribable. Only by transcending the printed page could song attain that most esteemed, elusive, and mystical appellation of "aria" that Parabosco attributed to Stampa.

Here I want to return to Einstein's assessment of Stampa and virtually all other Renaissance women singers as lascivious. For Einstein's view imposed on female music-making of the Renaissance a view that rent asunder mind and body through a romantic metaphysics in which the spiritual and corporeal are irreconcilable. The sixteenth century, to the contrary, viewed body and spirit in a continuous affiliation,[41] and saw female voices dispersed along this continuum. In salons, printed love dialogues, and lyric expression, the passions of the female voice slid along a mind–body continuum, especially when female subjects escaped simple classification at extremes of chastity or wantonness.

In several ways Stampa's position reminds me less of professed courtesans than of the *nacnis* of southern Bihar in East Central India who have been studied by Carol Babiracki.[42] Babiracki describes nacnis as kept women and semi-professional singer-dancers, who typically remain mistress to a single man over many years. In one of her primary cases, the poetic performance of the nacni is interwoven with the life she shares with her partner, as the two invoke images of themselves using the playful love lyrics of the divine couple Krishna and Radha. As in early modern Venice, the man who keeps a nacni as mistress can maintain and even enhance his own social position, though, unlike in Venice, she becomes casteless in the feudal society of rural East Central India. Her sacrifice of respectability and children makes for an inherently ambiguous relationship with the man who keeps her. The two are what the Bijaris call "non-social," or socially unofficial, the women are literally out-castes, and their union is said to be made for "private" reasons motivated by love, madness for music and dance, poverty, and sometimes devotion to Krishna.

Strikingly, the dynamics of a courtesan's or mistress's relationships were mobilized, like the nacni's, by the affect of her performances, which often invoked the established, pervasive idiom of Petrarch for the expression of love and the conflicts between spirit and flesh. A nacni's performances, Babiracki argues, are intensely affective because of her identification with the goddess Radha, even though the full consequences of her union for the sake of love put her in social disgrace. She becomes a "goddess" only to other performers and to her lover, who may idolize her (as Babiracki says) in an "inversion of normative gender roles [that] recalls the reversal of Radha and Krishna, whereby Krishna becomes the submissive devotee and Radha his powerful, even cruel goddess."[43]

That reversal recalls the poetic trope of the pitiless lady, Petrarch's unattainable goddess Laura, or even the elusive mistress of a rival peer. Not unlike nacnis, early modern courtesans and their like were products of a quasi-feudal, stratified system of patronage. In Venice, as that system threatened to crack under the pressures of early modernity, the courtesan's arts of speech, music, and manners, so susceptible to appropriation and imitation, became increasingly vulnerable to reaction, counteraction, and retaliation. Yet her virtuosity as a performer of rhetorical arts only gave her greater powers of seduction, power that in some cases was transformed through her reincarnation as the seventeenth-century diva in the new genre of Venetian opera. Detached from script, the courtesan's voice conjured up sensible worlds to which she had uncommon access. Special powers could accrue to her who could tap this affective world of sound. In Renaissance conceptions she gained power over harmonies and proportions with larger realms of sensory resonance, the immaterial glories of the voice affirming but eluding the material triumphs of the body.[44]

Notes

1. Important on the early layer of Italian courtesanship, complemented by music-making, are Monica Kurzel-Runtscheiner, *Töchter der Venus: Die Kurtisanen Roms im 16. Jahrhundert* (Munich: C. H. Beck, 1995); William F. Prizer, "Games of Venus: Secular Vocal Music in the Late Quattrocento and Early Cinquecento," *Journal of Musicology* 9 (1991): 3–56; and Shawn Marie Keener, "Virtue, Illusion, *Venezianità*: Vocal Bravura and the Early *Cortigiana Onesta*," in *Musical Voices of Early Modern Women: Many-Headed Melodies*, ed. Thomasin K. LaMay (Aldershot: Ashgate, 2005), chap. 5. On the practice and valence of women's music-making at the time see William F. Prizer, "Una 'virtù molto conveniente a madonne': Isabella d'Este as a Musician," *Journal of Musicology* 17 (1999): 10–49; Howard Mayer Brown, "Women Singers and Women's Songs in Fifteenth-Century Italy," in *Women Making Music: The Western Art Tradition, 1150–1950*, ed. Jane Bowers and Judith Tick (Urbana: University of Illinois Press, 1986), 62–89; and with specific attention to courtesans, William F. Prizer, "Wives and Courtesans: The Frottola in Florence," in *Music Observed: Studies in Memory of William C. Holmes*, ed. Colleen Reardon and Susan Parisi (Warren, MI: Harmonie Park Press, 2004), 401–15. I am grateful to him for sending me his newly published essay just in time to take account of it here.

2. *Opere in volgare*, ed. Mario Marti (Florence: Sansoni, 1961), 877–78. Bembo also had in mind the publicness of his words and their reception, since he had to establish the illegitimate Helena in patrician society, which he did by marrying her off to a Venetian nobleman in 1543.

3. *Gli asolani* (Venice, 1505), III, fol. vii^v. Cf. Gary Tomlinson, "Rinuccini, Peri, Monteverdi, and the Humanist Heritage of Opera" (Ph.D. diss., University of California at Berkeley, 1979), 37–43.

4. Gordon's essay in this volume makes clear how dominant Neoplatonism was in an early modern worldview.

5. *Gli asolani*, II, fol. vii^v.

6. Cf. Marco Equicola's *Libro della natura de amore* (Venice, 1525), Book V, fol. 171.

7. See Betussi, *Il Raverta* (Venice, 1544), esp. 19–45.

8. Quoted from Bernardino Tomitano, *Ragionamenti della lingua toscana*, rev. ed. (Venice, 1546), 461.

9. *Dialogo della infinità d'amore*, in *Trattati d'amore*, ed. Giuseppe Zonta; repr. ed. Mario Pozzi (1912; Rome: Giuseppe Laterza, 1975); in English as *Dialogue on the Infinity of Love*, ed. and trans. Rinaldina Russell and Bruce Merry, Introduction by Rinaldina Russell (Chicago: University of Chicago Press, 1997).

10. Salvatore Bongi, *Annali di Gabriel Giolito de' Ferrari*, 2 vols. (Rome: I Principali Librai, 1890–97), 1:193–95.

11. The correspondent was writing to the Marchesa Isabella d'Este of Mantua to keep her informed; see Rita Casagrande di Villaviera, *Le cortigiane veneziane nel Cinquecento* (Milan: Longanesi, 1968), 226.

12. Ibid., 221.

13. See *Dialogue on the Infinity of Love*, 79; *Trattati d'amore*, 211.

14. See, importantly, Paula Findlen, "Humanism, Politics, and Pornography in Renaissance Italy," in *The Invention of Pornography: Obscenity and the Origins of Modernity, 1500–1800*, ed. Lynn Hunt (New York: Zone Books, 1993), 49–108.

15. See Alfred Einstein, *The Italian Madrigal*, 3 vols., trans. Alexander H. Krappe, Roger H. Sessions, and Oliver Strunk (1949; Princeton: Princeton University Press, 1971), 1:94 ff.

16. Quoted in Edmond Vander Straeten, *La musique aux Pays-Bas avant le XIXe siècle: Documents inédits et annotés*, 8 vols. repr. in 4 (1882; New York: Dover, 1969), 6:221, vv. 122–24 and the full capitolo reproduced there. For analogues within injunctions against women's speech see chap. 6 below; and Jones, *The Currency of Eros*, chap. 1. See also Anthony Newcomb, "Courtesans, Muses, or Musicians? Professional Women Musicians in Sixteenth-Century Italy," in *Women Making Music*, 92; and idem, *The Madrigal at Ferrara, 1579–1597*, 2 vols. (Princeton: Princeton University Press, 1979), 1:app. 5, doc. 13.

17. On salon life see my *City Culture and the Madrigal at Venice* (Berkeley: University of California Press, 1995), part 1.

18. In Ortensio Landi's *Sette libri de cathaloghi* (Venice, 1552) she ranked with Polissena Pecorina and the elusive Polissena Frigera as one of three most noted female musicians of the modern era. Landi lists her as "Franceschina bella mano" (512). In the poetic anthology entitled *De le rime di diversi nobili poeti toscani*, ed. Dionigi Atanagi, vol. 2 rev. (Venice, 1565), fol. 11, she is addressed as "una virtuosa donna, che cantava, & sonava eccellentemente di liuto, detta Franceschina Bellamano" (sig. K/2 4). See also *Rime di Domenico Veniero*, ed. Pierantonio Serassi (Bergamo, 1751), xv and 37. Bellamano could sing "from the book" as well improvising or singing by heart, as seen in Pietro Aaron's *Lucidario in musica* (Venice, 1545), which cites her among Italy's renowned "Donne a liuto et a libro" (fol. 32). For further references to Bellamano see Einstein, *The Italian Madrigal* 1:447 and 2:843, who considered her—without evidence—to have been a courtesan.

19. In this my conclusions correspond to those of singer/scholar Sheila Schonbrun, "Ambiguous Artists: Music-Making among Italian Renaissance Courtesans (with Particular Reference to Tullia of Aragon, Gaspara Stampa, and Veronica Franco)" (D.M.A. thesis, City University of New York, 1998).

20. See *Ottaviano Petrucci, Frottole Buch I und IV: Nach den Erstlingsdrucken von 1504 und 1505 (?)*, ed. Rudolf Schwartz (repr. Hildesheim and Wiesbaden: Georg Olms and Breitkopf & Härtel, 1967). Petrucci's fourth book of frottole was published in 1505 (albeit without date).

21. See *The Bottegari Lutebook*, ed. Carol MacClintock, The Wellesley Edition, no. 8 (Wellesley, MA: Wellesley College, 1965), nos. 8, 31, 53, 56, 63, based on Modena, Biblioteca Estense, MS C311, no. 74, fols. 29–30; and *Aeri raccolti insieme . . . dove si cantano sonetti, stanze et terze rime*, ed. Rocco Rodio (Naples, 1577; = RISM 1577^8). The theorist Gioseffo

Zarlino attests to the continued practice in the mid-sixteenth century of singing sonnets on formulas, mentioning "those *modi* [i.e., *'arie'*] on which these days we sing sonnets or canzoni of Petrarch, or the verse of Ariosto"; *Le istitutioni harmoniche* (Venice, 1558), book iii, 79. Sonnets are included among the *arie* in Bottegari's lutebook. On the *madrigale arioso* see James Haar, "The 'Madrigale Arioso': A Mid-Century Development in the Cinquecento Madrigal," *Studi musicali* 12 (1983): 203–19, reprinted in idem, *The Science and Art of Renaissance Music*, ed. Paul Corneilson (Princeton: Princeton University Press, 1998), chap. 10 (from which I cite below); Howard Mayer Brown, "Verso una definizione dell'armonia nel sedicesimo secolo: Sui 'madrigali ariosi' di Antonio Barré," *Rivista italiana di musicologia* 25 (1990): 18–60; and John Steele, "Antonio Barré: Madrigalist, Anthologist, and Publisher in Rome—Some Preliminary Findings," in *Altro polo: Essays on Italian Music in the Cinquecento*, ed. Richard Charteris (Sydney: Frederick May Foundation for Italian Studies, 1990), 82–112. Melodic formulas also surface in other polyphonic madrigal settings of stanzas from Ariosto's early sixteenth-century epic *Orlando furioso*. As James Haar has shown in "Arie per cantar stanze ariotesche," in *L'Ariosto, la musica, i musicisti: Quattro studi e sette madrigali ariostechi*, ed. Maria Antonella Balsano with preface by Lorenzo Bianconi (Florence: Leo S. Olschki, 1981), the *Orlando* stanzas were recited for centuries by musical improvisers who continued to use traditional formulas for epic recitation; see also idem, "*Improvvisatori* and Their Relationship to Sixteenth-Century Music," in James Haar, *Essays on Italian Poetry and Music in the Renaissance, 1350–1600* (Berkeley: University of California Press, 1986), chap. 4. On Rocco Rodio's book and Petrarchan recitation in Naples, see Howard Mayer Brown, "Petrarch in Naples: Notes on the Formation of Giaches de Wert's Style," in *Altro polo*, ed. Charteris, 16–50. In Spain, during the 1530s there were books with pieces by Luis de Milán and Alonso Mudarra that offered sonnets by Petrarch arranged for voice and vihuela (the indigenous guitar-like instrument), like the *modi* of Petrucci, Bottegari, and Rodio; see Louis Jambou, "Sonnets de Pétrarque et chant accompagné a vihuela: Deux projets compositionnels distincts: Milan (1536) et Mudarra (1546)," in *Dynamique d'une expansion culturelle: Pétrarque en Europe, XIVᵉ–XXᶜ siècle. Actes du XXVIᶜ congrès international du CEFI, Turin et Chambéry, 11–15 décembre 1995*, ed. Pierre Blanc (Paris: Honoré Champion, 2001), 497–525.

22. In analyzing the dynamics of fame here I take inspiration from the astute work of Ann Rosalind Jones, *The Currency of Eros*, esp. 103–17.

23. The classic formulation of this poetic strategy is that of John Freccero, "The Fig Tree and the Laurel: Petrarch's Poetics," *Diacritics* 5 (1975): 34–40. For an intelligent recent analysis of Petrarch's poetics in various fifteenth- and sixteenth-century assessments see Gordon Braden, *Petrarchan Love and the Continental Renaissance* (New Haven: Yale University Press, 1999), esp. chap. 1, "Petrarchism," which claims that Bembo virtually invented the interpretation of Petrarch's poetizing as a solitary, autobiographical mode of poetic expression and gave it his own Neoplatonic overlay (94–101 and *passim*).

24. Fascinating in this regard is Prizer's account of a courtesan named Maria, a poet, singer, and quite possibly composer of the Roman and Florentine orbits, who sang songs "in the masculine role of seducer," addressing a man in a voice that would normally have been used to address a woman ("Wives and Courtesans," 412–13). Prizer notes that Maria thus "speaks" (by singing) to her client, yet does so on his behalf, "speaking for him of the desire she herself arouses." In keeping with the high/low dichotomies seen by Davies and others in this volume within courtesans' repertories (and repertories about them), Maria also sang frottole with bawdy texts, again envoicing the role of a man who in this case tries to "titillate" women.

25. Other variants use four phrases of music.

26. These are my own ornaments. Using the same tune, Schonbrun has made a contrafactum of a sonnet by the poet-singer Gaspara Stampa and provided ornaments that increase

in complexity and remoteness from the original tune through the second quatrain and espe-cially the two tercets, somewhat in the extravagant manner of written exemplars of monodic singing from around 1600. Cf. n. 31 below.

27. Singing and instrumental masters who wrote about ornamentation techniques in the period between the 1550s and 1580s show us nothing as lavish as Schonbrun offers, yet it seems to me likely that some courtesans would indeed have sung so elaborately if they were skilled enough to do so. Tullia would certainly be a candidate for such singing. The questions involved in such a matter are much too intricate to develop here. For a fundamental review of embellishing sixteenth-century music see Howard Mayer Brown, *Embellishing Sixteenth-Century Music* (Oxford: Oxford University Press, 1976), *passim* (and Introduction for a review of primary sources). It does seem evident that treatises dealing with vocal ornamentation dur-ing the sixteenth century, especially those written before the advent in about 1580 of what Anthony Newcomb calls the "luxuriant style" (*The Madrigal at Ferrara*), were often quite conservative, aiming to tame singers of overly ostentatious habits and mostly exemplifying stepwise passagework with few leaps and no consecutive leaps and with relatively regular forms of rhythmic organization.

28. Mod. ed. in Ernst Ferand, *Die Improvisation in Beispielen aus neun Jahrhunderten abend-ländischer Musik: Mit einer geschichtlichen Einführung* (Cologne: Arno Volk, 1956), 50–52. A vocal performance of the ornamented version has been recorded by Sara Stowe, soprano, and the group Sirinu, *The Cradle of the Renaissance: Italian Music from the Time of Leonardo da Vinci* (London: Hyperion, 1995), CDA66814.

29. See *The Italian Madrigal*, 2, chap. 12.

30. *Libro primo dei madrigali a 4 voci* (Venice, 1568). It is performed here with harpsi-chord accompaniment, using Einstein's transcription, which reduces the four voices of the original to an accompanied-song style version for soprano and keyboard (*The Italian Madrigal*, 3:322–25). For the text and translation, see the appendix.

31. *Le lettere di Andrea Calmo*, ed. Vittorio Rossi (Turin: Ermanno Loescher, 1888), book iv, 295–96; trans. quoted from Einstein, *The Italian Madrigal*, 2:843.

32. See Haar, "*Improvvisatori*," 83; and Nino Pirrotta, *Music and Culture in Italy from the Middle Ages to the Baroque: A Collection of Essays* (Cambridge, MA: Harvard University Press, 1984), *passim*.

33. Girolamo Molino also referred to Stampa in a poem to her first and main lover, Count Collalto di Collaltino, as a Siren ("Nova Sirena"); see Abdelkader Salza, "Madonna Gasparina Stampa, secondo nuove indagini," *Giornale storico della letteratura italiana* 62 (1913): 25–26; and for Ortensio Landi's praise of her musical prowess, ibid., 17–18.

34. See, most recently, Mary B. Moore, *Desiring Voices: Women Sonneteers and Petrar-chism* (Carbondale, IL: Southern Illinois University Press, 2000), chap. 3, "Body of Light, Body of Matter: Self-Reference as Self-Modeling in Gaspara Stampa."

35. As Jones points out (*The Currency of Eros*), courtesan-poets like Tullia d'Aragona and Veronica Franco sought out publication rather than avoiding it.

36. Translation by Justin Flosi and Courtney Quaintance from the program book for the concert by the Newberry Consort, *The Courtesan's Voice in the Italian Renaissance* (April 5, 2002), 14.

37. Both of these had been done by the late fifteenth-century singing star Serafino Aquilano, according to his contemporary biographer Vincenzo Calmeta. See *Vita del facondo poeta volgare Serafino Aquilano*, in Vincenzo Calmeta, *Prose e lettere edite ed inedite*, ed. Cecil Grayson (Bologna: Commissione per i testi di lingua, 1959). For relevant excerpts in English, see the passage translated in *Source Readings in Music History*, ed. Oliver Strunk, rev. ed. Leo Treitler (New York: Norton, 1998), part 3, *The Renaissance*, ed. Gary Tomlinson, 321–25, esp. 322.

38. For the essential form of the Ariosto formula as deduced by Haar from Arcadelt's polyphonic setting of *Chiare fresche*, see Haar, "The 'Madrigale Arioso," in his *Science and Art*, 226. Haar also makes a hypothetical extraction of the formula from each stanza of Petrarch's canzone set by Arcadelt, sometimes from the tenor voice and sometimes from the soprano. Most important for the history of song among Barré's *delle muse* prints is the *Primo libro delle muse a quatro voci, madrigali ariosi di Ant. Barre et altri diversi autori* (Rome: Barré, 1555 = RISM 1555²⁷), a volume that was reprinted many times over a thirty-year period.

39. Janet L. Smarr, "Gaspara Stampa's Poetry for Performance," *Journal of the Rocky Mountain Medieval and Renaissance Association* 12 (1991): 61–84.

40. A woman whose singing who bears some analogies with Stampa's as I reconstruct it here, especially in her general ability to manipulate song, improvisation, and polyphony, is Isabella Medici-Orsini, provocatively analyzed by Donna G. Cardamone in "Isabella Medici-Orsini: A Portrait of Self-Affirmation," in *Gender, Sexuality, and Early Music*, ed. Todd Michael Borgerding (New York: Routledge, 2002), 1–40.

41. Cf. Gary Tomlinson, *Music in Renaissance Magic: Toward a Historiography of Others* (Chicago: The University of Chicago Press, 1993), 202–3.

42. Carol M. Babiracki graciously shared with me her work on *nacnis* in the form of two unpublished papers: "Ideologies of Power, Gender, and Art in the Nacni Tradition of East-Central India," Annual Meeting of the Society for Ethnomusicology (Oxford, Miss., October 27–31, 1993), and "Gender and Religion in the Nacni Tradition of East-Central India," Annual Conference on South Asia (University of Wisconsin, Madison, November 4, 1994). Among Babiracki's published work in this area are: "What's the Difference? Reflections on Gender and Research in Village India," in *Shadows in the Field: New Perspectives for Fieldwork in Ethnomusicology* (Oxford: Oxford University Press, 1997), 121–36; and "The Illusion of India's Public Dancers," in *Women's Voices across Musical Worlds*, ed. Jane A. Bernstein (Boston: Northeastern Illinois Press, 2004), 36–59.

43. Babiracki, "Gender and Religion," 5. See the strategies of courtly love discussed in Flosi's essay in this volume, chap. 6.

44. See Gordon (chap. 9 below) for much fuller dealings with these issues. On male rivalries see the essays herein of Flosi, Quaintance, and Ruggiero, chaps. 6, 10, and 15.

On Hearing the Courtesan in a Gift of Song

The Venetian Case of Gaspara Stampa

We have seen that the repertories performed by Italian courtesans to such ac-claim are highly problematic for the modern scholar. Indeed there is hardly a single collection or even piece that can be said with absolute certainty to have been sung by a woman, courtesan or otherwise. In what follows I offer a case study designed to interrogate the much larger problem of the courtesan's lost music by look-ing at a set of polyphonic partbooks and proposing new possibilities for how female performance of solo song might be buried in written sources. My evidence is a four-voice collection of madrigals written by Perissone Cambio in Venice (fl. 1540–50) and dedicated in 1547 to the famous female poet, singer, and lute player Gaspara Stampa (1523–54).[1] Working backwards from a polyphonic madrigal book in order to uncover solo repertory is a relatively novel endeavor, as studies of women's solo reper-tories generally look directly at song-type genres like frottole and lute songbooks. My own study ostensibly addresses only the practice of a single female musician, but from it I extrapolate to a hypothetical cross-section of the repertories of Italian courtesans all told, raising various questions about how courtesans made their repertories and how their singing was regarded as cultural currency.

In the early twentieth century scholars often construed Stampa as a courte-san (as Feldman points out),[2] drawing obliquely in the absence of positive evidence on qualities she shared with courtesans of her time. Independent and unmarried, Stampa was a solo female performer acclaimed for her rhetorical powers to stir the feelings of a largely male audience. These biographical facts situated her ambiguously within Venetian society, where she moved outside the social spaces of marriage and convent that were traditional for respectable women. Yet it is precisely this situation that makes her case so valuable for recuperating the repertory of courtesans who, like her, thrived in male salons, outside the family structures of Venetian society. Perissone's four-voice madrigal book, I will argue, bears witness to one kind of reper-tory Stampa must have sung, and even furnishes clues to how she might have sung it—and indeed *prepared it* for singing—at the same time as it models the singing of her musical sisters, the courtesans of Venice.

Gaspara Stampa was trained to be a musical *virtuosa*, together with her sister Cassandra.[3] She was lauded as an "excellent musician"[4] and "divine siren"[5] by members of her social circles, who cited her "angelic voice" and her renowned performances of Petrarch's poems. These and other descriptions by prominent literati from Venice and elsewhere most often mention the quality of her voice and the power of her singing to move listeners, constructing her as a solo *cantatrice* rather than a member of a polyphonic ensemble (the famed Polissena Pecorina, active in Venice at the same time, was most renowned in the latter role). Yet the precise nature of Stampa's music-making remains unknown, since, except for the single description of her performance of Petrarch's "Chiare fresche" (see Feldman, chap. 4 above, 116), no specific references to her actual musical repertories survive.

Anecdoctal sources, by indicating that Stampa sang her own and perhaps others' poetry accompanied by her lute, do imply that she used melodic formulas (*modi*), repeating the essential tune for the different verses and stanzas of longer, multistanza poems with new ornamentation, harmonic substitutions, and melodic/rhythmic variations.[6] But sources of solo song are not the only place we can look for this lost repertory. Polyphonic literature cut across different performance media (notwithstanding its outer appearance). Adrian Willaert was designated in print as the intabulator of Verdelot's four-voice madrigals of the 1520s in an edition for lute and voice published in 1536;[7] and innumerable books anthologized intabulations of vocal polyphony either for voice and lute or for solo lute.

My experiment has been to transcribe several song-like madrigals from Perissone's partbooks "back" to solo song, thus exploring what Stampa or a singer like her might have done. While instrumental sources have long been scrutinized for traces of the art of solo improvisation (upon dance tunes or some other cantus firmus), polyphonic vocal sources, perhaps because of the prestige and perceived authority of the medium, less often serve as a point of departure in search of solo song.[8] The assumption underlying my methodology is that partbooks (the privileged medium for circulating music) contain the basic information for performance without necessarily prescribing the medium, which could take many different forms. A polyphonic composition could be performed "as written," that is by voices *a cappella*, or with instruments doubling the voices, by various combinations of voices and instruments (with or without doublings), for instruments alone, or for a solo voice accompanied by one or more instruments. Thinking of Stampa, who would probably have needed to "make" her repertory, and taking as my point of departure some of the more homophonic madrigals in Perissone's four-voice madrigal book dedicated to her, I recreate one process by which Stampa may have gotten her repertory for solo voice and instrument, that is, by arranging the voices of the four partbooks so that the soloist sings one of the voices (usually the treble) and a single instrument (whether lute, vihuela, clavichord, harp, or portative organ) sounds some arrangement of the other three. Although the format of Perissone's print is that of unaccompanied polyphony, several features in the individual voices indicate that the madrigals in it may indeed have been intended for Stampa (or others) to sing as solo song.[9]

STAMPA, SOLO SONG, AND POLYPHONIC MADRIGALS

Perissone dedicated his polyphonic collection to Stampa with a text that emphasizes her powers as a solo singer and even deploys metaphors that go beyond dedicatory conventions to reveal something of how her music-making was construed by her audience.[10]

> To the beautiful and talented Signora Gasparina Stampa:
>   Noble lady, well might I be reproved by the wise and learned composers of this sweet and admirable science—reproved in this science, yes, but no man in the world will ever be able to say that I have had little judgment in dedicating these notes of mine to your ladyship, however they may be. Because it is well known by now—and not only in this fortunate city, but almost everywhere—that no woman in the world loves music as much as you do, nor possesses it to such a rare degree. And thousands upon thousands of fine and noble spirits attest to this who, having heard your sweet harmonies, have given you the name of divine siren, remaining over time your most devoted servants, among whom I am as devoted as any. I come with this my little token and gift to refresh the memory of the love that I bear for your genius, begging that you deign to find me worthy to be placed where you place the innumerable throngs of those who adore and love your rare talents and beauties. And to your graces I commend and offer myself. Most devoted servant Pieresson Cambio.[11]

It is noteworthy that Perissone here invokes a Platonic metaphor of love as a binding force that makes harmony possible, and that he does so in a way that works on many levels. The metaphor begins by establishing a triangle between the protagonists of the publication: Perissone, Stampa, and Music. The three are brought together in the Boethian sense by Love: Stampa loves music; Perissone, with a musical offering, loves Stampa. In this Boethian construction, Love, the supreme power that holds the reins to the universe, bonds the three in proper relationship to one another within a shared universe.

But Stampa not only loves music, she possesses it; it resides in her. Sounding music, in the Platonic (and Neoplatonic) tradition, is the essential manifestation of cosmic harmony.[12] By possessing this harmony, by holding it inside her, Stampa also possesses some of this power to bind things to her. What is more, she is a divine Siren, an appellation that evokes the Homeric tradition of the temptress "Siren" with her uncanny ability to lure others, as well as the Platonic idea of Er, a cosmological vision wherein each planet is presided over by a Siren, each of whom sounds a single pitch. Gaspara in this construction is a singular figure whose virtue and harmony are so powerful that she is able to attract other beings to her, to bring other bodies into her solar system.[13]

Perissone, with his gift, thus establishes a bond with Gaspara. Yet the nature of the bond—and what he expected in return—remains unclear. From what we know about her social situation, Perissone was probably was not seeking from her a subvention for publication. It is possible that he hoped for some good words with members of her social circle, which included many members of the most prominent academy of vernacular letters in mid–sixteenth-century Venice, that of Domenico Venier. Perissone also draws attention to his own gender in the opening sentence of the dedication, speculating on how his publication will be received by his male colleagues while conjuring up a knowledgeable audience of men (and thus too a bevy of admirers for his dedicatee).

His gift, we are informed further down, is a reminder of his love for Stampa's musical talent—presumably her ability as a performer—and her power to attract and inspire devotion in "innumerable throngs" of male spectators and listeners. By virtue of the publicness of this gift, it will be judged by his colleagues on musical grounds. His text settings, voice leadings, and choice of stylistic register will all come under public scrutiny. But because of the giving of the gift, it will also be judged as a symbol of his bond with her, and seen as a tacit demand that she reciprocate. Moving one step further, if Stampa did perform this music as one form of reciprocation, any faults or weaknesses in the songs would be transformed by her transcendent powers of performance. In a certain sense, Perissone thus asks to become one of the planets that revolve in harmony around her, to be placed within her social circle, and to have his music issue forth from her. At the same time, her performative powers—that is, her powers to captivate and enchant listeners—offer protection to his own music.

The question remains, however, how specifically his dedicatee might have been directly involved with the music in Perissone's print. The opening madrigal of the collection provides a few answers. In general, first pieces of Renaissance song or poetic collections occupy a privileged position, often elaborating a formal dedication by praising the dedicatee's love, or ability, or munificence toward the subject matter. In the case of Perissone's print, the first madrigal, *Io mi son bella e cruda* (I am beautiful and cruel) is, interestingly, neither in the third person nor the masculine voice, nor does it praise the dedicatee's beauty or proclaim the male subject's love. Rather, a female speaker affirms her own paradoxical nature, a Petrarchan one that is simultaneously beautiful and cruel, and she does so arguably from a masculine perspective:

> I am beautiful and cruel
> And willingly cause the other's death
> I flee the one who desires me, and the one who flees I outrun,
> Full of pride and stripped of mercy.
> You whose heart is stirred up
> With the flames of love,
> Believe the hard truth in my eyes,
> That I am as cruel as I am beautiful.[14]

The poem expands the working metaphor of Perissone's dedication: that of Love as a binding force. The speaker reveals the nature of her power; her two attributes, beauty and cruelty, are opposing forces (attraction and repulsion), possessed in equal measure, which ultimately serve to hold her admirers at a distance. Of the twenty-three poems in the collection set by Perissone, only one other is unequivocally in the feminine voice, *Nel partir del mio ben sí part'Amore* (When my beloved departed, so did Love), while in another, *Se mai crud'a mei dolci pensieri* (If ever cruel to my sweet thoughts), the gender of the speaker seems purposefully ambiguous. By opening the collection with *Io mi son bella e cruda* in the not-so-common feminine voice, and thus reflecting still further on the speaker's feminine powers, Perissone places the gift in the mouth of the dedicatee, so to speak, while paying her a Petrarchan compliment.

It is as though Gaspara were enunciating and indeed announcing the contents of the collection. From here it is a small leap to imagining Gaspara singing some or all of the songs in the collection.

DISCERNING COURTESAN-LIKE SONG IN POLYPHONY

A few inherently musical aspects of Perissone's print mark it out among collections of its kind, as on close inspection the music reveals certain eccentricities of part-writing when compared with other four-voice madrigals. These eccentricities support the suggestion that some of the pieces in it probably had a double life as four-voice polyphonic madrigals and as accompanied solo madrigals.

Perissone's models for four-voice madrigals were essentially two: those of his teacher, Adrian Willaert, *maestro di cappella* at St. Mark's, and those of Willaert's contemporary (also an Italianized northerner) Cipriano de Rore, three of whose four-voice madrigals saw their first publication in Perissone's book, which preceded Rore's own first four-voice book by three years.[15] Both composers wrote four-voice madrigals marked by stepwise part-writing in all of the voices (leaps are usually confined either to points of imitation, where rhetorical emphasis is desired, or to cadential points) and a general similarity of compositional style shared by the three upper voices (the bass tends to be more angular since it provides harmonic support).[16]

Many of the four-voice madrigals by Perissone, by comparison, are strikingly odd in certain parts of their individual vocal lines. One of his two madrigals in the female voice, *Nel partir*, for example, begins with fairly stepwise inner voices (ex. 5.1).[17] Though it uses an octave leap in the tenor in measure 2, it is nevertheless singable, and as such emphasizes the main clause, *sì part'Amore*, love departs (companion website track 5):

Nel partir del mio ben sì part'amore	In the departing of my beloved, so Love departed
Et seco ne portò quei chiari lumi	And with him took those bright eyes
Che m'accesero il core;	That enflamed my heart;
Io sola altro non so che pianger sempre	Alone, I know nothing but to weep continually
La bella vista e i dolci suoi costumi.	For his beautiful image and his sweet demeanor.
Deh, iniquitoso arciero,	Oh! wicked archer,
Ferma l'amante mio che fugge sciolto;	Stop my lover, who flees unbound;
Guidami lui, guidam'il suo bel volto.	Lead him to me, lead his beautiful face to me.

The irregularities begin in measure 11 where the tenor sings *la bella vista* with a succession of leaps, including two pairs of descending fourths, the first pair separated by an ascending third and the second by no less than an ascending fifth (ex. 5.2). This was no printer's mistake, nor a compositional gaffe. Yet it is inelegant, very difficult to execute for the voice, and highly unusual by the idiomatic vocal norms of the time—something one would never find in Rore or Willaert, for example—all notwithstanding the fact that Perissone was known as a highly melodious composer. Furthermore, at the end of measure 14, the tenor makes a jump of an ascending sixth. It cannot be justified syntactically as it occurs in the middle of a grammatical unit, but rather clearly serves to prepare the perfect authentic cadence on *costumi* in the first half of measure 15 (ex. 5.3).

EXAMPLE 5.1. Perissone Cambio, *Nel partir del mio ben*, mm. 1–3. Transcription by Martha Feldman.

Finally, in the last three measures of the piece, the tenor traverses a minor seventh in the course of just three notes (ex. 5.4). In two swift bounds of consecutive descending fourths, the tenor has covered the interval of a seventh on its way to the cadence, even though two successive leaps in the same direction were considered undesirable, even unallowable, by contemporaneous contrapuntal norms of voice-leading, especially leaps of a perfect fourth.

I offer this comparison of Perissone's part-writing to the general stylistic norms of Franco-Flemish vocal polyphony not to establish criteria for value judgment. Instead I want to suggest that his approach to vocal writing in this four-voice madrigal

EXAMPLE 5.2. Perissone Cambio, *Nel partir del mio ben*, mm. 10–12. Transcription by Martha Feldman.

EXAMPLE 5.3. Perissone Cambio, *Nel partir del mio ben*, mm. 13–15. Transcription by Martha Feldman.

publication was different from existing norms because certain madrigals in it were intended to serve as solo as well as polyphonic songs. Even though *Nel partir*, when considered from the vantage point of Willaert's work, provides an extreme example of an unmelodious tenor, Perissone's tenor lines are rather eccentric throughout the print. Such eccentricities do not spoil his harmonies, but they do break contemporaneous rules of voice-leading. They allow us to infer that pieces of the kind were conceived harmonically rather than contrapuntally. Yet the procedure is so unusual that it is hard to believe that such pieces were conjured up with performance by multiple voices in mind at all, as would have been true for the polyphonic madrigal. Some of them could indeed have been written first as songs for solo voice with accompaniment, where the euphony of the chords would have been more important than the

EXAMPLE 5.4. Perissone Cambio, *Nel partir del mio ben*, mm. 23–25. Transcription by Martha Feldman.

propriety and interrelationship of the inner parts. The four-part vocal version could then be seen as a transcription that never fully erased the instrumental origin of the song's accompanimental lower voices, and that explains the dramatic oratorical repetition of the imperative, so evocative of oral recitation, in the last verse.

CONCLUSION

Several points suggest a close relationship between the repertory in Perissone's 1547 print and the solo singing of its dedicatee, Gaspara Stampa. The opening number, perhaps dedicatory, puts song in the feminine voice and elaborates one of the metaphors of the dedication. The oddities of part-writing in the inner voices suggest the possible harmonic (as opposed to contrapuntal) conception of songs in the collection. Perissone's oblique references to Gaspara's powers to engage her audience and her intrinsic musicality draw attention suggestively to her musical performance.

Most relevant here, much of the collection could very well have been performed by her, or just as easily by another female singer who got hold of it, and who might have performed it in Stampa's salon, that of Domenico Venier, or elsewhere.[18] In short, Perissone's 1547 book provides an exemplar, and a working musical method, for recreating the repertory of a contemporaneous courtesan whose music is otherwise lost in a haze of unwritten ephemera.

Notes

1. Perissone Cambio, *Il primo libro de madrigali a 4 voci* (Venice, 1547), ed. Martha Feldman (New York: Garland, 1989).

2. In this scholars were largely following the lead of Stampa's first biographer, Abdelkader Salza, "Madonna Gasparina Stampa secondo nuove indagini," *Giornale storico della letteratura italiana* 62 (1913): 1–101. Stampa's biography and the relevant literature is presented comprehensively in Maria Bellonci's introduction to Gaspara Stampa, *Rime*, ed. Rodolfo Cerielo (Milan: Rizzoli, 1976). The love affair recorded in Stampa's verses, together with her untimely death, provided fodder for many nineteenth-century scholars. Salza disputed previously held notions of Stampa as passionate but chaste. His representation of her as a courtesan, as Fiora Bassanese elaborates, was grounded in ambiguous evidence, namely, a posthumously published defamatory sonnet, her acquaintances, the dedication of works to her that Salza considered inappropriate for a respectable woman, more than one lover in her poetry and life, and her unmarried status; see Fiora Bassanese, *Gaspara Stampa* (Boston: Twayne, 1983), chap. 2, "Fiction and Reality."

3. See in particular Gioachino Brognoligo, "Gaspara Stampa," *Giornale storico della letteratura italiana* 76 (1920): 134–43; but also Bellonci, in *Rime*, 56, and Bassanese, *Gaspara Stampa*, 3.

4. Ortensio Landi, cited in Salza, "Madonna Gasparina Stampa," 29.

5. See Martha Feldman's introduction to Cambio, *Il primo libro de madrigali*, xiii.

6. Lynn Hooker, unpublished seminar paper, cited in Feldman, *City Culture and the Madrigal in Venice* (Berkeley: University of California Press, 1995), 106–107, and this volume, chap. 4, 114–18.

7. Philippe Verdelot, *Intavolature de li madrigali di Verdelotto: De cantare et sonare nel lauto*, arr. Adrian Willaert (Venice, 1536).

8. One notable exception is James Haar, "Monophony and the Unwritten Traditions," in *Performance Practice: Music before 1600*, ed. Howard Mayer Brown and Stanley Sadie (New York: Norton, 1990), 240–66. Haar finds evidence of monophony in repeated melodic patterns and declamatory rhythmic patterns in Jachet Berchem's polyphonic settings of Ariosto texts, for example; see especially pp. 255–57. See also other important writings of Haar's relevant to the subject cited above in chap. 4, n. 21. His interest, however, is mainly in how composers of polyphony were influenced by solo song and in how traces of solo song formulas can be found in polyphony, whereas mine is in discovering how a singer might have turned polyphony back into solo song.

9. My conclusion builds upon suggestions already made by Einstein, Haar, and Feldman that certain four-voice madrigals provide evidence of solo performance, despite the fact that they were circulated in the form of written partbooks. See Alfred Einstein, "Pseudo-monody and Monody," chap. 12 in *The Italian Madrigal*, 3 vols. (1949; repr. Princeton: Princeton University Press, 1971), 836–49, *passim*. Feldman points out the tuneful quality of Perissone's 1547 madrigal settings, suggesting that some of them may indeed be written versions of the improvised song practiced by Stampa and her fellow female performers. See Feldman, *City Culture*, 108–109.

10. Perissone's madrigal print is the only music known to have been dedicated to Stampa.

11. Cambio, *Il primo libro de madrigali*, xiii.

12. The topic of harmony and the Platonic and Neoplatonic tradition has been the subject of much musicological literature, including James Haar's dissertation, "Musica Mundana: Variations on a Pythagorean Theme" (Ph.D diss., Harvard University, 1960); Ann E. Moyer, *Musica Scientia: Musical Scholarship in the Italian Renaissance* (Ithaca: Cornell University Press, 1991); and Gary Tomlinson, *Music in Renaissance Magic: Toward a Historiography of Others* (Chicago: University of Chicago Press, 1993).

13. See below, chap. 9.

14. Translation mine, with suggestions by Bernardo Illari.

15. Feldman links some of Perissone's madrigals stylistically with Willaert's *Musica nova*, while Einstein suggests that Perissone's model was Rore. See Einstein, *The Italian Madrigal*, 439; and Feldman, *City Culture*, 109.

16. Adrian Willaert, *Musica nova* (Venice, 1559).

17. The listener may note discrepancies between the written polyphony and the lute transcription by looking at the score in Cambio, *Il primo libro de madrigali*, and comparing it aurally with the performance of *Nel partir* for lute and voice on the companion website to this volume (track 5).

18. See above, chap. 4, and below, chap. 10.

On Locating the Courtesan in Italian Lyric

*Distance and the Madrigal Texts
of Costanzo Festa*

In *The Gay Science*, Friedrich Nietzsche writes, "The magic and most powerful effect of women is, in philosophical language, action at a distance, *actio in distans*; but this requires first of all and above all—*distance*."[1] Jacques Derrida's reading of Nietzsche underscores this effect: "A woman seduces from a distance. In fact, distance is the very element of her power. Yet one must beware to keep one's own distance from her beguiling *song* of enchantment."[2] Derrida stresses action at a distance as intimately and essentially musical, a sympathetic vibration, a song. On this view a singing courtesan is doubly desirable, and openly courts desire, especially in the courtly urban salons of Renaissance Italy, where an amorous aesthetic so totally dominated by the Petrarchan poetics of loss relegated woman to an institutionalized absence. There, the paradox of action at a distance is personified in the form of the courtesan's voice. In the context of a poetics that denied them utterance, courtesans managed to modify conventional models and engage in meaningful lyric expression.

In this essay I explore the problem of voice and address in a single large corpus of madrigals from the 1520s and 1530s set to music by Costanzo Festa (1485–1540), an early master of the Italian madrigal, in a project I call "locating the courtesan." The courtesan appears in Festa's madrigal texts as addressee and speaker, and possibly even as author (three anonymous texts are written in the female voice). My study considers a more generalized musical representation of the courtesan's voice than De Rycke's (chap. 5), and rather than focusing on what she might have sung interrogates musical and poetic constructions both of and by her.

Most of the poems set by Festa remain unattributed and can largely be classified as "Madonna"-type madrigals addressed to an anonymous lady, which involve an irregular succession of verse lines, usually with the opening salutation "Donna" or "Madonna."[3] The ostensive social status of the woman serenaded varies greatly: in some she is a deified *donna* (or lady) or a patrician *damigella* (damsel), in others a refined *cortigiana onesta*, and in still others a debased *donna da bene* (woman of services, or prostitute).

Alongside the many graceful and elegant Petrarchan texts in his corpus are also a number of hybrid madrigals that Alfred Einstein likened to obscene *mascherate* or *canti carnascialeschi*.[4] For Einstein these were implicitly addressed to courtesans, as literary parodies that transferred the unnamed "Madonna into a lower and more vulgar sphere,"[5] such as the opening madrigal in Festa's *Vero libro*,[6] *Madonn', io son un medico perfetto*:[7]

> My Lady, I am a meticulous medic
> Who, without using irons or fire,
> Can cure every great ill in no time at all,
> And I come to you because I've been told
> That you have a large wound;
> And if you wish to be cured
> I'll put to good use a big probe,
> And I can tell you that it will surely cure you.
> I'll plunge it into the wound, and it has a liquor
> That heals with sweetness every pain.[8]

In the rare instances when a woman is named, she is so idealized (e.g., "Julia diva!")[9] that she seems more imaginary than real. Yet quite a few of Festa's settings do invoke real-world women, so it is reasonable to hypothesize that the "Madonna" of the more brazen texts was involved in some kind of sexual commerce: "I wish to return anew to that delight, / My lady, if it please you, / Because desire is undoing me, / And make of your soft flesh my bed."[10]

Even texts that do not name names sometimes participate, through crude syntax and subject matter, in a strain of madrigals that invoke common courtesans or prostitutes. Einstein reasoned that since madrigals were often "not always so direct, so outspoken and blunt," "the poems addressed to a courtesan, a *donna da bene*, ought to pass as homage to a patrician woman."[11] They operated incognito, in other words, blurring the boundary between the polite and the pornographic.[12]

How then can we read these texts? First there is the challenge of understanding how literary tropes mediate the courtesan's voice. In early sixteenth-century poetry, most texts followed the conventions of Petrarch's devotion to his muse Laura by addressing an unnamed female as *donna* or *Madonna*, often as idol or goddess. In *Ogni beltà, madonna, ch'io veggio*, for example, the speaker exclaims, "There is no mortal beauty that resembles yours, / for your countenance contains so many wonders / that now you appear a goddess, now a morning star."[13] Elevated to an almost Platonic ideal, all other women become mere imitations: "Every beauty, my lady, / that I see in the appearance of other women / seems to me no more than the shadings of gifted painters. / Yours is the only one / made on earth by nature, / that has seen the true form of beauty."[14]

Idealized, distant, and unattainable, this lady is universally faulted in Festa's madrigals for refusing to reciprocate the speaker's affection and fidelity. In *Madonn', il vostr'orgoglio*, the speaker declares: "My lady, your pride, / my pure fidelity, / my wretched fate, / have brought me so close to death. / . . . And against my will I tell you, / your unrelenting severity makes me wish / that I could free my heart."[15]

The male speaker is typically subordinated in direct relation to his lady's merits. His sufferings are as great as her beauty, his fiery torments as intense as her icy indifference: "Your beauty is the sun, the sun my flame, / of which I am well pleased, / for the torment should be equal to the beauty," he proclaims in *Madonna, al volto mio pallid'e smorto*;[16] and in *Madonna, io v'am'e taccio*, "Love will swear to you / that there is as much fire in me as ice in you."[17] The economy that governs the exchange is clear: by association, the value of the poet's lament is inflated to equal the beauty of the demi-goddess who inspires it.

Marrying the socio-sexual role reversal of troubadour lyric to the tenets of Neo-platonism within the Petrarchan aesthetic that prevailed around 1530, the poetic stance of these "Madonna" poems aggrandizes the speaker at the same time as it silences the Lady. The tradition exploits feudal hierarchies by positing a relationship in which the *domna* is installed as the *Seigneur*, whom the poet serves in the role of humble vassal. This seeming elevation of the woman's status actually allows the poet to control her response to his wooing, since the *Seigneur* must grant his vassal's request to fulfill the reciprocal rights and responsibilities of the feudal contract. Thus the lady of troubadour lyric is expected to reward her poet with the bliss of love's satisfaction once he has demonstrated sufficiently faithful service in song.[18] Further-more, the creation of the powerful, unfaithful, and unfeeling lady—a caricature of traditional masculine stereotypes—allows the male speaker to adopt the poetic po-sition of ultimate abjection: the conventionally feminized role of love's victim, the woman dying of unrequited love.[19] This reversed gender troping infuses such lyrics with great emotional and cultural appeal, presenting what Kathryn Gravdal has called the striking figures of "once-powerful men who, disempowered by love, suffer like women."[20]

Petrarch's poetry owes an enormous debt to the troubadour tradition, especially in effectively silencing the female love object (his Laura). In death Laura is the ab-sent object par excellence, "the woman who has disappeared from the public sphere only to reappear as the epitome of 'femininity,' the idealized woman whose absence" erects the poetic subject as he bemoans her loss.[21] Laura is more mirror than a sub-ject, "a brilliant surface, a pure signifier whose momentary exteriority to the poet serves as an Archimedean point from which he can create himself."[22] And as in troubadour lyric, it is precisely through Petrarch's glorifying of absence that the male poet attains poetic glory.[23]

Where does this leave women writers in the Renaissance who want to respond? They can hardly adopt the persona extolled by male poets—the silent, masculin-ized, distant *domna*—and when they do speak as faithful, long-suffering lovers, they are accused of being insufficiently so for "it would transgress the bounds of decorum for a female rhetor to confront her beloved as boldly as Petrarch does his."[24] Women writers were thus caught in a bind: if it was not proper for women to exploit their culturally appointed persona and real-life position as love's victims, then their poetry could never be deemed pathetic (or poetic) enough. It was ironically both more ap-propriate and more powerful for a man to proclaim "I sing like a woman" than for a woman to announce, "I sing *as* a woman."[25]

This paradox is foregrounded in the text of Festa's one six-voice madrigal, *Così estrema la doglia*, which I have identified in the corpus of Veronica Gambara (1485–1550), a noblewoman of Coreggio.[26]

So extreme is my suffering
That to such extreme harm no harm can come,
And in this way I am kept alive by it.
I would surely be dead by now,
But the pain I have in my heart, so harsh and hard,
Yields no place to death,
Nor can it increase or cause my woes to shrink.
Ah, pitiless attack!
How shall I make a defense
If you have filled my spirit and breast with so much anguish
That my enflamed soul cannot flee forth,
And I live in spite of myself?
But amid all my torments this is the greatest:
To be unable to lament my woes![27]

On one level this poem can be read as a typical "Madonna" ode, minus the salutation and in a female voice that bemoans the sufferings caused by her cruel lover. Various tropes of Petrarchan poetry appear: the anguish caused by the beloved equals the burning of the speaker's passion; the speaker cannot die or achieve satisfaction (a common erotic twist). However Gambara's speaker, while not going so far as to overtly plead for *pietate* (pity), a key Petrarchan trope, cunningly positions the word *dispietata* (pitiless) at the madrigal's metrical center. It is therefore possible to read it as an impassioned critique of the *poetic* "attack" against which she is defenseless because silenced.

Festa's setting only makes the problem worse by using a corrupted version of the text that strikes the central lament, "Ahi, dispietata offesa!" Moreover, it eradicates the poem's feminine voice, replacing the crucial feminine adjective, "viva" ("alive"), in the third line (all the more conspicuous because in rhyming position) with a construction requiring the first person singular in the present-tense subjunctive of "vivere" ("to live"), "convien ch'io viva" (thereby cleverly maintaining the rhyme scheme):

So extreme [is] my suffering
That the most extreme harm never comes,
And in this way *in the end I must live.*
I would surely be dead by now
But the pain I have in my heart, so harsh and hard,
Yields no place to death;
Nor can it increase or cause my woes to shrink.
[* * *]
How shall I make a defense
If you have filled my spirit and breast with so much anguish
That my enflamed soul cannot flee forth,
And so I live in spite of myself?
But amid so many torments this is the greatest:
To be unable to lament my woes![28]

Having neutralized the voice and eliminated its indictment of the "pitiless attack," Festa's version enacts the very rhetorical positions that Gambara laments, producing merely another "Madonna" madrigal in which the speaker "sings like a woman" to predictable effect. While we have little idea how many more "anonymous" texts in the masculine voice may prove to have been written by women, this example illustrates the problem of literary voice for sixteenth-century women and scholars who want to locate them.

What might such a voice sound like if spoken by a courtesan, and what clues would tell us whose it was? The answer lies, I suggest, in the problematic notion of distance. In the early sixteenth century, Italian women writers of patrician background tended to adopt the Petrarchan tradition to dispel the distance imposed on them as speaking subjects. Like Gambara, they bemoan their lack of voice and adapt male models of utterance to their own needs. Fifty years later the famed courtesan Veronica Franco approached distance very differently, embracing the Nietzschean power of action at a distance rather than seeking to dispel it. Yet far from rejecting completely the persona of the distant "Madonna," Franco deployed the courtesan's art of self-presentation to play with it, always maintaining a certain empowering distance on her own terms.

Often, for example, Franco brings the female speaker down to earth, openly celebrating sensuality and sexuality, instead of shackling herself to the role of love's victim. Proud, strong, and fierce, she retains stereotypically masculine traits that traditionally keep the "madonna" at a distance, and uses them to her advantage. In many of her *capitoli* (notably *capitolo* 13, "Non più parole: ai fatti, in campo, a l'armi"—an excerpt of which is performed to a melodic formula on the CD insert, track 6—and *capitolo* 16, "D'ardito cavalier non è prodezza") she appears as an armed warrior, ready to defeat her male rivals in war or words.[29] Thus she keeps the lady on her old Platonic pedestal, but gains from it a better vantage point from which to foil a man. Franco's female persona challenges a man to draw his weapon, only to remain a sword's length away.

The three texts in Festa's madrigals by female speakers deal with distance in ways that anticipate Franco's, suggesting that their authors, too, may be courtesans. Relevant here is the fact that during Festa's tenure in the Cappella Sistina he had intimate dealings with the wealthy Florentine nobleman Filippo Strozzi,[30] who was often in Rome on business. Strozzi helped Festa find a publisher for his music and was also godfather to his son. Richard Agee's analysis of the unedited Strozzi letters reveals that Strozzi more than once furnished Festa with texts for setting to music, including those of his brother Lorenzo, and that Festa asked Strozzi for such texts.[31]

Furthermore, Strozzi kept his own *villino* with live-in courtesans before the Porta San Gallo in Florence "for his own use and for the use of his friends, among them Lorenzo, Duke of Urbino, the father of the Catherine de Medici who later became Queen of France," as Einstein notes, continuing: "its occupants were some of the most celebrated courtesans of the day: Camilla Pisana, Alessandra Fiorentina, a certain Beatrice, and one Brigida. Camilla, Filippo's mistress, was also able to write poetry in the style of Bembo and Cassola[32] for which we may assume that Verdelot and Festa supplied the music."[33] When we consider Strozzi's letters together with Einstein's claim (admittedly undocumented but staked on the basis of an unequalled knowledge of the madrigal's cultural context) that Festa was among those furnishing music for verse of the famed courtesan-poet Camilla Pisana, there is strong reason to believe that a feminine-voiced madrigal text set by Festa was penned by her in the Strozzi *villino*.

All three texts bear marks of the courtesan's hand. In *Nasce fra l'herbe un fiore*, the most conventional, a woman compares her lover to the sun, by whose rising and setting she metaphorically lives and dies:

> Among the weeds a flower is born
> That so loves the sun that at its dawning,
> All laughing and beautiful, it opens itself and joyfully
> Feeds upon its splendor;
> But when, at the final hour,
> The sun takes its leave and sinks into the waves,
> The flower loses its strength, and hides itself completely.
> I who have lived so long from the living splendor
> Of your fair eyes, now deprived of those lights,
> Halfway between dead and alive,
> Am made blind, and if in my great pain
> I seek out comfort, yet I seek in vain,
> Because your being so far away
> Causes me to hear cries wherever I stray,
> And others' sighs redouble all my pain.[34]

The speaker adopts the troubadour role of love's victim, adapting the metaphor of the beloved as a mirror into which the subject gazes in self-admiration.[35] Here, however, Narcissus is a woman, able to see only through the beloved's eyes. Deprived of their sight, she goes blind. Moreover, she is less in love with self-beholding than with being beheld by her lover. She offers herself as a specular object, begging a man to look at her while knowing that his gaze brings desire.

By contrast, the speaker in *Amor ben puoi tu hormai* claims to regret the folly of her past, and swears off Love (Cupid) with his attendant ills:

> Love, well may you now
> Do to me the worst that you know how, and for my injury
> Use every art, your every force and fraud;
> For I have repented
> Of my former errors and ill-spent years,
> Which brought me only pain and troubles.
> Hence, now that I am free of them,
> I will live in liberty, since your arrow
> And flame will avail you little against me,
> As neither good nor ill, pleasure nor pain,
> Will I hope or fear from you ever again.[36]

Yet even after she sends Love away, the speaker constantly beckons him back. In a deft linguistic trope she tells Love she will not fall prey to his arts, all the while challenging him to seduce her. To incite desire, she manipulates throughout the distance between herself and Love—whether Cupid, real lover(s), or all potential lover-readers.[37]

The pattern continues in *Duro è il partito dove m'astringete*, where the female speaker refuses to satisfy her lover's desires but cannot deny them:

Hard is the decision you press upon me.
What, must I give you a yes-or-no answer?
To that I reply that I must not say yes,
That I see no way at all to satisfy you,
That gratifying your blithe desires would
Mean too much for me, and since it would cost me my honor,
Go slowly, and do not run with haste,
For dear is the beloved who is awaited with endurance,
And if in enduring you sense yourself becoming less firm,
Temper your ardor with my coldness.[38]

Here the erotic wordplay on *duro* (harsh or hard) and *durare* (to endure or harden) whets the same appetite it purports to want to sate. Aware of the power that traditional poetic models vest in the *madonna*'s indifference, the speaker knows that her *freddo* causes her suitor to burn ardently and uses this knowledge to maintain a position of control: the final couplet, "Et se durando non vi par star saldo, / Temprate col mio freddo il vostro caldo," means both "If you should become less steadfast while awaiting, bolster your resolve with my disdain" and "If in withstanding you should droop, harden your heat with my cold."[39] As the lover's desire is challenged it is also redoubled. But since the speaker also realizes the power of the traditional *madonna*'s silence, the entire poem reads as a non-answer as well. She speaks, but does not reply "yes" or "no," neither rejecting nor receiving her lover's demands and thus keeping him in desire, at attention, and under her command.

In addition to the many textual clues of a courtesan's hand (not just the envoicing of one), there is further historical evidence that Camilla authored these texts. Her thirty-three extant letters, all undated but written to her lover Strozzi and his friend (and her confidant) Francesco Del Nero while she was installed in the *villino*, attest to her literary pursuits: in one, she asks Francesco if he still has a certain book of her writings ("el mio libro") and implores that it "not be seen except among yourselves, because it has not been revised."[40] She then asks for his help in editing the book, "for without your aid I shall have nothing from it but shame."[41]

Describing in another letter to Del Nero (Machiavelli's brother-in-law) her desperate desire to see Filippo again, Camilla echoes the sentiment of *Nasce fra l'herbe un fiore*, saying that should she see him she "shall no longer care about dying, because I can receive no greater gift in this world. And just as privation causes me intolerable pain, so his presence expands my every joy and delight."[42] She further underscores the importance of seeing—and being seen by—Filippo (a key conceit in the poem) in a letter addressed to him: "Allow me, for my supreme solace, to see and to possess your sight ["possedere la tua vista"—both "see you" and "be the object of your gaze"], without which it is no longer possible for me to live."[43]

The metaphor of a flower growing among weeds ("Nasce fra l'herbe un fiore") is not found in Camilla's letters; however, she does employ the same verb, "pascere" ("to feed upon or graze"), used in the poem to link the flower's survival to the sun in depicting her own dependence on her lover, on whom her "every hope feeds and is nourished."[44] She portrays Filippo as the sun by whose light she lives: "Nor will I ever call all this night good until the longed-for day arrives when your clear brightness will restore to me the light of your desired splendor."[45] Further echoing the poem,

Camilla refers to another *cortigiana* in the *villino* who bemoans the absence of the beloved ("Alessandra likewise pines with me, and commends herself to you with endless sobs").[46]

Camilla's many references to both seeing and being seen by Filippo, to her hopes reviving with his return as with the rising sun, and to the laments of the other courtesans are all highly conventional, but recall precisely the tropes of Festa's madrigal *Nasce fra l'herbe*: deprived of her beloved's splendor and lights (eyes), the speaker is made blind and weeps with other lovers at his absence, but revives when her sun returns. The verses could well have been written by Camilla, perhaps during one of Filippo's long trips to Rome, or by another courtesan in a similar position.

The evidence, although sparser, is nevertheless stronger for the next two poems, which do not rely on such conventional tropes. Indeed, each is comparatively original in language and content, so the similarities to Camilla's letter-writing connect them to her more convincingly. Camilla's letters complain throughout of the suffering she has endured because of her love for Filippo: neglect, betrayal, disdain. In two instances, she describes her pains using nearly the same language as the second line of *Amor ben puoi tu hormai* ("Love, well may you now / Do to me the worst that you know how"): "We've been treated in such a way that we'll remember it all our lives. Do to us whatever evil you can . . . for we expect nothing but malice from you."[47] Closer still to the syntax of the poem, she writes on another occasion, when detailing to Francesco the efforts of an enemy to defame her: "But let each man do to us the worst that he can, for if my life is not taken from me, I do not believe there is anything that can remove from me my unceasing intention."[48]

The language in both letters resembles that of *Amor, ben puoi*, and in each a challenge is issued, although here Camilla's "intenzione" is to love Filippo always, whereas the poem's speaker vows never to love again. Still, the poem means to rekindle the very emotion to which she (ostensibly) bids farewell. If what we want are echoes of historical truth, we might find solace in the fact that Camilla by turns loved and left, was loved and neglected. In the end Filippo tired of Camilla, and she departed for Rome.[49] Could the poem have been a last plea? A farewell?

The most intriguing of the three poems is *Duro è 'l partito dove m'astringete*. Camilla's letters tell us that Filippo wanted to share her with his friends, and pressured her to offer herself to them for their pleasure, but she refused:

> I, who love him more than any other woman ever loved a man, resisted greatly, because, considering *how hard a decision he was pressing upon me* [che duro partito mi proponeva], I didn't have enough strength to see my every gift squeezed, kissed, grabbed, and enjoyed before my very eyes. And after I had battled greatly with myself I answered him that while in order to satisfy him I would be ready to cede, and would never wish to disturb his pleasure, I did not want to bring about my own death.[50]

Camilla states explicitly in prose the non-answer that *Duro è 'l partito* so artfully enacts in verse. "In the end, I neither promised nor denied him,"[51] she writes, explaining that in the interim afforded by this delaying tactic, she hoped to rekindle Filippo's love.

Once again, a locution and situation in Camilla Pisana's letters matches almost uncannily a key line from one of Festa's anonymous settings. And yet that anonymity is the last vestige of the mystery, the inaccessibility, indeed, the *distance* that gave the courtesan of early modern Italy her power: a power to find a voice, to make art of personal tragedy, and to create desire out of art.

Notes

1. Friedrich Nietzsche, *The Gay Science*, trans. Walter Kaufmann (New York: Vintage, 1974), 124.

2. Jacques Derrida, *Spurs: Nietzsche's Styles*, trans. Barbara Harlow (Chicago: University of Chicago Press, 1979), 49; emphasis mine.

3. Scattered among the eighty-seven madrigals in Festa's collected works are five settings of Petrarch sonnets, two of poems by Sannazaro, one each by Ariosto and Luigi Cassola, and some of minor poets. In all, however, Albert Seay was able to ascertain the authorship of less than 13 percent of the texts; Costanzo Festa, *Collected Works*, ed. Alexander Main and Albert Seay, 8 vols. (Neuhausen-Stuttgart: American Institute of Musicology and Hänssler-Verlag, 1962–78).

4. Alfred Einstein, *The Italian Madrigal*, 3 vols., trans. Alexander H. Krappe, Roger H. Sessions, and Oliver Strunk (1949; Princeton: Princeton University Press, 1971), 1:182.

5. Ibid., 1:175. Einstein points out that the profession of female addressees in similar verses set by Festa's contemporaries is either implicit or made explicit by the inclusion of names associated with courtesans: Isabella, Flaminia, Polissena, Tullia, and so forth.

6. Costanzo Festa, *Il vero libro di madrigali a tre voci di Constantio Festa* (Venice: Antonio Gardano, 1543).

7. Although attributed to him in numerous editions from the 1540s to 1560s, it is doubtful whether *Madonn', io son un medico perfetto* is actually Festa's. See *Collected Works*, ed. Seay, 7: xiii.

8. *Collected Works*, ed. Seay, 7:1–2. All translations here and below are mine.

9. Ibid., 8:40, from *Se i sguardi di costei*.

10. Ibid., 7:34–35, from *Non mi par che sia vero, madonna mia*.

11. Einstein, *The Italian Madrigal*, 1:182.

12. The fact that Festa's few bawdy texts satirize Petrarchan traditions of "Madonna" poetry does not make them any less rooted in those traditions.

13. Festa, *Collected Works*, 7:29.

14. Ibid., 7:28–29.

15. Ibid., 7:3–4.

16. Ibid., 8:53–54.

17. Ibid., 7:18.

18. Matilda Tomaryn Bruckner, "Fictions of the Female Voice: The Women Troubadours," *Speculum* 67 (1992): 869.

19. See Kathryn Gravdal, "Metaphor, Metonymy, and the Medieval Women Trobairitz," *Romanic Review* 83 (1992): 412.

20. Ibid., 413.

21. Juliana Schiesari, *The Gendering of Melancholia: Feminism, Psychoanalysis, and the Symbolics of Loss in Renaissance Literature* (Ithaca: Cornell University Press, 1992), 165; 167.

22. John Freccero, "The Fig Tree and the Laurel: Petrarch's Poetics," *Diacritics* 5 (1975): 39.

23. This poetic stance becomes further entrenched as Petrarchism becomes more Pla-

tonic through the influence of Pietro Bembo. Whereas Petrarch's Laura was at once idealized and real, unattainable and familiar, the Bembist-Petrarchan "madonna" becomes one or the other: either the untouchable super-human goddess or (in parody, satire, and invective) the all-too-available earthly whore.

24. William J. Kennedy, *Authorizing Petrarch* (Ithaca: Cornell University Press, 1994), 138.

25. Gravdal, "Metaphor," 411; 417. Later in the century a few women rejected this stance and proclaimed that they sang as men. See Margaret F. Rosenthal, *The Honest Courtesan: Veronica Franco, Citizen and Writer in Sixteenth-Century Venice* (Chicago: University of Chicago Press, 1992), esp. 177–97.

26. Neither Einstein nor Seay identifies this text, which was probably written before Gambara's 1509 marriage to Giberto X, Count of Correggio. By the age of seventeen Gambara was corresponding with Pietro Bembo, the leading Petrarchan of the century and her lifelong literary mentor. Her politically charged poetry was published in several mid-century collections of *Petrarchisti*. See Kennedy, *Authorizing Petrarch*, 135.

27. Così estrema è la doglia
ch'a così estremo mal mal non arriva,
e a questo modo me ne resto viva.
Sarei ben morta, omai,
ma 'l dolor ch'ho nel cor, sì grave e forte,
non da loco a la morte,
né accrescer può né sminuir miei guai.
Ahi, dispietata offesa!
Come farò diffesa
se m'hai sì pien d'angoscia l'alma e 'l petto
che fuor non può spirar l'anima accesa
e vivo al mio dispetto?
Ma fra tutti i martiri quest'è il maggiore:
non potermi doler del mio dolore!

Veronica Gambara, *Le Rime*, ed. Alan Bullock (Florence: Leo S. Olschki, 1995), 63–65.

28. Così estrema la doglia
Che così estremo mal mai non arriva,
E a questo mod'*alfin convien ch'io viva*,
Sarei ben'mort'hormai
Ma il dolore ch'ho nel core sì grave e forte,
Non da loco alla morte;
Né accrescer può né sminuir miei guai.
[* * *]
Come farò difesa
Se così ho pien d'angoscia l'alma e 'l petto,
Che non può spirar fuor l'anim'accesa.
E vivo al mio dispetto,
Ma fra tanti martir questo è il maggiore:
Non potermi doler del mio dolore.

Festa, *Collected Works*, 7:98–101; emphasis and asterisks mine.

29. Veronica Franco, *Poems and Selected Letters*, ed. and trans. Ann Rosalind Jones and Margaret F. Rosenthal (Chicago: University of Chicago Press, 1998), 132–37; 160–71. For the first four stanzas of the text and translation see the appendix.

30. On Strozzi see Martha Feldman, *City Culture and the Madrigal at Venice* (Berkeley: University of California Press, 1995), 24–30.

31. Richard J. Agee, "Filippo Strozzi and the Early Madrigal," *Journal of the American Musicological Society* 38 (1985): 231–32. Lorenzo's text, "Lieto non hebbi mai un giorno," appears among Festa's madrigals; see Festa, *Collected Works*, 7:16–17.

32. Luigi Cassola (d. ca. 1560), from Piacenza, was a poet of the textual *madrigali* (a specific kind of *poesia per musica*) active from at least 1530.

33. Einstein, *The Italian Madrigal*, 1:180–81.

34. Festa, *Collected Works*, 8:87–89.

35. See Gravdal, "Metaphor," 423.

36. Festa, *Collected Works*, 7:55–57.

37. Contrast the sincere contrition of Gaspara Stampa's "Mesta e pentita de' miei gravi errori." Stampa's sonnet is similar to "Amor ben puoi" but lacks any subtext of seduction.

38. Festa, *Collected Works*, 8:9–11.

39. This is a reference to humoral theory, according to which men were hot and dry and women cold and wet.

40. Camilla Pisana, *Lettere di cortigiane del Rinascimento*, ed. Angelo Romano (Rome: Salerno Editrice, 1990), 34.

41. Ibid.

42. Ibid., 49–50.

43. Ibid., 69.

44. Ibid., 68.

45. Ibid., 69.

46. Ibid., 48.

47. Ibid., 123.

48. Ibid., 110–11.

49. Camilla was registered in Rome as a tenant in the house of Giovanni Battista Candellataro during the papacies of Leo X and Clement VII (1517–26). See *Descriptio Urbis: The Roman Census of 1527*, ed. Egmont Lee (Rome: Bulzoni, 1985), 65–66 (nos. 3126 and 3214). She went on to become a muse of sorts to the young Pietro Aretino, who immortalizes her beauty in *La cortigiana* (II. xi) and in a 1541 letter to Angelo Firenzuola recalls a rather wild adventure he had at her house years earlier. See Pietro Aretino, *Lettere*, ed. Francesco Erspamer, 2 vols. (Parma: Ugo Guanda, 1995), 2:646. Also placing her in the capital is the coarsely satirical *Ragionamento del Zoppino* (1539), 70–71, which names Camilla as one of the stale, rancid-smelling whores of Rome (see below, chap. 10, n. 3).

50. Camilla Pisana, *Lettere*, 76–77; emphasis mine.

51. Ibid., 77.

On Music Fit for a Courtesan

*Representations of the Courtesan and Her
Music in Sixteenth-Century Italy*

For modern-day scholars it is hard to differentiate courtesans' music-making from women's musical traditions in general. Dawn De Rycke and Martha Feldman have elaborated on how courtesans' traditions of solo song, though orally transmitted, can be imagined in practice in the absence of a specific musical canon. By contrast, this essay explores courtesans' music and music-making as mediated through several compositional, visual, and poetic repertories that do not transmit the courtesan's voice directly but mediate it through various genres, especially paintings that associate specific musical genres with probable courtesan singers. In the process it confirms claims made by Guido Ruggiero and Courtney Quaintance later in this volume that the social register of Italian courtesans was routinely but ambiguously represented as both "high" and "low," and suggests that courtesans' music-making consisted likewise of an erudite or effete practice of performing markedly "lower" musical genres.

Giacomo Franco's *Habiti d'huomeni et donne venetiane* of 1610 depicts Italian courtesans engaged in various public and private activities. In an illustration entitled "Abito delle cortegiane prencipale" (fig. 7.1), Franco shows a courtesan playing a spinet with a young singer standing to her side. Sporting a fashionable haircut, pearls, and a low-cut dress with sumptuous sleeves, the courtesan distracts the singer from his music book while flaunting the accoutrements of the wealthy. As she performs, she gazes obliquely out of the print, enticing the viewer. Alongside other features, such as a visible *camicia* and discreetly beckoning hand gestures, this glance has been identified by art historian Christine Junkerman as a defining trope in the depiction of courtesans:

> Typically . . . the figure meets the viewer's gaze with a veiled or side-long look, from under partly closed lids, or over the shoulder, or with a strong bend of the head, . . . [she] may almost be said to flirt with a look that is at once direct and hesitant . . . to create a subtle yet unmistakable level of *active* engagement with the viewer and a seductiveness which is not part of standard portraiture.[1]

ABITO DELLE CORTEGIANE PRENCIPALE

FIGURE 7.1. Giacomo Franco, "Abito delle Cortegiane
Prencipale" (1610).

By using the plural "cortegiane," Franco claims that such music-making was endemic to women of the "type" courtesan. The scene appears to be a music lesson, a documented activity of some courtesans, including a purportedly Spanish courtesan living in Rome known as Isabella Ximenes who gave music lessons to a client before consummating sexual relations.[2] Franco's image reproduces neither the keyboard nor her probable hand position accurately, but it pointedly locates the courtesan within sophisticated society, in contrast to the more simply attired singer. The only notated music might well be in the singer's book. If so, the viewer would assume that the musicians perform a solo song for keyboard and voice, quite likely in a semiimprovisatory rendition. Importantly, Franco draws attention to the performative aspect of the scenario by using the courtesan's gaze to titillate the viewer while in the act of music-making. This produces conflicting class information that is central to the in-between, liminal identity of the early modern courtesan. Indeed it prefigures those stylized, sensual images that mix high culture, wealth, and suggested sexual availability constructed by promoters of popular musicians today to market their musical products.

BARBARA SALUTATI AND MACHIAVELLI

Unlike most women of the time, courtesans could forge financially and socially independent lifestyles, and some developed professional careers on the theatrical stage. Barbara Salutati ("La Barbara" or Barbara Fiorentina) built a theatrical career in Florence and was the courtesan-lover of Machiavelli from 1523 until his death in 1527.[3] The sixteenth-century art historian Giorgio Vasari described La Barbara as a "courtesan . . . beloved . . . for her beauty, for her good manners, and particularly for being a great musician and singing divinely,"[4] while Machiavelli himself described her in two letters that document his addition of five new *canzone* to his plays *La Clizia* and *La Mandragola* for proposed revival performances in 1526:

> I have dined these [past] evenings with La Barbara and discussed the comedy, so that she offered to come with her singers to provide the chorus between the acts; and I offered to write canzone suitable for the acts.
>
> She has certain lovers who could be in the way . . . [but I] assure you that she and I have made up our minds to come: we have written five new canzone suitable for the comedy, and they are set to music to be sung between the acts . . . If she is to come, you will need to send your servant here with two or three beasts of burden.[5]

Machiavelli represents La Barbara as a diva who not only demands physical luxuries and high wages for her singing but also contributes to the creative process. By citing "certain lovers who could be in the way," Machiavelli might allude to a social arrangement within courtesan culture by which some courtesans held contracts with customers who paid in installments for weekly services, sometimes with gifts rather than money. The courtesan might have even reserved the right to cancel appointments to meet an important foreigner who would pay a higher fee.[6]

The musical settings of the five canzone that Machiavelli and La Barbara wrote together were composed by Verdelot and survive in manuscript.[7] They are four-voice, homophonic madrigals that are typical of music performed between acts of comic plays at the time, and could easily be realized by performers as extemporized solo songs with instrumental accompaniment.[8] (A solo rendition of the madrigal *O dolce nocte* from *La Mandragola* can be heard on the companion website, track 7.)

In a portrait attributed to Domenico Puligo,[9] La Barbara appears as a *cortigiana onesta*.[10] An open partbook situated near a volume of Petrarch attests to her sophistication. The two visible pieces of music in the partbook include lines from the popular French chanson *J'ayme bien mon amy* on the left-hand page and a portion of an otherwise unknown motet setting of the Latin words "Quam pulcra es amica mea, et quam decora, vox enim tua" on the right-hand page.[11] The French piece, "I love my friend," is stylistically similar to O *dolce nocte*. Voiced in the first person feminine, it illustrates the kind of music La Barbara might have sung on the stage.[12] The Latin piece, "How beautiful you are my love and how lovely your voice," praises the courtesan through ecclesiastical allusion, but attempts to cover up the aspects of her profession deemed sinful by alluding to the Immaculate Conception of Mary. Interestingly, the motet text parallels verses from the Song of Songs used as antiphons at Vespers for the feast of the Immaculate Conception, at least in the fifteenth-century "Sicut lilium" Office compiled by Leonardo Nogarola: "Tota pulchra es Maria, et macula non est in te" and "Vox enim tua dulcis et facies illa tua decora nimis."[13] Moreover, the presence of the words "tota pulchra es" in sixteenth-century religious art signifies Mary as the Virgin of the Immaculate Conception.[14] The doctrine of the Immaculate Conception, that Mary was exempt from the stain of original sin from the first instance of her conception, was not accepted as church dogma until the nineteenth century. It was so controversial in the Papal States that it had even been forbidden to say the words "immaculate" and "conception" one after the other. Importantly, the doctrine does not proclaim that Mary was conceived by means other than human sexual intercourse, but rather that she alone among humans was free of sin from the time her soul was animated, and thus she did not require Christ's redemption. By including an Immaculist Marian reference in the music La Barbara holds, Puligo suggests that La Barbara likewise is neither sinful nor in need of redemption, and that her beauty ("tota pulcra") and sweet voice ("vox enim tua dulcis") are virtues. Indeed, transforming societal ideas of sin into virtues might be considered a prerogative of a *cortigiana onesta* such as La Barbara.

Elements in the background of the painting, such as the tower, suggest the iconography of St. Barbara and further "sanctify" La Barbara.[15] Finally, two Latin inscriptions in the painting extend the iconographic puzzle even further. The first, *meliora latent*, "better hidden," appears on the capital of the pilaster behind La Barbara. This might be seen as the motto of the painting, since Puligo conceals La Barbara's courtesanry by outrageously associating her with the Virgin Mary, as the Immaculate no less. The second Latin inscription, the line "tu, dea, tu praesens nostro succurre labori" from Virgil's *Aeneid*, runs along the front of the desk in the painting and, according to H. Colin Slim, invites the viewer to interpret La Barbara as a "goddess whose beauty and virtue sustain the endeavors of men."[16] Beyond this rich and complex iconographic puzzle, the two musical compositions in the painting juxtapose several dualities: Latin and French, sacred and secular, and church and street culture. By doing so, they delineate the paradoxical social nature of the *cortigiana onesta* as an assemblage of otherwise oppositional high and low cultural traits. La Barbara is at once a courtesan and the Virgin Mary, an opposition perhaps united only by the concept of "virtue."[17] Musically, the portrait associates a courtesan singer-actress with the popular French chanson repertory, and therein points out to a musically literate viewer the type of lighter polyphonic genre a courtesan might adapt for solo singing.

In a contrasting, well-known painting that also contains notated music (fig. 7.2), a young woman dressed elegantly though suggestively wears a bodice on which is inscribed "mal sta ascosto un bel sereno" (it is wrong to hide a beautiful face). Painted

FIGURE 7.2.   Sebastiano Florigerio, *Musical Conversation*. Munich, Alte Pinakothek.

in the mid-sixteenth century by Sebastiano Florigerio, the scene has traditionally been read as an allegory depicting the passage of time, but seems to show musical activity in a brothel as well, or instead.[18] My reading of the scene sees a courtesan, whose elegant dress and jewelry elevate her from the status of a common prostitute, along with her procuress-mother, amid a group of men, one of whom beats out the rhythm of a tactus. The music is Michele Pesenti's four-voice *canzona Alma gentil, s'en voi fusse equalmente*, published about 1520, a composition with a sixteenth-century madrigal text but music of the courtly frottola genre.[19] Here we see the courtesan making music not just for her clients but rather with her clients, in a popular genre generally associated with courts but in this case performed in the realm of the urban populace. Read literally, the image shows two of the men helping the courtesan learn her alto part.[20] Again, music associated with a courtesan in contemporaneous representation comes from the lighter genres that feature homophonic textures easily adaptable to solo singing.

MARCO FACOLI'S COURTESAN RUBRICS

In 1588, Marco Facoli published his *Il secondo libro d'intavolatura di balli d'arpicordo, pass'e mezzi, saltarelli, padouane, et alcuni aeri noui diletteuoli, da cantar, ogni sorte*

TABLE 7.1.   Marco Facoli, *Il secondo libro d'intavolatura di balli d'arpicordo, pass'e mezzi, saltarelli, padouane, et alcuni aeri noui diletteuoli, da cantar, ogni sorte de Rima* (Venice, 1588)

Pass'e mezzo Moderno in Sei modi	Aria della **Marchetta Schiavonetta**
Saltarello del Pass'e mezzo ditto in quattro Modi	Aria della Comedia Novo
Padoana dita la **Marucina**^a	Hor ch'io son gionto quivi
Padoana seconda dita la **Chiareta**	Aria della **Signora Michiela**
Padoana Terza dita la **Finetta**	Aria della **Signora Fior d'Amor**
Padoana Quarta dita **Marchetta** à doi modi	Aria da Cantar Terza Rima
Aria della **Signora Livia**	Napolitane:
Aria della Comedia	S'io m'acorgo ben mio
Aria della **Signora Cinthia**	Deh! Pastorella cara
Aria della **Signora Lucilla**	Tedesche:
Aria della **Marchetta Saporita**	La Proficia
Aria della **Signora Moretta**	L'Austria
Aria della **Signora Ortensia**	

^a Boldface mine.

de rima, a volume in which many of the titles of the short keyboard pieces bear the names of female characters, all purportedly courtesans, such as "Aria della Signora Ortensia" (see table 7.1). The collection contains a mixture of conventional dance pieces and lighter vocal compositions, some with the text removed. Some of these pieces may have been sung, but most would simply have been played on the harpsichord.[21] *Balli* were typically danced by amateurs in courtly settings, although the term became associated with theatrical entertainments, including *intermedi* and plays.[22] Collections such as Facoli's, however, were not necessarily used as dance accompaniments, but, if compared with music prints today, would have functioned like fakebooks or piano-vocal arrangements of selections from musicals intended for private rather than public performance. Using the keyboard arrangements in such a print, individuals could perform at home the dance and popular tunes they had heard at a theater or other musical venue, or simply have raw material for private musical entertainment.[23]

Scholars including Nino Pirrotta and Berthe Dedoyard, using work of the Paduan literato and philosopher Sperone Speroni as evidence, have recognized the *signore* and *marchette* named in the titles of thirteen of Facoli's pieces as references to courtesans.[24] Perhaps the titles refer to the (stage) names of specific actresses, some of whom were courtesans, as it seems they frequently adopted characteristic names, including Lucrezia, Isabella, Laura, Faustina, Giulia, Ortensia, Tullia, Livia, Cinthia, and Chiara.[25] Some of the names in Facoli's titles might also derive from sixteenth-century *commedie erudite*, including those of Livia from Aretino's *La cortigiana*, Lucilla from Aretino's *Talanta*, Cinthia, an *en travesti* role in Giambattista della Porta's *Cinthia*, and Ortensia, a stock courtesan character in the commedia dell'arte.[26] As seen in table 1, two of the pieces in Facoli's collection are specifically identified as tunes from the commedia dell'arte, as they are titled "aria della commedia" and "aria della commedia novo." Courtesans and other musicians, of course, feature prominently in the early iconography of the commedia dell'arte, and again this evidence points to a connection between courtesans, music-making, and the theater. The case for associating these brief pieces with courtesans is strengthened by Facoli's inclusion of several villanelle arranged for solo keyboard. Known also as the *napolitano* owing to its origins as a popular song in Neapolitan dialect, this lighter genre, usually performed by several singers together in a homophonic texture but also adaptable to solo singing, is unlikely to represent the music-making of a noblewoman but is stylistically consistent with the music that courtesans probably sang.[27]

Pirrotta took Facoli's collection to be an assemblage of the favorite tunes of individual courtesans.[28] Given that Facoli writes out different ornaments in different pieces, they could represent individual performing styles as well. However, as the tunes are otherwise not significantly differentiated from each other, I prefer to see them collectively as keyboard reductions representing the types of tunes courtesans sang, possibly on stage.[29] Each of Facoli's pieces ends with a virtuosic instrumental *ripresa*, an unusual feature in the *ballo* repertory. As the instrumentalist's role shifts from unobtrusive accompanist to solo virtuoso, the singer-actress seems to be given time to leave the stage, or at least pose onstage. If these pieces were originally conceived as purely instrumental compositions without reference to or accommodation of theatrical conventions, they would probably not include such incongruent codas, which can clearly be seen on the written page as stylistically distinct (ex. 7.1). Furthermore, a collection that characterized specific noblewomen almost certainly would not have included songs from the commedia dell'arte or villanelle.

Facoli's collection, though comprising dances, should not be considered only as representative of dance tunes, as some of them follow formulaic patterns for singing popular literary forms of the day. They might best be called sung dance or danced song.[30] Facoli's "Aria da cantar terza rima" constitutes yet another example of the untexted version of the genre of *modi* or *aeri* (*arie*) discussed by Martha Feldman (chap. 4) and Dawn De Rycke (chap. 5). Courtesans could have utilized the titled *aria* to extemporize musical settings of their clients' poetry on the spot, and because their musical phrase lengths correspond to conventional poetic meters most of them could also have been used as vehicles for semi-improvisation. Thus like the portrait of La Barbara, Marco Facoli's keyboard pieces illuminate courtesans' music-making by connecting stereotyped courtesan names, lighter musical genres, a theatrical context, and conventions of solo singing, the last involving ornamentation practices and vehicles for improvisation.

BANCHIERI'S MADRIGAL COMEDY

My final example, and the latest in historical time, is drawn from an early seventeenth-century satirical work. Adriano Banchieri's madrigal comedy *Barco di Venetia per Padova*, first published in 1605 and revised in 1623, synthesizes the various aspects of courtesans' music-making that I have discussed, including improvisation, lighter genres, and theatrical settings. The *Barco di Venetia* depicts a courtesan in the act of improvising an *ottava rima* and *risposta* with her suitor.[31] In this sometimes earthy satire, the courtesan's music is located in improvisatory and popular genres, and her earthy, humorous text reinforces commonly repeated biographical details of the stereotypical courtesan. Even though the work is parodic and its courtesan characters

EXAMPLE 7.1. Marco Facoli, *Aria della Signora Ortensia*, mm. 1–20.

are derived from popular stereotypes, I maintain that Banchieri's representation of courtesans' music-making nonetheless contains elements separable from its satiric content.

En route by boat from Venice to Padua, Banchieri's characters decide to pass the time by making music.[32] Among the travelers from various regions and cultural backgrounds are two courtesans, Ninetta and Rizzolina. While Ninetta is a minor character who does little but flirt with sailors and might be better described as a *meretrice* or *donna da bene* (roughly "whore"), Rizzolina associates with the gentlemen travelers rather than the laborers, and flaunts poetic and musical skills that Ninetta doesn't seem to have.

EXAMPLE 7.1. (*continued*)

   She is also Banchieri's most developed character. The name "Rizzolina" is derived from the commedia dell'arte character "Riciulina." Of the work's twenty numbers, Rizzolina sings four. In her first appearance she exclaims, following madrigals in the avant-garde style of Gesualdo, "non più, di grazia, simil Madrigali!" (no more madrigals like these, please). Immediately she introduces herself with a popular song, a villanella, the text of which pays compliment to her sexual and musical virtuosity. Thus while her proficiencies are extolled, her social standing is brought down by humor and musical preferences alleged to be her own, as she rejects erudite, courtly, avant-garde madrigals in favor of popular song.
   Yet despite her bawdy language, intended as entertainment within the play as the characters pass their time, as well as for the entertainment of the audience, Rizzolina is represented as a character worthy of respect. Following performances of madrigals in the styles of Marenzio and Spano, Rizzolina improvises her *ottava rima* as a singer would extemporize poetry within the boundaries of an *aria* or *modo*. Banchieri informs us that the passengers "enjoyed and paid great attention to" this music, which stylistically is also a villanella, the lighter polyphonic vocal genre popular from the 1530s into the early seventeenth century. The accompaniment consists of four other voices imitating the sound of the lute using syllables that allude comically to drunken passengers who speak German: "trinc tin tin" for the soprano, "trenc ten ten" for the alto, and "tronc" for the tenor and bass. The text follows the strambotto form (abababcc), which, like the villanella, was popularly cultivated decades before Banchieri. As Rizzolina "improvises," her hendecasyllabic text finishes a note before her musical phrase does, as if to suggest that she "messes up" a bit. Thus it literalizes an act of improvisation, as she needs to extemporize either by resinging

EXAMPLE 7.2. "Rizzolina canta e Orazio suona il lauto." Melodic excerpt, mm. 1–11, from Adriano Banchieri, *Barco di Venetia per Padova.*

the penultimate syllable or by slurring into the final pitch (ex. 7.2). Subsequently she adopts this motive at the end of each phrase, perhaps to show that her "mistake" was planned, even though the text underlay will sound awkward. She neither ornaments her melody nor continues with another verse. Her suitor's subsequent *risposta* draws upon her improvised frame by repeating her melody, the final rhyme of each of her lines, and the awkward text underlay.

Io mi recordo quando fui bambina	a	I remember when I was a little girl
Che la mia mamma mi facea carezze	b	That my Mama would caress me
E mi dicea: bella Rizzolina,	a	And said to me, "Pretty Rizzolina,
Se non par d'or quelle tue blonde trezze!	b	Aren't your blond tresses pure gold!"
Con le compagne poi sera e mattina	a	With partners then from dusk to dawn
Facea l'amor con lor ch'erano avezze	b	I would make love with those used to it,
Et imparai sì bene a far l'amore	c	And mastered the art of making love so well
Ch'à mill'amanti il dì rubavo il core.	c	That I stole the hearts of a thousand lovers a day.[33]

Rizzolina's text reinforces tropes that are stereotypical but whose basis lies in historical fact, including the relationship between the courtesan mother and her daughters. Banchieri tells us that Rizzolina's mother considered her a commodity even as a child. This corresponds to evidence that courtesan mothers sometimes introduced their daughters to courtesanry at the age of twelve or thirteen, and acted as procuresses who collected fees directly.[34] For example, Veronica Franco was the daughter of a courtesan and entered the profession while still living at home. Indeed a young girl's virginity was sometimes sold by her mother repeatedly to different clients for exorbitant prices. As for the blond tresses, comic prints show both courtesans and noblewomen bleaching their hair on sunny days using mirrors.

While Banchieri's text is for the comic stage and is not directly representative of the texts courtesans would actually have improvised in private spaces, the poetic form and style of music probably is. In his parodies of madrigals, Banchieri retains the musical and textual styles of his models, but exaggerates their poetic and syntactic conceits. When Rizzolina sings a madrigal in imitation of the composer Radesca, for example, her text mocks Petrarchan clichés:

Voi dite esser di foco	You say you are on fire,
E tutta ghiaccio sete.	And you are all ice.
Onde mai si trovò gelido ardore?	Wherever was such frozen passion found?

FIGURE 7.3. Giacomo Franco, "In questa maniera la state . . ." (1610).

Ah che mai non potete	Ah, you cannot possibly be on
Foco esser voi che tutta ghiaccio sete.	Fire, you who are all ice.

The fact that Rizzolina mocks Petrarchan verse in a comedy does not mean that composers were no longer writing music at the turn of the seventeenth century using straightforward Petrarchan tropes. We do witness Rizzolina presenting herself as a musically adept prostitute able to "ennoble" herself through musical performance and appearance, but going only as far as she can while still remaining "fun" for her suitors. The truth behind Banchieri's satire might also be glimpsed though his musical imitations of Marenzio and Gesualdo, which string together exaggerated though signifying clichés of their styles. Banchieri's one-dimensional verse lacks the subtleties of Petrarch, much as his courtesan characters lack the complexity of the true and venerated *cortigiana onesta*. Nonetheless, Rizzolina flaunts improvisational prowess in poetry and music utilizing lighter musical genres, a scenario that seems to translate historical reality into comedy.

In Banchieri's comedy, Rizzolina performs in public, and without the expectation of remuneration. Most representations of courtesan musicians, particularly paintings of courtesans playing the lute, imply a private space, while also suggesting a hidden clientele.[35] In prints, courtesans look out of windows at their suitors in the street below, and in sensuous half-length portraits, they appear suggestively disheveled in their boudoirs. In a stunning parallel to the *Barca*, Giacomo Franco depicts courtesan musicians performing chamber music on a large gondola in the Venetian lagoon (fig. 7.3). In this scene of Venetian water music, the women playing harpsichord, lute, and possibly a wind instrument behind the harpsichord are labeled as courtesans, and are joined by men playing wind and string instruments. Franco's image, like his illustration of the courtesan playing the keyboard, portrays courtesans as elements of "high" culture. While Banchieri-style earthy humor might color the revelers' conversation in the front-center gondola, the performing musicians lend an air of refinement to the scene. Are all of the women in the picture courtesans, or do noblewomen retreat in the covered gondolas? Is this mixed-gender ensemble amateur, or does it include professional women musicians, among them courtesans?[36]

Representations in various media, including visual art, instrumental music, and madrigal comedy, viewed together with supporting evidence, locate the courtesan along various axes of music-making. The courtesan, while retaining a refined appearance and cultivating musical talents as assets, uses her profession to extend the boundaries of music-making experienced by the noblewoman and draws praise from her audience. Representations associate her with lighter, secular genres, including the villanella, canzona, chanson, and semi-improvisational forms for extemporizing musical settings of poetry that would appeal to a greater range of listeners than avant-garde music would. The images, accounts, and compositions considered here reinforce the sense that music-making formed a significant aspect of a courtesan's identity. It shows, too, that inquiry into their musical practices can provide clues to understanding how courtesans assimilated elements of high and low culture to thrive within their own distinct milieu in early modern Italy.

Notes

1. Anne Christine Junkerman, "Bellissima Donna: An Interdisciplinary Study of Venetian Sensuous Half Length Images of the Early Sixteenth Century" (Ph.D. diss., University of California at Berkeley, 1988), 38–39.

2. Monika Kurzel-Runtscheiner, *Töchter der Venus: Die Kurtisanen Roms in 16. Jahrhundert* (Munich: C. H. Beck, 1995), 90. Presumably the music lesson was part of a package of services Ximenes offered her client.

3. H. Colin Slim, "A Motet for Machiavelli's Mistress and a Chanson for a Courtesan," in *Essays Presented to Myron P. Gilmore* (Florence: La Nuova Italia, 1978), 457–72. This essay has been reprinted in H. Colin Slim, *Painting Music in the Sixteenth Century: Essays in Iconography* (Aldershot: Ashgate, 2002), same pagination.

4. Giorgio Vasari, *Le vite de' più eccellenti pittori, scrittori e architetti*, 13 vols. (1568; Florence: Felice Le Monnier, 1846–57), 8:134.

5. H. Colin Slim, *A Gift of Madrigals and Motets* (Chicago and London: University of Chicago Press, 1972), 93. The first letter is dated October 20, 1525; the second, January 3, 1526. La Barbara's status as lover, courtesan, and author can be provocatively read alongside Jane Tylus's recent interpretation of *La Mandragola* as a staging both of feminine empowerment and rape that challenged mores of sixteenth-century society. See Jane Tylus, "Theater and Its Social Uses: Machiavelli's *Mandragola* and the Spectacle of Infamy," *Renaissance Quarterly* 53 (2000): 656–86.

6. Kurzel-Runtscheiner, *Töchter der Venus*, 157.

7. Newberry Library Case MS.-VM1578.M91, edited in Slim, *A Gift of Madrigals*.

8. On musical traditions in Italian theater of the time, see Nino Pirrotta and Elena Povoledo, *Music and Theatre from Poliziano to Monteverdi*, trans. Karen Eales (Cambridge:

Cambridge University Press, 1982). A transcription of Verdelot's O *dolce nocte* appears in Slim, *A Gift of Madrigals*, 333–35.

9. Puligo's painting resides in a private collection in Salisbury, England and was not able to be reproduced in this essay. Nonetheless, it is published in two readily available sources: Bernard Berenson, *Italian Pictures of the Renaissance: Florentine School*, 2 vols. (London: Phaidon, 1963), 2, pl. 1414; and H. Colin Slim, "A Motet for Machiavelli's Mistress," pl. 1, both pages unnumbered.

10. On the *cortigiana onesta* see Margaret F. Rosenthal, *The Honest Courtesan: Veronica Franco, Citizen and Writer in Sixteenth-Century Venice* (Chicago: University of Chicago Press, 1992).

11. Slim, "A Motet for Machiavelli's Mistress," 459. Slim recognized the identity of the French chanson and the reference to the Song of Songs, but did not connect them to the Immaculate Conception.

12. The full first stanza of the chanson is: "J'ayme bien mon amy / De bonne amour certaine / Car je scay bien qu'il m'ayme / Et aussi faictz je luy" (I love my friend with a good true love because I know well that he loves me and I do also him.)

13. I consulted the "Sicut lilium" office in numerous eighteenth-century liturgical prints, including the revised *Breviarium Romanum* (Madrid: De Mena, 1767). This is one of several offices used for the celebration in the sixteenth century, which was not recognized by the Universal Church at the time. Whether or not Puligo directly refers to this office, the "pulchra es" is enough to suggest Immaculist allusion. See *The Dogma of the Immaculate Conception: History and Significance*, ed. Edward Dennis O'Connor (Notre Dame, IN: University of Notre Dame Press, 1959), and Bonnie J. Blackburn, "The Virgin in the Sun: Music and Image for a Prayer Attributed to Sixtus IV," *Journal of the Royal Musical Association* 124 (1999): 157–95. Note that the Immaculate Conception of Mary does not refer to the conception of Christ. This was never a controversy for the Church. The issue at stake was not whether St. Anne (Mary's mother) was a virgin, but rather whether Mary was free of the sin of Adam and Eve from the moment her soul was animated by God, which could occur after physical conception. Deniers of the doctrine claimed that as she was a human, Mary's sin was redeemed by Christ.

14. For an introduction to the "tota pulchra" Immaculate Conception tradition in painting, see Suzanne L. Stratton, *The Immaculate Conception in Spanish Art* (Cambridge: Cambridge University Press, 1994), 39–45. Such images were painted or printed throughout Roman Catholic Europe, but with particular vitality in Spain and Spanish America.

15. On recognizing courtesan subjects through iconographic evidence, see Anne Christine Junkerman, "The Lady and the Laurel: Gender and Meaning in Giorgione's *Laura*," *Oxford Art Journal* 16 (1993): 49–58; David Rosand, "Venereal Hermeneutics: Reading Titian's *Venus of Urbino*," in *Renaissance Society and Culture: Essays in Honor of Eugene F. Rice, Jr.*, ed. John Monfasani and Ronald G. Musto (Ithaca: Cornell University Press, 1971), 263–80; and Eric Jan Sluijter, "Emulating Sensual Beauty: Representation of Danaë from Gossaert to Rembrandt," *Simiolus* 27 (1999): 4–45.

16. Slim, "A Motet for Machiavelli's Mistress," 461. My reading of the iconography is primarily based upon Slim's, although he does not directly attach it to La Barbara's status as a courtesan.

17. On the concept of the "virtuosa" see Fredericka H. Jacobs, *Defining the Renaissance Virtuosa: Women Artists and the Language of Art History and Criticism* (Cambridge: Cambridge University Press, 1997); and for *virtù* see Ruggiero in this volume, chap. 15.

18. Volker Scherliess, *Musikalische Noten auf Kunstwerken der italienischen Renaissance* (Hamburg: Musikalienhandlung Karl Dieter Wagner, 1972); Iain Fenlon, "Music in Italian Renaissance Painting," in *Companion to Medieval and Renaissance Music*, ed. Tess Knighton

and David Fallows (Berkeley: University of California Press, 1997), 189–210; and H. Colin Slim, "Two Paintings of 'Concert Scenes' from the Veneto and the Morgan Library's Unique Music Print of 1520," in *In Cantu et in Sermone for Nino Pirrotta on His 80th Birthday*, ed. Fabrizio Della Seta and Franco Piperno (Florence: Leo S. Olschki, 1989), 155–74. Only Fenlon connects the image with a brothel.

19. Walter H. Rubsamen, "From Frottola to Madrigal: The Changing Pattern of Secular Italian Vocal Music," in *Chanson & Madrigal: Studies in Comparison and Contrast*, ed. James Haar (Cambridge, Mass.: Harvard University Press, 1964), 51–72 and 172–242, at 67 and 213–18 (music).

20. This is my interpretation. Slim notes that this is the alto partbook, even though it uses the tenor clef. Possibly, the older woman represents an art patron outside the scene rather than a participant in the scene, as was a common practice.

21. Marco Facoli, *Collected Works*, ed. Willi Apel, Corpus of Early Keyboard Music, vol. 2 ([n.p.]: American Institute of Musicology, 1963). An incomplete edition is Marco Facoli, *Balli d'Arpicordo 1588*, ed. Friedrich Cerha, Diletto Musicale, no. 298 (Vienna: Doblinger, 1973).

22. Ingrid Brainard, "Ballo," *The New Grove Dictionary of Music and Musicians*, 2d ed., ed. Stanley Sadie, 29 vols. (London: Macmillan, 2001), 2:605–07.

23. The religious suppression of public theaters in Venice during the 1580s and 1590s may have created a market for collections of theatrical compositions that could be adapted to private amateur performances. See, for example, Gerolamo Priuli's diary entry of May 23, 1607, quoted in David Chambers and Brian Pullan, *Venice: A Documentary History, 1450–1630* (Oxford: Blackwell, 1992), 383–84.

24. Nino Pirrotta, "Commedia dell'Arte and Opera," *Musical Quarterly* 41 (1955): 305–24, and Berthe Dedoyard, "Des Musiques pour arpicordo de Marco Facoli à la découverte d'un testament inconnu," *Revue belge de musicologie* 41 (1987): 63–74.

25. Kurzel-Runtscheiner, *Töchter der Venus*. For example, she discusses fourteen courtesans named Lucrezia. Certain courtesan names were associated with specific cities—Lucrezia, for example, with Rome.

26. Douglas Radcliffe-Umstead, *The Birth of Modern Comedy in Renaissance Italy* (Chicago: University of Chicago Press, 1969).

27. An interesting literary parallel to Facoli's pieces is the fourth book of letters of Andrea Calmo, a playwright and early exponent of the commedia dell'arte. Each of them is addressed to a courtesan "Signora" with a fictitious though stereotyped name. Pirrotta, "Commedia dell'Arte," 309.

28. Ibid., 308.

29. The fact that some tunes are not ornamented is not necessarily problematic, according to Howard Mayer Brown, *Embellishing Sixteenth-Century Music* (London: Oxford University Press, 1976), 64, who claims that most instrumentalists but only some singers were skilled enough to ornament their music.

30. See also James Haar, *Essays on Italian Poetry and Music in the Renaissance, 1350–1600* (Berkeley: University of California Press, 1986), chap. 4.

31. Adriano Banchieri, *Barco di Venezia per Padova* (Rome: De Santis, 1969), and idem, *Barco di Venezia per Padova (Venezia, 1605)*, ed. Filomena A. DeLuca (Bologna: Ut Orpheus, 1998). Several commercial recordings are available.

32. Martha Wieand Farahat, "Adriano Banchieri and the Madrigal Comedy" (Ph.D. diss., University of Chicago, 1991). Farahat overlooks the role of courtesan characters in Banchieri's works.

33. Translations mine.

34. Kurzel-Runtscheiner, *Töchter der Venus*, 27–44.

35. Much has been written about images of lute-playing women, often believed to be courtesans. See, for example, H. Colin Slim, "Multiple Images of Bartolomeo Veneto's Lute-Playing Woman (1520)," in *Renaissance Cities and Courts: Studies in Honor of Lewis Lockwood,* ed. Jessie Ann Owens and Anthony M. Cummings (Warren, Mich.: Harmonie Park Press, 1997), 405–19.

36. Anthony Newcomb, "Courtesans, Muses, or Musicians? Professional Women Musicians in Sixteenth-Century Italy," in *Women Making Music: The Western Art Tradition 1150–1950,* ed. Jane Bowers and Judith Tick (Urbana: University of Illinois Press, 1986), 90–115.

PART III

POWER, GENDER, AND THE BODY

Royalty's Courtesans and God's Mortal Wives

Keepers of Culture in Precolonial India

The Indian courtesan pervades precolonial art, literature, mythology, texts on rituals, polity, pleasure, and law books in the three major religions founded on Indian soil. Yet as much as she captivates, she also eludes. Why? Because her actions, her character, her mystique, are relayed to us by outsiders to her world, or to traditional India. Her own voice has remained faint until fairly modern times. This essay introduces different voices that describe the Indian courtesan over a vast stretch of history. What becomes clear is that two options for power were open to the precolonial Indian woman: that of the sexually liberated and educated courtesan or the pure, sexually controlled, uneducated wife.

THE WIFE/COURTESAN DICHOTOMY

Abbé Dubois, a French missionary who lived and worked in India from 1792 to 1823, made up his mind that the cultivated Indian female existed, but she was not the Indian wife:

> A young girl's mind remains totally uncultivated though many of them have good abilities. In fact, what use would learning or accomplishments be to women who are still in such a state of domestic degradation and servitude? All that a Hindu woman need know is how to grind and boil rice and look after her household affairs which are neither numerous nor difficult to manage. Courtesans, whose business in life is to dance in the temples and at public ceremonies, and prostitutes, are the only women who are allowed to learn to read, sing or dance.

The Abbé's observations are corroborated by a contemporary Indian, Abdul Halim Sharar. In his history of the north Indian kingdom of Awadh, Sharar notes that it was the courtesans who sustained the high culture at Lucknow, the kingdom's capital. They kept alive the distinctive manners of Lucknow society and were instrumental in the development of Kathak dance and Hindustani music.[1]

I am prompted to cite these two testimonies by far more than a need to document the cultivated nature of courtesans in early nineteenth-century India. The Abbé's observations pertain to southern, or peninsular, India. His description of southern Indian mores is contained in his book *Hindu Manners, Customs, and Ceremonies;*[2] the operative word is "Hindu." Sharar, a novelist and journalist, wrote about the Muslim kingdom of Awadh in north India. These two observers, living and working in contrasting religious spheres at considerable geographic distance from each other, both imagined the courtesan as the keeper of culture. This overarching theme describes the courtesan not only of the precolonial period but also of prior ages.

Were all courtesans in India cultivated? Of course not. There were courtesans and prostitutes, as Abbé Dubois noted, and throughout Indian history specific Sanskrit terms were used to highlight distinctions between them.[3] The exceptionally civilized public woman, proficient in arts and endowed with winsome qualities, is called a *gaṇikā*. A *veśyā*, or specifically a woman called a *rūpajīvā*, is a prostitute, ranked below the *gaṇikā*, whose artistic talents she does not possess. A very low-grade prostitute (a "whore") is a *puṃścalī*, and a prostitute who is a slave is a *dāsī*, such as a *kumbhadāsī*, a "pots-and-pans" prostitute consigned to the most menial of tasks. A temple dancer, or religious courtesan, is called a *devadāsī*. The institution of the *devadāsī* can be traced in India from the third century B.C.[4] until it was finally outlawed in 1947. Unless otherwise stated, this essay concentrates on the *gaṇikā*, a secular courtesan, often associated with a royal court,[5] and the *devadāsī*, the temple courtesan, dedicated to the temple as god's mortal wife.

As may already be surmised, Indians liked nothing better than to name and classify, and this predilection extends to listing the arts that a *gaṇikā* should master. The *Kāmasūtra*, composed sometime between the early Christian era and the fourth and fifth centuries A.D., is perhaps the best-known source on courtesans and prostitutes of ancient India. Being a text with aphoristic rules on sexual relations between men and women, it devotes one section, part VI, to the courtesan (*veśyā*). Herein, the legendary author, Vātsyāyana, advises the courtesan to be skilled in the sixty-four arts that define a cultured person.[6] He lists them all and the list is daunting. Topping it are singing, playing on musical instruments, dancing, writing, drawing. Picture-making, trimming, and decorating are also to be studied. Some unexpected skills include knowledge of magic, tailoring, carpentry, architecture, chemistry, minerology, cock-, quail-, and ram-fighting, rules of society, and how to pay respects and compliments to others. In the aggregate, the sixty-four arts form a remarkable portrait of the civilized and knowledgeable elite in society. In fact, the text states this by saying that when the *veśyā* is proficient in these arts, and imbued with beauty, politeness, and virtue, she becomes a *gaṇikā*, and "receives a seat of honour in the assembly of men"; that is, she can discourse with men as their equal. The *Kāmasūtra* goes further: "She is moreover always respected by the king, and praised by learned men and her favour being sought for by all, she becomes an object of universal regard."[7]

Molding the sexualized female into a courtesan of character preceded the account in the *Kāmasūtra*. The *Arthaśāstra*, a text on Indian polity dating perhaps to the first or second century A.D. but containing information that may go back as far as the third century B.C., discusses the *gaṇikā*'s education because the state is to invest in her training and to profit from her success. *Gaṇikās*, *dāsīs*, and actresses are to be

FIGURE 8.1. One side of double-faced relief possibly depicting the courtesan Vasantasena (Kushan Period, 2nd century A.D).

taught singing, playing on instruments like the *vīṇā*, pipe, and drum, reciting, dancing, acting, writing, painting, reading the thoughts of others, manufacturing scents and garlands, shampooing, and the art of attracting and captivating the mind of others. The text proposes that the state bear the cost of this education and directly employ the recipients; in effect, the *gaṇikā* of the *Arthaśāstra* is to turn over her earnings to the state and to receive, besides the accoutrements of a glamorous lifestyle, a monthly salary from the king's treasury.[8] The *gaṇikā* in the play entitled *The Little Clay Cart* epitomizes the educated courtesan: independent, wealthy—and generous (see fig. 8.1).[9]

Her rigorous education can be inferred by the fact that she speaks Sanskrit whereas the others cannot, not even a brahman recently dragged into poverty. Her taste in architecture and the decorative arts is opulent and self-assured, as a visit to her mansion in act 4 of the play demonstrates. The mansion is preceded by eight courts. *Gaṇikā*s strolling through the third court have picture-boards in hand that are covered with all manner of scenes.[10] The fourth court reveals courtesans being trained in the arts of singing, dancing, playing musical instruments, and performing erotic plays. A visitor entering this court is amazed:

Oh, oh, oh! The drums are thundering like rain clouds under the hands of young
women. Brass cymbals are falling like the stars that fall from heaven when their
merit is exhausted, and the reed flute sighs sweetly like the humming of honey bees.
There with a blow of the hand a *vīṇā* is made to run like a mistress enraged by her
lover's jealous querulousness. And there the courtesans of the first degree, singing
sweetly like honey bees drunk with the attar of flowers, are dancing, and plays are
rehearsed, love plays all.[11]

Though none of the texts cited thus far (with the exception of that in n. 4) furnishes
an objective, historical account, each contains overlapping information regarding
the cultivated courtesan, indicating thereby that they may bear some semblance to
reality in these early periods. The *Viṣṇudharmottara Purāṇa*, a bit later, touches on
the connection between courtesans and painting.[12] It alludes to the way courtesans
(the *veśyā*) should be depicted in paintings; their proportions and their manner of attire ("flamboyant and erotic") are specified in III.43.24–25. The cumulative evidence
from these various sources has prompted one scholar to suggest that courtesans both
practiced (perhaps "dabbled in" would be more accurate) and fostered Indian fresco
paintings of the pre-medieval periods.[13] I would add that they also appeared in the
genre.[14]

Temple courtesans, *devadāsīs*, can also be traced back to early times. The third-
century B.C. Jogīmārā Inscription in Central India is perhaps the first to mention
a *devadāsī*. The lettering is engraved inside a cave and underneath paintings that
cover the vault of the cave.[15] And the *Arthaśāstra* says that when the temple service
of *devadāsīs* is finished, they can take up spinning (2.23.2). According to Desai's reading of the few available literary and travel accounts from about the eighth to twelfth
centuries A.D., the likely services these girls gave to the temple were singing, dancing,
and sexual gratification.[16]

In sum, the areas wherein literature claims that the secular and temple courtesans excelled during the first millenium A.D. appear to be the same as those they still
excelled in towards the end of the second millenium, when the Abbé Dubois made
his observations. The dichotomy he observed between the cultivated public woman
and the domestic wife is founded on customs long prevalent in traditional India. For
example, the *Kāmasūtra* has a separate section about the wife (part IV) that precedes
and contrasts notably with the section on the courtesan. Until colonial times, there
does seem to have been a split between females who are keepers of culture and females
who are keepers of the home.[17] The former are considered to be unmarried, unchaste,
attached to a matrilineal kin group, economically independent, and educated to a degree; the latter are recognized as being married, chaste, embedded in a patrilineal kin
group upon which the wife is economically dependent, and uneducated in spheres
unrelated to the home.[18] Whether, through the ages, this situation has a significant or
insignificant basis in reality depends upon how much credence one gives to literary
sources and traditional treatises on polity, law, love, the arts, and so forth, which may
express theoretical ideals or criteria more than factual realities.[19]

One such treatise, *The Law Book of Manu*, dating to around the second century
A.D., warns the virtuous on the evils of the virtueless: "Drinking (spirituous liquor),
associating with wicked people, separation from the husband, rambling abroad, sleeping (at unseasonable hours), and dwelling in other men's houses, are the six causes

of the ruin of women."[20] The evils *Manu* cites—drinking, promiscuity, and inattentiveness to the home—are infractions that narrow the gap between the world of the wife and that of the courtesan. These are, however, symptoms, not causes, of the dichotomy between wife and courtesan, just as education is symptomatic of a far greater divide. The apparent contrast between domestic degradation and urbane cultivation noted by the Abbé obscured the fact that the Hindu wife, confined though she was, had status in his day and throughout the first and second millennia A.D., according to traditional law. The same *Law of Manu* reveals the basis of her stature in a male-dominated society: "He who carefully guards his wife, preserves (the purity of) his offspring, virtuous conduct, his family, himself, and his (means of acquiring) merit" (*dharma*).[21] This passage recognizes that, from the point of view of the male, a married woman's power is her sexual purity. The commentator, who takes "*dharma*" as "religion" in the above verse, views an "unchaste woman" as one not "entitled to being associated in the performance of religious rites. For these reasons, if a man guards his wife, he preserves all these."[22] Herein lies the fundamental difference between the wife and courtesan, no matter how civilized the latter may be. Because of the bride's (or wife's) sexual purity, the husband knows his offspring are his, and the family he rears can maintain the necessary traditions that bring merit to his lineage: "As the male is to whom a wife cleaves, even so is the son whom she brings forth; let him therefore carefully guard his wife, in order to keep his offspring pure."[23]

To lead a traditional Hindu life, it is essential to be married and carry out familial obligations. The role of the wife is to continue the family line and enable it to perform life-cycle ceremonies. Upon these depend the social and religious merit (*dharma*) of the family. The traditional outlook was to consider only the virgin as marriageable. Since a woman was thought to be naturally libidinous, the unmarried girl, after puberty, needed to be guarded by the parents;[24] after marriage, the job passed on to the husband. Only the pure wife could prepare food for the family and cook the balls of rice offered in the all-important ancestor rites (*śrāddha*). Ideally, the legitimate son born out of a sanctified marriage could perform the *śrāddha* rites for the family's ancestors; if these rites were not done it was believed that at least three generations of ancestors would find no peace in the afterlife.[25] Traditional Hindu life is punctuated by other mandated life-cycle rites (*saṁskāras*),[26] which depend upon the proper behavior and actions of the wife, so that she may help her husband in performing domestic rituals.[27] Though familial rites revolve mainly around the male, the husband and/or sons, a wife is needed who is qualified to enable traditional rites, values, and social customs to survive. And survive they have. The *śrāddha* rite, still practiced today, goes back to ancient Hinduism; the same can be said of the *saṁskāras* and domestic rituals. The indispensable need for the sexual purity of the wife should have been her source of power for over two millennia—beginning sometime within the first millennium B.C. (with the formulation of the ancient Hindu rites, which were subsequently enshrined as duties in the theoretical law book of *Manu*), and continuing into contemporary times, as research conducted in the late twentieth century shows.[28] The basic dichotomy, in short, between the wife and the courtesan rests on the opposition between the keeper of the (pure) lineage and the keeper of culture, and this divide seems to describe the bookends of diametrically opposed realms of power open to the Indian female up to the colonial period and beyond.

It may surprise the Western reader that a cultivated courtesan could wield so much power and prestige throughout the millennia. The high regard accorded her in the *Kāmasūtra*, noted above, hints in that direction,[29] as do other literary works. In a Sanskrit farce attributed to King Mahendravarman I, who ruled in south India at the beginning of the seventh century A.D., the *gaṇikā* and her entourage are not the butt of ridicule; rather it is the ascetic brahman.[30] In Somadeva's eleventh-century work, *The Ocean of Story*, a tale called "King Vikramāditya and the Courtesan" recounts how Madanamālā's sensuality and magnanimity capture the heart of a king; but what prompts him to ask her to live with him is her loyalty, constancy, and selfless love for him.[31] Just as the power of the wife stems from the traditional values, customs, myths, and fantasies embedded in pan-Indic norms, so too do those of the courtesan. In the few instances where records reflecting the courtesan's thinking exist, a perspective becomes apparent which is quite different from the one revealed in traditional sources. Many ancient (and contemporary) societies considered the sexually awakened female as both auspicious and dangerous. The second section of this essay indicates that the Indian tradition had three archetypes so considered: the *gaṇikā*, the *devadāsī*, and the wife. This situation lasted until colonial times, when India was ruled by foreigners whose norms and codes were so different from those of traditional India that the latter lost ground. Then the courtesan's power was broken and her sphere of cultivation passed onto the virtuous wife and her daughters.

THE POWER OF THE SEXUALIZED FEMALE

Courtesans, especially the *gaṇikā* and *devadāsī*, had extraordinary customers. Kings and brahmans have already been mentioned. These are men from the two highest castes. Brahmans belong to the top, or priestly, caste, emphasizing learning, especially ritual knowledge; kings and lesser royalty formed the second, or ruling caste. Fact, fantasy, ritual exigencies, and poetic license all lead various sources to recount other, unusual paramours of courtesans as well.

An ascetic (*brahmacārin*) cavorts with a low-grade courtesan (*puṃścalī*) in an ancient Hindu (i.e., Vedic) ritual, the *Mahāvrata*, which probably celebrated the winter solstice. A *brahmacārin* is a high-born student of Vedic sacred knowledge; during the years of his studentship he is supposed to live a life of sexual abstinence. In one part of the *Mahāvrata* rite, the *brahmacārin* must exchange obscene insults with the whore. The *puṃścalī* cries to him: "you who have misbehaved! who have violated your vow of continence!," to which the *brahmacārin* answers: "shame upon you, depraved one! harlot! who washes off the village community, who washes off man's member!"[32] The sexual jibes may substitute for the act itself, for this part of the rite was supposed to promote fertility.[33] The procreative benefit resulting from an ascetic's encounter with a seductive female is a frequent motif in Indian mythology.[34] The seduction of Ṛṣyaśṛṅga (Sage "Antelope-horn") was so popular that versions are found in early Buddhist texts, in the Hindu epic (i.e., the *Mahābhārata*), in ancient stories (e.g., the *Padma Purāṇa*), in Chinese texts, and in Indian art.[35] The Sage was born when a doe ingested the seed of a Brahman ascetic living in the forest. She became pregnant and gave birth to a boy with a horn on his head (fig. 8.2).

FIGURE 8.2. Probably Ṛṣyaśṛṅga on a railing pillar (Kushan Period. 2nd century A.D.).

Ṛṣyaśṛṅga grew up practicing strict asceticism; so innocent and removed from females was he that he thought a seductress sent to break his chastity was some marvelous ascetic. In some versions the enticing female is actually an *apsaras* (heavenly nymph), or a princess, or a princess with her entourage of courtesans (as in fig. 8.3), or a courtesan with a troupe of prostitutes.

In all but the earliest versions, the continence of Ṛṣyaśṛṅga is so prolonged and strenuous that it causes drought in the land; for the release of rain, either Ṛṣyaśṛṅga's presence alone or the release of his seed is needed. To cause the latter is the job of the enticing female(s). Mythopoeic logic formulates an analogy, on the one hand, between the retention of sexual fluid and the withholding of fertilizing waters in nature, and on the other, the spilling of seed and the release of fertilizing rain. As part of this analogous thinking, courtesans, because of their unrestrained sexual life, can be regarded, in the Ṛṣyaśṛṅga legend and in other contexts, as valuable promoters of fecundity in nature, as well as in the human sphere. Thus, according to one Purāṇa, the *Viṣṇudharmottara Purāṇa* (II.21.6; 104.87), "the earth dug away from the housedoor of a prostitute was held to have absorbed her beneficent potency."[36] The

FIGURE 8.3. Ṛṣyaśṛṅga a surrounded by a princess and courtesans. Begram ivory.
Afghanistan (ca. 2nd century A.D.).

same *Purāṇa* (II.163.20) includes *gaṇikā*s of the first degree among a list of auspicious objects. And in another text of approximately similar age (*Viṣṇusmṛti* 63.29), courtesans are counted among those that cause good luck.

Frequent sexual coupling and the potency associated with that frequency seem to be a source of the courtesan's power. Myth, rite, and traditional lore recognize that sexual intercourse activates fertility and procreation. It follows therefore that the courtesan's carnal life promotes her own empowerment.

A glimpse at another source of her power can be caught in the late medieval songs sung by courtesans in parts of south India. A collection of short musical compositions, or *padam*s, recently translated from the Telugu, were composed mainly by the seventeenth-century poet Kṣetrayya for the sophisticated and talented courtesans who sang and danced in temples and courts before gods and kings.[37] These professionals were the *devadāsī*s, and possibly the *veśyā*s and *gaṇikā*s of the day. The poetry is devotional yet of a highly erotic content. As the courtesan sings, we ought to imagine the king, and even the god, cast in the role of lover. The poet voices, through the person of the courtesan, his own longing for a personal experience with god, giving the *padam*s a highly charged eroticism:

> Don't you know my house
> garland in the palace of the Love God
> where flowers cast their fragrance everywhere?
>
> Don't you know the house
> hidden by tamarind trees,
> in that narrow space marked by the two golden hills?
>
> That's where you lose your senses,
> where the Love God hunts without fear.[38]

The translators explain the reason why the courtesan is the perfect instrument by which the poet can express his hunger to experience god. It is not so much her boldness, her freedom from conventional constraints, her spontaneity and sensuality, as it is her particular knowledge of her lover that appealed greatly to the devotee's wishes. "Bodily experience becomes the crucial mode of knowing . . . the courtesan experiences her divine client by taking him physically into her body . . . there is this fascination with bodily knowledge of god."[39] Here, then, is another source of the courtesan's power, still based on her sexuality, though not only on the procreative energies released by her action, but also on the immediacy of the—erotically induced—knowledge of the divine she could claim.

A twentieth-century field study of the *devadāsīs* in the temple town of Puri, Orissa (in eastern India), describes the erotic atmosphere during a ritual temple dance, which I think sheds light on what actually happened when a dancer danced in the Hindu temple. The description is offered here as a way to explore how a dancer's sexuality can translate into physical knowledge of a king or a god. It is not offered as a direct explanation of the power of Kṣetrayya's courtesans since the time and circumstances between seventeenth-century south Indian temples and royal courts and the institutions and practices of nineteenth- and twentieth-century north India ought to be considerable.[40]

The Puri *devadāsīs* performed a daily midday ritual that brought them into intimate contact with the divine and his partial incarnation on earth, the king. The temple *devadāsīs*, also known as *gaṇikās* or *veśyās*, are themselves considered mortal embodiments of the god whose temple they serve. Indeed, they undergo an initial induction ceremony, after which they consider themselves married to the main deity of the temple. Thereupon they are believed to possess a share of divine sovereignty and to be the earthly embodiment of the god's divine consort. The god has absolute sovereignty over the temple land. Earthly temple servants have a share of that authority, and the king has the biggest earthly share. As such, a *devadāsī* can have sexual relations with those mortal men who partake of the divinity of her divine lord.

During sexual intercourse, the *devadāsī* produces the auspicious female life force; the female life force is her sexual fluid. The creative powers released by this life force assure prosperity, fertility, and well-being of the land. Just as, in myth, an ascetic, such as Ṛṣyaśṛṅga, can cause rain, good crops, and so on by finally spilling his powerful seed, so too it was believed that in dance the *devadāsī* brings on rains, harvests, and welfare by emitting her sexual fluid. Whereas the married woman's fluid makes her family and lineage thrive, the fluid of the *devadāsī* produced during her dance is available for the welfare of the devotees and embodiments of her divine lord.

"The dance is a divine sexual intercourse."[41] The way the dancer arouses eroticism is illustrated by the *devadāsī*'s sexual activity in the midday ritual at the Puri Temple. The dancer's active sexuality, her role as a courtesan, is announced by her costume, her ornaments, and her movements. All that she wears, from her tight-fitting choli (blouse) to the girdle upholding her sari skirt, clings to and accentuates her curves. Yet during the midday ritual, the *devadāsī* is not looked upon as a seductive woman but as a female power, a goddess. The Puri Temple is dedicated to the god Viṣṇu, whose presence resides in the temple's stationary icon. The *devadāsī* is referred to as the "mobile goddess," just as the king, the partial embodiment of

Viṣṇu, is considered the "mobile Viṣṇu."[42] During the midday ritual, the goddess, dancing for the assembled pilgrims, lets her potent sexual fluid fall to the ground. At the end of the dance, many of the pilgrims roll in the ground where her leavings have mixed with the dust. Marglin, the anthropologist who documents this midday ritual, offers an interpretation of the events: the *devadāsī*, transformed into the mobile goddess, has cosmic intercourse with her god; the production of sexual leftover is auspicious and beneficial for the land and its people.[43] Thus, the sexualized female during the midday ritual not only transforms into a goddess, but experiences union with god and produces, as a result, an actual substance charged with life-giving powers.

An early Buddhist text suggests that a courtesan achieves extraordinary power by doing her job faultlessly. The *Milindapañha*, probably composed at the beginning of our era, contains the story of Bindumatī, a courtesan who has the power to make the Ganges River flow back upstream.[44] She performed this feat by making a "Truth Act." A "Truth Act" is a formal declaration of the perfect execution of one's duties in life, prescribed according to one's particular position in the traditional social hierarchy. The king, who witnessed the miracle of the Ganges flowing upstream, exclaimed: "You possess the Power of Truth! You, a thief, a cheat, corrupt, cleft in twain, vicious, a wicked old sinner who have broken the bonds of morality and live on the plunder of fools."[45] What gives you the Power, the King asks. Her reply is that whoever gives her money, regardless of his caste, she treats them all exactly alike. Free from fawning and contempt, she serves the payer. This, she says, is the basis of her power to make the Ganges flow back upstream. The story not only connects the courtesan with the power that Indian custom ascribes to the potency of truth, but it also implies that the courtesan's job did not lie outside of the religiously sanctioned view regarding the different duties (*dharma*) for different strata of Hindu society.

There is an intriguing association, made in story and scholarship, between the courtesan and members of Hindu society who renounce all worldly connections in their quest of spiritual goals. The link probably rests on the fact that both courtesans and ascetics renounce family ties. As Marglin observes, with some surprise, the Puri *devadāsī*s are not referred to as outcastes; rather, her interviews conclude, once the women, recruited from different castes, had become *devadāsī*s, they were equated with the ascetic stage of life. This is the fourth stage of life, mentioned in such ancient Hindu treatises as *The Law of Manu*, wherein asceticism is described as being open only to males and considered to be an ideal that most men would not follow in their own lifetime. Likewise, Veena Talwar Oldenburg, who between 1976 and 1986 interviewed the descendants of Lucknow courtesans, finds that the stage of life closest to the courtesan's lifestyle is that of the fourth, or the ascetic's stage.[46] The divide between the courtesan and Buddhist renouncers could be narrow too (see fig. 8.4). The Buddhist Verses of the Eldresses (*Therīgāthā*) contain verses attributed to the courtesan Ambapālī (vv. 252–70). It was she who received the Buddha in the city of Vaiśālī as he toured and taught in northern India. The Buddha and his entourage stayed at Ambapālī's mango grove, and when she came to the garden and invited the Buddha and the brethren to take a meal at her house, he consented.[47] The commentary explains that she became a courtesan because in a former life she called an eldress (*therī*, a lady disciple of the Buddha) a *gaṇikā*.[48] According to the commentary, Ambapālī charged fifty pieces and so made her city of Vaiśālī very rich. (We are

FIGURE 8.4. Dancer and musicians. Cave 7 at Aurangabad, Maharashtra (ca. 6th century A.D.). Note that this sensuous female group is located on the left wall inside the main Buddha shrine.

reminded of the prescription in the *Arthaśāstra* that a *gaṇikā* should turn over her earnings to the government.) In the ca. sixth-century A.D. Tamil text *Maṇimēkalai*, the eponymous heroine decides to become a Buddhist nun just as her mother, the courtesan Mādavi, had decided earlier. Mādavi, a dancer in the great fifth-century Tamil poem *Śilappadigāram* ("The Jewelled Anklet"), vows to become a Buddhist nun when her beloved is executed for a theft he did not commit. *Maṇimēkalai*, more of a disputation on the ultimate worthiness of Buddhist doctrines than a narrative, sees the daughter follow the same religious path as the mother did.

The literature cited above, both fable and factual, and very varied—representing different religions, regions, and periods—nevertheless shows the tendency to emphasize the courtesan's sexuality. The focus of most of these accounts links a courtesan's power to her presence as a sexualized female. She is the temptress par excellence, and her faultless performance as a courtesan/prostitute correlates with the respect, cultivation, magic potency, even godliness she can achieve. Most of these accounts, it must be noted, are not primarily about the courtesan; when they focus on her, it is from an ahistorical point of view that sees her as a type, not a specific person. The *Kāmasūtra* belongs to this category, and so too do the *Arthaśāstra*, the *Mahāvrata* rite, *The Law of Manu*, the *Purāṇas*, the fictional accounts, and probably the Buddhist accounts. They are, most probably, masculine writings on the subject of a fascinating type—the powerful, dangerous female, not anchored to stabilizing and conventional norms. Even Marglin's interviews with the Puri *devadāsīs* and the

Puri ritual specialists sustain the view that a cultivated courtesan's power is derived mainly from her sexual activity. Another anthropologist, Saskia C. Kersenboom-Story, draws similar conclusions in her rather subjective book on the South Indian *devadāsī*.[49] The title of her work, *Nityasumaṅgalī*, announces the idealized orientation of the author. "Nityasumaṅgalī" means "a female who remains ever auspicious," and brings to mind the traditional view of the Indian wife who is considered auspicious while her husband lives and inauspicious upon his death. A *devadāsī*, being dedicated or "married" to a divine lord, has, as such, a husband who can never die, and is thus considered in Kersenboom-Story's book as "nityasumaṅgalī." Kersenboom-Story allies the *devadāsī*'s powers to her femininity in the ritual, connecting the *devadāsī* herself to the supreme goddess of the temple. Kersenboom-Story interviewed one *devadāsī* concerning her "marriage" ceremony, and others regarding the various arts they studied, which include (in addition to dance) literary texts and several languages.[50] In the end, she maintains that a *devadāsī* is not *like* a goddess but actually *is* a divinity. The *devadāsī-nityasumaṅgalī*, she says, is "a woman whose auspiciousness is lasting because she is the goddess."[51]

This view does not represent the total picture. A more complex image of the cultivated courtesan emerges from the few sources that analyze historical records or candid revelations provided by the courtesans themselves. Were it not for three such sources known to me, it would be easy to maintain that the unchanging power of the cultivated courtesan throughout Indian history relates to her function as a sexualized female. But this seems to be an incomplete assessment.

The first of these studies examines the conditions of South Indian temple women in the context of temple life during the Chola period, 850–1300 A.D.[52] The analysis is based on an exhaustive corpus of all Chola inscriptions that mention temple women. There are 304 pertinent inscriptions and they disclose a rather different story. First, it is noteworthy that in these Chola inscriptions, the temple women are not referred to as "dancers"; rather, the terms applied to them had meanings such as "devotee of God," "daughter of God," or, "woman of the temple."[53] The names reflect a relationship between the women and the temple that does not, apparently, hinge on feminine sexuality. "Temple women's relationships with the temple were secured not as a consequence of ritual function or professional skill—nor through inheritance or ceremonies of initiation or 'marriage' to the temple deity—but through their donations."[54] The inscriptions indicate that during the Chola period the most important undertaking of temple women was to make gifts to the temple. Orr, the author of the study, does not deny that Chola temple women were sexually active. Clearly they were, "given the references to their children in the inscriptions, but there is no hint that their sexual activity was significant to their identities or to their roles in the temple."[55] In their capacity as donors they established networks within the temple and could gain some rights and privileges; royal patronage was not a factor in their attainment of privileges. As such, the oft-quoted Chola inscription of Rājarāja I at the Tanjore Temple, used to indicate royal largesse and patronage since it mentions the king's transfer of four hundred dancing girls to this temple, is an anomaly. It is the only such event recorded in a Chola inscription, and therefore cannot be used as evidence of royal support for Chola temple women.[56] The inscriptions do suggest that Chola temple women had positions inflected by gender in the sense that they were different and more marginal than the positions occupied by temple males. But their identity as females was not due to their sexuality or their association or identification with female divine power. Indeed, Orr finds that the economic freedom of temple women, plus the limited power and connections they garnered for themselves within the temple structures, allowed them in later centuries "to have a continuing role in the life of the temple, eventually establishing themselves in hereditary positions as specialists in dance."[57] The results of Orr's study are quite different and more nuanced than studies of South Indian courtesans that are based on literary or theoretical writings.[58] Orr's findings caution that little about the life of the precolonial courtesan may actually be known until more rigorous historical accounts can be uncovered, or until credibly sensitive fieldwork can be undertaken for later periods.

Oldenburg's interactions and penetration into the world of the descendants of Lucknow courtesans represents just this kind of fieldwork. The tawa'if were patronized and became part of the powerful elite of Lucknow in precolonial times. These were certainly sexualized women who enjoyed luxury, privileges, property, and cultural engagement because of their liaisons with males in authority at Lucknow. As Oldenburg notes, these women, debased by the British, had consorted with kings and courtiers, enjoyed a fabulously opulent living, manipulated men and means for their own social and political ends, and had been the custodians of culture and the trendsetters of fashion (fig. 8.5).[59] Their descendants revealed to Oldenburg how these women had transformed themselves from diffident, fearful females at the time they entered a "salon" into assertive, propertied, independent, educated, and fiercely proud women.

The power they achieved resulted from a process implemented by the older women of a salon, who completely reversed the social perceptions (and thereby raised the confidence level) of the younger members. Instead of seeing themselves as objects dependent on the whims of males, they turned their outlook around. Through intense friendships among themselves leading to confessions of past grief, through private plays, jokes, raunchy songs downgrading heterosexual marriage, by mastering the art of deception with clients, the courtesans of a given salon freed themselves of the perceptions and expectations they encountered as children growing up in a society that fostered the role of the subservient female, be she daughter, wife, daughter-in-law, mother, widow. Yet the need for intimacy and love remained in their reconfigured world wherein they only pretended to love men. The extent to which Oldenburg was able to penetrate their private lives is perhaps most vividly demonstrated by the tawa'if admission to lesbian practices among themselves. In today's language, we might say that the source of power of these Lucknow courtesans stems from a recognition of their self-worth in private lives that they concealed from outsiders. Their pretense of succumbing to male fantasies would be hard to uncover were it not for the unusual interviewer who gains their confidence, or from their own literary writings.

The third source is one such rare literary voice. Binodini Dasi was a prominent actress of the Bengali theater at a time when the theater was undergoing extraordinary change. During the late nineteenth century, Bengali theater productions appeared on permanent, public stages; they were financed by financiers and presented by paid professional actors and actresses. Many of the latter were recruited from the

FIGURE 8.5. Nobleman
and courtesan on an
upper terrace. Opaque
watercolor on paper
(Lucknow, ca. 1820).
Photograph courtesy of
James Ivory.

prostitute quarters, as was Binodini Dasi. At the age of ten or eleven she was recruited, and worked as a successful actress for twelve years, starring in over fifty plays.
At the age of twenty-four she retired, and spent more than the next three decades
involved in a writing career during which she wrote two accounts of her life: *My
Story* (1912) and *My Life as an Actress* (1924). Her works must be considered courageous, honest, and remarkable. Though she had little formal education, she mustered
sufficient stamina to open her heart to an indifferent public whose hypocritical ways
she did not hesitate to criticize.

Dasi reveals not only her personal pain but also a fallacy in the wife/courtesan
dichotomy. In *My Story* she tells of her grief and despair after the death of her patron
of thirty-one years, whom she characterizes as having loved her, protected her, and
introduced financial stability into her life:

> Innumerable sighs hold together the heart of this luckless woman. An intolerable
> burden of pain has been covered by smiles, as despair fights hopelessness relentlessly
> day and night. How many are the unfulfilled longings, the wounds burning with
> pain that are alight in her heart; has anyone ever seen any of this? They become

prostitutes forced by circumstances, lacking shelter, lacking space; but they too, first come into this world with the heart of a woman. The woman who is a loving mother, she too belongs to the same species! But we have been struck against stone from the very beginning and like the bit of iron which becomes magnetized having been repeatedly struck against a magnet, likewise, we have been struck against stone, have turned into stone ourselves![60]

Dasi does not attribute the difference between the life of the wife and that of the courtesan to a difference of caste, deeds of a previous life and thus retribution, nor to moral superiority of the former over the latter. She blames economic and circumstantial inequalities between women who are otherwise sisters, some being luckier than others. Dasi's words stand in such sharp contrast with the other writings cited on this issue that we can only wonder how representative the others are. Accurate information, it would seem, on women's socio-economic positions may differ vastly and can well depend upon the gender and aim of the writer. Dasi is aware that in her own time some of the bourgeois lovers of courtesans by night turn into their severest denouncers by day. It is such hypocrites, writes Dasi, who prey on the defenselessness of courtesans, keeping them down, and thus unable to break out of their existence: "And it is these tempters of the helpless who become leaders of society and pass moral judgement on these insecure women in order to crush them at every step of their existence! . . . Nothing is lost for a man even if a hundred mistakes are made, but a woman is doomed if her step but falter one bit."[61]

Binodini Dasi was a remarkable actress, chosen to star in a play after only one previous theatrical appearance. She is also a courageous, captivating author.[62] Yet hers are not the proud, defiant words of a cultivated courtesan who conquered adversity and had the guts to write about her trials. Something had changed, and it is evident in Dasi's self-deprecating tone. The time is the early twentieth century, and the late nineteenth through early twentieth centuries are times when the cultivated courtesan is caught in a crossfire that reassigns traditional Indian culture away from its two archetypes, the courtesan and the *devadāsī*, to the third archetype, the wife.

One consistent feature in the precolonial texts examined above is that the cultivated courtesan and the *devadāsī* were both necessary and celebrated as keepers of, or contributors to, the artistic, cultural, and religious life of India. One nearly forgotten example of such an all-encompassing function is the eighteenth-century (so-called) Bani Thaniji, a poetess and courtesan or co-wife of Raj Singh (alias Nagari Das). Bani Thaniji was initiated into a temple in Vrindaban, near Mathura, Uttar Pradesh,[63] and she may have been the inspiration for the extraordinary female in Kishangarh paintings (fig. 8.6). What seems equally consistent is that India tended to link artistic and cultural involvement with sexual activity. Thus, an outlook running through precolonial literature, no matter what the genre, is that the cultivated woman is the public woman (fig. 8.7). The situation had not yet changed in the early nineteenth century in either the North or the South, according to the observations of Abbé Dubois and Abdul Halim Sharar, whose remarks opened this essay. But in 1856, the British captured Lucknow and annexed Tanjore, the cultural center of the South. They caused royal patronage to stop. The courtesans in the North lost employment in the sumptuous royal courts and the *devadāsīs* in both the North and the South lost prestige and employment. Under law, the British considered the *devadāsīs*

FIGURE 8.6.   Raja Sawant Singh and Bani Thani in a mango
grove (Kishangarh Miniature, ca. 1735–50).

as "temple prostitutes," and the courtesans and dancing girls ("*nautch* girls") in the
North also came to be considered as prostitutes. Photographs taken of courtesans
during this period represent them garbed as erotic curiosities with trapped, vacuous
stares facing a heartless lens (fig. 8.8). These photographs capture the cultivated
courtesan in the process of becoming objectified (fig. 8.9). Not only do the new rulers of India reduce her to the category of prostitute, but local reformers also work to
ostracize her and boycott her artistic appearances. Perhaps the most serious development towards elimination of the cultivated courtesan's power occurred after 1912,
with the decoupling of art and sex. Leaders in the Theosophical Society and A. K.
Coomaraswamy, the father of Indian art history, were actively engaged in transforming the erotic dances of the *devadāsīs* into Bharata Natyam ("Dance of the Nation"),

FIGURE 8.7. Courtesan. Painting on ivory (ca. 1825).

FIGURE 8.8. Courtesan with attendant.

FIGURE 8.9.   Courtesan with attendant.

and they encouraged girls from good families to learn and perform the dance.[64] A trend was set in motion whereby the definition of the cultivated woman would enter a new phase: the keeper of culture and the keeper of the (pure) lineage was to become one and the same.

Notes

1. Abdul Halim Sharar, *Lucknow: The Last Phase of an Oriental Culture*, trans. and ed. E. S. Harcourt and Fakhir Hussain (London: Paul Elek, 1975), 142, 145–47, 196, 276.

2. 3d ed. (Oxford: Clarendon Press, 1906), 336–37.

3. For a general discussion of these and other terms, see Moti Chandra, *The World of the Courtesans* (Bombay: Vikas Publishing House, 1973), 23–24, 33, 44–45; and Devangana Desai, *Erotic Sculpture of India: A Socio-Cultural Study* (2d rev. ed., New Delhi: Tata-McGraw Hill, 1975) (and see index therein for discussion of terms).

4. T. Bloch, "Jogīmārā Inscription," *Archaeological Survey of India, Annual Report*, 1903–4 (Calcutta, 1906), 128–31.

5. Note that in the Muslim court of Lucknow cited above she is called *tawaʾif*.

6. See *The Kāmasūtra of Vātsyāyana*, trans. Sir Richard F. Burton and F. F. Arbutknot (Mumbai: Jaico, 1976), 137 ff.; also 12–16. Jaina literature lists seventy-two arts (see Chandra, *The World of the Courtesans*, 38 ff.). These lists ought probably to be understood as conventionalized tropes intended to delineate, in broad strokes, the highly cultivated person.

7. *Kāmasūtra*, trans. Burton.

8. Cf. Chandra, *The World of the Courtesans*, 43–55; P. K. Gode, "The Role of the Courtezan in the Early History of Indian Painting," *Annals of the Bhandarkar Oriental Research Institute* 22 (1941): 24–37. For a ca. third-century B.C. statue of a royal courtesan exhibiting features mentioned in the *Arthaśāstra*, see my article now in press entitled "The Mauryan Gaṇikā from Ḍidargañj (Pāṭaliputra)," in the Maurizio Taddei Memorial Issue of *East and West* (forthcoming, 2005).

9. The date of the play is ca. A.D 400, but it seems to be an expansion of an earlier version written by another playwright. See J. A. B. van Buitenen, *Two Plays of Ancient India* (New York: Columbia University Press, 1968), 30–31, n. 10. The identification of the female on this second-century A.D. relief with the courtesan who is the heroine of this play has been made by C. Sivaramamurti, *Sources of History Illumined by Literature* (New Delhi: Kanak, 1979), 9–11.

10. Cf. van Buitenen, *Two Plays of Ancient India*, 102; Gode, "Courtezans," 30.

11. Van Buitenen, *Two Plays*.

12. Regarding the possible dating of the text, see *The Citrasūtra of the Viṣṇudharmottara Purāṇa*, ed. and trans. Parul Dave Mukherji (New Delhi: Indira Gandhi National Centre for the Arts, 2001), xxxi–xxxiii.

13. Gode, "Courtezans," 24–34.

14. For example, Cave 16 at Ajanta, sixth century, shows the remains of the Ṛṣyaśṛṅga story featuring the Ṛṣi, a princess, and her retinue of courtesans. See Klaus Fischer, *Erotik und Askese in Kult und Kunst der Inder* (Cologne: Du Mont, 1979), 136, fig. 85.

15. See Bloch, "Jogīmārā," 128–31. Note that the information in Desai, *Erotic Sculpture*, 107, differs from Bloch's analysis.

16. See Desai, *Erotic Sculpture*, 107, 201.

17. A clear statement of the opposing worlds in the nineteenth century is found in *When God is a Customer: Telugu Courtesan Songs by Kṣetrayya and Others*, ed. and trans. A. K. Ramanujan, Velcheru Narayana Rao, and David Shulman (Berkeley: University of California Press, 1994). Telugu is a Dravidian language dominant in the region from Chennai (Madras) to the borders of Orissa. See pp. 27–28.

18. See Frédérique Apffel Marglin, *Wives of the God-King* (Delhi: Oxford University Press, 1985), 2–6, 177–78; cf. *Kāmasūtra*, trans. Burton, chaps. 4 and 6; Veena Talwar Oldenberg, "Lifestyle as Resistance: The Case of the Courtesans of Lucknow, India," *Feminist Studies* 16 (1990): 259–87.

19. The uneven portrayal of the courtesan is evident in the compilation of hundreds of Classical Sanskrit texts by Ludwik Sternbach, *Gaṇikā-vṛtta-sangrahah, or Texts on Courtezans in Classical Sanskrit* (Hoshiapur: Viśveśvarānandasamsthāna-Prakāśanamandalam, 1953). Unfortunately, the author does not date his texts, but they generally agree on the dangerous, greedy, duplicitous character of the courtesan.

20. *The Laws of Manu*, in *Sacred Books of the East*, ed. F. Max Müller, 50 vols., vol. 25, trans. Georg Bühler (Oxford: Clarendon Press, 1886), IX.13, p. 329.

21. *Manu*, IX.7, p. 328. Note that the Sanskrit term translated as "merit" is *dharma*.

22. *Manusmṛti with Manubhāṣya of Medhātithi*, vol. 7, trans. Ganganath Jha (Calcutta: University of Calcutta, 1920–26), 6.

23. *Manu*, trans. Bühler, IX.9, p. 329.

24. Cf. A. L. Basham, *The Wonder that Was India*, 3d ed. rev. (London: Sidgwick and Jackson, 1967), 167.

25. Substitute provisions are possible, though less desirable; cf. A. L. Basham, *A Cultural History of India* (Oxford: Oxford University Press, 1975), 130.

26. Some of these rites take place at the birth of a child and celebrate the name-giving

ceremony, the first feeding of solid food, the first haircut, then educational rites for boys, next marriage rites, funeral rites, and *śrāddha*.

27. Ram Gopal, *India of Vedic Kalpasūtras* (Delhi: National Publishing House, 1959), 444.

28. Marglin, *Wives*, gives a fine analysis, based on interviews in Puri during the 1970s and 1980s on the contemporary basis of power of both the wife and the temple courtesan; see chaps. 2 and 3.

29. For a summary on the housewife in the *Kāmasūtra*, see Chandra, *The World of the Courtesans*, 78–79, and 85–93 for the courtesan in that text.

30. See King Mahendravarman, *The Farce of the Pious Courtesan; and A Farce of Drunken Sport*, ed. and trans. Michael Lockwood and A. Visnu Bhat (Madras: Tambaram Research Associates, 1991).

31. Somadeva's Kathā Sarit Sāgara, *The Ocean of Story*, trans. C. H. Tawney (London, 1924), vol. 3, chap. 38. Tawney cites references to inscriptions of courtesans as donors to temples, and to literary passages of courtesans as "intellectual, generous and of noble character" (p. 207). Madanamālā, the courtesan, is referred to as a *veśyā*; Tawney assumes she is a *gaṇikā*, the highest type of *veśyā*.

32. J. Gonda, "Ascetics and Courtesans," *Adyar Library Bulletin* 25 (1961): 78–102, at p. 80.

33. Ibid.

34. For treatment of the motif in early Indian mythology, see Wendy Doniger O'Flaherty, *Asceticism and Eroticism in the Mythology of Śiva* (Delhi: Oxford University Press, 1973), chap. 2.

35. Ibid.

36. Gonda, "Ascetics," 91.

37. See *When God Is a Customer*.

38. Ibid., 18.

39. Ibid.

40. The following account is based on the analysis of Frédérique Apffel Marglin, "Refining the Body: Transformative Emotion in Ritual Dance," in *Divine Passions: The Social Construction of Emotion in India*, ed. Owen Lynch (Berkeley: University of California Press, 1990), 212–36. Marglin analyzes the experience, knowledge, and reminiscences of the last quarter of the twentieth century from ritual specialists, practitioners, and informants.

41. Marglin, "Refining the Body," 224. It should be noted by those acquainted with South Asian religious developments that the midday ritual is part of a Tantric offering, and the followers of the Puri rituals are worshippers of female divine power, *Śakti*.

42. "Mobile" is to be understood as not fixed in one place, i.e. the *devadāsī* can move around in the dance.

43. This is a partial summary of the author's interpretation; it is condensed and abbreviated here for the non-specialist in South Asian religion and culture. For further details, see Marglin, "Refining the Body," 224, 230–32.

44. See E. W. Burlingame, "The Act of Truth (*Saccakiriya*): A Hindu Spell and Its Employment as a Psychic Motif in Hindu Fiction," *Journal of the Royal Asiatic Society* (1917): 430–67. The Bindumatī charm is in *Milindapañha* 122–23; Bindumatī is considered a *gaṇikā*.

45. W. Norman Brown, "The Basis for the Hindu Act of Truth," *Review of Religion* 5/1 (Nov. 1940): 37.

46. Oldenburg, "Lifestyle as Resistance," 277–79.

47. See *The Mahā-parinibbāna Suttanta* II. 16–20, in *Buddhist Suttas*, trans. T. W. Rhys Davids in *The Sacred Books of the East*, vol. 11 (1881).

48. Ria Kloppenborg, "Female Stereotypes in Early Buddhism: The Women of the Therīgathā," in *Female Stereotypes in Religious Traditions*, ed. Ria Kloppenborg and Wouter J. Hanegraaff (Leiden: Brill, 1995), 151–69.

49. Saskia C. Kersenboom-Story, *Nityasumaṅgalī: Devadāsī Tradition in South India* (Delhi: Motilal Banarsidass, 1987).

50. Ibid., 191.

51. Ibid., 197. The same author maintains this position in a subsequent short and well-intentioned essay on the function of the *devadāsī*; see Saskia C. Kersenboom, "Devadāsī Murai," *Rasamañjari* 2/2 (Aug. 1997), 55–64, at p. 60.

52. Leslie C. Orr, *Donors, Devotees, and Daughters of God: Temple Women in Medieval Tamilnadu* (New York: Oxford University Press, 2000).

53. Ibid., 162.

54. Ibid.

55. Ibid., 174.

56. Kersenboom-Story, *Nityasumaṅgalī*, 25–30. Perhaps the latest source to draw this erroneous conclusion is John Guy, "Indian Dance in the Temple Context," in Pratapaditya Pal, *Dancing to the Flute* (Sidney: The Art Gallery of New South Wales, Australia, 1997), 29.

57. Orr, *Donors, Devotees*, 171.

58. Compare, for example, Chandra, *The World of the Courtesans*, chap. 10, or Desai, *Erotic Sculpture*, 161–62, with Orr, *Donors, Devotees*.

59. Oldenburg, "Lifestyle as Resistance," 260.

60. Anupama Taranath, "Disrupting Colonial Modernity: Indian Courtesans and Literary Cultures, 1888–1912" (Ph.D. diss., University of California at San Diego, 2000), 300–301. Taranath is quoting from Binodini Dasi, *My Story and My Life as an Actress* (1912), trans. and ed. Rimla Bhattacharya (New Delhi: Kali for Women Press, 1998).

61. Taranath, "Disrupting Colonial Modernity," 305, quoting Dasi, 104–5.

62. Ibid., 306.

63. See A. W. Entwistle, *Brāj: Centre of Krishna Pilgrimage* (Groningen: E. Forsten, 1982), 209–10.

64. Taranath, "Disrupting Colonial Modernity," 306.

The Courtesan's Singing Body as Cultural Capital in Seventeenth-Century Italy

W hen courtesans trafficked in song, they engaged forces that were not just immaterial but material and that were altogether more potent than sex or money.
Itself a form of bodily exchange, song both enthralled and threatened the male admirer and the social fabric that surrounded him. Carrying an ambivalent but almost
magical power, the courtesan's singing voice moved from the mouth of the singer to
penetrate the ears of the unwitting (but often willing) male victim. Accosting body
and soul, song could force submission to any number of threatening temptations,
enticing a loss of control and reason that led to a wide variety of salacious activities.
Song, like love, could inflame the soul and arouse a violent carnal desire that might
come with fever, chills, and other remarkable effects.

This essay provides a musical context for the potentially pernicious effects of
courtesans' voices, and in so doing attempts to place the courtesan's song in a larger
sonic/sexual world—one constructed by philosophical, social, medical, and literary views of women. These understandings were grounded in the Neoplatonic and
Galenic discourses that had been passed down from the ancients and held sway well
into the seventeenth century. They were also grounded in the very close convergence
of music and love in early modern Italy. As demonstrated in previous essays in this
volume, the most famous courtesans of sixteenth-century Venice participated in a
variety of musical practices, of which singing was key to the performance of the
courtesan's self—an asset in her attempt to present the image of a cultivated lady and
a crucial enhancement of her sensual power. Building on the work of my colleagues
in this volume, who have made notable strides in reconstructing ephemeral traces of
the courtesan's voice, I explore cultural forces that rendered her song potent and argue that contemporary experiences of the bodily mechanics of song, love, and desire
coalesced to turn the courtesan's sung voice into a metonym of her sensuality. I also
position song as both embodied and symbolic capital; it enhanced the courtesan's
value both by increasing her sensuous capacities through its inherent lasciviousness
and by demonstrating her skills at an art that, in other contexts, might be socially
acceptable because it could improve soul, spirit, and intellect.

The discussions here of the courtesans' fitful access to power through singing and sexual prowess wrestle with her voice as both subject and object of desire. Rather than falling into the trap of those feminist scholars who try to turn historically subordinated populations into fully-fledged subjects, I want to suggest that the very confusion inherent in the courtesan's position within the dynamic of desire challenges the very notion of the early modern subject and some of the ideological tenets about it that early modern thinkers and their modern audiences have held as true.

THE RISK OF LOVE

The erotic forces of the courtesan's song stem from the assimilation of love and music that permeated art, literature, and philosophy in early modern Italy. Both love and music were unruly forces that could push their victims away from reason and into a state dominated by passions of the body, and both opened up spaces where courtesans, even when objects of desire, could assume a bodily agency generally denied to other women of their time. This particular constellation of music and love had its roots in the conventional Neoplatonic descriptions of love that informed the tradition of love treatises known as the *trattati d'amore*. The *trattati* posited love as a vehicle for a divine spiritual fulfillment, but also imagined it as a force that could entice the passions of the body, robbing the mind of reason and eventually threatening larger social orders. In her dialogue on the infinity of love, the Roman courtesan Tullia d'Aragona explained the problem of giving in to passions of the flesh as one of "subordinating reason, which ought to be the queen of the body, to the senses, and thus very quickly turn[ing men] from being rational . . . into being brute animals."[1] The Venetian Moderata Fonte, in her treatise *On the Worth of Women* (composed 1592), which is unique for its inclusion of solely female speakers, writes that "Desire in men is so powerful that their senses overpower their reason."[2] Explaining the risks of love, the satirist Pietro Aretino wrote: "I am truly more sorry for a man suffering from Love than for one dying of hunger or being wrongly hanged . . . the cruelty which assails a man in love is like a murder inflicted by his own faith, solitude, submission, and goodness."[3] Along similar lines Marco Venier writes of his love for Veronica Franco, "my suffering is more bitter than any death."[4] Love is a cruel fate acted upon an unwilling victim.

The despair of Venier and Aretino comes from the idea of love as a physical turmoil. Ficino explained that

> It also happens that those who have been trapped by love alternately sigh and rejoice. They sigh because they are losing themselves, because they are destroying themselves, because they are ruining themselves. They rejoice because they are transferring themselves into something better. They are also alternately hot and cold, like those whom a certain fever attacks. They are cold rightly, because they are deserted by their own warmth, and they are also hot, since they are enflamed by the splendors of the celestial ray.[5]

Totally losing themselves, lovers experience a radical confusion with physical and physiological ramifications. Tullia elaborates on the intense confusion caused by love as it was filtered through the Petrarchan metaphor of the icy fire: "Simultaneously they feel great heat and excessive cold. They want and reject in equal measure, constantly grasping things but retaining nothing in their grip. They see without eyes. They have no ears but can hear. . . . They are alive while dying."[6] She alludes to the physical consequences of a desire that will always remain unrequited and that leaves the lover wanting something that is impossible to have.

The almost violent consequences of love emerged from desire, a physical condition that caused an imbalance of humors. Tullia's "great heat and excessive cold" reflected a physical problem in a world that imagined good health to be dependent on maintaining appropriate body heat. In its pathological form, frustrated desire led to erotomania or love sickness, which incited a variety of unpleasant symptoms— a pale and wan complexion, fever, rapid pulse, facial swelling, decreased appetite, raging thirst, sighing, tears, insomnia, headaches, and madness. Fonte's interlocutor Corinna writes of failed methods to cure the malady by drinking the blood of the love object, but ultimately concludes that "Nothing except death can really cauterize and cure it." Thus when one of Veronica Franco's admirers wrote that "she has delighted the world in such a way that for love of her people burn and waste away," he was suggesting that Franco quite literally made her victims ill.[7]

Courtesans highlighted the practical similitude between the very experiences that Neoplatonists tried so hard to push apart, deliberately enticing both the splendor and the disgrace of desire. Their poetry and entertainments spoke the elevated language of Neoplatonic love but came infused with a tactile and physical component. Moreover, they performed both artistic and sexual services. This in effect corrupted the safe space of decorum and philosophical contemplation that supposedly kept the body under the rational control of the mind.

Expressing the reality of her life in philosophical terms, Tullia offered an alternative to the well-rehearsed dualisms of Neoplatonic love. Her dialogue refused the dichotomy between spiritual and physical love, reversing received oppositions and talking back to Neoplatonic authorities. For her, true love balanced physical and spiritual fulfillment with sex and enhanced the spiritual union of lovers, as "carnal pleasure" could cause love to "grow in intensity."[8] In a particularly pithy passage she writes: "Is anyone ignorant of the fact that the whole body and soul taken together are more noble and more perfect than the soul by itself?"[9] This statement of moral cosmology and physiology troubles the dichotomy between corporeal and spiritual love that her contemporaries worked so hard to uphold, and thus also blurs distinctions between virtuous and vulgar sounds.

Outside of philosophy, courtesans created a particularly perilous situation by purposefully engaging situations in which their intentions and actions could be read as either virtuous or vulgar and in which supposedly pure spiritual love ran head-on into the moral turpitude of sex. They exceeded the boundaries of a society obsessed with maintaining social order through the appearance of rigid class and gender lines. Feeling the threat of the courtesan, the senate decree of February 21, 1542 that regulated the clothing of women and especially "whores" complained that the latter could no longer necessarily be distinguished from the noble ladies they mimicked. Part of the confusion came from the shared costumes, on which Margaret Rosenthal has elaborated here (see chap. 2). They "go about openly in the streets and churches, and furthermore are so well dressed and adorned that on many occasions our noble and citizen women have been confused with them, the good with the bad, and not only by foreigners but also by those who live here."[10] The address of confused identity in his decree attempted to keep control of who was who, but also highlighted the problem of determining virtue. Pietro Aretino makes the confused identity abundantly clear in referring to Angela Zaffetta, who "more than any other has known how to put the mask of virtue (*onestà*) over the lascivious."[11]

With its power to penetrate body and soul, song, like love, was a sensuous experience that troubled the dichotomy between noble and base by its very nature. As with love, the similarity of sounds classified in both categories rendered sensuous sonorities dangerous, especially in the hands (or, more accurately, the mouths) of women. This potential led, on the one hand, to an understanding of music as an instrument of refinement and on the other to a distrust of music-making that dates back to St. Augustine and the Church Fathers and emerged from the idea that by viscerally stimulating the passions music could stimulate both listeners and performers to wanton emotions and actions.

Descriptions of courtesans' voices tend to portray their music as fearsome because seductive. Song allowed courtesans to take control of their listener/admirers by enticing them to lascivious thoughts and actions and forcing them to abandon reason. As Garzoni wrote, "Where do you think such songs, dances, jokes, parties, and so on come from but from the desire to seduce with angelic soprano voice and attract with divine sounds of harpsichord and lute."[12] For Garzoni, music leads men to suffer the destructive pangs of love. Making the seductive potential of music even clearer, the story by Giovanni Battista Giraldi of Tullia bemusedly seducing older men into dancing to her lute (cited in chap. 4 above) dramatizes her ability to make men lose control of themselves and all things female.

More generally, courtesans' voices, capable of ensnaring men, were frequently associated with sirens, recalling the mythological half-bird/half-woman creatures whose irresistible chants offered erotic pleasure by bewitching mortal men and forever detaching them from reason.[13] The anonymous text of a madrigal set by Willaert, *Amor, da che tu vuoi pur ch'io m'arrischi*, describes two courtesans thus:

> Love, since you wish me to risk
> Hearing and seeing
> Sirens and basilisks,
> Do me the favor,
> If the brilliance of two serene eyes
> Should melt me and I should fall prey
> To clever speech,
> Of having she who is to blame for this believe,
> By seeing and hearing, that I am dead.
> Noble and excellent pair,
> He who sees and hears you
> Just once
> And does not die of pleasure
> Can boldly go
> To hear and see
> The sirens of love and the basilisks.[14]

Willaert's text refers to two real women known as La Sirena and La Basilisca, who were popular sixteenth-century courtesans.[15] Their names stand for two deadly mythological creatures. Sirens, half bird and half woman, with their voices drew men to their enchanted island, where they were shipwrecked and died. In the *Odyssey* Circe says "the Sirens will sing his mind away on their sweet meadow lolling. There are bones of dead men rotting in a pile beside them and flayed skins shrivel around the spot."[16] The Basilisk, king of the snakes, conquered all other serpents with its hiss and could kill with both its look and breath. According to Pliny's *Natural History*,

> the Basilisci Serpentis (Basilisk serpent) also has the same power [to kill the Ca-
> toblepas by sight alone]. It is a native of the province of Cyrenaica, not more than
> 12 inches long, and adorned with a bright white marking on the head like a sort of
> diadem. It routs all snakes with its hiss, and does not move its body forward in mani-
> fold coils like other snakes but advances with its middle raised high. It kills bushes
> not only by its touch but also by its breath, scorches up grass and bursts rocks. Its
> effect on other animals is disastrous.[17]

The poet's use of the metaphor "to die," signifying both orgasm and death, suggests that their sounds provoked an utterly irresistible life-sucking pleasure and that for males to listen to and look at these ladies was profoundly exciting and dangerous.

Making a mockery of these conventional anxieties and associations, Aretino shows music falling definitively on the wrong side of the virtuous/vulgar dichotomy. His dialogues feature friars chanting in the process of seduction and famous, or, rather, infamous, courtesans like Angela Zaffetta serenading their lovers.[18] At one point, the midwife explains how courtesans of her day used singing to enhance her capital and to snare her victims.[19] "Songs were indeed much used, and those women who didn't know a bunch of the most beautiful and newest ones would have been ashamed."[20] Writing generations after Aretino, the Venetian Ferrante Pallavicino made this all very clear in *La rettorica delle puttane* (1673), a rhetorical textbook for prostitutes that positioned singing as a key tool for "whores" to use in seduction. Finding the ear an especially vulnerable orifice, he makes song into the ideal means for restoring a languishing lover with fresh vigor and new spirits.[21]

The sexual connotations of singing and its dangers can be traced to early modern understandings of vocal mechanics. When courtesans sang they made skilled use of mouths, tongues, and throats, all body parts that were used in sexual activity. Pallavicino makes the sexual connotations of singing perfectly clear when he merges his discussion of singing seamlessly into a discourse on the proper use of the tongue and lips in kissing, reminding readers of the erotics of body parts that make sound and serve as metonymic symbols of female sexuality. These understandings emerged from the still-reigning discourses of Galenic and humoral medicine that had been passed down from the ancient world and dominated medical practice and cultural understandings of the body well into the seventeenth century.[22] As I have argued elsewhere, the body parts used for speaking and singing directly affected those used for sex and reproduction. Early modern assimilations of voice and reproductive body parts linked the throat to the neck of the uterus, the mouth to female genitals, and the diaphragm to the womb. Singing required the rapid opening and closing of the glottis, which paralleled the motion of the uterus imagined to accompany orgasm.[23]

That what happened at one end of the body implicated the other end is made abundantly clear by the favorite Hippocratic method of testing fertility: having a woman sit over a head of garlic and checking her mouth for the pungent odor.[24] The French doctor/philosopher Jacques Ferand, writing in 1624, made a similar association when he claimed that chapped and dry lips indicated a "dry womb."[25] Intercourse was imagined to deepen a women's voice by enlarging her neck, "which responds in sympathy with the stretching of her lower neck." One could literally hear a woman's loss of virginity in her less pure, deflowered voice.[26]

This connection between orifices led to a state of anxiety about the woman's mouth. Since it was linked to the sexual organ and projected the sounds that caused carnality, the mouth itself became the locus of female sexuality.[27] The shared ability of mouths and sexual organs to swallow and consume made them analogous to one another: the vagina led to the womb and the mouth to the stomach. Both cavities could hold onto and process matter; the womb turned seed into a baby, which it then expelled, while the stomach turned food into the humoral materials that permeated the body and were expelled in the form of blood, breath, saliva, and other matter, *including voice*. The vagina consumed sexually and the mouth consumed gastrically. Yet the womb took the primary blame for producing the extra fluids that rendered women, with their leaky bodies, incontinent, excessive, and dangerous.[28] As they menstruated, lactated, and wept, women signified their inability to control their own bodies, their tendency to talk and desire too much.

Of the various leaky processes, menstruation caused the most anxiety, in keeping with writings that date back as far as the ancients and the Bible. Describing a menstruating woman, the Bible says that "Anyone who touches her will be unclean until evening. Anything she lies on in this polluted state will be unclean; anything she sits on will be unclean. Anyone who touches her bed must wash clothing and body and will be unclean until evening. Anyone who touches anything she has sat on must wash clothing and body and will be unclean until evening" (Leviticus 15:19–25). In the early sixteenth century Henry Cornelius Agrippa wrote that menstrual blood "makes dogs go mad if they taste it, and if they, in their madness, bite anyone the wound cannot be cured."[29] The Milanese doctor/philosopher Girolamo Cardano wrote: "From contact with this blood, fruits fail to germinate, wine goes sour, plants die, trees lose their fruit, metal is corroded with rust, and bronze objects go black. Any dogs which consume it contact rabies. The glue of bitumen, which resists both metal and water, dissolves spontaneously when polluted with that blood."[30] Given the similarity of mouth and womb and given that all fluids continually transformed into one another, early modern fears of menstrual blood suggest that the corruptive forces oozing out of the womb also affected the song that escaped women's mouths. The ancient gynecologist Soranus made this connection explicit by positing that "singing teachers" had less menstrual flow than other women and claiming that some women failed to menstruate because they were "barren singers or athletes in whom nothing is left over for menstruation, everything being consumed by the exercise."[28]

CHALLENGING CHASTITY

The participation of courtesans in musical life at once enhanced their sexual capital and the erotic connotations of song. Put a different way, that the public performance of writing, speaking, and singing caused problems for women who had no involvement in the sex trade only served to increase the erotic capital of those who did. The fact of courtesans' compromised chastity allowed them the freedom to participate in activities that would have damaged the ever-fallible reputations of more "noble" ladies.

In early modern Italy chastity was widely regarded as a woman's most valuable asset—one protected and owned first by her father and later by her husband. Lodovico Dolce's *Gli istitutioni delle donne*, first published in 1545 and one of the most popular tracts on noble women, reminds his readers that loss of virginity in the ancient world was punishable by death, a penalty he seems wholeheartedly to endorse.[32] Likewise, he made adultery tantamount to treason. Virginity was especially important in Venice, where the patrician class placed an extreme value on maintaining hereditary purity. A crucial asset in the preservation of the family line, it stood as a commodity to be bought by husbands and sold by fathers.

Chastity, or *castità*, a physical and moral category, depended on remaining completely untouched by intercourse, desire, or all manners of pollution from sex to dancing, eating spicy food, and reading lascivious books. Because of the vulnerability of women's virtue, most conduct books of the day required women to avoid overstimulating activities and limit reading and singing to things of a decidedly sacred nature. Fasting, cleanliness, regulated sleep, and avoiding luxurious clothing were seen as producers and signs of chastity— enjoying excess in any of these categories obviously meant the opposite. Explaining this intense vulnerability, Dolce made the unmarried girl's body analogous to a ship "floating in a sea of many dangers, all the orifices of which have to be closed so that these dangers cannot penetrate into the inner parts."[33]

The precariousness and value of a young lady's virtue prompted writings that ranged from prescriptive literature that restricted the activities of reading, writing, and education to carefully scripted texts that were usually moral or scriptural. If chastity reflected a woman's totally uncorrupted mind, excessive skills, desires, and displays could threaten virtue or raise her sexual capital. By using their sexuality to make themselves more attractive courtesans enacted a reversal of the normative notions of sexual capital. They turned their lack of chastity into an asset— manipulating and owning the value of their own bodies.

Singing served as a primary axis around which chastity and the lack thereof rotated. The accompanied song of courtesans required a complex set of skills, each of which could detract from virtue and enhance sexual capital (as Feldman and Davies show above, in chapters 4 and 7), doubtless involving considerable use of ornamentation in some instances. Making this kind of music required singing, reading, and writing, skills that exceeded the dabbling deemed appropriate for noble ladies, especially among those courtesans who wrote the words they sang—words that certainly did not fall within the narrowly virtuous confines dictated by the likes of Dolce.

The fifteenth-century controversy that emerged out of the writings of the Veronese Nogarola sisters suggests some of the ways in which skills that exceeded the boundaries of what was deemed pure enough for women took on decidedly sexual implications. Exceptionally well-educated, the sisters came under fire in an anonymous pamphlet detailing the vices of Veronese women. Responding to Isotta Nogarola's public display of her humanist education in a tract aimed at women in general, the author makes her out as an instrument of vanity, promiscuity, and general immorality by reading her supposedly grotesque intellectual display as a sign of excessive sexuality:

> I have believed the saying of numerous very wise men, "the woman of fluent speech is never chaste" . . . let me explain that before she made her body generally available for uninterrupted intercourse, she had first submitted to, and indeed earnestly desired, that the seal of her virginity should be broken by none other than her brother, to make yet tighter her relationship with him. By God! . . . [What inversions will the world tolerate] when that woman, whose most filthy lust knows no bounds, dares to boast of her abilities in the finest literary studies.[34]

Here the charge of incest effectively enhanced the charge of overabundant sexuality. The deviance of her excessive skills implies a sexual deviance and her learned nature makes it impossible for her to maintain chastity.

Speaking, and by extension singing, also caused trouble for women because it meant access to their bodies, as we know from conduct books like Castiglione's *Il Cortigiano*, in which female silence equaled chastity. In his 1555 treatise on wifely duties, Francesco Barbaro similarly wrote that "the speech of a noble woman can be no less dangerous than the nakedness of her limbs."[35] Explaining some of the problems in more detail, the early fifteenth-century writer Leonardo Bruni warned that "if a woman throws her arms around while speaking, or if she increases the volume of her speech with greater forcefulness, she will appear threateningly insane and requiring restraint."[36]

Singing was even more problematic than speaking for it necessarily involved hurling the voice with great force and other physical gestures, and had explicit sexual implications for women's chastity. Women who excelled in music-making were often assumed to be courtesans. These assumptions lingered well into the seventeenth century, as assaults on the virtue of Barbara Strozzi, singer and composer of eight volumes of vocal music published in Venice between 1644 and 1664, demonstrate. As Ellen Rosand has argued, a series of manuscript satires devoted to impugning Strozzi's Accademia degli Unisoni aims directly at its hostess's reputation. Describing Barbara's distribution of flowers to the academists, the satirist writes: "it is a fine thing to distribute the flowers after having already surrendered the fruit."[37] Even Anna Renzi, an opera singer whose chastity was frequently praised, was identified as a courtesan in an avid operagoer's program.[38]

Considering the lengths to which female singers who were not courtesans and their male patrons and families went to guard their virtue suggests that singing enhanced a courtesan's erotic, as well as artistic, capital. Patrons and families of professional singers in the sixteenth and seventeenth centuries worked to regulate the appearance, education, and morality of their charges, thus effectively containing their sexuality. Considering the lengths to which female singers who were not courtesans and their male patrons and families went to guard their virtue suggests that singing enhanced a courtesan's erotic, as well as artistic, capital. Patrons and families of professional singers in the sixteenth and seventeenth centuries worked to regulate the appearance, education, and morality of their charges, thus effectively containing their sexuality. Even in the case of "non-professional" musicians, women went to extreme lengths to keep their skills something of a secret. Fonte writes of a collective of noblewomen in which a woman with musical skills could sing, "taking up her lute or tempering her sweet voice with the sounds of a well-tuned harpsichord," only when she is certain that she is safe from the eyes and ears of anyone else.[39] In an extreme case, the Duke of Mantua did not allow the thirteen-year-old *virtuosa* Caterina Martinelli to sing at his court until she had undergone a virginity test.[40] On a more subtle level, women with intact virtue who wished to acquire a musical education almost always did so in their parent's homes, thus avoiding the unseemly implications of studying singing with a male teacher.

Until the 1580s few women actually sang in public for money, in large part due to associations with courtesans.[41] The creation of the Ferrarese *concerto delle donne* by the duke Alfonso d'Este in the 1580s began to change things, but these changes occurred in a framework that sheds light on the condition of courtesan singers. What differentiated the three original *donne*, Laura Peverara, Anna Guarini, and Livia d'Arco, from courtesans was a very specific performance context created by a constellation of social, economic, and musical forces. These women took part in the very same kind of music-making that heightened the sensuousness of a courtesan. Moving back almost forty years, we find Antonfrancesco Doni's *Dialogo della musica* (Venice, 1544) giving a representative description of an evening's entertainment like those in which the *concerto delle donne* participated, in which dialogues and civil conversation were often punctuated with musical entertainment.[42] The female interlocutor Selvaggia (evidently Doni's mistress Isabetta Guasca) generally initiates singing, reminding readers of the associations between women and music. In addition to the luxuriant virtuosic style for which they became famous, the women of the *concerto delle donne* often performed the *arie* or formulas for reciting poetry that courtesans made use of. Moreover, Tarquinia Molza, also one of the original singing ladies, received a classical education and was known, like many courtesans, primarily as a poet.[43] Her artistic skills thus paralleled those of Veronica Franco and Tullia d'Aragona, but, unlike courtesans, she and other members of the *concerto* seem almost always to have performed with book in hand, suggesting that their minds did not wander and that they did not themselves write the words or music or take inspiration from the setting by further ornamenting or otherwise elaborating it. Accounts of these women, admittedly carefully scripted, always remark that their musical gestures were invariably made to serve texts, not to enhance pleasure.[44]

The duke was committed to acquiring women whose reputations were beyond reproach and who had already established themselves as gentlewomen— women of at least an almost noble class. He took control of their sexuality by providing them with carefully chosen, nobly born husbands, a dowry, and a place to live within the palace. These fringe benefits rendered their salaries almost irrelevant and effectively assuaged the sexual implications of being paid to sing. Singers at court often had other jobs too. The singer Angela Zanibelli, for example, daughter and niece of court singers at Ferrara, served the marquis Enzo Bentivoglio's household as a weaver.[45] The difference in status between courtesans and the *concerto delle donne*, and the respective reception of their musics, also suggest that the performance of music and the women who performed it became mutually constitutive: virtuous women sang virtuous songs made by others whereas a woman already associated with sexual performance produced lascivious sounds that she herself had often created. While courtesans controlled their own voices and bodies (often in their own homes), exchanging their capital with listeners, the singing ladies used their voices to enhance the duke's status at his court.

In contrast to the performances of courtesans, those of the *concerto delle donne* were of "musica segreta," a quasi-public kind of music controlled by the duke and attended only by Este family members and their diplomatic and social guests. The existence of the *concerto delle donne* as the duke's artistic commodity allowed them to sing for distinguished listeners but still protected them from the "public" venues that courtesans frequented. Performing in a glorified private setting, controlled by the duke within the court itself and often in the duchess's chambers, confined their talents within the large extended family of the court. Their virtue was protected by their existence as part of the duke's capital and his control of their bodies and assets.

In another instance of controlled music-making by women, early modern Italy saw the cultivation of singing traditions within convent walls. As Robert Kendrick and Craig Monson have shown, nuns, especially in Milan and Bologna, sang from behind closed walls for very specific audiences. But while the tight structures of the courts allowed various dukes to control the sound their women made, the Catholic Church—as sound seeped out from grilled walls—never achieved that kind of success.[46] The carefully controlled performance situations of the nuns suggest what Monson has called an alternate "musica segreta," and yet nuns' performances also might be fruitfully interpreted alongside courtesans' performances as extreme versions of one another. Like courtesans, nuns were trained to sing and, like courtesans, singing added to their worth. Though entering an important convent required a substantial dowry, those who could sing could often do so with a very small dowry, or even none at all. While nuns trafficked in their virginity, courtesans trafficked in precisely the opposite. The spiritual ecstasy of nuns' singing and the sexual ecstasy of courtesans' songs rubbed up against one another especially in Venice, a city that imagined itself in terms of the seemingly contradictory images of the virginal body of Mary and the sensuous inviting body of Venus. If courtesans were symbols of Venice's luxury and beauty, nuns were symbols of its innate nobility.

SEXUAL PERFORMANCES AND CURRENCIES

By singing, courtesans such as Veronica Franco enacted desire viscerally, thus challenging—much as they did in writing—social mandates dictating that women act only as objects of desire, not subjects of it. Yet it is important to remember that courtesanship also demanded involuntary performances as part of selling, or at least marketing, the body. I do not want to forget that courtesans trafficked in their own bodies. Despite Franco's independent access to people, places, and activities, her letters contain traces of the kind of physical servitude that went with her trade. Her vehement letter to a mother who is considering making her daughter a courtesan scolds her for not protecting the young girl's virginity. "I've begged and warned you to protect her virginity."[47] Not unlike Dolce, Franco wants the mother to guard her daughter's most valuable possession—her chastity—by placing her in the Casa delle Zitelle, a charitable institution created as a refuge for poor unmarried girls to protect their chastity and thus prevent the loss of marriage potential. After dressing her daughter most chastely, Franco complains, her mother "let her show up with curls dangling around her brow and down her neck, with bare breasts spilling out of her dress, with a high uncovered forehead, and every other embellishment people use to make their merchandise measure up to the competition."[48] Franco's use of the word "merchandise" reminds us that courtesans functioned as objects of commerce, as she gestures toward the body as an icon of sexual capital. Further on she insists: "Don't allow the flesh of your wretched daughter not only to be cut into pieces and sold but you yourself to become her butcher,"[49] and remarks on the horrors of having to submit one's own body to occupation and ownership by others:

> It's a most wretched thing, contrary to human reason, to subject one's body and labor to a slavery terrifying even to think of. To make oneself prey to so many men, at the risk of being stripped, robbed, even killed, so that one man, one day, may snatch away from you everything you've acquired from many over such a long time, along with so many other dangers of injury and dreadful contagious diseases; to eat with another's mouth, sleep with another's eyes, move according to another's will, obviously rushing toward the shipwreck of your mind and your body—what greater misery? . . . Believe me, among all the world's calamities, this is the worst.[50]

Franco's critique highlights the courtesan's body as an object of contention and alienation: in eating with another's mouth and sleeping with another's eyes, the body is essentially removed from the subject.

While we must take seriously Franco's blunt analysis of her situation, it is important to remember that in some metaphorical way Venetians bought and sold young women's bodies every day. With its very tight marriage market, nobles exchanged their daughters for political clout and understood dowries as the financial make or break of the bride's pure, noble body. Such devil's bargains were also made on a regular basis with the church. Patricians unable to afford a high enough dowry to buy themselves a reputable son-in-law often forced their daughters into convents. Jutta Sperling estimates that by 1581 over 54 percent of Venice's noble women lived in convents, and usually not by choice.[51] What differentiates courtesans from nuns and wives, then, is that they sold themselves.

Hinting at this agency, Franco's published poetry articulates the courtesan's erotic power. Though her letter cited above dramatizes physical servitude and degradation, her poety highlights the courtesan's traffic in the more ephemeral currencies of poetry and ideas. Her writings demonstrate that she had access to poetic and other artistic means of projecting her own ability to manipulate her male lover. She could use her body to control her lovers in ways that other women could not:

I will make you taste the delights of love
When they have been expertly learned,
And doing this, I could give you such pleasure
That you could say you were fully content and at once fall more
    deeply in love,
So sweet and delicious do I become
When I am in bed with a man
Who, I sense, loves and enjoys me
That the pleasure I bring excels all delight.[52]

Franco's poem is remarkable for its time because she uses words to demonstrate her erotic prowess. That she wrote these lines explicitly for publication suggests that she intended to market herself as both a poet and a lover, the very opposite of the chaste images that noble ladies cultivated. Using the gift of language to express forbidden pleasure, she claims sexual power by giving and, presumably, withholding pleasure at will, even as she herself remains an object of desire. Her body brings her lover to a place where he will completely lose himself in desire—exactly what the Neoplatonists most feared. And she uses sexual pleasure as an instrument of power with the men who enjoyed her.

These considerations of the bodily activity of singing, the materiality of the voice, and differences of gender suggest that singing enacted an assertive sexual performance, one that exceeded even Franco's strikingly sexual prose. By singing, courtesans assumed a bodily and sexual agency that complicated the relation between active subject and passive object, proving it false. Received medical notions of the time distinguished men from women based on correlations between body temperature and social traits: women were colder and thus weaker, more lascivious, and less controlled than their superior and hotter counterparts.[53] Voice was directly related to temperament; hot breath produced deeper stronger voices and cold breath produced higher weaker voices. The deeper male voice, then, marked a noble character whereas the high voice reflected the imperfections of a vessel that was too cold, too weak, and too moist. Because singing required a naturally hotter body, the fact that women sang at all already threatened the precarious male/female continuum. Avicenna, an Arab medical writer who was widely read in early modern Italy, asserted that people with hot temperaments were "more fluent in speech and have a flair for music."[54] But hotter temperaments in women suggested excessive desire; young women were supposed to consume bland diets and engage in fasting, whose chilling effects regulated body temperature and effectively regulated sexual agency.

While normal breathing kept body heat consistent, singing, which required more heat and more air, set the precious balance off kilter by causing an unseemly rise in women's body temperature.[55] Moreover, the extra circulation of air and breath mimicked the excessive blood flow of sexual activity. Soranus, still read and followed in early modern Italy, wrote: "as the performance of the vocal function stimulates to an increased excretion the saliva which by nature accompanies the passage of the breath, in the same way during intercourse the associated movement around the female genitals relaxes the whole body."[56]

According to humoral doctrines, both vocal and sexual production depended on a rise in body temperature. Conception involved the use of erotic friction that heated both male and female participants up to their boiling points—ejaculation and orgasm. The sixteenth-century French doctor Ambrose Paré's much-quoted instructions for husbands on arousing frigid wives tells them to raise the furnace temperature with wanton words and caresses.[53] Paré, like the Neoplatonist and Petrarchan thinkers who dominated Italian philosophy, assumes that the wife sits still and silent while the husband entices her. She is not a creature of desire but instead exists as a means to propagation, which was not thought possible without orgasm. Courtesans did precisely the opposite, expressing and manipulating desire in ways that had nothing to do with reproduction and marriage. Their vocal exploits mirrored the frank sexuality that Franco, for instance, illustrated in her lyrics, and their sexual actions heated up their male lovers. Unlike Paré's passive objects, courtesans controlled the sexual situation with writing, speaking, and singing of desire and by literally raising body temperatures and manipulating voices.

In addition to mimicking the bodily motions of sex, singing enacted a bodily exchange whose currency was fundamentally physical, and embodied a social capital and penetrative force which had to be guarded against by male listeners. Often described in vocal treatises and accounts of singers as hard or soft, the human voice was understood as a kinesthetic entity that traveled from the mouth of the singer to the ear of the listener, where it worked a variety of physical and physiological transformations. Giulio Caccini, perhaps the most famous singing teacher of the early seventeenth century, described ornaments that "tickle the ear" of the listener—sounds literally move through the ear. The voice in these terms holds a penetrative and material power, one that in the mouths of courtesans became a commodity of exchange.

When the voice flowed out of the body it became something that could be exchanged, like the letters, books, and other currencies that courtesans circulated. It was a physical substance open for exchange that could increase a courtesan's sexual capital. Read in the material terms that dominated early modern Italy, the voice becomes an object of exchange between a courtesan and her audience, one of many circulating goods in which the courtesan traffics, and one that positions her both as a subject of patronage and a subject of power, thus complicating her role as object of desire. It is her voice that allows her, if only for a moment, to control the bodies and souls of her listeners. In early modern Italy conceptions of song and sensuality were inextricably linked, and courtesans by definition commercialized both. Not surprisingly, Venice, the capital of courtesanship, would also become the first space to commercialize music in the form of opera, a market system in which singers were paid for their services and their voices were rendered commodities on a free-exchange market. We know that early divas pursued musical careers outside the courts and parlors of the nobility, negotiated very complex contracts, and even earned enough money to put up their own dowries.[58] And perhaps courtesans who used the arts of song, rhetoric, costume, and makeup paved the way for female singers to enter a world of theatrical impersonation.

Notes

1. Tullia d'Aragona, *Dialogue on the Infinity of Love*, trans. Rinaldina Russell and Bruce Merry (Chicago: University of Chicago Press, 1997), 94.

2. Moderata Fonte, *Il merito delle donne*, ed. Adriana Chemello (1600; Venice: Eidos, 1988), 84.

3. "The Horrors of Falling in Love," letter to the Count of San Secondo, from Venice, June 24, 1537. Pietro Aretino, *Selected Letters*, trans. George Bull (New York: Penguin, 1976), 99; in Italian in Pietro Aretino, *Lettere*, ed. Paolo Procaccioli (Rome: Salerno Editrice, 1992), 228.

4. Veronica Franco, *Poems and Selected Letters*, trans. Ann Rosalind Jones and Margaret F. Rosenthal (Chicago: University of Chicago Press, 1998), 51.

5. Marsilio Ficino, *Commentary on Plato's Symposium*, trans. Sears Jayne (Dallas: Spring Publications, 1985), 52.

6. Tullia d'Aragona, *Dialogue*, 84.

7. Corinna quote from Fonte, *Il merito delle donne*, 171. Franco admirer quote from Franco, *Poems and Selected Letters*, 91, vv. 65–66.

8. Ibid., 102.

9. Ibid., 165.

10. *Venice: A Documentary History, 1450–1630*, ed. David Chambers and Brian Pullan (Oxford: Blackwell, 1992), 117.

11. Letter to Angela Zaffetta, December 25, 1537, in Aretino, *Lettere*, ed. Procaccioli, 609–11.

12. Tomaso Garzoni da Bagnacavallo, *La piazza universale di tutte le professioni del mondo* (Venice: Gio. Battista Somasco, 1589), 605.

13. For more on sirens, see Meri Lao, *Sirens: Symbols of Seduction* (Rochester, NY: Park Street Press, 1998). See also Linda Phyllis Austern, "Nature, Culture, Myth, and Musician in Early Modern England," *Journal of the American Musicological Society* 51 (1998): 1–49, and *Music and the Sirens*, ed. Linda Phyllis Austern (Bloomington: Indiana University Press, forthcoming 2005).

14. Amore, da che tu vuoi pur ch'io m'arrischi
In udir e vedere
Sirene e Basilischi,
Fammi gratia, signore,
S'egli avvien che mi strugga lo splendore
Di due occhi sereni, e ch'io sia preda
D'un ragionar accorto,
Che chi n'ha colpa creda
Che per udir e per veder sia morto.
Gentil coppia eccellente,
Chi vi mira et ascolta
Solamente una volta
E non mor di piacere,
Può gir arditamente
Ad udir e vedere
Le Sirene d'amor e i Basilischi.

Adriano Willaert, *Opera Omnia*, vol. 14, ed. Helga Meier, Corpus Mensurabilis Musicae, 3 (n.p.: American Institute of Musicology, 1977), 92. I have altered the punctuation.

15. The two women are named by Andrea Calmo in his fourth volume of letters devoted

to popular courtesans. Andrea Calmo, *Lettere*, ed. Vittorio Rossi (Turin: E. Loescher, 1888), 266–67.

16. Homer, *The Odyssey*, 12. 44–46; trans. Robert Fitzgerald (New York: Farrar, Strauss and Giroux, 1998), 210.

17. Pliny the elder, *Natural History*, 8. 33; trans. W. H. S. Jones (Cambridge, MA: Harvard University Press, 1963).

18. Pietro Aretino, *Dialogues*, trans. Raymond Rosenthal (New York: Marsilio, 1971).

19. Ibid., 362.

20. Pietro Aretino, *Ragionamento dialogo*, ed. Nino Borsellino and Paolo Procaccioli (Milan: Garzanti, 1984), 468 (translation mine).

21. See especially the fifteenth lesson of Ferrante Pallavicino, *La rettorica delle puttane* (1673), ed. Laura Coci (Parma: Fondazione Pietro Bembo, 1992). Wendy Heller discusses this in *Emblems of Eloquence: Opera and Women's Voices in Seventeenth-Century Venice* (Berkeley: University of California Press, 2003).

22. This reliance on humoral medicine is part of the humanist immersion in ancient texts of all kinds. For comprehensive studies of the impact of ancient medical practice on medieval and Renaissance Europe see Nancy G. Siraisi, *Medieval and Early Renaissance Medicine: An Introduction to Knowledge and Practice* (Chicago: University of Chicago Press, 1990); eadem, *Avicenna in Renaissance Italy: The Canon and Medical Teaching in Italian Universities after 1500* (Princeton: Princeton University Press, 1987); Ian Maclean, *The Renaissance Notion of Woman: A Study in the Fortunes of Scholasticism and Medieval Science in European Intellectual Life* (Cambridge: Cambridge University Press, 1980); and Giancarlo Zanier, "Platonic Trends in Renaissance Medicine," *Journal of the History of Ideas* 48 (1987): 509–19. Andrew Wear estimates that between 1500 and 1700 at least 590 different translations of Galen appeared in western Europe; see his "Medicine in Early Modern Europe, 1500–1700," in *The Western Medical Tradition, 800 BC to AD 1800*, ed. Lawrence Conrad *et al.* (Cambridge: Cambridge University Press, 1995), 253.

23. Bonnie Gordon, *Monteverdi's Unruly Women: The Power of Song in Early Modern Europe* (Cambridge: Cambridge University Press, 2004). Most obviously, the clitoris was known as a little tongue. These associations were handed down from the ancients. Galen understood the neck of the uterus as capable of opening and closing and the vagina as the door to the womb.

24. *The Medical Works of Hippocrates*, ed. John Chadwick and W. N. Mann (Oxford: Oxford University Press, 1950), 262.

25. Jacques Ferrand, *A Treatise on Lovesickness*, trans. David A. Beecher and Massimo Ciavolella (Syracuse: Syracuse University Press, 1990), 294.

26. As quoted from Hippocratic gynecology in Ann Hanson and David Armstrong, "The Virgin's Voice and Neck: Aeschylus, Agamemnon 245, and Other Texts," *British Institute of Classical Studies* 33 (1986): 97–100, at p. 99. The authors suggest that ancient Greek ideas about the physical signs of virginity stemmed from folk belief and held sway, along with Galenic medicine, well into the seventeenth century.

27. As other scholars have argued, a variety of discourses conflated sex organs with the mouth and positioned both as signs of female lasciviousness and unruliness. See Gail Kern Paster, *The Body Embarrassed: Drama and the Disciplines of Shame in Early Modern England* (Ithaca: Cornell University Press, 1993), and Peter Stallybrass, "The Body Enclosed: Patriarchal Territories," in *Rewriting the Renaissance: The Discourses of Sexual Difference in Early Modern Europe*, ed. Margaret M. Ferguson *et al.* (Chicago: University of Chicago Press, 1986), 123–42.

28. In addition to medical conflations of mouths and wombs, artistic representations conflate mouths with the damning abyss of hell and recall the medical associations by em-

phasizing the entrance to this dark and mysterious place. Barbara Spackman, "Inter musam et ursum moritur: Folengo and the Gaping 'Other' Mouth," in *Refiguring Woman: Perspectives on Gender in the Italian Renaissance*, ed. Marilyn Migiel and Juliana Schiesari (Ithaca: Cornell University Press, 1991), 19–35.

29. Cornelius Agrippa, *De occulta philosophia libri tres*, 1. 42; ed. V. Perone Compagni (New York: E. J. Brill, 1992), 162. Translation mine.

30. Quoted from Marcus Fiertz, *Girolamo Cardano*, trans. Helya Niman (Boston: Burkhauser, 1983), 99. Pliny the elder makes a similar statement; *Natural History*, 7. 15; ed. T. E. Page (Cambridge, MA: Harvard University Press, 1938), 2: 549.

31. Soranus, *Gynecology*, trans. Owsei Temkin (Baltimore: Johns Hopkins University Press, 1956), 133.

32. Lodovico Dolce, *Dialogo della istitutione delle donne* (Venice: Giolito, 1560), fol. 9ᵛ.

33. Ibid., fol. 9ᵛ.

34. A. Segarizzi, "Niccolo Barbo patrizio veneziano del sec. XV e le accuse contro Isotta Nogarola," *Giornale storico della letteratura italiana* 43 (1904): 39–54 and 50–54; the passage is translated in Anthony Grafton and Lisa Jardine, *From Humanism to the Humanities* (Cambridge, MA: Harvard University Press, 1986), 40.

35. Francesco Barbaro, "On Wifely Duties," in *The Earthly Republic: Italian Humanists on Government and Society*, ed. Ronald E. Witt *et al.* (Philadelphia: University of Pennsylvania Press, 1978), 205.

36. Cited in Grafton and Jardine, *From Humanism to the Humanities*, 33.

37. Cited in Ellen Rosand, "Barbara Strozzi, *virtuosissima cantatrice*: The Composer's Voice," *Journal of the American Musicological Society* 31 (1978): 241–81, at 251.

38. Claudio Sartori, "La prima diva della lirica italiana: Anna Renzi," *Nuova rivista musicale italiana* 3 (1968): 430–52, at p. 450.

39. Fonte, *Il merito delle donne*, 45.

40. Alessandro Ademollo, *La bell'Adriana ed altre virtuose del suo tempo alla corte di Mantova* (Città di Castello: S. Lapi, 1888), 39.

41. For a commercial recording of the Cantate, Ninfe leggiadrette e belle published in Marenzio's 1581 first book of madrigals, readers can listen to The Consort of Musicke, directed by Anthony Rooley: Emma Kirkby, Evelyn Tubb, and Deborah Roberts (sopranos), Mary Nichols (alto), Rufus Miller (tenor), Anthony Rooley (lute). Original Recording: *Concerto delle Donne: Madrigali* (Deutsche Harmonia Mundi, distributed by BMG Music, 1988, 77154-2-RC). Track 1.

42. Antonfrancesco Doni, *Dialogo della musica (1544)*, ed. Gian Francesco Malipiero (Venice: Fondazione Giorgio Cini, and Vienna: Universal Edition, 1965).

43. See Irma Jaffe, *Shining Eyes, Cruel Fortune: The Lives and Loves of Italian Renaissance Women Poets* (New York: Fordham University Press, 2002), 311–39.

44. On the *concerto delle donne* see Anthony Newcomb, *The Madrigal at Ferrara, 1579–1597*, 2 vols. (Princeton: Princeton University Press, 1980).

45. Stuart Reiner, "La vag'Angioletta (and Others)," *Analecta musicologica* 14 (1974): 26–88.

46. Robert L. Kendrick, *Celestial Sirens: Nuns and Their Music in Early Modern Milan* (Oxford: Clarendon Press, 1996), and Craig Monson, *Disembodied Voices: Music and Culture in an Early Modern Italian Convent* (Berkeley: University of California Press, 1995).

47. Franco, *Selected Poems and Letters*, 38.

48. Ibid.

49. Quoted ibid., 39.

50. Ibid.

51. Jutta Gisela Sperling, *Convents and the Body Politic in Late Renaissance Venice* (Chicago: University of Chicago Press, 1999), 3.

52. Franco, *Selected Poems and Letters*, 69.

53. Aristotle insisted that hot breath produced deeper, more noble voices and cold

breath produced higher voices; *Generation of Animals*, 5. 7; trans. A. L. Peck (Cambridge, MA: Harvard University Press, 1990), 342. Galen argued that drier, and thus more male, bodies made better sounds; *Galen: On the Usefulness of the Parts of the Body*, 1. 389; ed. Margaret Tallmadge May (Ithaca: Cornell University Press, 1968), 344.

54. Mazhar H. Shah, *The General Principles of Avicenna's Canon of Medicine* (Karachi: Naveed Clinic, 1966), 343.

55. Ferrand wrote that uterine frenzy led women to chatter incessantly and speak about sexual matters; *A Treatise on Lovesickness*, 263.

56. Soranus, *Gynecology*, 29.

57. As cited in Thomas Lacquer, *Making Sex: Body and Gender from the Greeks to Freud* (Cambridge, MA: Harvard University Press, 1990), 102.

58. For details see Beth L. Glixon, "Private Lives of Public Women: Prima Donnas in Mid-Seventeenth-Century Venice," *Music & Letters* 76 (1995): 509–31. For more, especially on the link between courtesans and their operatic representations, see Heller, *Emblems of Eloquence*.

Defaming the Courtesan

Satire and Invective in Sixteenth-Century Italy

In Pietro Aretino's fictitious *Dialogo* set in sixteenth-century Rome, Nanna, a veteran courtesan, cautions her young daughter regarding the inherent dangers in taking a literary man as a lover: "If there is a scholar present, approach him with a cheerful face, showing that you esteem him even more than the lord of the house . . . Why, all you need is for one of these types to write a book against you, and for the whole city to be gossiping about those dreadful things that men know how to say about women!"[1]

Nanna's concerns would not have been unfounded, since in sixteenth-century Italy, satiric poems, invectives, and dialogues on the vices of courtesans abounded. Even the most illustrious courtesans were the objects of pointed literary attacks that denigrated them through a figurative, unpaid use of their bodies. In *Il trentuno della Zaffetta* (The Zaffetta's Thirty-one; Venice, 1531) by the Venetian Lorenzo Venier, the poet subjects the famous courtesan Angela dal Moro—an intimate of the likes of Titian and Aretino—to a series of sexual assaults. Other writers often undermined the courtesan through a literary distortion of her body. Lorenzo's son, Maffio Venier, in a series of three poems in Venetian dialect written against the illustrious courtesan-poet Veronica Franco, uses obscene verse to transform Franco's body into a grotesque caricature: her breasts hang so low to the ground that he has heard she uses them as oars to row her gondola.[2] The anonymous *Dialogo dello Zoppino* (Paris, ca. 1539), on the other hand, neutralizes the allurements of Italian courtesans by de-eroticizing their bodies: "Do you really believe that because their chests are smooth, the skin on the rest of their bodies is smooth as well? Their skin is rough and wrinkled from too much handling, and their tits are so flat that they hang down like deflated sacks!"[3] Saturated with negative images of the courtesan's body, such texts also attack her moral integrity: time and time again, she is denounced as a liar, a thief, and even a witch.

Why did such texts seek to defame and humiliate courtesans? Given the often disturbingly violent nature of the texts I discuss here, it would be all too easy to view the courtesan as the passive victim of male aggression. Nonetheless, even as satiric texts depict the courtesan as both literally and figuratively overpowered, they also represent her as an active agent who is a dangerous threat to wealth, social status, and honor.[4] In this essay, I examine some of the most common negative tropes in Renaissance Italian literary representations of courtesans to show that defamatory texts are manifestations of a complex power dynamic between courtesans and literati that was played out in the public and private spaces of the city as well as on paper. Focusing on the push and pull between representational power—that is, the power of discourse—and pragmatic power at play in these texts, I suggest that male poets used the literary topos of the courtesan to negotiate a barrage of anxieties: from broad concerns about their social and economic status to more intimate worries about sexual prowess.[5]

Invectives against women began pouring from Italian presses sometime after 1527, when the brilliant satirist Pietro Aretino settled in Venice and published his scandalous *Sonetti lussuriosi*, a sequence of pornographic sonnets featuring some of Rome's most notorious courtesans. Along with Aretino's infamous courtesan dialogues, the *Ragionamenti* (1534–36), this text became archetypal for a circle of aspiring literary pornographers including Niccolò Franco, Antonfrancesco Doni, and the Venetian patrician Lorenzo Venier, whose two scurrilous invectives against Venetian courtesans, *Il trentuno della Zaffetta* and *La puttana errante* (The Wandering Whore) were published together in a single volume at Venice in 1531.[6]

La puttana errante targets Elena Ballerina, a Venetian courtesan whom Lorenzo accuses of having robbed him during one of his visits to her home. An obscene parody of Ariosto's famous epic *Orlando furioso* that transfers Ariosto's male protagonist to a female, the poem narrates the courtesan's sexual exploits as she wanders the Italian peninsula from Venice to Naples. In the opening lines of the first canto, she appears as a foil to Ariosto's errant knight, who "has done more with her cunt than Orlando did with his sword and lance."[7] The crass comparison with the armed knight, while outwardly intended as affirmation of Elena's lack of sexual restraint, implicitly measures her sexuality as weaponry. Ariosto's hero used a sword to wage his battles; the courtesan uses her sex.

In the final canto, Lorenzo overturns the stylized *donna angelicata* glorified by the Italian lyric tradition with a self-conscious play on the triumphal entry of Beatrice in Dante's *Purgatorio*. While Dante's angelic beloved made her entrance in a shower of flowers and accompanied by a celestial choir, Lorenzo's courtesan, crowned with thorns, artichokes, and borage leaves and infected with syphilis, is hauled off amid a jeering crowd of ne'er-do-wells to finish her days on the Ponte Sisto—the notorious bridge in Rome where only the poorest prostitutes plied their trade. The vulgar scene figuratively transforms Elena Ballerina, one of Venice's most sought-after courtesans, into a low-class, disease-ridden prostitute.

Lorenzo's other satiric poem, *La Zaffetta*, recounts in graphic and obscene detail the *trentuno* (thirty-one)—a pseudonym for gang rape—inflicted upon the Venetian courtesan Angela dal Moro by a procession of eighty peasants, fishermen, gondoliers, and other men of low social standing. In the opening stanzas of the poem, the author sets forth two reasons for its conception. First, he claims to want to confirm, once and for all, his own authorship of *La puttana errante*, which had been erroneously attributed to his teacher Aretino.[8] Second, he must make Angela's disgrace public in order to appease his friends, because "anyone who withholds words from his friends is no friend at all."[9] Addressing himself to the courtesan, the poet firmly ensconces himself in the old-boy network of Venetian patricians, feigning helplessness in the face of his posse's wishes: "You know that if someone wants to screw you he will do it both forwards and backwards. So what am I supposed to do if everyone wants me to make a poem out of your *trentuno?*"[10]

A likely motive for Lorenzo's literary attack on Angela Zaffetta is not revealed until the penultimate stanza of the poem, when the poet confesses that he—like his male protagonist—has also been scorned by the courtesan. Whether this passage actually evolved from some real historical incident, as some scholars have believed, is beside the point.[11] The *Zaffetta* is part of a centuries-old tradition of misogynist texts that use satire as their primary weapon. Thus, inherent in the very nature of the text is the satirist's conscious attempt to merge reality with fiction. The words achieve what the rapes would have: public defamation and humiliation of the courtesan. Angela pleads with her lover to keep her disgrace a secret, the author tells us, but in no time, "every brothel is full of talk of Angela, and the news of her *trentuno* has spread throughout Venice. In the entire city, not one man can be found who does not praise the man who did it to her."[12] The satirist here skillfully calls attention not only to Angela's disgrace, but also to his own accomplishment.

Lorenzo's poem suggests that another objective of the *trentuno* was to teach Angela a lesson and bring an end to her career. The poem's pedagogical function is evidenced when the author proposes Angela's misfortune as a warning to all courtesans who dare to refuse their noble lovers: "If some gentleman wants to screw you," advises Lorenzo, "think about Angela and her dishonor. By saying yes, you will pay him homage, and this, my dear whores, is the road to success."[13] Initially, Angela appears to have learned her lesson, begging her noble lover not to speak of the incident to anyone, and locking herself in the house "as if she were dead."[14] However, only six days after the rapes, the poet recounts bitterly, the courtesan was back on her balcony, "cheekier than ever."[15] By putting Angela back there, the poet rearticulates the power dialectic between courtesan and adversary: Angela's initial assertion of power—her rejection of the poet—prompts his retaliation, which is in turn followed by a reaffirmation of the courtesan's refusal to submit to her lover's will, a reaffirmation of her power, and a reassertion of the satirist's need to defame her, on and on in an endless regress.

Of course courtesans were also lauded by their male contemporaries for their beauty, charm, and conversational skill, sometimes by the very same men who elsewhere berated them. Sixteenth-century literary responses to courtesans—and to women in general—tended to be radically polarized, consisting at one extreme of highly idealized images of angelically chaste femininity and at the other of grotesque caricatures of mercenary, deceitful whores with voracious sexual appetites. Paradoxically, many writers even indulged in both tropes simultaneously. Lorenzo's brother, the Venetian senator and prominent literary patron Domenico Venier, is a case in point. In a sonnet entitled "Non è men del più bello Angelo in cielo" ("She is no less than the most beautiful angel in Heaven"), Venier praises the sublime beauty of Elena Artusi, a young woman who lived in Venice near the church of San Marcuola and probably had connections to Venier's group.[16] The same Elena, however, in a codex in Venetian dialect recently brought to light by Martha Feldman, is the object of bitter and sometimes obscene defamatory verse exchanged between Venier and a cohort, Benedetto Corner.[17] Following in the footsteps of the late medieval *tenzone*, the collection is organized as a poetic debate in which the two competitors elaborate on the amorous exploits of the lady in question, all the while vying for exclusive "ownership" of her. In one of the opening sonnets, Domenico sets forth the theme of Elena's moral integrity (or lack thereof), which dominates the collection: "And if nothing else, they [the two poets] know how to talk about a certain woman—I don't want to say a whore, but a lady who allows herself to be screwed."[18]

Later Domenico pens a fictitious dialogue between Elena and her mother in which the concerned mother takes her daughter to task for consorting with a certain Moresini. "You know," she chides, "these rumors are dangerous. These are the kinds of stains that cannot ever be washed away."[19] Indeed, many of Domenico's poems disguise themselves as attempts to protect Elena's reputation even as they denounce her for alleged sexual promiscuity and (ironically) condemn her angrily for resisting his sexual advances: "The fact that this broad is getting the best of me really gets under my skin. Why, she's tougher than Ancroia. Damn that bitch to hell!"[20]

Although Artusi was evidently not a "professional" courtesan—she was, rather, a married woman who probably exchanged sex for gifts of food and clothing from her noble admirers—she is targeted through a paradox that encapsulates the heart of Venetian literary responses to courtesans, who were alternately idolized and denigrated. The manuscript weaves together adulatory verse exalting her virtue and beauty with poems denouncing her as a mercenary, sexually voracious "puttana di natura" (whore by nature), willing to sell her body and soul for a new dress. In a later *sonetto dialogato*, Elena's maidservant attempts to turn away an eager suitor by telling him that her mistress is already occupied upstairs with the Moresini mentioned above. The persistent lover insists that the maidservant bring Elena downstairs to see him, and then manages to talk her into a quickie in the storeroom before she goes back upstairs. In this highly theatrical scene, reminiscent of early Venetian courtesan plays known as *commedie "alla bulesca,"* Elena is explicitly likened to a wily courtesan who has no qualms about sleeping with two men in one day in order to make a profit.

The association of courtesans with the cardinal sin of greed is commonplace in satires and invectives from this period, and sixteenth-century commentary on the mercenary motivations of courtesans burgeons into catalogues and lists—take, for example, the anonymous *Tariffa delle puttane di Venegia* (Venice, ca. 1535) and the *Catalogo de tutte le principal et più honorate cortigiane di Venetia* (Venice, 16th c.), among others. Indeed, in sixteenth-century Italy, developments toward capitalism were already well under way, and anxieties surrounding accelerations in the accumulation, circulation, and exchange of capital are certainly not surprising. Moreover, inherent in the figure of the courtesan, who by definition receives payment for her services, is an imbrication between the world of commerce and the murkier arena of sex and human desire.

The very fact that courtesans expected compensation for their services was clearly a major bone of contention for many Renaissance poets, who tended to represent courtesans as willing to do just about anything as long as they would be paid. Aretino has his fictitious Nanna confess frankly to her daughter Pippa that the "sweetness of scudi" is enough to make her overlook the obvious nuisances of her profession—even the bad breath and malodorous feet of her clients. Many other texts feature courtesans who are avaricious to the point of caricature. In Venier's *Zaffetta*, the courtesan selfishly harangues her admirers with outlandish requests for tokens of their admiration; at one point she even suggests that they buy her the "ca' Loredan," one of the most exquisite *palazzi* in Venice.

Similarly, an anonymous poem set to music as a four-voice madrigal by the Italianized Frenchman Jacques Arcadelt and published in his *Terzo libro* (Venice, 1539) has the courtesan herself brashly articulate her mercenary ways (companion website track 9). Words, she informs her lover, are worth nothing. Anyone who seeks to enjoy her company must be prepared to "put his hand in his purse:"

> If, as you always say, you find me beautiful,
> Then it shouldn't be too much trouble
> To put a few coins in my hand.
> If you were thinking of trying to trick me with your chatter,
> And pay me with words,
> You would never have me, not even with a thousand lances,
> Because this way we would be exchanging one crazy idea for another!
> But to him who desires to have his way with me
> Let this be said, for better or for worse:
> Put your hand often in your purse![21]

The poem, in the free form of the poetic madrigal, presents a heavily caricaturized, unilateral image of the female protagonist, who is motivated exclusively by her desire for material wealth. The purportedly nameless, ruthlessly mercenary courtesan in the madrigal could be a representation of Aretino's fictitious Nanna, or even a portrait of a real courtesan, such as Elena Ballerina, whom Lorenzo Venier accused of having stolen his purse in the middle of their love-making.

Another madrigal text set to music by Arcadelt (from *Il quarto libro di madrigali*, 1539) is also voiced by an anonymous male (companion website track 10). Following the tradition of paired challenge-riposte poems popular at the time, this one makes a direct response to the courtesan's demands in the text just quoted:

> Lady, among the most beautiful faces, honest and dear,
> Yours would rank as first
> If it weren't spoiled by your asking for money.
> If you want to be regarded above all others,
> As one hopes and believes,
> Don't ever ask anything of anyone,
> Because she who asks the most always seems the least beautiful!
> And though I, with great faith,
> Adore you as my goddess and my star,
> I pray you not to touch my purse![22]

The courtesan's face would be the loveliest among many beautiful and honest faces —an ideal of womanhood—were it not spoiled by her forthright requests for cash in exchange for her favors. The lover's attempt to silence the courtesan, "because she who asks the most always seems the least beautiful," invokes an image of the passive, silent lady of the courtly love tradition, codified by Petrarch in his *Canzoniere* and then reinforced by Pietro Bembo and his followers in the sixteenth century.[23]

The rules of courtly love that motivate the literary lover are even more apparent in the following poem by the musician-poet Girolamo Parabosco. Offended by the courtesan's demands for payment, the lover plays the troubadour: in place of material compensation, he offers his poems in exchange for her favors:

> Lady, I want to tell you,
> And this is God's truth:
> You don't love me one bit.
> Because asking one's lover for four or six *scudi* at a time
> Was never a sign or an act of love.
> I won't lie to you;
> With your art I would make of mine
> An exchange, a barter:
> So that, if you wish,
> You'll have *canzoni* and *madrigali* from me,
> And then you'll give me some of that which,
> Although it costs you nothing,
> You sell at such a high price.
> This way we will be equals.
> And if that deal doesn't suit you,
> I'll say: Best wishes!
> Because I'd rather take a vow of chastity
> Than spend four or six *scudi* on you.[24]

Parabosco, born in Lombardy to a bourgeois family, arrived in Venice in 1540. By 1551 he was appointed first organist of San Marco, one of the most prestigious musical posts in all of Europe, and was an intimate of numerous circles of literati, noble and non-noble. His peculiar position in Venetian society—at once inside and outside the privileged world of the nobility—may help explain why this and many of his other literary works play heavily on themes of class and status. For the lover in the poem, in fact, gift exchange is superior to cash payment: he wants to forget that his *Madonna* is a courtesan and thus earns her living by exchanging her favors for money. The other side of the coin, of course, is that the poet is not really the courtly lover that he'd like to be—since he's the one who has presumably initiated the transaction. Thus the author finds himself in the uncomfortable position of desiring the courtesan, yet being repulsed by monetary exchange, which constantly reminds him that she is not the woman-angel he ostensibly seeks. Nor can the courtesan, by virtue of her very profession, fulfill the poet's fantasy of a lover freely giving herself. What makes the courtesan–client relationship so complex is that, unlike that of the common prostitute, the courtesan's status as a commodity is mystified. Prostitutes sold only their bodies, while courtesans sold something else. The sumptuous palaces in which many courtesans lived, along with their costly clothing and erudite conversation, upheld the fantasy of idealized, refined femininity that their aristocratic clients sought.

Another poet, Antonfrancesco Grazzini, founder of the prestigious Accademia degli Umidi in Florence, presents a powerful image of the destructive powers of the courtesan in one of his carnival songs, tellingly entitled "Canto di giovani impoveriti per le meretrici" ("Song of the young men impoverished because of whores").[25] The title of the poem uses the word *meretrici*, a term usually employed to refer to common prostitutes and not to courtesans. The word is obviously meant not as a literal reference but a slur, since it is doubtful that men would have spent enormous sums of money on gifts for the low-class prostitutes described in the poem. The song has as its fictional singers a group of men who have fallen prey to the allurements of courtesans. In its opening lines, the singers point to the "false and deceitful beauty" of the courtesan as the source of her power to enchant and then manipulate her male victims. Here again, the courtesan is a selfish, mercenary manipulator who uses her powers of seduction to coerce her noble lovers into buying themselves into poverty to appease her "dishonest desires."[26]

Having cast the courtesan as a malevolent, destructive force and themselves as the innocent victims of her seductive powers, the singers present to their listeners a series of examples of men ruined by their association with courtesans: "Some men don't go out except in the dead of night, others have fled to the countryside . . . and still others were once prelates, rich and worth something, but now they are tainted and miserable because of the wicked whores."[27] More overtly than in any of the other texts we have examined, the male poet in this carnival song expresses a sense of subjection and helplessness. It is the courtesan who, with her bewitching beauty, false though it may be, transforms men who were once wealthy and politically powerful into miserable social outcasts. The song reverses the common trope of the courtesan's body riddled with sores as punishment for her sins. Indeed, here it is the men who are "so tainted with pains and boils and wounds that they cannot find a hospital that will admit them."[28] The courtesan's body, though apparently untouched by disease, is the implicit cause of men's scourge.

In an ironic inversion of the conclusion of Venier's *Zaffetta*, Grazzini's closing lines warn young men of the dangers associated with courtesans. While Venier hoped that Angela's *trentuno* would teach other courtesans to be obedient to their noble lovers, Grazzini uses the tragic example of the ruined noblemen to discourage other men from consorting with courtesans. The only things that can come of such trysts, the men lament, are "Exile, poverty, torment, tears, anguish, and torture."[29] What is intriguing about this poem is that the courtesan is explicitly represented as a significant adversary who clearly has power over her male "victims." By denouncing her as a dangerous temptress, a siren who first lures men to her and then destroys them, Grazzini acknowledges that it is the courtesan who has the upper hand.

In sum, literary attacks on sixteenth-century Italian courtesans suggest that their male contemporaries viewed them as threatening yet desirable adversaries. In an era characterized by intense social and economic instability, authors deployed the figure of the courtesan to comment on issues of identity, both societal and personal. As Margaret Rosenthal has argued, some writers may have had professional reasons for their jealousy and insecurity as women entered the literary sphere and made use of the new power of print.[30] However, a closer look at texts such as Venier's *Zaffetta* reveals another, more primitive motive for the denigration of the courtesan: unfulfilled desire.[31] To put it as René Girard does, "Only someone who prevents us from satisfying a desire which he himself has inspired in us is truly an object of hatred."[32]

Indeed, Venier's poem puts forth an image of an idealized, obedient courtesan: "It would be a pleasure to say: I love a woman who is happy to serve me, and comes running to me when I call her."[33] When the courtesan refused to come running, Venier and other sixteenth-century poets responded with satire. Yet even as male writers sought to defame and disempower the courtesan, she emerged from their texts an independent, powerful woman who refused to conform to male expectation and desire. The very fact that she was considered threatening enough to be the subject of such forceful condemnation is evidence in itself of her power, a power to seduce the poet, a power to accept or reject him, and ultimately, the power to destroy him.

Notes

1. Pietro Aretino, *Ragionamento-Dialogo*, ed. Carla Forno and Giorgio Barberi Quarotti (Milan: Rizzoli, 1998), 323–24. English translations mine.

2. Maffio Venier, *Il libro chiuso di Maffio Venier (La tenzone con Veronica Franco)*, ed. Manlio Dazzi (Venice: Neri Pozza, 1956), 30. On Franco's poetic battle with Maffio Venier, see Margaret F. Rosenthal, *The Honest Courtesan: Veronica Franco, Citizen and Writer in Sixteenth-Century Venice* (Chicago: University of Chicago Press, 1992), 153–97.

3. *Il Dialogo dello Zoppino de la vita e genealogia di tutte le cortigiane di Roma*, ed. Gino Lanfranchi (Milan: L'Editrice del Libro Raro, 1922), 52.

4. For more on how courtesans were imagined and feared in Renaissance Italy, see Guido Ruggiero's essay, below, chap. 15. Ruggiero emphasizes the fact that while courtesans were sometimes perceived as destroyers of wealth, status, and *virtù*, they were also granters of these elements, since they selected and rewarded only the most worthy men. The two courtesan invectives by Lorenzo Venier, discussed below, are telling examples of how Renaissance poets responded when they were not "selected" by courtesans.

5. By foregrounding the power dialectic at work in sixteenth-century courtesan satires, I do not mean to discount the implications of genre, a subject with which I cannot deal at length in this essay. The discursive strategies deployed in these texts are informed by their participation in a centuries-old tradition of misogynist literature that goes back at least to the philosophical and medical theories of the ancient Greeks. Indeed, sixteenth-century satirists justified and bolstered their literary attacks on specific courtesans by deploying anti-woman topoi (all women are greedy, sexually voracious, and incapable of fidelity, to name a few) drawn from the misogynist tradition. Another important element of genre that I do not discuss here is the bawdy humor inherent in most of these texts. Indeed, literary wit is an important part of sixteenth-century satires on women: the burlesque caricatures, vitriolic lists of women's vices, and obscene anecdotes in satiric texts were commonplace, and one gets a sense that some authors may have been engaging in a game of one-upmanship.

6. On early editions and reprints of the poems see Lorenzo Venier, *Il trentuno della Zaffetta*, ed. Gino Raya (Catania: Tirelli, 1929), xii–xiii.

7. Lorenzo Venier, *La puttana errante: Poème en quatre chantes de Lorenzo Veniero* (Paris: Isidore Liseux, 1883), 12.

8. Venier, *Il trentuno della Zaffetta*, 7.

9. Ibid., 7.

10. Ibid.

11. See, for example, Lynne Lawner, *Lives of the Courtesans: Portraits of the Renaissance* (New York: Rizzoli, 1987), 74. I am not aware of any evidence that would support the historical reality of Venier's satire or of the practice of the *trentuno* in early modern Venice. However,

there are several references to Angela's *trentuno* in other sixteenth-century texts. The earliest of these that I am aware of is in the second, heavily revised version of Aretino's comedy *La cortigiana* (IV, 8), completed in 1534. An anonymous text, *La tariffa delle puttane di Vinegia* (Price-list of the Whores of Venice), first published in Venice in 1535 and then reprinted in Antonio Barzaghi's *Donne o cortigiane? La prostituzione a Venezia: Documenti di costume dal XVI al XVIII secolo* (Verona: Bertani, 1980), also mentions Angela's disgrace. In the *Dialogo dello Zoppino* (attributed to both Aretino and the Spanish priest Francisco Delicado), probably published in 1539, Zoppino claims to have participated in a *trentuno* inflicted upon another courtesan called "Lorenzina dal forno" (p. 66).

12. *Il trentuno della Zaffetta*, 59.

13. Ibid., 63.

14. Ibid., 59.

15. Ibid., 61.

16. In *De le rime di diversi nobili poeti toscani raccolte da M. Dionigi Atanagi*, book 2 (Venice: Ludovico Avanzo, 1565), fol. II[r].

17. London, British Library, Add. MS 12197 (hereafter BL 12197). See Martha Feldman, "The Academy of Domenico Venier, Music's Literary Muse in Mid-Cinquecento Venice," *Renaissance Quarterly* 44 (1991): 496–97, esp. n. 51; Tiziana Agostini Nordio, "Poesie dialettali di Domenico Venier," *Quaderni veneti* 14 (1991): 33–56; and Massimo Frapolli, "Un microcanzoniere di Domenico Venier in antologia," *Quaderni Veneti* 33 (2001): 29–68.

18. "E si no sarà d'altro el so parlar, che d'una, basta, no voi dir puttana; Mo d'una donna, che se fa chiavar." BL 12197, fol. 1[v].

19. "E ti sa, che ste zanze no sta ben, / ste macchie no se puol cussi lavar." Ibid., fol. 13[r].

20. "El me vien pur la gran stizza, / Ch'una femena me soia: / L'è pi dura, ch'un'Ancroia; / Maliazo sia sta chizza." Ibid., fol. 3[r]. The "Ancroia" that Venier is referring to is probably the virtuous heroine of the anonymous *Libro de la regina Ancroia*, a low-styled chivalric romance that was reprinted ten times in Venice between 1479 and 1589. See Marina Beer, *Romanzi di cavalleria: Il "Furioso" e il romanzo italiano del primo Cinquecento* (Rome: Bulzoni, 1987), 186, 208, 226, 236, and 286.

21. *Sì come dit'ogn'hor bella vi paio*, in Jacob Arcadelt, *Opera omnia*, vol. 4, ed. Albert Seay ([Rome]: American Institute of Musicology, 1968), 56–58. For the Italian text see the appendix.

22. *Donna, fra più bei volti honesti e cari*, in Arcadelt, *Opera omnia*, vol. 5, ed. Seay, 41–43. For the original Italian see the appendix. This text is also found in Francesco Corteccia's *Libro primo* (Venice: Scotto, 1544). I am indebted to Martha Feldman for pointing out that the rhyme schemes of this pair of poems are identical (AbACdCEeFF), along with some vocabulary—most notably, the final word of both poems is "scarsella" (purse)—an observation that confirms my thesis that the second poem was written as a riposte (*risposta*) to the first.

23. Indeed, female speech was one of the key issues of the *querelle des femmes*, the literary debate on the nature of woman that began with Christine de Pizan's *Book of the City of Ladies* (1405) but roiled throughout all Europe for over three centuries. A good, chaste woman, according to influential treatises on marriage and family such as Francesco Barbaro's *De re uxoria* (1415) and Leon Battista Alberti's *I libri della famiglia* (1433–37), was characterized by her ability to hold her tongue.

24. Girolamo Parabosco, *Rime di M. Girolamo Parabosco* (Venice, 1544), fol. 65[v].

25. Antonfrancesco Grazzini, *Canti carnascialeschi del rinascimento*, ed. Charles S. Singleton (Bari: Laterza, 1936), 421–22.

26. Ibid., vv. 1–10, p. 421.

27. Ibid., vv. 25–31.

28. Ibid., vv. 44–45, p. 422.

29. Ibid., vv. 48–49.

30. See Rosenthal, *The Honest Courtesan*, 15.

31. On Renaissance fears regarding the disastrous consequences of sexual love for courtesans see below, chap. 15.

32. René Girard, *Deceit, Desire, and the Novel: Self and Other in Literary Structure*, trans. Yvonne Freccero (Baltimore: Johns Hopkins University Press, 1965), 10–11.

33. *Zaffetta*, 65.

The Masculine Arts of the Ancient Greek Courtesan

Male Fantasy or Female Self-representation?

The literature and vase paintings of ancient Greece represent courtesans in a variety of poses and social situations, raising the hope that for this very small group of women we may have enough evidence to talk about their lives in some detail. This hope is, however, repeatedly dashed by scholars who rightly worry about the difficulty of hearing real female voices in male-authored texts or seeing real women's lives represented clearly in paintings commissioned and executed by males.

But ancient depictions of courtesans—both literary and graphic—do not fit the usual pattern, because they include a number of puzzling scenes in which courtesans are shown performing skills or arts that traditionally belong to the domain of men. As we shall see, when faced with such anomalous scenes, scholars repeatedly suggest that for one reason or another, a male painter or a male poet or writer has created a fantasy or a mirage that has no grounding whatsoever in reality. Taken individually, these arguments about male fantasies are highly plausible in explaining a glaring anomaly and each is useful in isolation. But as a group the anomalies suggest that there might in fact be something special about the social condition or position of courtesans themselves that allows them to generate such images and thereby to represent themselves, as women rarely do, in the historical record of ancient Greece.

In this brief study I will argue that a consistent and peculiar feature of the courtesans of Athens and perhaps elsewhere in the ancient Greek world is the manner in which they co-opt various "arts"—symposiastic, rhetorical, ritual, and so on—that are otherwise associated almost exclusively with men; and that they do so in order to assert their own autonomy and independence in a culture that has no real concept of the autonomous and independent woman. I will also suggest that like the men they imitate, they too were often either practitioners or consumers of the literary and graphic arts and thus had more control than we think over the images found there.[1] In what follows, I will focus on three different kinds of masculine arts pursued by Athenian courtesans: (1) an aggressive form of male magic used to drive a young man from his home, (2) the game *kottabos* and a whole repertory of other typically male gestures performed at the symposium, and (3) male verbal wit—both poetical and rhetorical—performed at the symposium. With regard to this last section I shall go on to suggest that many or most of the small number of female poets from ancient Greece may in fact have been courtesans and that the existence of courtesan poets may even have been responsible for the amazingly wrongheaded idea circulating during Roman times that Sappho herself was a courtesan who killed herself out of unrequited love for one of her male lovers.

I shall quote a brief anecdote in order to frame my argument that courtesans were able—unlike any other women in Athens—to control the production and perhaps even the reception of their images. In his *Memorabilia*, Xenophon tells how Socrates hears about the great beauty of an Athenian hetaera named Theodote and goes with some friends to visit her,[2]

> a beautiful woman who was ready to keep company with anyone who pleased her. One of the bystanders remembered that the beauty of this woman was beyond description and that painters visited her in order to paint her portrait and that she revealed to them as much of herself as was honorable (*kalos*). So they [i.e., Socrates and friends] went to Theodote's house and when they found her posing for a painter, they began to watch.

Note that although I have followed the usual translation of the word *kalos* in this passage as "honorable," it has, in fact, a wide range of meanings and can also mean "beautiful," "noble," or "of fine quality." A few lines later in the dialogue, Xenophon reports that "Socrates noticed that she was sumptuously adorned, that her mother at her side was also wearing fine clothes and jewelry and that she had many lovely looking maid-servants also well looked after and that her house was lavishly furnished." Socrates at first glance assumes that Theodote is a wealthy landowner, but later learns that she supports herself on the gifts of her male friends (*philoi*), that is that she is a courtesan.[3]

I shall return to this scene again in this essay, but for the present we need to ask ourselves: if Xenophon's general description of this rich courtesan is true—and most probably it *is* true, given the usual verisimilitude that both Plato and Xenophon use in framing their dialogues—and if by some miracle one of these paintings of Theodote had survived from antiquity, would we be justified in claiming that the image of her in that painting was solely the creation of a male artist based on flights of his fantasy? Or for that matter, is the description just quoted from Xenophon entirely his fiction? I suspect not, for it is clear from the passage itself that Theodote both limits the access of men to her home (she keeps company with those who please her) and when posing for a painting carefully reveals only what is *kalos* about herself. This anecdote, then, illustrates my thesis in very brief compass: that some of the most successful courtesans may have been able, because of their independent position in the Greek city and because of their wealth, to control their own lives and their own images as well.

CASE NO. 1: THE ARTS OF EROTIC MAGIC

More than a decade ago, my teacher Jack Winkler put his finger on a startling inconsistency regarding the ancient evidence for the use of an aggressive erotic spell that aimed at forcing unwilling victims from their houses and into the arms of the person perform-ing the spell.[4] He noted that in more than seventy of the eighty extant examples of actual spells of this type—those inscribed on lead tablets or papyri—a man was the agent and a woman the victim, as we can see in these three different examples:[5]

> Burn, torch the soul of Allous, her female body (= sexual organs?), her limbs, until she leaves the home of Apollonius.

> Goad the tortured psyche, the heart of Karosa, whom Thelo bore, until she leaps forth and comes to Apalos . . . do not allow Karosa herself, whom Thelo bore, to think of her [own] husband, her child, drink, food, but let her come melting for passion and love and intercourse, especially yearning for the intercourse of Apalos . . . in this very hour, immediately, immediately; quickly, quickly.

> Seize Euphemia and lead her to me, Theon, loving me with crazy desire, and bind her with inescapable bonds, strong ones of adamantine, for the love of me, Theon, and do not allow her to eat, drink, obtain sleep, jest or laugh but make her leap out [i.e., of her house] . . . and leave behind her father, mother, brothers, sisters, until she comes to me.

We can see how in each of these cases a man uses a magical incantation to burn or torture a woman until she leaves the home of her parents or husband. Winkler noted, however, that the literary evidence seemed to show precisely the opposite: that women were the primary users of such spells. Thus, for example, in a well-known poem by Theocritus a courtesan named Simaetha narrates and performs a spell of this type:[6]

> Delphis brought me trouble, and I for Delphis burn this bay. And as these bay-leaves crackle loud in the fire . . . so too may the flesh of Delphis waste in the flame!
>   Iunx,[7] drag to my house the man I love!
> As with the goddess's aid, I melt this wax, so straightway may Delphis of Myndus waste with love . . .
>   Iunx, drag to my house the man I love!

In her incantation Simaetha uses sympathetic magic to burn and melt her lover Delphis,[8] who she suspects is at the home of a rival; the refrain of her incantation, moreover, reiterates her overall goal: "drag to my house the man I love!" A literary epigram by a retiring courtesan named Niko similarly describes a powerful *iunx*-wheel that "knows how to drag [she uses the same verb as Simaetha] a man from across the sea and young men from the women's quarters."[9]

Lucian gives us another look at the kind of magic used—or in this case commis-sioned—by courtesans, when he has a courtesan named Bacchis describe a spell that she once paid an old witch (*pharmakis*) to perform:[10]

> She [i.e., the witch] hangs these [i.e., the clothes or hairs of the man] from a peg and heats them up with burning sulfur, sprinkling salt over the fire, and says in addition the names of both people, his and yours. Then she brings out from her bosom a *rhombos* and whirls it round while speaking with a rapid tongue some incantation of barbaric and frightening names . . . And not long afterwards . . . he came to me led by the incantation—despite the fact that his buddies had told him off and Phoebis, the girl with whom he was living, kept pleading with him.

Like the real spells quoted earlier, the witch hired by Bacchis uses sympathetic burning magic to force her lover away from the house of another courtesan and back to
her. Here, as in the case of Simaetha and Niko, a male Greek author represents a
courtesan performing or paying for a ritual designed to torture and burn a past or
potential lover and thereby "drag" him to her against his will.

We can see quite clearly, then, the disparity that troubled Winkler: the hard
evidence suggests that in real life men regularly used this kind of violent spell to get
at women residing in the households of other males, whereas the literary texts repeatedly show us women, not men, performing these same rituals. Winkler suggested
that the literary representations—some of which probably derive ultimately from
the Athenian comic stage—were little more than male fantasies, which result when
male authors project their own bad behavior onto women. He argued, moreover, that
this process involved a double psychological projection whereby lovesick persons try
to project their own terrible symptoms of pain, madness, and irresistible yearning
onto the female object of their desire and at the same time take on the beloved's
own aloofness and imperviousness to such pains.[11] I have pointed out elsewhere that
Winkler formulated the problem brilliantly but that his explanation faltered on a
number of points, only one of which is of concern here: in nearly every one of these
literary descriptions of erotic magic the agent is not simply a female, but a courtesan
in whose arsenal these aggressive spells seem to be a traditional weapon.[12] Space does
not permit me to recount here the full argument, but only to note that courtesans
co-opt such spells from men because from time to time they (like male seducers and
adulterers) need surreptitiously to force a reluctant lover away from the home of
his parents, his spouse, or another courtesan. Such behavior fits into a much larger
pattern of courtesans competing with older males to become the aggressive lovers
of wealthy younger men. This idea is, at first glance, quite odd, since the role of an
aggressive older male—that is, the *erastēs* who pursues younger men in homoerotic
courtship—is the centerpiece of a Greek's representation of himself as quintessentially male. In fact, in the dialogue of Xenophon quoted earlier, Socrates and the
courtesan Theodote joke about the fact that they both are "hunting" after the same
kinds of young men (3.11.7–17): "Socrates," exclaimed Theodote, "why don't you
become my partner-in-the-pursuit (*sunthēratēs*—that is, of young men)?"

A little further on in the same dialogue, when the conversation turns to love
spells, Socrates even jokes that he uses love magic to ensure that his favorite young
men come to him and stay by his side (3.11.15–18):

> "Indeed, do you also know how to do these things [that is, use love magic], Soc-
> rates?" she said.
>
> "Why else," he said, "do you think that Apollodorus here and Antisthenes
> never leave me? And why do you think that Cebes and Simmias come from Thebes?
> Know well that these things do not happen without many love-potions, incanta-
> tions, and *iunges*."
>
> "Do, then, lend me your *iunx*," she said, "so that I may draw it against you
> first!"
>
> "But by Zeus," he said, "I wasn't planning to be drawn to you, but rather I want
> you to come to me."

The joke here turns on the conceit that the notoriously ugly Socrates is always surrounded by good-looking young men, and therefore must be using magic to keep some by his side and force others to travel long distances, like the *iunx* of the courtesan Niko, which was able to drag men to her home from other women's bedrooms and even from across the sea. Indeed, the tongue-in-cheek argument at the end of the sequence nicely illustrates the kind of confusion in gender roles that the Greek courtesan generates: both Theodote and Socrates insist on using the *iunx* against the other.

Joan Burton and others have shown, in fact, that the lovesick Simaetha in Theocritus' poem also acts very much like an aggressive male lover (*erastēs*) when she falls in love with Delphis the first time she sees him walking home from the gymnasium with his chest glistening with sweat.[13] In my book I argue that this anomalous attitude and stance of courtesans like Theodote and Simaetha makes more sense if we understand that they—because they live outside of the direct control of a male citizen and because they have a house and an independent income—were either socially constructed as males by the men with whom they interacted or perhaps even aggressively co-opted and fashioned this image for themselves.

CASE NO. 2: COURTESANS PLAY *KOTTABOS*

Let me turn now to a pair of enigmatic red-figured Athenian vase paintings of the late sixth century B.C. that depict all-female symposia, again a startling idea since these symposia were the bastion of elite male privilege and self-identity, from which most women were rigorously excluded. The images in question depict women mimicking the dress and activities of men at a symposium: the pair in the upper register of fig. 11.1, for example, recline on pillows, drink, converse, and play a game with wine cups called *kottabos*, which involved hooking a finger or two in one of the handles of a drinking cup and hurling at a suspended target the sediment or lees that collected at the bottom of their cups of unfiltered wine. In fig. 11.1, the women are dressed precisely like male symposiasts: they bare their upper bodies and casually drape a himation over their lower parts. In fig. 11.2 we see a larger scene of four entirely naked courtesans, each one labeled with a name that is appropriate for a courtesan: two are drinking wine, one is playing an aulos, and a fourth is about to make a toss in the *kottabos* game (she is in the bottom right corner). In the late 1980s two German scholars, Ingeborg Peschel and Carola Reinsberg, suggested that these pictures—like the named figures of men on similar cups in similar scenes—probably represented real courtesans, who—they conjectured—held such all-female parties in their homes.[14] More recently, however, some skepticism has been voiced about the realism of these scenes, and Leslie Kurke has suggested that the vases were in fact made for "the gaze of (male) symposiasts, who enjoyed seeing their own activities mirrored in those sexually available female companions."[15] In short, like Winkler, she believes that these vases merely depict male fantasies about courtesans performing a series of typically male activities.

I can, of course, sympathize with the current dissatisfaction with Peschel and

FIGURE 11.1. Hydria painted by Phintiasm ca. 520 B.C.

Reinsberg, who at times seem to take a very simplistic view that if a scene is painted on a vase, it must have happened in real life. On the other hand, it does not seem a priori impossible to me that wealthy courtesans like Theodote might have held such drinking parties for their friends and that they may also have commissioned a set of drinking cups and pitchers to commemorate these parties and at which to use them—precisely as wealthy elite males did. I also think Peschel and Reinsberg are probably closer to the truth in the case of these two vases in particular, because they use inscriptions in a way that clearly links the images on the vase to the real world. The painting of the two women in fig. 11.1 appears on the shoulder of a vase whose main scene (on the belly of the vase, shown in the lower register of fig. 11.1) portrays a young man and a boy in a music lesson with a bearded instructor. The young beard-less man who sits holding the lyre (he is second from our right) is labeled with the name "Euthymides." In the scene of the two women on the upper panel, moreover, an inscription informs us that the courtesan on the left is saying: "For you, beautiful Euthymides, [I cast] this." The connection is greatly emphasized on the vase itself, because these are the only inscriptions and because the figure named Euthymides is positioned directly below the woman who speaks his name—indeed, the elbow on which she reclines is about an inch and a half above his head. We know from other sources that in this game of *kottabos* the success of a throw was often believed to be predictive: if an older man successfully hit the target after dedicating his throw to a lover, he would also be successful in his pursuit of that particular young man (a bit like plucking the petals of a flower and saying "he loves me, he loves me not"). The close connection between the two scenes in fig. 11.1 is thus rather humorous:

FIGURE 11.2. Psykter ("Wine cooler"), painted by Euphronius, ca. 520 B.C.

while the young man is slaving away at his music lessons, these two courtesans are drinking at a symposium and one of them is thinking about him, presumably in an erotic fashion.

In fig. 11.2, there is a similar use of inscription: the naked courtesan about to make her *kottabos* toss is identified by an inscription as Smikra, who says: "I toss this one for you, Leagros." As in the other painting, this inscription seems to connect this scene closely with an individual living in Athens at the time of its manufacture. Indeed, the object of Smikra's affections is well known to us: the phrase "Leagros is beautiful!" is inscribed on at least forty-five other pots from this same time period and scholars have inferred that this Leagros must have been an extremely attractive young man.[16] We usually understand that vases inscribed with such compliments were gifts or at least compliments to the young man. In light of this social practice, what are we to make of the inscriptions in figs. 11.1 and 11.2? Kurke suggests that these scenes were not commissioned or owned by courtesans, but rather by men who share their own longing for the same beautiful youth. In this reading, the generalized male fantasy of courtesans holding their own symposia is much more focused, for the inscriptions reveal that these same males have projected onto Smikra their desires for Leagros. Like Winkler's interpretation of the literary scenes of courtesans performing male forms of magic, this is a highly plausible explanation, but here, too, the evidence for the existence of wealthy, autonomous courtesans in Athens suggests a more straightforward reading of the scene of Smikra playing *kottabos*: the vase was commissioned by her as a compliment for or a declaration of love to Leagros. In having done so, of course, Smikra, like the wealthy men who commissioned similarly inscribed pots or cups, was clearly positioning herself as an aggressive hunter and seducer (*erastēs*) of the most beautiful young man in town.

We know, in fact, that in some situations courtesans did feel themselves in direct competition with older males who pursued the same young men. I have already discussed the jokes between Theodote and Socrates about their shared interest in and methods for pursuing handsome young men, and Lucian relates the story of yet another courtesan named Chelidonion, whose lover Clinias has been sent by his parents to study philosophy day in and day out with an older man. Here Chelidonion is speaking to a woman friend:[17]

> But Dromo [i.e., the boy's slave] says that Aristaenetus [the boy's teacher] is the sort who's fond of boys, and, by pretending to teach them, keeps company with the most handsome youths, and has now got Clinias on his own . . . he's reading with him amorous discourses addressed by the philosophers of old to their pupils, and is all wrapped up with the boy.

Chelidonion herself is undeterred and plans a counterattack to win her lover back. The situation described here is, in fact, similar to the scenario suggested by the inscriptions to Euthymides on the vase in fig. 11.2, where the same two worlds of a young Athenian man are contrasted: his music lessons with a bearded older man and the house of the unnamed courtesan who dedicates her shot in *kottabos* to him.

CASE NO. 3: RHETORIC AND POETRY AT THE SYMPOSIUM

Finally, I close by discussing—very briefly, since James Davidson has already covered much of this territory in his essay in this volume (chap. 1)—the repeated image that we get of well-educated courtesans successfully participating in the competitive games of wit and verbal skill at the symposium. The most astounding fact about the Athenian courtesans of the fifth and fourth centuries B.C. is the high level of education that some of them seem to have received. Machon, for example, an early Hellenistic author, collected anecdotes (*chreiai*) about witty Athenian courtesans who in their banter are able to quote and parody famous lines of Euripides and Sophocles in a very sophisticated way that reveals close knowledge of the original text.[18] And indeed, the famous thirteenth book of Athenaeus' *Deipnosophistae* is filled with tales of witty courtesans verbally sparring and one-upping their male companions. This high level of education and sophistication seems to be at the heart of the confused biography of Aspasia, the mistress—and eventually the wife—of the Athenian leader Pericles. Most scholars believe that as a young woman she emigrated to Athens from the city of Miletus and began a career as a courtesan; she was, moreover, famed for her intelligence and her mastery of rhetoric. Some ancient authors claim that she taught rhetoric and was an acclaimed writer of public speeches for her male friends—including Pericles and Socrates. (In one Platonic dialogue, the *Menexenus*, Socrates quotes from memory a speech that he claims to have learned from her.)

In recent years some scholars have suggested that this later biographical tradition is a mirage or fantasy based on quotations from hostile comic poets and that we really know very little about this woman, and certainly not enough to ascertain that she was a courtesan.[19] The question is a vexed one that I shall sidestep here by declaring myself agnostic. But if we accept the persistent stories of her great intelligence, her high level of education, her independent financial resources, and her famed oratorical ability, we can make another argument: that even if Aspasia was not a courtesan, the fact that she was quite easily and repeatedly assumed by later authors to be one speaks precisely to the point I wish to make, namely that wealthy, educated women living in classical Athens were simply assumed to be courtesans, since other women were not taught the kinds of literary skills they were able to acquire.

With erudite and combative Renaissance poets like Veronica Franco in mind,[20] it is interesting to note that Aspasia was also said to have composed poetry:[21]

> The clever Aspasia, to be sure, who was Socrates' teacher in rhetoric, says in those hexametrical verses that have been handed down as hers [which Crates' student Herodicus quotes]:
> Socrates, I have not failed to notice that your heart is smitten with desire for the son of Deinomarche and Clinias. But pay attention to me if you wish to be successful in your suit. Don't disregard my message, but obey me, and it will be much better for you . . .

And thus the noble Socrates goes off "hunting" with the woman of Miletus as his teacher of eros (*erotodidaskalos*).

The poem, which I have not quoted in full, goes on to give Socrates explicit advice about seducing young men and—if it is genuine—was most likely performed at a symposium not unlike those that included the songs and mimes discussed by James Davidson in this volume. It is especially noteworthy that in this anecdote Aspasia is treated as an expert in the art of seducing (literally "hunting") young men, much the same as Theodote, who as we saw earlier, invites Socrates to join her as a fellow hunter of young men.

There is, in fact, scattered evidence (most of it late) for several courtesan-poets:[22] Charixena (an aulos player, who composed erotic verse), Glauce of Ceos (a citharist in the court of Ptolemy II), Nossis of Locri (who wrote among other things erotic "Locrian songs"), and Theano of Locri (who also composed Locrian songs). Athenaeus also mentions a Spartan poetess (*poiētria*) named Megalostrate, a contemporary of Alcman, who was famous for attracting her lovers by conversation. Praxilla, a female poet of the early classical period, was said to have composed scolia and drinking songs, both of which were traditionally sung at the symposium, and for this reason, several scholars have suggested that she, too, was a courtesan.[23] The most surprising member of this group, however, given the undeniably homoerotic content of her poetry, is Sappho, who according to Athenaeus and several other writers, died out of love for one of her male lovers.[24] It is hard to know what to make of such a strange assertion, but like the charge that Aspasia was a courtesan we can certainly understand the logic that drives it: since Sappho performed solo songs or poems and since nearly all monodic poetry composed by males in this same period was performed at symposia for their male peers and comrades, it seems obvious, unless proven otherwise, that the symposium was the site for Sappho's performances as well. And since most female performers in this context were either slaves or courtesans,[25] it is quite reasonable that Greeks in the later periods—presumably those who had not taken the time to read Sappho's poems carefully—might assume that she, too, was a courtesan.

CONCLUSION

I hope I have shown here that some of the literary and graphic evidence for courtesans belongs in a special category of representation, for despite their gender some courtesans—and I grant that it was probably a small number—were in a position (thanks primarily to their wealth and independent status) to control the production and even the reception of their images, very much like the male elites whom they emulated and indeed with whom they competed. There is widespread literary evidence that courtesans co-opted the magic spells of men, either performing them themselves or paying for others to do so. Does this constitute evidence of a male fantasy? Perhaps, but the existence of female poets and performers at symposia (some of them courtesans) leaves open the possibility that some of these literary scenes of courtesans using erotic magic may have themselves been created by courtesans. Indeed Davidson's essay proposes that Theocritus' poem about the elaborate erotic spell of Simaetha may have imitated this kind of short performance of a courtesan at a symposium. In my second case, the images of courtesans playing *kottabos* similarly co-opt male gestures and dress, and—as the inscriptions on the two vases reveal—there is reason to believe that such images were produced for wealthy courtesans as a way to fashion themselves as autonomous males who could make erotic claims on handsome young men like the other *erastai* of the city. In my third case, I suggested briefly that the tradition of courtesans as witty and combative conversationalists likewise embraces the less well-documented evidence for courtesans as the producers of symposiastic poetry, such as elegies, scolia, and drinking songs, which were also traditional vehicles for male self-representation and competition. Wealthy courtesans, in short, seem to have occupied a unique place in Athenian society, from which they could influence and control the way in which they were represented in the sources that have come down to us. These images—like those of elite males who called themselves *kaloi k'agathoi* ("the beautiful and the good")—can, of course, be combative, manipulative, and exaggerated. But as Xenophon reveals about Theodote and the men who came to paint her, the courtesan, like her male counterparts, was in a special position financially and socially that allowed her to control the access men had to her home and her body. Indeed, we are told that she apparently revealed to her adoring public only as much as she deemed to be *kalos*—a word that notoriously means "beautiful," "noble," and "good" and would seem in this context to refer to her own self-positioning as one of the elites of Athens.

Notes

I would like to thank the editors of this volume for organizing the splendid conference at which this essay was first presented and for their helpful comments and suggestions on the later written version.

1. This essay is part of a larger, on-going project in which I argue that some Greek courtesans—the wealthy and successful ones—were consistently seen in Athens as anomalous males, because they were the autonomous heads of their own "all-female households" and because they took advantage of their wealth and influence to fashion themselves as aggressive, powerful figures in their own right—just like elite males. Another part of the project will appear as "Lysistrata the Priestess or the Courtesan? Female Stereotypes in Aristophanes' *Lysistrata*," in *Prostitutes and Courtesans in the Ancient World*, ed. Christopher A. Faraone and Laura McClure (Madison: University of Wisconsin Press, Madison, forthcoming 2006).

2. Xenophon *Memorabilia* 3.11.1–4.

3. James Davidson, *Courtesans and Fishcakes: The Consuming Passions of Classical Athens* (London: HarperCollins, 1997), 120–30, *passim*, gives a thorough and thoughtful discussion of this encounter.

4. Jack Winkler, *The Constraints of Desire: The Anthropology of Sex and Gender in Ancient Greece* (New York: Routledge, 1990), 71–98, esp. 82–90.

5. I give here three illustrative examples dating to the second and third centuries A.D. For relevant bibliography and discussion see Christopher A. Faraone, *Ancient Greek Love Magic* (Cambridge, MA: Harvard University Press, 1999), 3–4 and 59–63. In general the evidence and arguments that I deploy here are drawn from chap. 2 of this book: "Spells for Introducing Uncontrollable Passion," 41–95.

6. Theocritus *Idyll* 2.23–32, in *Theocritus*, trans. A. S. F. Gow (Cambridge: Cambridge University Press, 1952), ad loc. with minor revisions. In what follows I give a brief selection and synopsis of the evidence and arguments assembled in Faraone, *Love Magic*, 55–68 and 149–60. For the growing scholarly consensus that Simaetha is clearly represented as a courtesan, not some noblewoman down on her luck, see ibid., 153–54.

7. The *iunx* (pl. *iunges*) addressed in the refrain here and referred to in several of the literary treatments of erotic magic cited below has a long and complicated history. It originates as a "bird bound to a four-spoked wheel" (Pindar, *Pythian Ode* 4.214), that is, a device designed to torture a bird as an effigy for the victim. In later periods, however, the bird disappears altogether and the *iunx* is reduced to the wheel alone, and seems designed to spin and disorient the victim like a whirling top; see Faraone, *Love Magic*, 56–58 and 64–69.

8. Throughout this essay I use the neutral term "lover" to refer to the client-boyfriend of a courtesan. In ancient Greek discourse, courtesans referred to these men discreetly as "friends" (*philoi*) and they themselves were referred to politely as hetaerae, the female equivalent of the *hetairoi*, who were a man's "boon companions" and "best friends." But the traditional and often quite nasty invective of classical Athens (extant, for example, in comedy and public speeches) frequently cast these relationships as purely commercial ones and would refer to the same women as whores (*pornai*). See Davidson, *Courtesans and Fishcakes*, 109–27, and Leslie Kurke, *Coins, Bodies, Games and Gold: The Politics of Meaning in Archaic Greece* (Princeton: Princeton University Press, 1999), 176–87, for the best recent discussions with full bibliography.

9. *Palatine Anthology* 5.205; see Faraone, *Love Magic*, 151–53 for a full discussion.

10. Lucian of Samosata, *Dialogues of the Courtesans* 4.1.

11. Winkler, *Constraints*, 82–90.

12. Faraone, *Love Magic*, 82–85.

13. Joan B. Burton, *Theocritus' Urban Mimes: Mobility, Gender, and Patronage* (Berkeley: University of California Press, 1995), 43–44, which cites earlier bibliography.

14. Ingeborg Peschel, *Die Hetäre bei Symposion und Komos in der attisch-rotfigurigen Vasenmalerei des 6.–4. Jahrhundert v. Chr.* (Frankfurt: P. Lang, 1987), 70–74 and 110–12, and Carola Reinsberg, *Ehe, Hetärentum und Knabenliebe im antiken Griechenland* (Munich: C. H. Beck, 1993), 112–14.

15. Kurke, *Coins, Bodies*, 205–8.

16. Ibid., 207.

17. Lucian, *Dialogues of the Courtesans* 4.1.

18. Machon, *Chreiai* 168–73, 226–30, and 405–10 (Sandbach). See Leslie Kurke, "Gender, Politics, and Subversion in the *Chreiai* of Machon," *Proceedings of the Cambridge Philological Society* 48 (2002): 20–65 for a full discussion.

19. Madeleine M. Henry, *Prisoner of History: Aspasia of Miletus and Her Biographical Tradition* (Oxford: Oxford University Press, 1991), for the full argument and bibliography.

20. Margaret F. Rosenthal, *The Honest Courtesan: Veronica Franco, Citizen and Writer in Sixteenth-Century Venice* (Chicago: University of Chicago Press, 1992), 9–10, describes the performative nature of the Renaissance Italian courtesan, who like her male counterparts, the courtiers, relied heavily on debate, invective, and other forms of verbal competition to make a name for herself. This tension shows up occasionally in Greek materials in the competition between the courtesan and the male philosopher, for which see my discussion above and Leslie McClure, *Courtesans at Table: Gender and Greek Literary Culture in Athenaeus* (London: Routledge 2003), 103–4.

21. Athenaeus 219 C–D. See McClure, *Courtesans*, 83–84.

22. McClure, *Courtesans*, 85–86, for further discussion.

23. See Athenaeus 594 A, for Praxilla's *scolia*, which were known to Aristophanes and are quoted on an Athenian vase of 470 B.C.; see McClure, *Courtesans* 86, for discussion.

24. Ibid., 85.

25. See Davidson's essay in this volume, chap. 1.

PART IV

EXCURSUS: GEISHA DIALOGUES

The City Geisha and Their Role in Modern Japan

Anomaly or Artistes?

INTRODUCTION: THE WORLD'S FIRST MODERN WOMEN

From the very beginning of their history, geisha were always a profession entirely separate from courtesans as they were conceived of in Japan. They originated in eighteenth-century Japan, both inside and outside the pleasure quarters, and were defined as "entertainers" or "artistes": the word *gei-sha* literally means "arts person." The courtesans of the pleasure quarters (known as *tayu* in seventeenth- and eighteenth-century Kyoto and *oiran* in eighteenth- and nineteenth-century Edo [Tokyo]) offered their bodies as currency—though very often at a price too high for all but the wealthiest and most powerful men to afford. The geisha conversely were defined as selling music, singing, and dancing.

Thus the traditional roles of the courtesan as understood in the West were divided. In Japan, courtesans provided sexual fantasy and also sexual favors when they chose to do so, while the geisha took the role of entertainer. But the division was never totally clear-cut. The fact that the geisha originated in the pleasure quarters inevitably colored the way in which they were perceived by the rest of society.

As for prostitutes, they filled the lower ranks of the demimonde. In English there are two principal terms for women who sell sexual favors—"courtesans" and "prostitutes"—whereas in Japan there were many terms denoting different ranks of prostitute and courtesan, suggesting that it was a large, thriving, and variegated industry.

Courtesans and geisha called the separate reality which they inhabited the *karyukai*, the "flower and willow world." Present-day geisha continue to use the term. The courtesans were the colorful "flowers" while the geisha were "willows," modest and quiet but strong and resilient, able to bend with the winds of fate. Up until World War II geisha served as a pool of potential mistresses in an age when all self-respecting Japanese men were expected to have one or several as an indication of their wealth and power (rather like having a Porsche today). But they have always maintained that they are primarily professionals; they are artistes.

Within the geisha world there is a strict gradation of ranking. The top ranks are the grand dowagers of the Gion district of Kyoto, who consider themselves a world apart even from the lower-ranking geisha districts of the same city. In all there are five geisha districts (*hanamachi* or "flower towns") in Kyoto, of which three (Gion, Pontocho, and Kamishichiken) have a grander pedigree and reputation than the others (Gion Higashi and Miyagawa-cho); five in Tokyo, of which four (Shimbashi, Kagurazaka, Akasaka, and Yoshicho) are classier and one (Asakusa, situated in the working-class East End of Tokyo) lower ranking; and one or more in almost every other Japanese city.

At the opposite extreme are hot-spring geisha who work in the spa resorts and, as far as most Japanese are concerned, are little better than prostitutes. These are the geisha that Miho Matsugu writes about in her essay (see chap. 13).[1] They cater to office workers on holiday—a far less exclusive clientele than their Kyoto sisters, and are much less ruinously expensive. They may well supplement their income by selling sex. Nevertheless they are not the same as prostitutes. Hot-spring geisha too are trained to be skilled dancers and musicians. City geisha, particularly the high-ranking geisha of districts like Gion, do not consider them geisha at all and would be horrified to be mentioned in the same breath. Except where specified, my essay refers to city geisha who consider themselves professional entertainers, representing the mainstream geisha tradition.

In 1999 I spent several months living among the geisha in several different cities. I began my research in Kyoto, where the geisha tradition and arts are most fully maintained. Breaking into the geisha world required great patience; I had to use my years of experience of living in Japan to become part of the landscape, rather as if studying wildlife. I took a room in a small inn in one of the geisha districts and bided my time. Day after day I would be seen on the street, in the local coffee shop, at tea ceremony classes, and even at the hairdresser's where the geisha get their hair done. Little by little I made friends. Eventually, after a couple of months, the geisha began to invite me into their homes.

I made contact with geisha of different ranks—not just the grand dowagers of Gion but also geisha in the much-despised Miyagawa-cho in Kyoto. I was befriended by Tokyo geisha and spent time in their geisha houses, and I met geisha in the cities of Fukuoka and Kanazawa. I also made a trip to Atami to meet hot-spring geisha and participated in a teahouse party there—though if I had revealed this to any of the city geisha I knew, they would never have spoken to me again.

The fact that I was an outsider and a temporary visitor to their culture and their country made it possible for geisha to talk to me and to reveal things that they would not have revealed to Japanese. I have never come across a Japanese woman who has had a similar experience and suspect that perhaps a Japanese woman would not want to. Most Japanese of either sex are very suspicious of geisha and of Western interest in them. They regard them as one of the three irritatingly clichéd images that Westerners have of Japan, alongside cherry blossoms and Mount Fuji. Most Japanese have never met a geisha and are not at all interested in them. One Japanese woman friend asked me, "Why do you want to write about the bad side of Japan?"[2] Even if a Japanese woman did wish to meet geisha—as a journalist or a scholar—I suspect that as a fellow countrywoman she would find the geisha world considerably more firmly closed than it was to me. In any case, it requires vast amounts of patience, determination, and time—and usually quite a lot of money—to overcome the geisha's resistance to outsiders.

To fevered Western imaginings, "geisha" embodies all the allure of the mysterious East. The very word conjures up an image of doe-eyed maidens who chatter charmingly, pour men's drinks, laugh at their jokes, and satisfy their every desire. "Demure," "submissive" (the favorite adjective for geisha), these women are everything that their tough, politically correct Western sisters are not—or so the myth goes.

But geisha are, in fact, very unlike our Western imaginings. Far from being demure, the geisha I got to know during my research ranged from formidable dowagers who mix on equal terms with the most powerful men in Japan (and whom one would not dare for one second suggest had ever been prostitutes) to charismatic dancers and musicians on a par with Gelsey Kirkland and Darcy Bussell or Jessye Norman and Josephine Baker, and self-assured, accomplished young women who see the geisha training as a kind of finishing school.

There is thus an enormous gulf between the geisha's self-image and the way in which the rest of the world sees them. As far as the geisha are concerned, they are artistes not far removed from ballerinas or opera singers, who spend their lives perfecting their art, be it music, singing, dancing, or the art of conversation. In contrast, those outside their closed world—both Japanese and Western—often dismiss them as prostitutes. Cognoscenti today often assert that, to the contrary, they are far from prostitutes. But in Japan the truth is never that simple. As one geisha told me, theirs is not a world of "yes" and "no" or black and white.

Indeed one wonders why Westerners are so fiercely wedded to their notion of geisha. The concept is intimately tied up with the creation of the Western image of the "orient." Madame Butterfly, the fictitious geisha who kills herself for love of a Western man, embodies this Western fantasy. Her story was inspired by fact but was shaped into its best-known melodramatic form by a succession of Western males, beginning with the amateur American writer John Luther Long, who wrote the original short story "Madame Butterfly" in 1898, which inspired the librettists Giuseppe Giacosa and Luigi Illica and the composer Giacomo Puccini to create their famous opera. "Madame Butterfly" has shaped our stereotype of Japanese women and of geisha (and is the source of considerable irritation among Japanese); yet it has virtually nothing to do with the reality of the tough independent Japanese women who actually pursue the profession of geisha.[3]

Part of the explanation for Westerners' continuing fascination with geisha is that there is no equivalent of the geisha's profession in Western society nor any direct translation for the word "geisha" in English.

In fact, as I discovered to my surprise when I went to live among them, geisha lead lives not very different from those of modern Western women. When I first lived in Japan, I discovered that, as an unmarried career woman, I had almost nothing in common with the Japanese women I knew. They were housewives who had married in their twenties and devoted themselves to their children. They spent their time cleaning, cooking, and dealing with family finances and hardly ever saw their husbands. They asked me so frequently why I was not married that I too began to wonder why I was the odd one out.

When I met the geisha I discovered that in Japan there were kindred spirits after all. I felt thoroughly at home among them, far more than I ever had among Japanese housewives. For a start, geisha never asked me why I was not married. If a geisha marries, she gives up her geisha status, so no one can be a wife and a geisha at the same time. Some geisha have children; but if they do, the children rarely see their fathers. Far from being domestic, geisha have maids to clean and cook; one of the axioms of geisha life is that geisha can't cook.

Instead their lives are centered around their careers, perfecting the classical Japanese music and dance which is their profession. And while in the past most were supported by a *danna*—a patron who was very often also their lover—these days the average geisha supports herself; not a million miles, in fact, from the life of a modern Western woman who has chosen to forego married life in order to focus on a career which she feels passionate about. Given that the geisha have pursued this lifestyle ever since their origins in the eighteenth century, they could claim to be the world's first modern women.

"DO THEY OR DON'T THEY?": ORIGINS OF THE GEISHA

In many ways the geisha world is like a photographic negative, the looking-glass image of "real" Japan. All the usual rules are subverted. It is a topsy-turvy world, not surprisingly, for the geisha world arose out of the pleasure quarters, which were set up specifically to provide an escape for men from drab everyday life into a colorful alternative reality.

In the early seventeenth century, long before the word "geisha" was coined, the precursors of the geisha—actresses-cum-prostitutes—were strutting their stuff on stages set up in the dry bed of the River Kamo in Kyoto. In those days the line between acting and prostitution was very thin, as in Shakespearean and even Victorian England (whence the music hall song, "Don't put your daughter on the stage, Mrs. Worthington"). The most original of all, a woman named Izumo no Okuni, electrified her public by cross-dressing. She performed erotic dances and saucy sketches wearing brocade trousers and an animal skin jacket like a dashing young man about town. Sometimes she even dressed as a priest. Soon there were troupes of courtesans performing risqué dances across the country and providing other services after the show.

To describe this new and exotic form of performance, people used the word *kabuku*, "to be wild and outrageous." From this they coined the word *kabuki* for her dances. This was the beginning of the kabuki theater.

Being unafflicted by Judeo-Christian guilt, the Japanese had no concept of sin, and therefore of sex being sinful. Rather than sin, the set of beliefs we refer to as Shinto focused on the concept of purity. Among the samurai of traditional Japanese society, sex with women was considered polluting and debilitating; a man who had sex with a woman risked becoming effeminate himself. The purest form of love, the closest Japanese equivalent to the Western notion of romantic love, was love for beautiful boys. Daimyo warlords had page boys and many samurai devoted their affections to younger warriors. It was commonplace and unremarkable for men who could afford it to frequent male brothels. Eighteenth-century Japanese were flabbergasted when they heard reports that Westerners not only disapproved of male-on-male sex but punished it by death.[4]

Only men were expected to feel romantic affection. Apart from youths, the other suitable objects of a man's affection were prostitutes, courtesans, geisha, or other inhabitants of the demimonde—the pleasure quarters. It was highly inappropriate for a man to feel or express affection towards non-"professional" women such as his wife.[5]

Compared to buttoned-up Western ways, attitudes to sex and sexuality—for men—were extraordinarily lax. So long as a man married and produced an heir, he could do virtually anything he liked in his private life. Any man who could afford it and who was so inclined had at least one mistress. Daimyo normally kept harems. And the shogun—the generalissimo who was the effective ruler of the realm—was expected to offer his services to several dozen concubines whose main function was to ensure the production of a male successor.

This was a society that embraced sexual delights. Where sex was concerned there was no guilt and no holds barred. No orifice, practice, or person was out of bounds except ordinary "non-professional" women, which included a man's own wife.

Pleasure was considered desirable not only for men but also for women. Connoisseurs studied ancient Chinese pillow books such as the *Records of the Bedchamber*, which advises that the "man must always first engage [his partner] in protracted gentle play to harmonize her mood with his and make her feelings respond."[6] *Shunga*—"spring pictures," woodblock prints depicting erotic activity—showed men supping a woman's vital *yin* juices, which they believed ensured long life. The manuals detailed the different ways—some listed thirty, others forty-eight—in which the "Jade Stalk" might penetrate the "Cinnabar Cleft" and move within it. But none of this applied to women other than denizens of the pleasure quarters.

In those days, according to the neo-Confucian code which governed society, it was unthinkable to marry someone you loved. As Naomi Tamura wrote in *The Japanese Bride* as late as 1904: "It is very clear that we do not marry for love. If a man is known to have broken this rule, we look upon him as a mean fellow, and sadly lacking in morality. His own mother and father would be ashamed of him. Public sentiment places love for a woman very low in the scale of morals. . . . We place love and brutal attachment on the same plane."[7] Marriage was a political bond between families; young people of good family married a person chosen by their parents and had no choice in the matter. Procreational and recreational sex were quite separate. The function of marriage was to produce offspring and sex was expected to cease once that had been fulfilled. It was unsuitable for a man to enjoy sex with his wife, which was for procreation only.

For sexual enjoyment and romantic attachment, men went to professionals in the arts of love—the courtesans. There was plenty of sex for sale, both male and female, and no stigma against men buying it. In fact, a man who could afford to frequent the pleasure quarters and did not do so would be considered a miserable fellow indeed and probably a skinflint. It is rather misleading to apply modern Western attitudes to such a society and to suggest, as Miho Matsugu does in her essay, that geisha, courtesans, and prostitutes were "exploited . . . and oppressed." The conceptual framework of the times was entirely different, and I doubt if the women of the pleasure quarters would have thought of themselves in that way at all.

François Caron visited Japan with the Dutch East India Company in 1639. He observed: "One Man hath but one Wife, though as many Concubines as he can keep; and if that Wife do not please him, he may put her away, provided he dismiss her in a civil and honorable way. Any Man may lie with a Whore, or common Woman, although he be married, with impunitie; but the Wife may not so much as speak in private with another Man, without hazarding her life."[8]

The shogunate, the government of the day, was thus not at all concerned with questions of morality. It was, however, extremely worried about anything that might undermine law and order. In 1647, after brawls between samurai over particularly desirable women, actresses were banned from the public stage. Women's kabuki was replaced by young men's kabuki. But the problem remained the same, with beautiful young actors offering sexual favors to their largely male audience. So that in turn was banned and replaced by adult men's kabuki, as we have it today (in which, instead of women dressing like men, men take the parts of women).

To maintain order and keep an eye on courtesans and prostitutes and their potentially trouble-making clients, the shogunate had already rounded up as many street women as possible. They installed them in government-sponsored pleasure quarters, which, along with the kabuki theaters, were known as the "bad places." It was recognized that these were places where men could go to let off steam. They thus played an essential part in maintaining the stability of society.

The pleasure quarters quickly turned into glamorous entertainment hubs offering far more than just sex. The first was the Shimabara in Kyoto, founded in 1589. But the greatest was the Yoshiwara just outside Edo (Tokyo), which formed the focus of men's lives, fantasies, and desires from 1656, when it was established, until well into the nineteenth century.

As Timon Screech shows in this volume (chap. 14), the Yoshiwara was located in a grassland a good-sized journey from the city, to protect decent folk from its heinous influence. At its height it housed 3,000 courtesans and prostitutes in a walled town with a single gate, lined with streets of elegant restaurants and banqueting houses. It was called the Nightless City because—as in Las Vegas today—customers lost track of time and entertainment went on around the clock. There men went to while away the evening with fine food, drink, music, and dancing. They were entertained by beautiful and charming women with whom, if they were lucky, they might be able to enjoy a sexual encounter. Perhaps that too is not unlike Las Vegas today. The top ranks of courtesans were at liberty to choose whether or not they slept with their suitors. Men often ruined themselves trying to win their favors.[9]

The early courtesans were highly accomplished women who would entertain their male customers by singing, dancing, and playing music. Many were also renowned poets, fine calligraphers, and accomplished practitioners of the tea ceremony. But gradually they became more specialized, and a new profession, of pure entertainer, arose. Around the turn of the eighteenth century the first entertainers appeared in the pleasure quarters, calling themselves geisha. These early geisha were men. Like the jesters of Shakespeare's time, their job was to entertain the customers who waited—sometimes days or weeks—to see the most popular courtesans. The customers paid, wined, and dined them while they entertained with bawdy conversation, song, and dance. Visiting the pleasure quarters was a huge expense.

Around 1760 women began to join their ranks and quickly outnumbered the men. The first recorded woman to used the word "geisha" of herself was an Edo prostitute named Kikuya. Having made a reputation for her shamisen playing and singing, she decided to make entertaining her full-time profession.[10]

Soon tea-brewing women in the Gion district of Kyoto, who served tea and sold sexual favors on the side, were beginning to call themselves geisha, along with other similarly ambiguous professions—sake-serving women, dancing girls, and others. It was a way of acquiring respectability and asserting that they were professionals. It was not long before the word "geisha" was used primarily of women.[11] Geisha were free spirits. Their skills at music and dancing gave them independence. They came and went as they pleased and relied primarily on their arts, rather than their bodies, for their living. Nevertheless, unofficially they might seek to supplement their income by selling sexual favors—though in the pleasure quarters, at least, this was strictly proscribed, not for reasons of morality but in order to protect the courtesans' business.

The courtesans, conversely, gorgeous though they were, were caged birds, literally imprisoned within the walled pleasure quarters. There, sex was their monopoly. The geisha were strictly forbidden to steal their customers. While courtesans were famous for their beauty, multi-layered kimonos, and ornate, heavy headdresses, geisha were initially chosen from among plainer women. They were legally obliged to wear simple hairstyles and modest kimonos. A courtesan wore her huge obi (cummerbund) tied in a huge knot in front of her, implying that it might be untied if a man was lucky and wealthy enough. Geisha conversely wore small obi, tied at the back, like ordinary townswomen (fig. 12.1).

Geisha who worked outside the pleasure quarters, in the town, however, could do as they pleased. Often they supplemented their income with prostitution, but there remained a firm line between prostitutes and geisha. Geisha who engaged in prostitution had to have two licenses—one for prostitution, the other for entertaining.

Over the years the gaudy courtesans fell out of fashion. The more modest geisha came to be seen as far more chic and desirable for well-heeled customers. By the nineteenth century they were the heart of the demimonde, the "floating world" celebrated in woodblock prints and kabuki plays. Before the advent of the movies, geisha and kabuki actors were superstars whose affairs were followed with avid curiosity by the public. If a famous city geisha appeared in a particular color or pattern of kimono, the ordinary women of the town would quickly follow suit. In their fame, influence, and ability to set trends, geisha were strikingly similar to the courtesans of Renaissance Venice whom Margaret Rosenthal describes in her essay in this volume (chap. 2). Trendy young rakes vied to be seen in their company. They were Japan's first modern women, in control of their own destinies in a way that wives could never be.

But, along with kabuki actors, they remained social outcasts, on the bottom rung of the hierarchy. Ordinary folk might be their fans and admirers, but they could never actually marry them. Geisha usually married outcasts like themselves—

FIGURE 12.1. An actress dressed in the costume of a courtesan
raises a bowl of sake to her lips. The large "apron" in front of her,
embroidered with flowers, is actually the loose end of her enormous
knotted obi. Her tortoiseshell and coral headdress weighs ten pounds
and is far more ornate than the hair ornaments worn by geisha.

kabuki actors or sumo wrestlers, who made up the entertainment industry. It was
indeed—as in the Victorian West—a case of "Don't put your daughter on the stage,
Mrs. Worthington."

Wives, chosen for their pedigree, came from suitably upper-class families and were
expected to be quiet and modest, devoted to their home and children. The word for
someone else's wife (not one's own) was and is *oku-san*, the "honorable person inside."
According to the marriage code drawn up in the late nineteenth century, one of the

seven acceptable grounds for divorcing your wife was if she talked too much.[12] For romance and sparkling conversation, men of means frequented the geisha quarters.

Geisha were usually working-class, either the children of geisha themselves or girls from poor families—samurai or merchant families that had fallen on hard times, as well as peasant families—who had been sold into the profession and were therefore burdened with a debt which they would eventually have to repay to their owners, their new "families," through their work. To sell one's daughter was not considered a terrible or cruel thing to do. Rather, it was a way of providing a girl from a disadvantaged background with a chance in life. Like modeling today, becoming a geisha was and is a way in which a girl could rise from a lowly background to mix with the most powerful and wealthy men in the land, solely on the basis of her beauty and talents.

The 1920s were the heyday of the geisha. There were about 80,000 geisha throughout Japan including 10,000 in Tokyo alone. Since the war, however, the options available to both Japanese women (who might once have become geisha) and to Japanese men (who would have been their customers) have much increased. Today there are probably only 4–5,000 geisha in the whole of Japan.

The final blow was the outlawing of licensed prostitution in 1958—though geisha, who were not considered to be prostitutes, were not outlawed. Thereafter, if sex occurred, it was a private matter. Nowadays, to the outside world, the geisha insist firmly that their job consists only of music and dancing and absolutely nothing else. If that is not the truth, they are certainly smart enough to ensure that no one will ever find out.

In Japan courtesans have long since died out, though there are still some women who practice the courtesan arts and dress in the courtesan costume. There are nonetheless clear parallels to be seen between geisha and the hetaerae of ancient Greece, the courtesans of Renaissance Venice, or other courtesans at other times and places around the world. Like them, geisha are highly accomplished women whose profession includes music, singing, dance, and the arts of entertaining and pleasing men.

But if geisha are indeed courtesans, then they are courtesans who are also adepts at the art of spin. In order to survive as a profession in the modern world, geisha have had to reshape their public image to accord with contemporary notions of propriety. Geisha will tell you that their job has nothing to do with sex; a prime example is Mineko Iwasaki's recently published *Autobiography of a Geisha*. But this is not exactly true. They are not prostitutes in the sense that they have no need to sell themselves cheap. But their profession certainly includes an erotic edge.

Geisha are mistresses of the art of teasing and flirtation. Their job description does not include the selling of sexual favors on a one-off basis for cash and most earn so much as performers and entertainers that they have no need to do so; in any case, they are far too canny to devalue themselves in this way. They do, however, form a pool of potential mistresses. A man who wishes to do so may take on a geisha as a mistress, negotiating a complex contract with the owner of the *ochaya* (teahouse) where he is a regular customer, who will act as an intermediary with the *okami-san* (owner) of the *okiya* (geisha house) where she lives. He will usually provide her with an apartment and an income, fund her dance classes and stage appearances, and pay for her kimonos. When he is not around she remains independent and free to do as she pleases.

Hot-spring geisha, as described in Miho Matsugu's essay in this volume, are a different story. As we have seen, for most Japanese the term is virtually synonymous with "prostitute"; and city geisha strongly object to their being considered geisha at all. They are nonetheless accomplished dancers and entertainers, though of a lower order than city geisha. In modern Japan, they are working women who have chosen to make their living this way; they are no longer sold as in Kawabata Yasunari's heart-rending novel or Masuda Sayo's harrowing autobiography. They too deny that the selling of sexual favors is part of their job; nevertheless it is generally assumed that that is in fact the case.

Even at the highest levels, geisha have always had an ambivalent position on the edge of society. On the one hand, their profession is considered little higher than prostitution and they originally sprang from the bottom classes of society. But on the other, like the hetaerae of ancient Greece, geisha in the elite districts are trained to be the companions of brilliant and powerful men. Many prime ministers have taken a geisha as their lover and sometimes as their wife. Often wealthy men, forced by their fathers into an unhappy first marriage with a woman of "suitable" background, get a divorce as soon as they become powerful and independent in their own right. They are then free to marry the woman of their choice, who may well be a geisha whom they have met at a teahouse party. Several of Japan's top executives are married to ex-geisha, as is at least one recent ambassador to the United States.

WHO AND HOW: BECOMING A GEISHA

In the past there were two ways to become a geisha. Either you were born into it and began your training in dance and music at the age of six years, six months, and six days; or you came from a poor family and were sold by your parents into a sort of slavery in a geisha house as young as four or five. Such women had to spend many years repaying their crippling debts, a process that was usually accomplished by the sale of their virginity.

Present-day Japan is extremely prosperous, and the wealth is fairly evenly spread. Even in remote rural communities, no one is desperately poor. It seems unlikely that any family today is so poor that they need to sell their daughters. The most recent case I heard of a girl being sold was in the early 1970s. The modern young women I met told me they had chosen to become geisha—often against their parents' wishes—because they loved the way that geisha look or wanted to pursue their studies in traditional music and dance.

One *maiko* (trainee geisha, literally "dancing girl") whom I got to know well was called Harumi. Her father was a carpenter, her mother a taxi driver. As a child she had yearned to become a geisha. Her father strongly opposed the idea but her mother sympathized with her. When she was thirteen her mother arranged an interview with Haruta, the *okami-san* (proprietress) of the Haruta geisha house in the Miyagawa-cho geisha district of Kyoto. She was accepted. When she left home at thirteen, she gave up her old identity and family, rather like a young teenager leaving home to join the Bolshoi Ballet—giving up her family to follow a dream. Her parents were reassured that she would be taken care of and protected by her new "family." Her new name, Haru-mi, "Spring Beauty," indicates that she belongs to the

Haru-ta, "Spring Field," house. She also calls the proprietress "Mother." Here she has a five-year apprenticeship, much akin to any apprenticeship in Japan. Her "Mother" provides accommodation, food, and kimonos. In exchange, when she performs at a teahouse party, the Haruta geisha house (which has made the booking) receives the fee, from which she is given pocket money; she may also keep tips. The most important bond of her career is with her "older sister," a senior maiko named Haruka ("Spring Flower"). Haruka is her friend, confidante, guide, and mentor and bears the responsibility if she does something wrong.

When I met her she was fifteen and in the second year of her five-year training. She was learning the Kyoto lilt and the forms of speech peculiar to the geisha world. She also learned how to keep conversation light and entertaining and how to behave in front of customers and within the hierarchical geisha world. And she was beginning what geisha say is a lifetime study: the geisha arts.

THE GEISHA ARTS

Geisha begin their study of music and dance, the geisha performing arts, as maiko but continue to practice and develop throughout their lives. Outsiders may think that a geisha's job is primarily to interact with men. But as far as a geisha is concerned, the basis of her life and work is her art.

When women performers were banned from the kabuki stage in 1645, they went underground and became "parlor actresses." Kabuki actors, who are male, perform on the public stage. Geisha also act, but in private, to a select group of customers. The arts of geisha and kabuki are intimately connected. Geisha perform dances, scenes, and excerpts from the kabuki repertoire. The most austere school of geisha dance, the Inoue school (practiced in the Gion district of Kyoto), derives from the slow-moving, aristocratic Noh. But most geisha dance is far more closely linked to the lively, colorful kabuki theater.

The "wild and outrageous" performances with which Izumo no Okuni shocked the populace of seventeenth-century Kyoto have evolved into a stylized, subtle, and controlled form of dance. Unlike ballet, it is not athletic but slow, graceful, and enormously disciplined, more like tai chi. Every dance tells a story through gestures so allusive that only a connoisseur can read the symbolism. A tiny hand gesture indicates reading a love letter, holding the corner of a handkerchief in one's mouth shows coquetry and sleeves are much used for dabbing tears. This is not exclusively a women's dance; the same dances are performed by men in the kabuki theater. Whether performed by women or by male actors playing the parts of women, the dance communicates femininity by the smallness of steps and the limited range of movements. Put simply, it is the only way to dance while wearing a heavy wig and a kimono which binds the legs (fig. 12.2).

The dances are accompanied by music and songs. The key instrument is the shamisen, a three-stringed banjo-like instrument played with a plectrum that originated in Okinawa. In woodblock prints, a woman carrying a shamisen is almost certainly a geisha. The distinctive melancholy plink plonk of the shamisen can be heard alongside the flute in the instrumental rendition of Ataka no Matsu (the Pine

FIGURE 12.2. A geisha from the Asakusa geisha district in Tokyo performs a dance as part of a formal entertainment. She is fully made up and wears a kimono suitable for summer; the fan also communicates that it is summer. As an adult geisha, she wears only simple hair ornaments.

Tree of Ataka) on track II of the companion website to this book. (This is a popular traditional tune in which the flute player expresses his yearning for his lost love, a typical subject for a geisha song.) The shamisen—like the piano or the violin—takes years to master. Maiko like Harumi can dance prettily even if they have not mastered the crisp movements that mark the adept. But only a veteran can play the shamisen with precision, confidence, and passion. As the number of geisha declines, good shamisen players are harder and harder to find. This in itself is a threat to the continuation of the geisha world. There are of course plenty of non-geisha players of the shamisen—amateur women and also men; but traditionally the geisha world is a closed community. For the geisha their profession is a calling and a lifestyle, not simply a job. It would be very alien to employ someone from outside the community.

Besides the disciplines of dance, song, and the shamisen, the geisha repertory includes the small hourglass-shaped shoulder drum (*ko-tsuzumi*), the larger floor drum (*taiko*), and the flute (*fue*). Maiko take regular examinations and give public performances.

In the past a party at a teahouse with geisha was a participatory affair. The customers were themselves adepts at singing and dancing and enjoyed showing off their skills. These days such men rarely exist. Appreciating the music and dance of the geisha is an acquired art. One reason why the geisha world is under threat is because the kind of men who in the past would have appreciated these arts no longer do.

Besides the performing arts, several courtesans and geisha from the past were poets who wrote rather melancholy poems. Others painted pictures that gave a glimpse into their lives very different from the highly eroticized depictions of geisha and courtesans in ukiyo-e woodblock prints, which were almost invariably produced by male artists. Some compose music. The stirring Miya Sama chorus in *The Mikado* is actually a war song composed by a nineteenth-century geisha to be sung by samurai as they marched into battle. W. S. Gilbert and Sir Arthur Sullivan hijacked it in its entirety (and without acknowledgment).

A LIVING WORK OF ART: GEISHA CHIC

The pinnacle of the geisha's art is the creation of herself, both physically and as a persona, in which she transforms herself into a living work of art.

One of the most popular geisha in the Miyagawa-cho district is Koito. The daughter of a news agent and a hairdresser, she has been a geisha for twenty years, since her early teens. She is an astute businesswoman who owns her own geisha house and trains maiko in the geisha arts. I sat in several times while she prepared herself for the evening's entertainment. The full makeup is worn by all maiko but by geisha only for formal entertainments, like putting on an evening dress. Maiko visit the hairdresser once a week and spend hours having their hair back-combed and lacquered into an elaborate sculptural creation. To sleep they place hard wooden pillows under their necks so as not to crush their hair. A geisha like Koito, conversely, wears a wig. She can put on or take off her geisha identity at will (see fig. 12.2 above).

To begin the transformation, Koito covered her face in a perfect oval of thick white makeup. It was as if she had put on a beautiful but expressionless mask, like a Noh mask. She left an edge of skin unpainted at the hairline. (Young trainee geisha need help to do this; older women like Koito use a floor-level dressing-table mirror and a hand mirror.) This line of bare flesh is, according to Japanese men, extremely erotic, hinting at the naked woman behind the mask.

In the past, when candlelight was the only lighting, the white makeup gave women's faces a magical, almost supernatural glimmer. Lead-based, it had a devastating effect on the skin; geisha looked like old women before they were thirty. Some geisha and also kabuki actors who played women died of lead poisoning. Today the white makeup is harmless, made by Shiseido.

Next Koito painted in eyebrows shaped "like a moth's wings" and outlined her eyes in black. Then she whitened her back, leaving a fork of bare flesh at the nape of the neck, considered the sexiest part of the body in Japan. The unpainted tongue of skin supposedly depicts a woman's private parts (fig. 12.3). Lastly she painted in a tiny rosebud mouth, using a stick of safflower lipstick. She had become a compilation of markers of femininity—woman embodied. As she put on her makeup, her persona too began to change. She was stepping into the role, as an actor does. Whereas she had been down to earth and straightforward, she became coquettish, speaking in a coy, girlish voice.

Then came the kimono. Both the choosing and the wearing of a kimono is an art, she explained. A geisha has to be expert at choosing the perfect kimono for the season and the occasion—a kimono with a plum blossom design in February, for example, a wisteria pattern in June, or a chrysanthemum border in the autumn. Like a maestro in any art, once the geisha has mastered the rules, she can improvise to express her individual taste.

First Koito put on several layers of under kimono. It was June, so she then chose a dark blue kimono with a pattern of wisteria to evoke the season. Around it she wound a heavy brocade obi, which covered her from armpit to hips, concealing all hint of her female shape. At the front the kimono was crossed almost to the throat. But it curved low at the back of her neck, focusing attention on the tantalizing tongue of unpainted flesh. This was an eroticism of concealment and mystery. It left almost everything to the imagination, making every tiny glimpse of the flesh beneath all the more piquant.

In the past in Japan, sex appeal was all to do with mystery. Far from revealing swathes of naked bosom, midriff, or leg like a Hollywood star on Oscar night, the epitome of desirability was the geisha, swathed in layer upon layer of sumptuous fabric, with just a hint here and there to remind a man of the frail flesh beneath.

It is a mode of allure and glamour of which modern women can also see the advantages. Among much else, the publication of Arthur Golden's phenomenally successful novel *Memoirs of a Geisha* led to the rise of "geisha chic." The collections of 1999 were full of kimono-like creations that swaddled the body. That summer Madonna appeared at the Grammies in a garment described as a kimono, with long flapping sleeves and a plastic "obi." The fad, like all fads, has passed. But it has inspired a reconsideration of the role of mystery in feminine allure.

PLAYING A ROLE: GEISHA AT NIGHT

The geisha districts constitute a little world separate from the rest of Japan. Outside their streets of dark wooden houses, men are in charge. They dominate the corporate and political worlds and most of the public professions. Though much is changing in

FIGURE 12.3. A maiko in the Gion district of Kyoto shows the unpainted nape of her neck. Her own hair has been swept up into the complex style of the maiko. The loose end of her stiff brocade obi hangs down behind her.

Japanese society, the majority of women still marry and—whether or not they have jobs—have full responsibility for the house, family finances, and child-rearing.

In the geisha districts, conversely, women are in charge, on the surface, at least. The geisha houses are matriarchal, run by "mothers," not "fathers." The men there tend to be service employees: barmen, dressers, and music and dance teachers. Rather than hoping for a boy child, geisha hope for a girl to continue the mother's profession. Boy children pose a problem and are often sent off to be brought up by their fathers.

One geisha commented to me rather contemptuously that the only men in the geisha district are barmen or the husbands of those "mothers" who are married. Community decisions are made by women—by an association of "mothers" who make up the *kaburenjo*, the geisha union. Each of the geisha districts has a union. However, most of the clerks who work in the union offices are men, so the geisha world is not strictly a women's world.

But the male customers are only customers. Their money may fund the whole enterprise, but that does not give them control over it, any more than shopping in a supermarket gives one control over the supermarket. When they enter the *ochaya*, the teahouse that is the geisha's workplace (the *okiya*, which I have translated as "geisha house," is her home), they step inside a fantasy realm where they can become little boys or imagine themselves Casanovas. For them it is a world of play, a realm entirely separate from the everyday world. But the geisha are at work. Topics like work and family are never discussed. It is the geisha's job to create this fantasy world and—like the sirens enticing Ulysses—to try and make it so seductive that a man will never want to leave. This is business for the geisha, it is their living; and the longer a man stays, the more money he will spend.

When geisha marry, they stop being geisha. Rather like nuns, the two roles are mutually exclusive. Rather than marry, many are supported by a *danna*, "patron." These tend to be elderly men who can afford to support a geisha (or two, or three) as well as their wife and children. Among Japanese of the old school it is still a sign of success to be wealthy and powerful enough to do so.

Until World War II, every geisha assumed that she would have a *danna* to provide her with a house, pay for her kimonos and dance classes, and give her a regular allowance. These days *danna* are hard to find. Few men have the disposable income to support a high-maintenance mistress; and those who do may prefer to spend their money on a fast car or a European skiing trip. Only some twenty percent of geisha are supported nowadays by *danna*.

THE TEAHOUSE

In Japan, the real decision-making in the worlds of business and politics takes place at night. Daytime is for a display of democracy, for earnest discussions in which a final decision is never reached, or for implementing a decision that has already been made. But in the evening, after sake and dimmed lights have eroded natural Japanese shyness and barriers, bonding occurs and everything is resolved. At the highest levels of society, one of the places where decisions are made that might shake the political or financial landscape is in the country's geisha houses. Entertaining lies at the heart of the business and political worlds in Japan. Of course, such entertaining would be intolerably dull were it not spiced with the company of women. This role is likely to be taken not by men's wives but by geisha, who are trained to do the job. In this respect geisha may be seen as perfectly groomed equivalents of high-society hostesses or corporate wives.

Until recently, and maybe even today, geisha were far more than just cosseters of men's egos or sexual partners. When a man went to a geisha house, he encountered women whom he had known for many years, who were old friends and maybe lovers. They were women he could talk to and even ask advice of. As well as having a good time, he might also discuss problems of the work place, political problems, or even the Japanese economy.

Geisha never give direct advice. Japan is a country where the ex-geisha wife of a business magnate is admired because, people say, "she is clever enough never to let a man realize how clever she is." The essence of feminine skill is to make a man think that it is he who has had a brilliant idea. But a geisha could prod the finance minister, for example, cooing, "How clever of you to think of raising the interest rates!" much like the deliciously feminine American southern belles who rule the roost while convincing their husbands that it is they who are both brilliant and in control. Such a mode of behavior will be totally familiar to the writers and readers of books like *The Surrendered Wife* and *Woman Power* (anathema though such an approach might be to feminists).[13]

Generally the geisha's job is to keep the conversation light. Rather than showing off their wit and intelligence or discussing the latest newspaper reports, their skill lies in their ineffable femininity, their ability to make a man feel that he is masterful and brilliant, the handsomest, most sexy man alive.

A young Tokyo geisha who became a friend of mine was an excellent golfer and frequently went out with customers to play golf. Her aim, she explained to me, was—of course—to make sure the customer won. She had to play as well as possible. If it was too easy to beat her, he would not feel that he was a great golfer. But if she played well, then at the end of the game he would feel that he was truly a brilliant golfer. Similarly the geisha aims to make every man feel that he is irresistible, not to show off her own attractions or conversation skills.

Having spent the evening telling each man how handsome he is and how much in love with him they are, they will almost certainly say "Goodbye" with a chaste peck on the cheek.

GEISHA AND SEX

Everything about a geisha—her makeup, the louche way in which she wears her kimono, her dance—offers the promise of the erotic. But it is a promise that is very seldom kept, at least among city geisha. It is about enticement and desire, not about realization. It is a game, a flirtation—but it takes place only within the bounds of the teahouse; it has no reality outside. For a geisha to make herself any more accessible would be to decrease her own high value.

Once a geisha has painted her face, she is an actress playing a role, as Japanese men recognize. When she tells an ancient company chairman that she is madly in love with him, he knows perfectly well that this is a charming game. Only Westerners—who usually come from far more buttoned-up societies—take it seriously. Westerners who have attended geisha parties often report that geisha are uniformly of pensionable age, for the simple reason that, when a teahouse proprietress hears that Westerners are to be among the guests, she delegates the most experienced and least tempting geisha to attend to these customers, who may seriously misunderstand what their job is all about.

Nevertheless the currency is love and that is dangerous if a geisha is dealing with a handsome young customer. Like anyone else, a geisha can do as she likes in her spare time and may strike up a relationship if she feels like it.

Until the outlawing of licensed prostitution in 1958, the rite of passage that marked a maiko's entry into adulthood was *mizuage*, the selling of the maiko's virginity for a sum reportedly equivalent to the cost of a small house. Geisha in their sixties and seventies told me that they had undergone this around the age of thirteen. For them the experience was an ordeal on the same order as circumcision for youths in societies where it marks the coming of manhood. For them it marked the coming of womanhood. And, like circumcision, they gritted their teeth and prepared themselves for an uncomfortable experience but an unavoidable mark of passage in order finally to come of age. It was not surrounded with the opprobrium with which underage sex would be regarded today in the West; in fact the concept of underage sex probably did not yet exist. Romeo and Juliet (who were thirteen or fourteen), along with women in Japan and in the West, were until fairly recently considered adults from puberty. In Japan, if a girl did not become a geisha, she would be undoubtedly be married to a man she did not know around that same age.

After the ceremony the geisha's coming of age was marked by a new hairstyle, new style of kimono, and new footwear, material markers of her sexual transformation. She was now an adult. One geisha remembered that she had been so plain that there were no volunteers to deflower her. At fourteen, when her fellow geisha were dressed as adults, she had yet to be deflowered and still wore a child's kimono, which she found extremely galling.

Theoretically all that came to an end in 1958. In this day and age young women choose to be maiko or geisha; there are plenty of other professions open to them. Elderly geisha are extremely concerned that the geisha world and its traditions may die out. They would not risk forcing a young girl to do anything against her will, which would encourage her to leave. The traditional strict training has ceased; a trainee geisha's life is easier than it ever was in the past.

ANOMALY OR ARTISTE? DO GEISHA HAVE A FUTURE?

Ever since geisha pranced into the pleasure quarters with their shamisens in the mid-eighteenth century, no one has ever been able to answer the question, "Do they or don't they? Are they or aren't they?" It is this ambiguity that makes them so tantalizing and gives them such an intense appeal. Today there are still plenty of young women who want to become geisha. They are attracted by the glamour, the money, and the chance to meet wealthy and powerful men. They also still have a role to play in society.

The great question is what will happen when the baby-boom generation—which has grown up dining in French restaurants, playing golf, and flying to Paris and New

York—reaches the age at which men traditionally reward themselves for a lifetime's hard work with what in the past was always considered the pinnacle in female company—the geisha. To entertain in a teahouse is also the ultimate sign of status, power, and wealth. But the up-and-coming generation may no longer value geisha in the same way. If that is the case, the profession may indeed die out.

If geisha disappear, they will take with them much of Japan's traditional culture, of which they have become the custodians. Already the silk weavers and kimono manufacturers of Kyoto are in difficulties. Without geisha, there may not be enough purchasers of kimonos, fans, wooden clogs, and wigs to keep these industries alive. There will be only amateurs and kabuki professionals to continue the traditions of music and dance.

Some cities—such as Kanazawa, on the Japan Sea coast—have become so worried about their geisha communities that they now subsidize them. In effect the geisha there have become civil servants who give public performances in exchange for a grant from the public purse. But in opening their doors to the public, they have given up their exclusivity, mystery, and erotic edge. They are artistes—but no more than that.

If geisha lose their mystery, they lose that special quality that makes them geisha. Turning the harsh light of day on these fragile creations of the night is like trying to analyze sex appeal: the second you examine it, it disappears. It is their ambiguity and magic that make geisha what they are. They are not so much custodians of national tradition (as Miho Matsugu argues) as the personification of femininity and beauty, women who have chosen to transform themselves into walking works of art. Indeed, if geisha are to survive, they need to remain both anomaly and artistes.

Notes

1. One hot-spring geisha wrote her autobiography: Sayo Masuda, *Autobiography of a Geisha*, trans. Gaye G. Rowley (New York: Columbia University Press, 2003).

2. For the full story of my research, see Lesley Downer, *Women of the Pleasure Quarters: The Secret History of the Geisha* (New York: Broadway Books, 2001).

3. For the development of the Madame Butterfly story and the way in which it shaped stereotypes of Japanese womanhood see Lesley Downer, *Madame Sadayakko: The Geisha who Bewitched the West* (New York: Gotham Books, 2003), 198–20. Also Jan van Rij, *Madame Butterfly: Japonisme, Puccini, and the Search for the Real Cho-Cho-San* (Berkeley, CA: Stonebridge Press, 2001).

4. See Timon Screech, *Sex and The Floating World: Erotic Images in Japan, 1700–1820* (London: Reaktion Books, 1999), 287–88.

5. There is a brilliant discussion of romantic feeling in Japan in Takayuki Yokota-Murakami, *Don Juan East/West: On the Problematics of Comparative Literature* (Albany: State University of New York Press, 1998).

6. Quoted in Nicholas Bornoff, *Pink Samurai: Love, Marriage, and Sex in Contemporary Japan* (London: GraftonBooks, 1991), 133.

7. Naomi Tamura, *The Japanese Bride* (New York: Harper & Brothers, 1904), 2; quoted in Downer, *Women of the Pleasure Quarters*, 301.

8. François Caron, *A True Description of the Mighty Kingdoms of Japan and Siam* (Am-

sterdam, 1648; London: Samuel Brown and John de l'Ecluse, 1663); repr. ed. C. R. Boxer (London: Argonaut Press, 1935). Caron (1600–73) lived in Japan from 1639 to 1641, where he fathered an illegitimate child.

9. See Cecilia Segawa Seigle, *Yoshiwara: The Glittering World of the Japanese Courtesan* (Honolulu: University of Hawaii Press, 1993).

10. See Downer, *Women of the Pleasure Quarters*, 102–3.

11. There are still five or six male geisha who perform in Tokyo. See Downer, *Women of the Pleasure Quarters*, 95–100.

12. The others were jealousy, sterility, adultery, disobedience to parents-in-law, larceny, and severe disease. See Downer, *Women of the Pleasure Quarters*, 69–71.

13. Laura Doyle, *The Surrendered Wife: A Practical Guide to Finding Intimacy, Passion, and Peace with Your Man* (New York: Simon & Schuster, 2001); Laura Schlessinger, *Woman Power: Transform Your Man, Your Marriage, Your Life* (New York: HarperCollins, 2004).

In the Service of the Nation: Geisha and Kawabata Yasunari's *Snow Country*

GEISHA AND MODERNIZATION

The Oxford English Dictionary defines the geisha as a "Japanese girl whose profession is to entertain men by dancing and singing; loosely, a Japanese prostitute."[1] Many geisha, to the contrary, define themselves as professional artistes, and take pride in dedicating their lives to the traditions of Japanese art and culture.[2] Yet as I will argue, particularly before the end of the war in 1945, geisha often performed many of the same services as prostitutes. To understand geisha and their current status as cultural symbols, it is important to acknowledge this tension between the sex work that many geisha performed throughout parts of history, and their denial of it. The insistence on the part of many geisha both now and then that they are not prostitutes is a rejection of the stigma that has historically marginalized these women and kept them from being seen as self-supporting, skilled workers.[3] If they are now national symbols, it is because their former ignominy as entertainers and sometimes prostitutes, exploited by the state and oppressed by society, has today been replaced with the "prestige" of representing the artistic tradition of the same state and society that once oppressed them.

This transformation is evocatively revealed in the canonical novel by Kawabata Yasunari, *Snow Country*, which I explore later in this essay. But to begin unraveling the geisha's origins, a brief look at the complex history of female performers in Japan is in order. Various terms such as *yūjo* and *geisha* have been used throughout Japanese history to refer to women whose performances bridge art and sexual labor,[4] reflecting their shifting locations in Japanese society. In ancient imperial Japan, up to approximately the tenth century, the imperial court recognized the skills of female performers who were thought to have a shamanistic ability to communicate with spirits and gods. The court rewarded their expertise in religious performances by designating their skills as "professional." In doing so, the emperor gave these women special privileges, such as freedom to travel and exemption from taxes. By the late tenth century, such women (known as *yūjo, kugutsu,* and *shirabyōshi*) had formed their own households, often matrilineal and independent socio-economic units, and professional communities.⁵ Supported by their close association with the emperor, they appear in historical records as "belonging to the court" in a sense linguistically close to the English term "courtesans," and it was not unusual for them to be mothers of high-ranking ministers.⁶

After the late thirteenth to fourteenth centuries, the ancient imperial system was weakened by the rise of the samurai class. Female sexuality began to be commercialized as a market economy developed; the sexual labor of female entertainers became legally subject to economic exploitation and their profession came to be seen with disdain.⁷ Hence the ancient courtesans' political power and socio-economic status declined. In 1587, the samurai-led government established a licensed pleasure quarter in Kyoto where those women who engaged in sexual labor were enclosed (see chap. 14). In the early seventeenth century, the Tokugawa regime established a licensed pleasure quarter in the new capital of Edo, and in the eighteenth century, when women in the districts began to specialize in the sex business and lost their artistic repertories and skills, geisha emerged to take over the role of entertainers.⁸

Though the government officially prohibited geisha from selling sex, sex was nonetheless often part of their work. Geisha were governed by contracts similar to those for prostitutes, by which male family heads transferred the women to their new owners.⁹ Thus, when the United States and Britain criticized Japan for its slave trade in female prostitutes in 1872, the modern government, headed by an emperor newly restored to power in 1868, emancipated not only "prostitutes" (*shōgi*) but also "geisha" (*geigi*)¹⁰ from their contracts under the old regime. In fact, authorities saw geisha as being almost identical to prostitutes, as shown in a proposal by the Ministry of Law that the Tokyo government incorporate prostitutes under the official name of *geisha.* Importantly, the capital decided to maintain the line between geisha and prostitutes in order to prevent the "shamefulness" of the latter from attenuating the "beauty" of geisha.¹¹ In other words, the authorities purposely legitimated the hierarchical division of elite and lower classes among these underprivileged sex workers.

In 1872, a new licensed geisha system made possible the instantaneous production of many geisha. The central government authorized local governments to give separate licenses to geisha and prostitutes that allowed them to work "voluntarily" for their employers in designated districts and required them to be tested for syphilis. Differences in the licenses maintained the "honored" status of geisha. For example, the laws of one prefecture required licensed prostitutes to take the syphilis exam three times a month. Geisha had to be tested only once a month.¹² Nevertheless, the very fact that geisha were required to be tested at all reveals an assumption that sex work was deemed to be part of their job.¹³ While geisha were also tested in shamisen-playing¹⁴ and dancing, for geisha who specialized in selling their services to all but the highest classes in Tokyo such skills were less important than sex appeal when it came down to getting the license and making money for the geisha house.¹⁵ This licensed geisha system lasted until the defeat of Japan in 1945.¹⁶

ILLUSION OF EQUALITY

In the late nineteenth century authorities exploited geisha's labor to promote state policies of industrialization and militaristic expansion. "Sake, women, and shamisen are privileges for men as well as symbols of local economic prosperity," said supporters of a policy to increase licensed pleasure districts in the 1890s.[17] National development denoted the promotion of the capitalist economy together with the military invasion of other Asian countries such as Taiwan, Korea, and China.

Historian Fujime Yuki suggests that geisha served in several ways to support empire-building. First, taxes on geisha including the license fee were an important source of income for state and local governments. Second, businesses that demanded geisha brought large profits to local economies. Third, the military relied heavily on geisha's services, including sex, to boost the morale of soldiers and officers and foster aggression that in turn would be productive on the war front.[18] Indeed, there was a direct connection between the army and geisha. After the Japanese army invaded Shanghai in 1932, the military began recruiting women to cater to soldiers' sexual needs in overseas "comfort" stations. The army specifically recruited geisha for officers. Their "Japaneseness"—in costume, hairstyle, makeup, and artistic skills—helped them to be seen as "better" than either Japanese prostitutes or non-Japanese women.[19]

In the meantime, modernizing and militarizing the nation helped swell the geisha labor pool. Steep tax increases to fund nation-building projects destroyed economically vulnerable farmers' lives. Numerous farmers had to give up their lands and become tenant farmers or leave their villages. Many of these abjectly impoverished families had to sell their daughters into prostitution. In this way, geisha were a byproduct of the imperialist endeavor, as well as a resource for it. What is important here is that for daughters from destitute families, becoming geisha was their "best" alternative. And their customers shared that viewpoint. What, then, gave geisha their elevated status?

Sex was certainly not the geisha's only appeal. Geisha were more valuable than licensed prostitutes because they skillfully offered a pleasurable space and time for ordinary men, who enjoyed talking, drinking, singing, dancing, and playing games in a group.[20] The hedonistic banquet with geisha in attendance functioned as a social outlet for working- and middle-class Japanese men by allowing them to express their discontent within an economic system dominated by the rich and powerful. Geisha's anachronistic and hyperbolic "Japaneseness" was important to this end. Japanese men, who more or less rejected westernized modern life as expensive and its attitude as arrogant, could form male solidarity through geisha that neither the experience of Western modernity through café waitresses nor individualized sexual acts with prostitutes could provide.

For middle-class men and workers, to be able to buy the services of a geisha for an evening was a symbolic act of democratization and modernization. "Mass-produced" geisha, the products of social inequality and patriarchal sexism, were paradoxically a vehicle for providing the illusion of equality for men. They could make middle- and working-class men as well as farmers feel like instant connoisseurs of the "flower-and-willow" banquet dominated by politicians, rich people, and elite urban intellectuals.[21] Interacting with geisha, these men could elevate their class status, attempt a slight revenge against the dominant class, and experience what it is to be a "Japanese" man.

Geisha played a double role—providing both art and sexual labor—which originated in the class division of high and low among themselves. The lower the status of a given geisha and the clientele she served, the more likely she would be expected to provide sexual services; the more a geisha provided sexual services, the more she was seen as lower class. High-class geisha in urban areas may also have used sex, but they mainly left that function to prostitutes and geisha without artistic skills.[22] Translating the autobiography of Masuda Sayo (b. 1925), a former geisha who worked in a hot-spring resort in the 1930s and 1940s, literary scholar Gaye Rowley explains:

> The romanticization of geisha life as dedicated principally to the pursuit of traditional arts ignores the poverty that drove many parents to indenture their daughters to geisha houses. Such romanticization also erases certain geisha from the collective memory and overlooks the bottom line of the whole geisha business. The geisha thus erased are hot-spring-resort geisha, and the bottom line of the geisha business is, of course, sex for money. At the glamorous high end of the geisha world, in the Pontocho and Gion districts of Kyoto and Shinbashi in Tokyo, sex may seem a less obtrusive aspect of the geisha business. But at the lower end, in a hot-spring resort like Suwa where Masuda worked, sex with geisha was the expected end of every evening.[23]

It is important to note that the licensing system did not differentiate between the lower and higher ends of the geisha continuum; under the law, all geisha were seen as potential prostitutes.

Thus geisha were not just players of a double role, but deployed as figures of cultural authenticity in imperial Japan, helping to energize wartime nationalism. Through the provision of sexual-cultural entertainment to soldiers and workers, geisha contributed to the project of modernization: capitalist development, militarist expansion, and empire-building.[24] In the mid-1930s, in between the Japanese army's invasion of Manchuria (1931) and its entering the war against China (1937), some writers and scholars began developing an aesthetic and theory of geisha as symbols of the nation. I will consider *Snow Country* by Kawabata Yasunari (1899–1972) in this context in order to show how lower-class geisha-prostitutes were transformed into symbols of authentic Japanese beauty.

SHAMISEN SCENE FROM *SNOW COUNTRY*

Snow Country is the story of Komako, a geisha who works at a hot-spring resort, and her affection for Shimamura, a traveler from Tokyo.[25] She becomes a geisha to pay the medical bills of her childhood friend and former lover. This novel is usually read as a lyrical account of traditional Japanese beauty because of the geisha's self-sacrificing femininity in the countryside. The novel, which helped Kawabata win Japan's first Nobel Prize in Literature in 1968, was written from 1934 to 1948, when Japan was at war and then under occupation. The historical context of war is absent from the mainstream reading,[26] but Kawabata's strategic sketch of reality does not allow history to be expelled from the text.

Although its geisha heroine makes this novel quintessentially Japanese to our eye, it should be made clear that Kawabata's use of a hot-spring geisha was new, and surprised many of his contemporary critics. Few novelists wrote about these lower-class, underprivileged geisha as beautiful heroines. As a prominent modernist and one of Japan's most influential writers, Kawabata invoked her in the service of a new national aesthetic, since his main strategy was to represent imperial Japan—the supreme object for enthusiastic self-identification by Japanese people—which he located in the geisha's self-sacrificing and innocent beauty.

Kawabata's accounts of Komako's profession, body, rooms, hobbies, fashion, and social relationships accurately reflect the countryside geisha's idiosyncratic everyday life in the 1930s. One scene in particular superimposes art and sexual labor on the geisha against the backdrop of national beauty. The scene has Komako playing the shamisen for Shimamura as he visits her room, but also portrays the intrusion of modernity into the romanticized realm of traditional geisha arts in the mid-1930s. Unable to practice the traditional method of learning music by ear from a teacher because of her life in a remote village, Komako instead learns new songs from printed written music and by listening to the radio.[27] The text thus suggests that "mass-produced" geisha like Komako on the margins of a modernizing society could attain quintessential Japaneseness through reproducible means. The unorthodox style of her cultural practice first makes Shimamura ridicule Komako, but soon he recognizes it as a new form of "art" that he has never seen before.

"A chill swept over Shimamura. The goose flesh seemed to rise even to his cheeks. The first notes opened a transparent emptiness deep in his entrails, and in the emptiness the sound of the samisen reverberated" (p. 71).[28] Shimamura resists the music produced by the unsophisticated geisha, yet as her "notes went out crystalline into the clean winter morning, to sound on the far, snowy peaks," he is haunted by her "wild strength of will" (p. 72). By the time Komako plays her third song, Shimamura gives in to feeling "relaxed and warm" (p. 73) and we get to one of the most erotic descriptions in the novel. The moment her shamisen overwhelms Shimamura, Komako's face grows utterly sensual. "The high, thin nose was usually a little lonely, a little sad, but today, with the healthy, vital flush on her cheeks, it was rather whispering: I am here too. The smooth lips seemed to reflect back a dancing light even when they were drawn into a tight bud; and when for a moment they were stretched wide, as the singing demanded, they were quick to contract again into that engaging little bud. Their charm was exactly like the charm of her body itself" (p. 73).

The blissful state of mind achieved by Shimamura helps prove the surprising cultural authenticity offered by the countryside geisha.[29] The elite male avant-garde critic of both traditional Japanese and Western dance, on whom the third-person narrator focuses exclusively, is the embodiment of the intellectual sophistication of Tokyo. Shimamura finally finds an ideal muse in the countryside geisha. Through the lens of his interiority, we see how Komako conquers Western modernity and uses it to build authentic geisha art. Komako is thus naturalized as a symbol of the beauty of imperial Japan, seen not as a violent and oppressive nation but as one in which people endured many hardships and rendered great service and sacrifice. Komako, though indigenous to the hot springs, carried the imprint of national beauty.

The description of Komako's lips in the shamisen passage is striking not only because of its eroticism but because of the gap between what Komako is—a hot-spring geisha—and what she is sublimated into by Shimamura: the nation. But more striking is the process by which the spectacle of transformation is inscribed on her face.

Komako is described as having "smooth lips." The Japanese phrase *ano utsukushiku chi no namerakana kuchibiru* would be translated as "those beautifully smooth-blood lips," a string of words that makes little sense on its own.[30] The pronoun "those" points us back to a very similar passage, from the first of Shimamura's three trips to the countryside: "The high, thin nose was a little lonely, a little sad, but the bud of her lips opened and closed smoothly, like a beautiful little circle of leeches" (p. 32). This is Shimamura's first discovery of Komako's beauty right after he admits his sexual desire for her. Eliding her lips with leeches, Kawabata created a new metaphor for Komako as a sexual object.

We are guided by the word "those" to transpose "leeches" from the description of Shimamura's first journey into the shamisen scene. There is complicity between Japanese grammar, our shared memory as readers, and our collective subconsciousness. It is hard to deny that what connects her "lips" and "leeches" is the dominant association of women with primitive nature as opposed to civilized culture, as well as the assumption of female sexuality as grotesque.[31] Kawabata knew the leech was disgusting,[32] but nevertheless used it to convince the reader of Komako's beauty.

In fact, the use of the leech is no idle metaphor, but was based on Kawabata's microscopic observations of the creature. A leech has thirty-four segments regardless of sub-species or length.[33] Japan's most common leech is about three or four centimeters long.[34] Komako's lips, scored with tiny creases, are thus likened to a three- to four-centimeter-long leech covered by about five hundred rings. Because of the wavy effect produced by the numerous surfaces of the rings, her lips glisten even when they are still.[35] Kawabata's indifference to the leech's vile reputation and his fascination with similarities of form transfigures the grotesque into the beautiful.

His description of the geisha's social position was equally microscopic, yielded by paying a real geisha in order to study her as an object. The model for Komako, Kodaka Kiku (1915–99), was the daughter of a blacksmith who had nine sisters and brothers.[36] Because her family was poor, Kodaka was sent to become a geisha when she was nine years old. When she was thirteen, she moved as a geisha to the village Kawabata later visited. As I have noted above, villages such as Kodaka's flourished as war and military expansion accelerated, bringing troops and industry to remote areas and contributing to the development of a sex industry. During his stay in the most expensive room at the most expensive local inn, Kawabata would call Kodaka in the evening and have her play shamisen while he wrote. Kawabata would send his writings to his publishers from the inn. He did not ask her consent to use her for his novel. She learned that she was the inspiration for Komako after his installments were published, not from the author but from critics and writers who came to take her picture.[37]

What strikes me is that Kodaka might never have served as his model had it not been for the war, which encouraged the development of the entertainment industry in her town. It was seen as normal literary practice for an established male novelist to use a subject in this way. Far from bringing the matter to the courts,[38] Kodaka quit being a geisha, married a man in a nearby town, and became a kimono tailor. The only way Kodaka expressed any criticism was by burning a copy of the novel when she married. The book was covered with red ink marks, including comments such as "I did not say that" and curse words in the margins.[39]

Kawabata's text was thus shaped by the war, which forced underage girls into sex labor. A historical knowledge of the state's exploitation of geisha guides us to read the novel as a compelling testimony of geisha's sexual labor in the 1930s. Consider the following passage: "The first physical examination she had had here—she thought it would be as when she was an apprentice geisha, and she bared her chest for a tuberculosis check. The doctor laughed, and she burst into tears—such were the intimate details she went into" (p. 105). The passage clearly refers to the state-required gynecological exams for geisha.

The institution of the licensed geisha, the state's exploitation of geisha in the service of the war, and the strength of Kodaka's humanity are all conditions enabling this text to produce a quintessential Japanese beauty that is still valid today.[40] I have argued that this novel takes the exploited geisha and makes her into an emblem of Japan in the service of national expansion and modernization. Kawabata's aestheticization of these socio-political conditions blocks the possibility of criticism. Imagining the wartime violation of the geisha's human condition, however, I think that we can feel the weight of their struggle. I suggest that understanding geisha in their historically complex role of both artistes and sometime prostitutes provides a new sense of their path to becoming national symbols.

Notes

1. 2d ed. (Oxford: Clarendon Press, 1989), 4:419.

2. Iwasaki Mineko (b. 1949), the model and source for the best-selling American novel *Memoirs of a Geisha* by Arthur Golden (1997), claimed "although some geisha quarters did engage in prostitution, most did not, and the perception that all geisha sleep with their clients is absolutely false. We are proud, accomplished women who have absolute rights over our own bodies"; Gary Tegler, "'Memoirs of a Geisha': Muse Vents Spleen at Author," *The Japan Times*, May 1, 2001. It should be noted that geisha entertain not only men but some women as well—for example, Queen Elizabeth was hosted at a geisha party in Kyoto in 1975, as Iwasaki notes in Iwasaki Mineko with Rande Brown, *Geisha: A Life* (New York: Washington Square Press, 2002), 266.

3. Mainstream scholarship on Japanese women's history has excluded geisha and other sex workers from female professions. See Fujime Yuki, *Sei no rekishigaku: kōshō seido, dataizai taisei kara baishun bōshihō, yūseihogohō taisei e* [History of sexuality: from the licensed prostitution and illegal abortion system to the Prostitution Prevention Act and the Eugenic Protection Act system] (Tokyo: Fujishuppan, 1998), 27–28.

4. It should be noted that "art" is translated into at least two Japanese words: *geijutsu* and *gei*. While the former usually refers to the Western and high arts, the latter covers traditional Japanese arts, including popular or "low" cultural practices excluded by the term *geijutsu*. This is the *gei* in geisha.

5. Narahara Junko, "Chūsei zenki ni okeru yūjo kugutsu no 'ie' to chōja" [The household and riches of *yūjo* and *kugutsu* in the early medieval period of Japan], ed. Ishizaki Shoko and Sakurai Yuki, *Nihon joseishi ronshū*, vol. 9: *Sei to karada* [Collections of articles on Japanese women's history, vol. 9: sexuality and body] (Tokyo: Yoshikawa kobunkan, 1998), 7.

6. Amino Yoshihiko, *Chūsei no hinin to yūjo* [The "non-humans" and yūjo in the medieval period] (Tokyo: Akashishoten, 1994), 190–91.

7. Ibid, 220–21.

8. Geisha were both female and male, but the former became more popular. Komori Ryūkichi, "Geisha," in *Kokushi daijiten* [Great dictionary of Japanese history], vol. 5, ed. Kokushi daijiten henshū iinkai (Tokyo: Yoshikawa kobunkan, 1985), 38; Miyamoto Yukiko, "Yūjo," in *Kokushi daijiten*, vol. 14 (Tokyo: Yoshikawa kobunkan, 1993), 273.

9. Hayakawa Noriyo, *Kindai tennōsei kokka to jendaa* [The modern imperial state and gender] (Tokyo: Aokishoten, 1998), 189–97.

10. The term *geigi* technically means female while *geisha* includes both men and women.

11. Hayakawa, *Kindai tennōsei kokka to jendaa*, 200–201.

12. Since local governments had the decision-making power in legal practices, rules varied by region. For example, the case I refer to above is based on Fujime Yuki's research on the Gunma Prefecture. Fujime says that no other prefectures mandated the exam for geisha in 1914 (*Sei no rekishigaku*, 102). Morisaki Kazue, however, shows that the Fukuoka Prefecture started a mandatory exam for geisha in the mid-1870s ("Sekushuariti no rekishi" [History of sexuality], ed. Okuda Akiko, *Onna to otoko no jikū: nihon joseishi saikō* [Time and space for women and men: reconsidering Japanese women's history], vol. 5 [Tokyo: Fujiwara shoten, 1995], 157–58). The Flower and Willow Disease Prevention Act of 1927, also known as the Law for the Prevention of Venereal Diseases, subjected geisha and other sex workers nationally to mandatory gynecological exams, according to Fujino Yutaka, *Kyōsei sareta kenkō: Nihon fashizumuka no seimei to karada* [Forced health: lives and bodies under Japanese fascism] (Tokyo: Yoshikawa kobunkan, 2000), 195.

13. Based on international standards promulgated by the International Convention for the Suppression of the Traffic in Women and Children (1921), the League of Nations' Commission of Enquiry into Traffic in Women and Children in the East conducted a survey of the Japanese prostitution and geisha systems in 1931 and criticized the government for legalizing trafficking and the working conditions of geisha, as forced prostitution violated their human rights. The report described geisha working to pay off their parents' debts, and girls under twenty-one being forced to be prostitutes behind the shield of the adoption system. Onozawa Akane, "Kōshō seido haishi mondai no rekishiteki ichi" [A historical position of the prohibition of licensed prostitution], *Rekishigaku kenkyū* 764 (2002): 9–10.

14. Also spelled *samisen*.

15. Hirota Kazuko, *Shōgen kiroku, jūgunianfu, kangofu: senjō ni ikita onna no dōkoku* [Testimonial documents by military comfort women and nurses: lament of women living on the battlefield] (Tokyo: Shinjinbutsu ōraisha, 1975), 64. This is an interview with a geisha in the 1970s recalling life in 1939.

16. The Japanese government stopped the geisha business in 1943 as the war became fierce (Morisaki Kazue, *Kaishun ōkoku no onnatachi: shōfu to sanpu niyoru kindaishi* [Women in the kingdom of prostitution: modern Japanese history through female prostitutes and pregnant women] [Tokyo: Takarajimasha, 1993], 187). In 1946, the General Headquarters of the Supreme Commander of the Allied Powers (GHQ) ordered the invalidation of all laws related to licensed prostitution out of concern over sexually transmitted diseases (Shiga-Fujime Yuki, "The Prostitutes' Union and the Impact of the 1956 Anti-Prostitution Law in Japan," trans. Beverly L. Findlay-Kaneko, *U.S.–Japan Women's Journal*, English Supplement 5 [1993], 7). Technically all laws under the Imperial Constitution were abrogated in 1947 under the new Constitution.

17. Morisaki, "Sekushuariti no rekishi", 161.

18. Fujime, *Sei no rekishigaku*, 87–115.

19. Yoshimi Yoshiaki, *Comfort Women: Sexual Slavery in the Japanese Military during World War II*, trans. Suzanne O'Brien (1995; New York: Columbia University Press, 2000), 100–103 and 194–95. Yoshimi cites an example from Hirota's *Shōgen kiroku*. The U.S. army during the Occupation used geisha for higher-ranking officers (John Dower, *Embracing Defeat: Japan in the Wake of World War II* [New York: Norton/The New Press, 1999], 300).

20. The number of geisha increased about ninefold from 8,651 in 1884 to 79,348 in 1925. During the same period, the number of licensed prostitutes almost doubled from 28,432 to 52,886 and a new type of prostitute called serving women totaled 48,974 (Kusama Yaso'o, "Baishōfu shōkaiseido to jukyūjōtai: 1" [The prostitution management system and situation of demand and supply (1)], ed. Isomura Eiichi and Yasuoka Norihiko, *Kindai nihon no donzoko* [The bottom of modern Japan] [1928; Tokyo: Akashi shoten, 1992], 121).

21. For modernization in the business of geisha, see Inoue Shoichi, *Ai no kūkan* [Space of love] (Kadokawa shoten, 1999), 68–130.

22. Fukuda Toshiko, *Yoshiwara wa konna tokoro de gozaimashita* [Yoshiwara was this type of place] (Tokyo: Sekai shisōsha, 1993), 94–101

23. Gaye G. Rowley, translator's introduction to Sayo Masuda, *Autobiography of a Geisha* (1957; New York: Columbia University Press, 2003), 6–7.

24. Geisha also organized overtly in the war effort. See Fujino, *Kyōsei sareta kenkō*, 192–93, who explains that geisha in one district in Osaka organized such activities as patriotic folksinging and visits to injured soldiers.

25. Kawabata Yasunari, *Snow Country*, trans. Edward Seidensticker (New York: Knopf, 1956). Hereafter I cite page number references to the English translation in the text.

26. The absence of war may be attributed in part to censorship, first by the Japanese government and then by the U.S.-led occupation. In fact, some scholars claim that the absence of war in the novel was a form of "passive resistance" against the dominant ideology (Ienaga Saburo, *The Pacific War, 1931–1945*, trans. Frank Baldwin [New York: Pantheon Books, 1978], 205). I argue that the war is present in the novel but the mainstream reading has made it invisible. Examining Kawabata's social position and extra-textual activities in the wartime literary world, we need to recognize the socio-historical and ideological significance of the novel in contemporary cultural imperialism. See Roy Starrs, "Writing the National Narrative: Changing Attitudes toward Nation-Building among Japanese Writers, 1900–1930," in *Japan's Competing Modernities: Issues in Culture and Democracy, 1900–1930*, ed. Sharon A. Minichiello (Honolulu: University of Hawai'i Press, 1998), 206–27; and also Charles Richard Cabell, "Maiden Dreams: Kawabata Yasunari's Beautiful Japanese Empire, 1930–1945" (Ph.D. diss., Harvard University, 1999).

27. Kineya Yashichi IV (1890–1942) invented notation for shamisen music, and popularized shamisen and nagauta through radio in the 1920s and 1930s (Gunji Katsuyoshi, "Chūkai" [Annotation], Kawabata Yasunari, *Yukiguni* [Snow Country] [Tokyo: Shinchosha,, 1947], 152).

28. Komako plays *Kanjinchō*, a song from a kabuki play, which was popular during wartime because of its theme of loyalty to one's master. After the war, the occupation government banned it for the same reason. See Marlene J. Mayo, "To Be or Not to Be: Kabuki and Cultural Politics in Occupied Japan," in *War, Occupation, and Creativity: Japan and East Asia 1920–1960*, ed. Mayo and J. Thomas Rimer with H. Eleanor Kerkham (Honolulu: University of Hawai'i Press, 2001), 273 and 279.

29. For a discussion of Komako's shamisen and cultural authenticity, see also Saeki Junko, *Yūjo no bunkashi* [A cultural history of Japanese courtesans] (Tokyo: Chuo koronsha, 1987), 223.

30. Kawabata Yasunari, "Yukiguni" [Snow country], *Kawabata Yasunari zenshū*, vol. 10 (Tokyo: Shinchosha, 1999), 60.

31. See also Tajima Yoko, "A Rereading of *Snow Country* from Komako's Point of View," trans. Donna George Storey, *U.S.–Japan Women's Journal* (English Supplement no. 4, 1993), 47.

32. Kawabata wrote that he gave permission to Seidensticker to omit the repetition of the leech metaphor for her "lips." According to the author, Seidensticker had suggested that "the word 'leech' would give an unpleasant impression to the Westerners," to which Kawabata adds, "indeed to Japanese too" (Kawabata, "Furui nikki" [An old diary], *Kawabata Yasunari zenshū*, vol. 28 [Tokyo: Shinchosha, 1982]: 90–91 [1959]).

33. Maki Sachiko, "Hiru" [Leech], *Daihyakka jiten* [Great encyclopedia], vol. 12 (Heibonsha, 1985), 762.

34. Imajima Minoru, "Chisuibiru," in *Nihon daihyakka zensho* [Encyclopedia Nipponica 2001], ed. Akiba Takashi, 2d ed. (1987; Tokyo: Shogakukan, 1995), 248.

35. While Seidensticker translates the phrase *hiru no wa* as "a circle of leeches," implying the shape of her mouth, I propose to translate it "rings of a leech," to disclose Kawabata's strategy.

36. Hirayama Mitsuo, *Kawabata Yasunari "Yukiguni" jiten* [Encyclopedia of Kawabata Yasunari's *Snow Country*], 2d ed. (Saitama: Mochinaga kikaku, 1998), 29. Muramatsu Tomomi, *Yukiguni Asobi* [Playing with Snow Country] (Tokyo: Kobunsha 21, 2001), 148. Kodaka's comments are introduced in *Asahi shimbun*, October 18, 1968 and April 17, 1972.

37. "Shōsetsu 'Yukiguni' hiroin no moderu Kodaka Kiku san no shōgai" [The novel *Snow Country*'s heroine Ms. Kodaka Kiku's life], *Mainichi shimbun*, February 21, 1999.

38. Iwasaki sued Golden for "breach of contract and a tarnished reputation" in 2001 (Alyssa Kolsky, "Real Geisha, Real Story," *Time Asia*, November 25, 2002, http://www.time .com/time/asia/magazine/article/0,13673,501021202–3938130,00.html, accessed February 12, 2004). The case was closed on February 14, 2003 after a "voluntary dismissal," according to records at the U.S. District Court for the Southern District of New York.

39. Kodaka's husband, Hisao, said "it was filled with red lines that showed where it differed from the facts" (*Asahi shimbun*, October 18, 1968).

40. On the exploitation and negation of geisha as a human subject by male Japanese writers in their novels, see Kanai Keiko, "Kiku otoko, kataru onna, kaku dansei sakka: Tokuda Shusei 'Shukuzu' o yomu" [A man who listens, a woman who narrates, and a male writer who writes: reading Tokuda Shusei's *Shukuzu*], ed. Egusa Mitsuko *et al.*, *Dansei sakka o yomu: feminizumu hihyō no seijuku e* [Reading male writers: toward the maturity of feminist criticism] (Tokyo: Shinyōsha, 1994), 67–96.

PART V

FANTASIES OF THE COURTESAN

Going to the Courtesans

Transit to the Pleasure District of Edo Japan

This essay addresses the process by which males accessed female courtesan enclaves during Japan's Edo Period (1603–1868). It proposes that men were transformed and so prepared for the transient joys of the pleasure world through rituals of transit from the city proper to the pleasure districts, and were reconnected to civic life upon their return home the following morning. In tracing this transit, I dwell more on the culture of proleptic expectation than on the courtesans per se, and the voices heard are more male than female, the subjectivities of the courtesans themselves existing in the hinterland.

The city of Edo (modern Tokyo) had been established as the seat of the Tokugawa warrior family in 1590, and at the installation of Tokugawa Ieyasu as shogun, in 1603, it became the de facto center of the realm, gradually ousting the pre-eminence of Osaka and Kyō (modern Kyoto). In 1657, a devastating fire swept Edo, and in response to it, the city was redesigned. Firebreaks were added and the center of night-time revelry, the district known as the Yoshiwara ("field of reeds" but rewritten to mean "happy fields"), was removed to an outer location. The Yoshiwara became the New Yoshiwara. Though other locales, called "hill places," were available for sexual release, only the Yoshiwara was licensed by the shogunate, imbricated into their city, and deemed a legal entity. Edo was demographically male-dominated and filled with men passing through, both points crucial to its scale and style. The Yoshiwara was off-limits to Edo's female population.

The new Yoshiwara was some 4 km from the city center. This prudent separation also indicated displeasure, for displacement was to the northeast, which was regarded as the vector of geomantic pollution. A significant cluster of prophylactic and purificatory temples had been set in the northeast to protect the city magically, and the Yoshiwara was now positioned behind them along with homes of pariahs, execution grounds, and abattoirs—collectively known as "vile places"—such that its malevolence, like theirs, might be blocked out.

The domain of pleasure was not "vile" to all. Generally, it was referred to as the Floating World, an ancient Buddhist term indicating the ephemerality of all things, but in Edo times used in distinction to the "fixed" world of responsibility and labor. The good householder, whether samurai or merchant, would leave Edo in one frame of mind and arrive at the Yoshiwara in quite another. The structure of the route assisted in his psychological transformation, I propose, as the cultural encrustations on the journey served as the real *cordon sanitaire* around the quarter, separating it far more emphatically from the city than any intervening distance could have secured.[1]

In its post-1657 location, the Yoshiwara operated for over two hundred years.[2] The quarter has, of course, a real history, and this has been written by others.[3] The documentation adduced here is that of myth: it propounds an aura to overlay the place and color the experience of it. Collectively this is known as Floating World literature. The real lives of the indentured women (abused, diseased), or for that matter of the male visitors (duped, diseased), are seldom part of its orbit, whereas celebrations of amorousness and beauty invariably are. Important genres are novellas set in the districts (*sharebon*) and faddish poems (*senryū*); all are written by men, are mutually referential, and in the case of senryu are anonymous, or survive under untraceable pseudonyms. A wealth of visual material also exists in "pictures of the Floating World," both paintings and prints.

GOING TO THE YOSHIWARA

Four routes were available from Edo to the Yoshiwara (fig. 14.1). The first two began in Asakusa. One took the Bridle Path from the Sensō-ji temple until it joined a levee, which in turn led to the Yoshiwara's Great Gate. Alternatively, the man could track through the semi-rural Naka-tanbo area, meeting the same levee part-way along.[4] There was not much to choose between these options; either made sense if one was already in the northeastern part of the city. Thirdly, one left from Ueno, by the Kan'ei-ji temple, which housed several shogunal graves and was a better starting point from the plush official residential districts; the road led toward Minowa, but a path veered off before Senjū, joining the levee again. The fourth way was to begin at the Willow Bridge in downtown Edo and go up the Sumida—usually called the "Big River"—as far as Imado, joining the levee at its opposite end.

The fourth route was the most traveled, and alone gave rise to the canopy of writing and visual recreations treated in this essay. The river route was also the most distancing, for to walk was common but to be boat-bound unwonted. The river was extensively trafficked, with recreational and business uses, but the affluent classes that frequented the Yoshiwara would take boats on the Big River infrequently and probably never for other than visiting the Yoshiwara. For them what was encountered along the way was thus germane to anticipating the district. Quotidian river-users might see the same things without registering any of the same meanings.

AT THE WILLOW BRIDGE

The Willow Bridge was on the Kanda, a smaller stream that flowed into the Big River some meters on. Its arch, or just its head, can be seen in many Floating World pic-

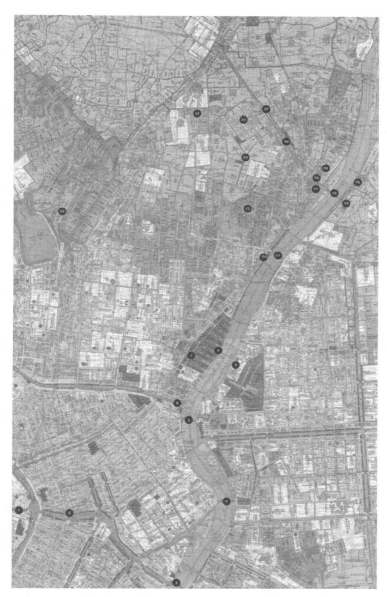

FIGURE 14.1. Northeast Edo.

Key:

1. Edo Castle
2. Nihon ("Japan") Bridge
3. Eitai ("Eternal") Bridge
4. Sin'ō ("New Great") Bridge
5. Ryōgoku ("Two States") Bridge
6. Yanagi ("Willow") Bridge
7. Shogunal Storehouses
8. Topsy-turvy Pine

9. Pasania Tree
10. Komagata ("Foal-form") Hall
11. Azuma ("Eastern") Bridge
12. Sensō-ji Temple
13. Kan'ei-ji Temple
14. Mimeguri ("Three Rotations") Shrine
15. Takeya Ferry

16. Mokubo-ji Temple
17. Mt. Matsuchi
18. Imado
19. Imado Tile Kilns
20. Nihon Embankment
21. Emon ("Clothing") Slope
22. The Yoshiwara
23. Umamichi ("Bridle Path")
24. Shōtji Temple

FIGURE 14.2. Chōbunsai Eishi, *The Willow Bridge*. From *Scroll of the River Sumida*, ca. 1780s. Handscroll, ink and color on paper with gold cartouches.

tures (fig. 14.2). The Kanda was celebrated for the stand of willows along its length, planted in the mid-eighteenth century, after erection of the bridge, the renaming of which necessitated a previous Willow Bridge elsewhere in the city becoming the Old Willow Bridge.[5]

The Kanda Willow Bridge was a major center of waterboat hire and a point of departure to many places. But as the Yoshiwara trip was made at night, there would be small risk of meeting other customers. The only destination apart from the Yoshiwara would be the Fukagawa, a "hill place" across the river. Some 700 boats might be tied up, awaiting customers.[6] Female agents accosted men and escorted them to the boats.

Floating to the Yoshiwara was unlike floating anywhere else, even for those used to river travel, for the boat was of a special type. Thin and high-speed, it had been devised for night-time revelers. Some said it looked like a leaf dropped on the water, but generally it was thought to resemble a boar's tusk. River vehicles tended to be collective ferries for crisscrossing Edo's narrow moats. Noisy and lumbering, their insides were a random sample of society.[7] "Boar's-tusk boats" were, uniquely, for private hire. Their maximum load was three (plus the waterman), but for speed most men rode alone, facing forwards, waterman behind.

This created one of the most solitary experiences a person would ever know, for in Edo the poor were rarely far from a busy street, and the rich seldom free of servants. Darkness would accentuate an uncanny isolation, important for initiating a mood of stillness in opposition to the gregariousness of the quarter.

As boar's-tusk boats were unstable it was necessary to keep still, so the man would adopt the *agura*, a relaxed version of the Lotus Position used by Buddhist images. For all that this was common, it was remarked that the Yoshiwara visitor began his trip in a sort of Buddha's bodily hexis.[8] Transit was silent and pitch black, now also meditational. As the eyes grew used to the darkness, features on the bank could be discovered, in a gradual awakening.

Invocation of Buddhahood, at the outset of the journey, was decidedly relevant. Yoshiwara denizens were seeking pleasures while knowing them to be false. The vanity of all pleasure was an axiom of Buddhism, but the Floating World, by its very label, recognized this lack of durability. Thus, it was argued, time spent with the courtesans was an affirmation, not a denial, of the credo that what was called pleasure was actually meaningless. Many parallels—equations, not antinomies—were established between the world of pleasure and the unhoused, untied world of the truly Enlightened. Under this logic, it was the fixity of civic life that was in error. The courtesan and Buddha were proposed as alike, for both eschewed home, procreation, filiality, and established karmic ties. Pictures supported this equation. Suzuki Harunobu, the first commercial multicolored printmaker, showed a boar's-tusk boat on its way to the Yoshiwara, poled not by a crusty waterman but by a courtesan; the client is not the typical pleasure-seeker, but Boddhidharma, legendary founder of Zen (fig. 14.3). The woman, not just beckoning him to the quarter, is actually conveying him there, while the cleric views his face in flowing water, a long-standing metaphor for vanity, preening himself for the night ahead. There is no need to shun pleasure once its fleetingness is accepted—in fact, clinging to false fixity is worse.

As the boat moved off from the bridge, the man would think of these conundrums, but also of something more. Willows had an established symbolism, relevant to his objective. Their tangled branches, trailing in confusion, were compared to the unkempt tresses of a disquiet woman. Buddhas have stilled their cravings, and courtesans (in myth) are impervious to love; both are free of unrest. The disquiet woman in Edo lore was the daughter of a good house, deranged through passions that she could neither attain nor shed. At death, such females did not become extinct, but were propelled back into life as ghosts, and willows were their abode. The willows at the bridge recalled the powerful hearts of women, and the destructiveness they could wreak, when thwarted, on self and others. This offered a warning to the pleasure-seeker, who was someone's intended if not already someone's husband. Willow symbolism would resurface twice more before the Yoshiwara was gained.

THE BRIDGES

The Kanda entered the Big River some distance upstream of Edo Bay. One therefore missed many of the famous sites of the lower reaches. The Bridge of Two States (*Ryōgoku-bashi*), the sole river crossing when built in 1658, was alone visible to the Yoshiwara-bound, a few score meters downstream. The boar's-tusk boat did not go beneath it, but turned in the other direction, and headed upstream. The Yoshiwara visitor's purpose was not to bridge the gap between Edo's two constituent states, and bind the shogunal city together, but find the seam of no-man's land between. The trip to the courtesans ran along a borderline, detached and judicially unaccounted for. As a senryu verse went, recognizing this liminality,

Two states,
Moving between them -
The speed of it![9]

FIGURE 14.3. Suzuki Harunobu, *Boddhidharma in a Boar's-Tusk Boat*, 1765–70. Multi-color woodblock print.

Bridges were everywhere in Edo, a city of waterways. But just as most boats were for cross-moat hops, most bridges spanned narrow canalized waters. The Two-States and two other bridges further downstream were unwonted in dimension. Their construction had been feats of a significant order, built by the shogunate to assist traffic but also to boast its regulatory power.

A colossal bridge was a gift from the government to the people; as welcome as the elements of the season but unlike them, it too was not natural but created. The Tokugawa not only built, rebuilt, and named their bridges with ceremony, but centered their entire city on one, erected in 1603, the year the shogunate was declared. This last was relevant to the courtesan-goer on account of its name: Nihon Bridge.

The etymology is unsure, as *nihon* has two possible meanings. Either it is "two pathways," signifying a width that allowed dual files to pass together (a rarity), or, more cogently, "Japan." From the apex of Nihon Bridge people could look down a carefully planned vista—one of Edo's few—to the towers of the shogunal castle, soaring slightly to the right, and Mt. Fuji contrapuntally to the left. Nihon Bridge was a gift from the authorities, but also linked their power with the natural world in a complementary pair. The specific relevance to the Yoshiwara visitor was that the levee leading to the Great Gate was called Nihon Embankment. Men accessed the Floating World by taking the government's prime iconic trajectory and throwing it over a different body of water. We shall return to this below.

It was significant that the Yoshiwara trip began after all three Big River bridges were passed (Two-States Bridge only was seen but even it not gone under).[10] The boar's-tusk boat led the visitor away from the securities of regulated civic life that they represented. It pushed hard against a current that sought to drive it back to the city's workaday world.

The unspanned condition of the upper parts of the river was altered in 1774, with the erection of the Big River Bridge, which acquired the name Azuma Bridge.[11] This added a further leg of interpretation to the symbolic topography of the Yoshiwara trip. "Azuma" meant the eastern part of Japan (as viewed from Osaka and Kyō, in the west); it encompassed the two states that faced each other across the river, as well as six others. The name had been common in antiquity, but by Edo times was historicizing and romantic. To be in "Azuma" was to be back in the olden days, which, however, predated the building of Edo and creation of the Tokugawa state: "Azuma" had always meant the east as wilderness. Azuma Bridge took the government-built bridges of downstream and upset them, obliterating the shogunate—not through revolution or war but anachronism—less erased than not yet there. This sense of the irrelevancy of the status quo was enhanced by the practical fact that Azuma Bridge had been erected with local funding, not a shogunal grant.[12]

At Azuma Bridge, the Tokugawa dispensation was gone. Shortly after, the boat would pull over to the right-hand bank, and the man would disembark.

BUILDINGS AND TREES

Given that only one bridge was passed under (before 1774 none at all), it is unsurprising that bridges were not the prime punctuations of the Yoshiwara route. Other features were emphatically present.

Having pulled into the Big River, boats would initially hug the bank. They were punts and the pole could not reach bottom in center stream. Shogunal godowns soon came into view on the left at an area known as Kuramae ("in front of the storehouses") or Mikura ("august storehouses"). By day the area was alive with longshoremen, loading and unloading. By night it was quiet. The waterborne passenger could see that the castle was well provided for, but that all had now taken their rest. Such was the Tokugawa social contract: the state exacted, but returned with a gift of rest. The man, however, was wide awake, expectant. He was out of kilter, for his night would be wantonly spendthrift with no respite at all.

It was taboo to depict government. No portraits or sculptures dotted Japanese cities, and the shogunate used what has been called an iconography of absence.[13] With city vistas, occlusions such as swirling clouds concealed the castle too. Not to

FIGURE 14.4. Chōbunsai Eishi, *The Topsy-turvy Pine.* From *Album of the River Sumida*, 1804. Ink and color on silk.

hide would incur the serious charge of lèse-majesté. Even the shogun's storehouses were treated with circumspection, and pictures offer their shapes concealed in haze (fig. 14.4).

Where possible, such sites went not just undepicted but unseen. It was impossible to conceal the castle turrets (which, at Nihon Bridge, though there only, were part of the visual encoding), but most shogunal spaces were fenced and walled. The Kuramae wharves were invisible from the city side. As the man viewed them from the river, he knew he had a special vision, never vouchsafed from fixed land, only available to the floating, viewable as all good things slept.

Planted in the middle of the wharves was a pine tree. Pines, like willows, were common around Edo, and like them had figurative meanings. As long-living evergreens, pines were signifiers of fortitude, permanence, and a range of lordly qualities. The Tokugawa planted pines to denote their spaces, hence they set one centrally at their stores. But if pines were the ultimate fixed trees (impervious to passage of seasons and years), the Kuramae pine was peculiar: right but also wrong, correct but also perverse. In keeping with the reordering of norms being undergone by the man en route, this tree was *upside down*. Popularly known as the "top and tail"—or to paraphrase somewhat, the "topsy-turvy" pine, its branches bent far out and down across the water, so that its head was truly below its heels— it might have somersaulted completely had stakes not been placed in the water to restrain it. A more perfect icon of inversion could not be hoped for. There was a pun here, for *shubi* meant both "topsy-turvy" and "[amorous] success."[14] The man was on his upside-down way to purchase sexual excitement, but the pine that announced this grew within the river's main shogunal site. This tree embodied an imbalance that was accepted and even legitimated by the regime that had, after all, licensed the courtesan district. On the trip to the Yoshiwara, the government withdrew its controlling prerogatives. The tree would perhaps right itself in the morning when the workforce returned and fixed norms reasserted their priority, although the man (asleep on the return journey) would never know.

Contrast was here allowed with another tree, preternaturally erect: a fine pasania, or sweet acorn, gracing the palace of the Matsura family, daimyos (regional rulers) of Hirado, directly across from Kuramae. This soaring tree formed the first of three lofty points on the Yoshiwara route (the others being Azuma Bridge and a rocky outcrop called Matsuchi). Boats would take bearings from the tree, then "dash like an arrow towards it," as was said.[15] The pasania's current meaning came from pivoting against the inverted pine; "otherwise," wrote one man on going past, "just growing there on the land you wouldn't find much to say about it."[16] The Matsura were an old established family, but by no means supreme among the daimyo, and a witty remark was that the tree was higher in esteem than the proprietor himself. With pasania and pine, nature and culture did not quite align, as the boat sped between. But order was momentarily superseded, not annulled.

The pasania/pine axis was a crossing point too, for here was one of the Big River's traversing facilities, the Omiyabashi ferry. It did not run at night, but its lateral shuttle bound daimyo and shogun (local and general rulers) together.

The pasania also had a symbolism of its own. It recalled the medieval general Minamoto no Yorimasa, promoted from the fourth to the third court rank (a giddy honor), aged seventy-five; he had written a verse punning "fourth court rank" on its homophone "pasania." The poem, which remained well known, professed a desire to give up officialdom and flee the world of fixity:

> These tidings of my elevation –
> Were it not for them,
> Just gathering pasania acorns
> Beneath trees,
> Is how I would pass through the world.[17]

An anonymous senryu writer referred to Yorimasa's verse and produced the following:

> The pasania!
> But where I am heading now is also
> A hidden village.[18]

Yorimasa had sought the obscure, rural life, but "hidden village" was also a fixed epithet for the Yoshiwara.

RELIGIOUS TENETS

The next feature fell some distance on. It was an unusually shaped edifice known the Foal-form Hall (Komagata-dō). Though part of the Sensō-ji temple, it was discontiguous with it owing to Azuma Bridge. Like its head temple, the Komagata-dō enshrined an image of Kannon, the bodhisattva of salvation, here in his manifestation with a horse's head. It ushered in the host of religious institutions that were collected in the northeast of the city, where the boat had now arrived.[19]

Opposite the Sensō-ji was the shrine of Mimeguri, literally "three turns" of ritual circumambulation. Having passed along the seam of the two states and between the linked trees, the traveler now ran the gauntlet of Buddhist temple and Shinto shrine. The two were also in harmony, and to prove it, a crossing was made here too, by the Takeya ferry.

The Tokugawa had once patronized the Sensō-ji, but early in the seventeenth century had transferred it to the people and built the Kan'ei-ji at nearby Ueno for themselves.[20] Similarly, Mimeguri, though old, was no high-flown institution, as its principal icon was the lowly fox-god Inari. Importantly, foxes were held to be capable of metamorphoses such that they entered the human world (as was plain to see), but also disappeared into the other world too. They had no stable form. The man underwent his own shift, transferring from water to land, as he would alight at this point.

Mimeguri itself was a confused and confusing place. Like foxes that came and went, the shrine was both there and somewhere else. Although of normal structure, an earthen embankment had been raised in front to prevent flooding. From the water, only the crossbars of the shrine gate could be seen (fig. 14.5). It looked only high enough for an animal to slink through. The bank had of course been built up to hide the gate, but in a typical Floating World reversal, some preferred to imagine the gate had dropped down. One of many verses reads:

> You'd think
> The gate had
> Sunk into the embankment.[21]

The Takeya ferry connecting Mimeguri and the Sensō-ji had formerly been called the Matsuchi ferry, after the outcrop on the right-hand bank with a hall enshrining Shōten, who, somewhat ironically for the boat-based man, was the divinity of matrimonial felicity. His iconography inextricably fused male and female forms. It was said that wives looked askance at pilgrimages to the Sensō-ji and Mimeguri, since all too often the male devotee was actually planning a trip to the Yoshiwara. But the Matsuchi hall was anxious for the man himself, as he thought of marriage bonds that the Yoshiwara inevitably loosened. Matsuchi was once taller, but had

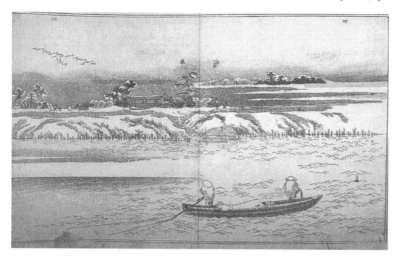

FIGURE 14.5. Kitagawa Utamaro, *Mimeguri Shrine*. Illustration to Yadoya no Meshimori, Ehon gin sekai, 1790. Multicolor woodblock book illustration.

been partially leveled to build Nihon Embankment.[22] One could surmise, therefore, that it was by the lowering of marital aspirations that passage to the Yoshiwara had been effected. Over-reliance on "fixed-world" ties was error, and in Edo, where marriages were arranged, this rode for falls.

One more riverine cluster merits consideration. The visitor would normally disembark on the left-hand bank of the Mimeguri-Matsuchi axis; "swift-boats have no business beyond the shrine gate," it was said.[23] But some men went a few extra minutes upstream to take in another place.

Azuma was a wilderness and the area that became Edo lacked "poetic pillows," or the sites of literary renown, which studded older areas and accorded prestige to landscape.[24] Edo had but one such significant site, at the very ancient Hashibae ferry, which connected hamlets to the right and the northern part of Asakusa to the left.

The tenth-century *Tales of Ise* (*Ise mongatari*), one of the sourcebooks of literary geography, told of a courtier and companions, who, lost in exile, had come here, and while being taken across the river had heard the cry of an unfamiliar bird, which they were told was called a "capital bird." In the words of the *Tales*,

> As they boarded to cross, the ferryman chivvied them along as it was nearly nightfall. All felt mournful, the more so because their lovers were far off in Miyako [the capital]. Just then, a white bird with red beak and legs, about the size of a snipe, came down to splash in the water and catch fish. None of them had seen such a bird before, and it was so unfamiliar that they enquired of the ferryman, who replied it was a "miyako bird." Taking the lead from its name, they called out an appeal, "Oh miyako bird, are the ones we love alive or not?" Right there, in the boat as they were, they burst into tears.[25]

To visit the Hashibae ferry was to reaffirm Edo's (rather tenuous) relevance in cultural history. For pleasure-seekers who did not wish to extend their trip, but who wanted a cachet of culture, a teashop at the point of disembarkation by Matsuchi was called The Capital Bird.[26]

The protagonist of the *Tales* had been exiled because of an inappropriate liaison with a shrine maiden who, the next morning, had written:

Did you come,
Or did I go?
I cannot tell.
Was it a dream or not?

He had responded with similar equivocation. Edo's chief point of validation was a place that questioned sexual relations.

The Hashibae ferry had its right-hand jetty at the temple of Mokubo—an institution that had grown up around a grave that marginally postdated the *Tales*, and so unlike the ferry, its fame did not derive from the exile's story. Its literary celebration was in a fifteenth-century nō play by Motomasa entitled simply *The River Sumida* (*Sumida-gawa*). It was old, but still in the repertory. The playwright's dramaturgical strategy was to build around the "Capital bird" incident, such that an audience could not follow without knowledge of the prior text. He told of a woman who came to the crossing, mad and distracted. As the boatman took her over, together with another passenger, he recounted the story of the origin of the grave, said to be still fresh and not yet enhanced by the Mokubo-ji. The woman realizes it is that of her son, whose abduction by slave-drivers has driven her to insanity, and whom she is desperately seeking.

But to the Yoshiwara-goer, the Mokubo-ji fitted into a Floating World sequence too. The Willow Bridge had alerted him to the fearsomeness of female passion; Mt. Matsuchi had referred (precariously) to the regulation of sentiment through marital ties; the *Tales* pointed to the fruits of broken codes; now a grave evoked the tenacity of females in the maintenance of families. This was quite overwhelming, and perhaps it was lucky that this region was an optional extra.

The play was about the mad woman, and the son does not appear (though some versions have his disembodied voice crying from within the mound). She is unnamed, in the patriarchal manner of the times.[27] The boy is named Umewaka (a given name), literally, "little plum." A fourth tree thus joins the willow, pine, and pasania. Plums blossom in winter when the season is cold, and aged, gnarled trees produce the best flowers. The blossoming plum conveyed a sense of maturity and fortitude, which was supposed to equate with the human male. (By contrast, cherries are finest on younger trees, and buds open only when warm, so they denoted women.) The man in the boat, even if he went so far, would see no plums at the Mokubo-ji, for Umewaka had died before his time, and on top of the grave was a willow, not a stand of them, as at the bridge, but a single tree, standing for one specific mother and her son.

NIHON EMBANKMENT

Just beyond Matsuchi, the boat pulled into the left-hand bank and entered San'ya Canal; immediately it passed under San'ya Bridge, spanning the bourne with the Big River.[28] People noted that this bridge was often passed under but seldom passed over, so of all bridges it was the most perverse.[29] Those going under were heading to the Yoshiwara; those crossing over were heading for the tile-kilns, an uncouth environment to the city's wealthy, and one where work, they said, drowned out the poignant cry of the capital bird.[30] Past the bridge, at Imado, a man stepped ashore in a scurry of sixty or seventy boathouses.[31] Here he would wait for friends who had traveled up separately.

From Imado to the Yoshiwara was 1 km, or eight *chō*, and so one-fourth of the trip. If the river portion of the journey had served to displace and distance the man from civic norms, progression along the embankment proposed to heighten his civic status, another dimension of this realignment. One could walk, but it was preferable to hire a palanquin, hundreds of which awaited customers. Boar's-tusk and palanquin and were the twin vehicles of passage. Both were peculiar to the Yoshiwara, for just as a boar's-tusk was scarcely used other than for the ride there, the palanquins were also of a special type. The common Edo chair was an open platform slung from a pole and supported on the shoulders of two men. Important personages would ride in grander affairs, enclosed to prevent their being seen. Yoshiwara palanquins were known as a "four-handers," as two extra chairmen were hired for running in relay. Other than speed, the palanquins were special in being enclosed (except for a small grill). The effect was to ride along this bit of "Nihon" as a man of superior status, upgraded, and quite detached from "fixed" reality.

In the 1780s, the "four-hander" was introduced into Edo itself, where it acquired the name of "Yoshiwara palanquin." It was used by men desiring a raffish look. But by civil directive, windows had to be inserted.[32]

One of many verses on Nihon Embankment reads:

Nihon–
Eight *chō*
Then the world of sage-women![33]

This road led somewhere unexpected, for sages are not beings of the human world. The embankment wrinkled space. To the visitor, inside the unseeing palanquin, distance was all in the mind.

The land to either side of the embankment was marshy—neither water nor land. The path was a line of in-betweenness, athwart definitions. Many verses elaborated the altering sense of transit:

A great snake!
Nihon Embankment
Is transformed into a serpent![34]

This is a pun, as "great snake" (*uwabami*) is homophonous with "heavy drinker." Alcohol is mind-altering, and the man would consume a lot in the quarter. He now slid along the path and shed the skin of citizen to reveal that of sybarite. The embankment acquired the name of the "road of transformations" (*bakemono no michi*).[35] At the end of it, the man was not the person he had been before.

The enclosed palanquin had initially been intended for samurai, fearful of being criticized for extravagance. The easiest way to deflect the charge, however, was to change clothes. Removing the twin swords and starched upper garment that denoted a samurai would allow him to melt into the mass of townsmen. Swords were forbidden in the quarter, so these had to be consigned somewhere anyway. Along the embankment, left-luggage huts sprang up. But in a society of status-dependent dress, to lose the badge of rank was to lose the rank itself. A man might leave Imado as a samurai and arrive at the Yoshiwara as a commoner. Both samurai and townsmen became just *people*.

For another category of persons, namely monks, undetected entry into the Yoshiwara was not just for dignity but a necessity, for they were banned. The badges of clerical status were the monastic robe and the shaven pate. While vestments were easily checked, an absence of hair was harder to conceal, though as physicians also shaved their heads, mutation from monk to doctor served the trick, and in the huts priests would swap cassocks for medical robes. Ribald comments are not hard to find on (to impose an English pun) the furtively unfrocked.[36] One verse parodies a classic by Bashō, written when he had been midway between the Sensō-ji in Asakusa and the Kan'ei-ji in Ueno, and suddenly heard a temple bell. Bashō had wondered:

> In a cloud of blossoms
> The sounding bell—is it from Ueno?
> Is it from Asakusa?[37]

Everyone knew this verse. The parody went:

> Along the Embankment
> The walking physician—is he from Ueno?
> Is he from Asakusa?[38]

Of course it was not a physician at all, but a monk from the Sensō-ji or Kan'ei-ji.

A sustained parody on the warping effects of Nihon Embankment was offered by Sharaku-sai Manri in a novella of 1771 entitled *Modern Foibles* (*Tōsei anabanashi*), which set the "transformations" into an absurdist entomological context:

> If we consider the transformations going on in the world today, we see things like mosquito larvae sprouting wings and flying off as mosquitoes, maggots growing wings and taking off as flies, and caterpillars changing into butterflies. Courtesans transform into ordinary girls and [allowing them to exit the quarter] head off for a spree; men transform into women and get known as "female experts" [kabuki]; samurai drop off two swords at a boatmen's hut and transform into normal townsmen; monks change into physicians.[39]

As a Floating World writer, Sharaku-sai sympathized with Yoshiwara institutions, but saw their danger: a butterfly may be more beautiful than a larva, but upon losing its carapace it is vulnerable and does not live. Floating is fleeting (and here the pun works in English and in Japanese).[40] The Yoshiwara was an inversion of reality, not an alternative to it, and it was quite unsustainable in the long term.

After some fifteen minutes along the embankment, a path descended to the left. This was known as Clothing Slope. Sumptuary laws forbade luxurious garments, but these were allowed to pass in the Yoshiwara, and a man here might pull out a fancy tunic, or reverse what he was wearing to reveal a gorgeous lining.[41] People entered the quarter with their social selves, quite literally, inside out.

The slope was crooked, tracing the form of a chevron, or dog-leg. The shape replicated the appearance of entrances to government checkpoints. All main highways had barriers approached by this configuration, ostensibly to prevent their being stormed, but the dog-leg soon became a hallmark of progression from the open to the overseen, from freedom to surveillance. The man arriving at the Yoshiwara felt the weight of an impending bureaucratic nightmare—a sensation accentuated by the quarter's Great Gate and the moat and stockades around it, which did resemble the entry to a checkpoint. Once within, though, this flipped, and instead of special severity came special relaxation.

At the top of Clothing Slope were two more sights. To the right was a signboard, not unlike those seen about town, detailing regulations and directives, but here posted with the bylaws of the quarter; it was a final reminder that the Yoshiwara was licensed, subject to condition, and the license could be revoked. Opposite this, on the left, was a single willow, which bore the name of the Looking-backwards Willow; in the morning, visitors would turn repeatedly as they wended their way back to Imado. The trip, which had begun under willows, ended with one too. Note, however, that the last willow took its relevance from the *return* trip; it was as if not seen at evening, and it hung, pending, like the unpredictable power of women, until next morning when it closed the chapter.

At the bottom, on the slope, all had to alight as palanquins were not permitted through the gate. Men would emerge somewhere better than where they had gotten it. It was like being reborn, they said, in paradise. From San'ya there were two roads: one leading to the kilns and on to the execution grounds, a district commonly known as "The Bones" (*Kotsu*); the other was the embankment leading to Yoshiwara. The first led to the inferno, the second to bliss:

> The roads to paradise
> And hell
> Divide at San'ya Bridge.[42]

The man would not forget that the Foal-form Hall, and entire Sensō-ji, were dedicated to Kannon, the divinity who proffers the lotus bud within which the deceased is transported to the Pure Land. The man had entered the palanquin at dirty Imado, his dead, civic body bound inside the palanquin's calyx, and this now opened at the Yoshiwara entrance in a land of perfection. It was proverbially said that paradise was "fifty times one hundred million leagues" away, which played into the length of Clothing Slope, together with the flat stretch that led up to the gate itself, which measures fifty *ken* (1 *ken* = ca. 10 m), which were collectively known as Fifty-ken Street. The Nihon Embankment had effected the ultimate "transformation"—from mortal to immortal life.

SEASONS AND MYTHS

The flat stretch at the bottom on the slope accommodated a row of shops, thirteen to the right and twelve to the left. Originally dealing in face-concealing hats, they switched to selling refreshments or trinkets. In the late eighteenth century, the seventh on the right was occupied by the famous Tsurube soba noodle shop, while the seventh on the left was that of a dealer in Floating World books and prints, so highly pertinent to this essay.[43] The owner was Tsutaya Jūzaburō, an innovative newcomer whose publications had become industry benchmarks. In 1782, he bought the rights to the *Yoshiwara Guide* (*Yoshiwara saiken*), a biannual compendium published continuously since 1718. This acquisition made him chief circulator of the information, but also the mythology of the quarter.[44] Visitors would leaf through his volumes, and consume the representations before taking empirical soundings. Being at the gate meant all patrons of the courtesans passed by. But the location had its limitations too, for not all men went there, and no women could. The year after buying the *Guide*, Jūzaburō therefore secured a shop in Edo proper, greatly expanding access, but, importantly, breaking the dyke between the Floating World and the fixed (which his prints, bought in Fifty-ken Street and taken home, had already caused to leak).[45] The shogunate had expelled the quarter, but now courtesan culture swept back. No little consternation was caused the authorities by the thought that its sanctions should so easily be collapsed.[46] One senior official harrumphed that it had become the norm for mothers to dress their daughters in fashions they could only have learned of through prints, and which, "though pretty, make the girls took like trainee courtesans from the pleasure district."[47] Decrying the intrusion of the Floating World into the fixed was as old as the district itself, but voices were raised ever more strongly.

Such Floating World prints and paintings are among the sublimest works of Japanese art, and have been intensively studied. Depictions of the *journey* to the Yoshiwara have not been examined as a group, but must detain us briefly. Views of the Sumida had been produced since Edo came into being. In the 1780s Chōbunsai Eishi, a Floating World artist and, unusually, also a senior samurai, popularized the theme and made it his own.[48] He began with experiments in various panoramic formats, capturing movement upstream. No less a figure than the emperor's elder brother procured one in 1800, taking it back to Kyō, and showing it to his grandmother, the abdicated empress.[49] Surely prince and lady would have wished to dwell on the beauties of the river, and there is no evidence that the painting included illustration of the "vile places." But given Eishi's Floating World orientation, it was only to be expected that he adapt the formula to give a reduced stretch of Sumida, from the Willow Bridge to Imado only, and add on a second element of Nihon Embankment, Fifty-ken Street, and the quarter itself. From a genre of views of the Sumida was spawned a genre of depictions of trips to the Yoshiwara.

The figures shown making the transit in Eishi's pictures are often not humans, but the Lucky Gods (*fukujin*). As these divinities featured as New Year's ornaments, he may have intended his work as part of the New Year's festivities (cf. fig. 14.2). Alternatively, the point may have been to make the pictures equally enjoyable to samurai and townsmen (who could not identify with pictures of each other). Nanpo's story prompted the renowned Yoshiwara rake Marishima Chūryō to publish two years later

FIGURE 14.6. Kitagawa Kunisada, illustration to Ota Nanpo, Kakurezato no ki, 1836. Monochrome woodblock book illustration.

The Lucky Gods' Snakes and Ladders (*Fukujin sugoroku*), the title of which alludes to the Japanese snakes and ladders board, which is in the form of a journey. Both books were unillustrated, but may have been Eishi's prompts.[50] Nanpo's manuscript was not published until 1836, at which time pictures were made to accompany it by the Floating World print designer Utagawa Kunisada, who culled them (as he properly pointed out) from the then deceased Eishi's originals (fig. 14.6).

As Edo grew and its fame spread, pictorial guides and albums of city views came into being. For completeness, these covered several of the Yoshiwara trip's punctuation marks, and referred to (though seldom showed) the quarter too. One example is Utagawa Hiroshige's *One Hundred Famous Views of Edo* (*Meisho edo hyakkei*) of 1857. The large number of images—which exceed the stated number by sixteen—show aspects of the Yoshiwara transit, three of which merit examination (Imado, Nihon Embankment, and the Great Gate; fig. 14.7).[51] The first shows the disembarkation point of Imado, across the water, the boat- and teahouses illuminated for the night, and the entry to San'ya Canal jammed with boar's-tusk boats. A geisha—a musician, not a courtesan, and so allowed to exit the quarter—walks by. We will return to this image.

The Nihon Embankment view shows men scurrying on foot and conveyed in palanquins, between the huts. The levee runs through the not-water/not-land of the marsh, and a skein of geese flies overhead across the moon. Conventionally, large full moons denote autumn, and so, though not all of Hiroshige's *Hundred Views* contain a season, this clearly does. In Edo, fall was a time of long and warm nights, and if

FIGURE 14.7. Utagawa
Hiroshige, *Nihon
Embankment*. From his series
Edo meishō hyakkei, 1857.
Multicolor woodblock print.

Hiroshige does not show the rain that often accompanied them, others did. Indeed,
autumn rain was the general mode for depicting the embankment. Rain erodes division between the moisture of water and the dryness of land, and, as a "female" (*yin*)
element, it nicely drenched the male (*yang*) figures that hurry onward. The seasonal
association was supported further along the embankment by the Shōtō-ji, a temple
famous for its maples, which attracted tourists when the foliage was red. Out of season, a verse suggests, the embankment offends.

> The Shōtō-ji
> What? Dead leaves?
> You don't stop.[52]

It is a marked feature of Japanese verse to prefer a definite seasonal anchor. An entire
vocabulary of "seasonal words" was created. Not to be locked seasonally into place
made a site tricky to refer to in literary terms.

Thirdly, Hiroshige's depiction of the gate shows it in the morning, as men are
leaving, hostesses accompanying them as far as the exit. It is now springtime. The

Yoshiwara was quintessentially a place of cherry blossoms, they being the prime icons of female beauty. Among the thousands of pictures of the Yoshiwara, barely one is set in a season other than spring.

The autumn of the embankment and the spring of the quarter thus created a pair which echoed a common division in Japanese art. Domestic screens, for example, which came in left and right sections, often showed these two seasons, climatically the best, omitting frigid winter and sweltering summer. But on the way to the Yoshiwara, season is inverted, with autumn *preceding* spring.

Nanpo had written of the Lucky Gods: "having forgotten to go under the spring blossoms, they determined to go before the autumn moon"[53]—that is, in summer. Most likely this was to fit with the autumn and spring that would come later. But he also nods at the radiance of the shogunal presence in Edo's center, associated with brilliant sunshine. To constitute a full year, winter had to be unaccounted for, and so willy-nilly Imado came to be accorded that season, although in Nanpo's joke, its being always in the present might have been grounds for extracting it. Hiroshige's set does indeed give Imado in winter, with figures wrapped warmly and a chill, cloudless sky. The whole stretch of river around San'ya was most often rendered under snow (see fig. 14.5 above).

If the 3 km from Edo to Imado is summer, the 1 km from Imado to the Yoshiwara unfolds in a sequence of winter–autumn–spring. This reversal of true order is corrected the next morning when the returning man leaves the Floating World, autumn–winter, shogunal summer greeting him when back in Edo.

More common in less ambitious series than Hiroshige's, or in ones showing only the Yoshiwara journey (his set shows the whole city), was to omit central Edo. In any case the shogunal sites could not be openly depicted. A long-established pictorial theme was "Snow, Moon, and Blossoms" (*setsugekka*), referring to winter, autumn, and spring. Triptychs worked best, and as they were hung with their "first" element in the center (snow), their second to the right (moon) and third to the left (blossoms), the triad became seasonally correct, running from right to left (as normal in East Asia) autumn–winter–spring. The final land-based segment of the trip therefore conformed to proper iconography, allowing the fixed world back, only once beautiful—this was a representation of the world, not a rendition of actual fixity.

Verses or pictures can take liberties with fact, adjusting seasons to fit received rules. But nature copies art. One could hardly orchestrate a descent of snow or geese, but it was practice in the Yoshiwara to manipulate real cherries in springtime. The Yoshiwara arrogated the highest beauty to springtime, yet warped it, for the quarter's trees "floated" literally, as they were not enracinated in the soil, but carted in for blossomtime, then carted out again:

> Year on year, age on age
> To call the customers in,
> They plant them out.[54]

But if the blossoming planting was shown and written on, the removal of the bare leaves some weeks later was passed over invisibly and in silence. Green cherry trees were a representational solecism, as pathetic as a too-young plum.

TIME

For most people the trip from central Edo to the Great Gate must have taken some two hours. Edo time-telling, however, differed from the modern system, and requires elucidation as it affected the sense of elapse along the journey's transit. An Edo hour was called a *koku* or, more poetically, a *toki*, and was equivalent to two of today's hours; thus, a day and a night was twelve not twenty-four, each announced by a bell. Koku had no formal internal divisions, but clappers would be struck four times, marking not quarters but sixths, as they did not sound at the beginning or end of the koku, thus sounding every twenty-four minutes.[55] Koku were numbered 9–4 in descending order (there were no koku 3–1), then returned to run 9–4 again, one set falling in daylight and one in darkness.

The Yoshiwara visitor would leave Edo during the last daylight koku (9–11 p.m.). The Great Gate closed at the beginning of the first (ninth) darkness koku, or 11 p.m. It would not do to arrive late and find oneself shut out (although in practice a postern was kept open for the tardy). But so that men did not abscond, it was established that the Yoshiwara—which twisted everything else—would also twist time. The last daylight koku began in the normal way, but the four internal clappers were omitted.[56] This long stretch of silence was broken only at the end of the koku, by the bell, but it did not ring the next proper koku (the first of darkness), but rang the last of daylight again.[57] In modern terms, 11 p.m.—1 a.m. became loose, with its subdivisions removed, and was then replayed, only after which time was released to move on again. The typical man who took two modern hours in transit from Edo to the Yoshiwara would, therefore, arrive *at the same moment* he had left. Few people had chronometers to check elapse for themselves (imported pocket watches existed but for obvious reasons were of little use), and so the journey that was so replete with meaning was utterly devoid of time. Being on the water, none of Edo's timebells and certainly none of its clappers would be audible. After the koku repeated, the gate was locked, severing all permeability between the Floating World and the fixed, at which point time was allowed back into operation and one koku was jumped.

This would have been a disorienting experience, but the sense of slippage was not unique: at the other side of Edo, time was variable in the other direction: Shinjuku, the point of entry for shogunal retainers, had a bell that rang ahead of time, lest officials arrive late for duty.

THE SPACE INSIDE

Within the Yoshiwara, life took on new forms, but it should be noted that its pleasures were not necessarily freedoms. Civic laws might be suspended and hierarchies obscured, but self-generated codes were firmly in place. No one wished to offend, for fear of being branded a lout (*yabo*). To become knowledgeable in the mores of the quarter required frequent visits, and those who attained this were known as *tsūjin*, literally, "those who had made trips [to the Yoshiwara]."

It was *having made the journey* that created and defined them. *Tsūjin*—among whom were Eishi, Nanpo, Chūryō, and the anonymous writers quoted above—were the ones who confected the visual and literary iconography of the Yoshiwara, and transit to it.

Some called this space the "world of sage-women" and thought of it as paradise. Others called it the "State of Yoshiwara" as if it were a daimyo's domain.[58] But here was Japan nonetheless, only under distortion and accessed in a bobbing boat down the Embankment of Japan that unfolded as a parody of Edo's iconic core. Legislation required that Yoshiwara architecture be of a standard kind, and the streets look no different from those of the real city.[59] To the authorities, the Yoshiwara was just an unfortunate and tedious necessity accompanying the power center of the realm. But to its denizens, the Yoshiwara became all Japan. Plans were issued plotting the quarter over a map of Japan—making a topography that was useless for orientating oneself, but one that postulated the courtesan district as a replacement, though, of course, a fleeting one, for reality.[60]

THE RETURN

In about 1795, Tsutaya Jūzaburō published a set of prints by Kitagawa Utamaro entitled *Twelve Toki in the Blue Towers* (*Seiryō jūni toki*); "blue towers" was a poetic term for any courtesan district, but Utamaro meant the Yoshiwara.[61] The prints show home-goings taking place during the sixth koku of darkness (5–7 a.m.), which the print poetically refers to as the toki of the Rabbit (fig. 14.8).

Utamaro shows no customer, for the print-buyer would see himself in that role, as a courtesan with tousled hair hands him back his tunic. The garment is de-reversed, its fineness hidden. An inscription can nevertheless be discerned on the lining, reading "Rinshō," that is, Suzuki Rinshō, a fashionable artist known personally to Utamaro.[62] Probably in the same year, 1795, Tsutaya published a novella by the best-selling Shikitei Sanba, illustrated by Utamaro, referring to a consummately attired man who goes to the Yoshiwara in a tunic lined with a painting by Hokusai.[63] The reversal at Clothing Slope has now been de-reversed for return to Edo. The lining shows Boddhidharma, the legendary founder of Zen (already encountered in Harunobu's print). After a night in the Yoshiwara, the man had reached a state of detachment from this-worldly care akin to Buddhist enlightenment, although it is internalized, as it were, as his clothes are turned back, and he hides his knowledge of "floating" truths, as work calls.

All was transience. The man had escaped family for just one evening, but the courtesan had left domesticity for good, and for one brief night she had led him nearer to the karmically noiseless state of, as it was called, "fleeing the home," in her case, literally done.

The visitor left the quarter, Clothing Slope now seeming unnecessarily named.[64] He would look back at the willow as he dragged himself (or was carried) to Imado, perhaps remembering singing a song such as *Yuki* (*Snow*; track 12). The tile furnaces were already stoked, and their billows obliterated much of the scenery, so that the sites, so pregnant as harbingers of floatation, no longer seemed even to exist, as the moist rain of evening gave way to dry, all-swathing smoke.[65] The man would board a boat, lie down, and sleep his way back to Edo. The trip upwards had been pegged all

FIGURE 14.8. Kitagawa
Utamaro, *Hour of the Rabbit*.
From his series Seirō jūni toki,
1794. Multicolor woodblock
print.

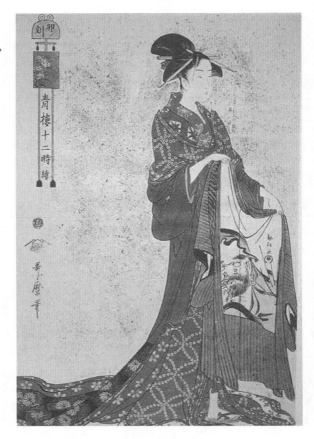

along its route, but the return was often unseen. The experience was like viewing a
handscroll backwards (one of Eishi's, perhaps), where the rewinding process did not
require attention because it was uninteresting once the pictures had been enjoyed in
correct sequence. Those who did stay awake would comment on how, for example,
the pasania looked much better to the right than to the left.[66] But most men were
recumbent:

> The morning boar's-tusk:
> Boddhidharma,
> And a *pari-nirvana* too.[67]

The man lay in the horizontal pose adopted by the Buddha as he entered Nirvana.
Again,

> The going boar's-tusk carried an aspirant;
> The returning boar's-tusk has
> The Buddha in Nirvana![68]

At his return destination, the reveler would be awakened by the waterman, and open
his eyes beneath swinging branches of willow.[69]

Notes

1. I have offered some preliminary thoughts on the topic; see Timon Screech, "The Edo Pleasure Districts as 'Pornotopia,'" *Orientations* 33 (2002): 36–41. See a short collection of *senryū* verses in Watanabe Shin-ichō, "Yoshiwara e no michi," *Kokybungaku: Kaishaku to Kanshō* 473 (1971): 8–22; this issue of *Kokubungaku* was subsequently published independently, as *Senryū Yoshiwara fūzoku zue*, ed. Satō Yōjin (Tokyo: Chibunkaku, 1972).

2. There were occasional temporary relocations after fires, but none was enduring.

3. The fullest account in English is Cecilia Segawa Seigle, *Yoshiwara: The Glittering World of the Japanese Courtesan* (Honolulu: University of Hawai'i Press, 1993).

4. See Nanakubo Hiroshi, "Shin-yoshiwara kaiwai," in *Kokubungaku: Kaishaku to Kanshō* 473 (1971): 8255–62.

5. Nakano Tatsurō, *Edo sumidagawa kaiwai* (Tokyo: Miyoi, 2000), 95.

6. Watanabe, "Yoshiwara," 13.

7. This was not only the experience of ferries but also their iconography; see Timon Screech, *O-edo ijin ōrai* (Tokyo: Maruzen, 1995), 3–8, with illustration.

8. See below, n. 69.

9. *Ni ka koku no mannaka o yuku sono hayasa*; see Watanabe, "Yoshiwara," 14.

10. One further bridge did exist upstream, at Senjū, but was very much farther on and irrelevant to the Yoshiwara experience.

11. This is now the bridge's official name. See *Edo bungaku chimei jiten*, ed. Hamada Giichirō (Tokyo: Tōkyōdō, 1973), 20–21 and 78.

12. Ibid., 20.

13. See Timon Screech, *The Shogun's Painted Culture: Fear and Creativity in the Japanese States* (London: Reaktion Books, 2000), 112–18.

14. The meaning of "success" has been noted in English before, but not that of "topsy-turvy"; see Henry Smith, *One Hundred Famous Places in Edo: Hiroshige* (London: Thames and Hudson, 1986), cat. no. 61.

15. *Chokibune wa mina shiinoki e ya o hanasu nari*; see *Edo bungaku*, ed. Hamada, 205.

16. *Shiinoki wa kude wa omoshiroku nai ki*; see ibid.

17. *Noborubeki tayori nakereba kinomoto ni shii o hiroite yo wo wataru ya*; in *Shinpen kokushi taikei* (Tokyo: Kadokawa, 1987), 5:1168.

18. *Shiinoki wa ima mo kakurete yuku todoko*; see Watanabe, "Yoshiwara," 17.

19. *Edo bungaku*, ed. Hamada, 174.

20. For a history of the temple see Nam-lin Hur, *Prayer and Play in Late Tokugawa Japan: Asakusa Sensōji and Edo Society* (Cambridge, MA: Harvard University Asia Center, 2000).

21. *Dote e torii ga merikonda yō ni mie*; see *Haifū yanagi daru zenshū*, ed. Okada Hajime (Tokyo: Sanshdō, 1999), 3/192 [hereafter HYDZ].

22. *Edo bungaku*, ed. Hamada, 439.

23. *Hayaibune torii yori saki yō wa nashi*; see *Shodai senryū sen kushū*, ed. Chiba Osamu (Tokyo: Iwanami, 1986), 2/47.

24. For this phenomenon see Edward Kamens, *Utamakura: Allusion and Intertextuality in Traditional Japanese Poetry* (New Haven: Yale University Press, 1997).

25. Anon (atrib. Ariwara no Narihira), "Ise monogatari," in *Shin Nihon koten bungaku taikei* (Tokyo: Iwanami, 1997), 89–90. The connection between the anthology verses and the narrative is traditional, and probably not historically valid. For a translation of the full work, see H. Jay Harris, trans., *The Tales of Ise* (Rutland, VT: Tuttle, 1972).

26. *Edo bungaku*, ed. Hamada, 385.

27. Tradition accorded her the given name Hanako, although this is an addition to the story; see Ishino Hiromichi, "Esoragoto" (1803), in *Enseki jusshū*, ed. Mori Senzō, 8 vols. (To-

kyo: Chūō Kōronsha, 1980), 6:269; for a full translation of the text see *Artistic License*, trans. Timon Screech (Hollywood, CA: Highmoonoon, 2003).

28. The span was known as either San'ya Bridge or Imado Bridge.

29. *Imado-bashi ue yori shita o hito tōru*; see Nanakubo, "Shin-yoshiwara," 259.

30. *Kawara shi wa shitafuri suru miyakodori*; see ibid., 260.

31. Nakano Mitsutoshi, "Edo no yūri," in *Zusetsu edo no koten* (Tokyo: Shiseisha, 1989), 18:123.

32. Watanabe, "Yoshiwara" 10.

33. *Nihon o hatchō yuku to sennyo kai*; see HYDZ 10/285.

34. *Uwabami mo nihon tsutsumi hebi ni bakeshi*; see Nanakubo, "Shin-yoshiwara," 251.

35. Sharaku-sai Manri, *Tōsei anabanashi*; see Nakamura Yukihiko, "Gesaku-ron," in *Nakamura Yukihiko chōbetsu-shū* (Tokyo: Chūō Kōronsha, 1982), 8:124.

36. *Nakajuku no mae o genzoku o waratte'ku*; see HYDZ 2/173.

37. *Hana no kumo kane wa ueno ka asakusa ka*; see *Nihon koten bungaku taikei* (Tokyo: Iwanami, 1962), 45:53.

38. *Dote o yuku isha wa ueno ka asakusa ka*; see HYDZ 5/189 and 5/292.

39. Quoted in Nakamura, "Gesaku-ron," 124.

40. *Uki* means both "floating" and the sadness that comes from impermanence.

41. See below, n. 69.

42. *Gokuraku to jigoku no michi wa san'ya-bashi*; see HYDZ 6/98.

43. A plan giving names of the shops is contained in the *Yoshiwara saiken* for 1775; for a convenient illustration see Nakano, "Edo no yūri," 131.

44. Hiraki Museum of Art, *Yoshiwara saiken: edo bijo kurabe* (Yokohama: Hiraki Ukiyo-e Foundation, 1995), 112.

45. Matsuki Hitoshi, *Tsutaya Jūzaburō: edo geijutsu no enshutsuka* (Tokyo: Nikkei Shinbunsha, 1988), 41–71.

46. See Screech, *The Shogun's Painted Culture*, 113–18.

47. Moriyama Takamori, "Shizu no odamaki," in *Nihon zuihitsu taisei*, 20 vols., series 3 (Tokyo: Yoshikawa Kōbunkan, 1974), 22:240.

48. Kobayashi Tadashi, "'Sumidagawa ryōgan zukan' no seiritsu to tenkai," *Kokka* 1172 (1993). Naitō Masato, "Chōbunsai Eishi no iwayuru 'yoshiwara-gayoi zukan' ni tsuite," in *Nikuhitsu ukiyoe taikan*, ed. Kobayashi Tadashi (Tokyo: Kōdansha, 1996), 3:240–47.

49. Naitō, "Chōbunsai Eishi," 240. The man was Myōhin no miya ("prince-abbot of the Myōhin").

50. It is also possible that Nanpo copied Eishi, although Nanpo's genius tends to suggest the innovation was his.

51. The set also includes views of the Topsy-turvy Pine, the Hashibae ferry and kilns, and the Mokubo-ji. For reproductions see Smith, *One Hundred Famous Places*. For illustrations of the Great Gate, see Screech, "Edo Pleasure Districts," 40.

52. *Shōtō-ji nani karetsuba to sugu tōri*; see ibid.

53. Ota Nanpo, "Kakurezato no ki," 317.

54. *Toshidoshi saisai kyaku o yobu tame ni ue*; see Osaka Hōichi and Segawa Yoshio, "Yoshiwara nenchū gyōji," in *Kokubungaku: Kaishaku to Kanshō* 473 (1971): 83.

55. This is schematic. In practice, koku were of variable length as six fell in daylight and six in darkness, so they had to be adjusted accordingly using complex calculations.

56. Ibid., 264.

57. The material in the remainder of this paragraph and in the next is derived from Mitamura Engyō, "Jikoku no hanashi," in *Mitamura Engyō zenshū*, 8 vols. (Tokyo: Chūō Kōronsha, 1975), 7:265–68.

58. There were many such terms, including "Arinsu Land" (from the patois of the quarter).

59. Seigle, *Yoshiwara*, 23.

60. An illustration of "Yūkoku zu" (State of Play) appears in an undated joke book (*kokkeibon*) by Tōbu Maji Yūkan, *Eitai yūri zasshō*; reproduced in Nakano, "Edo no yūri," 132.

61. For the date, see Shogo Asano and Timothy Clark, *The Passionate Art of Utamaro* (London: British Museum Press, 1995), 137.

62. Utamaro and Rinshō collaborated on the poetic (*kyōka*) anthologies *Haru no iro* (1794) and *Yanagi no ito* (1797); for Rinshō, see Screech, *Shogun's Painted Culture*, 127.

63. Shikeitei Sanba (Kitagawa Utamaro, ill.), "Tatsumi fugen," in *Nihon meichō zenshū* (Tokyo: Nihon Meichō Zenshū Kankkai, 1929), 12:590. Hokusai is referred to as Sōri, the name he used 1795–98. Since the print series cannot be dated precisely, elapse between it and the sharebon is unsure; the latter was published in 1798 (thus probably written in 1797) and the former is said to be ca. 1795; see Clark and Asano, *The Passionate Art*, 1:137. "Tatsumi" was a nickname for the Fukagawa unlicensed quarter; thus the novella does not refer to the Yoshiwara, although the larger contention holds.

64. *Emonzaka kaeri ni tsuketa na de wa nashi*; see Nakano, *Edo sumidagawa*, 245.

65. *Asa-gaeri imado no kemuri ni torimakare*; see HYDZ 2/194.

66. *Hidari yori migi ni miru shii omoshiroi*; see Watanabe, "Yoshiwara," 17.

67. *Modoru choku daruma mo areba ne-jaka ari*; see HYDZ 1/21.

68. *Yuku choki wa zazō kaeru choki ne-jaka*; see HYDZ 12/192.

69. *Okite miriya yanagi no shita ni tsuite iru*; see Watanabe, "Yoshiwara," 20.

Who's Afraid of Giuliana Napolitana?

Pleasure, Fear, and Imagining the Arts
of the Renaissance Courtesan

In 1562 the young Venetian noble Luigi Dolfin visited the noted Florentine courtesan Giuliana Napolitana, and after making a deal with her that she would come sleep with him at his lodgings, he left her four gold scudi[1] and went about his business, one imagines anticipating with pleasure his night of pleasure. Such were the prerogatives of men, upper class and rich. They could buy the artful services of beautiful, cultured, and desirable women and in the process confirm their place on top of society as well as their power and masculinity. But the smooth power of wealth and status in this case was overturned by the young and, strange as it may sound, equally powerful Giuliana. Her power, however, is less easily recognizable because it lies in places where many are not used to looking for such things: in gender, sex, and ultimately in fantasy and illusion, perhaps her most developed arts as a courtesan. But make no mistake: her power was no illusion, as Luigi Dolfin, with all his more traditional social, economic, and masculine power, learned to his regret.

His first hint of this came when Giuliana did not show up for their night together. When he returned to her lodgings to demand his due, she flatly rejected him, surrounded by a host of mocking admirers. Needless to say, Dolfin was outraged, but being a moderate man he decided to seek redress from the Florentine authorities. And, in fact, Florence, like most other major Italian cities, had a court that was concerned with the disciplining of sexual mores and prostitutes, the Onestà. Prostitutes were supposed to register with the Onestà and cases of their illegal activity and misbehavior were regularly handled by this court.[2] But if Dolfin expected that he would find justice there, he ruefully admitted that he found little: "Thinking that there I would be given the correct and good justice, it turned out instead that I saw clearly the unmeasured and open favors given to her . . . ."[3] It seems that when Dolfin entered the court he discovered Giuliana already there "accompanied by some 150 young men making a great din all to my dishonor." Allowing for some hyperbole, it still seems evident that the judge's countenancing such a fracas was not a good sign for Dolfin's suit. Moreover, he reported that Giuliana bantered with the judge, who assured her that he would have no patience with the Venetian's complaints, perhaps a sign that some inter-city as well as sexual rivalries were at play. In fact, the judge was as good as his word, for we learn of these events because Dolfin's suit was rejected and he appealed his case to a higher court.

Before the higher court he secured some redress for the dishonor he had suffered. Giuliana was ordered "to go and sleep with him and give him the use of her body as is the custom in such relationships." But even in granting Dolfin's right to have the object purchased, we see that Giuliana was no "common" prostitute and not so easily bought, for she was given the option of refusing Dolfin if she repaid him his four scudi. It is not clear what Giuliana decided, but it is clear that she was a match for Dolfin and, tellingly, her body was hers to dispose of as she wished, not the common property of all men, as was regularly claimed for "common" prostitutes.[4] Crucially, however, Luigi Dolfin had been humiliated publicly and perhaps for a moment was even forced to recognize a weakness in that invisible armor of prestige and social place that made men of the Renaissance social elite virtually invulnerable to those below them. I would suggest that Dolfin learned to his regret that even he had to be afraid of Giuliana Napolitana.

But the European Renaissance loved to play with reversals. And the dangerous, evil courtesan, who had to be handled with care, was certainly in the Renaissance imagination the flip side of the brilliant, cultured, beautiful courtesan, who was so attractive as a companion. Matteo Bandello writes in a novella of the famous Roman courtesan Imperia, whom he portrays as the personification of everything fine and beautiful that the aristocratic world of the Renaissance had to offer. Her lodgings, as her name suggested, were virtually imperial: "her house was furnished in a manner that was all carefully planned so that whatever foreigner entered, seeing the furniture and the discipline of the servants, would believe that here lived a princess."[5] In fact, she was the perfect match in grace, style, and manners for the elite men who visited her. And in many ways she was the mistress who made the man, her lovers marked out as true aristocrats merely by being accepted into her company. The point is emphasized by the typically "Bandellian" twist that ends the tale. Attracted by reports of Imperia's grace and beauty, the Spanish ambassador to the Pope visited her regal quarters and was awed by what he saw. After a while, feeling the need to spit, he searched in vain for a suitable place amid all that elegance and finery, clearly feeling on trial. Finally, inspiration saved him and he rose to the occasion spitting in the face of one of her servants. Underlining his brilliant and witty solution to his dilemma, as a man of refinement and manners, he suavely apologized to the servant: "I hope you don't mind [young man], but your face is the most base thing here."[6] Exactly. Imperia was a courtesan who artfully offered just what an upper-class patron sought—an elegance, grace, and *virtù*[7] not merely to match his own but crucially to reinforce and demonstrate it—and the Spanish Ambassador did just that.

Here we are faced with a seeming contradiction. Renaissance courtesans threatened honor, status, and *virtù*, as the case of Giuliana Napolitana and many other cautionary tales from literature and the archives reveal, yet at the same time they demonstrated and even bestowed honor, status, and *virtù* with the help of their arts, as the tale of Bandello's Imperia and many other sources report. We might well ask which picture is correct: was the courtesan the dangerous destroyer of aristocratic males or their artful fashioner? Well, for once the answer is straightforward even if it is not simple. She was both. In an intriguing and revealing dance of reversals it was often those very things that were most attractive about her that could quickly become most dangerous. And that meant in turn that in life, literature, and imagination the courtesan's beauty, grace, and *virtù* were always on the edge of becoming ugliness, coarseness, and dishonor.[8]

In this essay, then, I would like to look at a few areas where attraction for the courtesan easily became fear, beauty quickly slid into ugliness, and the honest aristocratic courtesan could rapidly turn into the demeaning, dishonoring whore—a dream/nightmare that haunted the imagination of the Renaissance. And I should emphasize that I am less concerned in what follows with the real lives of courtesans (a topic which I have considered elsewhere) than with the way they were imagined and feared at the time.[9] One risk, however, of not discussing again the negative aspects of their lives is that one may get the impression that this essay gives too much power or too much glamour to courtesans at the expense of acknowledging the real dangers and real limits they faced. Hopefully the reader will be distant enough from the Renaissance fears and imaginings I discuss here to see them for what they are, another set of often overlooked but crucial realities that in their own way reflect and had an impact on the arts of the Renaissance courtesan.

A second disclaimer is in order. Recent scholarship has tended with good reason to stress the economic nature of prostitution. Viewing such practices in an economic rather than a moral light has deepened our understanding. But it has limited it as well, for the imagination and fear involved in such relationships was about much more than money. Even at the level of an economic transaction it is all too easy to fall into an anachronistic vision that sees the prostitute selling a commodity, her body, like many another Renaissance entrepreneur. Yet things were much more complex, especially when it came to the courtesan. In turn, less emphasis has been placed on the reverse side of this economic relationship: aristocratic men, when they paid for a courtesan, were buying a series of things that went well beyond a prostitute's body, as the title of this volume suggests. Still, even at the level of buying "the use of [a courtesan's] body, as is the custom in such relationships," one must remember that at the time there was much less added value, meaning, or moral stigma involved in such an act than one might assume. The European Renaissance accepted slavery, servants' and workers' bodies were used with a freedom difficult to imagine today, and, most notably, using someone else sexually was more a normal act than an abnormal one. Even in an institution as central and morally sanctioned as marriage, the ideal of the "marital debt" wholeheartedly supported by the Church encouraged the notion that individuals gave their bodies to their spouses for their use.[10] In what follows, then, this essay attempts to add complexity and nuance to the discussion of what was exchanged economically between a Renaissance courtesan and her client by focusing on what was imagined and feared in such exchanges; but it also considers a series of other exchanges that were perhaps even more significant than money in the fears and imaginings of the times.

First off, Renaissance courtesans were imagined as beautiful, graceful, refined —objects of rare value like Imperia—and conveniently for the desires of an aristocratic male, they could be bought. The price could sometimes be high, but it should

be remembered that upper-class males of the Renaissance displayed their wealth
and power by purchasing rare and acclaimed beauty wherever it could be found,
and courtesans provided a particularly interesting opportunity to buy. In essence a
courtesan was a truly beautiful luxury good, much like a work of art, and perhaps for
many noble patrons easier to appreciate and enjoy.

But there was a more sinister side to this economic understanding of the courtesan, and again Matteo Bandello, true to his dark imagination, provides a telling tale.
Setting his story in Venice, a city famed for its avaricious ways, he reports:

> In Venice there . . . [is] an infinite number of whores, who as in other cities are
> called with honest language courtesans. One notes there, however, an [unusual]
> custom . . . namely that there are courtesans who will normally have five or six Ve-
> netian gentlemen for their lovers. Each of these men has a night of the week when
> he goes to dine and enjoy her. But the day belongs to her. . . . If it should happen
> that some outsider arrives with a fat purse and asks to spend the night with her she
> accepts him . . ."[11]

Seemingly a perfect example of the commercialization of aristocratic sex, a sophisticated contractual relationship permitted a form of sexual time-sharing that gave a
courtesan a secure income and the opportunity to maximize her profits from time to
time with outsiders.

This account of sharing courtesans, in Venice at least, was not just a reflection
of the dark imagination of Bandello or his anti-Venetian sentiments. There are many
accounts of this practice in the archival records of the city, where courtesans refer
to groups of upper-class men who keep them. One notable example is the courtesan
Andriana Savorgnan, who in the late 1570s and early 1580s was shared by, among
others, the nobles Santo Contarini, Piso Pisani, Filippo da Canal, the Count Scipio
Avrogado, as well as the substantial commoner Paolo Robazzo, along with several
ecclesiastics, only to dump them all to marry the noble Marco Dandolo and create a
scandal that kept the city abuzz for months.[12] In fact, it appears this practice continued well into the seventeenth century, for in 1646 a functionary of the Papal Nuncio
in the city wrote a report to the Pope about the many sins of the Venetians and
noted, "What is really amazing, however, is to consider how four or six men together
and peacefully keep a woman in whose house they drink and play. . . . Thus they
build their friendship where normally one would expect jealousy and animosity."[13]

In Bandello's tale, however, a youthful Milanese gentleman fell victim to this
system. Young and well off, he came to an unnamed but evidently noted courtesan,
expecting to buy her, but instead found himself the protagonist of a cautionary tale.
From the first Bandello suggests that if his young gentleman had stuck with the more
sensible whores of Lombardy (a note of chauvinism perhaps, as Bandello himself was
a Lombard) his wealth would have sufficed to secure the object of his desire. Right
from the start, then, Bandello implies that such a relationship should be merely
economic, yet he clearly imagines and fears that that is not the case, at least not
with Venetian courtesans. Cutting to the heart of the matter, he relates: "She, . . .
seeing him richly dressed and looking like a man ready to spend, realized that he was
a pigeon ready for plucking; thus, she began to play him, making eyes at him and
giving him many sweet looks."[14] Over a period of three months she slowly plucked

him clean, leaving him desperate and penniless—a perfect reversal of the bright Renaissance image of attractive, cultured, graceful courtesans who could be bought like any other beautiful object. And in the end, with her artful ways she turned this noble consumer of beautiful objects into the object consumed.

This fear of the courtesan's ability to destroy wealth and the wealthy is ubiquitous in Renaissance literature. Perhaps best known is Pietro Aretino's account in his *Sei giornate* of the training of young Pippa by her mother Nanna to be as refined a whore as possible, reaching for the status of a courtesan. In Aretino's tale, Pippa's grace and learning are largely shams to cover a carefully cultivated trade in selling virginity over and over again, furnishing expensive lodgings over and over again, and extorting as many expensive gifts as possible over and over again; in sum, maximizing profits at the expense of wealthy victims. But such scams were not limited to literature; they were a frequent aspect of sexual commerce. Governments were regularly concerned with protecting men from falling victim to such artful schemes. Authorities were particularly worried about young notables mortgaging their future inheritances to unscrupulous moneylenders working in conjunction with high-level prostitutes and courtesans—thus losing not only their own wealth but that of their families.[15] Clearly, when it came to the economic aspects of the courtesan, attractive objects could easily become dangerous predators.[16]

The courtesan, however, was much more than a luxury good; a crucial aspect of her attractiveness was her intimate relationship with status. As her very name suggests, to some degree the courtesan was associated with courts. Clearly she was not the lady of court imagined by contemporary mavens of court etiquette like Baldassare Castiglione or Giovanni della Casa. In their vision of how the court should function, the aristocratic ladies of court selected the graceful, mannered, perfect courtiers and rewarded them with their favors—but that game of power and status was complicated beyond such ideals by jealous husbands, families anxious to protect the honor of their daughters, and upper-class mores that made it difficult for the court woman to reward courtiers "honestly." It might be suggested as well that many court ladies were less refined and less capable of living up to this role than the ideal allows, just as recent studies have shown that many men at court fell far short of the mannered and moderate demeanor envisioned by literature.

Enter the courtesan, a theoretically refined, elegant woman, with educated tastes who while she may not have frequented the court was frequented by the men of court as well as men who attempted to imitate courtly ways. Unlike the aristocratic court lady, she could select and *reward* with her arts the "perfect" courtier, a man with the grace, wit, and *sprezzatura* called for by the new etiquette manuals. And nicely, although the competition for her favors could be portrayed as open, the rich and powerful could assume that they had a real advantage, even if they did not quite live up to courtly ideals. In sum, the courtesan as an arbiter of status might seem ideal for men at court and perhaps beyond the court as well.[17] In both Bandello tales cited above, an underlying fear turned on the power of the courtesan to select the best men. Imperia's imperial ways made her fit to select such men; and the unnamed Venetian courtesan rejected the inexperienced, Milanese nobleman because he was not worthy. Selection/rejection: Giuliana Napolitana's rejection of Luigi Dolfin was not just a matter of loss of money or a beautiful object, it was a much more telling loss of status. Once more, fearing Giuliana made eminent sense.

But again there were deeper issues involved in the fear of a courtesan's power to select, for hand in hand with the power to confirm status went the broader power to confirm or call into question one of the key evaluative terms of behavior in Renaissance Italy: *virtù*. *Virtù* was intimately related to status because at one level it was simply that set of behavioral characteristics that made one man better than another. In fact, a great deal of time and psychic energy was consumed evaluating who had *virtù* and who did not; and, needless to say, the complex calculations of *virtù* drive many a plot and character portrayal in Renaissance literature as well.[18] What makes this complex dynamic of social and cultural evaluation harder for us to see is the fact that *virtù* varied across class and gender lines and changed dramatically over time. Most notably for upper-class males of the early Renaissance *virtù* turned on reason (verging at times on cunning), calculation, a moderation of passion (especially the violence that was associated with an earlier warrior nobility), and control; as the fifteenth century progressed and the Renaissance became more aristocratic, *virtù* came to be associated with more aristocratic values like grace, mannered behavior, a certain nonchalance labeled *sprezzatura*, and an easy, game-like playful approach to a wide range of activities. The earlier vision is easily seen in Boccaccio's *Decameron* where clever and cunning characters seem invariably to win, and violent or foolish ones are the designated victims of humorous and often cruel jokes (*beffe*); the classic later vision is perhaps best articulated in Castiglione's *The Courtier* where, as noted above, the perfect courtier is selected and rewarded by the court lady.

In literature the disciplining potential of *virtù* is particularly apparent. Perhaps because the discourse of *virtù* was so deeply embedded in culture, literary texts constantly returned to it—with an unending subtle analysis of who had *virtù* and the honor and status that went with it. But, of course, such discussions in literature were merely part of something much larger: a whole complex apparatus and discourse that was so central to Renaissance life that it might well be labeled "the Renaissance regime of *virtù*." Much like other more recognized regimes, the regime of *virtù* ruled people's lives, but because its rule was informal and largely organized in the social arena rather than the political, it has been less noted. Nonetheless, its power comes through strong and clear when we look at how the period imagined the attractions and dangers of courtesans. For at the heart of their ability to select rather than accept their clients lay the assumption that they too were evaluating the *virtù* of those men who sought to be their lovers. When Luigi Dolfin was publicly rejected and shamed by the "hundreds" of young men who crowded into the court of the Onestà, this was no mere insult or slight: it was a public moment that proclaimed his lack of *virtù*. Beyond the political world of the Onestà, beyond wealth and power, beyond status, Dolfin understood that he had been tried by Giuliana and her friends in the regime of *virtù* and lost. But Dolfin was not alone in this position, for crucially in the Renaissance imagination winning a courtesan's favor put into play one's place in this regime—a potentially dangerous game to play and perhaps even more troubling to imagine. Of course, once again money, power, and status would presumably favor those who possessed them. But if one was insecure about one's place—and given the fluidity of the discourse of *virtù* and its inherently unstable nature, we might posit that insecurity was the name of the game—it was easy to fear the worse and, as Dolfin's case illustrates, all too easy at times to experience it.

In one area, however, Renaissance fear of the courtesan may well have been especially troubling: the sexual. Sex was a principal domain of the courtesan, of course, and for many upper-class men of the Renaissance it was a highly contested territory where sliding and conflicting codes of morality, sin, and ideal behavior often put their sense of honor and *virtù* at risk. This was especially true for young men of the upper classes who led a sexual life that was often highly problematic. Perhaps most significantly, they married late and lived through a long period of rather indeterminate sexuality often labeled adolescence, but better thought of as *gioventù* (youth), as it was more regularly called. This period could stretch from puberty at age twelve or thirteen on to marriage at age thirty or beyond.[19] Across this period of time it was assumed that males would be first sexually passive and androgynous (or even feminine) and many would be involved in passive relationships with older males, based on education, patronage, sex, or all of the above. As they grew older and matured, developing facial and body hair, gaining more economic and social independence and power, and becoming more "masculine" in the eyes of contemporaries, it was assumed that they would become active sexually, that is, more interested in dominating and penetrating their sexual partners, whether they were female or male.

But it seems clear, reading the literature and the court records, that this transition from passive to active male was often troubled and a cause for concern and fear. First, legitimate female partners were virtually unavailable short of marriage, and for upper-class males marriage was ideally reserved for later in life. From a young aristocrat's late teens until his late twenties or early thirties keeping a concubine, victimizing lower-class women or servants, penetrating younger boys, or paying lower-class prostitutes were all common expedients for demonstrating an active adult sexuality. But "common expedients" expresses the problem well—all these expedients were common and to a greater or lesser degree demeaning. Moreover, as the Renaissance upper classes became more aristocratic and mannered and newer visions of *virtù* gained sway that stressed more graceful, mannered, and even passive behavior for adult males, it may be that such expedients became even more "common" at the same time as it became more necessary to demonstrate the active, aggressive behavior still associated with adult male sexual status. Be that as it may, sexual performance was a crucial aspect of *virtù* for young men, and performing successfully, given the options for doing so, was not easy.

Enter the courtesan, imagined. On the positive side, with her mastery of the art of sex, with her carefully cultivated manners and gentle ways, she was the ideal person to guide young aristocrats through this difficult transition. Her whole art could be seen as aimed at training them to fulfill their active sexual role as adults and providing this in a way that reinforced the broader social and cultural context of aristocratic society. No need to become involved with common whores, the wives and daughters of the lower classes, or worse yet, the wives and daughters of one's own class. From a Renaissance perspective, who could imagine a better solution to a difficult situation?

But, of course, yet again the perfect solution had its reverse. Who could fail to imagine how dangerous it would be to give this power over young men to courtesans? Bandello's story involving the young noble from Milan makes this perfectly clear, and with tragic symmetry. Having been rejected for three months, his would-be young lover in the flower of his *gioventù* decides to make the ultimate public gesture to demonstrate his love—to commit suicide in her quarters before her and her other lovers, should she refuse him again. In the face of his threat, she denies him one last time. So, dramatically he drinks down a poisonous draught, a potentially courageous act that might confirm his unrecognized manliness. But true to his spectacular lack of *virtù*, the poison does not act immediately and Bandello comments wryly, "she, thinking it a joke, [just] laughed." With her final demeaning laughter ringing in his ears he returns home to die "without anyone noting it." Bandello's "without anyone noting it" is literally a dead giveaway, for the regime of *virtù* was fundamentally a social one in which *virtù* was evaluated in public. Our young noble's dramatic gesture was lost precisely because it went unnoticed.[20] Instead of making a successful transition to adult male status, he was literally cancelled from the regime of *virtù* by a courtesan and died unnoted—truly a nightmare reversal for the Renaissance and light years from a simple economic transaction that failed.

This mad love leading to suicide reveals one last set of dangers that a courtesan posed for the Renaissance, namely her ability to make some men lose self-control and perhaps at a deeper level literally to lose themselves in love. In a curious way this might be seen as a reversal of a classic theme of love imagined, that fine love of medieval literature. The pure love for a woman that allowed a man to transcend himself and literally give his soul to another had a long tradition that was often evoked in the Renaissance, most notably in Petrarchan conceits of love poetry and the Neoplatonic enthusiasms that reworked them. But in real life Petrarch's perfect love, Laura, remained more often a dream than a reality, and transcendence in love between humans was rare. Still in a curious way the courtesan came closer than many women to fulfilling this dream. Her special status as non-wife and chosen love, outside the everyday world of marriage, children, and family concerns, along with her aura of grace, beauty, and learning, could make her an ideal site for imagining fine love. But once more, the opposite was true as well, for it was easy to see the courtesan as the clever fabricator of a mad love that caused men to lose their self-control and literally, in a destructive passion, to lose themselves.

Here again life and literature coincide in an interesting way, for one of the most powerful political thinkers of the Renaissance, none other than Niccolò Machiavelli, outlined the dangers and pleasures involved in succumbing to such love both in his letters and in his comedy *La Clizia*. Machiavelli's letters consistently express his respect and affection for his wife Marietta; but his love and passions were reserved for a series of mistresses and courtesans, most notably the courtesan La Riccia and the noted singer and courtesan Barbara Salutati.[21] Referring to himself as an old man having reached his mid-forties—a vision of old age shared by his correspondents—Machiavelli saw that love for a courtesan *still* had the potential to be a mad passion that could threaten everything a mature man should hold most dear: family, wealth, status—and even, I would suggest, a patriarch's very sense of self.

An evocative reflection of this is found in letters that Old Nick exchanged with his friend Francesco Vettori in 1514. At the time Vettori was serving as Florentine ambassador to the pope, and Machiavelli, it appears, hoped that his friend might be able to help him gain favor with the Medici and a return to the active political life which he longed for after his fall from power in 1512. But Vettori, as was frequently the case in their letters, interrupted their discussions of political power to talk about the power of love, which fascinated them both equally. For Vettori had fallen suddenly in love with a young woman named Costanza, the daughter of an upperclass Roman widow, noted for her loose morals. Apparently this widow had not been averse to profiting from sharing her refined favors—not unlike a courtesan—and as her daughter came of age had selected Vettori as a potential lover to launch the young girl in a similar career. After describing the mad passion that had wrenched him out of his tranquil life as a diplomat in Rome, Vettori remarks "and because I have seen you [Niccolò] several times in love and saw how much you suffered, I have resisted as much as I could . . . [but] I don't know if I will be strong enough to hold out."[22]

This was not an idle concern or an empty reference to Machiavelli's loves, for in his correspondence and apparently in his conversations with his male friends, Machiavelli took care to present himself both as a master strategist of politics *and of love*, as well as a passionate lover—even occasionally mocking the way his passions overwhelmed him. Suggestively, however, that presentation of the sexual side of himself seems to have been so important to Machiavelli that at times he elevated it from the private realm of friendship to the more public arena of literature and theater, most notably perhaps in his later comedy *La Clizia*, which deals with a similar theme about the mad passion of an old man for a young woman. There the lead character, an old man who has lived a successful life of moderation and *virtù*, much like Vettori, has totally lost control of himself in an all-consuming passion for a young woman who is his ward, Clizia. What has especially attracted the attention of Machiavelli scholars to this comedy is the fact that the old lover in the plot seems to evoke Machiavelli himself and his love for the young singer and courtesan Barbara Salutati, with whom he was passionately involved when he wrote this comedy. Even the name of the main character suggests this association—Nicomaco. Clearly the ring of Nicco-lò Machiavelli is there, but there seems also to be a playful reference to the Greek meaning of the name Nicomaco, victor in battle; for (to get ahead of the story) Nicomaco is a man who loses in a humiliating way what he is seeking, young love, but wins ultimately by retaking control of himself and his life.[23]

As the play opens, Nicomaco has been reduced to utter foolishness by his mad passion for young Clizia. Not only does he upset his whole world for this love—alienating his wife and son and demonstrating a total lack of *virtù*—he seems literally bent on destroying himself and his family for it. Against all his wife Sofronia's sage counsels, and totally out of line with the wisdom expected of old age, Nicomaco tries to play the lion when he is no longer capable of doing so and even foolishly fails at being the fox, too blinded by love to see what is happening. But unfortunately for his mad desire, the rest of the characters in the play have not lost their senses, and in the dark of the bedchamber designated for the consummation of Nicomaco's passion and the plot, they have substituted for Clizia a robust male servant. Entering the bed with hope, Nicomaco tries to answer Natalie Davis's famous question for the early modern period, "Who's on Top," in the affirmative for old men, but quickly finds that the tables have been reversed at his expense. Beaten, and perhaps worse, by this servant, Nicomaco regains his senses and literally himself, albeit a bit the worse for wear. But up to that point the kind of mad love that a man, and especially an older man, could feel for a courtesan had caused Nicomaco literally to lose himself—perhaps the ultimate danger of courtesans and one that Machiavelli knew well from personal experience.[24]

In fact, in his earlier reply to Vettori's letter, Machiavelli picks up that very theme, but turns it on its head, putting such dangers in a surprisingly positive light: "because you are dismayed by my example, recalling what the arrows of Love have done to me, I must tell you how I have handled myself with Him [the God of Love]. In fact, I have let Him do as he pleases . . . and I have found that He has stroked me more than if I had [attempted to] destroy Him. . . . So say: 'Go ahead Love, guide me . . . I am your slave."[25] Although it might sound strange coming from the man who normally advocated an aggressive, Cesare Borgia-style approach to life, here Machiavelli counsels his friend Vettori to take the passive, submissive role with the masculine God of Love and literally give himself up to his passion and become Love's slave as he, Machiavelli, has done with his own courtesan loves. Fine love perhaps, but needless to say, many Renaissance men, when they considered this prospect in terms of the passions that they felt for a courtesan, were considerably less sanguine about letting themselves go. And, of course, Machiavelli a decade later in *La Clizia* would humorously turn the tables and play on those fears himself, perhaps having realized, as he moved into his fifties, that passivity in one's relationships with courtesans was as dangerous as passivity with that other feminine power that he lusted after—*Fortuna.* Whether Machiavelli had learned his lesson or not, his imaginative alter ego Nicomaco learned it the hard way; and as his name suggests, he gave up on such passions to become the victor in the battle for *virtù,* regaining his very self.

No wonder that literature and law, moralists and immoralists tried to reduce relationships with courtesans to mere economics. No wonder that many tried to label courtesans "common" whores, thus denying them a deeply feared power to act as social arbiters and select the best. No wonder their power over *virtù* was decried and denied. No wonder many feared that courtesans, rather than educating youths in sex, might well destroy them. But the deepest fear of all was the danger of losing self-control and perhaps even one's own self in the love of a courtesan. For that old dream of fine love, the noble passion that transcended self, became, when reversed, the mad passion for a dangerously beautiful, graceful, and refined courtesan—in a word, all that the courtesans' arts seemed to offer. "Devil or angel?" as the Bobby Vee lyric of the 1950s asked, was literally the question. In the imagination of the time the Renaissance courtesan was quite simply, over and over again, both. As a result the wise man was well and truly afraid of Giuliana Napolitana.

Notes

1. A scudo was a coin used widely in sixteenth-century Italy, of varying value depending on who coined it and the amount of gold or silver it contained. Usually, however, it was a considerable sum. For example, a Venetian gold scudo was worth slightly more than a ducat at the

time. In a fascinating article on the financial situation of a Venetian courtesan, Kathy Santore notes that according to the *Catalogo de tutte le principal et più honorate cortegiane di Venetia* of ca. 1565, the average price asked by a courtesan for her favors ranged from 1 to 30 scudi and that one-third of the women listed there charged more than 8 scudi; see Santore, "Julia Lombardo, 'Somtuosa Meretrice': A Portrait by Property," *Renaissance Quarterly* 41 (1988): 44–83, at 46. This might make Giuliana seem rather inexpensive, but this supposed catalogue of prices must be used with care as its status as an actual list of prices is problematic. More telling is the fact that one could rent a substantial house for 40–50 scudi a year, as Santore reports. Thus, Giuliana could have earned a year's rent with ten such evenings.

2. It seems clear, however, that the most powerful prostitutes, like our courtesan Giuliana herself, regularly avoided this requirement, presumably with the support of important patrons and protectors. In fact, these lists of registered prostitutes are probably quite inaccurate, because the lower level of workers in the profession also seem to have avoided registration. Moreover, as these lists were compiled in large part for collecting taxes many would have attempted to avoid being registered.

3. Florence, Archivio di Stato, Otto Suppliche, Register 2241, n. 412, March 17, 1563. For more on the Onestà see Michael Rocke, *Forbidden Friendships: Homosexuality and Male Culture in Renaissance Florence* (New York: Oxford University Press, 1996), 28–32; on the Otto where Dolfin eventually brought his complaint about his mistreatment before the Onestà see John K. Brackett, *Criminal Justice and Crime in Late Renaissance Florence, 1537–1609* (Cambridge: Cambridge University Press, 1992), 17–25.

4. In most larger Renaissance cities in the sixteenth century there was a wide range of prostitution that included part-timers at the bottom who drifted in and out of the profession moved by economic necessity; registered prostitutes who worked in large, usually public brothels; registered prostitutes who worked outside of brothels but usually for a procurer or procuress; more independent unregistered women, often with a protector who allowed them to avoid the costs and problems of being registered; and finally courtesans. What set the courtesan apart and on top of this hierarchy will be discussed further below. For a more complete discussion of these categories and their implications see Ruggiero, *Binding Passions: Tales of Magic, Marriage, and Power at the End of the Renaissance* (Oxford: Oxford University Press, 1993), 24–56 and especially 33–37.

5. Matteo Bandello, *Le quattro parti de le novelle del Bandello*, ed. Gustavo Balsamo-Crivelli (Turin: UTET, 1924), pt. 3, novella XLII.

6. Ibid.

7. At the most straightforward level *virtù* was that set of behaviors that made one person better than another in the Renaissance. This crucial concept will be discussed more fully below.

8. There is a famous portrait by Giorgione in the Accademia di Belle Arti in Venice that is quite out of step with most Renaissance depictions of women there. The picture represents a broken-down old woman who looks the viewer boldly in the eye. Her portrait is accompanied by the motto "col tempo," "with time." Most easily seen as a commentary on aging and especially the aging that will take away the beauty of once beautiful women, one wonders if this is not also a commentary on the fate of courtesans. With time the Imperias and Giulianas would become broken old women while, tellingly, the rich noble males who saw this portrait would know that they would remain rich and powerful, if anything becoming more rich and powerful as they left their youthful days behind and took up the mantle of family patriarchs. "Col tempo," dangerous courtesans would be put in their place.

9. See Ruggiero, *Binding Passions*, 24–56, 88–129, as well as idem, "Marriage, Love, Sex, and Renaissance Civic Morality," in *Sexuality and Gender in Early Modern Europe*, ed. James Grantham Turner (Cambridge: Cambridge University Press, 1993), 10–30. Several of the

examples used in this essay are also discussed in those works, but there more with an eye to illuminating the life of prostitutes at the time.

10. The concept of the marital debt was central to the medieval and early modern Catholic vision of marriage. Essentially it required that spouses give the use of their body to their partners when asked. The key here was that rather than being willing to have sexual intercourse, the person who rendered the marital debt would be free of sin because they gave their partner the use of their body out of a sense of duty and not for their own sexual pleasure.

11. Bandello, *Novelle*, pt. III, novella XXXI.

12. Ruggiero, *Binding Passions*, 24–56 and esp. 32–33.

13. Quoted in Giovanni Scarabello, "Le 'signore' della repubblica," in *Il gioco dell'amore: Le cortigiane di Venezia dal Trecento al Settecento* (Milan: Berenice, 1990), 11–35, at pp. 25–26.

14. Bandello, *Novelle*, pt. III, novella XXXI.

15. In fact, governments were concerned enough about the practice to pass laws against it and attempt to limit it by prosecuting those who took advantage of the situation. For a rich and thoughtful analysis of this problem see Baccio Rustichelli's late sixteenth-century report to the Florentine government on this problem in *Miscellanea Medici*, busta 29, inserto 22, fols. 2^v–7^v. For Venice and regulations related to such scams, and the consequent riches that courtesans were able to flaunt, see Scarabello, "Le 'signore' della repubblica," 18–21. Youthful schemes to secure funds for sexual escapades were also a popular topos in Renaissance comedies. One of the most humorous examples of this, although it does not involve a courtesan, can be found in Ludovico Ariosto's *La Lena*. In that comedy the perennially under-funded young gentleman, Flavio, needs money to pay Lena in order to gain access to the woman he loves. His servant Corbolo works out a complex scam to trick the young man's father into unknowingly financing the escapade. In the end, thanks to Corbolo's quick thinking and an unexpected turn of good fortune, Flavio wins his love and eventually marries happily as well—the traditional happy ending required by the genre. Off the stage presumably things often did not work out so well.

16. Of course it should not be forgotten that prostitutes in the Renaissance were much more likely to be the victims of economic exploitation. One fact, however, that normally made the courtesan different from poorer and more exposed "common" prostitutes was the fact that she usually had a powerful protector or a group of powerful protectors whose favor kept her relatively safe from such depredations. Still, if those protectors withdrew their support, even the courtesan could become a victim, as the tale of the infamous *trentuno* discussed by Quaintance in this volume suggests (see chap. 10).

17. Just how far beyond court life this might extend is suggested by the famous encounter between the future king of France Henry III and the perhaps most famous courtesan of the age, Veronica Franco. While visiting Venice Henry went out of his way to meet with the noted poet and beauty and the event was celebrated by all—not just Franco, but also Venice and the future king. For Franco see Margaret F. Rosenthal, *The Honest Courtesan: Veronica Franco, Citizen and Writer in Sixteenth-Century Venice* (Chicago: University of Chicago Press, 1992), and for the meeting with Henry pp. 102–11.

18. For a further discussion of this see my "Mean Streets, Familiar Streets; or The Fat Woodcarver and the Masculine Spaces of Renaissance Florence," in *Florence: Revisioning the Renaissance City*, ed. Roger Crum and John Paoletti (Cambridge: Cambridge University Press, forthcoming).

19. The discussion that follows echoes the analysis first suggested in my book *Boundaries of Eros: Sex Crime and Sexuality in Renaissance Venice* (New York: Oxford University Press, 1985), 159–61; for a discussion that ties the analysis to Renaissance comedies see the introduction to *Five Comedies from the Italian Renaissance*, trans. and ed. Laura Giannetti

and Guido Ruggiero (Baltimore: Johns Hopkins University Press, 2002), xxxiii–xl and the comedies themselves.

20. Bandello, *Novelle*, pt. III, novella XXXV.

21. See the thoughtful discussion of this aspect of Machiavelli's correspondence with Vettori in John Najemy, *Between Friends: Discourses of Power and Desire in the Machiavelli–Vettori Letters of 1513–1515* (Princeton: Princeton University Press, 1993), esp. 263–68 and 288–94. On Salutati's musical connection to Machiavelli see Davies in this volume (chap. 7).

22. Machiavelli, *Opere*, 3 vols., ed. Corrado Vivanti (Turin: Einaudi, 1999), 2:308; letter of January 18, 1514. My reading here has been much influenced by Najemy's in *Between Friends*, 258–71.

23. This Greek reading of the name Nicomaco has been often suggested, but I am particularly influenced here by Ronald L. Martinez's important article, "Benefit of Absence: Machiavellian Valediction in *Clizia*," in *Machiavelli and the Discourse of Literature*, ed. Albert Russell Ascoli and Victoria Kahn (Ithaca: Cornell University Press, 1993), 117–44, at p. 132. Although our readings might be seen as almost diametrically opposed—he sees the play as virtually a tragedy because of its unhappy ending (featuring Nicomaco's beating and failure to have Clizia) and I read it as a comedy with Nicomaco's winning out in the regime of *virtù* because he does not get Clizia—his reading is compelling. In fact, the play could be read both ways today, and perhaps could have in the Renaissance as well. The key to the difference between our readings turns on the understanding of *virtù*. For Martinez it is a concept that has endured in Mediterranean culture from antiquity through the Renaissance (see p. 136) whereas, as noted above, I see it as a term that evolved and changed in the Renaissance. As a result, Martinez sees Nicomaco's inability to have Clizia as a failure of his sense of his own *virtù* (where *virtù* is the timeless concept of male power and dominance), while I see Nicomaco's failure to have what he wants as less important than his rediscovering and returning to *virtù* (i.e., the moderation and control of self and emotions combined with an active approach to life that drives Machiavelli's vision of political action and correctly ordered society).

24. Zeitlin notes in this volume (chap. 2) that men in seventeenth-century China who formed around the emperor were often portrayed as neglecting other crucial aspects of their lives while under the spell of a courtesan. This raises the issue of whether or not fear of a loss of self is a more general phenomenon. Certainly the fear of a loss of self-control is often associated with the passions of sexual desire, but I would argue that the sense of self is a more culturally specific phenomenon and thus the fear of losing oneself in sex in general or for a courtesan will turn on more culturally specific keys. In Machiavelli's play the self that is lost turns on the loss of *virtù*, status, wealth, and patriarchal control—all crucial to a specifically Renaissance vision of self.

25. Machiavelli, *Opere*, 2:310; letter of February 4, 1514.

PART VI

COURTESANS IN THE POSTCOLONY

The Twentieth-Century "Disappearance" of the Gisaeng during the Rise of Korea's Modern Sex-and-Entertainment Industry

The history of the vanished Korean female professional entertainer known as gisaeng is riddled with ambiguities. These arise from the inherent social-structural ambiguity of Korean (and many other) traditional female entertainers who have operated outside of established morality but in a way that often reinforces the conventions they seem to subvert. The ideological contexts in which gisaeng are remembered are no less ambiguous: as symbols of national culture, as pre-modern symbols of the oppression of women, and as early examples of emancipated females. Some scholars understand the gisaeng to have been a kind of sex worker or a prostitute,[1] while many others insist that the gisaeng were entertainers, forbidden from selling their bodies, who only became involved in sex work under Japanese colonialism (1905–45).[2]

This essay cannot begin to resolve these contradictions and ambiguities, but rather outlines the historical conditions for their emergence by looking at the social transformation of gisaeng institutions and the concept of the gisaeng over the course of the twentieth century. The essay is based on bibliographic resources and on my six months of fieldwork in 1997 on the twentieth-century history of one group of female performers with ties to the gisaeng legacy.[3] It follows up on the conversation begun by ethnomusicologist of Korea Byong Won Lee in his 1979 essay on the modern history of the gisaeng, and draws on recent groundbreaking scholarship by a specialist in women's music, Kwon Do-Hee.[4] My own contribution is to show the role of South Korea's modern sex-and-entertainment industry in the gisaeng's transformation, while providing some preliminary remarks on the important gap between the history of the gisaeng themselves and the history of the concept of gisaeng.

The rapidly changing backdrop of twentieth-century Korea—which witnessed its colonization by Japan, the division into North and South, more than forty years of South Korean military rule, and the rapid industrialization of the country under the neo-colonial steering of the United States—saw the court entertainers called gisaeng pressured into a modern colonial and postcolonial sex-and-entertainment industry even as they attempted to resist absorption by it. After the *idea* of the gisaeng was assimilated into the sex industry by the era of the 1970s, efforts began to retrieve and memorialize the historical gisaeng as a lost national cultural treasure. Some of the women at work in the world of the gisaeng were absorbed by the high-class tiers of the sex-and-entertainment industry. Others struggled on their own as laborers, and still others, with difficulty, remained performers by starting private organizations or joining national arts institutions, especially during the South Korean traditional music revival, which began in the 1960s. This essay is only a starting point in an examination of this story. It ends by proposing that the lurking question of "what happened to the traditional female entertainer" elsewhere in the world might best be answered by looking to the development of modern sex industries and to concurrent canonizations of national tradition.

FEMALE ENTERTAINERS IN ANTIQUITY AND EARLY MODERN KOREA

Paintings and written documents suggest that professional female entertainers have existed in Korea since the Three Kingdoms Period (57 B.C.–A.D. 668). In the Goryeo Dynasty (A.D. 918–1392), female entertainers danced and sang in the court and at countrywide festivals. Some gisaeng were conscripted or sold from poor families, but most were drawn from the hereditary *cheonmin* outcaste class. Many inherited their roles from their gisaeng mothers, and most were state slaves.[5] Under Goryeo, gisaeng were often selected as kings' concubines and given noble rank. But due to the neo-Confucian prescriptions of the Joseon Dynasty (1392–1910), the gisaeng lost much of this class mobility and were demoted in status. Records of illicit intercourse involving the gisaeng were kept in the Joseon court[6] and the gisaeng seem to have engaged in sex work primarily by becoming concubines or mistresses. The line between entertainment and sexual labor was ambiguous, however, so the gisaeng institution contradicted neo-Confucian codes that disapproved of the sensuous female entertainer. Certain kings attempted to abolish the system but ultimately failed, lacking sufficient central authority; some of the most doctrinaire neo-Confucian leaders embraced the gisaeng system wholeheartedly.[7]

In extreme phases, Neo-Confucian doctrine mandated the separation of the sexes in the court. This created a need for skilled female professional entertainers and other professional women. Women were needed to serve as nurses to female members of the court, who could not be touched by male doctors. The court mediated this problem by allowing blind male musicians to perform for women, but went through phases where even this was not allowed, thus requiring female instrumentalists. Throughout the Joseon Dynasty gisaeng cultivated their talents in music, dance, calligraphy, poetry, nursing, and textile crafts. There were also classes of professional female entertainers who entertained commoners, the itinerant traveling groups called *sadangpae*, many of whom engaged in prostitution.

In the late nineteenth century—the twilight of the Joseon Dynasty, which ruled from 1392 until 1910, professional female entertainers performed for the ruling class, the small class of *jungin* ("middle people") bureaucrats, and commoners. Kwon Do Hee describes female performers of this time as divided into three classes: entertainers attached to the court (gisaeng, *yegi, ginyeo,* or *gwangi*), private female entertainers (*sampae*) who performed for the aristocratic and middle classes, and itinerant group performers (*sadangpae*) who performed for commoners.[8] The Hanyang (Seoul) court and other regional government centers trained gisaeng in government schools called *gyobang* or *gyobangcheong;* and some gisaeng operated privately outside the confines of state circles. The *sampae* were entertainers and hostesses who sang *japga* (literally "miscellaneous songs," narrative songs mostly sung seated) and *sijo* (aristocratic song poems) to entertain their customers, and unofficially practiced prostitution.[9] The troupes of itinerant female singers called *sadangpae* that toured the country specialized in folk songs and standing dance songs (*ipchang*) and traded sex for money or goods.[10]

Korea emerged from several hundred years of isolation and entered a new era of rapid societal change and economic development as Japan forced Joseon to sign the unequal Treaty of Ganghwa in 1876. The traditional middle classes (*jungin* and regional bureaucrats) and the growing merchant class gained power. And as the clientele of the private *sampae* entertainers prospered, so did the institution of the *private* high-class female entertainer. At the same time, as the court was gradually weakened by foreign imperial encroachment, the numbers of court gisaeng dwindled.

With private entertainers having gained power, scholars and the public in the early twentieth century began to consider both court and private high-class entertainers to be gisaeng.[11] This was reflected in the terminology *ilpae, ipae, sampae gisaeng* (first-, second-, and third-rank gisaeng), first spelled out in print by Yi Neunghwa in his *Joseon hae'eohwasa* [A history of the flowers that understand speech][12] of 1927.[13] According to Yi, below the court gisaeng was a second rank (called *eun'geunja* or *eun'gunja*) consisting of women who performed elite repertoires and "secretly practiced prostitution," or who had become concubines (*cheob*). Members of the third grade of women (*sampae*) were called *changnyeo* (prostitutes); they were engaged primarily in prostitution and singing folk songs to entertain their customers in drinking houses. Many scholars have adopted this vision of the third rank (*sampae*) of gisaeng,[14] which sounds at odds with Kwon Do-Hee's description of the third-rank *sampae* as private entertainers of the middle and upper classes. This is because this categorization, and the ranking system, written in 1927, are interpretations of the turn-of-the-century gisaeng world from the standpoint of neo-Confucian morality in the era of its colonial modernization. The proponents of that morality, rich in all its contradictions, tried earnestly to insulate the highest ranks of gisaeng from the flourishing colonial sex industry. The schema that labels the *sampae gisaeng* as a "prostitute who entertains her clients with folk songs" is based on a long-standing view of Korean traditional music as split into folk and art traditions, an ill-suited bifurcation that generally forces middle-class genres of music such as *jwachang* (ballads sung in a seated position and epic songs) down into the folk music category, and categorizes female entertainers as either artists or prostitutes, virtuous or sinful women. But the taxonomy is nonetheless an attempt to understand the impact of the burgeoning private-sector entertainment industry on the turn-of-the century gisaeng.

FEMALE ENTERTAINERS IN THE COLONIAL
ENTERTAINMENT INDUSTRY

The Japanese colonial government (1910–45) disbanded the government offices that supported the official gisaeng. After 1918 female government entertainers went into private gisaeng guild-run schools that were called *gwonbeon* (from the Japanese term *gyoban*),[15] which were overseen by the colonial government. There formerly state-employed female entertainers mixed with the private *sampae*, and the distinction between state and private gisaeng disappeared. The private schools dispatched entertainers to drinking houses, restaurants, banquets, radio stations, recording companies, and theaters, so that female professional entertainers were involved in the development of two connected entertainment arenas: a public scene of mass media and theater performances and a private room culture geared toward entertaining colonial elites, which was centered in private homes, upscale restaurants, and drinking houses.[16] The gisaeng were a major force in the growing colonial public culture, as some of the first recorded performers in Korea (beginning in the early 1900s), as well as regular performers on state radio, which began in 1927 (see fig. 16.1), and in famous stage venues such as the first modern theater, Seoul's Won'gaksa, where they began giving concerts of court songs and dance in the first decade of the new century.[17] In these various ways the gisaeng became some of the most powerful figures for disseminating the musical forms of the emergent public culture.

The face of this new public culture was also deeply affected by rural gisaeng traveling to Seoul via the new colonial railway system. The repertories of southwestern gisaeng gained popularity in the public arena as the popularity of Central/Western regional styles waned, lingering on in private performance contexts where, as local genres, they relied on local patronage. The new mobility brought about by the transportation system and migration into the cities brought many commoner girls into the gisaeng schools, changing the traditional hereditary nature of gisaeng institutions.

As the court and aristocracy lost power, gisaeng performed more for colonial bureaucrats and Japanese and Korean merchants, and so they broadened their store of repertories. The curriculum of the private schools featured Japanese language, geisha instruments including koto (Japanese zither) and shamisen, and popular genres of Korean traditional music, those liked by bureaucrats and regional elites. Whereas before the only repertories that the gisaeng and the *sampae* shared were aristocratic genres such as song-poems (*sijo*), the private schools assimilated *sampae* (third-rank) repertories, including elite and traditional middle-class "miscellaneous song" (*japga*) genres.[18] Colonial urbanization and the development of mass transit gave rise to an influx of northwestern and southwestern female entertainers to Seoul after 1910, and as they went into private schools and as the pop-cultural popularity of their genres spread beyond regional boundaries, regional genres were also added to the curriculum. The gisaeng began to learn regional "miscellaneous song" genres and "folk art" genres such as *pansori* (epic song improvisation) and *sanjo* (solo instrumental improvisation) that were formerly performed mainly by *gwangdae* (itinerant professional male entertainers). Some gisaeng even learned the standing dance songs of the itinerant *sadangpae*, as the old social institutions supporting these genres also collapsed and as the popularity of these genres grew in the new urban public culture.

Broadcasting from Korean Division of Keijo Radio Station

FIGURE 16.1.   Staged photo of two gisaeng dancing and playing janggo
(hourglass drum) at state-operated Keijo (Seoul) Radio (1935/6).

The private gisaeng guild/school became, for a time, one of the central institutions promoting, developing, and preserving Korean traditional music, with a staff of male instructors and some retired gisaeng.

The pressure of the booming colonial sex-and-entertainment industry on the institution of the gisaeng was to be the central factor in its decline. Like all state-managed and elite social scenes in the colonial era, the gisaeng industry would provide a healthy source of collaborators, especially those, like the *sampae*, who had less allegiance to the Korean king than the former state-slave gisaeng. Also, while this industry was upper class, it was connected by bureaucracy to the system of licensed industrial prostitution introduced by the Japanese.[19] Gisaeng were registered and monitored by the colonial government much as prostitutes were, more and more high-ranking gisaeng were forced into sex work, and, according to Pak Jeongae, the principle of "sell one's talent, not one's body" gradually fell away.[20] In the Asia-Pacific War some gisaeng were even fed into the military sex industry, sent to the fronts to entertain Japanese officers and enlisted men, and many seem to have been forced into the military sexual slavery of the so-called "comfort women" system.[21]

As the institutions of the gisaeng collapsed into a popular colonial entertainment industry, the percentage of time that female professional entertainers devoted to the traditional arts steadily declined, and as it did, gisaeng traditions suffered. The industry increasingly demanded modern popular repertories, and the emerging strata of star female performers of popular music was composed in large part of gisaeng or former gisaeng. The gisaeng school, focused as it was on producing young women for men's entertainment, was not designed as an atmosphere in which women could mature as artists. In order to dedicate themselves solely to performance, some women joined the state-sponsored Joseon Eumak Hyeop'hoe (Joseon Music League), which focused on court music, or the Yeongeuk Munwha Hyeop'hoe (Theater Culture League), which focused on folk and popular forms, especially those of the southwest. Doing so, these women gained a measure of independence from the gisaeng schools, hard-wired as they were to the entertainment complex.[22] This was the first of many moves of the gisaeng to distance themselves from the institutions of the colonial gisaeng and the growing sex-and entertainment industry.

THE FEMALE PROFESSIONAL ENTERTAINER AND THE POSTCOLONIAL FLOURISHING OF THE SEX-AND-ENTERTAINMENT INDUSTRY

In 1945 the United States military divided the Korean peninsula in half, giving half of the spoils of war to the Russians, who had swept over to fight the Japanese in northern Asia toward the end of the Asia-Pacific war. The American military government in South Korea officially outlawed prostitution in 1946,[23] and abolished the gisaeng's private schools and special entertainment zones in 1947.[24] But the occupying government inherited the sex-and-entertainment industry that had flourished in the colonial period and participated in it, only with less state supervision. The U.S. army moved into former Japanese military bases in close proximity to the famous prostitution districts. And as radical militarization of the peninsula went forward in anticipation of the Korean War (1950–53) and its aftermath, new sex-driven "camp towns" sprang up around bases. The war, which completely demolished many parts of the country, including Seoul, and which killed more than three million Koreans, drove countless widows, orphans, and destitute girls and women into the sex industry. In 1953, the year of the cease-fire, a government report gave the number of "prostitutes," which we can assume to include all female entertainers, at about 350,000; surveys indicate that in the 1950s and 1960s about 60 percent of all sex workers worked in the vicinity of American military bases. In 1962, the Korean government designated "special zones" as entertainment quarters, effectively legalizing prostitution near American and Korean military bases and other districts in Seoul.[25]

    The number of sex workers surrounding the American military dropped dramatically with the decrease of the American military presence, but the "camp towns" around American military bases north of Seoul and elsewhere are active to this day. Nowadays many women working in the industry are foreigners, mainly from the Philippines and the countries of the former Soviet Union, trafficked into South Korea typically with promises of factory or domestic work or simply abducted and sold into the sex industry. And although the general poverty of Korean society made the development of a large sex industry for Korean males an impossibility until the 1970s and especially the 1980s, prostitution was to become a general feature of South Korean military culture, and eventually a general feature of South Korean society.

In elite circles, the room culture industry of private restaurants and resorts continued to entertain the new international military, business, and political elite much as it had in the colonial period. Elite "gisaeng restaurants" (*gisaengjib* or *yojeong*) sprang up all over Seoul. Some of the most famous were the government favorite Samcheonggak, nestled in the hills in Seoul's northern Samcheong District, where the famous North–South Korean Red Cross talks were held in 1972, and which hosted at least one American president, and the nearby Daewongak, managed by the *gwonbeon*-trained and very famous gisaeng Kim Jaya.

At houses like these, former gisaeng seem to have worked mostly in a managerial capacity. The young women who danced, sang, and performed for and with patrons are today generally regarded not to have been "real" gisaeng owing to the limited extent of their artistic training, although many of their proprietress/teachers were trained in the gisaeng schools during the colonial period. The girls and women working in the gisaeng houses were generally drawn from the massive numbers of poor young women who came to urban areas seeking employment during South Korea's rapid authoritarian state-capitalist industrialization, as were the majority of women working in the sex industry in general.

As the new international elite consisted of Japanese businessmen, American and Korean businessmen, politicians, and military personnel, the repertory now included Japanese, American, and Korean popular songs, as well as Korean folk and other traditional pieces. Performances were of three kinds: staged shows for guests, rounds in which women and guests would take turns singing, and couples dancing. In 1966, Jerry Jackis, formerly of the U.S. State Department, published an account of his experience in one of these "gisaeng houses," deep in the mountains north of Seoul, most likely one of those discussed above:

> Up and up we climb through the trees and the great boulders, until we finally reach our very own *kisaeng*[26] house, or "jib." Awaiting us are four *kisaeng* girls, standing in the small wooden floored entry room, called the "maru." They are dressed in hand embroidered, varied colored, traditional Korean style costumes, the long skirt called "chima," and the blouse, "chogori." Their very low bows, reserved for special guests, including foreigners, symbolize their high regard for us. With smiles and gestures of welcome, they greet us in Korean. . . .
>
> At the steps of the maru, we are helped by the girls to remove our shoes and we are led into a medium size room where there are no chairs, no tables, only a number of hand embroidered red cushions to sit on . . . So there we are, four men and each of us with his own gisaeng girl beside him, sitting on the floor in a circle smiling politely at each other. Soon our cigarettes are lighted and we start asking the inevitable questions to break through the cultural barrier . . .
>
> The table . . . includes five bottles of the finest Scotch whisky, which are immediately opened and highballs with ice are served. It is the job of the ever-pleasant *kisaeng* girl to keep our glasses full and to help us eat with silver chopsticks.
>
> Actually, all I do is sit and just open my mouth to receive food and drink what my *kisaeng* girl feeds me. . . .
>
> Our inhibitions and worldly cares melt away and we all start singing at the top of our voices. Try to imagine us singing the popular song "Never on Sunday," and an American of Greek extraction in our group doing a Greek folk dance, much to the delight of all present.

After this, three Korean girls appear to entertain us by doing a Korean folk dance. They dance to the music of a "kayagum," a flute and a Korean drum called "changgo."[27] The drum is beaten by an elderly woman, or "ajumoni," who hits the drum with a stick held in her left hand and with the palm of her right hand.

After the departure of the dancers, large drums mounted on stands are set up, two facing each other and one in the background facing us. Soon the drum girl appears and with two sticks in her hands begins beating the drums, first slowly and then faster and faster. She beats the drums while dancing, keeping in step with the music and occasionally hitting the rim of the drum making a clicking sound in contrast to the booming of the drums.[28]

Then the floor is cleared and three musicians step up and immediately the saxophonist plays, as most of us expected, Korea's "second national anthem," "Danny Boy."

At this musical signal, the *kisaeng* girls get up and induce us all to dance. After a while, we could not be induced to stop dancing. The *kisaeng* girls are marvelous dancers, who can fox trot, waltz, two step, and even twist.

Sheer exhaustion convinces us that even good things must come to an end. So while all of us, Koreans and Americans alike, holding hands, stand up and sing "Arirang," we end another wonderful evening. I hope Korea's unique *kisaeng* parties will never disappear.[29]

Despite the contemporary tendency to consider all of the women working in gisaeng houses in the 1960s and onwards as "mere" call girls or prostitutes as opposed to performing women, music and dance were a central feature of the so-called "gisaeng party" (a term in use since mid-century) at that time. There were hierarchies of different types of women, variously skilled in conversation and songs in multiple languages, couples dancing, traditional dance, or instruments, even to the extent of performing the elegant *seungmu*, a Buddhist monk's drum dance that gisaeng had been performing since the colonial period.

In the 1960s, as the Japanese economy strengthened, a Korean sex tourism industry targeted specifically at Japanese tourists developed, attracting hundreds of thousands of primarily lower- and middle-class Japanese men to Korea each year. 1,825 Japanese visited Korea in 1962, but by 1978 that number had increased to 667,319, and Japanese statistics showed that in 1976 98 percent of male visitors to Japan were unaccompanied by women.[30] Women, once again poor rural migrants, were drawn or driven into the industry, and the government and civil society encouraged them to dedicate themselves to sex-and-entertainment labor for the good of the nation. The government took to listing the numbers of large "gisaeng houses" in their tourist literature distributed in Japan. Men bought sex-tour packages in Japan at travel agencies.

The sex-tour industry took its model from the gisaeng party like the one that Jerry Jackis recounts above. The industry was dubbed "gisaeng tourism" and thereby the idea of the contemporary gisaeng was married to the figure of the industrial sex worker.[31] On a typical tour, men would travel in a group to a large gisaeng house, where they were attended by individually assigned gisaeng. During the meal a few women with artistic training would perform short staged music and dance numbers. The evening would then be given over to rounds of singing and dancing, before shuttles would take the couples to hotel rooms, all part of the package. In 1973 the government registry listed around 40,000 of these entertainers/sex workers.[32]

As the South Korean economy boomed in the 1980s and the Japanese yen lost value against the South Korean won, "gisaeng tourism" began to fade, or rather to be exported elsewhere. Sex tourists, now including many Korean men, took their money to Thailand, the Philippines, and other parts of southeast Asia. Sex tourism, as the industrial production of sex, made the same long-range migration from Japan, to Korea, and then to southeast Asia that other industries made. The sex-tourism industry also faded from view because it was under fire from civic groups, whose growing outrage coincided with the emergence of a comfortable middle class. As the sex-tourism industry faded it relocated to Jeju Island, far from Seoul and the centers of public morality and surveillance, and use of the term gisaeng in the sex-and-entertainment industry basically disappeared.

Despite the decline in the international trade in South Korean women's sex-and-entertainment services starting in the late 1970s, the South Korean sex-and-entertainment industry flourished from that time onward and diversified largely with South Korean capital and in the interests of South Korean men, paralleling the "miraculous" growth of the economy, the growing numbers of South Korean men with disposable income, and the growth of the middle class. By the 1990s, men could easily find sexual services and female company (either employees or call girls) in high-class room salons, cabarets, nightclubs, bars, karaoke rooms, beer halls, coffee and tea houses, video booths, motels and hotels, tourist restaurants, saunas and bathhouses, barbershops, massage parlors, and phone rooms (where men phone posted numbers of girls and women).[33] The special prostitution districts such as Seoul's Miari and Cheongnyangri, where women wait behind glass windows on display, have expanded rapidly as well. In early twenty-first-century South Korea, female entertainment and prostitution are ubiquitous, stratified, and accessible to all classes.

The colonial sex-and-entertainment industry and the gisaeng tourism industry rented Korean women dressed in traditional or neo-traditional clothes, and with other cosmetic trappings of tradition, to an international clientele. But the industry that caters to South Koreans trades more on contemporary ideas of South Korean and foreign femininity. There is still a handful of places that claim to be *yojeong*, where the women who pour drinks, sing songs, and provide witty conversation wear Korean traditional clothes instead of Western-style dresses, and sometimes give limited performances of Korean traditional music. One or two of these places have been in operation since the colonial period, and their function remains much the same: catering to an international clientele of men with money and power.[34] Some of them advertise on-line, proclaiming the elegance, beauty, and obedience of their *agashi-tim* (teams of young women), and some sites are available in English and Japanese.[35] But many of the old *yojeong* ("gisaeng" houses), like Samcheonggak and Daewongak, closed down due to financial difficulties in the late 1990s.

As Cheng has noted, men who visit prostitutes or patronize the entertainment industry in South Korea are involved in a complex ritual of collective transgression of public decorum, a ritual of social bonding. For many men, for whom military service is universal and compulsory, this training starts in the military, when senior soldiers take them to prostitutes. So at the same time as they learn to kill, men are trained into smooth participation in the sex-and-entertainment industry, as a rite of initiation and collective social transgression in a time of danger.

In the high-class entertainment world this rite of manhood is part of the emotional core of business dealing. Most high-rollers who have been to South Korea on business have been taken into the female sex-and-entertainment industry in Seoul, as business culture depends on room culture to make public relationships intimate, making a business deal a matter of a temporary, quasi-familial relation, even for businesswomen, as *U.S. News and World Report* relates:

> when the 30-something blond saleswoman from AT&T turned up in Seoul, her hosts didn't want her to feel slighted. They couldn't help the fact, however, that gisaeng boys were impossible to come by. Would their guest mind a girl? "Absolutely not," she assured them. The rest of the evening, Carleton "Carly" Fiorina got the full gisaeng treatment: food, alcohol, and copious flattery. The hostess "just changed some of the adjectives," Fiorina recalled in an interview.[36]

Not only corporate but also political and military deal-making takes place with the aid of the entertainment industry: "Two flamboyant former nightclub owners that Northrop hired as consultants to represent it in South Korea spent $90,000 a month in the mid-1980s entertaining South Korean government officials at saloons, hostess bars and Korean-style geisha houses in an effort to sell the firm's F-20 jet fighter."[37]

THE SOUTH KOREAN TRADITIONAL CULTURAL REVIVAL AND THE EMERGENCE OF THE NEW FEMALE PROFESSIONAL ENTERTAINER

As the sex-and-entertainment industry developed throughout the immediate post-World War II period, the highly trained professional female musicians or dancers formerly known as gisaeng were either pressed into this industry, struggled on at the margins of society, or banded together in unions for the promotion of their art forms. The burgeoning of private performing groups to support the traditional arts following liberation from colonial rule in 1945 was squashed with the outbreak of the Korean War in 1950. The female performers who led the revival of *seodosori*, a collection of north-western Korean professional folk songs gathered together in the gisaeng schools in the early twentieth century, had all been trained in the Pyeongyang Gisaeng Gwonbeon (Pyeongyang gisaeng school) during the colonial period, and several had worked as gisaeng. (*Seodosori*'s signature song, *Sushimga*, can be heard on the companion website accompanying this volume, track 13.) But in the destroyed economy of the post Korean War era, performances were rare and recording was shut down. The new South Korea was an authoritarian society that encouraged citizens to forsake long-standing ways of doing things in the interests of high-speed industrial capitalist development. There was no infrastructure for, or interest in, learning traditional art, so surviving gisaeng were unable to live from teaching. They worked as maids, ran shops in public markets, and performed other odd jobs, until a tiny apparatus of state support grew in the 1960s.[38]

A very small number of court artists, mostly men, enjoyed a small means of support even through the war, with the South Korean founding of the *Gugnip gugagwon* (literally the "National Center for National Music," but now translated as the "National Center for Korean Traditional Performing Arts") in 1951. Early in its post-war history, the National Center began to admit women.

Beginning in the 1960s, the South Korean military government, with the firm support of dictator Park Chung Hee, began to take an interest in canonizing national culture in the face of the massive social revolution brought on by South Korea's state-driven race to economic prosperity, and as a source of legitimacy vis-à-vis the North, which has attempted to modernize and revolutionize Korean traditional arts by developing traditional instruments, music, and dance according to principles deemed "scientific" or "rational," or just in imitation of the West. In 1962, the South Korean Government promulgated the Cultural Property Protection Law, in order to safeguard against the disappearance of historical objects and late Joseon Dynastic cultural forms. The National Center created a branch for folk music and dance in the late 1960s, and these two institutions, together with the National Center-affiliated National Music High School, became the core of the canonization effort. As of 1996, the government had authorized ninety-seven categories of "intangible cultural assets," referring to artistic abilities, and 173 people were designated as "Human Cultural Assets," the official bearers of these traditions. Master singer O Bongnyeo, whose student, Kim Gwangsuk, sings *Sushimga* on the companion website, track 13, was one such person, who studied with prominent gisaeng in Pyngyang (see fig. 16.2). The Human Cultural Assets are musicians, dancers, theatrical performers, artists, and ritual

FIGURE 16.2. O Bongnyeo, Human Cultural Asset for the northwest lyric song tradition (*seodosori*), in concert with her students, 1997. Left to right: Yi Jinyeo, Yu Jisuk, O Bongnyeo, and Shin Jeongae.

specialists, among others. Each chooses a successor to her or his title, who eventually ascends to the master's position after the master's death. Although the stipend given to master artists and their apprentices is small, appointment as a Human Cultural Asset establishes an artist as the preeminent master of her or his art form and allows him or her to charge high rates for lessons.

The gisaeng played a prominent role in the institutionalization of Korean traditional art forms in South Korea. Many of the women who gained status as Human Cultural Assets were former gisaeng or had been trained in colonial-era gisaeng schools, but they were given the title of "researcher" or "performer"; and the same was true for the women at work in the National Center—indeed, many women who were appointed as Cultural Assets were given a seat at the National Center as well. The gisaeng were also quite active in forming private organizations to promote the traditional arts, forming numerous *hagwon* (studios) and even such large organizations as the *Gugak yesul* (National Music and Art) High School, founded around 1964 and still functioning today.[39] These women carried colonial gisaeng lineages back into national institutions again, and, freed from the economic pressures of the marketplace and the threat of sexual labor, the women were now subjected to the new pressures of national culturalism. For one, this meant unspoken injunctions to be discreet about the gisaeng and the colonial past, the sexual frankness of folk music, and so on. But also, a performer had to struggle to prove the value of her art form and her virtuosity as an artist; in folk and middle-class musical genres, performers added complex ornamentation to their songs or instrumental music and borrowed aristocratic musical elements (for example, tempo and ornamentation) to increase the prestige of their musical forms.

However much the institutions heading the canonization of national culture and the performers themselves sought to resurrect traditions of the late Joseon Dynasty free of the taint of Japanese colonialism, modernity, or the aura of change, the colonial gisaeng legacy continues to exert a profound influence on that national canon. The post-Korean War institutionalization of traditional music concretized many elements of performance practice that were basically new to the twentieth century and that were put in place by gisaeng in the era of their colonial privatization and their participation in the new public cultures (through theater and radio) and room cultures. The gisaeng and their female students continue, in new national institutional contexts, to perform *pansori* (solo operatic storytelling) and other genres that were formerly performed almost exclusively by men; and in the National Center, the category of "folk song" is entirely dominated by women, and really refers not to songs of "the folk" or the peasantry, but rather to the professionalized folk songs and middle-class vocal pieces that the gisaeng performed at the turn of the century and through the colonial period.

The place of the gisaeng in the official national-cultural story is strategically vague. The effort to preserve the cultural forms of the gisaeng has not been an effort to canonize the gisaeng legacy as a chapter in the history of Korean traditional arts, despite its centrality to traditional art practice. Several developments were byproducts of the social juncture and conceptual conflation of the gisaeng with sex workers: the gisaeng label disappeared from the public discourse on traditional arts, perform-

FIGURE 16.3.   Singer Yi Jinyeo, inheritress of the northwest lyric song
tradition, performing in Seoul, fall 1997.

ers spoke of their former status as gisaeng reluctantly and with much ambivalence,
and the historical gisaeng, while absorbed by the canons of national culture, disappeared from their discourses.

The figure of the female professional "researcher" or "performer" neatly merged
the gisaeng tradition with the institution of modern South Korean womanhood,
with its standard obligations of marriage and family, and with its conventions of
relatively voluntary rather than hereditary participation. The performers I worked
with in the late 1990s have no hereditary connection to the gisaeng and have chosen
performance as a means of life, although many of them, such as Yi Jinyeo (see fig.
16.3), still come from poor families. Most are married and treat their career as other
women do, as a means of contributing to the family or gaining a measure of financial
or social independence.

As "gisaeng tourism" faded in the 1980s and popular consciousness began to
remember the historical separation of the gisaeng from the sex industry, performers
spoke somewhat more openly about their teachers' pasts as gisaeng as pride in the
tradition began to flourish. Despite the fact that most of the singers I have worked
with are married modern women, several of them consider their own intelligence,
frankness, performative power, and emotions to be the inheritance of gisaeng lega-
cies. Some performers and numerous other women told me that had they been born
in the Joseon Dynasty, they would certainly have become gisaeng. For some, then,
the gisaeng has become again not wholly a symbol of the oppression of women but a
cultural hero or prototype of modern, independent womanhood.

CONCLUSIONS

In many places in the modernizing world, the traditional role of the female entertainer seems to have disappeared or to be disappearing. As the preceding pages have
shown, the traditions of Korean female entertainment have not really disappeared,
but they have mutated into two currently unrelated streams: a massive sex-and-
entertainment industry concerned with popular entertainment and a national culture of female "performers" or "researchers" who continue to perform selected repertories of the colonial-era *gisaeng*. The modern-day female music star, who evolved
out of a colonial public cultural scene that prominently featured the gisaeng, can be
considered a third stream—just one topic among many that warrants further historical investigation. But the institution as such has disappeared, and as in China, India,
Europe, and elsewhere, the traditional female entertainer is remembered ambiva-
lently and her "disappearance" is seen as an inevitability of modernization, a tragedy
of colonialism, or a result of new generalized models of feminine propriety, often
imported from western Europe or North America.[40]

In Korea the traditional arts of the gisaeng were finally absorbed by the canons
of national culture in the era of sex industrialization. The concept of the gisaeng, on
the other hand, was absorbed into that sex industry and has been slowly salvaged.
So in South Korea those new notions of female propriety imported in part from the
West must be seen to have emerged against the backdrop of the growing sex industry
in the colonial period and under military-state-led capitalist development post-1945.
Those notions accumulated, in part, as Korean people became aware of the sex industry, and as they took concrete measures to keep themselves or their daughters out
of that industry. The new female propriety was one ideological means of preventing
this participation or ostracizing participants. Twentieth-century colonial and neo-
colonial industrialization saw the simultaneous emergence of several phenomena
that gave birth to conflicted notions of South Korean female propriety: the concentration of masses of poor girls and women seeking work in urban industrial centers;
the rise of new classes of working men with disposable cash; the rise of sex work as a
state strategy for the accumulation of foreign capital; the radical militarization of the
Korean peninsula and the development of a military sex market; and the development of a business culture that did its business by trading women's charms, talents,
and bodies.

The attitude that conflated gisaeng with sex workers developed with progressive
pressure on the gisaeng to enter the high-class layer of the pleasure industry, and
out of the efforts of the gisaeng to distance themselves from that industry. Once the
conflation was complete, the women began to distance themselves from the gisaeng
tradition itself. Gail Hershatter has described a similar social and discursive swallow-
ing of Shanghai courtesan traditions by a modern sex industry, and evidence points
to a similar process in India as well.[41] So the pressure on institutions of traditional
female entertainment to assimilate into modern sex industries and the ideological
conflation of the female entertainer with the sex worker seem to be the crucial common denominators in the so-called disappearance of the role of several of the world's
traditional female entertainers. The issue, then, is not just that the traditional female
entertainer became archaic in the era of women's liberation or immoral in a new era

of female Christian virtue, but also that traditional entertainment systems became outdated means of exploiting women for male pleasure.

Notes

I would like to thank the editors of this volume for encouraging me to develop my short conference presentation into an essay and for their assistance in the process. I would also like to thank Drs. Byong Won Lee and Yi Bohyeong for sharing their extensive knowledge of the gisaeng with me. I am especially indebted to Kwon Do-Hee, without whose groundbreaking scholarship and guidance I would not have been able to write this article. I am deeply grateful to the singers I worked with: my teachers—the late Human Cultural Treasure O Bongnyeo and current Human Cultural Treasure Kim Gwangsuk—as well as Yi Jinyeo and Yu Jisuk. I thank my University of Chicago colleagues Heekyoung Cho, Christine Y. Hahn, Suzy Kim, Albert Park, and Yoon Sun Yang for their comments.

1. See chap. 2 of Heisoo Shin, "Women's Sexual Services and Economic Development: The Political Economy of the Entertainment Industry and South Korean Dependent Development" (Ph.D. diss., Rutgers University, 1991).

2. For this view, see Pak Jeongae, "Nalgoshipeun 'nongjungjo': iljesidae gisaeng iyagi" [Caged birds who want to fly: the story of the gisaeng in the Japanese colonial period], in *20-segi yeoseong sageonsa* [Events in twentieth-century women's history], ed. Gilbakksesang (Seoul: Yeoseong sinmunsa, 2001), 77–89, at p. 79.

3. See Joshua D. Pilzer, "Post-Korean War Change in *Sŏdosori*, a Northwest Korean Vocal Genre in Contemporary South Korea" (M.A. thesis, University of Hawai'i, 1999).

4. For Byong Won Lee, see "The Evolution in the Role and Status of Korean Professional Female Entertainers (*Kisaeng*)," *World of Music* 21 (1979): 75–81. Kwon Do-Hee's scholarship has focused on the late nineteenth- and early twentieth-century gisaeng: see her "Reorganization of Musical Groups in the Beginning of the 20th Century," *Dongyang eumak* 20 (1998): 269–87; "20-segi gisaeng ui eumaksahoesajeog yeon'gu" [A music-sociohistorical study of the twentieth-century gisaeng], *Han'guk eumak yeon'gu* 29 (2001): 319–344; and "19-segi yeoseong eumakgye ui gudo" [The makeup of nineteenth-century women's musical scenes], *Dongyang eumak* 24 (2002): 5–17. Recently her work has begun to embrace the postcolonial period. See Kwon Do-Hee, "The Female Musicians Activity since the Dissolution of the Gisaeng Guilds," in *Proceedings of the Seventh International Asian Music Conference: Korean Music Viewed from In and Out* (Seoul: Seoul National University, 2003), 177–90.

5. See Lee, "The Evolution in the Role and Status of Korean Professional Female Entertainers," 75.

6. See Pak Jongseong, *Baekjeong gwa gisaeng: joseoncheonminsa ui du eolgul* [The baekjeong and the gisaeng: two faces of the outcaste during the Joseon Dynasty] (Seoul: Seoul National University Press, 2003), 256–69.

7. For a brief English-language review of the gisaeng in pre-twentieth-century Korea, see the relevant chapter in *Women of Korea: A History from Ancient Times to the Present*, ed. and trans. Yung-Chung Kim (Seoul: Ewha Women's University Press, 1976).

8. See Kwon, "19-segi yeoseong eumakgye ui gudo." The term *sampae*, which literally means "third group," i.e., third-rank gisaeng, appears to be an early twentieth-century term retroactively applied to this group. It seems likely that in the late nineteenth century these women were already conflated as gisaeng, and the term *sampae* was designed to distinguish them from state entertainers (see the discussion of Yi Neunghwa's history of Joseon Dynasty gisaeng below).

9. See Lee, "The Evolution," 79–80.

10. Yi Bohyeong, personal communication.

11. Kwon Do-Hee, personal communication.

12. This is a metaphor for female entertainers.

13. Yi Neunghwa, *Joseon hae-eohwasa* [A history of the Joseon Dynasty gisaeng] (1927; repr. Seoul: Dongmunseon, 1992). The time of origin of this three-tiered categorization, by which entertainers who practiced prostitution and those who did not are described with the same qualified term, gisaeng, is immensely controversial. Some scholars have treated the distinctions as hundreds of years old or more (see Lee). Pak Jeongae, a contemporary feminist, claims that the distinctions arose to distinguish artisan gisaeng (ranks 1 and 2) from the prostitute, an institution recently imported from Japan (see Pak Jeongae, "Nalgoshipeun 'nongjungjo,'" 80).

14. For instance, Lee, "The Evolution," 79–80.

15. Kwon, "Reorganization."

16. "Room culture" refers to the widespread practice of socializing in small rooms in private inns and restaurants, which, at least since the colonial period, has often involved professional women serving drinks and entertaining men with conversation and performance.

17. Kwon, "Reorganization," 271.

18. Tanabe Hisao records an official curriculum of the central *gwonbeon* in Pyeongyang in his *Chosen ongaku chosa kiko* [Field survey of Joseon music] (Tokyo: Ongakunotomosha, 1970), 19. Such "low" genres are not listed in Tanabe's record of the Pyeongyang school curriculum, but my fieldwork with Human Cultural Treasure O Boknyeo, a student at this school, has shown that middle-class genres of Korean traditional music and elaborate versions of folk songs were taught there. Yi Changbae also corroborates this in his *Han'guk gachang daegye* [General introduction to Korean traditional song] (Seoul: Hongin Munhwasa, 1976), 273.

19. See Song Youn-ok, "Japanese Colonial Rule and State-managed Prostitution: Korea's Licensed Prostitutes," *Positions* 5 (1997): 171–217.

20. Pak Jeongae, "Nalgoshipeun 'nongjungjo,'" 79.

21. Numerous references to gisaeng forced into sexual slavery can be found in the testimonies of the former comfort women. See Han'guk jeongshindae munje daechaek hyomuihoe and Han'guk jeongshindae yeon'guhoe, *Gangjero ggulyeogan Joseonin gunwianbudeul* [Korean women forcibly conscripted for military sexual slavery] (Seoul: Hanul, 1997), and Han'guk jeongshindae yeon'guhoe and Han'guk jeongshindae munje daechaek hyomuihoe, *Jungguk euro ggulyeogan Joseonin gunwianbudeul* [Korean women dragged off to China for military sexual slavery] (Seoul: Hanul, 1995).

22. Kwon surveys female participation in these organizations in "The Female Musicians Activity," 180.

23. Kawamura Minato, *Gisaeng: mal haneun ggot* [Gisaeng: talking flower] (Seoul: Sodam, 2001), 23.

24. Ibid., 299.

25. John Lie, "The Transformation of Sexual Work in 20th-Century Korea," *Gender and Society* 9: 310–27, at pp. 316–17.

26. Jackis follows the McCune–Reischauer system in transliterating "gisaeng," hence "*kisaeng.*"

27. The *gayageum* is a twelve-string plucked zither with movable bridges. It is rested on the lap and plucked with the right hand while the left hand presses the strings to produce interior notes, vibrato, and other kinds of microtonal shading. The flute is probably a *daegum*, a large flute made of irregular bamboo. One of the holes of the *daegum* is covered in a river reed, so that when it is blown the reed vibrates, producing a distortion effect. The *janggo* is a barrel-shaped drum, typically covered in cow, horse, or dog hide.

28. This dance is a variant of the popular *seungmu* (monk's drum dance), which the gisaeng have been custodians of for most of the twentieth century.

29. Jerry M. Jackis, "Korea's Unique *Gisaeng* Party," in *The Feel of Korea*, ed. In-hah Jung (Seoul: Hollym, 1966), 171–75.

30. Lie, "The Transformation of Sexual Work," 318.

31. See Korean Church Women United, *Gisaeng gwangwang* [Gisaeng tourism] (Seoul: Korean Church Women United, 1983), and Korean Church Women United, *Proceedings of the International Seminar on Women and Tourism* (Seoul: Korean Church Women United, 1988).

32. Lie, "The Transformation of Sexual Work," 319.

33. See also Cheng Sea-Ling, "Assuming Manhood: Prostitution and Patriotic Passions in Korea," *East Asia: An International Quarterly* 18, no. 4 (Winter 2000), 40–78, at p. 48.

34. Lie, "The Transformation of Sexual Work," 319.

35. See www.daboyojung.co.kr, www.oginam.co.kr, and the extensive www.sul-zip.com ("www.drinking house.com").

36. August 2, 1999, p. 44.

37. *Los Angeles Times*, August 15, 1988, p. 1.

38. See Pilzer, "Post-Korean War Change."

39. Kwon Do-Hee, personal communication.

40. Jennifer Post, for instance, in her article on the death of Indian courtesan traditions, concludes that the fragmenting of traditional life under British colonialism and a new, West-inflected sense of female propriety brought about the disappearances of the *devadasi* (temple-affiliated courtesan) and *ganika* (court-affiliated courtesan); see her "Professional Women in Indian Music: The Death of the Courtesan Tradition," in *Women and Music in Cross-Cultural Perspective*, ed. Ellen Koskoff (Urbana and Chicago: University of Illinois Press, 1989), 97–109.

41. See Gail Hershatter, "Courtesans and Streetwalkers: The Changing Discourses on Shanghai Prostitution, 1890–1949," *Journal of the History of Sexuality* 3 (1992): 245–69, and eadem, *Dangerous Pleasures: Prostitution and Modernity in Twentieth-Century Shanghai* (Berkeley: University of California Press, 1997). On India, see Asha Ramesh and H. P. Philomela, "The Devadasi Problem," in *International Feminism: Networking against Female Sexual Slavery: Report of the Global Feminist Workshop to Organize against Traffic in Women, Rotterdam, the Netherlands, April 6–15, 1983*, ed. Kathleen Barry, Charlotte Bunch, and Shirley Castley (Rotterdam: Global Feminist Workshop to Organize against Traffic in Women, 1984), 82–87.

Female Agency and Patrilineal Constraints

Situating Courtesans in Twentieth-Century India

SITUATING THE ISSUE

From at least 1800 until after Indian independence, courtesan singer-dancers (*tawa'if*) were at the center of elite entertainment in feudal and mercantile-colonial milieus of India, performing at courts and presiding over reenactments of court assemblies in salons that became the first public venue for Hindustani art music. Ostensibly free from the constraints of patrilineal kinship, these women enjoyed cultural and personal prominence as well as wealth and influence, and they could set musical trends.

However, during the decade following Indian Independence (1947), the courtesans' voices and contributions were all but erased by the nationalist bourgeois reform movement that culminated in a ban on salons enforced by police raids. Princely States were abolished in 1952, and All India Radio, which had consciously taken over musical patronage from the princes, banished all (women) performers "whose private life is a public scandal."[1] As a result, tawa'if and their multifaceted art all but disappeared from the cultural scene apart from nostalgic representations in literature and films. Few primary sources are left beyond early recordings, reminiscences by their patrons and musicians, and the conflicted career paths of a few women who could adapt themselves to the modern concert stage. Few of the women themselves have spoken.

Until their banishment, courtesans and their salons had been a central locus of Indian elite culture for at least a century, and until today they retain a unique presence in the cultural imagination of literature and film. Courtesan establishments were a prominent part of the urban scene all over northern India. Uniquely, they were operated by women who were capable of managing their art for their own benefit, many growing rich in the process. Given their well-established socio-economic as well as musical moorings, why did the courtesan's art and agency disappear rather than metamorphose into a different practice, just as the salons themselves had emerged from court performances?

In other words, how viable was these women's agency? Did Indian courtesans need courts for their art to survive? True, the salon successfully replaced the court. But did its courtly ritual require the validating presence of courts and aristocratic patronage? Could the courtesans' art not be transplanted onto the concert stage, like the classical art of the male singers who were their masters? Or was the barrier to bourgeois respectability insurmountable for these women? Was it the official condemnation of courtesans' morals and their banishment from government patronage at All India Radio that erased their art? Or did their music not measure up to the reformist canon of classical music? Under what conditions did a very few exceptional courtesans continue to perform on the public concert stage, and to what musical effect?

Recent initiatives addressing these issues have been prompted by specific concerns both for the courtesans and for their music. Musical progressives have been working to have courtesans' music restored to, or at least de-indexed from, the classical canon;[2] feminists and social activists are supporting the women's autonomy and freedom from exploitation.[3] My own study of Begum Akhtar's brilliant post-salon career demonstrates the possibility of success for such transformative efforts—she became a concert performer of her own music and a national icon of feudal culture (listen to companion website track 14 and see the appendix).[4] A few others, notably Siddeshwari Devi and now her daughter Savita Devi, became teachers at music academies.[5]

The exceptional story of Begum Akhtar has raised crucial questions about the way female agency worked within the patriarchy of quasi-feudal productive relations. I want to explore (in the literal, unfinished sense of the word) the issue of individual agency of North Indian courtesan-singers on the margins of a thoroughly patrilineal society. My nexus of questions is: How *socially* viable was the courtesans' "loose matrilineality" within patrilineally controlled Indian society? Traditional kinship studies suggest that the viability of these "non-wives" was predicated on the seclusion of respectable elite women to maintain reproductive control over feudal property. Has the abolition of feudal courts eliminated this social niche for courtesans? Or did control over her performance venue in the salon put a courtesan in control of her musical production and thus ensure her continued viability beyond feudal patronage? Above all, could courtesans produce and reproduce themselves as professional performers without the traditional ties of dependence with hereditary male musicians who had the social organization to do both? Finally, under what social and musical conditions were courtesans able to transcend social and gender boundaries creatively and why were they nevertheless prevented from participating in the bourgeois reform of classical music, despite the fact that they had been the most prominent bearers of that art?

To address these questions I want to problematize the courtesan's individual agency by situating it in the quasi-feudal nexus of productive relations—musical as well as economic—that tie her in contradictory ways to hierarchically opposed male constituencies, both marked by patrilineality and patriarchy: the patrons who consumed her music, and the musicians who taught and accompanied her. The challenge is to expand the traditional humanist perspective on the "art" of the courtesan to the social dimensions of its existence by examining the place and scope of courtesans as agents within a social universe of musical production and its economic base.

Following my earlier adaptation of a Marxist mode-of-production perspective on the feudally based music-making nexus of male hereditary professional musicians,[6] I propose here to focus particularly on the crucial site of the salon as the locus of female-controlled musical production and surplus appropriation as the site where women controlled musical production, as well as the profit or surplus value that the music generated. This means expanding the mode-of-production concept in two ways. To begin with, the quasi-mercantile dimension of the salon must be accommodated conceptually within the feudally based musical economy of northern India.[7] The second and conceptually overarching expansion is to factor the impact of gender into the social relations of musical production.[8]

First, however, a context needs to be sketched of historical sources and of courtesans themselves as I was able to experience them and their patrons, thanks to my encounters with eloquent participants in that remarkably gendered musical culture. Unlike the exclusively historical focus of most courtesan-related studies, my project is motivated and influenced in important ways by these experiences of the courtesan milieu during its last phase, and on continuing personal contact with some of its performers and patrons. Their performances and remembrances are a treasure of oral history that enables me to center my exploration on the heyday of the twentieth-century salon culture of Lucknow. I thus admit to a frankly personal involvement with the world of Hindustani music and women, being deliciously situated among both musicians and patrons, including some present and former courtesans. Their words are central to my understanding. So is their silence, in the case of courtesans who have reasons for non-disclosure that I deeply respect.

My thinking turned to these challenges in response to a now famous article by Veena Oldenburg.[9] A historian originally from Lucknow, she elicited an astonishing insider account of resistance against patriarchal domination from a group of Lucknow courtesans, which she described in an essay entitled "Lifestyle as Resistance." Based on their earning capacities, these women were able to invert their society's patrilineal control over women, by assigning men the role of service providers in their families and by treating patrons strategically as a source of income. Oldenburg draws a picture of a functionally feminist (and affectively lesbian) self-sufficiency. In social terms, what I see here is a "loose matrilineality" that extends familial solidarity to the biologically unrelated women who have joined a propertied senior courtesan and her daughter in an extended family setting. What stands out is the senior woman's prosperity and her social prominence as the leader of the hereditary courtesan community in Lucknow, a position that has been held by prosperous women since at least the mid-nineteenth-century *chaudhrayin* (fem. of *chaudhri*, the standard term for the leader of a village or a professional caste group, including musicians). Oldenburg's account does not address these women's hereditary identities as performers, though the chaudhrayin's daughter is a well-known singer who later replaced courtesan songs with the popular group genre of qawwali.

When Oldenburg's piece appeared, I realized that this was the household that I too had visited some years earlier, but to a distinctly different effect. Mine was a search for the courtesan's art, and it resulted in the very special treasure of a private performance and video recording that I was able to make of the daughter's singing in the intimate setting and style of her familial training, though accompanied by the larger group of musicians she now performs with.

What made it possible to have this performance held in a courtesan's home, albeit in the daytime, despite the permanent ban on such performances? My own patronage was mediated, thanks to a common friend, by a landed gentleman who had an already existing quasi-familial patronage link to the artist. His late father had had a permanent liaison with the chaudhrayin and he therefore continued a benevolent relationship with the daughter as his half-sister—another aspect of patriarchy and perhaps also a reason for the continuing prosperity of the chaudhrayin's family. Together we walked into the crowded old section of the city and were received with warm courtesy. The gentleman and our friend were comfortably seated in the rather small room upstairs, facing the performers; I was further back, perched on the balcony railing in order to gain a wider angle for my camera, though not wide enough to show my two companions, the patrons of the event. Male patrons were clearly an important constituency in this courtesan household, even if they remained in the background of her performing career.

The second male constituency were her accompanists, traditionally an intimate ensemble of sarangi (bowed string) and tabla supporting the singer and typical of the quasi-domestic intimacy of performances shared with one or two special patrons. The proliferation of instrumentalists in her ensemble was notable, because it provided a built-in enactment of the female artist addressing her singing to a collectivity of men, sometimes also reinforced by a second woman singer and/or a dancer. "Holding court" has been one of the historical settings for the enactment of courtesan performances in salons as well as in feudal courts, in addition to performing in intimate privacy. The two settings correspond directly to the two feudal social spaces that are literally built into the palaces ("forts") of the Mughal kings in the form of courts for "general" and "special" audiences, respectively (darbar-i-'am = "general court," darbar-i-khas = "special court")—a standard architectural feature of Indo-Muslim forts and palaces.

What is the connection between this 1984 enactment of a salon performance and feudal culture? Lucknow is situated in the feudal heartland of Colonial India located in the fertile Gangetic plain, where British colonial authority sustained feudal agriculture with numerous local courts and surrounding princely states.[10] Thus throughout colonial rule this erstwhile royal capital continued to be a cosmopolitan center of feudal culture where courtesans continued to enjoy elite support.[11] Tawa'if performances also remained the quintessential courtly display of high culture-cum-entertainment in the Princely States until they were abolished in 1952, five years after Indian Independence. Sustained by feudal incomes, these courts could remain unperturbed by metropolitan bourgeois condemnation, especially since several of them financed public musical institutions like music colleges and some even expected courtesan singers to become students or teachers there.[12] Landed (as well as commercial and industrial) wealth continued as an economic and social force sustaining salons, along with private patronage.[13]

It was in these regions of longest feudal domination, often deemed "backward," that I had the opportunity to access the milieu of cultivated music-making as it existed in Lucknow and other urban centers away from metropolitan centers in which Western influence and Victorian values held sway over rising professional and bourgeois elites. In addition, a rich historical record makes it possible to situate this salon culture more broadly within the preceding feudal/colonial context of cultural and economic production in the region. Taking the 1984 performance as a starting point. I ask whether the tawa'if's practice has remained meaningfully linked to feudal culture. The question is of more than historical interest; it is of both semiotic and social relevance to interrogating the post-feudal life of this practice. I begin by sketching a historical frame based on sources for the feudal and post-feudal courtesan, keeping in mind her dual male constituencies of patrons and musicians.

COURTESANS AS CONSORTS:
TAWA'IF AND FEUDAL PATRONS

A rich pictorial and literary record attests to the historical prominence of women musicians who consorted with and danced and sang for royalty, elite patrons, and even for British officers of the East India Company. Dating mainly from the eighteenth century, numerous court paintings depict women performers either in a standing or dance position, facing a seated princely patron who may have courtiers standing by him. They show the formal framing of courtesans, their appearance, and the distant but intense communication between the noble patron resting on a throne-like seat, at times surrounded by courtiers. The woman in turn may have male instrumental accompanists standing behind or even following her.[14] Another style of painting depicts a more intimate setting with both patron and courtesan seated, he on a raised platform with bolsters, she on the floor facing him as a performer. Numerous intimate scenes also depict the patron consorting playfully with a courtesan on his dais.

Prominent because of their accessibility to Western readers, accounts by visiting Europeans report on courtesan performances as early as the seventeenth century. Like paintings, these descriptions tend to privilege the visual since these authors lacked the familiarity and comprehension to relate to the words or their musical setting. What these sources do make clear, however, is that formal performances by female singers and dancers were the standard entertainment for honoring guests, and visitors were obligated to be present and offer appropriate appreciation for what was obviously considered the most prized cultural performance at courts across northern India.

In vernacular literature (Persian, followed by Urdu in the eighteenth–nineteenth centuries), the pre-Victorian period is represented in chronicles of courtiers and princes that give at least a formalized sense of social milieu and dynamic between courtesans and their patrons. Courtesans are mentioned collectively and also as individuals. Abu'l Fazl, the sixteenth-century court chronicler of Akbar the Great, identifies musicians, including women singer-dancers, by their community, suggesting hereditary identities, although matriliny is not even hinted at.[15] Kanchan/kanjar are the dominant groups mentioned; these are also identified as tribes, implying an endogamous (patrilineal) community in which women are professional performers. Whether named or not, early tawa'if are often assigned a regional origin from Kashmir or other northwestern locations that are already associated with fair-skinned beauty in classical Farsi poetry, and explicitly so in what is claimed to be the earliest Indian novel written in Farsi, by Hasan Shah.[16]

The standard Urdu-Persian term for courtesan, tawa'if, encapsulates these social characteristics, though it appears to be of more recent usage and designates profession and status rather than a particular communal origin. Tawa'if[17] literally means "tribe, community," while also implying people who move about, wander, and settle. Hasan Shah's novel provides an account of just such a troupe of women entertainers with male managers and accompanists traveling in search of patronage and ready to settle in their large tent where they find it.[18] A somewhat related identifier is the Farsi term *deredar* (lit., tent-dweller), specifying the highest-ranking category of courtesans (*deredar tawa'if*) and referring to the royal tents of military chiefs and rulers and perhaps also to their own movable dwelling place.[19] Etymologically, linguistically, and historically, courtesans were clearly a part of the Persianate cultural environment created in northern India by the Muslim ruling class.

A different treatment is found in the literary and historical accounts of particular courtesans who stand apart from references made to undifferentiated social groupings. Paralleling the careful paintings of courtesans at courts, these women are clearly presented as individuals, and as performers. Their social identity is not assigned but rather construed by association with their patrons, if only temporarily so, much like wives who are invested with the social identity of their husbands. An example is the vividly illustrated account in Persian of the travels of King Jahandar Shah with his consort, the singer Lal Kunwar. Of somewhat later origin is the equally remarkable romance between a singer/dancer in an East India Company officer's establishment and his literary scribe Hasan Shah in the autobiographical novel mentioned above.[20]

What emerges from these and other sources is that pragmatically and functionally a tawa'if could share her patrons' social life, but her very function also kept her subsumed within the feudal nexus of performers as hereditary service providers—a trusted, beloved, admired servant, but a servant nonetheless. As for her lack of paternity, it was irrelevant, since her heterosexual interaction was extra-familial and thus by definition could not result in legitimate offspring.

This does not mean that noble patrons did not acknowledge or even own the children of their consorts.[21] That this social valuation continued is confirmed by my experience with Zarina Parveen, which shows that daughters, and sometimes sons, were provided with musical training. One of several known examples is the daughter of a singer for whom her noble patron in Baroda had engaged Abdul Karim Khan as a teacher in the 1920s.[22] When the teacher eloped with his pupil the noble tried in vain to have her return "home."[23] And in the 1930s Begum Akhtar was regularly asked to set to music and perform the poet Natiq's verses at Lucknow's annual poetry festival, because he was generally acknowledged to be her father.[24]

COURTESANS AS INDEPENDENT PERFORMERS:
SALON CULTURE

Strongly overlapping with patronage at court, courtesans holding court and performing in their own residence are mentioned as early as the 1730s in a contemporary account of Delhi's cultural life.[25] In the eighteenth century these venues were either urban salons or tents that rendered a tawa'if mobile and capable of joining military patrons—including commanders of the British East India Company's army. But as an institution, salons gained widespread prominence from the nineteenth century onward. The most detailed and evocative account of salon life by novelist/historian Hadi Ruswa suggests that nineteenth-century courtesan establishments were, at least ideologically speaking, supplemental to courtly performances.[26] Landed nobles remained the dominant patrons, while money from trade and other sources—including colonial offices—brought patrons lacking, but also learning, the culture of tawa'if patronage, including courtly deportment and the sophisticated idiom of Urdu poetry. Ghazal poetry of numerous Urdu poets most eloquently conveys the affective dimension of salon interaction. The British, too, continued to patronize salons, at least in the feudal environment between Calcutta and Lucknow.[27] This included travelers "in search of the picturesque" like Mrs. Belnos or Fanny Parkes, who describe in detail what the British categorically called "nautch" (from Hindi *nach*, i.e., dance), since they did not understand the songs and their poetic meanings, which underlie the dance.[28]

From the nineteenth to mid-twentieth century, the urban salon or *kotha* (lit. "villa") enjoyed increasing prominence as the first venue for Hindustani art music that was accessible to the growing commercial and colonial elite cadres outside the control of princely hosts. Elite salons maintained decorum and attendance was strictly screened so as to retain the character of an elite gathering. But money also enabled untutored wealthy men to visit, if not to join, the elite gatherings there. The increasing shift of feudal patronage to the locale of the salon was paralleled by the rise of mercantile wealth as well as the powerful impetus of reform and the rise of nationalism. Salons proliferated in urban centers across northern India and Pakistan, and they continued to flourish in large numbers even during the years of World War II when war contractors generated an upsurge in patronage.

Most remarkable about salons is the fact that courtesans themselves managed and even owned the salon venue, notwithstanding the fact that major feudal patrons sometimes owned the building or provided other forms of support for the tawa'if—though there is little information about the economy of such ownership. The courtesan in turn had to comply with patrons' preferences in performance, but she could exercise control over proceedings and also over who should be admitted to the performance. Control, finally, enabled courtesans to have family members live in their establishments, especially daughters, real or putative, who could become singers, but also sons and brothers who attended to service tasks and even served as subsidiary musical accompanists.[29]

SALON CULTURE IN THE TWENTIETH CENTURY

As a locus for social/musical heterosexuality, the salon served feudal patrons when in urban residence, along with merchants and colonial functionaries, who together formed a feudal-mercantile urban elite.[30] The unprecedented scope for female agency afforded by the salon within a thoroughly patrilineal/patriarchal society needs to be rendered explicit, because it stands in stark contrast with the subsequent turn toward public concerts that were essentially inspired by bourgeois notions of stage performance controlled by (male) managers. The tawa'if's independence was indeed singled out in contrast to respectable women suffering from male oppression, but such independence could not pass the test of Victorian social norms.[31] Already by the late nineteenth century, tawa'if and their dance became morally stigmatized by the "anti-nautch" movement of missionaries and middle-class social reformers.[32] Half a century later, nationalist musical reformers simply followed suit, with the aim of replacing bad courtesans with good wives, especially on the Radio, so that "respectable" middle-class women could perform there.[33] Starting before the turn of the twentieth century, the expansion of middle-class music-making by both men and women accomplished a gradual bourgeois takeover of relations of musical production, both in music education and on the concert stage. Gradually, music-making as a gendered field of cultural production was eliminated as cultural capital increasingly accrued to male and female musical performances on the public stage.[34]

After independence in 1947 "a new public tradition which did not distinguish between male and female roles" superseded the gender-specific performances of professional women under feudal patronage,[35] and their musical repertory became marginalized within the gamut of "classical" (*klassiki*) music as it was reconceptualized by bourgeois scholarly and institutional consensus. The evocative text-oriented genres long cultivated by courtesan singers—thumri, dadra, and ghaza—were now defined as "light" or "semi-classical" genres sung to "light" and "mixed" ragas, in contrast to the fully "classical" khayal and dhrupad, which form the core genres of pure raga music that alone came to constitute the classical canon. Equally important, dancing and the miming of poetic content became detached from singing even while dance (and mime) retained their status among the three "branches" of *sangit*, the inclusive classical concept of Indian music.

Overshadowed by the triumphal march of musical reform in the twentieth century, the remarkable story of women music-makers and their gender-specific musical voice took the span of another generation and the impetus of the women's movement to gain scholarly and institutional attention. Recent historical research is opening up eloquent archival material on women musicians of the last two centuries, mainly rooted in Urdu literature and courtly paintings,[36] but also of English provenance, highlighting "the demise of the nautch girl" and the subsequent "decline" of professional women performers.[37] A special impetus comes from feminist initiatives that include women-centered perspectives on courtesans as well as temple dancers (*devadasis*).[38] And a pioneering effort was made in 1984 to assemble long-retired (and often impoverished) hereditary singer-dancers at India's premier arts academy,[39] although after decades of (respectable) silence few were still able to sing, or willing to speak of their life as courtesans.[40] The event brought into stark focus the social collapse of the courtesans' cultural capital and their overt musical deference to male hereditary musicians who, in contrast to the women, have retained their primacy as musical experts and teachers.

Much work is yet to be done to open the doors shut by the official, essentially male, history of Indian music. But the strong moral antagonism cultivated in Victorian British as well as Indian writings against professional women performers has indelibly marked present-day historicizing efforts toward achieving a culturally appropriate perspective on the cultural and social role of courtesans. "Appropriate" here must mean: in the terms of the milieus that grounded courtesans culturally and sustained them socially, and free from the bourgeois resignification of courtesans as "fallen women." To achieve such a perspective is a formidable challenge, given the historical permeation of colonially generated Victorian values among dominant Indian elites and their institutions in the metropolis, including the state itself. And even the most positive twentieth-century representations of feudal milieus, particularly in Urdu, cannot help but speak in reaction to the long-dominant "anti-nauch" discourse, if only through attempts at rehabilitating courtesan heroines as innocent victims—a favorite plot in films (*Pakeeza*, *Zindagi ya Tufan*) as well as literature.[41]

A major challenge is that such cultural representations—apart from the tawa'if themselves—are invariably authored from the vantage point of male patrons. Furthermore, the very media of painting and literature typically serve elite representation. My own work is no exception: even as a female and thoroughly acculturated musician, my own relationship with former courtesans, like that of other female scholars (e.g., Post), has never transcended the confines of middle-class female respectability and connoisseurship that I have inevitably represented. On the other hand, there are now feminist scholars who explicitly represent courtesans from a position of solidarity[42] and who offer a woman-centered identification of the courtesan's repertory with her agency.[43] Their work not only challenges the moralist bourgeois condemnation of courtesans by the likes of social reformers such as Mrs. Fuller, it also puts into question the feudal nostalgia that often colors representations of courtesans in literature and film.

Still, the issue of voice and representation clearly remains a strategic challenge in any discourse by and about courtesans. Agency can be found only in a few exceptional voices of retrospection from women who successfully negotiated the transformation into classical twentieth-century concert performers, the most outstanding one being an autobiographical account by Gangubai Hangal (even if translated and perhaps edited).[44] Alternatively, one untapped locus of agency is the courtesan's performance in which she literally enacts her rule over her court of elite patrons, making her art her primary tool of domination. Her performance is also the most accessible site of her interaction not only with patrons but with her male musicians. What kind of a tool is this art, and what empowerment does it contribute in the courtesan's relationship with both these male constituencies?

TAWA'IF AS PERFORMERS

By all accounts, Indian courtesans have been performers by definition, although they were not necessarily so named. The earliest accounts strongly identify tawa'if with the performance of poetry: they sang, mimed, and danced poems. Persian and Urdu ghazals were the privileged currency of elite conviviality that included enriching conversation with spontaneous recitation of verses from a shared repertory of classical and contemporary poems. Every account of courtesans performing is studded with ghazal verses from classical poetry as well as from the tawa'if's own personal repertory.[45] Poets traditionally asked tawa'if to sing their poems, to their mutual enhancement.[46] The performance of poetry, from informal conversation to formal presentation, was a central enactment of North Indian elite culture, then, and tawa'if were central participants in it.

In performance, the ghazal art song has been the tawa'if's most widely appreciated vocal genre. Musically more valuable, however, was the tawa'if's improvisational art music, which she sang to short poems in Hindi, notably thumri and dadra. Her other Hindi song genres were derived from regional songs evocative of her feudal patrons' local roots. The tawa'if's dance encompassed the two classical aspects of Indian dance: expressive miming (*bhav*) of the song and virtuosic rhythmic movements or "pure" dance (*nrittya*). Together they constituted the most directly physical way for the tawa'if to embody both the text and the music of her performance.

How did these performances "go"? Sources on court performances offer scant information about the process beyond the visual depiction of courtesans dancing and singing in court assemblies and intimate settings. Musical matters are left out, beyond the sight of instruments and a few expressive hand gestures, but poetry, including poems composed for tawa'if (*tawa'ifi*) by recognized poets, has been recorded and published, though not explicitly identified.

More is known about the content of performances held by courtesans in their own establishment, since they have lasted until what is today still living memory. Moreover, they were attended by elite members outside the control of princely hosts, among them writers and poets. Salon audiences have been vividly described and remembered as court-like assemblies observing rank and etiquette, but here the courtesan herself presided over the court, even while she was serving the patrons in her audience in performances that in fact paralleled the court ritual. The continued use of the term *mujra* ("seven salutations") for these performances in the twentieth century clearly attests to the cultural capital accruing to this courtly model, if not to its literal enactment.

This continuity is evident from oral reminiscences shared by erstwhile patrons and poets who offered me concrete and evocative depictions of the mujra as enacted in Lucknow salons between the 1920s and 1940s. What follows is a composite sketch of a performance drawn from such living memories. It is here that cultural-musical relations of production were enacted and rendered observable.

COURTESAN PERFORMANCES OBSERVED

Mujra is symbolic of total submission before a royal patron. The deep obeisances which the tawa'if executes in an entreating and artful gesture introduce her display of artistic mastery, and of herself as a desirable female. For the mujra is really a heightened musical frame for a dialogue between one woman and many men—but only the tawa'if is privileged with the language of song. Her answers come from patrons in multiple forms through gestures, exclamations, and material rewards. Underlying this unequal discourse is an asymmetry of power that is tempered with gentility. The patron requests and the tawa'if complies, while the instrumentalists frame and facilitate compliance. A Lucknow patron recalls: "Whatever you made a request (*farmaish*) for is what was performed. Anything."[47] Within a song, improvisational musical structures serve the very purpose of responding flexibly to the listeners' preferences. What the audience has come for, in the words of Lucknow poet and patron Umar Ansari, is *ruhani ghiza* (literally: soul food), an essential emotional-spiritual nourishment that is inherent in music.[48]

Dancing initially entails, for both dancer and musicians, a standing position appropriate in the presence of patrons who are, by definition, superior in status. For the mujra event is a *darbar*, or ranked assembly, where status is validated, and also a *maidan* (field of battle) where rivals assemble and compete for the queen's favor. Indeed, paintings as well as descriptive accounts of eighteenth- and nineteenth-century court performances show how the model of actual court performances continued to inform twentieth-century salon etiquette.[49] Just as in the feudal court assemblies, the tawa'if awaits or elicits the permission (*ijazat*) of her superiors, and only then, followed by her musicians, does she sit down to present the songs that speak to her listeners' special preferences: thumri, dadra, and, above all, ghazal for Urdu speakers with Muslim cultural affinities, but also Hindi genres like *hori*, *kajri*, and *chaiti*, depending on the listeners' affinities with either Muslim or Hindu culture.

From an entreating inferior, she now becomes queen of the *mahfil*, the candle (*shamma'*) among moths (*parvane*), and the proud target of their rivalry. She is the cupbearer (*saqi*) of the wine of ecstasy, but also the killer who wields the dagger (*khanjar*) of cruelty. Aesthetically and affectively, her listeners, the patrons, become her lovers, ardent, helpless, and silent. But her songs speak for them as well as to them. She is the voice not only of love (*'ishq, muhabbat*) but also of the lover (*'ashiq*), his suffering and his delights. An assembly of rivals is by definition a place of suffering, a contest of desire for a woman untrammeled by the constraints of patrilineal kinship ties.

It is the tawa'if's unencumbered identity as a woman that enabled the courtesan to produce a sensual gendered cultural experience for her male patrons in return for the rewards they offer. But producing the music is different. Very much present in the performance were the courtesan's musicians, who provided her singing with melodic and rhythmic support on the bowed sarangi and the paired tabla (and earlier also on the sitar). Far more than mere accompanists, these men were in fact indispensable as co-producers of the tawa'if's performance, both in an immediate and in a more global sense.

PRODUCING THE PERFORMANCE:
COURTESANS AND MUSICIANS

Production is here understood to be more than staging the proceedings of a cultural event. The focus is on the relations of production as a diagnostic of what it takes to produce and sustain the mujra as an ongoing cultural practice. The concept of production is collective and functional, and the concept of social relations serves to identify the locus of control over the music that is being produced.

As highly accomplished performers, tawa'if were professionally trained and spent years studying and practicing their art. This training was in the hands of hereditary musicians who also provided the tawa'if's instrumental accompaniment. Sarangi and tabla players functioned as her teachers for voice and dance respectively. Sarangi players, in particular, have been uniquely identified with teaching courtesans as well as guiding their singing in performance, and even with managing their engagements. These instrumentalists belonged to endogamous patrilineal communities of male hereditary professional musicians who have been the exclusive heirs to Hindustani art music. An ongoing association existed between them and tawa'if as masters and students, and tawa'if accepted their authority, collectively referring to them as Khan Sahib (Respected Sir; literally: Chief). This is reflected in accounts of Begum Akhtar and others, and it was evident as recently as 1984, during the Women Music Makers festival. Tawa'if themselves may have learned from their mothers or other courtesans informally, but their acknowledged masters were always men with a hereditary musical pedigree.

As accompanists the musicians of course played a subordinate role, but they received a fixed share of the income (usually 25%) and the sarangi player, at least, often lived in the establishment.[50] The relationship was ongoing and hereditary, with sons taking their father's place, although few courtesans had hereditary successors.

Why did tawa'if owners of salons not simply hire accompanists and, above all, teach their own daughters or granddaughters, avoiding the inevitable dependence on hereditary male musicians? In order to contextualize this question it is helpful to examine the social conditions of this musical production in the wider context of class and heredity that has continued to characterize Indian feudalism up to the twentieth century.

Feudal musical production in India comprised ties of patron–client relations between controllers/appropriators and "laborers" or servants—even if given a chiefly title like Khan Sahib, that is, musician. Paternalistic, even affective, ties between patron and servants were balanced by a strict opposition between their functions: a patron[51] listened to the music he had his musicians perform, but by definition did not perform himself, while his musicians had the duty to provide the patron with the music he wanted to hear. An ideology of land control as the source of wealth, and of labor as having low social value, legitimized the feudal appropriation of the value generated by labor, be it agricultural or musical. According to the same ideology, rewarding the laborer was seen as benefaction rather than a redistribution of value that was created by labor in the first place. Thus feudal rewards were considered a patron's personal gift to the musician, not a payment keyed to a musical service. Salon performances operated on a similar pattern, in which each patron presented his remuneration as a personal gift to the singer, in a style that also evokes offerings made by courtiers to their superiors.[52]

The means of production for music obviously includes a musician's instrument and skills; it also, crucially, includes the venue for the creation of a performance. Venues were of course totally controlled by the feudal patron, enabling him to appropriate the value or "cultural capital"[53] produced by the musician. In order to qualify for productive relations with patrons, musicians themselves were responsible for producing and reproducing their professional skills. This took place through long-term teaching and learning within endogamous "brotherhoods" (*bradri*) of patrilineal families who protected, and still protect, their professional knowledge by marrying within their community. While active performers were engaged elsewhere, earning support for their families, their children were raised and taught by senior relatives, enabling them in turn to perform at courts and support the community of their elders, wives, and children.[54]

INSERTING GENDER

For male musicians, their endogamous patrilineal kinship organization has clearly been a functional aspect of musical production. For female musicians, gender difference profoundly affected both the production of music and their own reproduction. In terms of class and professional function, tawa'if are producers and can be classed with other feudal servants. Like male musicians, they became subject to feudal beneficence as reward for professional service. But the courtesan's presence in an assembly of men introduced an extra dimension of sensuality and heterosexual attraction that placed her in a potential relationship of personal and social intimacy with individual patrons. As a potential consort, she was subsumed by patrilineal society into a patron's entourage and then became his adornment. This was possible because she had the competence to transcend her service class and to affirm this new status through her cultivated deportment, wit, and conversational literacy in addition to her musical competence.[55] Whether in a feudal court or in her own salon, the courtesan acted the part of a higher class and received commensurate material rewards, certainly far beyond those of her male professional counterparts. In short, feudal and sexual ties became blurred.

The fact is that the gender position of consort is by definition unstable. In contrast to the patron's wife, her role is reproductively irrelevant and the gendered space she occupies lies on the margins of the patrilineal system of reproduction that is controlled through female seclusion within a propertied patron's family, leading to a de facto functional separation between the reproductive and the social and musical heterosexuality of wife and courtesan respectively. Functioning as a focal point for conspicuous consumption, social competition, and reaffirmations of social ranking, the tawa'if's social role and individual position was of necessity dependent on the male patron class.

Even while socially advantaged as individuals, courtesans also continued to depend collectively on men of their own class of hereditary professional musicians. As her teachers and accompanists, these musicians were in a position to act as her musical managers. Historically and functionally grounded, such musical dependence continues to find expression in gestures of formal deference by courtesans acknowledging the dominant musical position of hereditary (male) professional musicians as the teachers of professional female singers.

Why were tawa'if not trained within their own families and why, as elders, did they not take on the role of teachers? Not enough is known about courtesan families and communities, but what emerges, based on recent conversations, is a lack of numbers and a generational structure that amounts to a lack of stable and localized communities that could serve as home base for female musicians. The major issue is reproduction. Since courtesans by definition could not be married or have "families," their very success with patrons meant that they could not be recognized as having their own hereditary or affinal family ties. This in turn affected their access to the means of musical reproduction: namely, to male master musicians.

INDIVIDUAL AGENCY—COLLECTIVE CONSTRAINTS?

Individually courtesans were elevated by noble patrons as great artists and individuals, but collectively they shared the inferior status of specialized feudal servants. As owners and managers of salons, however, tawa'if have collectively enjoyed an autonomy that is entirely exceptional among women in their society, as was noted a century ago and has been again in the present.[56] Would courtesans not be ideally suited to the project of feminist emancipation?

In 1984 when Rita Ganguly brought surviving courtesans from across the country into Delhi to celebrate and acknowledge their art, most could no longer sing after decades of silence. I saw for myself how impoverished some of them were: the once splendid Mushtari Bai lived in squalor in a dark Old Delhi attic and had not sung in many years. I did not see an extended household with younger relatives providing for their mothers. And very few of these old courtesans had daughters who sang and could support their mothers. Others had sons who prospered in business, but kept little contact with their mothers. Most of all, what struck me with its absence was reference to wider kin and community links. This situation contrasts sharply with that of the courtesans' male accompanists, whose hereditary community continues to be overtly represented by a far-flung network of practicing musicians, including youngsters.

Zarina Parveen (fig. 17.1)[57] and other courtesans have targeted the loss of the *kotha* (salon) as the root cause of their demise (listen to companion website track 15 and see the appendix). I tend to agree with them, for economic and social reasons alone. The *kotha* was in fact the first public concert venue of broad attraction, and, remarkably, it was run entirely by women. This situation surely became an issue of control for nationalist reformers and their governmental backers. And the loss of landed estates and courtly patronage also greatly reduced those patrons' support for the salons themselves. This amounted to a substantive loss, because members of the elite feudal class were paramount patrons who kept other men away from controlling the women they patronized. Since the control of venues is tantamount to controlling the major means of producing a performance, feudal patronage of the tawa'if—not just her

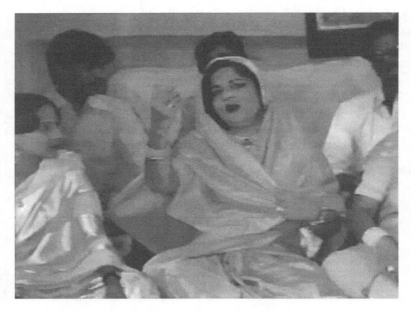

FIGURE 17.1.   Master singer Zarina Parveen of Lucknow offers a traditional
ghazal performance, videorecorded by Qureshi (August 1984).

particular performance—created the infrastructure for her to sell her performances
to others while controlling the major means of musical production: the salon itself.

MATRILINEAL TIES AND POST-SALON STRATEGIES

Are courtesans matrilineal? Veena Oldenburg believes so, and indeed the matriline
is invariably the only lineage identity courtesans have been assigned by others. But
lineality is a construct invoked or denied strategically, and the absence of patrilineality does not equal matrilineality. Personal encounters in the post-salon present
suggest some strategies employed by individual women to configure kinship around
female solidarity. I have also heard a courtesan flatly deny that a famous courtesan
was her mother, even though this was a piece of common knowledge put forward
twice by the interviewing hostess of a performance that was being recorded at a
prestigious Arts event for Pakistan's National Lok Virsa Heritage Label. On the other
hand, the famous Pakistani singer Malka Pukhraj publicly promoted her daughter
Tahira Syed as a singer and toured the world with her. Other courtesans, including
Begum Akhtar herself, have emphasized, if not identified, their fathers and pointed
out that their fathers encouraged them to become singers, thus projecting patrilineal
legitimation for being a performer.

   In actual practice, active lineal ties for courtesans have remained maternal. This is most obvious in the traditional courtesan household of Lucknow's Zarina Parveen, whose mother was the head of the household of several women and their children while husbands and brothers remained in the background, even when I visited there along with my husband. Begum Akhtar, too, was raised by her mother, and after engagements at various courts she and her mother lived in her own house in Lucknow where she entertained and boldly drove around in a black Packard wearing slacks. But once she married Barrister Abbasi, she accepted the patrilineal rules of upper-class respectability, and therefore could not receive her matrilineal relatives in her new patrilineal household. Begum Akhtar had to compromise her matrilineal ties to the extent of having to camouflage the existence of her young daughter as a "niece" so that the girl could stay in her house. And she could only visit her natal family in the anonymity of a *burqa*, because any public sign of their existence was evidence of her disreputable lack of patrilineal identity and thus self-control.

This contrasts with the situation of courtesans who have married hereditary musicians and accompanists. One singer, the wife of a famous instrumentalist, has her sister live with them and her other relatives visit them freely, even though they are Hindus and the husband a Muslim. She has, however, given up singing in public, and he earns well. In another marriage of a Muslim courtesan singer to a hereditary musician, also Muslim, the wife has continued to raise her two daughters "in her people's way," that is, outside of domestic seclusion, even after she married a hereditary instrumentalist whose own milieu requires female seclusion. I saw these teenage girls sing and freely socialize with male visitors in their home while their stepfather kept his own daughter-in-law in strict seclusion in the kitchen of the same small apartment. He explained to me that his wife was following the norms of her community (*qaum*), he those of his. For these and other singers, marriage can be seen as cementing the courtesan's traditional musical partnership with her teacher/ accompanist. At the same time she becomes locked into the patrilineal class status of her husband, thereby compromising her potential social mobility as a courtesan. But her professional scope as a singer, as well as that of her musician husband, is clearly enhanced.

In maintaining female agency outside patriliny the issue is, in the end, one of economic power. Capital assets are what enable Zarina Parveen and other courtesans of means to maintain their independent social arrangements; in other words, some of these elite courtesans became entrepreneurs who can afford to live with or without music. But these may well be high-profile exceptions. We now need to hear from less fortunate courtesans whose only livelihood remains their traditional calling. Amelia Maciszewski's important new research on the self-help organization Guria clearly demonstrates their dependence on men to access the assets of patrilineal power structures. Denial or assertion, alliance at upper or lower class levels, the underlying social fact is that for North Indian and Pakistani courtesans agency has been contingent and linked in one way or another to patrilineal validation.

This exploration suggests that female agency is indeed constrained by the dominant social system of patrilineality. It was the post-feudal salon that provided courtesans with a unique, if limited, niche for systemic female control over the means of musical and even material production, if only in a narrow, domestic sense. The violence with which the bourgeois Indian nation state eradicated this niche raises questions about the gender factor that must widen the usual focus on sensuality and its control in heterosexual relations. Could the female-controlled management of salon establishments have been seen as a systemic negation of patriarchal control itself? On an individual level, did salon culture open to women artists a social domain of agency vis-à-vis men, to the point of a transgressive blurring of class boundaries? And, not to be forgotten, did the absence of stable social conditions of reproduction most directly undermine patriarchal norms as well as the viability of the salon itself, including the courtesan's arts?

Marx, and prevailing Marxist social analysis, did not consider it within its all-male purview to bring gender into its conception of production; indeed, Marx's own attention to kinship extended to class, but not to gender.[58] In this study I have attempted to explore the convergence and tensions between the two, in searching for a relevant frame for situating North Indian courtesans and their lasting social legacy as women, as well as their cultural legacy as performing artists. I have also attempted to factor in the social style and "cultural capital" represented by feudal court patronage in order to show its impact on post-feudal salons, both in the form of landed patronage and cultural validation. My hope is that an approach embodying structure as well as agency should offer meaningful new ways for understanding the life of these women and for listening to their remarkable music.

Notes

Research for this study owes much to the late Begum Akhtar, Zarina Parveen, the late Umar Ansari, Saleem Qureshi, Abdul Qavi Zia, Khaliq Ahmad, and many others for sharing their memories with me.

1. In the famous 1954 dictum of the Broadcasting minister B. V. Keskar, quoted in H. R. Luthra, *Indian Broadcasting* (New Delhi: Publications Division, 1986).

2. See Vidya Rao, "Thumri and Thumri Singers," in *Cultural Reorientation in Modern India*, ed. Indu Banga and Jaidev (Shimla: Institute of Advanced Study, 1996), 278–315.

3. See Veena Talwar Oldenburg, "Lifestyle as Resistance: The Case of the Courtesans of Lucknow," *Feminist Studies* 16 (1990): 259–88; *Women as Subjects: South Asian Histories*, ed. Nina Kumar (Calcutta: Stree, 1994); Rita Ganguli (-Ganguly), "Bai Theke Begum [From courtesan to wife]," *Desh* 63/64 (1996): 73–93; Amelia Maciszewski, "Stories about Selves: Selected North Indian Women's Musical Biographies," *The World of Music* 43 (2001): 139–72; and eadem, below, chap. 18.

4. Regula Burckhardt Qureshi, "In Search of Begum Akhtar: Patriarchy, Poetry, and Twentieth-Century Indian Music," *The World of Music* 43 (2001): 97–137.

5. Siddeshwari Devi taught at the National Arts Academy (Bharatiya Kala Kendra), Savita Devi at Delhi University. Both were exceptional appointments for courtesan singers, speaking to their artistic eminence.

6. Regula Burckhardt Qureshi, "Confronting the Social: Mode of Production and the Sublime in (Indian) Art Music," *Ethnomusicology* 44 (2000): 15–38; and eadem, "Mode of Production and Musical Production: Is Hindustani Music Feudal?" in *Music and Marx: Ideas, Practice, Politics*, ed. Regula Burckhardt Qureshi (New York: Routledge, 2002), 81–105.

7. Christopher Alan Bayly, *Rulers, Townsmen, and Bazaars: North Indian Society in the Age of British Expansion, 1770–1870* (Cambridge: Cambridge University Press, 1983).

8. See Gayle Rubin, "The Traffic in Women: Notes on the 'Political Economy' of Sex," in *Toward an Anthropology of Women*, ed. Rayna Reiter (New York: Monthly Review Press, 1975), 157–210; repr. in *Women and Revolution: A Discussion of the Unhappy Marriage of Marxism and Feminism*, ed. Heidi Hartmann and Lydia Sargent (London: Pluto Press, 1981); and Sumita Chakravarty, *Nationalism and Identity in Indian Popular Cinema, 1947–1987* (Austin: University of Texas Press, 1993).

9. Oldenburg, "Lifestyle as Resistance."

10. The so-called *ta'alluqdar* system inspired by its British counterpart. Princely states were under indirect British rule and internally autonomous.

11. Vivid oral accounts exist of Lord Butler supporting and presiding over annual song recitals by courtesan singers (Abdul Qavi Zia, pers. comm., 1992).

12. Susheela Misra, *Music Makers of Bhatkhande College* (Calcutta: Sangeet Research Academy, 1985).

13. In still-feudal regions of Pakistan such private patronage continues to this day, although urban salons have been curtailed even in that country as well.

14. This representation is of colonial provenance.

15. Abu al-Fazl ibn Mubarak, *The A'in-I Akbari*, trans. H. Blochmann, ed. S. L. Goomer, 2d ed. (Delhi: Aadiesh Book Depot, 1965).

16. Written in Persian in 1790 but extant only as *Nishtar: Naval* in a nineteenth-century Urdu translation by Anjum Kasmandvi (Lahore: Majlis-e-Taraqqi-e-Adab, 1973), Hasan Shah's valuable source has been translated into English by writer Qurratulain Hyder, changing the title from *Nishtar* (= *nashtar*, "the surgeon's knife") to *The Nautch Girl: A Novel* (New Delhi: Sterling Paperbacks, 1992).

17. The term is a plural derivative of the Farsi (Arabic) *ta'if* of no earlier than eighteenth-century provenance.

18. See Hasan Shah, *Nishtar*; and idem, *The Nautch Girl*, trans. Hyder.

19. Abdul Halim Sharar, *Lucknow: The Last Phase of an Oriental Culture*, trans. and ed. E. S. Harcourt and Fakhir Hussain (London: Paul Elek, 1975).

20. Hasan Shah, *The Nautch Girl*.

21. Unfortunately, my pre-nineteenth-century sources do not contain such information.

22. When Abdul Karim Khan subsequently eloped with his pupil, the noble tried in vain to have her brought back "home." She eventually established a school in Bombay.

23. Jayantilal S. Jariwalla, *Abdul Karim: The Man of the Times* (Bombay: Popular Book Depot, 1973).

24. Qureshi, "In Search of Begum Akhtar."

25. Dargah Quli Khan, *Purani Dehli ke Halat* [An account of Old Delhi; original Farsi manuscript in Urdu], trans. Khwaja Hasan Nizami (Delhi: Mahbub Press, 1949).

26. Mirza Hadi Ruswa, *Umrao Jan Ada* [The Courtesan of Lucknow], trans. Khushwant Singh and M. A. Husaini (Bombay: Orient Longmans, 1961).

27. Qureshi, "In Search of Begum Akhtar."

28. See Fanny Parkes Parlby, *Wandering of a Pilgrim in Search of the Picturesque, During Four-and-Twenty Years in the East* (London: P. Richardson, 1850); and Mrs. Belnos, *Twenty-four Plates Illustrative of Hindoo and European Manners in Bengal* (London: Smith and Elder, 1832).

29. See Oldenburg, "Lifestyle as Resistance"; Ruswa, *Umrao Jan Ada*; and Shah, *Nishtar*, trans. Kasmandvi.

30. Bayly, *Rulers, Townsmen, and Bazaars*.

31. Mrs. Marcus B. Fuller, *The Wrongs of Indian Womanhood* (Edinburgh: Anderson and Ferrier, 1900).

32. Pran Nevile, *Nautch Girls of India: Dancers, Singers, Playmates* (New Delhi: Ravi Kumar, 1996).

33. David Lalyveld, "Upon the Subdominant: Administering Music on All India Radio," unpublished paper, 1998.

34. Pierre Bourdieu's concept of fields of cultural production is useful for this major shift within the realm of production and productive relations. See his *The Field of Cultural Production*, ed. Randal Johnson (New York: Columbia University Press, 1993).

35. Jennifer Post, "Professional Women in Indian Music: The Death of the Courtesan Tradition," in *Women and Music in Cross-Cultural Perspective*, ed. Ellen Koskoff (New York: Greenwood, 1992), 97–109, at 104.

36. See Hasan Shah, *Nishtar*; idem, *The Nautch Girl*, trans. Hyder; Khan, *Purani Dehli ke Halat*; Sharar, *Lucknow: The Last Phase*; Mirza Jaffar Quadim Husain, *Lukhnau ki Akhri Bahar* (New Delhi: Taraqqi-yi Urdu Biyuro, 1981); and Ruswa, *Umrao Jan Ada*.

37. See Jennifer [Post] Quinn, "Marathi and Konkani Speaking Women in Hindustani Music, 1880–1940" (Ph.D. diss., University of Minnesota, 1982); eadem, "Professional Women"; Joep Bor, "The Voice of the Sarangi: An Illustrated History of Bowing in India," *National Centre for the Performing Arts Quarterly Journal* 15, nos. 3 and 5, and 16, no. 1 (1986–87): 9–183 (inclusive); and Nevile, *Nautch Girls*.

38. See Amrit Srinivasan, *Reform or Conformity? Temple "Prostitution" and the Community in the Madras Presidency* (New Delhi: Kali for Women Houdou, 1988); Oldenburg, "Lifestyle as Resistance"; and Maciszewski, below, chap. 18.

39. *Women Music Makers of India Seminar* (New Delhi: Bharatya Kala Kendra, 1984).

40. The Seminar was organized by Rita Ganguly, herself a student of Begum Akhtar and Siddeshwari Devi, the senior hereditary singer from Benares who also taught at the sponsoring academy of the event, Bharatiya Kala Kendra.

41. See Ruswa, *Umrao Jan Ada*; Shah, *Nishtar*, trans. Kasmandvi; and idem, *The Nautch Girl*. *Pakeeza* (1971) was directed by Kamal Amrohvi, and *Zindagi Ya Toofan* (1956?) by A. K. Abbas.

42. Ganguli, "Bai Theke Begum"; Oldenburg, "Lifestyle as Resistance"; Carol Babiracki, "What's the Difference? Reflection on Gender and Research in Village India," in *Shadows in the Field: New Perspectives for Fieldwork in Ethnomusicology*, ed. Gregory F. Barz and Timothy J. Cooley (New York: Oxford University Press, 1997), 121–36; and Maciszewski, below, chap. 18.

43. E.g., Rao, "Thumri and Thumri Singers."

44. *Gangubai Hangal*, ed. S. L. Bhyrappa and Ashok Ranada (Hubli: Academy of Performing Arts, 1988).

45. See Shah, *The Nautch Girl*; Ruswa, *Umrao Jan Ada*; and Vikram Seth, *A Suitable Boy* (London: Phoenix House, 1993).

46. Regula Burckhardt Qureshi, "How Does Music Mean? Embodied Memories and the Politics of Affect in the Indian Sarangi," *American Ethnologist* 27 (2000): 805–38.

47. Ansari in Qureshi, "How Does Music Mean?"

48. Umar Ansari (pers. comm., 1992). Sufis also use this concept to explain *sama'* (listening to music for spiritual purposes); see my *Sufi Music of India and Pakistan: Sound, Context, and Meaning in Qawwali* (Chicago: University of Chicago Press, 1995), first published in 1987 by Cambridge University Press. See also Amin Nun, "Ruh ki Ghiza," in *Bazgasht (Sarguzisht)* (Karachi: published by author, 1991).

49. This is well exemplified by a painting depicting Raja Balwant Singh of Jammu and Musicians (dated 1748; Victoria and Albert Museum, IS 24–1974).

50. Jariwalla, *Abdul Karim*.

51. Significantly, even post-feudal concert audiences continue to be called patrons.

52. The notion of payment as a gift for musicians rather than payment for music—either of which could take the form of cash—survives among traditional hereditary musicians up to

the present day, as manifest in the offering practices still taught to disciples within the community. See Qureshi, "Mode of Production," 98–99, and Lowell Lybarger, "The Tabla Solo Repertoire of Pakistani Panjab: An Ethnomusicological Perspective" (Ph.D. diss., University of Toronto, 2003).

53. Pierre Bourdieu, *Distinction: A Social Critique of the Judgement of Taste*, trans. Richard Nice (Cambridge, MA: Harvard University Press, 1984).

54. This process of musical production continues to operate among some hereditary musicians today, though in greatly reduced numbers.

55. A role that is familiar from ancient Greece to feudal Japan and Europe.

56. Fuller, *The Wrongs of Indian Womanhood*; and Oldenburg, "Lifestyle as Resistance."

57. I gratefully acknowledge the artist's generosity in sharing her art with me and offer my sincere thanks to Mr. Khaliq Ahmad for making this recording possible.

58. Of course, ignoring gender is itself a gesture of patriarchy.

Tawa'if, Tourism, and Tales

The Problematics of Twenty-First-Century Musical Patronage for North India's Courtesans

INTRODUCTION: TAWA'IF (COURTESANS) AND THEIR NEW PATRONS

The stage in the prestigious Shri Ram Centre of Art and Culture in New Delhi was sparsely decorated. At the backdrop hung a banner with colorful Hindi script announcing the sponsor organization, Guria Sansthan, and the event, Guria Mahotsav. Beside this was Guria's logo, a sketch of a doll's head with the word "Guria" emblazoned across it and a rooftop above. At the top of the banner beckoned the words "Come, let us unite for tawaif-s [women in prostitution/ courtesans] and their children." Below it stood a mantle lined with "Guria"-emblazoned doll's head trophies, which looked as though they were bobbing in a breeze.

The emcee introduced Bombay filmmakers Mahesh Bhatt and Tanuja Chandra, the festival's guests of honor, each of whom spoke briefly. Meanwhile singers Aruna Devi and her daughter Chandni, surrounded by their accompanists (tabla, harmonium, and sarangi players), sat quietly on their performance space on the floor, ready to begin. The emcee then announced that ten-year-old Chandni from Benares would begin with a ghazal composed by the respected Urdu poet Faiz Ahmed Faiz. With her ghazal (companion website, track 16), Chandni set the mood of the festival: the irony of survival in the courtesan community.

. . . In this way my silence echoes,
Crying as if an answer were coming from each direction.
Duty is the right path to my final destination.
Wherever I arrive, may I find success . . .

The couplet Chandni sang with the grace and feeling of someone much older seemed to speak of "the pain of longing and . . . the silence of isolation . . . in the kothas [courtesans' salons]"[2]—not unlike the atmosphere where she was growing up. Yet, she and others in her community remain dedicated to their means of survival, which many of them consider their duty.

This essay has emerged from fieldwork I conducted in April–May 2001 and January–February 2003 in Delhi, Calcutta, Muzaffarpur (Bihar), Benares, and Jaunpur (Uttar Pradesh); in Muzaffarpur in collaboration with my research associate Arup Sen Gupta in October 2001; and throughout from my ongoing communication with Ajeet Singh, Guria's founder and president. In it, I examine how a group of North India's tawa'if (courtesans—low-status professional women musicians and dancers) are adapting to changing musical patronage in the twenty-first century, using their music and dance as a tool for empowerment. Juxtaposing ethnographic accounts with qualitative analysis of performance practices and oral narratives of several professional women musicians and a few men who hail from provincial cities and towns in eastern Uttar Pradesh and western Bihar, I open up exploration of a number of issues.

During the past several years an important presence in the lives of these women has been the NGO Guria Sewi Sansthan ("doll help/service collective," hereafter Guria), dedicated to the upliftment not only of members of various clans and castes of tawa'if but also of prostitutes, as an initiative for profound social change.[3] Guria embodies above all a dialectic about courtesans and prostitutes between its mainstream advocates, represented by the organization's director, grassroots social activist Singh, and its members, who belong to the tawa'if community. Guria is also a revivalist force. Its members work together to preserve the regional performance traditions of tawa'if through "festivalization" on a national level, whereby the organization presents its socially denigrated member-performers and their devalued performance traditions on the public stage in mainstream venues. In doing so, the initiative strives to override the stigma attached to its members' profession and performance repertory by using performance to recontextualize and thus reaffirm their artistic identity. Guria Festivals as cultural shows, and their participants—represented to the public homogenously as "WIP" (Women in Prostitution)—are configured in an antihierarchical manner that opposes vertical differentiations.[4] Nevertheless, questions remain about who controls particular aspects of the means of production that provide the public space in which tawa'if are challenging stereotypical negative images of themselves and their art—something that raises questions in turn about Guria's conflation of tawa'if with sex workers.

Courtesans in India bear a legacy of valuable musical and cultural contributions, as well as aesthetic and social privilege. In postcolonial, post-feudal North India the music and dance in which courtesans traditionally specialized remains vibrant, but has been taken over by non-hereditary musicians and performed on the concert stage. The courtesan tradition is thus in danger of dying, its bearers facing severe social marginalization. Except for the outstanding few who have been accepted as mainstream artists, tawa'if lead a precarious existence, living in poverty- and crime-ridden red-light districts where the present-day clientele is more interested in sex than songs, and the songs "patrons" wish to hear often have little, if anything, to do with the rich traditions these women embody.

Still, there is a flicker of hope among members of the Guria "family," as represented in the narratives and performances recounted in these pages. Through their music, talk about music, and talk about themselves, tawa'if play the role of organic intellectuals,[5] providing a meta-commentary to and about their extended community, and proposing, in the genre of oral literacy criticism, certain challenges to the order of things.[6]

LOCATING THE TAWA'IF

Professional women musicians from low-status hereditary communities in North India and Pakistan, generally called baijis or tawa'ifs,[7] differ from devadasis in South India in their performance context, intent, and patronage. While the performance context of devadasis was religious (e.g., the Hindu temple or associated place of religious worship) and their patrons were those members of the community who supported the temple to which they were attached, baijis and tawa'ifs traditionally performed in secular contexts and were patronized by royalty, feudal aristocracy, and the late nineteenth- and early twentieth-century bourgeoisie. Those who were born before India's independence (1947) were able to undergo intensive training in classical and light-classical music and dance under highly knowledgeable male teachers. They devoted themselves to the rigorous practice of their art and, later, to its performance before knowledgeable, mostly male listeners from whom they received patronage (not excluding romantic liaisons with one or more of them).[8] Many women of the post-independence generation(s), however, have (or have had) little or no access to the training and opportunities necessary to pursue and succeed in a "mainstream" musical career. Rather, they struggle to make a living with their performance in their respective localities, frequently supplementing this income with sex work. This survival strategy, ironically, only serves to reaffirm their negative status.

Even though the diffuse community of courtesans is highly stratified with respect to the type of performance executed by members of each subgroup and the degree of their sexual availability, the subgroups frequently coexist in adjacent quarters and sometimes even intermarry. Members of the greater community acknowledge solidarity among themselves as one extended *biradri*, or occupational brother/sisterhood.[9]

The English word "courtesan" fails to capture the diversity of this community in South Asia, which runs the gamut from highly trained and refined court musicians/dancers/poets to street performers who entertain at festivals and weddings, instead creating a discursive stereotyping or "totalizing."[10] Furthermore, the British colonialists' lack of understanding of this simultaneous diversity and solidarity, and their frequent insensitivity to these women's performance traditions, led them to impose the Victorian label "prostitute" on female members of the community (and, whenever possible, to interact with them in this way). The majority of mainstream post-colonial Indians have adopted the term "prostitute" along with the judgmental attitude it indexes to refer to courtesans of all types. Several have tried to prove the point that these women are indeed prostitutes by interpreting ancient texts that elaborate on how these women are bearers of culture yet morally suspect because they do not fit neatly into the South Asian patriarchal system as economically dependent and monogamous wives.[11]

One of the aims of this essay is to unpack the terms "courtesan" and "prostitute" and notions about them through an ethnography of the performance process and event as well as narratives about (and by) the performance, the performers, and the patrons. Another is to examine the relations of production among the performers and the Guria administration, in particular Ajeet Singh. In doing so, I open up the question, albeit in a preliminary way, of how the cultural integrity of the courtesan tradition,[12] identified through its continued cultivation and renewal of a body of repertory and performance practices consisting of a variety of genres that originate from several historical points (feudal, colonial, post-feudal, and postcolonial), may be challenged in the Guria frame by expectations of authenticity and/or respectability informed by dominant Indian middle-class values.[13] This study is a tale of tawa'if, cultural tourism, and postcolonial and postmodern *taluqdars* (patrons).

Muzaffarpur, Bihar, is a provincial market town with a large courtesan quarter and red-light district known as Chaturbhujastan, which continues to be fully opera-tive and contains the remnants of the once lively tawa'if culture. In one household three generations of women musicians—Chandni, her mother Aruna Devi, and Aruna's mother Kali Dasi—all lived together until Kali Dasi died in January 2003, leaving behind her daughter and granddaughter. Aruna and Chandni maintain their identity as tawa'if who are relatively high on the socio-musical ladder of their com-munity and acknowledge themselves as members of Guria. They were the first to enlighten me about the existence of this organization during my visit to their home in February 2000, leading to the present exploration of what difference Guria is mak-ing in such women's lives.

Aruna (aged forty-something) and the teenaged Chandni, accomplished singers, share their house near the main crossroads of the quarter with numerous other family members. Kali Dasi, who virtually ran the household until shortly before her death at about age eighty, practiced a classical, semi-classical, and traditional regional reper-tory and elegant performance style that evoked the late feudal patronage she had en-joyed during her career.[14] Aruna Devi is a sought-after professional singer of popular ghazal, devotional songs, and regional songs in the Bhojpuri language, and charming, precocious Chandni frequently accompanies her in performance.

Aruna, who demonstrated increasingly versatile musicianship and dignified en-trepreneurial sense each time we met, pointed to several doll's-head-shaped trophies inscribed with the word "Guria" on the mantle across the room (see fig. 18.1, show-ing Chandni and Aruna with director Singh seen partially in the foreground). This organization, she said, presents music festivals in various big cities in which they pay tawa'ifs quite well to perform on a concert stage with dignity (*izzat se*). Chandni had also performed at these festivals with her mother. In this way, Aruna went on, the organization is trying to keep the musical traditions of tawa'if alive, so that they don't have to do "dirty work" (*galat kam*).[15] This new information, which I learned from tawa'if themselves, was remarkable in that it was the catalyst for revitalizing a women's performance tradition that had nearly fallen into oblivion. The catalyst "link" is complicated, however, in being achieved within a new, quasi-paternalistic relationship—in this case, between tawa'if and festival organizers—that is, simulta-neously empowering yet reminiscent of the feudal one between benevolent patron and dedicated service professional.[16]

FIGURE 18.1. Vocalists Chandni Devi and her mother Aruna looking at
Guria director Ajeet Singh in Muzaffarpur.

SURVIVAL AND THE STAGE

How are Guria's women musician members using the NGO space—the Guria
"family"—to construct, reaffirm, and reinvent their identities as historical beings
and artists? What are the social relations and relations of production that obtain in
their mobilizing social change and negotiating their positions in a rapidly transforming provincial milieu that is increasingly bombarded by the media and the marketplace with images of globalization? Where is their performance situated in this? An
examination of how individuals have predicated issues of identity (which necessarily include social marginalization) in their narratives and enacted them through
song lyrics, genres performed, and self-presentation on stage can yield insights into
their adaptive strategies and their meta-commentaries on these strategies. Through
their musical practice, which includes social relations, these women both create and
articulate a discourse about how they are negotiating their survival as they cross
socio-musical borders, moving between the *mujra* (the salon performance, where an
intrinsic part of their artistic appeal consists of catering to the male gaze) and the
socially "respectable" music festival, markers of the marginal and the mainstream.
Despite their socio-musical liminality, they embody and project a certain cultural
"authenticity" by virtue of their identity as tawa'if.[17]

Through the vital identity markers of live performer (tawa'if), text, and musical sound, "authenticity" is indexed to audience members at the same time as it is
recontextualized, reaffirmed, and sanitized in the festival frame.[18] The celebratory,
respectable concert stage provided by the Guria collective allows the performer to
use the tactility of her performative "self"—her voice and body—to manipulate
both individual emotions and social situations. This process is both dialogical and

mimetic, involving the citation, presentation, and reception of artistic, gendered, socially stigmatized selves. At once cathartic and cryptic, the staged process embodies
an ongoing tension between that which is revealed and that which is concealed,[19] not
unlike the songs these women sing. This process is also contingent on, and indicative
of, asymmetrical relationships of production into which the women enter with the
sponsors and consumers of the festivals.

On a pragmatic level, these professional women musicians are small-time entrepreneurs, often operating female-centered family businesses at the margins of
society—not unlike hereditary artisans. Through their craft of music and dance and
their social behavioral relationships, they provide sensual pleasures, but also (again)
provide a meta-commentary on their identity and condition, as well as on gender
relations in South Asia all told. They do so in terms meaningful and financially
profitable to themselves and attractively resonant to their audiences, patrons, and
clients. The narratives and vignettes in these pages provide glimpses of how several
tawa'if are mobilizing the Guria festivals as new working contexts for disseminating
this layered meta-commentary to the mainstream. Their stories tell of survival in
which much has been lost, yet something remains to be gained.

*Enthusiastic applause arose from the audience in the nearly full hall. There were
male and female students and novice journalists; middle-aged, middle-class men;
and families of various social classes, some wearing distinctly rural-style clothing.
A few women in the back of the hall were dressed and made up for their upcoming
stage performance.*

*Chandni followed her opening ghazal with a folk song, typical of her native
region in the North Indian states of Bihar and Uttar Pradesh. Its simple lyrics
evoked the spring month of Phagu, a time when rural men often traveled away in
search of work, leaving their women and children at home. The voice in the song is
that of a young girl dreading separation from her soon-to-be-absent lover, wondering whether to wait for him or go on with her life (which may mean accepting
another suitor)—a common theme in texts inspired by bhakti (popular devotional)
discourse.*

How will the days pass?
Tell me the solution.
Today I found
The passing of Phagun in his face . . .
On this bank is the Ganges, on the other is the Jamuna.
I'm caught in the middle—don't make me choose . . .

Musically gifted, adolescent Chandni, growing up in a lineage of courtesan singers, may be at a similar crossroads (metaphorically represented by the facing banks
of the rivers Ganges and Jamuna), soon to choose among the career of a singer, an
arranged marriage, or the pursuit of a mainstream education.

*Chandni's mother Aruna then followed with two songs, each beginning with a brief
alap, or free rhythmic/melodic introduction. First she sang a magadhi in the style*

*of a light-classical "dadra" song, then followed with a folk song of her region.
In the magadhi (companion website, track 17), she boldly and evocatively sang
bhakti-derived lyrics depicting a woman's surrender to her paramour, poeticized
as the Lord Krishna. The song's melody clearly corresponded to the Hindustani
raga Pilu, whose constant shifts between major and minor intervals are sonic
icons of coy restlessness. The somewhat rhythmically sparse tabla accompaniment also reflected a light-classical aesthetic. Aruna elaborated the song with
light-classical bol banao, or melismatic stretching of syllables of key words in the
text to enhance their emotional impact. In the second song, her tight-throated
voice was flirtatious in tone, as she playfully chided her man who had returned
from afar about the quality of gifts he had brought her.*

With her choice of repertory (a light-classical and folk song), dignified performance demeanor and appearance (a simple white sari draped modestly around her
shoulders, simple jewelry, and the red vermillion powder worn by married Hindu
women adorning the part in her hair),[20] Aruna sought to draw attention to her vocal
virtuosity rather than her body. Her intention of projecting an image of "respectability"
and artistic expertise indicated her understanding of the appropriate self-presentation
on the Guria festival stage, as well as her own position within the socio-musical hierarchy of her community. On the other hand, she used her regional identity to connect
with the audience by exploiting with ease and immediacy tropes of rural nostalgia (and
playfulness) in her distinct "folk" treatment of the Bhojpuri song.

A gradual shift in patronage of Hindustani music has occurred in the past century—from semi-private courtly patronage by feudal lords, to similar patronage by
wealthy bourgeoisie, and finally to patronage by government institutions and a largely
middle-class public. This "democratization of patronage" supports the performance of
Hindustani music and dance in the public concert hall, mostly in urban centers. Paradoxically, public performance on the concert stage by "respectable" women has now
become socially sanctioned, while women from courtesan backgrounds have become
vilified by the mainstream public with the exception of a few outstanding performers
who have mostly laundered their images. The courtesan has thus lost her court—the
(quasi) feudal, if exploitative, patronage that once supported her art no longer exists.[21]
Lack of patronage and social ostracism have forced most tawa'if to the margins, where
their entanglement in a complex web of poverty and crime generally prevents them
from gaining access to, or even seeking, non-exploitative contacts or performance
opportunities.

Additionally, although both the recording and film industries—points of access to
upward socio-musical mobility—have the potential to constitute a new kind of "court,"
many women from courtesan communities in provincial cities and towns, isolated and
marginalized, simply have not had access to these alternatives. Finally, recorded music
disseminated by a grass-roots cassette industry, as well as initiatives to prohibit the
hiring of "dancing girls" at weddings and other events, are challenging the demand for
these women's live performance at social functions with increasing frequency. In this
scenario, a performer's talent becomes less relevant than her survival, which requires
resourcefulness, creativity, and resilience, very often in the face of severe exploitation.

Although the conflation of courtesans with prostitutes is problematic, Guria President Ajeet Singh's field research has revealed chilling facts about the predicament of women who were traditionally courtesans that support this conflation. Most of the eastern districts of India's northern states of Uttar Pradesh (U.P.), Madhya Pradesh (M.P.), and Bihar have numerous large red-light areas in which various castes and clans of low-status hereditary professional performers, such as Gandharvas, Deredars, Bedias, Nats, Kanjars, and Mirasis, reside. A considerable number of women from among these communities routinely practice prostitution nowadays, although historically many were professional specialists in vocal music and dance. From the eighteenth to the mid-nineteenth centuries they were patronized by provincial royalty, and from the mid-nineteenth through the first half of the twentieth century by landed gentry—*taluqdars* and *zamindars*—who controlled the local surplus economy. Today, female artists residing in almost all the red-light areas of U.P., Bihar, and M.P. make up between 10 percent and 60 percent of the population.[22] While for courtesan performers of earlier generations, sexual relations with one (or an exclusive few) of their patrons were somewhat incidental to their primary relationship with art, the opposite is very frequently the case today.[23]

VENUES AND EXPECTATIONS

Guria members and volunteers, under the leadership of Ajeet Singh, have organized Mahotsavs (Music Festivals) at elite venues in several cities in northern India: one time each at Murari Lal Mehta Auditorium in Varanasi (Benares), Nagari Natak Mandali in Kabir Chaura, Varanasi, and Bharat Bhavan in Bhopal; and four times at Shri Ram Centre for Art and Culture in the cultural-and-arts district of New Delhi. Singh's rationale behind choosing high-status, nationally known venues for the Mahotsavs is revival and upliftment (endorsed by the development agencies whose funding has supported the endeavor): to give national exposure and prestige to the festivals and their performers in order to attract a "respectable" audience. Moving the festival venue to Shri Ram Centre was a major breakthrough for Guria, creating for the audience and media an image of the festival that was distinct from that of a "prostitutes' dance." Accessing these venues is straightforward: Guria rents them with funds budgeted for production expenses, similar to what is done by any other presenter.[24]

By means of this "festivalization" process, Guria the collective is seeking to undermine the distinction between high and low culture, presenting socially denigrated performers and their devalued performance traditions in mainstream venues. The growing audience for these festivals includes intellectuals, members of the media and arts communities, and social activists of both genders, alongside middle- and lower-middle-class men who are either ex-kotha-goers or would-be salon-goers who prefer the safety, anonymity, and free entrance at the festivals. Thus, Singh is strategically deploying (and challenging) the pervasive discourse of "globalization and liberalization" to enable the performers' positioning "in the right slot" of patronage.[25] That is, the Guria Festivals as cultural shows have begun to attract the attention of the media, a diverse audience, as well as both national and international funding agencies. Guria's intent is to continue to secure and expand a new, postcolonial patronage for an endangered performance tradition that is historically and aesthetically rich. Significantly, Singh controls this aspect of the means of production, facilitating access to the public space where tawa'if are challenging stereotypical negative images of themselves and their art.[26]

MUSIC, SEX, AND SURVIVAL: ISSUES OF VOICE

At the press conference before the 8th Guria Mahotsav on April 14, 2001, in a seminar room off the auditorium at Shri Ram Centre, the themes projected by Singh and the festival's guests of honor, Bombay filmmakers Mahesh Bhatt and Tanuja Chandra, were hope, survival, and choice. Here, some fifty journalists interrogated Singh's and Guria's objectives and goals, but were most interested in Singh's, Bhatt's, and Chandra's positions regarding the profession of prostitution and its role in society. After a discussion lasting some forty-five minutes in which the three denounced moralizing and supported increased awareness, Bhatt summed up the conference with his endorsement of Singh's and Guria's mandate: to provide these women with a choice so that they are not forced to do sex work for survival.

Typical of the asymmetrical power relations inherent in such a gathering, none of the performers was present at the press conference, nor did any of the journalists seem concerned about interacting directly with the women performers, their families, and their accompanists. The talk was entirely about them and about the issue of prostitution and was directed to privileged members of society, not to the persons the discussion was supposed to affect, as if the women were fetishes in a moral debate. The key participants (performers, their families, and their accompanists) huddled in rather dirty, scantily furnished dressing rooms just outside the auditorium, eating and chatting, hurriedly rehearsing, applying final touches to their costumes, hair, and makeup, or playing cards to pass the time before going on stage.

THE FESTIVAL

> *Sixteen-year-old Meena Tabassum followed Chandni's and Aruna's performances by singing qawwali, her speciality. Accompanied by men playing harmonium, tabla, nal (small barrel drum), and the zither "benjo," she alternated in a shrill, sometimes slightly off-key voice between singing qawwali verses and reciting witty, ironic couplets in a heightened speech rhythmically punctuated with little shouts, illustrating her lyrics with hand gestures. Often she rested her hand on the harmonium beside her, signifying her tawa'if identity: metaphorically "holding court" over both her accompanists and her audience.*

The couplet in her first qawwali conflated patriotism and respect for the simultaneous strength and vulnerability of women, presumably those members of the communities Guria serves—a take from off-center on the notion of the Indian Woman as a symbol of national identity.[27] She challenged the power of the elite, taunting and exhorting them to beware of the supposed power of their actions, which is both transparent and fragile, like glass.

If you make a house of glass,
Beware that your reputation isn't ruined.

Having voiced a warning, her tone softened. Unlike the brittle inflexibility of the privileged, the female Guria member (and her social peers) is malleable, vulnerable, and breakable, like clay. Thus she is capable of surrendering, whether to the beloved, the divine, or to political ideology.

I am in your hands,
I am a doll of clay.
Those who give their blood for the earth of their country,
For them there is a bed of flowers in heaven.

Sensual reward in heaven is offered to those who are willing to risk their heart, money, and reputation for the doll of clay. The doll of clay relates in a loosely metaphoric way to the homeland, sacrifice for which will bring rewards.

The eyes of cowards cannot scare me;
I know well how to compete with a storm . . .

Cowards represent the oppressors, the storm the exploitative social nexus against which a woman like herself is now empowered to fight and survive.

Her next song, a popular qawwali, elegantly articulated one of Guria's mottos: hope and adaptation in spite of struggle. It also warned the self-satisfied privileged to change their attitude toward and treatment of the disenfranchised. Finally, it strongly suggested that exploitation is almost unavoidable in an intimate relationship between a socially marginalized woman and someone from the mainstream—an oral, literary articulation of social criticism from inside the community (as referred to above).

To keep the air fresh
You have to leave a certain path
Even if you close the door.
Keep the window open
To absorb suffering
Is the first rule of love. . . .
Between beauty and love
There is a wall of gold and silver.
If the direction you're looking is a crime
Stop looking in that direction . . .

Following several other performers, Zeenat Jahan, a middle-aged qawwali singer (referred to metonymically as a "qawwala") from Muzaffarpur, came on stage with her ensemble, which consisted of a harmonium, two nals, and a benjo. Zeenat began with a brief alap in a melody related to the Hindustani raga Shivaranjani (which also shifts between a major and minor third, giving its "unsettled" feeling). Her powerful, husky voice was rich and lyrical, although initially a bit ragged in the high pitches. Her facial expressions were relaxed, and her assertive gestures embodied the ecstatic mood and identity of qawwali and qawwali singers: arms stretched straight forward or upwards, with palms upturned, or one hand in a loose fist with the index finger pointing upwards,[28] again often resting her hand on the harmonium beside her in a show of "holding court."

Zeenat opened with a popular selection that tells of the wandering, ephemeral lifestyle of a Sufi in search of divine truth (and strongly suggests the often insecure, peripatetic life of a tawa'if in search of patronage).

*I've come to your city
As a wanderer.
To meet you, just once,
give me a chance.
Where is my destination?
Where is my address?
By morning you have to leave me
And go somewhere
To think about this.
For one night give me a chance.*

She emphasized the line "Give me a chance" by repeating it several times during the performance, as if making an appeal to the audience and organizers of the festival, a kind of stylized expression of hope.

Zeenat's skill and senior status as a qawwala were evident in several ways: she controlled the tempo and dynamics of the ensemble; the harmonium player did not interrupt her at any time; and there were no catcalls from the audience, only excited applause and *vah vahs* acknowledging the meaningfulness of both the lyrics and her presentation of them. When she and her ensemble broke into the couplet that comprised the "punch line" of her second song, below, they repeated it numerous times with slight variations, subtly increasing the speed and volume in a manner that created a high level of intensity, visibly exciting the audience—the objective of a qawwali performance.[29] The couplet offered both a piece of advice and a challenge to take the leap of mutual trust, a notion that resonates with the mission of Guria.

*If you have faith in me, I will have faith in you.
If you are unjust, then I will be unjust.*

In sum, apart from a few folk dances from western and southern regions and Aruna's magadhi, genres performed by the women were three: ghazal, qawwali, and Bhojpuri folk. Except for Zeenat, who is an Urdu speaker, and some folk dancers from South India, the performers were all native speakers of the Bhojpuri dialect of Hindi spoken in eastern Uttar Pradesh and western Bihar states. For the clientele, many of whom are also Bhojpuri speakers who understand Urdu-influenced Hindi (or Hindustani) in popular qawwali and ghazal texts, ghazal signifies "high culture"; qawwali expresses ecstatic devotion and/or social commentary; and Bhojpuri songs feed nostalgia about regional rural culture. Chandni's and Aruna's performances stood out in terms of their levels of skill and expressive refinement. The text of the ghazal sung by Chandni was composed by a historically esteemed poet, and her presentation of it was consistent with the dignified milieu it signified. Aruna's restrained, somewhat virtuosic performance of a magadhi in dadra style evoked the devotional/romantic mood of light-classical music; the quiet playfulness of her Bhojpuri contrasted with the more overt coquettishness of regional songs performed by the other artists. Zeenat's performances on both days stood out in terms of her skill and powerful presentation.[30]

The singers perform these items of repertory in various contexts, from the Guria festival to small-town weddings and other rural functions to salon performances. Singh, along with several seasoned participants such as Aruna, seeks out performers for festivals and informally "auditions" them to check their competence and the appropriateness of their repertory and presentation for the purposes of the festival. Hindi film songs[31] or songs whose lyrics are vulgar are not allowed; the women's gestures are monitored to make sure they are not too seductive. (In Singh's words, they are not on stage to seduce anyone.)

Another indication of these women's "traditional" backgrounds is their identifying in interviews direct female relatives who have professionally performed any of the above-mentioned genres and/or semi-classical ones,[32] and thus identifying individually with a particular musicians' caste (Gandharva, Mirasi, etc.).[33] Nevertheless, male members of the audience often respond to them viscerally, viewing the performance as a spectacle for the male gaze, if one recontexualized in a manner intended to celebrate the performer's authenticity as an artist and hence her worthiness of respect.

Thus, in addition to the pragmatic considerations behind the women's choice of repertory, it is important to look at the performances (and narratives) as a kind of "oral literary criticism."[34] Some of the women sang songs with lyrics that suggest that even among members of this collective, individuals have unequal access to material and symbolic resources (in this case, musical and literary material and training). Although diverse points of view exist, at least some performers are bound together in their conscious attempt to give voice, individually and collectively, to a disenfranchised group. The self-affirmation, expression of irony, and (in some cases) challenge conveyed by the women's narratives and performances all suggest that some may be using song toward a subtle poetics of subversion,[35] as evidence in the next section shows.

IDENTITY, VOICE, AND CHANGE

Among members of the broadly diffuse courtesan community the tawa'if have their own perceptions of their identity, caste, and sub-caste distinctions, and recognize problems in Guria's portraying the women participants in the festival as "Women in Prostitution." Several recurring themes and words emerged: *peshavali*, literally "professional women," a term used colloquially to refer to women whose primary work is sex, versus *gane-bajane vale*, female singers who are courtesans; *izzat*, or respect; *galat kam*, or wrongdoing (which includes dishonorable work, i.e., sex work); and *majboori*—necessity or extenuating circumstances, carrying with it a feminist notion of contingencies. These themes and their apparent allusion to some sort of grassroots poetics of resistance, or oral literary criticism, are addressed in the account and narratives below.

In Muzaffarpur, Aruna's younger sister Baby (a non-musician but active, informed listener), their mother the late Kali Dasi, and Sajan Bharati, regular accompanist at the festivals and son of another elder tawa'if, Daya Kumari, assembled to discuss the most recent festival. It was marriage season, and Aruna was away, performing at weddings in neighboring towns. Aruna and family not only feel positive about the Guria festivals and proud to be a part of them, but they also identify themselves as authorities with a socio-musical status superior to many other members—and are perceived by others as such.[36] For Sajan, who accompanies many vocalists on benjo, the Guria festivals constitute a step in socio-musical upward mobility that takes him away from modest engagements at small-town weddings and social events to the perceived glamour of urban concert halls. He was not concerned about the homogenization of sex workers with tawa'if because he felt that the opportunities Guria provides to aspire toward the "limelight" outweigh the disadvantages.

In the muddy red-light district of Jaunpur known as Mohalla Shogav Mohammed, which borders a large bazaar selling all kinds of clothing, jewelry, and household utensils, is the salon of Roshan Jani, a musician in her fifties who resides there with her twenty-three-year-old daughter, Afsana. In mid-afternoon, a slow time during the official hours of operation for the kothas in the neighborhood (8:00 a.m. to 8:00 p.m.), she had time to talk. The signboard above the salon's "store front" announced the mother–daughter team as qawwali singers. Women like Roshan Jani and Afsana rent small rooms, called affis ("offices"), overlooking narrow, busy streets such as this one, to conduct their business, paying a fee to landlords that fluctuates between "high" and "low" season—the former corresponding with marriage season.[37] Upon our introduction to one another, Roshan Jani greeted me with a statement that poignantly articulated both her plight and her empowerment within it: "We are the queens of the night [rat ki rani],[38] but when daylight comes we become just like garbage. Yes, do talk to me, for I, too, am a human being!"[39]

Roshan Jani's daughter Afsana and their neighbor Neelam, in her late twenties, both participated in the April 2001 Guria festival in Delhi for the first time. Both young women recounted that, although initially nervous performing on stage before several hundred people, they quickly realized what a profound difference this experience had made in their lives. Neelam enthusiastically spoke of the sense of empowerment and her hope the Guria festivals had provided her and her "sisters" but was also matter-of-fact about her apprehension regarding the reality of their situation: "Performing on stage is something completely different. The respect there . . . there's no comparison between that and performing here [in the salon]. But doing one program like that a year doesn't make our problems go away. There's so much pressure on all of us sisters, you can't imagine. We all suffer, no doubt. But if that [Guria concerts] can become a part of our lives, maybe we can even leave this lifestyle [prostitution combined with performance] and lead that one [performance only]."[40]

Although she expressed deep appreciation for the enhanced respectability Guria performances offer and continued willingness to accept subsequent invitations to perform at future festivals, Neelam's concerns are pragmatic. Her choice of lifestyle (and that of many others in her community) is a consequence of having to make a living—and, for the present time, performance that includes sex work appears to be the way to do so. Moreover, as discussed earlier, survival for the members of this community is fragile, caught in a cycle of exploitation that includes police interventions, greedy landlords, dealings with neighborhood "mafia," and often-dishonest clients.

In her salon, Roshan Jani's qawwali, sung in a warm, slightly off-key, world-weary voice, summed up the irony of their lives:

It wouldn't even take a moment
To burn the slum. . . .
It takes centuries
To build a road
Even if a poor girl does it.
What can she do
but give her life
to save her honor . . .?

Through these simple lyrics, Roshan Jani delineated the limits of her world: her class (tawa'if), gender, cultural background (lower-class Muslim from semi-rural North India), and her placement within it (her unique life history, including her musical identity). Repeating the couplets numerous times with slight variations, echoed by her accompanists, she articulated the precariousness of their situation. Indeed, these marginalized people live in the slums, both pragmatic and metaphoric, of their society, where their earnings, health, and safety, as well as their self-respect and artistic tradition, are constantly at risk. Their struggle is multifaceted, all-pervasive—yet they must continue in order to survive. In this way, Roshan Jani strategically deployed her identity as a qawwala, using both music and talk as an exhortative conversation with her visitors, enabling a cordial but critical social process to take place among a vastly diverse group of people.

For Aruna, also a veteran performer, Guria provides some hope of continued earnings in the future, as her age advances. She remarked: "We should get a chance—to teach in some school. A school like this—if you people [Singh and associates] start one—would give us some chance to earn. After all, from where would we earn in order to live? We are also getting on in age, and soon no one will pay attention to us."[41] Moreover, Aruna's desire to transmit her artistic knowledge (*kalavidya*) to younger members of the community reflects an empowered consciousness regarding the importance of the tradition of which she is part. She understands Singh's financial limitations and acknowledges that he has thus far kept his promise to provide two or three engagements a year for her and others.

Additionally, despite the hope she and her family derive from their membership in Guria as regular performers and festival advisers, Aruna, proud of her family's socio-musical status, considers the conflation of their artistic identity with that of prostitutes problematic:

We are not *peshadars* [literally, "professionals," a word used colloquially to mean prostitutes], to whom one customer after another would come . . . we haven't done that till now. . . it's better to die of hunger. We want people to come here who will listen to at least a few *cheez* [classically based songs], so that we can make our living. . . . We are musicians (*gane-bajane vale*), not prostitutes (*peshadar*).[42]

Meena Tabassum, a budding young qawwala, rents a room with her father, the nal player and leader of her ensemble, in the home of Aruna Devi and family. She voiced both a sense of solidarity with her fellow members and thoughtful insight into the conditions of poverty that often force women into prostitution. With regard to Guria's "Women in Prostitution" banner hung as backdrop to the stage, she remarked: "I feel it's all right . . . because *we all become one during this time*. As it is, people don't understand that we women belong to different categories. We are all seen through the same eyes—I mean that *we are all women*."[43] Despite her young age, Meena understands what it means to be an object of the male gaze. She seemed aware that the label "Women in Prostitution" may be used by the Guria organizers to "sell" the performances as spectacle, attracting an audience to unknown artists and thus exercising control over the means of production. Yet, the "communitas" she experienced with the other festival participants somehow erased class/caste distinctions and made the event a kind of assertion of women's agency, for her a transformation that occurred during performance, within the festival frame.[44] Although she claims that the "category" she belongs to does not include sex work, she knows that an important aspect of her marketability at this early point in her career is her physical attractiveness. Nevertheless, she noted that middle-class Guria festival organizers were insensitive about the circumstances that lead women into prostitution: "They too have mothers and sisters at home. They never think that if tomorrow times are bad for them, they'd have to do this work too. I mean, when there's nothing to eat, there's no one to look after you, then one has to do this work."[45]

For Meena, as for many other women in her larger community, getting into prostitution is a matter of survival. Like her elder colleague Roshan Jani, Meena (in the couplets below) deployed her skills as a qawwala to critique the bitter irony of their situation:

> Only after being hurt countless times have I understood this secret:
> That it's a world of betrayal and a time of selfishness.
> The routine of coming and going is old,
> That which is called the world is a temporary address.
> Before surrendering the heart to anyone
> One must save the mirror [of one's heart] from the "city of stone" [the stonehearted].

The first couplet speaks of the resignation that is actually a revelation experienced following one's loss of innocence and then disillusionment. The second evokes the South Asian/Sufi trope of impermanence, which necessitates continual peregrination. The third refers to the first, envoicing a resolve to protect onself against betrayal.

Seasoned qawwala Zeenat Jahan, a Mirasi woman in her forties whose mother, grandmother, and maternal aunts were all singers trained in semi-classical music, offered her own analysis of the qawwali "Vafa karenge vafa karoge—jafa karenge jafa karoge" ("If you have faith in me, I will have faith in you—If you are unjust to me, I will be unjust to you"), which she had sung in the festival performance in Delhi. She began her analysis with an explanation of how such lyrics can be deployed as ammunition in a musical duel (*moqabala*), common among performers sharing the stage, regardless of gender. When secular qawwali is performed by a woman and man (or men), the rivalry is intensified to the point of ritual hatred (presumably because of the inherent power struggle between genders). At some point, one side gives in and asks for friendship and mutual cooperation,[46] to some extent an embodiment of the Sufi notion of surrendering to the mystical *yar*, or friend/lover/divine.

Linking the couplet to the issue of Guria's labeling festival participants as Women in Prostitution, Zaneet offered a meta-commentary that engaged with the questions raised throughout this essay. She began with a polemic against the post-feudal patriarchal society that blames women of her community for their disenfranchisement. This society, she quipped, has configured professional women music-makers as *galat*, or dishonorable, something Guria festivals have, to some extent, made a "show" of in order to cater to the "tourist gaze" of mainstream audiences. Zeenat lashed out against the double standard that neither questions the respectability of these women's patrons/clients nor takes into consideration the extenuating circumstances, *majboori*, of their needing to survive without male support. *Majboori*, she exclaimed, can force an honorable person into a *galat jagah*, or a wrong, dishonorable position. Nevertheless, she acknowledged the power of solidarity among Guria's members to advocate recognition of these marginalized artists' professionalism by the mainstream. For Zeenat, the space provided by the Guria festival is both an opportunity and a challenge for her (and her musical peers/sisters) to maintain her honor as a female hereditary musician by reaffirming her identity as a qawwala through performance. In her words:

> I told Aruna, "look sister, we'll certainly perform on that stage . . . Because I'm from a musicians' gharana I must sit on that stage and keep that honor intact! . . . I earn my living as an artist . . . and I perform my qawwala artistry there! And a woman's respectability—I guard that for myself too. It's not a small matter . . . maintaining it on that stage."[47]

While she did not blame Singh personally for the essentialist gloss, she felt it reflected a privileged, male chauvinist attitude.

> There's no need to say that everyone who's on that stage does that [sex work]! People from good families also sit on that stage, don't they? . . . Why have they gotten into this? They have some majboori, that's why! First look at the majboori—they [the Guria organizers] are just seeing what they've become. Take, for example, a girl from a rich family—what can't she do? She'll do it openly [perform and lead a controversial personal life]. And here . . .a bai [tawa'if] . . . [performs for clients] at her home. She deserves respect as much as the woman who does it publicly![48]

Zeenat's narrative eloquently sums up the simultaneous empowerment and irony that Guria Sewi Sansthan encapsulates. Through her performance of qawwali at the April 2001 festival and her reflexive analysis of it, she strongly echoed the sentiment of "If you have faith in me, I will have faith in you—If you are unjust to me, then I will be unjust to you."

In these pages, I have opened up the question of how the courtesan tradition's cultural integrity, identified through its members' dynamic practice and renewal of a body of repertory and performance practices consisting of various genres that have several historical points of origin, may be challenged in the Guria frame by expectations of authenticity and/or respectability informed by the mainstream Indian middle class. Encouraged by the discourse of empowerment they have gained through membership in Guria (despite its echoes of patriarchal patronage), these tawa'if are using their bodies and voices to perform music, text, and dance in a layered manner, thus invoking feminist (auto)biographies, histories, and gender and class politics to voice resistance as a poetics of oral literary criticism, simultaneously negotiating their socio-musical identity.

The members of Guria Sevi Sansthan have created the Guria Festivals as cultural shows in hopes of extending a new postcolonial patronage to a historically and aesthetically rich but endangered performance tradition. The results of a decade of effort made by Singh and the members are evident in the forms of media attention, a diverse audience, and funding from humanitarian organizations within and (recently) outside India. This has begun to make a difference in the lives of the women served and their community, by virtue of the emergent transformation of consciousness that coexists with their accumulated experiences as participants in the initiative. To what extent this initiative will make a pragmatic, far-reaching difference in their lives depends to a large extent on the ability of the collective process to sustain itself, ultimately from among the women participating in it—a long-term goal of Guria. They have now taken important first steps. The tale of tawa'ifs as postcolonial artists and independent "micro-entrepreneurs"[49] is at an emerging stage as a complex coexistence of several issues: the women's strategies of cooption, the mainstream's simultaneously patronizing and valorizing attitude toward the women's situations, the women's strategies of alternately subtle and explicit subversion, and the hope and passion that motivates Guria's diverse, diffuse members.

Notes

1. Chandni (actually thirteen at the time) and her mother, Aruna Devi, although residents of Muzaffarpur, Bihar, claim Benares as their ancestral home. Thus they locate themselves as members of the Benares *gharana*, or stylistic community, of hereditary professional musicians, an important validation strategy for musicians, including tawa'if.

2. Anees Jung, *The Asian Age*, April 29, 2001.

3. Founded in 1994 by Singh, a man in his thirties who is the only son (among four sisters) of a well-to-do aluminum-rolling mill owner in Benares, Guria is a proactive feminist self-help organization whose members consist of tawa'if (many of whom hail from matrilineages of professional musicians), their children, their musical accompanists, sex workers, and

several social activists from the mainstream. Guria's head office is in a small suite of rooms on the roof of the Singh family home in Benares; the organization also has a presence in Raisen, Madhya Pradesh, the home of some of the performers.

4. See John Urry, *The Tourist Gaze* (London: Sage Publications, 1990).

5. The following individuals' comments, elicited through personal communication, appear in the text, their names abbreviated as follows: Aruna Devi (AD), Ajeet Singh (AS), Arup Sen Gupta (ASG), Daya Kumari (DK), Kali Dasi (KD), Madhuri Devi (MD), Meena Tabassum (MT), Neelam Devi (ND), Roshan Jani (RJ), Shweta (S), Zeenat Jahan (ZJ).

6. Kirin Narayan, "The Practice of Oral Literary Criticism: Women's Songs in Kangra, India," *Journal of American Folklore* 108 (1995): 243–64.

7. Various other names exist for subgroups, some of them referring to some aspect of the women's performance, such as *nacni* (lit. female dancer, referring to folk theater actresses), others being clan or sub-caste names, such as Kanjar and Bediya.

8. See above, chap. 17.

9. AD (10/2001). See also Fouzia Saeed, *Taboo! The Hidden Culture of a Red Light Area* (Oxford: Oxford University Press, 2002); Prakash Tandon, *Punjabi Century* (New York: Harcourt, Brace, and World, 1961).

10. See Chandra Mohanty, "Under Western Eyes: Feminist Scholarship and Colonial Discourses," in *Third World Women and the Politics of Feminism*, ed. Chandra Mohanty, Ann Russo, and Lourdes Torres (Bloomington: Indiana University Press, 1990), 51–80.

11. See, for example, Suresh Chandra Banerji and Ramala Banerji, *The Castaway of Indian Society: A History of Prostitution in India* (Calcutta: Punthi Pustak, 1989).

12. Cf. Deborah Root, *Cannibal Culture: Art, Appropriation, and the Commodification of Difference* (Boulder, CO: Westview Press, 1996).

13. Correspondence with Kaley Mason, May 31, 2002.

14. See Kali Dasi's oral history in my "Our Stories, Our Songs: North Indian Women's Musical Auto/biographies" (Ethnographic video, 2000); and eadem, "Multiple Voices, Multiple Selves: Song Style and North Indian Women's Identity," *Asian Music* 32 (2001): 1–40.

15. AD (2/2000).

16. See above, chap. 17.

17. The case of Guria's female artists includes issues of peregrination as necessary for survival, reclamation of language, various tropes of sexuality and intimacy, collective solidarity to combat exploitation by members (men and women) of the mainstream and of their own community. All of these resonate with the notion of "borders," literal or metaphoric, as sites of feminist epistemics. At issue, too, is their positioning just outside the canonical Hindustani musical "center," with which they sometimes simultaneously maintain intimate socio-musical ties. See Jane Duran, *Worlds of Knowing: Global Feminist Epistemologies* (New York: Routledge, 2001), and Deborah A. Gordon, "Border Work: Feminist Ethnography and the Dissemination of Literacy," in *Women Writing Culture*, ed. Ruth Behar and Deborah A. Gordon (Berkeley: University of California Press, 1995), 373–89. Furthermore, their socio-musical marginality generally makes "mainstream" professional music-making such as concert performances, music festivals, studio recording, etc. virtually inaccessible to them (Maciszewski, "Multiple Voices, Multiple Selves").

18. Cf. Thomas Turino, "Signs of Imagination, Identity, and Experience: A Peircian Semiotic Theory for Music," *Ethnomusicology* 43 (1998): 221–55.

19. Mary Ellen Jacobs, Petra Munro, and Natalie Adams, "Palimpsest: (Re)Reading Women's Lives," *Qualitative Inquiry* 1 (1995): 327–46.

20. She is partially supported by a benefactor who lives nearby, an instance of what Kamala Visweswaran (*Fictions of Feminist Ethnography* [Minneapolis: University of Minnesota Press, 1993]) calls being married "differently."

21. Regula Burckhardt Qureshi, "Mode of Production and Musical Production: Is Hindustani Music Feudal?" in *Music and Marx: Ideas, Practice, Politics*, ed. Regula Burckhardt Qureshi (New York: Routledge, 2002), 81–105; eadem, "In Search of Begum Akhtar: Patriarchy, Poetry, and Twentieth-Century Indian Music," *The World of Music* 43 (2001): 97–137; eadem, "Confronting the Social: Mode of Production and the Sublime for (Indian) Art Music," *Ethnomusicology* 44 (2000): 15–38.

22. Evidence of this abounds in literature (e.g., Somnath Chakravarti, *Kolkatar Baijibilas* [Calcutta: Bookland Pvt. Ltd., 1991]); Saeed, *Taboo!*; Amritlal Nagar, *Yeh Kothewaliyan* [Allahabad: Lokbharati Prakashan, 1964]); documentary and "docu-feature" films (e.g., Ismael Merchant, *The Courtesans of Bombay* [1983]; and Meera Nair, *Salaam Bombay* [1989]); and personal narratives (e.g., AS ongoing; RJ (5/2001); MD (5/2001, 2/2000); AD and KD (8/1997, 2/2000, 5/2001, etc.).

23. AS (7/2002, 9/2002, 2/2003).

24. AS (5/10/2001). Audience members at the Guria festivals probably resemble those attending folk music festivals or cultural shows more than those attending concerts of classical music, although a strict distinction cannot be made.

25. See Urry, *The Tourist Gaze*. This flattening of distinctions sometimes causes discomfort among the participants, a point that is discussed in the tawa'if's narratives below.

26. I will deal with questions regarding reception by the press at Guria Festivals in another essay.

27. E.g., Partha Chatterjee, *The Nation and Its Fragments* (Delhi: Oxford University Press, 1993).

28. The movement and lines created by these gestures are largely straight and two-dimensional, in contrast to the more curvaceous, delicate ones derived from the *ada* vocabulary.

29. See, for example, Edward O. Henry, "The Rationalization of Intensity in Indian Music," *Ethnomusicology* 46 (2002): 33–55.

30. Both in their forties, Zeenat and Aruna were the oldest singers performing at this festival.

31. ZJ, MT to ASG (10/10/2001 and 10/9/2001); ND, RJ (5/14/2001, etc.).

32. ZJ, AD, KD to ASG (10/10/2001 and 10/9/2001, etc.).

33. ZJ, AD, KD to ASG (10/10/2001 and 10/9/2001, etc.).

34. Narayan, "The Practice of Oral Literary Criticism."

35. See Gloria Raheja and Ann Grodzins Gold, *Listen to the Heron's Words* (Berkeley: University of California Press, 1994).

36. They identify themselves as belonging to the Gandharva caste, one that holds relatively high status in this region, as does Sajan's mother Daya Kumari (AD and KD to ASG, 10/8/2001; DK, 6/1996). Kali Dasi frequently enjoyed the honor of lighting the votive lamp to inaugurate festivals.

37. RJ (5/10/2001).

38. *Rat ki rani* also refers to a type of sweet-smelling jasmine that blooms at night.

39. RJ (5/10/2001).

40. ND (5/14/2001).

41. AD to ASG (10/9/2001).

42. AD to ASG (10/9/01).

43. MT to ASG (10/9/2001), emphasis mine.

44. Cf. Carol Babiracki, "Courtesan Traditions of North India: Cutting through Conventional Concepts," paper presented at the Annual Meeting of the Society for Ethnomusicology, 1994.

45. MT to ASG (10/9/2001).

46. ZJ to ASG (10/10/2001).

47. 10/10/2001.

48. 10/10/2001.

49. Kaval Gulhati (president of Unniti Foundation, a U.S.-based non-profit organization involved in South Asian women's development), personal communication (5/2002).

Appendix: Companion Website Notes and Texts

Visit the Companion Website at
www.oup.com/us/thecourtesanarts

Username: Music2
Password: Book4416

The musical pieces included here exemplify some of the music-making carried out by courtesans discussed in this volume.

Track 1. "Zao luo pao," aria from *Peony Pavilion*   Chapter 3
Written by Tang Xianzu, performed by Yuan Anpu. Gaoting Company, 1926.
2'41"

Text and translation:

> Yuanlai chazi yanhong kaibian, si zhe ban dou fu yu tuijing weiyuan. Liangchen meijing naihe tian, shangxin leshi shuei jia yuan. Zhao fei mu juan, yunxia cuixuan; yusi fengpian, yanpo huachuan, jinping ren te kan di zhe shao guang jian.

> (*Spoken*) Without visiting this garden, how could I ever have realized this splendor of spring!
> (*Sung*) See how deepest purple, brightest scarlet
> open their beauty only to dry well crumbling.
> "Bright the morn, lovely the scene,"
> listless and lost the heart
> —where is the garden "gay with joyous cries?"[1]

Track 2. "Hao jiejie," aria from *Peony Pavilion*   Chapter 3
Written by Tang Xianzu, performed by Yuan Anpu. Gaoting Company, 1926.
2'49"

Text and translation:

> Bian qingshan tihong liao dujuan. (Na)[2] chamo wai yansi zui ruan. (Na) mudan sui hao, tuo chun gui zen zhan de xian. Xian ning mian. (Ng) shengsheng yanyu ming ru jian. Lili ying sheng[3] liu de yuan.[4]

To the tune "My Dear Girl"

> The green hillside
> bleeds with the cuckoo's tears of red azalea,
> shreds of mist lazy as wine fumes thread the sweetbriar.
> However fine the peony,
> how can she rank as queen
> coming to bloom when spring has said farewell!
> Idle gaze resting there where the voice of swallow shears the air
> and liquid flows the trill of oriole.[5]

Tracks 1 and 2 are the two famous arias from *Peony Pavilion* ("Black Gossamer Robe" and "My Dear Girl") that the courtesan Li Xiangjun rehearses during her singing lesson in *Peach Blossom Fan*. The singer heard here is Yuan Anpu (1904–93), a male amateur who specialized in female (*dan*) roles. This version comes from the 1926 recording issued by the Gaoting Company, downloaded from http://www.dongdong qiang.com. It represents one of the few extant recordings of *kun qu* performed in the "pure singing" style, which, at least in modern practice, strictly adheres to the correct pronunciation of linguistic tones, even when doing so conflicts with the tune pattern. To the contemporary ear, accustomed to the more harmonious style of stage performance singing where tones are altered to fit the tune pattern and grace notes are added to smooth the melody, this recording sounds a bit bumpy. Because of the strictness of the rules governing "pure singing" practice, however, it is possible that this recording preserves a *kun qu* vocal style from earlier periods.

Seven of the next eight examples (tracks nos. 2-7, and 9-10) are performed by the Newberry Consort, directed by Mary Springfels. All were recorded in December 2004 especially for this volume. The performers are David Douglass, violin; Ellen Hargis, soprano; John Lenti, lute; Ken Perlow, viola da gamba; Mary Springfels, viola da gamba; Craig Trompeter, viola da gamba.

Track 3. *Dolce mio ben, dolce colomba mia*   Chapter 4
Music by Baldissera Donato, Text anonymous.
Performed by The Newberry Consort.
2'13"

Text and translation:

> Dolce mio ben, dolce colomba mia,
> se 'l veder voi m'ha tolto
> dispetto e gelosia,
> tolto non mi fia già che quel bel volto
> dentr'al mio cor non sia,
> e ch'io non porti nella ment'impresso
> quel che veder non puon gl'occhi d'appresso.
>
> O my sweetheart, my sweet dove,
> if spite and jealousy

have taken the sight of you away from me,
your beautiful face is still in my heart,
and I still carry imprinted in my mind
that which my eyes cannot behold nearby—
and this cannot be taken away from me.[6]

This anonymous Petrarchan plaint to a lost lover, set by the Venetian Baldissera Donato and published in his *Secondo libro de madrigali a quattro voci* (Venice, 1568), represents what Alfred Einstein called "pseudo-monody" to describe instances of homophonic polyphony with highly decorated treble parts, characteristic of accompanied song. The soprano part of *Dolce mio ben* features a kind of ornamentation that was otherwise rarely notated before the seventeenth century, but the lower voices are predominantly chordal. Pseudo-monody represents the packaging up of a style that allowed courtesans and other virtuosic singers to display their skills at embellishing texts when singing with several other voices and/or instruments. Such pieces could also have been performed with lower parts adapted for an accompanying instrument, as heard in this performance by voice and lute.

Track 4. "Chiaro e famoso mare" (first stanza) sung to Arcadelt's *Chiare fresche e dolci acque*   Chapter 4
Music by Jacques Arcadelt, text by Gaspara Stampa.
Performed by The Newberry Consort.
2′17″

Text and translation:

Chiaro e famoso mare,
sovra 'l cui nobil dosso
si posò 'l mio signor, mentre Amor volle;
rive onorate e care
(con sospir dir lo posso),
che 'l petto mio vedeste spesso molle;
soave lido e colle,
che con fiato amoroso
udisti le mie note,
d'ira e di sdegno vòte,
colme d'ogni diletto e di riposo;
udite tutti intenti
il suon or degli acerbi miei lamenti.

Shining and famous sea
upon whose noble back
my lord reposed as long as Love desired;
Honored and lovely banks
—I say it with a sigh—
that often looked upon my tender heart;
Sweet shore, beloved hills
that harkened to my notes
breathed forth in tones of love,

empty of wrath and scorn,
but filled with all delight and gentle peace:
Now hear with fixed attention
the sound of my distressful, sad lamenting.[7]

This performance plays with the remains of lost oral practices by substituting the poet-singer Gaspara Stampa's canzone "Chiaro e famoso mare" of the mid-sixteenth century for the poem it glosses, Petrarch's "Chiare fresche e dolci acque." In 1555 Arcadelt's music for "Chiare fresche"—a madrigal cycle setting each stanza as a separate piece—was published in the first book of *madrigali ariosi* by the Roman printer Antonio Barré. Barré's book was rife with melodic formulas of the kind we identify with courtesans' singing, and these formulas (as James Haar has shown) found their way into Arcadelt's entire cycle. As such our reworking of Arcadelt's setting using Stampa's text represents a whimsical endeavor to give voice to a poem for which Stampa was justly famous both as a poet and as a singer. The text fits Arcadelt's music exactly as Petrarch's does, since in composing her poem she based its form entirely on that of Petrarch (doubtless so she could sing both to the same music), as Lynn Hooker discovered. Though Arcadelt's original as printed is all-vocal, soprano Ellen Hargis here sings with the accompaniment of a viol ensemble, suggesting something closer to the manner in which Stampa herself might have sung this when she accompanied herself on the lute (cf. fig. 7.2). In preparing to sing their repertories, courtesans probably often readied performances in a process not totally unlike Arcadelt's much more composerly one. Many would have fleshed out in advance of performance the accompanied melodies they used, melodies often associated with traditions for singing for Petrarch's lyrics, with worked-out accompaniments.

Track 5. *Nel partir del mio ben*   Chapter 5
Music by Perissone Cambio, text anonymous.
Performed by The Newberry Consort.
1'55"

Text and translation:

> Nel partir del mio ben sì part'Amore
> et seco ne portò quei chiari lumi,
> che m'accesero il core.
> Io sola altro non so che pianger sempre
> la bella vista e i dolci suoi costume.
> Deh, iniquitoso arciero,
> ferma l'amante mio che fugge sciolto,
> guidami lui, guidam'il suo bel volto.

> In the departing of my beloved, so Love departed
> and with him took those bright eyes
> that enflamed my heart;
> Alone, I know nothing but to weep continually
> for his beautiful image and his sweet demeanor.
> Oh! wicked archer,

stop my lover, who flees unbound;
lead him to me, lead his beautiful face to me.[8]

This madrigal was published in Cambio's *Primo libro de madrigali a 4* (Venice, 1547), a book of four-part madrigals that was dedicated to the famed Gaspara Stampa. It is one of only two madrigals in the collection written in the female voice. The published four- part vocal version could have been performed by a solo voice with lute accompaniment, as featured here in a transcription by Dawn De Rycke.

Track 6. Bottegari's tune for a *terza rima* sung with Veronica Franco's capitolo "Non più parole" (excerpt)   Chapter 6
Music by Cosimo Bottegari, text by Veronica Franco.
Performed by The Newberry Consort.
1′06″

Text and translation:

> Non più parole: ai fatti, in campo, a l'armi,
> ch'io voglio, risoluta di morire,
> da sì grave molestia liberarmi.
>   Non so se 'l mio "cartel" si debba dire,
> in quanto do resposta provocata:
> ma perché in rissa de' nomi venire?
>   Se vuoi, da te mi chiamo disfidata;
> e se non, ti disfido; o in ogni via
> la prendo, ed ogni occasïon m'è grata.
>   Il campo o l'armi elegger a testia,
> ch'io prenderò quel che tu lascerai;
> anzi pur ambo nel tuo arbitrio sia.

>   No more words! To deeds, to the battlefield, to arms!
> For, resolved to die, I want to free myself
> from such merciless mistreatment.
>   Should I call this a challenge? I do not know,
> since I am responding to a provocation;
> but why should we duel over words?
>   If you like, I will say that you've challenged me,
> if not, I challenge you; I'll take any route
> and any opportunity suits me equally well.
>   Yours be the choice of place or of arms,
> and I will make whatever choice remains;
> rather, let both be your decision.[9]

In this poem, a capitolo in terza rima (three-line stanzas), Franco presents herself as an armed warrior ready to conquer her male combatant with words and deeds. Here Franco's text is sung to a melodic formula from Cosimo Bottegari's lutebook of 1574, compiled a year before Franco's poem was published. Much of the courtesan's repertory seems to have been recitational, using patterned, repetitive tunes like this one. These melodic formulas, sung over repeated chord and bass patterns, were reused for any number of poems that followed the prescribed syllabic and metric patterns of the relevant poetic genre. The first few stanzas of this long poem are heard here performed by soprano and lute.

Track 7. *O dolce nocte*　　　　　　　　　　　　　　　　　　　Chapter 7
Music by Philippe Verdelot, text by Niccolò Machiavelli.
Performed by The Newberry Consort.
1′46″

Text and translation:

> O dolce nocte, o sanct'
> hore nocturn' et quete,
> ch'i desiosi amanti accompagnate;
> in voi s'adunan tante
> letitie, onde voi sete
> sole cagion di far l'alme beate,
> Voi, li giusti premii date
> a l'amorose schiere, a voi amiche,
> delle lunge fatiche;
> Voi fat'o felice hore,
> ogni gelato pect'arder d'amore.
>
> O sweet night, O blessed
> nocturnal and still hours
> that wait on ardent lovers;
> in you so many
> delights are joined
> that you alone make souls happy.
> You bestow gifts
> upon the companies of lovers, friends of yours,
> deserved by long trials.
> You, O happy hours, make
> every chilled breast glow with love.[10]

This theatrical declamatory madrigal, with text by the famous Niccolò Machiavelli and setting by Philippe Verdelot, is preserved in a set of illuminated partbooks given to Henry VIII of England around 1527 and now held at Chicago's Newberry Library, where they are widely known as the Newberry Partbooks. Machiavelli wrote "O dolce nocte" as part of the intermedi tucked between acts of his play *La Mandragola* (The Mandrake, ca. 1518), inspired by his courtesan lover Barbara Salutati. This kind of four-voiced homophonic madrigal worked well when performed by a soloist with instrumental accompaniment, as it is here with a consort of viols.

Track 8. *Cantate ninfe*　　　　　　　　　　　　　　　　　　　Chapter 9
Music by Luca Marenzio, text anonymous.
Performed by The Consort of Musicke, directed by Anthony Rooley: Emma Kirkby, Evelyn Tubb, and Deborah Roberts (sopranos), Mary Nichols (alto), Rufus Miller (tenor), Anthony Rooley (lute). Original Recording: *Concerto delle Donne: Madrigali*

(Deutsche Harmonia Mundi, distributed by BMG Music, 1988, 77154–2-RC). Under license from The SONY BMG Custom Marketing Group, SONY BMG Music Entertainment.
1'24"

Text and translation:

> Cantate, ninfe leggiadrette e belle,
> i miei novelli ardori,
> e scherzate e ridere insieme Amori
> con la mia Filli in queste parti e in quelle.
> Cantate e di piacer gioie tutti,
> c'ho d'amor colto i desiati frutti.

> Sing, graceful and beautiful nymphs,
> of my new ardors,
> and Cupids, joke and laugh together
> with my Phyllis, in this part of the countryside and that.
> Sing and be joyous everyone,
> for I have harvested the desired fruits of love.[11]

Luca Marenzio's madrigal on an anonymous text, published in his first book of madrigals for six voices in 1581, serenades the voices of the famous "three ladies" of Ferrara, known as the *concerto delle donne*, and provided an opportunity for them to display their talents. The virtuosic upper parts of this six-voice madrigal reveal skilled individual voices as well as the remarkable ensemble work for which the ladies were famous. In this piece Marenzio uses the so-called luxuriant style to embellish small motives, especially as an element of word painting.

Track 9. *Sì come dit'ogn'hor: bella vi paio*   Chapter 10
Music by Jacques Arcadelt, text anonymous.
Performed by The Newberry Consort.
1'53"

Text and translation:

> Sì come dit'ogn'hor: bella vi paio,
> non vi paia fatica
> darm'un poco alla man qualche danaio.
> Se voi pensasti pur tenermi in ciance
> et pagar di parole,
> voi non m'havrasti mai con mille lancie,
> che sempre scambierem folle con folle!
> Ma chi godermi vole,
> sia vi ditto per sempre o brutta o bella,
> metta spesso le man'alla scarsella!

> If, as you always say, you find me beautiful,
> then it shouldn't be too much trouble
> to put a few coins in my hand.

If you were thinking of trying to trick me with your chatter,
and paying me with words,
you would never have me, not even with a thousand lances,
because this way we would be exchanging one crazy idea for another!
But to him who desires to have his way with me
let this be said, for better or worse:
Put your hand often in your purse![12]

This madrigal comes from the extensive repertory of songs, texts, and caricatures of various sorts that degraded and defamed courtesans. The anonymous text, undoubtedly written by a man, then set by Arcadelt and published in his third book of madrigals for four voices (Venice 1539), has the courtesan articulate her own mercenary ways—one of the many sides of courtesanship that was often slandered in derogatory literature. Published as a madrigal with four singable parts, it is sung here in historically characteristic fashion by a soprano accompanied by viols.

Track 10. *Donna, fra più bei volti honest'e cari*   Chapter 10
Music by Jacques Arcadelt, text anonymous.
Performed by The Newberry Consort.
1'51"

Text and translation:

Donna, fra più bei volti honest'e cari,
il vostro saria 'l primo,
se 'l chieder non guastasse de denari.
Se volete d'ogni altro esser corona
come si spera e crede,
non chiedete de nulla mai persona,
che gli è men bella sempre chi più chiede!
Et se io con molta fede
Vi adoro per mia diva et per mia stella,
Di gratia non toccate la scarsella!

Lady, among the most beautiful faces, honest and dear,
yours would rank as first
if it weren't spoiled by your asking for money.
If you want to be regarded above all others,
as one hopes and believes,
don't ever ask anything of anyone,
because she who asks the most always seems the least beautiful!
And though I, with great faith,
adore you as my goddess and my star,
I pray you not to touch my purse![13]

This madrigal text, set by Arcadelt in his *Quarto libro di madrigali* for four voices (Venice, 1539), gives voice to an anonymous male. In the tradition of the paired challenge/riposte poems that were popular at the time, the poet here responds directly to the courtesan envoiced in the previous selection, claiming that she would be an exemplum of the ideal beautiful woman were it not for her mercenary ways. In print, this piece was also presented as all-vocal polyphony (like all vocal music of the time). It is performed here, like its companion madrigal, *Sì come dit'ogn'hor: bella vi paio* (track 10), with soprano Ellen Hargis accompanied by viols.

Track 11. *Ataka no Matsu* (The Pine Tree at Ataka) (1769)   Chapter 12
Hirokazu Sugiura, shamisen, Kôhachiro Miyata, shakuhachi. Original recording: Ensemble Nipponia, *Japan: Kabuki and Other Traditional Music*, Elektra Nonesuch H-72084 (1980). Produced under license from Nonesuch Records.
3'14"

This popular tune was adapted by Fujita Kichiji for nagauta, the extensive musical accompaniment for the Kabuki theater. The nagauta ensemble consists of several shamisen (three-stringed plucked lute), vocalists, flute (shakuhachi), and percussion. Because geisha give large stage performances similar in nature to those of the Kabuki, nagauta is also the mainstay of geisha musical study and geisha study it even today. The piece is performed here with only flute and shamisen.

Track 12. *Yuki* (Snow) (excerpt)   Chapter 14
Music by Minezaki Kôto. Keiji Azechi, kokyu; Kunie Fujii, voice and shamisen. Original Recording: *Keiji Azechi plays Kokyu*, Camerata 25CM-447-8 (1997).
4'03"

Translated text:

> When I brush away
> The flowers, and the snow—
> How clear my sleeves become!
>
> Truly it was an affair
> Of long, long ago.
> The man I waited for
> May still be waiting for me.
>
> The cry of the mandarin duck
> Calling for his mate
> From his freezing nest
> Makes me feel sorrowful.
> The temple bell at midnight
> Wakes me
> From my lonely reverie.
>
> It makes me sad to hear
> That distant temple bell.
> When the patter of hail
> Reaches my pillow,
> I seem to hear, somehow,
> His knocking on my door again.

> And less and less am I able
> To dam up my tears,
> Freezing now
> Into icicles.
> I no longer care about
> This hard, bitter life.
> I'm only sorry that
> I still can't think of
> My former lover as sinful.
> Ah, the discarded sorrows![14]

This excerpt exemplifies the musical mood of the New Yoshiwara, what a male patron might have sung with the *tayu* courtesan's accompaniment. Originally from China, the kokyu is a two- or three-stringed fiddle played in an upright position with a horsetail-strung bow (similar to the Chinese *er-hu*). Here the kokyu forms an ensemble with the shamisen, as heard on track 11. The song narrates the story of a geisha of the pleasure quarter of Osaka. The whole poem is reproduced here, but the performance is heard only through the first few lines. This piece was composed in the latter half of the Tenmei era of the Edo period (1781–89).

Track 13. *Sushimga/Yeokkeum Sushimga* (Song of Sadness /Extended Song of Sadness)
Chapter 16
Kim Gwangsuk, voice. Jang Deokhwa, janggo. Original recording: *Nostalgia: Traditional Folksongs from the Western Province of Korea* (EMI EKLD-0068). Reproduced by permission of the artists. Unauthorized reproduction forbidden. Copyright 2001 by Kim Gwangsuk and Jang Deokhwa.
6′25″

Translated text:

> If I could visit my beloved
> In dreams as often as I like
> The stone road before her gate
> Would turn to sand.
> The more I long for my lover's flowered face,
> The less I know what to do.

Sushimga (Song of Sadness) and its faster companion piece *Yeokkeum Sushimga* (Extended Song of Sadness) come from a collection of folk ballads and songs called *seodosori* (northwestern song) from the northwestern provinces of the Korean peninsula in what is now South Korea. The repertory was collected in the late nineteenth century at the northwest gisaeng schools. Many of the songs became popular in the early part of the twentieth century, as performed by famous colonial-era gisaeng and semi-professional male entertainers. In 1969 the South Korean government made *Sushimga* and one other song from *seodosori* an "Intangible Cultural Treasure." The song is now generally performed in South Korea by professional female folksingers with North Korean ancestry, and it is known for its impressive vocal technique and melodic subtlety, most notably the microtonal shading of pitch. Here "Human Cultural Treasure" Kim Gwangsuk performs perhaps the best-known, canonical version of the piece. She brings to it her unique personal style, characterized by gravity, and her subtle manipulation of pitch, but also her tandem virtuoso shadings of timbre and dynamics. She is accompanied by janggo, an hourglass drum.

The texts of *seodosori* center around meditations on separation from loved ones and the evanescence of life. They take inspiration from several principal sources: Korean and Chinese legends; Buddhist and indigenous shamanist figures and ideas; and events in the lives of their composers. Although the origins of the opening, best-known verse are unknown, it takes on a particular poignancy in the context of the lives of many nineteenth- and early twentieth-century female professional entertainers, who expressed their lack of physical freedom and social mobility in song.

Track 14. *Is ishq ke hathon se* (So strong is the grip of this love) Chapter 17
Begum Akhtar, voice; Nizamuddin Khan, tabla. Original recording: *Begum Akhtar (Live Bombay)*, Makar (MAKCD030).
17′28″

Text and Translation:

> Is ishq ke hathon se hargiz na ma*far dekha*
> Itni hi barhi hasrat jitna hi u*dhar dekha*
>
> Tha khel sa pahle ishq, lekin jo khuli ankhen
> Duba hua rag rag men who tir-e-*nazar dekha*
>
> Who ashk bhari ankhen aur dard bhare nale
> Allah na dikhlae jo waqt-e-*sahar dekha*
>
> Jate rahe dam bhar men sare hi gile shikwe
> Us jan-e-taghaful ne jab ek *nazar dekha*
>
> Tha ba'is-e-ruswai har chand junun mera
> Un ko bhi na chain aya jab tak na *idhar dekha*
>
> Yun dil ke tarapne ka kuchh to hai sabab akhir
> Ya dard ne karwat li, ya tum ne *idhar dekha*
>
> Mathe pe pasina kyun? Ankhon men nami kaisi
> Kuchh khair to hai, tum ne kya hal-e-*Jigar dekha*
>
> So strong is the grip of this love that I could see no escape from it.
> My desire increased beyond bounds the more I looked toward her.
>
> At first love was like a game, but as my eyes opened
> I saw that the arrow of her glance had pierced every vein in my body.
>
> My eyes are full of tears, my moans are full of agony.
> May God preserve others from what I suffered when I saw the dawn of separation.
>
> In an instant all my complaints vanished
> When she who personifies indifference suddenly fastened her eyes upon me.

Although my infatuation caused me ill repute,
She could not rest until she had cast a glance at me.

Something must be causing the sudden fluttering of my heart.
Is it a stab of pain, or is it that you turned your gaze toward me?

Why the perspiration on your forehead, why are your eyes moist with tears?
May God preserve us! Have you at last noticed Jigar's suffering?[15]

This live recording features Begum Akhtar, one of few tawa'if who made the transition from the salon to the public concert stage. She is best known for her sophisticated mastery of Urdu poetry and light-classical music. Ghazals, widely used in Muslim cultures in south Asia are composed of several independent couplets with a unified rhyme scheme: *aa, ba, ca,* etc. Those like the one heard here were the mainstay of the courtesans' repertory, so every account of courtesans' performances features descriptions of ghazal verses from classical poetry as well as their own personal compositions.

On this recording, made on January 16, 1953 during a private performance for a patron, Akhtar sings a ghazal art song. The song is richly beautiful, filled with musical sighs and flirtations upon a wonderfully courtesanish and artful poem. The ghazal, by the favorite twentieth-century poet Jigar Muradabadi, is a perfect "mujra" poem, embodying the symbolic of total submission before a royal patron. Like all ghazals, it consists of self-contained couplets with the opening and each concluding line sharing the same rhyme syllable and a monorhyme (underlined in the Urdu text). The meter is identical throughout: – – <u> / <u> – – – – / – – <u> / <u> – – (represented verbally by the Arab-Persian metric *fa'ulun mufa'ilun, fa'ulun mufa'ilun*). The last couplet incorporates the nom de plume of the poet, Jigar (literally "liver," "seat of feelings," "heart"). The translation aims to convey the remarkable range of meanings contained in the single monorhyme *dekha* (seen, noticed, looked, etc).

The melody is loosely set in raga *Khamaj* (not a raga *malika* or cycle garland of ragas, as sometimes asserted), and the metric cycle is *kehrva*, an eight-beat cycle. Rhyming and non-rhyming lines correspond musically to the *asthayi* (concluding, lower tessitura) and *antara* (intermittent, higher tessitura) portions of the song.

Track 15. *Daulat-e-aish-o-masarrat* (The world around me is blessed)   Chapter 17
Zarina Parveen, in a small private gathering at her residence; Bahadur Khan, sarangi; S. Singh, tabla. Soundtrack from a video recording made by Regula Burckhardt Qureshi in Lucknow, 1984.
17′05″

Text and translation:
Introduction:

Zindagi di thi to jine ka *maza kyun na diya*
Meri qismat men yeh aram *bhala kyun na dia*

Khayal tha keh kabhi ham *bahar dekhenge*
Gale men phir teri bahon *ka har dekhenge*

Sirf du'a karte zaban se na *gila karte hain*
Tum salamat raho ham to yeh *du'a karte hain*
Tum hath utha kar mujhe is tarha se koso
Dekhnewale yeh samjen ke *du'a karte hain*

You gave me life, then why not give me the pleasure of life?
Why could you not bestow this blessing on my fate?

I had hoped that I too would see the blossoming of spring
And once again see the garland of your arms around my neck

My tongue utters no complaint, only prayer.
May you live long, that is my prayer.
Raise your hands when you curse me, so that
People think you are raising your hands in prayer.

Ghazal:

1.
Daulat-e-aish-o-masarrat hai *zamane ke lie*
Ek ham hi rah gaye dard *uthane ke lie*

The world around me is blessed with pleasure and happiness;
Only I am left with the burden of pain.

2.
Dusri sans na ae yeh du'a do mujh ko
Dil men sochun bhi agar tum ko *bhulane ke lie*

Pray that I may never take another breath
If I even think of ever forgetting you.

3.
Faida kya hai gham-e-dauran jo tu dar dar jae
Ham hi kya kam hain tere raz *uthane ke lie*

Why do you go from door to door for solace?
Why don't you trust that I can keep your secret?

4.
Saqiya thori si mai dekh bachae rakhna
Kam aegi mujh ko hosh men *lane ke lie*

O cupbearer, make sure to keep a little wine aside for me.
It will help bring me back to my senses.

[repeat of opening:]
Daulat-e-aish-o-masarrat hai *zamane ke lie*

The world around me is blessed with pleasure and happiness.[16]

Zarina Parveen is Lucknow's preeminent courtesan singer, coming from a lineage of leading women musicians. In this performance she sings while delicately miming the poetic and musical content, accompanied vocally by her sister, who is also a dancer.

Her performance is sustained by the traditional ensemble of sarangi and tabla, both played by hereditary musicians. The bowed sarangi supports the voice and provides elaborated melodic interludes while the tabla articulates the musical meter throughout, showing intermittent virtuosity. Zarina has recently married and retired from performing.

This ghazal song begins with a recitative-like introduction of two rhyming couplets and a quatrain (*qat'a*) with the rhyme scheme *aaba*. The ghazal itself follows a single rhyme scheme (italicized in the text below) and a single meter: – <u> – – / <u> <u> – – / <u> <u> – – / <u> <u> – (*fa'ilatun fa'ilatun fa'ilatun fa'ilat*). The same meter governs the introductory verses, except for the second couplet, whose meter is: <u> – <u> – / <u> <u> – – / <u> – <u> – / <u> – <u> – (*mafa'ilun fa'ilatun,' mafa'ilun failun*). This song presents the simpler poetry used in recent years to address more diverse audiences than the ones courtesans addressed during the feudal pre-independence era.

The melody draws on features of raga *darbari*; the tala (in Sanskrit, "clap," or musical meter) is *kehrva*, an eight-beat cycle for representing the poetic meter. Rhyming and non-rhyming lines (or concluding and initial lines in the introduction) correspond musically to the *asthayi* (concluding, lower tessitura) and *antara* (intermittent, higher tessitura) portions of the song.

Track 16. Chandni's ghazal   Chapter 18
Field recording by Amelia Maciszewski, made at a festival of Guria Sevi Sansthan [Doll help/service collective], Shri Ram Centre of Art and Culture, New Delhi, April 14–15, 2001. 5'02"

Text and translation:

> . . . Aaye kuchh avr
> Kuchh sharab aaye
>
> Uske bad aaye
> Jo izaab aaye
>
> Kar rahaa thaa ghame jahaan ka hisaab
> Aaj tum yad behisab aaye
>
> Is tarah hamari khamoshi goonji
> Roya har simt se javaab aaye
>
> Pharz thi rah sarpasar manzil
> Ham jahaan pahoonchhe kamyab paye
> **
>
> Let some clouds come, and then some wine.
> After that may whatever punishment come.
>
> Yesterday the suffering of that place was expected.
> Today your memory came unexpectedly.

In this way our silence echoes,
Crying from every direction for an answer.

There was hope of reaching the destination.
Wherever I arrive, I will find success.

Is tarah hamari khamoshi goonji
Roya jaise har simt se jabab aye
Pharz thi rah sarpasar manzil
Ham jahan pahunchhe kam yab paye . . .

. . . In this way my silence echoes,
crying as if an answer were coming from each direction.
Duty is the right path to my final destination.
Wherever I arrive, may I find success . . .[17]

The thirteen-year-old Chandni performed this song at the Guria festival in New Delhi. Along with her mother Aruna Devi (heard on track 18) and her late grandmother Kali Dasi, she comes from Muzaffapur, Bihar, and claims Benares as her ancestral home. She is accompanied by tabla, harmonium, and sarangi. The ghazal was composed by the Urdu poet Faiz Ahmed Faiz. The festival and performances were put on to benefit tawa'if and their children. Chandni sings of the pain and longing that permeated the community of women in which she was raised.

Track 17. Aruna's *magadhi* in dadra style   Chapter 18
Field recording by Amelia Maciszewski, made at a festival of Guria Sevi Sansthan, Shri Ram Centre of Art and Culture, New Delhi, April 14–15, 2001.
5′27″

Text and translation:

Kahe maare naina bar sabro?
Sab koi bandhela sine bandh parhe
Uji guji badliya
Sainya barhe jhoole lal sabro

Why are you making eyes at me, o dark one?
You're captivating everyone with your arrogance.
The dark clouds gather;
The lover pushes the swing out, little dark one.[18]

Chandni's mother, Aruna, follows her daughter by singing in the Bhojpuri language a *magadhi* in dadra style. The magadhi is a song form from the region known as Magadh. In it she boldly and evocatively sings lyrics derived from devotional poetry (*bhakti*) that depict a woman's reluctant surrender to the amorous glances and advances of a Lord. The poetic tropes allude to the antics of the Hindu god Krishna, his consort Radha, and the Gopi cowherds with whom he cavorts.

The *magadhi* begins with a brief alap, or free-rhythmic melodic introduction similar to that performed in semi-classical music. The pitch collection and melodic movement of this selection clearly correspond to that of the Hindustani raga *Mishra Pilu*, and the tabla accompaniment, in the six-beat cyclic pattern dadra, is more restrained than other times. While singing this song, Aruna performs a somewhat virtuosic *bol banao*, the melismatic stretching of syllables of key words in the text to enhance their emotional impact—again, a treatment reminiscent of classical and semi-classical music.

Notes to Appendix

1. Translated from scene 10 by Cyril Birch, *The Peony Pavilion* (Bloomington: Indiana University Press, 1980), 44–45. Translation of tune titles added by Judith T. Zeitlin.

2. All words in parentheses have been added by the singer and do not appear in the original text of the aria.

3. The word sung here as "sheng" on this recording has been changed from the character "ge" in the original text of this aria.

4. Original Chinese from Tang Xianzu, *Mudan ting* [Peony Pavilion], ed. Xu Shuofang and Yang Xiaomei (Beijing: Renmin daxue chubanshe, 1993), 47–48.

5. Translation by Birch, *The Peony Pavilion*, 44–45.

6. Translation from Alfred Einstein, *The Italian Madrigal*, 3 vols., trans. Alexander H. Krappe, Roger H. Sessions, and Oliver Strunk (1949; repr. Princeton: Princeton University Press, 1971), 3:lvi.

7. Translation by Laura Ann Stortoni and Mary Prentice Little, eds., in *Gaspara Stampa: Selected Poems* (New York: Italica Press, 1994), 54–55.

8. Translation by Dawn De Rycke with Bernardo Illari.

9. Translation by Ann Rosalind Jones and Margaret F. Rosenthal, eds., in *Veronica Franco: Poems and Selected Letters* (Chicago: University of Chicago Press, 1998), 132–33.

10. Translation by H. Colin Slim, ed., in *A Gift of Madrigals and Motets*, 2 vols. (Chicago: published for the Newberry Library by the University of Chicago Press, 1972), 2:441.

11. Translation from *Concerto delle Donne: Madrigali* (Deutsche Harmonia Mundi, distributed by BMG Music, 1988) 77154-2-RC (unattributed).

12. Translation by Courtney Quaintance.

13. Translation by Courtney Quaintance.

14. Translation by Tsuge Gen'ichi, cited from http://www.komuso.com/pieces/Usu_Yuki.html (accessed February 5, 2005).

15. Translation by Regula Burckhardt Qureshi.

16. Translation by Regula Burckhardt Qureshi and Saleem Qureshi.

17. Translation by Amelia Maciszewski.

18. Translation by Amelia Maciszewski.

Selected Bibliography

The bibliography that follows contains selected items from the essays in this volume, emphasizing those that deal specifically with courtesans. Items are grouped into the categories Primary Sources (including textual editions, translations, and scores) and Secondary Sources, the latter with subsections Ancient Greece, Early Modern Italy, East Asia, and South Asia.

Primary Sources

Alciphron, *Letters of the Courtesans*.

Arcadelt, Jacob. *Opera omnia*. Ed. Albert Seay. [Rome]: American Institute of Musicology, 1965.

Aretino, Pietro. *La cortigiana* (Venice, 1534).

————. *Dialogues*. Trans. Raymond Rosenthal. New York: Marsilio, 1971.

————. *Lettere*. Ed. Francesco Erspamer. 2 vols. Parma: Ugo Guanda, 1995.

————. *Lettere*. Ed. Paolo Procaccioli. Rome: Salerno Editrice, 1992.

————. *Ragionamento-Dialogo*. Ed. Carla Forno and Giorgio Barberi Quarotti. Milan: Rizzoli, 1998.

————. *Selected Letters*. Trans. George Bull. New York: Penguin, 1976.

————. *Sonetti lussuriosi* (Venice, 1534).

Athenaeus. *Deipnosophistae*. Book 13.

Banchieri, Adriano. *Barco di Venezia per Padova (Venezia, 1605)*. Ed. Filomena A. Peluca. Bologna: Ut Orpheus, 1998.

The Bottegari Lutebook. Ed. Carol MacClintock. The Wellesley Edition, no. 8. Wellesley, MA: Wellesley College, 1965.

Calmo, Andrea. *Le lettere di Andrea Calmo*. Ed. Vittorio Rossi. Turin: Loescher, 1888.

Cambio, Perissone. *Il primo libro de madrigali a 4 voci*. Venice, 1547. Ed. Martha Feldman. New York: Garland, 1989.

Caron, François. *A True Description of the Mighty Kingdoms of Japan and Siam*. London: Samuel Brown and John de l'Ecluse, 1663. Repr. ed. C. R. Boxer. London: Argonaut Press, 1935.

Castiglione, Baldasar. *The Book of the Courtier (1528)*. Trans. George Bull. New York: Penguin Classics, 1986.

The Citrasutra of the Visnudharmottara Purana. Ed. and trans. Parul Dave Mukherji. New Delhi: Indira Gandhi National Centre for the Arts, 2001.

Dasi, Binodini. *My Story and My Life as an Actress* (1912). Trans. and ed. Rimla Bhattacharya. New Delhi: Kali for Women Press, 1998.

Il Dialogo dello Zoppino de la vita e genealogia di tutte le cortigiane di Roma. Ed. Gino Lanfranchi. Milan: L'Editrice del Libro Raro, 1922.

Dolce, Lodovico. *Dialogo della istitutione delle donne*. Venice: Giolito, 1560.

Doni, Antonfrancesco. *Dialogo della musica* (1544). Ed. Gian Francesco Malipiero, with transcriptions by Virginia Fagotto. Venice: Fondazione Giorgio Cini and Vienna: Universal Edition, 1965.

Equicola, Marco. *Libro della natura de amore*. Venice, 1525.

Facoli, Marco. *Collected Works*. Ed. Willi Apel. Corpus of Early Keyboard Music, 2. [Rome]: American Institute of Musicology, 1963.

Feng Menglong. *Feng Menglong quanji* [Collected works of Feng Menglong]. Ed. Wei Tong-xian. 43 vols. Shanghai: Shanghai guji chubanshe, 1993 (including *Taixia xinzou* [The celestial air played anew]).

Ferrand, Jacques. *A Treatise On Lovesickness*. Trans. David A. Beecher and Massimo Cia-volella. Syracuse: Syracuse University Press, 1990.

Festa, Costanzo. *Collected Works*. Ed. Alexander Main and Albert Seay. 8 vols. Neuhausen-Stuttgart: American Institute of Musicology and Hänssler-Verlag, 1962–78.

————. *Il vero libro di madrigali a tre voci di Constantio Festa*. Venice: Antonio Gardano, 1543.

Franco, Giacomo. *Habiti delle donne veneziane*. Venice, 1610.

Franco, Veronica. *Poems and Selected Letters*. Ed. and trans. Ann Rosalind Jones and Margaret F. Rosenthal. Chicago: University of Chicago Press, 1998.

Fuller, Mrs. Marcus B. *The Wrongs of Indian Womanhood*. Edinburgh: Anderson and Ferrier, 1900.

Gambara, Veronica. *Le Rime*. Ed. Alan Bullock. Florence: Olschki, 1995.

Ganika-vrtta-sangrahah, or Texts on Courtezans in Classical Sanskrit. Ed. Ludwik Sternbach. Hoshiapur: Viúveúvarānandasamsthāna-Prakāúanamandalam, 1953.

Hou Fangyu. *Hou Fangyu ji jiaojian* [Literary works of Hou Rangyu]. Ed. Wang Shulin. Zhengzhou: Zhongzhou guji chubanshe, 1992.

Iwasaki Mineko with Rande Brown. *Geisha: A Life*. New York: Washington Square Press, 2002.

The Kāmasūtra of Vātsyāyana. Trans. Sir Richard F. Burton and F. F. Arbutknot. Mumbai: Jaico, 1976.

Kawabata Yasunari. *Snow Country*. Trans. Edward G. Seidensticker. New York: Knopf, 1956.

Kong Shangren. *Taohua shan* [Peach blossom fan]. 1699; Beijing: Renmin chubanshe, 1980.

Khan, Dargah. *Purani Dehli ke Halat* (original Farsi manuscript in Urdu). Trans. Khwaja Hasan Nizami. Delhi: Mahbub Press, 1949.

The Laws of Manu. In *Sacred Books of the East*. 50 vols. Ed. F. Max Müller. Vol. 25, trans. Georg Bühler. Oxford: Clarendon Press, 1886.

Lettere di cortigiane del Rinascimento. Ed. Angelo Romano. Rome: Salerno Editrice, 1990.

Li Yunxiang [Weilinzi, pseud.], compiler. *Seductive Courtesans of Suzhou* (1617).

Lucian of Samosata. *Dialogues of the Courtesans*.

Machon. *Chreiai*.

Machiavelli, Niccolò. *Opere*. 3 vols. Ed. Corrado Vivanti. Turin: Einaudi, 1999.

Mahendravarman, King. *The Farce of the Pious Courtesan; and A Farce of Drunken Sport*. Ed. and trans. Michael Lockwood and A. Visnu Bhat. Madras: Tambaram Research Associates, 1991.

Mallanaga, Vatsyayana. *Kamasutra*. Trans. Wendy Doniger and Sudhir Kakar. Oxford: Oxford University Press, 2002.

Manusmrti with Manubhasya of Medhatithi. Vol. 7. Trans. Ganganath Jha. Calcutta: University of Calcutta, 1920–26.

Masuda Sayo. *Autobiography of a Geisha.* Trans. Gaye G. Rowley. New York: Columbia University Press, 2003.

Mubarak, Abu al-Fazl ibn. *The A'in-I Akbari.* Trans. H. Blochmann. Ed. S. L. Goomer. 2d ed. Delhi: Aadiesh Book Depot, 1965.

Pallavicino, Ferrante. *La rettorica delle puttane.* Ed. Laura Coci. 1673; Parma: Fondazione Pietro Bembo, 1992.

Parkes Parlby, Fanny. *Wandering of a Pilgrim in Search of the Picturesque, during Four-and-Twenty Years in the East.* London: P. Richardson, 1850.

Pearl, Cora. *Grand Horizontal: The Erotic Memoirs of a Passionate Lady.* Ed. William Blatchford. New York: Stein and Day, 1983.

Petrucci, Ottaviano. *Frottole Buch I und IV: Nach den Erstlingsdrucken von 1504 und 1505 (?).* Ed. Rudolf Schwartz. Repr. Hildesheim and Wiesbaden: Georg Olms and Breitkopf & Härtel, 1967.

Qingtiao yishi [pseud.], compiler. *Huapin jian* [Categories of flowers]. 17th century.

Ruswa, Mirza Hadi. *Umrao Jan Ada* [The courtesan of Lucknow]. Trans. Khushwant Singh and M. A. Husaini. Bombay: Orient Longmans, 1961.

Satō Yōjin, compiler. *Senryū Yoshiwara fūzoku zue* [Illustrated compendium of Yoshiwara customs]. Tokyo: Chibunkaku, 1972.

Shah, Hasan. *The Nautch Girl: A Novel.* Trans. Qurratulain Hyder. New Delhi: Sterling Paperbacks, 1992.

Somadeva. *Kathā Sarit Sāgara, The Ocean of Story.* Trans. C. H. Tawney. London 1924.

Stampa, Gaspara. *Rime.* Ed. Rodolfo Cerielo. Milan: Rizzoli, 1976.

Sun Zhongling. *Dongguo ji* [The eastern city wall]. In *Guben xiqu congkan* [A series of old editions of plays]. 2d ser. Shanghai: Shangwu yinshuguan, 1955.

Tang Xianzu. *Mudan ting* [Peony pavilion]. Ed. Xu Shuofang and Yang Xiaomei. Beijing: Renmin daxue chubanshe, 1993.

———. *The Peony Pavilion.* Trans. Cyril Birch. Bloomington: Indiana University Press, 1980.

Theocritus, *Idyll.*

Tullia d'Aragona. *Dialogo della infinità d'amore.* In *Trattati d'amore del Cinquecento.* Ed. Giuseppe Zonta. 1912; Bari: Laterza, 1967. Repr. ed. Mario Pozzi. Rome: Giuseppe Laterza, 1975.

———. *Dialogue on the Infinity of Love,* ed. and trans. Rinaldina Russell and Bruce Merry. Chicago: University of Chicago Press, 1997.

Vecellio, Cesare. *Degli habiti antichi, et moderni di diverse parti del mondo.* Venice, 1590.

Venier, Lorenzo. *La puttana errante: Poème en quatre chantes de Lorenzo Veniero.* Paris: Isidore Liseux, 1883.

———. *Il trentuno della Zaffetta.* Ed. Gino Raya. Catania: Tirelli, 1929.

Venier, Maffio. *Il libro chiuso di Maffio Venier (La tenzone con Veronica Franco).* Ed. Manlio Dais. Venice: Neri Pozza, 1956.

Veniero, Domenico. *Rime di Domenico Veniero.* Ed. Pierantonio Serassi. Bergamo, 1751.

Verdelot, Philippe. *Intavolature de li madrigali di Verdelotto: De cantare et sonare nel lauto.* Arr. Adrian Willaert. Venice, 1536.

When God Is a Customer: Telugu Courtesan Songs by Ksetrayya and Others. Ed. and trans. A. K. Ramanujan, Velcheru Narayana Rao, and David Shulman. Berkeley: University of California Press, 1994.

Willaert, Adrian. *Opera omnia,* vol. 14. Ed. Helga Meier. Corpus Mensurabilis Musicae, 3. Rome: American Institute of Musicology, 1977.

Xenophon, *Memorabilia.*

Yu Huai. *Banqiao zaji* [Miscellaneous records of the Wooden Bridge District]. Ed. Li Jintang. Shanghai: Shanghai guji chubanshe, 2000.

Zhang Mengzheng, compiler. *Qinglou yunyu* [Stylish verses of the green bower]. Hangzhou, 1616; facsimile ed. in *Zhongguo gudai banhua congkan hebian.* Shanghai: Shanghai guji chubanshe, 1994.

Zhang Xu, compiler. *Caibi qingci xiqu congkan* [A series of rare editions relating to drama]. In *Shanben* [Love lyrics of stylistic brilliance], vol. 75. [1620s].

[Zhou Zhibiao] [Wangyuzi, pseud.], compiler. *Wuji baimei* [Seductive courtesans of Suzhou] (1617).

Secondary Sources: Ancient Greece

Beard, Mary, and John Henderson. "With This Body I Thee Worship: Sacred Prostitution in Antiquity." *Gender and History* 9 (1997): 480–503.

Burton, Joan B. *Theocritus's Urban Mimes: Mobility, Gender, and Patronage.* Berkeley: University of California Press, 1995.

Cooper, Craig. "Hyperides and the Trial of Phryne." *Phoenix* 49 (1995): 303–18.

Davidson, James. "*Liaisons Dangereuses*: Aphrodite and the Hetaera." *Journal of Hellenic Studies* 124 (2004): 169–73.

———. *Courtesans and Fishcakes: The Consuming Passions of Classical Athens.* London: HarperCollins, 1997.

Faraone, Christopher A. *Ancient Greek Love Magic.* Cambridge, MA: Harvard University Press, 1999.

———. "Lysistrata the Priestess or the Courtesan? Female Stereotypes in Aristophanes' *Lysistrata*." In *Prostitutes and Courtesans in the Ancient World.* Ed. Christopher A. Faraone and Laura McClure. Madison: University of Wisconsin Press, Madison, forthcoming 2006.

———. *Talismans and Trojan Horses: Guardian Statues in Ancient Greek Myth and Ritual.* Oxford: Oxford University Press, 1992.

Faraone, Christopher, and Laura McClure, eds. *Prostitutes and Courtesans in the Ancient World.* Madison: University of Wisconsin Press, Madison, forthcoming 2006.

Hamel, Debra. *Trying Neaira: The True Story of a Courtesan's Scandalous Life in Ancient Greece.* New Haven: Yale University Press, 2003.

Henry, Madeleine M. *Prisoner of History: Aspasia of Miletus and Her Biographical Tradition.* Oxford: Oxford University Press, 1991.

Kurke, Leslie. *Coins, Bodies, Games and Gold: The Politics of Meaning in Archaic Greece.* Princeton: Princeton University Press, 1999.

———. "Gender, Politics, and Subversion in the *Chreiai* of Machon." *Proceedings of the Cambridge Philological Society* 48 (2002): 20–65.

———. "Pindar and the Prostitutes." *Arion* 42 (1996): 49–75.

Laurence, Ray. *Roman Pompeii: Space and Society.* London: Routledge, 1994.

Lewis, Sīan. *The Athenian Woman: An Iconographic Handbook.* London: Routledge, 2002.

Llewellyn-Jones, Lloyd. *Aphrodite's Tortoise: The Veiled Woman of Ancient Greece.* Swansea: Classical Press of Wales, 2003.

McClure, Laura. *Courtesans at Table: Gender and Greek Literary Culture in Athenaeus.* London: Routledge, 2003.

Ogden, Daniel. *Polygamy, Prostitutes, and Death: The Hellenistic Dynasties.* London: Duckworth, 1999.

Peschel, Ingeborg. *Die Hetäre bei Symposion und Komos in der attisch-rotfigurigen Vasenmalerei des 6.–4. Jahrhundert v. Chr.* Frankfurt: P. Lang, 1987.

Pirenne-Delforge, Vinciane. *L'Aphrodite grecque: Contribution à l'étude de ses cultes et de sa personnalité dans la pantheon archaïque et classique.* Kernos Suppl., 4. Liège: Centre International d'Étude de la Religion Grecque Antique, 1994.

Reinsberg, Carola. *Ehe, Hetärentum, und Knabenliebe im antiken Griechenland.* Munich: C. H. Beck, 1993.

Winkler, Jack. *The Constraints of Desire: The Anthropology of Sex and Gender in Ancient Greece.* New York: Routledge, 1990.

Secondary Sources: Early Modern Italy

Ademollo, Alessandro. *La bell'Adriana ed altre virtuose del suo tempo alla corte di Mantova.* Città di Castello: S. Lapi, 1888.

Barzaghi, Antonio. *Donne o cortigiane? La prostituzione a Venezia: Documenti di costume dal XVI al XVIII secolo.* Verona: Bertani, 1980.

Bassanese, Fiora. *Gaspara Stampa.* Boston: Twayne, 1983.

Brognoligo, Gioachino. "Gaspara Stampa." *Giornale storico della letteratura italiana* 76 (1920): 134–43.

Brown, Howard Mayer. *Embellishing Sixteenth-Century Music.* Oxford: Oxford University Press, 1976.

———. "Women Singers and Women's Songs in Fifteenth-Century Italy." In *Women Making Music: The Western Art Tradition, 1150–1950,* ed. Jane Bowers and Judith Tick, 62–89. Urbana: University of Illinois Press, 1986.

Cardamone, Donna G. "Isabella Medici-Orsini: A Portrait of Self-Affirmation." In *Gender, Sexuality, and Early Music,* ed. Todd Michael Borgerding, 1–25. New York: Routledge, 2002.

Casagrande di Villaviera, Rita. *Le cortigiane veneziane nel Cinquecento.* Milan: Longanesi, 1968.

Chambers, David, and Brian Pullan, eds. *Venice: A Documentary History, 1450–1630.* Oxford: Blackwell, 1992.

Chojnacka, Monica. *Working Women of Early Modern Venice.* Baltimore: Johns Hopkins University Press, 2001.

Cohn, Samuel K. *Women in the Streets: Essays on Sex and Power in Renaissance Italy.* Baltimore: Johns Hopkins University Press, 1996.

Einstein, Alfred, *The Italian Madrigal.* 3 vols. Trans. Alexander H. Krappe, Roger H. Sessions, and Oliver Strunk. 1949; repr. Princeton: Princeton University Press, 1971.

Feldman, Martha. *City Culture and the Madrigal at Venice.* Berkeley: University of California Press, 1995.

———. "Cortigiane e donne da ridotto: petrarchismo, tradizione orale e scale sociale." In *Il Petrarca e la musica,* ed. Andrea Chegai and Cecilia Luzzi. Lucca: LIM, 2005.

Ferand, Ernst. *Die Improvisation in Beispielen aus neun Jahrhunderten abendländischer Musik: Mit einer geschichtlichen Einführung.* Cologne: Arno Volk, 1956.

Findlen, Paula. "Humanism, Politics, and Pornography in Renaissance Italy." In *The Invention of Pornography: Obscenity and the Origins of Modernity, 1500–1800,* ed. Lynn Hunt, 49–108. New York: Zone Books, 1993.

Glixon, Beth L. "Private Lives of Public Women: Prima Donnas in Mid-Seventeenth-Century Venice." *Music & Letters* 76 (1995): 509–31.

Gordon, Bonnie. *Monteverdi's Unruly Women: The Power of Song in Early Modern Europe.* Cambridge: Cambridge University Press, 2004.

Heller, Wendy. *Emblems of Eloquence: Opera and Women's Voices in Seventeenth-Century Venice.* Berkeley: University of California Press, 2003.

Jacobs, Fredericka H. *Defining the Renaissance Virtuosa: Women Artists and the Language of Art History and Criticism.* Cambridge: Cambridge University Press, 1997.

Jaffe, Irma. *Shining Eyes, Cruel Fortune: The Lives and Loves of Italian Renaissance Women Poets.* New York: Fordham University Press, 2002.

Jones, Ann Rosalind. *The Currency of Eros: Women's Love Lyric in Europe, 1540–1620.* Bloomington: University of Indiana Press, 1990.

Junkerman, Anne Christine. "Bellissima Donna: An Interdisciplinary Study of Venetian Sensuous Half Length Images of the Early Sixteenth Century." Ph.D. diss., University of California at Berkeley, 1988.

————. "The Lady and the Laurel: Gender and Meaning in Giorgione's *Laura*." *Oxford Art Journal* 16 (1993): 49–58.

Keener, Shawn Marie, "Virtue, Illusion, *Venezianità*: Vocal Bravura and the Early *Cortigiana Onesta*." In *Musical Voices of Early Modern Women: Many-Headed Melodies*, ed. Thomasin K. LaMay, ch. 5. Aldershot: Ashgate, 2005.

Klapisch-Zuber, Christiane. *Women, Family, and Ritual in Renaissance Italy*, trans. Lydia Cochrane. Chicago: University of Chicago Press, 1987.

Kurzel-Runtscheiner, Monica. *Töchter der Venus: Die Kurtisanen Roms im 16. Jahrhundert.* Munich: C. H. Beck, 1995.

Lawner, Lynne. *Lives of the Courtesans: Portraits of the Renaissance.* New York: Rizzoli, 1987.

Moore, Mary B. *Desiring Voices: Women Sonneteers and Petrarchism.* Carbondale, IL: Southern Illinois University Press, 2000.

Newcomb, Anthony. "Courtesans, Muses, or Musicians? Professional Women Musicians in Sixteenth-Century Italy." In *Women Making Music: The Western Art Tradition 1150–1950*, ed. Jane Bowers and Judith Tick, 90–115. Urbana: University of Illinois Press, 1986.

————. *The Madrigal at Ferrara, 1579–1597.* 2 vols. Princeton: Princeton University Press, 1979.

Poli, Doretta Davanzo. "Le cortigiane e la moda." In *Il gioco dell'Amore: Le cortigiane di Venezia dal Trecento al Settecento: Catalogo della mostra*, ed. Alfredo Bruno. Milan: Berenice, 1990.

Prizer, William F. "Games of Venus: Secular Vocal Music in the Late Quattrocento and Early Cinquecento." *Journal of Musicology* 9 (1991): 3–56.

————. "Wives and Courtesans: The Frottola in Florence." In *Music Observed: Studies in Memory of William C. Holmes*, ed. Colleen Reardon and Susan Parisi, 401–15. Warren, MI: Harmonie Park Press, 2004.

Renaissance Characters. Ed. Eugenio Garin. Trans. Lydia G. Cochrane. Chicago: University of Chicago Press, 1988.

Rosand, David. "Venereal Hermeneutics: Reading Titian's *Venus of Urbino*." In *Renaissance Society and Culture: Essays in Honor of Eugene F. Rice, Jr.*, ed. John Monfasani and Ronald G. Musto, 263–80. New York: Italica Press, 1971.

Rosand, Ellen. "Barbara Strozzi, *virtuosissima cantatrice*: The Composer's Voice." *Journal of the American Musicological Society* 31 (1978): 241–81.

Rosenthal, Margaret F. *The Honest Courtesan: Veronica Franco, Citizen and Writer in Sixteenth-Century Venice.* Chicago: University of Chicago Press, 1992.

Ruggiero, Guido. *Binding Passions: Tales of Magic, Marriage, and Power from the End of the Renaissance.* Oxford: Oxford University Press, 1993.

————. "Marriage, Love, Sex, and Renaissance Civic Morality." In *Sexuality and Gender in Early Modern Europe*, ed. James Grantham Turner, 10–30. Cambridge: Cambridge University Press, 1993.

Salza, Abdelkader. "Madonna Gasparina Stampa, secondo nuove indagini." *Giornale storico della letteratura italiana* 62 (1913): 1–101.

Santore, Kathy. "Julia Lombardo, 'Somtuosa Meretrice': A Portrait by Property." *Renaissance Quarterly* 41 (1988): 44–83.

Schonbrun, Sheila. "Ambiguous Artists: Music-Making among Italian Renaissance Courtesans (with Particular Reference to Tullia of Aragon, Gaspara Stampa, and Veronica Franco)." D.M.A. thesis, City University of New York, 1998.

Simons, Patricia. "Portraiture, Portrayal, and Idealization: Ambiguous Individualism in Representations of Renaissance Women." In *Language and Images of Renaissance Italy*, ed. Alison Brown, 263–311. Oxford: Clarendon Press, 1995.

Slim, H. Colin. "A Motet for Machiavelli's Mistress and a Chanson for a Courtesan." In *Essays Presented to Myron P. Gilmore*, 457–72. Florence: La Nuova Italia, 1978.

Sluijter, Eric Jan. "Emulating Sensual Beauty: Representation of Danaë from Gossaert to Rembrandt." *Simiolus* 27 (1999): 4–45.

Smarr, Janet L. "Gaspara Stampa's Poetry for Performance." *Journal of the Rocky Mountain Medieval and Renaissance Association* 12 (1991): 61–84.

Spackman, Barbara. "Inter musam et ursum moritur: Folengo and the Gaping 'Other' Mouth." In *Refiguring Woman: Perspectives on Gender in the Italian Renaissance*, ed. Marilyn Migiel and Juliana Schiesari, 19–35. Ithaca: Cornell University Press, 1991.

Sperling, Jutta Gisela. *Convents and the Body Politic in Late Renaissance Venice*. Chicago: University of Chicago Press, 1999.

Stallybrass, Peter. "The Body Enclosed: Patriarchal Territories." In *Rewriting the Renaissance: The Discourses of Sexual Difference in Early Modern Europe*, ed. Margaret M. Ferguson, Maureen Quilligan, and Nancy K. Vickers, 123–42. Chicago: University of Chicago Press, 1986.

Secondary Sources: East Asia

Amino Yoshihiko. *Chūsei no hinin to yūjo* [The "non-humans" and yūjo in the medieval period]. Tokyo: Akashishoten, 1994.

Bornoff, Nicholas. *Pink Samurai: Love, Marriage, and Sex in Contemporary Japan*. London: GraftonBooks, 1991.

Bossler, Beverly. "Shifting Identities: Courtesans and Literati in Song China." *Harvard Journal of Asiatic Studies* 62 (2002): 5–37.

Cabell, Charles Richard. "Maiden Dreams: Kawabata Yasunari's Beautiful Japanese Empire, 1930–1945." Ph.D. diss., Harvard University, 1999.

Cheng Sea-Ling. "Assuming Manhood: Prostitution and Patriotic Passions in Korea," *East Asia: An International Quarterly* 18, no. 4 (2000): 40–78.

Dai Ning. "Ming Qing shiqi Qinhuai qinglou yinyue wenhua chutan [A preliminary exploration of Ming and Qing dynasty musical culture in the Qinhuai pleasure district]." *Zhongguo yinyuexue jikan* 3 (1997): 40–54.

Downer, Lesley. *Madame Sadayakko: The Geisha who Bewitched the West*. New York: Gotham Books, 2003.

————. *Women of the Pleasure Quarters: The Secret History of the Geisha*. New York: Broadway Books, 2001.

Fujime Yuki. *Sei no rekishigaku: kōshō seido, dataizai taisei kara baishun bōshihō, yūseihogohō taisei e* [History of sexuality: from the licensed prostitution and illegal abortion system to the Prostitution Prevention Act and the Eugenic Protection Act system]. Tokyo: Fujishuppan, 1998.

Fukuda Toshiko. *Yoshiwara wa konna tokoro de gozaimashita* [Yoshiwara was this type of place]. Tokyo: Sekai shisōsha, 1993.

Golden, Arthur. *Memoirs of a Geisha: A Novel*. New York: Alfred Knopf, 1997.

Hamada Giichirō, ed. *Edo bungaku chimei jiten* [Dictionary of Edo literary topography] (Tokyo: Tōkyōdō, 1973).

Hayakawa Noriyo. *Kindai tennōsei kokka to jendaa* [The modern imperial state and gender]. Tokyo: Aokishoten, 1998.

Hershatter, Gail. "Courtesans and Streetwalkers: The Changing Discourses on Shanghai Prostitution, 1890–1949." *Journal of the History of Sexuality* 3 (1992): 245–269.

———. *Dangerous Pleasures: Prostitution and Modernity in Twentieth-Century Shanghai*. Berkeley: University of California Press, 1997.

Hirota Kazuko. *Shōgen kiroku, jūgunianfu, kangofu: senjō ni ikita onna no dōkoku* [Testimonial documents by military comfort women and nurses: lament of women living on the battlefield]. Tokyo: Shinjinbutsu ōraisha, 1975.

Idema, Wilt L., and Stephen West. *The Moon and the Zither: The Story of the Western Wing*. Berkeley: University of California Press, 1991.

Inoue Shoichi. *Ai no kūkan* [Space of love]. Kadokawa shoten, 1999.

Ishino Hiromichi, *Artistic License* (1803). Trans. Timon Screech. Hollywood, CA: Highmoonoon, 2003.

Jackis, Jerry M. "Korea's Unique Gisaeng Party." In *The Feel of Korea*, ed. In-hah Jung, 171–75. Seoul: Hollym, 1966.

Kamens, Edward. *Utamakura: Allusion and Intertextuality in Traditional Japanese Poetry*. New Haven: Yale University Press, 1997.

Kanai Keiko. "Kiku otoko, kataru onna, kaku dansei sakka: Tokuda Shusei 'Shukuzu' o yomu" [A man who listens, a woman who narrates, and a male writer who writes: reading Tokuda Shusei's *Shukuzu*]. In *Dansei sakka o yomu: feminizumu hihyō no seijuku e* [Reading male writers: toward the maturity of feminist criticism], ed. Egusa Mitsuko et al., 67–96. Tokyo: Shinyōsha, 1994.

Kawamura Minato. *Gisaeng: mal haneun ggot* [Gisaeng: Talking flower]. Seoul: Sodam, 2001.

Kazue Morisaki. *Kaishun ōkoku no onnatachi: shōfu to sanpu niyoru kindaishi* [Women in the kingdom of prostitution: modern Japanese history through female prostitutes and pregnant women]. Tokyo: Takarajimasha, 1993.

Ko, Dorothy. *Teachers of the Inner Chambers: Women and Culture in Seventeenth-Century China*. Stanford: Stanford University Press, 1994.

Kolsky, Alyssa. "Real Geisha, Real Story." *Time Asia*, November 25, 2002.

Kwon Do-Hee. "The Female Musicians Activity since the Dissolution of the Gisaeng Guilds." In *Proceedings of the Seventh International Asian Music Conference: Korean Music Viewed from In and Out*, 177–90. Seoul: Seoul National University, 2003.

———. "Reorganization of Musical Groups in the Beginning of the 20th Century." *Dongyang eumak* 20 (1998): 269–87.

———. "19-segi yeoseong eumakgye ui gudo" [The makeup of nineteenth-century women's musical scenes]. *Dongyang eumak* 24 (2002): 5–17.

———. "20-segi gisaeng ui eumaksahoesajeog yeon'gu" [A music-sociohistorical study of the twentieth-century gisaeng]. *Han'guk eumak yeon'gu* 29 (2001): 319–44.

Lam, Joseph S. C. "The Presence and Absence of Female Musicians and Music in China." In *Women and Confucian Cultures in Premodern China, Korea, and Japan*, ed. Dorothy Ko et al., 97–120. Berkeley: University of California Press, 2003.

Lee Byong Won. "The Evolution in the Role and Status of Korean Professional Female Entertainers (*Kisaeng*)." *World of Music* 21 (1979): 75–81.

Lie, John. "The Transformation of Sexual Work in 20th-Century Korea." *Gender and Society* 9 (1995): 310–27.

Liu, Marjory Bong-Ray. "Tradition and Change in *Kunqu* Opera." Ph.D. diss., University of California at Los Angeles, 1976.

Mao Wenfang. *Wu.xingbie.guankan: Mingmo Qingchu wenhua shuxie xintan* [Things, gender, and visuality: writing culture in the late Ming and early Qing]. Taibei: Xuesheng shuju, 2001.

Morisaki Kazue. *Kaishun ōkoku no onnatachi: shōfu to sanpu niyoru kindaishi* [Women in the kingdom of prostitution: modern Japanese history through female prostitutes and pregnant women]. Tokyo: Takarajimasha, 1993.

Narahara Junko. "Chūsei zenki ni okeru yūjo kugutsu no 'ie' to chōja" [The household and riches of *yūjo* and *kugutsu* in the early medieval period of Japan]. In *Nihon joseishi ronshū*, vol. 9: *Sei to karada* [Collections of articles on Japanese women's history, vol. 9: Sexuality and body], ed. Ishizaki Shoko and Sakurai Yuki, 3–20. Tokyo: Yoshikawa kobunkan, 1998.

Ōki Yasushi. *Chūgoku yūri kūkan: Min Shin shinwai gijo no sekai.* Tokyo: Seidosha, 2002.

———. *Fū Bōryū sanka no kenkyū.* Tokyo: Keisō shobō, 2003.

Okuda Akiko, ed. "Sekushuariti no rekishi" [History of sexuality]. *Onna to otoko no jikū: nihon joseishi saikō* [Time and space for women and men: reconsidering Japanese women's history], vol. 5. Tokyo: Fujiwara shoten, 1995.

Onozawa Akane. "Kôshô seido haishi mondai no rekishiteki ichi" [A historical position of the prohibition of licensed prostitution]. *Rekishigaku kenkyû* 764 (2002): 2–40.

Pak Jeongae. "Nalgoshipeun 'nongjungjo': iljesidae gisaeng iyagi" [Caged birds who want to fly: the story of the gisaeng in the Japanese colonial period]. In *20-segi yeoseong sageonsa* [Events in twentieth-century women's history], ed. Gilbakksesang, 77–89. Seoul: Yeoseong sinmunsa, 2001.

Pak Jongseong. *Baekjeong gwa gisaeng: joseoncheonminsa ui du eolgul* [The *baekjeong* and the gisaeng: Two faces of the outcaste during the Joseon Dynasty]. Seoul: Seoul National University Press, 2003.

Pilzer, Joshua D. "Post-Korean War Change in *Sŏdosori*, a Northwest Korean Vocal Genre in Contemporary South Korea." M.A. thesis, University of Hawai'i, 1999.

Qian Qianyi. *Liechao shiji xiaozhuan.* 2 vols. Beijing: Zhonghua shuju, 1983.

Rij, Jan van. *Madame Butterfly: Japonisme, Puccini, and the Search for the Real Cho-Cho-San.* Berkeley: Stonebridge Press, 2001.

Ropp, Paul S. "Ambiguous Images of Courtesan Culture in Late Imperial China." In *Writing Women in Late Imperial China*, ed. Ellen Widmer and Kang-i-Sung, 17–45. Stanford: Stanford University Press, 1997.

Saeki Junko. *Yūjo no bunkashi* [A cultural history of Japanese courtesans]. Tokyo: Chuo koronsha, 1987.

Screech, Timon. *Artistic License.* Hollywood, CA: Highmoonoon, 2003.

———. "The Edo Pleasure Districts as 'Pornotopia.'" *Orientations* 33 (2002): 36–41.

———. *Sex and The Floating World: Erotic Images in Japan, 1700–1820.* London: Reaktion Books, 1999.

———. *The Shogun's Painted Culture: Fear and Creativity in the Japanese States.* London: Reaktion Books, 2000.

Seigle, Cecilia Segawa. *Yoshiwara: The Glittering World of the Japanese Courtesan.* Honolulu: University of Hawai'i Press, 1993.

Shiga-Fujime Yuki. "The Prostitutes' Union and the Impact of the 1956 Anti-Prostitution Law in Japan." Trans. Beverly L. Findlay-Kaneko. *U.S.–Japan Women's Journal*. English Supplement 5 (1993): 3–27.

Shin Heisoo. "Women's Sexual Services and Economic Development: The Political Economy of the Entertainment Industry and South Korean Dependent Development." Ph.D. diss., Rutgers University, 1991.

Song, Youn-ok. "Japanese Colonial Rule and State-Managed Prostitution: Korea's Licensed Prostitutes." *Positions* 5 (1997): 171–217.

Tamura, Naomi. *The Japanese Bride*. New York: Harper & Brothers, 1904.

Tegler, Gary. "'Memoirs of a Geisha' Muse Vents Spleen at Author." *The Japan Times*, May 1, 2001. Also at http://www.japantimes.co.jp/cgi-bin/getarticle.pl5?nn20010501k3.htm, accessed November 13, 2005.

Vinograd, Richard. *Boundaries of the Self: Chinese Portraits, 1600–1900*. Cambridge: Cambridge University Press, 1992.

Watanabe Shin'ichiro. "Yoshiwara e no michi [The road to Yoshiwara]." *Kokubungaku: Kaishaku to Kanshō* 473 (1971): 8–22.

Women of Korea: A History from Ancient Times to the Present. Ed. and trans. Yung-Chung Kim. Seoul: Ewha Women's University Press, 1976.

Wong, Isabel. "Kunqu." In *Garland Encyclopedia of World Music*, vol. 7, ed. Robert C. Provine et al. New York: Garland, 2002.

Writing Women in Late Imperial China. Ed. Ellen Widmer and Kang-i-Sung. Stanford: Stanford University Press, 1997.

Yi, Neunghwa. *Joseon hae-eohwasa* [A history of the Joseon Dynasty gisaeng]. 1927; repr. Seoul: Dongmunseon, 1992.

Yokota-Murakami, Takayuki. *Don Juan, East/West: On the Problematics of Comparative Literature*. Albany: State University of New York Press, 1998.

Yoshimi Yoshiaki. *Comfort Women: Sexual Slavery in the Japanese Military during World War II*. Trans. Suzanne O'Brien. 1995; New York: Columbia University Press, 2000.

Yuki, Fujime. *Sei no rekishigaku: kōshō seido, dataizai taisei kara baishun bōshihō, yūseihogohō taisei e* [History of sexuality: from the licensed prostitution and illegal abortion system to the Prostitution Prevention Act and the Eugenic Protection Act system]. Tokyo: Fujishuppan, 1998.

Yuki, Shiga-Fujime. "The Prostitutes' Union and the Impact of the 1956 Anti-Prostitution Law in Japan." Trans. Beverly L. Findlay-Kaneko. *U.S.–Japan Women's Journal*. English Supplement 5 (1993).

Secondary Sources: South Asia

Abbas, Shemeem Burney. *The Female Voice in Sufi Ritual: Devotional Practices of Pakistan and India*. Foreword by Elizabeth Warnock Fernea. Austin: University of Texas Press, 2002.

Babiracki, Carol M. "Courtesan Traditions of North India: Cutting through Conventional Concepts." Paper presented at the Annual Meeting of the Society for Ethnomusicology, 1994.

———. "The Illusion of India's Public Dancers." in *Women's Voices across Musical Worlds*, ed. Jane A. Bernstein, 36–59. Boston: Northeastern Illinois Press, 2004.

———. "What's the Difference? Reflections on Gender and Research in Village India." In *Shadows in the Field: New Perspectives for Fieldwork in Ethnomusicology*, ed. Gregory F. Barz and Timothy J. Cooley, 121–36. New York: Oxford University Press, 1997.

Banerji, Suresh Chandra, and Ramala Banerji. *The Castaway of Indian Society: A History of Prostitution in India*. Calcutta: Punthi Pustak, 1989.

Bloch, T. "Jogīmārā Inscription." In *Archaeological Survey of India, Annual Report, 1903–4*, 128–31. Calcutta, 1906.

Chandra, Moti. *The World of the Courtesans*. Bombay: Vikas Publishing House, 1973.

Chakravarty, Sumita. *Nationalism and Identity in Indian Popular Cinema, 1947–1987*. Austin: University of Texas Press, 1993.

Desai, Devangana. *Erotic Sculpture of India: A Socio-Cultural Study*. 2d rev. ed. New Delhi: Tata-McGraw Hill, 1975.

Doniger O'Flaherty, Wendy. *Asceticism and Eroticism in the Mythology of Śiva*. Delhi: Oxford University Press, 1973.

Fischer, Klaus. *Erotik und Askese in Kult und Kunst der Inder*. Cologne: Du Mont, 1979.

Ganguli, Rita. "Bai Theke Begum [From courtesan to wife]." *Desh* 63/64 (1996): 73–93.

Gode, P. K. "The Role of the Courtezan in the Early History of Indian Painting." *Annals of the Bhandarkar Oriental Research Institute* 22 (1941): 24–37.

Gonda, J. "Ascetics and Courtesans." *Adyar Library Bulletin* 25 (1961): 78–102.

Gopal, Ram. *India of Vedic Kalpasūtras*. Delhi: National Publishing House, 1959.

Husain, Mirza Jaffar Quadim. *Lukhnau ki Akhri Bahar*. New Delhi: Taraqqi-yi Urdu Biyuro, 1981.

Kersenboom-Story, Saskia C. "Devadāsī Murai." *Rasamañjari* 2/2 (Aug. 1997), 55–64.

———. *Nityasumaṅgalī: Devadāsī Tradition in South India*. Delhi: Motilal Banarsidass, 1987.

Kloppenborg, Ria. "Female Stereotypes in Early Buddhism: The Women of the Therīgathā." In *Female Stereotypes in Religious Traditions*, Ed. Ria Kloppenborg and Wouter J. Hanegraaff, 151–69. Leiden: Brill, 1995.

Maciszewski, Amelia. "Multiple Voices, Multiple Selves: Song Style and North Indian Women's Identity." *Asian Music* 32 (2001): 1–40.

———. "Our Stories, Our Songs: North Indian Women's Musical Auto/biographies." Ethnographic video, 2000.

———. "Stories about Selves: Selected North Indian Women's Musical Biographies." *The World of Music* 43 (2001): 139–72.

Marglin, Frédérique Apffel. "Refining the Body: Transformative Emotion in Ritual Dance." In *Divine Passions: The Social Construction of Emotion in India*, ed. Owen Lynch, 212–36. Berkeley: University of California Press, 1990.

———. *Wives of the God-King*. Delhi: Oxford University Press, 1985.

Merchant, Ismael, director. *The Courtesans of Bombay*. Merchant Ivory Productions. Released January 1983. Dir. and Produced by Ismael Merchant.

Misra, Susheela. *Music Makers of Bhatkhande College*. Calcutta: Sangeet Research Academy, 1985.

Mohanty, Chandra. "Under Western Eyes: Feminist Scholarship and Colonial Discourses." In *Third World Women and the Politics of Feminism*, ed. Chandra Mohanty, Ann Russo, and Lourdes Torres, 51–80. Bloomington: Indiana University Press, 1990.

Nair, Meera, director. *Salaam Bombay*. Mirabei Films Production; presenter Film Four International, NHDC-Doordarshan Cadrage, S.A. La S.E.P.T.; Producer and director Mira Nair. Original release 1988.

Nevile, Pran. *Nautch Girls of India: Dancers, Singers, Playmates*. New Delhi: Ravi Kumar, 1996.

Oldenburg, Veena Talwar. "Lifestyle as Resistance: The Case of the Courtesans of Lucknow." *Feminist Studies* 16 (1990): 259–88.

Orr, Leslie C. *Donors, Devotees, and Daughters of God: Temple Women in Medieval Tamilnadu*. New York: Oxford University Press, 2000.

Post, Jennifer. "Professional Women in Indian Music: The Death of the Courtesan Tradition." In *Women and Music in Cross-Cultural Perspective*, ed. Ellen Koskoff, 97–109. New York: Greenwood, 1992.

Post Quinn, Jennifer. "Marathi and Konkani Speaking Women in Hindustani Music, 1880–1940." Ph.D. diss., University of Minnesota, 1982.

————. "Professional Women in Indian Music: The Death of the Courtesan Tradition," in *Women and Music in Cross-Cultural Perspective*, ed. Ellen Koskoff (New York: Greenwood, 1992), 97–109.

Qureshi, Regula Burckhardt. "Confronting the Social: Mode of Production and the Sublime in (Indian) Art Music." *Ethnomusicology* 44 (2000): 15–38.

————. "How Does Music Mean? Embodied Memories and the Politics of Affect in the Indian Sarangi." *American Ethnologist* 27 (2000): 805–38.

————. "In Search of Begum Akhtar: Patriarchy, Poetry, and Twentieth-Century Indian Music." *The World of Music* 43 (2001): 97–137.

————. "Mode of Production and Musical Production: Is Hindustani Music Feudal?" In *Music and Marx: Ideas, Practice, Politics*, 81–105, ed. Regula Burckhardt Qureshi. New York: Routledge, 2002.

Ramesh, Asha, and H. P. Philomela. "The Devadasi Problem." In *International Feminism: Networking against Female Sexual Slavery: Report of the Global Feminist Workshop to Organize against Traffic in Women, Rotterdam, the Netherlands, April 6–15, 1983*, ed. Kathleen Barry, Charlotte Bunch, and Shirley Castley, 82–87. Rotterdam: Global Feminist Workshop to Organize against Traffic in Women, 1984.

Rao, Vidya. "Thumri and Thumri Singers." In *Cultural Reorientation in Modern India*, ed. Indu Banga and Jaidev, 278–315. Shimla: Institute of Advanced Study, 1996.

Rubin, Gayle. "The Traffic in Women: Notes on the 'Political Economy' of Sex." In *Toward an Anthropology of Women*, ed. Rayna Reiter, 157–210. New York: Monthly Review Press, 1975. Repr. in *Women and Revolution: A Discussion of the Unhappy Marriage of Marxism and Feminism*, ed. Heidi Hartmann and Lydia Sargent. London: Pluto Press, 1981.

Saeed, Fouzia. *Taboo! The Hidden Culture of a Red Light Area.* Oxford: Oxford University Press, 2002.

Shah, Hassan. *The Nautch Girl: A Novel.* Trans. by Qurratulain Hyder. New Delhi: Sterling Paperbacks, 1992.

————. *Nishtar.* Trans. by Anjum Kasmandvi. Lahore: Majlis-e-Taraqqi-e-Adab, 1973.

Sharar, Abdul Halim. *Lucknow: The Last Phase of an Oriental Culture.* Trans. and ed. E. S. Harcourt and Fakhir Hussain. London: Paul Elek, 1975.

Srinivasan, Amrit. *Reform or Conformity? Temple "Prostitution" and the Community in the Madras Presidency.* New Delhi: Kali for Women Houdou, 1988.

Srinivasan, Doris Meth. "The Mauryan Ganika from Didarganj (Pataliputra)." Maurizio Taddei Memorial Issue of *East and West.* Forthcoming 2005.

Taranath, Anupama. "Disrupting Colonial Modernity: Indian Courtesans and Literary Cultures, 1888–1912." Ph.D. diss., University of California at San Diego, 2000.

Women Music Makers of India Seminar. New Delhi: Bharatya Kala Kendra, 1984.

Index

Page numbers in boldface indicate a primary discussion of the topic.

Printed and bound by CPI Group (UK) Ltd, Croydon, CR0 4YY